The Irvines and Their Kin: Revised by the Author in Scotland, Ireland and England; a History of the Irvine Family and Their Descendants. Also Short Sketches of Their Kindred, the Carlisles, Mcdowells, Johnstons, Maxwells, Gaults, Mcelroys, Etc., from A.D.

Lucinda Boyd

THE IRVINES
AND - THEIR - KIN

A History of the Irvine Family and their Descendants. Also short sketches of their Kindred, the Carlisles, McDowells, Johnstons, Maxwells, McElroys, Etc., from A. D. 373 to the present time. ∴ ∴

"A Wonderful Storehouse'

Compiled by L. BOYD.

8vo.   9¾ x 6¾.   -   -   -   432 Pages.

CLOTH, Gilt Top, ∴ ∴	$ 5.00
HALF MOROCCO, Gilt Top, ∴	10.00
LEATHER, ∴ ∴ ∴ ∴	25.00

R. R. DONNELLY & SONS COMPANY,
PUBLISHERS, ✐ ✐ ✐ ✐ CHICAGO.

Announcement

☖ ☖ ☖

We beg to announce the production of a new and revised edition of *"The Irvines and Their Kin."* The author made a special trip to Scotland, England and Ireland, and remained for a year among the Irvines of the present-day. By close contact and association with the descendants of this glorious family there is brought to the work the warmth and glow of an original setting, an intimate knowledge of character and characteristics in no other way obtainable. On the canvas of the present is painted the scenes of the past in striking colors. Primarily historic, the work abounds in anecdote and story, illuminating to a marked degree the lives of the people with whom it deals.

Revised from ancient records and data not to be obtained in America, the history appeals with force to all members of the family. Yet at no time is the narrative dry or dull.

There is an account of the Scottish Border in early times as an introduction to the history of an old Dumfriesshire family, which will be found of absorbing interest. The derivation of the Irvine name, the Irvings of Drum, the Irvines or Irwins or Irvings of the Old and New Country, clan contemporaries in Scotland, furnish some idea of the nature and scope of its contents.

The work is profusely illustrated. As the frontispiece is given a portrait of the late John Bell-Irving, Laird of White Hill, to whom the chieftainship of the Hoddom branch of the Irvings descended from the Dukes of Hoddom. Other portraits are those of Hon. Mr. Justice Irwin, C. S. I., Rangoon, Burma, Farther India; Robert Irwin, Sr., Mrs. Elvira Irwin Farber, the

Hon. Henry J. Farber, Jr., the Hon. John G. Carlisle, President Roosevelt, Benjamin Harrison, Washington Irving, Andrew Jackson and a score of others, all members of this distinguished family.

A number of views of scenes and places in the old World serve to supplement and interpret the narrative. In addition to the illustrations, several plates, or "Family Trees," are furnished complete to the present generation. Coats of Arms are given in profusion.

The work contains a catalogue of the clan contemporaries in Scotland and contemporaries in America, arranged by states and cities, affording a ready reference.

Such a work can not fail to enlist the interest of hundreds of Americans, descendants of this house, and we feel sure it will meet with a ready sale.

We should be glad to have you order on the blank hereto attached.

For Sale by

The Robert Clarke Co., ⁄ Cincinnati.

R. R. Donnelly & Sons Co., ⁄ Chicago.

L. Boyd, ⁄ ⁄ Cynthiana, Ky.

ORDER BLANK.

L. BOYD, Cynthiana, Kentucky;

You may send to my address ...., ... *cop.* ..... *of*

THE IRVINES AND THEIR KIN,

By L. BOYD,

8vo. *Illustrated.* Handsomely Bound. Cloth, $5.00. Half Morocco, $10.00. Leather, $25.00.

(Draw a line through the binding not desired.)

Name..

Address ....

Date..................

THE IRVINES
AND THEIR KIN

The late John Bell-Irving, Laird of Whitehill, to whom the Chieftainship of Hoddom branch of the Irvings descended from the Dukes of Hoddom. His son, John Bell-Irving, Laird of Milkbank, succeeds him.

THE IRVINES

AND THEIR KIN

REVISED BY THE AUTHOR IN SCOTLAND,
IRELAND AND ENGLAND

A HISTORY OF THE IRVINE FAMILY AND THEIR DESCENDANTS.
ALSO SHORT SKETCHES OF THEIR KINDRED, THE CAR-
LISLES, McDOWELLS, JOHNSTONS, MAXWELLS,
GAULTS, McELROYS, ETC., FROM A. D. 373
DOWN TO THE PRESENT TIME.

COMPILED BY
L. BOYD

Mrs. Lucinda Jean (Rogers) Boy

———

CHICAGO
R. R. DONNELLEY & SONS COMPANY
1908

TO
MRS. ELOIRA IRWIN FURBER,
CHICAGO, ILLINOIS,
JOHN BELL IRVING, ESQ.,
LAIRD OF WHITE HILL, MILKBANK, ETC., SCOTLAND,
AND HON. R. T. IRVINE,
VIRGINIA,
THIS BOOK IS GRATEFULLY DEDICATED
BY L. BOYD.

CONTENTS

———

PREFACE.

To the Irving Clan, Greeting:

I have the honor to belong to this Clan, the most numerous on the globe; but not to the Clan militant, as my forbears did. No. If a trumpet should sound "To Arms!" to-morrow, I might mount and ride; but not to the cannon's mouth. But ever since I could read, I have been a hero-worshiper, and have admired the brave men who faced death in its most awful forms, in battle by sea and land, and have been proud to learn that the Irvines were second to none on any field.

The Erinvines warred with the Romans, A. D. 373, and ever since that time they have fought, and many have fallen, on all the battle fields of the world.

They were as dauntless as any when Bruce was crowned, 1306, and one, Baron Irving, of that date, protected him when he fled from Edward Longshanks, King of England. How they fought and fell at Hardlaw, 1411, history relates, and at "Fatal Flodden Field" the ground ran red with their best blood. Says an ancient Chronicle: "Here all the male Irvines of the House of Bonshaw, who were able to carry arms, were killed, and few of that House were left to preserve the name, except those unborn."

The ancestor of the Canadian Irvings, Jacob Æmilius, was wounded at Waterloo; he was a gallant officer who was honored by his country.

I hope the Irvines who read this history will understand that the titled Irvines are not of more distinguished descent than those of the Clan who bear the same name. Says history: "Of these Irvines of Bonshaw are the most part of the Scotch Irvines descended, and those of Ireland in a very near line." (Dr. Christopher Irvine, Historiographer to King Charles II., and Historian of Scotland.)

Men of the Irvine Clan: Allow me to appeal to you to make my American Irvine Book a success. I have crossed the ocean and visited Scotland, Ireland, and England, to gather data to make my history as comprehensive as possible. I have compiled all that is of importance, from A. D. 373 down to the present time. It has been the fond hope, and the toilsome work of years, to embalm the deeds of your ancestors in undying form. I have used my best endeavors to accomplish what I have so longed to do. If my book pleases you, then my hopes will have found fruition.

THE IRVINES, IRVINS, IRVINGS, ERVINES, ERWINS OF THE OLD COUNTRY AND THE NEW.

I place the Irvines, etc., of the old country, first, in order to prove the immutable law of hereditament. The germ of life in man is like the seed of the thistle, that may be borne thousands of miles and fall into rich loam, and it will come up a thistle, as all of its fathers were. It may be warped by strong winds, or increased in size by the rich nourishment of its new home, but it will still bear the unmistakable marks of its ancestors, and wounds, if one handle it too roughly. The same courage and strength of mind that the ancestors of the Irvines of the old country displayed on many a battlefield have been repeated by their descendants in this new land. The same ability in literature, statesmanship, and theology, that characterized many an Irvine of the old country, has distinguished the Irvines of America.

The training and easy living of many generations of pure-blooded men make aristocrats. The ease that wealth and careful training of many generations of aristocrats give, enervates and depletes them. They diminish in size and strength, and lose, in a measure, their hardihood and capacity to endure, but never lose the distinctive characteristics of their race.

Read the long list of honors won by the Irvines of Scotland, England, and Ireland, and then follow their descendants, from 1729 when they first landed in Pennsylvania, down to the present time, and be convinced that the law of hereditament in man is as immutable as the law that governs the animal and vegetable worlds. Is not the blood in man as strong to paint its likeness, from generation to generation, as the sap that colors the rose on its tree, with unchanging fidelity, from year to year and from age to age, in all climates and in every land?

County Antrim, Ireland, has furnished five Presidents to the United States:

First — Andrew Jackson, whose father was born at Ballahill, near Carrickfergus Castle (now a fortress), County Antrim, Ireland, and emigrated to America and settled in Tennessee, near Fort Bledsoe, near where Gallatin now stands. Andrew Jackson was born there, and became President of the United States. He is related to

IRVINGS OF HODDOM

Irvine.
IRISH BRANCH

Irwin
CAMLIN.

IRVINGS OF BONSHAW

Alexr. Irvine Esqr. of Drum

DE LA CHEVOIS T IRWIN
C.M.G.
IRVINES OF CASTLE FORTAGE

the Irvines as follows: Sarah Jackson, sister to President Andrew Jackson's grandfather, married Frances Craig; the daughter of Sarah Jackson and Francis Craig, Anne by name, married Alexander Irvine, son of Robert Irvine and Elizabeth Wylie, his wife. The son of Anne Craig and Alexander Irvine married —— Gault, whose family were of the nobility, and lived at Glenoe, Ireland, where his three sons, William, Christopher, and Andrew, were born. Alexander Irvine, with his wife and three sons, emigrated to Bedford county, Virginia, where, shortly after his removal, he and his wife died on the same day, and were buried in one grave. The Virginia Irvines reared Andrew, who was a lad when his parents died, and the Pennsylvania Irvines reared Christopher and William. All three of the sons of —— Gault and Alexander Irvine were in the war of the American Revolution.

Second — President Benjamin Harrison's grandfather, four times removed, Benjamin by name, came to Pennsylvania, 1642, lived at Ballamena, County Antrim, Ireland. John Scott Harrison married Elizabeth Irwin.

Third —'President Theodore Roosevelt is descended from the great house of Drun, Aberdeen, [North Britain. (Pedigree in full elsewhere.)

The ancestors of Andrew Johnston lived at Ballamena, County Antrim, Ireland.

The ancestors of President Garfield lived at Lisburn, County Antrim, Ireland.

President McKinley's ancestors lived at Dervock, County Antrim, Ireland.

There is no district in all Ireland so rich in armorial bearings as the neighborhood of Larne. The churchyards of Carncastle, Glynn, and Raloo abound with them. The churchyard of Raloo is overgrown with long grass and weeds, so as to be almost inaccessible. But one may pull aside obstructions and remove lichens from the tall gray tombstones; trace the arms carved upon them, and read the names of the Craigs, M'Dowells, Crawfords, Boyds, and others. In the churchyard of Raloo, Margaret McDowell lies buried. She was the wife of Ephraim McDowell, and daughter of Robert Irvine.

There is an old book, more than six hundred years old (I was told), that I found at Fair Hill, near Larne. It had belonged to successive sextons for hundreds of years, from the dates it contained, the last one being 1775, and giving a description of the flag adopted by the American Colonies. It is written in longhand, and has pen-pictures of the Coats of Arms of the Carlisles, Earls of Kilmarnock, McDowells, Irvines, Johnstons, Crawfords, and Blairs, and many others not connected with this history. In the beginning of the book this appears, written in a clerkly hand:

"*Nobilitatis virtus non stemma*" (virtue, not pedigree, is the mark of nobility).

Says this same old chronicle: "A son, who was named James, was born to Christopher Irvine, shortly after he fell at Flodden Field. He had two sons, Robert and John, who fled to Ireland in time of the English persecution, and settled at Glenoe. John afterwards removed to Cushandall and became a Presbyterian minister. John Irvine had two sons, one named Abram, the other Robert, who went to America, and Robert Irvine, Sr., had sons who went to America.

Robert Irvine built a house, in 1585, of red limestone, roofed in by slate. It stands just outside of the village of Glenoe. Passing down the one long street of that village, bordered on each side by tall stone houses, once the property of the Irvines and McDowells, one is struck by the good repair in which they remain, after withstanding the storms of centuries. The blacksmith-shop of Ephraim McDowell looks as if he had laid his hammer down but yesterday, and gone with his brothers-in-law, Alexander Irvine (not his brother-in-law then, as Ephraim was a mere lad, as was Alexander Irvine also), to Londonderry to fight for "The Faith" behind the weak walls, in time of the famous siege. Ephraim was fifty years old when he came to America.

I followed the narrow, rocky street until I came to the mills, once belonging to the Irvines, Wylies, and McDowells. The mill-wheels are still now, and moss and rust-covered, and the mills are open to the night-birds, and afford homes for tramps, who sometimes seek lodging in that picturesque spot.

The Ballyvallog furnished the water power that turned these wheels of the many mills, so sadly silent now. It is a narrow stream and runs across a beautiful brae, falling seventy-five feet into a well-shaped opening in solid rock, into a pool that no plummet has ever fathomed. From this pool the water leaps over an immense stone that crosses the space at the bottom of the opening of this well, formed by nature, and just opposite the waterfall. The village of Glenoe is the most silent place I ever saw. If any business is carried on there, I couldn't discern it. It seems but a monument of the long ago.

SHAW CARNCASTLE

GOD'S PROVIDENCE IS
MY INHERITANCE

VINCER VEL MORI

McDOWELL

TRUSTY AND TRUE

McELROY

GAULT   ARMS.

MOTTO: Laudem implebitur.

VOLO NON VALEO

Carlisle

BOYD
CONFIDO

History should be painted as a stern goddess, with Truth on her right hand and Memory on her left, while in the background should appear Tradition, like a wandering light glimmering along the quicksands of oblivion, and in the foreground should stand an angel pointing to the future.

—SORROWS OF NANCY.

ACCOUNT OF SCOTTISH BORDERS IN EARLY TIMES.

A short account of the conditions of the Scottish Borders before the Union may perhaps be of interest as introduction to the history of an old Dumfriesshire family.

This sketch consists largely of extracts and quotations from well-known authorities, and refers more particularly to the Western Marches.

Even from the earliest historical times, the Borders were the scenes of constant conflicts; no sooner had the country been overrun and settled by one race of invaders than another invasion took place with fresh bloodshed; struggle succeeded struggle, till by the end of the twelfth century the inhabitants consisted of an extremely mixed race, descended chiefly from Picts, Scots, Saxons, Norwegians, Danes, and Normans.[1]

After the Norman Conquest of England, large numbers of Saxons fled into Scotland, and later on various powerful Normans also settled there and obtained large estates, both on the English and Scottish borders.

There had been frequent wars between England and Scotland in the twelfth century, but Richard I of England, before starting for the Crusade against the Saracens, made such friendly arrangements with Scotland that for a period of nearly one hundred years there were very few outbreaks between the two countries. This condition of affairs lasted until the death of Alexander III in 1294. By that time numbers of nobles owned large estates in the Border counties of both England and Scotland.[2] Friendly relations prevailed and frequent intercourse between the two countries was carried on without let or hindrance. The similarity of language also helped to promote cordial relations. The Scotch language, from early times up to the end of the fourteenth century, was almost the same as Northern English, though with a number of words derived from races who still spoke Gaelic, or Celtic, after it had been abandoned in all England except Wales.

[1] Buckle's History of Civilization in England, vol. 3, ch. i. McDowall's History of Dumfries, ch. i.

[2] See Scott's "Tales of a Grandfather," vol. 2, ch. iv.

Later on, when Scotland became the ally of France during the wars of independence, a large number of forms and words were adopted from the French. These must be distinguished from the Norman French already introduced into both England and Scotland by the Norman Conquest.[1]

On the death of Alexander III the relations between the two countries became entirely changed. Edward I trumped up old claims to the feudal sovereignty of Scotland, which had been renounced by Richard I, and determined to make himself master of the country. Buckle graphically describes the result, as follows:

"In 1290, Edward I determined to avail himself of the confusion into which Scotland was thrown by disputes respecting the succession to the crown. The intrigues which followed need not be related; it is enough to say that in 1296 the sword was drawn and Edward invaded a country he had long desired to conquer. But he little recked of the millions of treasure and the hundreds of thousands of lives which were to be squandered before that war was over. The contest that ensued was of unexampled length and severity, and in its sad course the Scotch, notwithstanding their heroic resistance and the victories they occasionally gained, had to endure every evil which could be inflicted by their proud and insolent neighbor. The darling object of the English was to subjugate the Scotch, and if anything could increase the disgrace of so base an enterprise it would be that having undertaken it, they ignominiously failed."[2]

The English invaded Scotland, burnt and destroyed the whole country as far north as Frith of Forth, in 1296, 1298, 1310, 1314, 1322, 1336, 1346, 1355, and 1385. During that time the country was constantly overrun and castles and towns laid waste.

The agricultural laborers either fled or were murdered, and the fairest parts of Scotland became a wilderness, overgrown with briers and thickets.[3] Thousands died from want and starvation, and on the authority of contemporary authors, some of the starving inhabitants were even driven to cannibalism.[4]

The inhabitants of the Borders being thus prevented from tilling the ground, or from any other peaceful employment, were

---

[1] See Introduction to Pitscottie's Chronicles, Scottish Text Society Edition, p. 132.

[2] Buckle, vol. 3, ch. i.

[3] Buckle, vol. 3.

[4] Buckle's Leslie.

1. Ruins of Woodhouse.   3. Blackyett House, an old watch-tower.
2. Staple Towers.   4. Merkland Cross.
                  5. Robgill Tower.

driven to inaccessible places in the hills and moor, and were forced to take cattle and other provisions where they could get them. Forming themselves into strong bodies of armed men, all mounted, they made constant forays into the neighboring parts of England, burning and pillaging wherever they went and returning home by the most secret paths and byways, known only to themselves.

The following extract is from Leslie's account of the Borders, and taken almost verbatim:

"They get their living by stealing and reiving, but they are averse to shedding blood, but are not particular whether they steal from English or Scottish.[1] They live chiefly on flesh, milk, and cheese; they do not care much for bread and little for wine.[2] Their buildings are merely huts of sods and branches and they do not care much if they are burnt. They also build strong castles, all made of earth called Peils, which cannot be burnt, and are difficult to destroy.

"Some of the great nobles do not openly take a share in the booty, but they do not like to break with the reivers, as they are useful in time of war.

"When the princes of the country come against them, they take to the hills and morasses, and from there to the woods and rivers. Their horses are light and active, and being unshod they can go over the bogs and marshes where other men could not follow. They have a great contempt for those who go on foot, therefore they are all horsemen, and provided they have good horses and clothes for their wives, they care little about their household gear.

"The old writers say that the Scottish men were in the habit of eating men's flesh, but that ought not to be attributed to all the Scots, but only to the wild men of Annandale.

"They believe that in times of necessity, by the laws of nature, all goods are common, but that slaughter and such like injuries are against the laws of God. They are very revengeful, and will resent any injury against any of the clan. But they are true to their word and hold any of their number in scorn who would go back on his word.

"They are still good Catholics and are fond of singing about the exploits of their ancestors and are never more fond of praying than when driving a prey.

[1] See History of John Leslie, translated into Scottish by James Dalrymple.
[2] Scottish Text Edit., 1888, vol. 1, pp. 97–103.

"The man who can best lead a foray and knows all the by-paths is considered a man of great parts, and is held in great honor."

Froissart speaks of their qualities as soldiers as follows:

"The Scots are both hardy and much inured to war. When they make their invasions into England they march from twenty to twenty-four leagues without halting by day and night. They are all on horseback except the camp followers. They carry no provisions of bread or wine, for their habits of sobriety are such in times of war that they will live for a long time on flesh half sodden and drink river water without wine. They have no use for pots and pans for they dress the flesh of the cattle in the skin. They take none with them, being sure to find plenty.[1]

"Under the flaps of their saddle each man carries a broad plate of metal; behind the saddle a bag of oatmeal. When they have eaten too much of the sodden flesh and their stomachs appear weak and empty, they place the plate over the fire, mix with water their oatmeal and make a cake or biscuit which they eat to warm their stomachs. It is therefore no wonder that they perform a longer day's work than other soldiers.

"The knights are well mounted on large bay horses; the men on little Galloway hackneys, which they never tie up or dress but turn immediately, after the day's march, into the pastures."

The Scots seem to have used as war instruments of music long cows' horns,— see Froissart. "The Scots made such a blasting and noise with their horns, that it seemed as if all the devils in hell had been there."

These horns must not be confused with bagpipes; according to Francesque Michel, bagpipes were introduced into Scotland from either England or France, where they had been in common use for a long time. They seem to have been first used in war during the sixteenth century.[2]

In these warlike days foreign trade was small and manufactures of any kind scarcely existed. Even the weapons and armor which they used had to be imported from abroad. There were numerous laws against exporting horses, cattle, and all provisions into England, but trade with France and Flanders seems to have been encouraged. The only trade of any importance seems to have been salting salmon, and there are numerous Acts regarding the

[1] Vol. 1, ch. xvii.

[2] See critical enquiry into the Scottish language, by Francesque Michel, p. 225.

industry. There were laws fixing the close season; another passed in 1469 prohibits all fishing for three years in tidal waters, to prevent depletion. Other laws dealt with size of barrels and branding of same.[1]

The rivers of Esk and Annan were exempted from the close season on account of the proximity of the English making such regulations useless.

The selling of salmon to Englishmen was prohibited except the English bought it in Scotland for "English gold."

The punishment for breaking the fishing laws was, for first offense, 10 to 40 shillings, and for third offense, death. It may well be imagined that on the borders little or no attention was paid to these laws, or in fact to any others.

There also seems to have been a small trade in hides and codfish. How little the trade of Scotland amounted to is shown by the fact that at the time of the Union, in 1707, the total export trade of Scotland was under £100,000. Up to the seventeenth century, rents were chiefly paid by feudal service and in kind. Fletcher of Saltourne, writing in 1690, says that the poor state of the country was largely due to all rents being paid in kind.

The continued wars with England had greatly weakened the power of the king and proportionately strengthened the powers of the nobility.[2]

The Borders had to bear the first brunt of all English invasions, and so well were they prepared and so used to war that in twenty-four hours from 10,000 to 20,000 men, all armed and mounted, could be raised and assembled by the wardens. When the English invasions became less frequent the Scottish kings made desperate efforts to reduce the power of the nobles and generally to restore order in the Borders. Their services as guardians of the Marches against the English were less often required, and the constant feuds and depredations on the more peaceable inhabitants in the Middle Counties of Scotland became intolerable to the Scottish monarchs, and numerous Acts were passed to bring the Borders into order. The Border and Highland clans were usually classed together in these Acts, probably on account of their general lawlessness, but in constitution and habits the Highland and Lowland clans were altogether different.

[1] See The Laws and Acts of Parliament, by Sir Thomas Murray of Glendook, Edinburgh, 1682, pp. 3, 21, 45, 84, 106, 401, and 433.

[2] See Robertson's History of Scotland, vol. 1, pp. 18–25.

In the Highlands the entire clan was absolutely at the sole command of the chief.

"The chief could determine what king, what government, what religion, his vassals should obey; his word was the only law they respected; a complete devotion to his interests, an absolute obedience to his commands, was the first and almost the single article of their moral code." [1]

In the Borders the conditions of things were entirely different; no traces of any such blind devotion to clan chiefs or leaders can be found. The mixture of the races on the Borders produced a race that was conspicuous for its dogged independence and dourness and insubordination to all authority.

The need for mutual protection, the expectation of mutual benefits to be obtained, and the obedience of a feudal tenant to his landlord probably formed the basis of the Border clans.

The Normans and Saxons who early settled on the Borders introduced the feudal system, traces of which still existed in Scotland till the middle of the nineteenth century.

Robertson remarks that "many years after the declension of the feudal system in the other kingdoms of Europe, and when the arms and policy of princes had everywhere shaken or laid it in ruins, the foundation of that ancient fabric remained in a great measure firm and untouched in Scotland." Thus, the purely clan system of the Highlands was largely interfered with by the great power of the feudal barons.[2]

Up to the middle of the fifteenth century, the Douglasses were all-powerful in Dumfriesshire. After their fall the chief families were the Herries, Maxwells, and Johnstons.

During the long feuds between the Maxwells and Johnstons, which lasted with short intervals for nearly one hundred years, culminating in the battle of Dryfe Sands, 1593, men of the same clan were to be found fighting on both sides, especially amongst the Irvings, Carruthers, Bells, and Armstrongs. Thus, the Irvings of Bonshaw, being related to the Laird of Johnston, took his side, while others in Lower Annandale, being feudal tenants of the Maxwells of Hoddom and Castlemilk, were to be found fighting for the Maxwells.[3]

[1] Leckie's History, vol. 2, ch. vi.
[2] Robertson's History of Scotland, book 1, p. 29.
[3] Johnston's Historical Families of Dumfriesshire, p. 122; McDowall's History of Dumfriesshire, p. 250.

When Regent Murray made a military progress through the border with a large force, with the object of punishing outlaws, numerous heads of families had to give security, or pledge themselves as security, for those under them. Thus, Edward Irving became security for "the haill Irvings, of Bonshaw, their bairns, tenants and servants, and John Irving became security for such numbers of Irvings of Hoddom as shall be declairit that day." Habby Irving became security for the Irvings of Trailtrow.[1]

In 1547, Lord Wharton burnt the town of Annan and the whole of Annandale, and amongst a large number of others the following heads of branches of clans, including both Johnstons and Maxwells, surrendered to him and became security for those under them. "Christie Irving, of Bonshaw, 103, Rythie Irving, called the Duke's Richie, and those under him, 121, Christie Irving, 74, Wat Irving, 22."[2]

There are many similar records of the heads of families becoming security for their immediate dependents, but there are no contemporary records of any one chief on the West Marches ever having given such bond for the whole number of branches of same clan.

In this respect the Border clans are in marked contrast to the Highlands, where the clansmen followed their chiefs as one man.

It seems, therefore, extremely unlikely that any of the smaller clans, such as the Irvings, Bells, and Carruthers, ever had any single chief whom they recognized as the actual leader or chief of all the different branches of the clan; there are no contemporary records pointing that way. The fact that so many different clans inhabited the same valley made any such control almost impossible.

The Lairds of Johnston probably more nearly resembled the Highland chieftains than any others on the Western Marches.

McDowall says, "By the middle of the fourteenth century an immense number of families bearing the Johnston name were to be found in Annandale, all counting kinship with the Laird of Lockwood, their relation towards him being in every respect more like that borne by Highland clansmen to their chief than the feudal vassalage of Norman origin that generally prevails throughout the Lowlands."[3]

There is an old bond of man rent in existence, dated 1555, by which twenty-six different Johnstons bind themselves to follow

---

[1] Register of Privy Council of Scotland, vol. 2, pp. 48–49.
[2] Calendar of Scottish Papers, Bain, 1547–1563.
[3] McDowall's History, pp. 261, 262.

the Laird of Johnston. The mere fact that such a bond was thought necessary shows the radical difference between the Highland and Lowland clans.

After the union of the crowns in 1603, the Borders ceased to be the scene of constant outbreaks. The men who had made war their only business did not easily accommodate themselves to the new condition of affairs, and their condition became most precarious; the wardens of England and Scotland acted together, and cattle-thieving and raiding were put down with a strong hand.

The Grahams of Debatable Land were sent in a body to Ireland; numbers and numbers of the outlaws were banished from the country. Hundreds of men accustomed to no other trade but war went to the Continent as soldiers of fortune. Thus, during the thirty years war in Germany, 1618 - 1648, many of the most prominent generals on both sides came from Scotland. There were Scotch regiments in Germany, Holland, France, and Sweden.

But the troubles of the Borders were not yet over. The attempt to introduce the Episcopacy into Scotland proved as difficult a task as the former attempt to conquer the country. In no part of Scotland were the religious persecutions more severe than on the Borders and West of Scotland, and most abominable outrages and cruelties were perpetrated by Claverhouse, Dalzell, and his followers.

The revolutions in 1689, when William III became King of England and Scotland, and the political union of the countries in 1707, at last brought relief to the blood-stained district. Even then, the inhabitants, being so long accustomed to a wild, warlike life, were unable to settle down to peaceful pursuits and to take advantage of the free trade with England and the colonies which the Union gave to Scotland. It was not until late in the eighteenth century that the Borders began to recover from the effects of centuries of turmoil and trouble, and gave signs of becoming what it now is, one of the fairest and most prosperous districts in the United Kingdom.

The old inhabitants of the Borders were a wild and lawless race, the product of the times they lived in, but it was largely to their courage and perseverance that the Scotch were able to so long maintain their independence, and finally to demand, and at last secure, honorable and fair terms of union with England, a union which resulted in immense benefits to both countries and more particularly to the Borders.

> "The knights are dust
> And their good swords are rust;
> Their souls are with the Saints we trust."

The Hon. Mr. Justice Irwin, C. S. I. (Companion to the Star of India), Rangoon, Burma, Farther India.

PART I.

DERIVATION OF NAME.

(Copied from Dr. Christopher Irvine's " Family of the Irvines," 1678.)

The Erevine, or contracted, Irvine, cometh from the ancient Celto-Sythick Erinvine, or Erinfeine, which signyfieth a true, or stout, Westland man; for Erin, both in the old Galick Welsh and old Galick language signyfieth "the West" (and therefore Ireland is at this day called Erin, both by the ancient Inhabitants and by those of Albin, because its situation is west from Albin). Veine, or feine, signifyeth "himself," which, by way of Excellency, is as much as to say a resolute man, etc.

ORIGINAL SETTLEMENT OF THE IRVINGS, IRVINES, IRWINS, ETC., IN IRELAND AND SCOTLAND, AND THEIR POSSESSIONS THERE.

When the clans of the Galick Nations came from the West Coast of Spain and seated themselves in the East coast of Erin (Ireland), and in the West Hills and Isles of Albin, from Sabrin to the Promontorium, Oncas (now Farohead) which is the utmost point of Strath-navern and most North Promontory of Scotland, then the Erinveines, or Erinfeins, came to both these Islands.

The Silures of South Wales were of these Colonies, as Tacitus affirms, and the Brigantes, both of Albin and Erin, were the same, as all men acknowledge. The Brigantes of Erin had their Seats in the East Coasts, and the Erivines, a great family of them, possessed and gave name to a great Barony that to this day bears their name Ouvon, or Ouvine, which continued in their family until Strongbow's conquest (in the reign of Henry the Second of England).

The Brigantes of Albin did possess the North parts of Wales, and all the Countries of (now) England and Scotland from Wales to Clyde, *ad Glotee æstauarium.*

The family of the Ervinvines, amongst them, had their seat in that part of Albin that is now called Cuninghame; they gave their name to the river and to their palace, which is now called the Town of Irvine; they remained possessed thereof until the banishing of the Albin-Scots by the Romans, after the death of Eugenius the First, their King, about the year A. D. 373.

The Expulsion and Return of the Erivines into Albin with Fergus the Second.

Eugenius, the first King of Albin-Scots, being killed in battle (with many of the nobles) by the joint forces of the Romans, Picts, and Britons, the Roman General, Maximus, seized the Scottish territories in Albin, and banished the natives out of the continent. Ethodius, brother to the late King, with his son, Ethus, and nephew, young Fergus, attended by divers of the chief Clans (amongst them the Erinvines), being banished, sailed for Scandia, where they were kindly received by the King thereof, out of hatred of the Romans. These Albin Scots, assisted by the Irish Scots, having made several attempts to recover their liberty and possessions, were at length totally subdued, and the Irish forced to return to Erin, whereby, all hopes of recovering their native country being lost, Fergus remained many years in exile. At this time the Northern nations, making several incursions into the Roman provinces, especially into Hungary and Gaul, greatly annoyed the Romans. Fergus, now grown to man's estate, joined them, with the exiled Scots, and went to the Hungarian Wars, where the Irvines that were in the expedition, and one of the principal Clans of the Scots, greatly distinguished themselves under their valiant commander Fergus, and left that noble family, which to this day are Earls (or counts), and do carry the name of Erin (as before said), and own their origin from the Scottish Irvines, that served against the Romans in the train of Fergus, in the Hungarian Wars. There is likewise another family, still in Spain, that bears the same name of Ervin, and is supposed to be the original of all.

The Picts and Scots being both weary with the tyranny of the Romans, joined in recalling Fergus (whose heroic actions had acquired him great reputation among them), in hopes, by his means, to recover their lost liberties. He accepted the invitation, and returning to Albin, was made King of the Scots by the name of Fergus the Second. With him the Erevines returned, and were restored to their ancient possessions in 104, as were the other exiles.

Besides the lands the Irvines possessed on the South side of the Clyde, and on the North Side, in Grangebarge, they had the Lands of Dule, and their chief habitation was in the Castle Garth.

These lands lie on the North Side of the river Tay, from the rise thereof until it joins with the Tummel. It is commonly called Strath Tay.

CRINUS EREVINE, THE FOUNDER OF A ROYAL LINE IN SCOTLAND AND OF THE KINGS OF THE NAME OF IRVINE

We read in history that Crinus (or Crine) Erevine, to whom aforesaid possessions belonged by right of inheritance, was Abthane of Dule (the highest title of honor then in Scotland), and Seneschal and Collector of the King's Rents in the West Isles, and a man of great note and authority in those days. And to this day the church of Irvine, where he lies interred, is called after him — Aphthin Dull, corruptly, for Abthan Dule. Crine Irvine, in the year 1004, married Beatrix, eldest daughter and heiress of Malcolm II., King of Scotland (as Joannes Major, or Mr. Maine, a Doctor of the Sorbonne, and our first printed History of Scotland relates on the 41st leaf and 2nd page). By her he begat Duncan I., King of Scotland, who mounted the throne 1034. So that all the Kings of Scotland, from Malcolm II., until John Balliol, were Irvines, and male descendants of the said Crine Erevine and Beatrix, Heiress of Scotland (except McBeath the usurper, who was son to the younger daughter of Malcolm). Duncan I., being treacherously slain by McBeath in 1040, that usurper held the government until he was, in 1057, slain by Malcolm III., called Kenmore. But he (Kenmore) was dethroned by Duncan II. (natural son of Malcolm III.), who was dispossessed by Edgar, legitimate son of said Malcolm III., by Margaret, sister to Edgar Atheling. He was succeeded by his brother, Alexander I., called the Fierce, in 1107. His brother, David I., mounted the throne in 1124. He was succeeded by Malcolm IV., his grandson, in 1153; he by William the Lion, his brother, in 1165; he by Alexander II., his son, 1214; he by his son Alexander III., in 1249; who, dying without male issue, and his granddaughter, Margaret of Norway, dying on her passage to Scotland, the crown was disputed by John Balliol and Robert Bruce, both descended, in the female line, from David Erevine, Earl of Huntingdon, brother to Malcolm IV. and William, Kings of Scotland.

This famous contest is too well known to require recounting, as also, the injustice of Edward Longshanks, King of England, who was chosen referee by the contending parties, and upon what dishonorable terms to Scotland he awarded the Crown to John Balliol, until that great Prince, Robert the Bruce, shook off the bondage under which Scotland lay, and restored the monarchy to its former lustre. From this record, it appears that the Ervines reigned in Scotland, in the male line, from 1034 to the death of Alexander III., in 1285, and in right of the female line to this day.

Crine Erevine, or Irvine, being dead, and his patrimony falling to his son, King Duncan, the country was called Cuninghame, that is in the old Pictish language (or Barlea), Koningshame, the King's habitation (several of the Kings of that race residing here), which country was by his successors given to several families.

The Settlement of the Irvings in the Borders and the Origin of the Family of Bonshaw.

About this time, the several families of the Albins sent the most stout and able men of their Clans to the Borders to defend the same; first in the reign of Fergus II., against the Romans and Britons, and afterwards against the Saxons or Sessions, now called English; among the rest Irvines were sent, brothers to the former Abthanes. They took up their first habitation upon the river Esk, between the White and the Black Esk, and built their first habitation, which to this day is called Castle Irvine, or Irvine's Hall; ruinous now. Below the Langham, the brook and oak wood still carry the name of Irvine Wood and Irvine Burn. From thence, by marriage, the eldest of that family got the lands of Bonshaw, and many other lands there, and married into the best families in the South of Scotland.

"From the time that the Bruce had recovered the independence of Scotland, and driven out the armies of England from Scottish territory, a spirit of hostility began to pervade the borders of both Kingdoms, which gave rise to a chronic system of border warfare. A warlike temper amongst the Borderers caused them to frequently turn their swords against each other, without regard to nationality, by which private feuds were engendered between Scottish families within their own borders, in addition to their national hostilities against the English beyond. So that property in that part of Dumfriesshire came, for the most part, to be held by the sword, and the West Marches became a kind of separate Dominion, outside the sway and protection of the government of the kingdom."

The authority of the Crown, in order to suppress this lawlessness, made use of forfeitures and confiscations, to bring the Borderers to order. But the power of the State being in the hands of the

nobility, these measures ended usually in conferring these forfeited lands, by royal grants, upon influential nobles — who showed
the lawless spirit which then existed, "When might made right."

By forfeiture, consequently, the greater part of Dumfriesshire
fell into the hands of the Crown.   In the Fifteenth century, a great
portion of these possessions were made over to the families of Douglas and Hume.   And at the beginning of the Sixteenth century,
extensive grants were made to the Maxwells, a Border family and
Clan which had then come into much favor at Court.

During these commotions the Irvines suffered greatly.   Their
possessions, lying on the front line of Border warfare, not only were
they exposed to their enemies within their own country, but were
also exposed to the invasions of the English, as the Scotch border
on that side lay open to England.   So, therefore, as other families
gained in power, they lost ground, under the continual devastations,
burnings, "reift and slaughter," to which they were subjected,
and in meeting which all their energies and resources became
exhausted; and as they frequently turned their failing forces against
the Crown, or those who held its authority, when they were defeated
they were punished as rebels and their lands confiscated.

Christopher Irvine, Laird of Bonshaw, who was head of the
family in the beginning of the Sixteenth century, commanded an
body of light horseman. of tenants, retainers, clansmen, etc., in the
last expedition of King James IV. into England, which ended in the
disastrous battle of Flodden Field, Sept. 9, 1513, where Laird
Christopher fell, with the most of his followers.   After Flodden
Field, the English invaded and desolated the Border regions of
Dumfries, which then became a scene of much disorder.

The war with England which led to the battle of Solway Moss,
November 24, 1542, proved disastrous to the Scottish Marches,
as the death of King James V. took place directly afterwards, and
the English army, following up their victory, occupied portions of
Dumfriesshire, wasting and plundering the whole country.   For
many years after this time, this devoted territory remained
reduced to great distress.

In 1547 King Henry VIII. of England died, and the war broke
out with renewed violence.   The Protector, The Duke of Somerset,
in order to enforce the marriage of Mary, Queen of Scotland, with
Edward VI. of England, tried to subjugate Scotland, and to quell
the hostility of the Borderers of Dumfriesshire, which, for a time,
was annexed to England.   In order to make headway against the

powerful English armies, they were forced to give their adherence to the Crown of England, and submit, unwillingly, to the English yoke. In the course of this war, Bonshaw was taken, plundered, and burned to the ground, all excepting the tower, which had been built in 900 A. D., and was so constructed that fire could injure it but very little, the floors, only, being of wood.

From 1550, peace prevailed between England and Scotland, but the Borderers did not at once reap all the benefits of this change. The cessation of national hostilities led at first to a revival of family feuds hitherto held in check by the long war with England.

A hereditary feud existed between the Irvines and the Bells, a powerful Border clan, who had the support of the Carlyles, another Border family. For a time the Irvines had the advantage over these two clans, which was lost, however, about the middle of the century mentioned above. The Irvines, besides these and minor hostilities with other clans, had also a feud with the Maxwells, the most powerful of the West Border clans. The grants made by the Crown to the Maxwells included Eskdale, Ewisdale, Wauchopdale, etc., lands confiscated, that had once belonged to the Irvines. This brought the Irvines and the Maxwells into collision, and was the origin of the feud between them. But so great was the power of the Maxwells, supported as they were by the Crown, that they were quite a match for any other of the Border families, and their preponderance of influence threatened to overturn the balance of power in Dumfriesshire. The Johnstons, the strongest of the other Border clans, were also aroused against the Maxwells, and, with the Irvines and other lesser clans, combined to withstand them. An alliance was formed of the greater part of the East Dumfriesshire families, including the Johnstons, the Carlyles, the Irvines, the Bells, the Elliotts, the Graemes and the Armstrongs, under the leadership of Johnston, to oppose the Maxwells and the families of West Dumfriesshire who supported them, and the contest filled all Dumfriesshire with civil war during the remainder of the century.

An old Scottish poet (1490–1567), Sir David Lindsay, thus commemorates the Irving Clan:

> "Adew! my bruthir Annan thieves
> That holpit me in my mischevis;
> Adew! Grossars, Vicksonis and Bells,
> Oft have we fairne owrthrench the fells:
> Adew! Robsons, Howis and Pylis,
> That in our craft has mony evilis:
> Littlis, Trumbells and Armstronges;
> Adew! all thieves that me belangis;

> Bailowes, Erewynis and Elwandis,
> Speedy of flicht and slicht of handis;
> The Scotts of Eisdale and the Gramis,
> I haif na time to tell your nameis."

When the period of the Reformation had spread widely over England and Scotland, owing to the distracted state of the Western Borders, the turbulent spirit of these Borderers who were carrying on war with each other prevented them from investigating doctrinal questions, and they regarded the controversy from a political standpoint. As their enemies, the English, were Protestants, they took the side of Rome, and when the war broke out between Queen Mary and her insurgent subjects, the Irvings adhered to her cause, as did all the principal families of the Western Marches, including the Johnstons and Maxwells. On this account, the Earl of Murray Regent of Scotland, after having defeated and driven Queen Mary into England, led an army into Dumfriesshire to subdue the chieftains and their clans. The submission he obtained by this measure, however, was only temporary. The Borderers still remained loyal to Queen Mary, and when opportunity offered, again took up arms in her behalf.

A conspiracy was organized, not only throughout Great Britain, but in foreign countries as well, inflamed by zeal for the church of Rome, which broke out in a dangerous rebellion of the Roman Catholics in the North of England. When Elizabeth had subdued these, she turned her attention to crushing the Borderers of the Western Marches of Scotland. English armies invaded that region, contrary to the peace that had existed between the two kingdoms, and laid it waste with fire and sword. On that occasion, Bonshaw was again taken, sacked, and burned.

Edward Irving was a turbulent chieftain, as were all the lairds or chieftains of that period. He was succeeded by his son, Christopher Irving, a still more dauntless and daring chieftain than his father, who was known to the Borderers as "Black Christie," on account of the black armour which he wore. He entertained King James VI. at Bonshaw Tower in 1588.

The war between the Johnstons, Irvings, and their clans, and the Maxwells occupied the West Marches during the concluding portion of the sixteenth century. Lord Maxwell had reached the summit of his power, when, as Lord Warden, he was enabled to denounce his enemies as traitors, and wield the authority of the Crown against them. In 1584 Dumfriesshire was reduced to a desert waste. Lockwood Castle was besieged, taken, ravaged, and

then burned to the ground.   Lockwood was the residence of Laird
Johnston, but he escaped harm in the battle and fled to Bonshaw
Tower, of which place, at that time, Christopher Irving was laird
and chieftain.   Maxwell then laid siege to Bonshaw, which, however, was able to hold out until terms of peace were agreed upon
through the mediation of the English Lord Warden.

As long as the Maxwells remained the strongest party,
King James VI. (of gentle memory) was on their side.   But after
the Johnstons and Irvings defeated them, then King James
made Johnston the Lord Warden of the Marches.

But such were the oppressions practiced in retaliation on the
Maxwells by Johnston and his clans, that King James, on his accession to the throne of England, in 1603, adopted the measure of
destroying the iron yetts, or gates, of the border castles.   But still,
for a hundred years, the old lawless spirit lived on in the hearts of
the Borderers.   (It slumbers in this, the twentieth Century, but it is
not dead.)

We have a list of the several branches of the Annandale Irvings
and their fighting forces contained in Bishop Nicholson's *Leges
Marchiarum:*

"On the West Borders the following barons and clans gave
pledges to Lord Wharton, Warden of the English Marches, that they
would serve the King of England, with the number of followers
annexed to their names, in 1574:

Lairds.	Annsdale 1574.	Lairds.	
Kirkmighel	222	Patrick Murry	203
Rose	165	Christie Murry of Coveshawe	102
Hempsfield	163	Cuthbert Urwin of Robgill	34
Home-Ends	162	The Urwins of Senerbeck	40
Wamfray	102	Wat. Urwin of Bonshaw	120
Dunwoody	44	Jeffrey Urwin of Woodhouse	93
Newby and Gratney	122	William Urwin of Kirkonnel	184
Timmel	102	James Urwin of Stapleton	74

Again, from Bishop Nicholson in *Leges Marchiarum:* "There
is no place in Scotland or England which contains so many monu-
ments of feudal times as the banks of the Kirtle and its vicinity."
There are Bell Tower, Kirconnel Abbey, Blacket (Blackyett) House
Tower, Bonshaw, Robgill, Woodhouse and Stapleton Towers, with
the ruins of Red Hall and Fleming Towers; the beautiful Cross
at Merkland, the cross for fair Helen at Kirkconnel churchyard,
and the wonderful Cove House, all within the circuit of a few miles.

All once belonging to the Irvings, and, tradition says, all were connected by tunnels. Just below the north battlement of Bonshaw Tower is a strange shaft, built in the wall of the Tower, and leading far below the huge foundation stones. One who drops a lighted torch in this narrow stone shaft may watch it die out at an immeasurable distance below, perhaps in the tunnel that still connects the castles or manor houses that once belonged to the Irvings.

Fair Helen Irving of Kirkconnel! No sadder love story was ever written than that of fair Helen. She had two suitors, of whom she preferred the one named Fleming. One evening Helen and her accepted lover were walking by Kirtle Water, when Helen saw her rejected lover, on the opposite bank of the river, level his gun at Fleming. She covered her lover's heart with her own, and receiving the shot meant for him, fell dead at his feet. Some records have it that Fleming avenged Helen's death at once; others that Fleming met the murderer on a battlefield in Spain and shot him to death. Be that as it may, Fleming left his native land for years after Helen's death, and did not return until he was old and gray. None knew of his return until he was found dead by Helen's grave one morning. He was buried beside her. Their tombstones are exactly alike, long and narrow, lying even with the ground, and touching their full length. Time, rain and lichens have long since effaced the inscriptions traced on these stones with loving, pitying care, but the ghost of a sword is still to be seen on Fleming's stone. Sir Walter Scott and Wordsworth visited these graves, and each embalmed the fate of the lovers in verse.

The old Kirk is in ruins now. The roof is fallen in, and but one wall is left standing, from which the pilgrim may surmise what a goodly church it once was. I climbed the moss-grown steps to the entrance door, and looked within. All trace of flooring had disappeared. Heaps of stones and mortar, covered by rank weeds and grass, marked the place where hundreds of years ago a congregation knelt when prayer was wont to be offered up. This was the church that Helen and her lover attended. I wondered where she sat, and where Fleming. As I turned to the stones that covered this unfortunate pair, and which are well cared for, I could but whisper: It is the intangible, not the material, that is immortal, even in this life. Since these two unfortunates were laid to rest, towers and castles have fallen; churches lie in heaps of moss-grown ruins; kings have died and been forgotten, but this Border love tale is still retold, and will be for centuries to come.

1. Hoddom Castle, Seat of Laird   2. Milkbank, Seat of Laird John Bell
   Brooke.   Irving.

PART II.

INTRODUCTION.

Faint notices — not very reliable we fear — are given by pedigree-makers respecting some Nithsdale families of this early time.

Nuath, son of Coel Godhebog, a Cumbrian prince who flourished before 300, owned lands in Annandale and Clydesdale, it is said, which were named, after him, Caer-nuath or Carnwath. If this statement could be relied upon, it would be no very bold hypothesis to say that the River Nith also, owes its name to the son of God-hebog. One of Nuath's descendants, of the fourth generation, Loth, a Pictish King, formed a strong encampment along the base of the Tynwald Hills, which bore the appellation of Barloth. The second son, Gwallon, built a chain of forts extending from Dryfes-dale to the vicinity of Lochmaben, the designation of which is still preserved in the existing farm of Galloberry.

Gwallon's sister, Thenelis, was the mother of the celebrated Kentigern, or St. Mungo, whose name is retained by a Dumfriesshire parish. Marken or Marcus, brother of Loth, had a son named Kinder; to him belonged the district which now forms the parish of Newabbey, and which was at first called after him, Loch Kinder. A son of Kinder, Yrein or Yrvin, owned lands in Eskdale which bore his name; and to him it is that the prolific family of the Irv-ings, who, ages afterwards, flourished in Annandale, and often held civic rule in Dumfriesshire, owe their origin.—*History of the Burgh of Dumfries.*

Irvine, a surname of ancient standing in Scotland, supposed to have been originally Erevin, the latter word derived, according to some antiquaries, from the Celtic-Scythic Erin-vine or fein, that is, a stout Westland man; Erin, west, and vine or fein, a strong, resolute man.

Nisbet (*System of Heraldry*, vol. II. App. p. 69) says that when the colonies of the Gauls came from the west coasts of Spain, and seated themselves in the east coasts of Erin and in the west hills and islands of Albyn, the Erevines came to both these islands.

In the latter country, they had their seats in that part of Ayrshire called Cunningham, and gave their name to the river, and to their own part of residence, now the town of Irvine. One of them, Crine Erwine, was Abthane of Dull, and Seneschal and Collector of all the King's rents in the Western Isles. He married the princess Beatrix, eldest daughter of Malcolm II., and was father of Duncan I., King of Scotland.

Some of this family went south to Dumfriesshire, and settled on the river Esk. (*The Scottish Nation*, by William Anderson.) When the Irvings first came to the Scots border to form a Border guard, they appear to have entrenched themselves at Auchenrivock, on the banks of the Irving Burn, near Langholm, where they had a tower, a fragment of which still remains. They quickly spread from Eskdale to Annandale, where they could watch the various fords of the rivers and also the crossings of the Solway. About 1550 they occupied most of the country from the Esk to Gretna, up the valleys of the Sark and Kirtle, along the shores of the Solway and Annan, up that river to Hoddom, and as far north as Burnswark Hill in Annandale. Their chief towers and strongholds at that time were: Bonshaw, Woodhouse, Robgill, Cove, Starkheuch, Sark, Gretna, Kirkconnel, Kirkpatrick, Redhall, Stapleton, Luce, Turnshaw, Trailtrow and Hoddom. They seem to have intermarried chiefly with their neighbours, the Grahams, Johnstones, and Bells, and to have assisted each other in their various raids and clan fights.

IRVINGS OF HODDOM.

There is no accurate account of when the ancestors of the Irvings called "Dukes of Hoddom" first came to lower Annandale, but it was probably some time in the Twelfth century. That part of the clan which settled in Hoddom is supposed to have had its first stronghold where Hallguards now stands, at the bend of the Annan, above Hoddom bridge. Their old burying ground is immediately below the bridge, where Kentigern (St. Mungo), the patron Saint of the Irvings, is said to have had a chapel; and within a short distance are still the Duke's pool on the Annan, — famous for its salmon, — the Duke's meadow, the Duke's mill, etc.

In "*Acta Dominorum Concilii*, November 6, 1490," there is

reference to "John Irvin callit the Duc," who was up before the Bishops of Glasgow and Aberdeen, Chancellor Earl of Buchan, Lords Gray, Oliphant, and Drummond, for some offence; John Lindsay of Wauchop and William Grahame of Moskeswray becoming surety for the Duc.

The word Duke, or Duc, as above written, may have meant leader or chief, but it was evidently of French origin. When Archibald, Earl of Douglas, entered on a military campaign and joined the Scottish Legion in France, in 1420, the Douglases held lands in Hoddom, and his force being composed entirely of Borderers, the leader of the Irvings was probably honoured with the military title of Duc. Be that as it may, however, the name was applied to the head of the Hoddom Irvings for some two hundred years.

The Douglas Book refers to an interesting marriage contract between Andrew Herries, son of Herbert, Lord Herries of Terregles, and Janet of Douglas, in 1495, affecting certain lands in Hoddom formerly belonging to Archibald, Earl of Douglas. This marriage was probably the origin of the Herries connection with Hoddom.

In 1528, the injuries committed by the Scots upon the West March of England are referred to in Bruce Armstrong's History: "The xxx day of May tymlie in the morning the Amstrongs with the Irwens of Hoddom, Scottismen, com to the ground betwixt Eske and Levon, and there brunt all the houses hereafter mentioned," etc.

In 1545, Duke Ritchie of Hoddom is mentioned as having 142 followers. (Calendar of State Papers.) In 1552, among the Scottismen sworn to defend the Kynge's Majesty was Rychie Irwin, called Duke's Rychie (son of the Duke), and those under him, 127 men, the fighting strength of the clan then sworn being given at 431 men. When William, Lord Herries, died in 1547, Hoddom, of which Knockhill formed part, was left to his three daughters — Lady Agnes, who married John, Master of Maxwell, afterwards Warden of the West Marches; Lady Katherine, who married Stewart, son of Sir Alexander Stewart, of Garlies, and Lady Janet, who married James Cockburn, of Stirling, Knight. Lady Agnes, in February, 1549, got a crown charter of the third part of the £20 land of Hoddom, her sisters getting the other two-thirds. On the 20th May following (1549), Lady Agnes made over to Richard Irving her charter, which ran as follows: "To all the sundry, etc.:

Agnes Herries, eldest daughter and one of the three heirs of that noble and potent Lord William Herries, and spouse, to John, Master of Maxwell (afterwards Lord Warden), with the express consent and assent of my beloved husband, for the good and faithful services done to him and me by our well beloved Richard Irving (called of old, Duke Richie), and to be done in time to come, and me being willing and most earnestly desiring thankfully to reward the said Richard, etc., not only to have given and disponed, and by-this our present charter confirmed, but also by these present gives, grants, and by this present charter confirms to the said Richard, his heirs and assigns, all and haill, that third part of all and haill my twenty pound land of old extent of Hoddom, extending to one ten merk land of old extent, with its pertinents, lying within the parish of Hoddom, and stewartry of Annandale, etc., to the said Richard Irving (otherwise called Duke Ritchie), his heirs and assigns, of me and my heirs and assigns, in feu and heritage forever.

"In its haill, meaths and marches, both old and divided, as they lie in length and breadth, in valleys, plains, muirs, mosses, ways, paths, waters, stanks, rivers, meadows, pastures, and pasturages, mills, millheads, with their sequels, hawking, hunting, fishing, turfs, peats, coals, cunnings, cunningards, dewes, dewcots, smith-smidies, brooms, whins, woods, frogs, bushes, timber trees, quarries, freestone and whinstone, with courts with their appertenants, bloodwilts, and the marchel mulievum, etc., etc., beneath the earth, and above the earth, far and near, belonging or any ways known to appurtain and belong to the said third part of the forsaid twenty pound land, etc.

"Therefore, yearly, the said Richard Irving, his heirs and assigns forsaid, to me my heirs and assigns, waived and relief of the foresaid lands with their pertinents with the marriage of the heir when it shall happen, etc.

"I, the above named Agnes Herries, with consent and assent of my said husband, binds and charges us, our heirs and assigns, to acquit and forever to defend all and haill the foresaid third part of the twenty pound land, etc. to the said Richard Irving, his heirs and assigns foresaid, to be free, safe and sure at all hands and against all deadly.

"In witness thereof, I have subscribed this my charter, and appended my seal, together with the seal and manual subtz of the said John, Master of Maxwell, my said husband. In token of his consent and assent to the premises, at Dumfries, the twenty day of May, and year of God one thousand five hundred and forty-nine, before these witnesses — John Hayparth, David Maxwell, John Maxwell, Cuthbert Irving of Rogill (Robgill), and Mr. John.

"David Neaper, notar public *sic subtz*, Agnes Herries, led on the pen by David Neapar, notar, *sic subtz*, David Neaper, notar, *sic subtz*, John Maxwell."

The twenty pound land was the whole of what belonged to Lord William Herries in Hoddom, except the ten pound land of Ecclefechan. His eldest daughter, Agnes, got one third, and that is what is represented by the ten merk land of Knockhill, White Hill (so far as lies in Hoddom) and Duke's Close. From the fact that Cuthbert Irving, of Robgill, and his son John were witnesses to the charter on behalf of Richard Irving, they were probably near connections, whilst Richard and John occur elsewhere as family names among the Robgill Irvings.

Blean's map, 1660, rather indicates the Duke's Tower as having been on the site of Hallguards, but Knockhill, less than a mile away, was afterwards their residence. The Tower is also called "Duke of Hoddom's" on Moll's map, 1725.

The valuable services more recently rendered by Richard Irving to Lord Maxwell were probably in connection with the driving of Lords Wharton and Lennox over the Border in 1548, after the disastrous battle of Solway Moss, where Lord Maxwell's father was taken prisoner; besides, the Hoddom Irvings had a grievance to redress, as appears from Lord Wharton's letter, September 6, 1544, wherein he records the result of his expedition across the West Marches of Scotland thus: "Burnt the town of Crookedmoore, the Maynes of Hoddolm, the towns of Hodholme, Suplebank, Peelstells, laird Latymers lands, the townes of Bushe, Bonelands, Holme and Crooke, and all the Peeles houses, corn and sheds within Hodholm.

"The same burnt the townes of Middleby and Haglefleigham, and all the Peeles houses, corn and sheds in Middleby, and in their return burnt Bonshaw, Robgill and all the Peeles houses, sheds, and corn in their way; 4 Scots slayn."

In 1545 Duke Richie of Hoddom, in addition to having 142 followers of his own, had also, in time of need, the support of his neighbours, the Irvings of Luss, Pennesax, Turnshaw, Trailtrow, etc., the two latter places being just across the Annan from Hoddom. It is on record that the Irvings of Trailtrow kept up the bale fires on Trailtrow Hill before the Watch Tower of Repentance was built by Lord William Maxwell, afterwards Lord Herries, about the year 1560. In 1541 Habby of Trailtrow had two sons, John and Dick, and their grant of Wardpark adjoining the beacon, is still known by that name. Earl William of Douglas is referred to in 1448 as having appointed a warden to erect, maintain and fire the beacons on the approach of the English by way of the Solway fords.

The Duke of Hoddom was a supporter of Queen Mary, and fought at the battle of Langside in 1568. Lord Herries was in command of the Horse, consisting entirely of Borderers. Mary was defeated and fled to England, where, after being long imprisoned, she was executed by order of Elizabeth. The adherents of the unfortunate Queen were afterwards treated very severely, and James VI. and Regent Murray, on their march from Hawick to Dumfries via Langholm and Hoddom, when they lay in camp at castle Milk for two days, visited the Queen's sympathisers with no gentle hands.

On October 28, 1569, in a summons to appear before James VI., with Murray encamped on the Watersof Milk, Adam Carlisle, of Brydekirk, and John Irving, younger son to the Duke, "oblissit them to enter the Duke aldar (senior) in Dumfries on Sunday to ly as pledge for sic nowmer of the Irvings of Hoddom as sal be declarit that day, under pane of 2000 merks."

James Douglas, of Dumlanrig, had also to be surety for Bonshaw and Trailtrow, and Alexander Stewart of Garlies, for Turnshaw. (Register of Privy Council of Scotland.)

In 1570, Lord Scrope, the English Warden, made a raid into Dumfriesshire, by order of Queen Elizabeth, to punish those who had supported Queen Mary. On April 21st of that year, Scrope reported that he had "burned the Tower of Hoddom-Maynes, Trailtrow and other places; took and cast down the Castles of Carlavrock, Hoddom, and Dumfries, and burned Dumfries to the blackness of ashes." Hoddom appears to have been mixed up with most of the Border raids and feuds of those times. In 1578, as the result of some controversy between Jonne Irving, the Duke, and Alexander Carlyle, of Brydekirk, both were imprisoned in Dumfries, Carlyle being kept there for twenty-two months, Irving being let out on bail. Carlyle was the brother of Lord Carlyle of Torthorwald, and it was from him that Jaffray Irving got a charter of Luss (Luce) in 1545.

In the same year there is a complaint by John Johnstone, of that ilk, Warden, that "James Douglas of Dumlanrig, along with the Carlyles and Irvings of Mulflats (Hoddom) and Turnshaw, Scottish outlaws; also the Grahams of Esk, together with the brother of Rosetrees Hutcheon, the Graham's son (who married a Irving of Hoddom), with divers other broken men, went to the house of Bonshaw and there by force and way of weir enterit therein and masterfully set at liberty and did take with them certain Bells and Irvings, to the number of eighteen, notorious robbers, which were warded by the said Warden in the Tower of Bonshaw."

In 1551 there were offers made by Edward Irving, of Bonshaw, George Graham, of Renpatrick, and John Irving, of Knockhill, to the Laird of Johnstone and to the "wyif and bayrnes of the late William Johnstone of Hayhill, their Kin etc., on behalf of certain Irvings and Grahams who had slayn the said William." The John Irving of Knockhill, mentioned in the above, had two sons, Richard and John. Richard succeeded to Knockhill, and John to White Hill and Duke's Close.

In 1583 John Urwin of Whitehill, called the Duke's John (the Duke's son), is referred to in a list sent by Musgrove, the Commissioner, to Lord Burghley as being one of the well-known Border Riders and ill-doers. This John, commonly called "Jock O' Milk," the subject of the Old Border ballad, "Duke of Milk," and who was celebrated as a rider and raider, is made the subject of a conversation between James VI. and George Heriot in the "Fortunes of Nigel:"

"D'ye mind, for thou wert in most of our complots, how we were fain to send sax of the Blue-banders to harry the Lady of Logan house's dewcot and poultry yard, and what an awfer plaint the poor dame made against Jock O' Milk and the thieves o' Annandale, wha were as sackless of the deed as I am of the sin of murder?"

"It was the better for Jock," said Heriot, "for if I remember well it saved him from a strapping at Dumfries which he had well deserved for other misdeeds."

"Ay, man, mind ye that," said the King, "but he had other virtues, for he was a tight huntsman, moreover, that Jock O' Milk, and could holloa to a hound till all the woods rang again."

"But he came to an Annandale end at last, for Lord Torthorwald ran his lance out through him."

In 1592 this John was wrongly imprisoned in Carlisle Castle

for half a year, and Maxwell, the Warden, complained of it to the King.

In March, 1593, Richard Lowther, the English Warden, refers to him in the following letter to Lord Burghley: "My son and servants, while on the watch for Scottish thieves, took four, one named John Irving, of whom I had before been written to by my Lords Hamilton and Carmichael (Scottish Warden), and of whom the Lord Herries complained while in London. I sent Irving to Lords Hamilton and Carmichael, whom I wished to pleasure, rather than to Herries, and I hope you will approve." (Callander Border Papers.)

In the Book of Carlaverock the following appears about the Irving's respite by James VI., to Sir James Johnstone and eight score others, for the slaughter of John, Lord Maxwell, Warden, December 1593, including John Irving of Lus; Habbie Irving, of Turnshaw; Richie Irving in Staikcleugh, and Eskie Irving, his brother; William Irving, called Kange;[1] Edward Irving, of Bonshaw, and his sons.

Robert Graham, son of Hutcheon Graham, of Netherby (son of Long Will who was banished from Scotland and came to the debatable ground on the Esk about 1516), married an Irving of Bonshaw, and was slain, leaving a son George, of Renpatrick. Richard Graham, another son of Hutcheon, married an Irving of Hoddom. A sister of the above Richard married William Armstrong, alias Kynmont Willie, and a son, named Hutcheon, married a daughter of John Armstrong of the Hollas. A daughter of William Graham also married a Bell in Scotland, and was the mother of William Bell, alias "Redde Cloke," a principal with Buccleugh. Those relationships account for the active assistance rendered to Buccleugh by the Grahams, Bells, and Irvings at the rescue of Kynmont Willie from Carlisle Castle, in 1596, where he had been wrongly imprisoned by Lord Scrope, the English Warden, in time of truce. The said rescue nearly led to war with England, which was only avoided by the giving up of Buccleugh; also two Armstrongs, two Irvings, one Bell, one Carlyle, one Graham, and one Johnstone, as pledges on behalf of Scotland, and others on behalf of England, for the future peace of the Borders. Buccleugh appears to have remained in England until February, 1598, having meanwhile found favor with Elizabeth for his daring

---

[1] The word Kange was frequently used as an alias in connection with certain Irvings in olden days, but its meaning has not been ascertained.

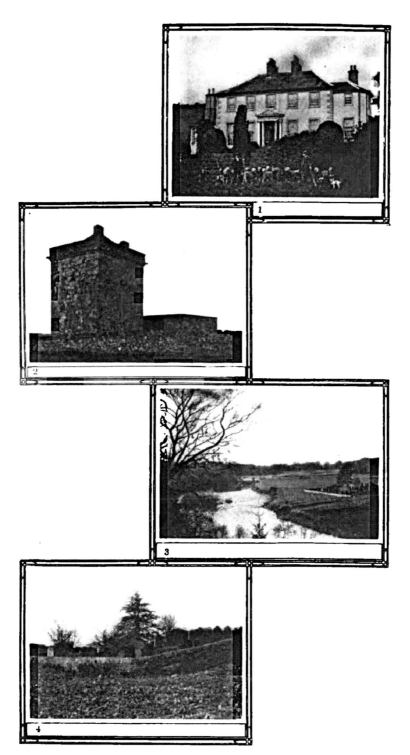

1. Knockhill, part of the old charter granted to Duke Richard Irving of Hoddom.
2. Repentance Tower. An ancient watch-tower with beacon on top. It commanded a view of the fords of the Salway. The Tower was in charge of the Irvings of Hoddom, who lighted the beacon when the English were seen crossing the Salway.
3. Hoddom old Kirkyard.
4. The old burying place of the Irvings of Hoddom.

in having undertaken such an enterprise as the attacking of Carlisle Castle with a force of a few hundred men.

After Buccleugh's adventure, the following is Scrope's and Musgrave's schedule of munitions wanting and needful for the better defence of the castle and town of Carlisle: Corne powder 1 last, muskets furnished 30, pikes 50, black bills 200, bows 100, sheafs of arrows 200, Flanders corselets, complete, 50, horsemen's stores 50. (Callander Border Papers.)

After the union of the two thrones of England and Scotland, the Borderers, being no longer able to make raids into England, were for a number of years in a transition state, and during that period the Irvings seem to have acted up to the good old rule of "He shall take who has the power, and he shall keep who can," as the Law Courts contain many examples in which the Dukes of Hoddom and their followers figured, of which the following are a few:

"John Irving, of Turnshaw, having been transferred from Edinburgh Castle to James Chene, of Streloch, and escaped from him, forfeited 3000 merks."

"Richard Irving of Robgill, William Irving of Skallis, and fifty others, destroyed goods belonging to Maxwell of Nether Rodick."

"Complaint of Herbert Maxwell of Cavens against Ritchie Irving in Hartildill, and James Irving of Trailtrow, outlawed."

"Decree of Bessie Miller and others against Jock Armstrong and Jock Irving, in Starkheuch, on a charge of spuilzie and slaughter."

In 1610 — "Suspension of horning (outlawry) obtained against Lady Newbie and Richard Irving of Hoddom by the laird of Johnstone."

"John Maxwell of Conheath and Robert Herries of Hillilour, for Elizabeth Stewart, Ladie Newbie, 1000 merks, and for Richard Irving, Duke of Hoddom, 500 merks, to answer before the Council on the 24th the complaints against them by Sir James Johnstone of Dunskellie for intromitting with the corns growing on the lands of Newbie." Elizabeth Stewart was wife of John Johnstone of Newbie and sister of Stewart of Garlies.

"Richard Irving of Knockhill is a witness in a trial."

In 1614, "Minute book of progress — suspension of Lawbarrowis, Richard Irving against the Lord Herries." In the same year "John Irving, called the long laird of Hoddom, and his son, the young laird of Hoddom, were tried for raiding. The elder was acquitted; the younger was banished the land."

On June 21, 1621 — "Complaint of Robert Maxwell, of Dinwoodie, how the laird of Wamfran and others, and Richard Irving, called the 'young Duke of Hoddom,' came and destroyed his peats and chased his cattle with the butt ends of their lances, so that some of them were left dead on the ground, and others broke their legs. Had to find security."

In 1622,— "Caution by Richard Irving of Knockhill that Andrew Murray of Moryquat shall not molest John Gibson in Kirkwood; bound in 300 merks.'

In 1622,— "James Irving of Cleucheid (Mount Annan) acted himself as cautioner and souertie for Edward Irving, son to Jaffray, of Robgill."

"Court held in Dumfries, February 12, 1823,— Wat Bell, in Middleshaw, became cautioner in 500 merks for Jok Bell."

"Jaffray Irving becomes cautioner in 500 merks for David Irving, in Middleshaw." (In St. Mungo adjoining White Hill.)

"Willie Bell, called Reidcloak, becomes cautioner in 1000 merks that Robeine Bell and Jok Bell, in Carruthers, Middlebie, will appear in next court."

"Court held in Dumfries 1623."

"Pannell consists amongst others of Richard Irving, called Gawines Richie."

"George Colthart, charged with resetting and maintaining Richie Irving, in Wodhouse, and Jaffray Irving, of Robgill, fugitives and outlaws. (Acquitted.) "

"On April 23, 1623, Court held in Dumfries. John Irving, called 'lang laird of Hoddom,' James Irving, his brother, and J. Johnstone, his spouse, are accusit for airt and pairt of the thifteous steilling of seven gaitt furth of the lands of Brockshaw at several times, pertening to Elizabeth Hardie, and for the cruel burning of one barn of corne bair quheit and ry purtaining to William Bell, in Holmhead (now Bankside). (Acquitted.)"

"At a court held at Jetborough, August 28, 1622, John Irving, young laird of Hoddom, was accused of steilling Ky out of the lands of Gimmenbie and tuk them to a sheep house in Hoddom. (Acquitted.)"

"At the same court held at Jetborough, August 28, 1622, 23 persons declared fugitives and outlaws for no appearance, amongst others John Irving, called Ritchie's Jokkie, in Bankhead."

"At a court held in Jetborough April 19, 1623, John Elliot, that came from Carleill, and Edward Irving, son of Lang Will of Hoddom, acted themselves to depart presently from Scotland and never to return without the license of the Lords of Council under pane of death."

As already stated, Richard Irving succeeded to Knockhill, and John (Jock O' Milk) got White Hill. Richard, who was in most of the troubles of the times, died about 1620, and was succeeded by his son Richard, known as "the young Duke." This Richard left three daughters: Margaret, · Barbara and Janet. Meanwhile "Jock O' Milk's" son, John Irving, married a Johnstone (probably of Newbie), and their son, John Irving of White, Hill, married Margaret Irving, of Knockhill. Barbara married William Johnstone, of Myrhead (Lockerbie), and Janet married George Irving, of Braes (Bonshaw family). John Irving, of White Hill, son of the above John Irving and Margaret Irving, married Mary Bell, of Middlebie, which parish belonged almost entirely to the Bells at that time, and on behalf of his mother and two aunts, signed a disposition of the lands of Knockhill to George Johnstone, son of Andrew Johnstone, of Lockerbie, in 1665.

The tenor of the disposition to George Johnstone in 1665 set forth: "Imprimus. A disposition to John Irving, aier, or at least having right, to Margaret Irving, his mother, lawful daughter to Richard Irving, of Knockhill, his father, of the ten merkland of Knockhill, to Mr. George Johnstone, dated ye 19 day of October, 1665.

"Item: A disposition ye 2 day of July, 1672, ye said John Irving, the first disposition or disposer of, to the said Mr. George, Johnstone, and disposition to Barbara Irving, lawful daughter to Richard Irving, of Knockhill, with consent of William Johnstone, of Myrehead, her husband, to the said Mr. George, date ye 24 of November, 1665, of ye said lands of Knockhill.

"Item: Disposition Janet Irving, lawful daughter to Richard Irving of Knockhill, with consent of George Irving of Braes, her husband, dated 4th day of October 1665, to ye said George Johnstone, of the said lands of Knockhill."

George Johnstone, to whom Knockhill was disponed, and described as a son of Andrew Johnstone, of Lockerbie, was probably a grandson of the Johnstone who fought at Dryfesands (December 6, 1593), and whose wife, who was an Irving, was said to have killed Lord Maxwell by knocking out his brains with the keys of the castle when he lay wounded on the field. He married Isabel Weir, daughter of Archibald Weir, of Edinburgh, and Elizabeth Hamilton, in 1670, but died in 1672 leaving an only son Andrew.

This boy's mother married again (1675) John Stark, of Killera-mont, in Ayrshire.

In 1702, John Irving, of White Hill, son of John Irving and Mary Bell, married Isabel Stark, a daughter of this second marriage, so that Andrew Johnstone and John Irving's wife were half-brother and sister.

The disposition of the lands had already been settled, but a claim in connection with the marriage settlement (tochergood) of Isabel Stark, due by Knockhill to White Hill, began in 1672, was only finally settled between Andrew Johnstone and William Bell-Irving in 1794, so that it kept its legs for no less than 122 years.

JOHN IRVING, who married Isabel Stark, was concerned with the management of James Douglas of Dornock's extensive estates as long as he lived, and was evidently a good business man, for in 1743 he gave most valuable and detailed evidence as to the rentals and boundaries of the surrounding properties, before the commissioners in connection with the enclosing of the common lands in Hoddom. Dornock was the second son of the Earl of Queensberry, and was brother of Kellhead. He married Philadelphia, daughter of Sir James Johnstone, of Westerhall, and his son, Archibald Douglas, who married Jean, daughter of Sir Patrick Maxwell of Springkell, sold the Dornock estate, and bought that of Castlemilk, which John Irving continued to manage. In 1743, John Irving feued the lands of Northcroft, Etterickholm, Norwood and Manes Castle in St. Mungo, from Dornock, but they seem to have been disposed of later. Holmfoot, on the Milk, which he also feued from Dornock in 1738, and which adjoins White Hill, is still in possession of the family. In 1745, John Irving was much in sympathy with the Jacobite rising, and his name is returned in the following list of rebels by the Supervisors of Excise on May 7, 1746:

"John Irving, of White Hill, was active in pressing horses for the service of the rebels, and threatening the constables who would not assist. James Leslie Johnstone, of Knockhill, and Andrew Johnstone, his son, carried arms with the rebels from the time they left Edinburgh till they dispersed. William Johnstone, of Locker-bie, Edward Irving, of Wyseby, William Irving, of Gribton, and James Irving, his son, were also implicated."

John Irving was not banished, probably on account of his age, sixty-three, but he maintained a number of Prince Charlie's followers until his death, and as he went surety for their good behaviour, he more than once got into trouble through their singing of Jacobite songs in Ecclefechan. James Johnstone, son of Andrew, obtained possession of Knockhill in 1722, after his return from the West Indies, to which place he had been banished in 1715, for having joined the rebellion of the Earl of Mar in that year, and fought at the battle of Shriemuir and Falkirk. In 1736 a bond was granted on Knockhill by this James Johnstone in favour of John Irving, of White Hill, and his spouse, Isabel Stark, but Johnstone never fulfilled his part of the contract, and the matter drifted on till 1745, when Andrew Johnstone, his son, enlisted in Prince Charlie's army, and James himself, being suspected of giving aid to the rebels, had to fly the country. Andrew, who had fought at Preston Pans and Culloden, was taken prisoner, tried, and condemned to be executed at Carlisle, but was afterwards pardoned and deported to the West Indies. When under sentence of death he wrote the following letter to John Irving, of White Hill, 1746:

"DEAR SIR—I am informed that you have done all that lay in your power, to assist me in my present situation, but according to the advice of my lawyer, I pled guilty, hoping to be recommended to mercy, but I am afraid that little will be shown to any but such as can make interest at Court, either for pardon or transportation.

"May God Almighty prosper you in all your undertakings, for showing as much humanity as you have done to him, who did not deserve it at your hand."

In a subsequent letter, after he had got a transportation pardon, he wrote again in the following terms: "I am daily expecting to leave this place for Liverpool, in order to embark for transportation, and God knows I am ill provided for it." He then goes on to mention having applied to numerous friends in vain, and makes a request to Irving, of White Hill, to make an advance to him, in which he very readily complied.

John Irving subsequently entered into possession of the lands of Knockhill, but commiserating the unfortunate position of James Johnstone, and his son, Andrew, he allowed the tenants to make payments to them from time to time, and also himself assisted them with money, as appears from their letters, whilst Johnstone's daughters and a younger son, James, continued to live at the Mains of Hoddom.

John Irving and Isabel Stark left a son John, who was also mixed up in the Rebellion. He never took any action against Johnstone with regard to the deed until 1765, when Andrew, having returned from the West Indies, where he had prospered, he brought an action for payment before the Court of Session, but Johnstone having soon afterwards returned to the West Indies, nothing was done in the submission of the case.

This John Irving died unmarried in 1777, and left a will dated June 12, 1773, by which "he bequeathed in favours Agnes, Mary and Philadelphia Irvings, my Sisters germain, in life rent for their liferunt use allenarly during their joint lives, and the life of the longest liver, except the share of the said Mary Irving, as after mentioned, exclusive always of the *jus marite* of their respective husbands (Mary Irving married Thomas Bell in 1743); and to William Bell, writer to the signet in Edinburgh, my nephew, and the heirs of his body; failing, to John Carruthers, of Braes, also my nephew, and the heirs of his body; whom failing, to John Carruthers of Denbie, and my nephew, son to Mary Carruthers, sister to the said John Carruthers, of Braes, and my nieces and the heirs to his body; whom failing, to my heirs and assignees whatsomever, heritably and irredeemably, all and whole my lands of Whitehill, and Duke's Close, lying in the parish of Hoddom, and shire of Dumfries, as also all and whole my lands of Holmfoots of Whitehill, lying in the parish of St. Mungo."

The successors were to take and bear the surname and designation of Irving of Whitehill, and make Whitehill their place of residence, and those succeeding to them in virtue thereof, shall do the like. He also bequeathed all debts due to him, and particularly a "debt due to me out of the estate of Dornock (Douglas); another debt due out of the lands of Cocket Hill, being share of the estate of Rammerscales (Bell); another due to me out of the estate of Knockhill (Johnstone); another due to me out of the estate of Castlebank (Rae), as also a debt due to me by John Carruthers, of Holmains (whose mother was an Irving); another due to me by Bonshaw (Irving), and also another due to me by Janet Knox of Kirkconnel (whose mother was an Irving)." His heirs were also to erect a handsome monument upon the graves of "John Irving and Isabel Stark, my Father and Mother, in Hoddom old Kirkyard," where he was also interred.

After the death of Thomas Bell, his son, William Bell (who married Mary Irving) assumed the name of Irving, and ever since the family name has been Bell-Irving. The Bells, known as the Bells of Milk, were for generations settled on the Water of Milk, and took part in all the feuds and forays of the Borders. Will Bell, the son of Thomas Bell and Mary Irving, who assumed the name of Bell-Irving, was the grandson of George Bell of Strands (now Milkbank),[1] Skellyholm (now Glenholm), Nutholmhill, Bankside, and Middleshaw.

Agnes Irving married John Carruthers of Braes; her daughter married John Carruthers of Denbie, and their son, Colonel Carruthers, succeeded to that property.

As already mentioned, the close relationship between the Johnstones and Irvings led to a long lawsuit between the lands of Knockhill and Whitehill as to the division of the property, Whitehill having a claim of over £4,000 on Knockhill. As previously stated, the disposition of the lands had already been settled but the claim in connection with the marriage settlements of Isabel Stark was still open, and was only finally arranged between William Bell-Irving and Andrew Johnstone in 1794.

Andrew Johnstone pulled down the old Tower, and, with its remains, built the present house of Knockhill in 1772. He lived to a great age, and died about 1798 or 1799. After his death, Knockhill was sold, and his "good and ladylike widow," who survived him a few years and lived at Bankside, excited the talk of the more bigoted Presbyterians at the scandal of having the burial services of the Episcopal church (to which she was strongly attached) read by a most worthy Scotch Minister at her burial in Hoddom Kirkyard. Since that time Knockhill has passed through the hands of the Lascelles, Scotts, Harpes, and Brooks, and is now the property of Mr. J. E. Brooks of Hoddom Castle.

WILLIAM BELL-IRVING'S name was on the list of those in Hoddom who, in 1792, responded to the Duke of Queensberry's invitation to assist the government in repelling all foreign enemies; and to assist the civil magistrates, whenever called upon, for the purpose of suppressing all riots and tumults which might arise in the County of Dumfries. He married, in 1769, Margaret Dempster, daughter of Andrew Dempster of Castle Hill, Edinburgh, a merchant and magistrate of the town, bearing the honorary title of "Keeper of the Keys of the City Gates."

As it may be of interest to some of his descendants, the following

---

[1] Their old tower is shown on Blean's Map, 1660.

is a letter from William Bell to his wife, care of Mrs. Dempster, Castle Hill, Edinburgh:

"BANKSIDE, Oct. 25, 1772, Sunday morning.
"MY DEAR MEG,—

"I hope you won't blame me for not having wrote sooner. I expected to have heard from you how our little son Jock is [John Bell-Irving] and Mary [afterwards Mrs. Byers]. I trust they are both well. My father and mother were vexed that Mary has not been brought out here; in particular my mother, who is very anxious to see her.

"I got safe home, but not so soon as I intended, owing to the horse I had from Edinburgh turning lame at Linton, where I was obliged to hire another horse to Moffat, where I stayed till my own horse was sent up.

"Mr. Hall at Know, whom I saw at Moffat on his way to Edinburgh, promised to call upon you, but as he was to be hurried perhaps he neglected it. All friends are well, and my Uncle Whitehill [John Irving] and I were for the first time at Denbie yesterday. Jock [John Carruthers] was from home, but we saw his wife and mother [formerly Agnes Irving of Whitehill], who send their most respectful compliments to you. The child [afterwards Colonel Carruthers of Denbie] is thriving pretty well. Mrs. Carruthers has praised you much for the kindness you showed her when in Edinburgh. They took three days by the road to reach home. I hope you are well, and making a good nurse, and that Jock is thriving. We have had most monstrous bad weather, which has almost ruined all the corns, but my father [Thomas Bell] had everything in before it turned quite so bad. You know my father is expeditious and careful, so all the better for us. I wish I could follow his example. There is the same want of cash in this country as with you in Edinburgh.

"Pray did the dinner with Mr. Cowan and the oyster feast hold good — was you there? and did the lovely Jean charm the company with her singing? I hope she and all your uncle's family are well — pray present my most respectful compliments to them, and also Miss Gordon and your mama. You will be dull Meg, only little Jock will divert you, and I will be in town in three weeks or less, I imagine.

"My father proposes finishing the other part of our house [Bankside] this spring. All the hewn stones are here — he goes through with things when he takes them in hand, and does not allow them to stick in the middle.

"Pray, have you heard from Mrs. Coventry's people. My mother is sitting by me just now; she is anxious to hear from you as I am; pray write on Wednesday first.

"My Uncle and Aunt, Mrs. Hall [probably Philadelphia Irving, who married the then Laird of Balgray], present their most respectful compliments to you and your friends in Edinburgh.

"My Uncle has been asking what sort of a child little Jock, his name son, is; if he is a fine boy; but he is scarce of cash at present, else would have sent him some; however, there is a good time coming. For want of room I am obliged, my dear Meg, to conclude, and wish you and your little ones well till I have the pleasure of seeing you and them.

"I am, my dear Meg, your affectionate husband,

"WILL BELL."

As stated elsewhere, the writer assumed the name of Irving on the death of his Uncle Whitehill. His wife, Meg, died suddenly, three years after the date of this letter, at the age of twenty-seven, as is to be seen on the tombstone in St. Mungo Kirkyard.

On William Bell-Irving's death, in 1808, he was succeeded by his son, John Bell-Irving, who served in the Border Yeomanry during the Wars of Napoleon. He married, in 1802, Margaretta Ogle, daughter of Captain William Ogle, who at that time occupied Knockhill, son of Henry Ogle of the Causey Park family, Northumberland, a scion of the ancient noble house of Ogle, of Ogle and Bothall Castle, Northumberland, whose wife, Jane Rutter, was a daughter of William Rutter and Margaret Lowther, a niece of the Earl of Lonsdale.

The old spirit of litigation seems to have been inherent in him, for it is told of him that he had no less than sixteen lawsuits going on at one time. With these, and twelve children to bring up he must have had his hands full. He died in 1849, at the age of seventy-eight, leaving his property of Whitehill, Duke's Close, Holmfoot and Bankside jointly to his two eldest sons, William Ogle and John. The following letter is from John Bell-Irving to his son William Ogle Bell-Irving, who was at that time in practice as a Surgeon at Lamberhurst, Sussex.

"Bankside, Sept. 4, 1841.

"My dear William,—

"It gives me infinite satisfaction to know that I will soon have the pleasure of seeing you at Bankside, after so long an absence, but I must confess it would have been doubly so if you could have brought my dear daughter-in-law alongst with you, a person for whom I have the highest possible respect, but I am afraid this desirable object cannot be accomplished at this time, the season being so far advanced and the weather so wet and stormy. However, I fondly cherish the hope that I will yet again see her before I am called to another world.

"The Victoria steam ship sails from Liverpool on the 21st September, at one o'clock in the morning, when either John or I will meet you; if all is well, you will arrive at Annan waterfoot at between two and three o'clock afternoon.

"I do not know what you will do for a pointer, they are so bad to be got at this season of the year. . . . There is a fine covey of pheasants on the croft at Bankside; I see them almost every morning. I have no doubt that partridges are plentiful, and I think there are hares in abundance. We are all well at Bankside when I write this. I am only a little deaf, myself, but you perhaps can do me some good in that way when I see you. I hope George is well. Give my best respects to him and your amiable wife and

"I remain, my dear William, your ever affectionate Father,

"John Bell-Irving.

"Your Mother desires me to mention that she is quite disappointed that your wife is not coming with you — write immediately and let us know what day you are coming, as your Mother says she will think every day a week till you arrive. J. B.-I."

The present house of White Hill is built exactly on the boundary of the parishes of Hoddom and St. Mungo, but a previous house, dated 1721, and the site of the old Tower, the last remains of which disappeared some sixty or seventy years ago, were in Hoddom, and a little nearer the river Milk, the erratic course of which was the cause of much litigation, till it was finally diverted, early in the last century, into one channel further east than its original course.

William Ogle Bell-Irving was born, in 1806, at Scarborough Castle, where his father was quartered at that time. He took up his residence at Bankside after the death of his father, and died there in 1897, in his ninety-first year. He married Sarah, daughter of Richard Owen Stone, of Mayfield, Sussex, who predeceased him, and died without issue. No one was more popular in Annandale than the "Doctor," as he was called, for he adopted the medical profession in his younger days, and practised for a number of years in the South of England. He was a well-known politician, a keen sportsman, a crack shot, a great salmon fisher, a successful courser, and his name will always be associated with "Fusilier," the ancestor of most of the best greyhounds of the present day.

JOHN BELL-IRVING, the recent Laird of White Hill, etc., was born in 1813, and was the only survivor of the family of twelve, in his ninety-first year. He was educated for the law in Edinburgh, but after taking up his residence at White Hill he became widely known as one of the most enterprising and successful agriculturists in the South of Scotland. He was a J. P. for the County of Dumfries for over half a century. His name was ever associated with the sports of a country gentleman, and he was the only one left of the group of original founders of the Dumfriesshire Fox Hunt, established about fifty-nine years ago. He married, in 1843, Mary Jardine (sister of Sir Robert Jardine, Bart., of Castle Milk), daughter of David Jardine, of Muirhousehead, Applegarth — whose wife was Rachel Johnstone, daughter of William Johnstone, of Dalton Hook, Lockerbie. The venerable and much respected couple celebrated their Diamond Wedding (sixty years) on November 13, 1903. When they were married, in 1843, there were no railways into Scotland, so that on their honeymoon they went South by the mail packet from Annan waterfoot to Liverpool, and returned by mail coach from York. He passed away in the following year at the age of 94. They had issue:

1. John, born February 2, 1846.
2. David Jardine, born August 12, 1847.
3. William Ogle, born July 8, 1851.
4. Andrew, born July 9, 1855.
5. James Jardine, born December 24, 1857.
6. Rachel Johnstone Jardine, born August 12, 1844.
7. Margaretta Ogle, born April, 16, 1849, died March 11, 1850.
8. Margaretta Ogle, born June 1, 1853, died 1899.
9. Mary, born May 13, 1860.
10. Jessie Elizabeth, born July 6, 1862.

1. JOHN, of Milkvale, Lockerbie, was born in 1846 and resides at Mount Annan, Annan. He was educated at Edinburgh and on the Continent. He went out to China in 1872, and was for a number of years a partner in the well-known mercantile firm of Jardine, Matheson & Co. of Hongkong, China, and Japan; was a Member of the Legislative Council of Hongkong, Director and Chairman of the Hongkong and Shanghai Banking Corporation, and many other public companies. He has been a J. P. for the County of Dumfries since his return from China in 1889. He married in Hongkong, September 27, 1884, Isabella Thornton, niece of Lady Marsh, wife of Sir Wm. H. Marsh, K. C. M. G., who was then Administrator of the Government of the Colony. She was daughter of Henry Thornton, whose wife was Louisa Bannerman MacKenzie. (See Clans Gairloch and Kintail.) Their children are:

(1). John, born January 3, 1888.
(2). William Ogle, born July 31, 1889.
(3). Mary Louisa, born July 12, 1885.
(4). Bella, born August 10, 1886.
(5). Elsie Helen, born December 17, 1890.

2. DAVID JARDINE, of Winterhopehead, Middlebie, which property he recently purchased from Major Francis Carruthers, of Dormont, whose ancestor, Francis of Dormont, became heir to William Bell of Winterhopehead through his marriage with a Bell in 1634,— was born in 1847; he resides at Bankside, St. Mungo, Lockerbie; is a J. P. for the County of Dumfries; a well known sportsman and agriculturist, who has spent most his life in Annandale by reason of a gunshot accident to his right hand. He married first, in 1876, Bessie, daughter of William Bryden; she died in 1879 leaving one son.

(1). William, born May 12, 1878.

He married secondly, in 1884, Hetty, daughter of George Lea.

3. WILLIAM OGLE, born 1851, now of Milkbank, Lockerbie — which property he bought in 1895 from his cousin Henry. He went out to India in 1874, where he joined the mercantile firm of Jardine, Skinner & Co. of Calcutta; in which firm he has been for many years a partner. He was presi-

dent of the Bank of Bengal, and other companies in India. After he retired from India, in 1897, he built the present mansion house of Milkbank, where he now resides. He is a J. P. for the County of Dumfries.

4. ANDREW, born in 1855. Obtained a Commission in the Royal Artillery in 1875; served in the Afghan campaign in 1878-1880; was at the Defence of Kandahar and battle of 1st September; mentioned in despatches — medal with clasps. During the South African War, 1899–1902, was in command of the 11th Brigade Division R. F. Artillery; operations in the Orange Free State, including actions at Poplar Grove, Dreifontein, Vet River and Zand River; operations in the Transvaal, including actions near Johannesburg, Pretoria and Diamond Hill. Was also in action at Belfast; mentioned in despatches; Queen's medal with five clasps; Distinguished Service Order; King's medal with two clasps. Retired from the army in 1903 as Lieutenant-Colonel.

5. JAMES JARDINE, born 1857, resides at Minto House, Hawick. Was a partner in the firm of Jardine, Matheson & Co. Member of the Legislative and Executive Councils of Hongkong, and was Chairman and Director of numerous public Companies. He married in Hongkong, in 1890, Eva Gertrude, daughter of Benjamin Piercy of Marchwill Hall, Wrexham, and Macomer, Sardinia. Knight Commander of the Crown of Italy, and has issue:
   (1). Ethel Mary, born October 4, 1891.
   (2). Eva Margaretta, born July 20, 1893.

8. MARGARETTA OGLE, born in 1853; married, in 1878, Francis Joynson, of Newpark, Annan. She died in 1899.

9. MARY, born May 13, 1860, married March 24, 1886, Thomas Erskine Cochrane, Commander R. N., son of Colonel W. M. Cochrane (see Dundonald Peerage), and has issue:
   (1). Mary, born November 18, 1889.
   (2). Jessie Edith, born July 18, 1891.
   (3). Daisy Bell-Irving, born July 22, 1894.
   GEORGE BELL-IRVING, the third son, was born January 7, 1817. Was an eminent surgeon and for many years had an exten-

sive practice at Great Stanmore, Middlesex. He afterwards retired and spent the later years of his life at Sunny-bank, Hayfield, Sussex. His favourite recreation was coursing, and he owned some noted greyhounds amongst others, "Iron Shot," "Iron Shell" and "Iris," — the latter of which ran up for the Waterloo Purse, whilst "Iron Shell" ran into the last four for the Cup. He married, first, in July, 1843, Anna Maria, daughter of Henry Leaves Johnson, and granddaughter of Richard Owen Stone, of Mayfield. She died in October, 1852. His family are:

1. Isabella Alice, born 1844.
2. Elizabeth Margaretta, born July 20, 1847.
3. Anna Maria, born November 25, 1848.

1. ALICE, married Rev. Arthur Henry Cumming in 1868, who has been rector of Loftus-in-Cleveland, Yorkshire, for many years, and has issue:

(1). Edward Nolan, born December 8, 1870.
(2). Evelyn George Arthur, born April 10; died August, 1872.
(3). George Bell-Irving, born August 13, 1871, died January 27, 1899.
(4). Muriel Anna Charlotte, born September 29, 1869; married William Brown of Arncliffe Hall, Yorkshire, August 1, 1900, and has —
    (a). Margaret Helen, born November 18, 1903. (This is the first of a new generation.)
(5). Dorothy Margaret Alice, born July 20, 1875.
(6). Stephanie Mary Christin, born December 26, 1879.
(7). Marjorie Gertrude Heather born August 23, 1881.

George Bell-Irving married, secondly, in 1879, Florence Barclay, daughter of Hugh Barclay, of Surbiton. He died on November 24, 1896, at the age of seventy-nine years.

HENRY OGLE BELL-IRVING of Milkbank, St. Mungo, the fourth son, was born in 1819. He spent the early years of his business life in Georgetown, British Guiana. After his marriage, in 1851, he engaged in the West Indian business in Glasgow, and lived near there for several years, removing subsequently to Milkbank, where he resided with his family till his death in 1864. He was a keen sportsman, and took an active interest in greyhound coursing, fox hunting, otter hunting, curling, and other outdoor sports. He married, June 30, 1851, Williamina McBean, daughter of Duncan

McBean, of Tomatin, Inverness-shire (see McBean Clan), and died April 30, 1864.   Their children were:

1. Henry Ogle, born January 26, 1856.
2. Duncan, born October 2, 1857.
3. William, born June 7, 1862.
4. Jane McBean, born May 10, 1852.
5. Margaretta Ogle, born November 11, 1853.
6. Sara, born January 29, 1859 ; died January 23, 1904.
7. Adriana, born June 16, 1861.

1. HENRY OGLE BELL-IRVING of Vancouver, British Columbia, sold Milkbank in 1895 to his cousin, William Ogle.   He qualified as a Civil Engineer at Carlsruhe, Germany, and after four years' practice in England, went out with his brother William to Western Canada in 1882, where he joined the staff of the Canadian Pacific Railway.   He remained in the service of this company till the line was completed through the Rockies to the Pacific Coast in the autumn of 1885.   After his marriage, in 1886, he settled with his wife in Vancouver, British Columbia (then a village of 700 inhabitants), and engaged in business there, which business he still carries on.   In Vancouver he has filled the posts of Chairman of the Board of Works (Municipal Council), President of the St. Andrew's and Caledonian Society, and was for two years (1895 to 1897) President of the Board of Trade, which he also represented as their delegate at the Fifth Congress of Chambers of Commerce of the Empire, held in Montreal in 1893.   He married February 11, 1186, Marie Isabel del Carmen Beattie, daughter of Richard Hudson Beattie of St Michael's Torquay. Their children were born as under:

(1). Henry Beattie, March 25, 1887.
(2). Richard, May 31, 1888.
(3). Roderick Ogle, January 15, 1891.
(4). Malcolm McBean, April 9, 1892.
(5). Allan Duncan, August 28, 1894.
(6). Æneas McBean, May 3, 1898.
(7). Isabel, August 16, 1889.
(8). Anita Helen, July 7, 1893.
(9). Mary McBean, April 26, 1896.

2. DUNCAN, after completing his education at Heidelberg University, went out to Georgetown, British Guiana, with the intension of joining his uncle in business there. Business being uncongenial, he went off on an exploring expedition into the interior of the colony and succeeded in reaching the watershed of the Amazon, passing Mount Roramia on the way. On his return, he came home and qualified as a surgeon at St. Thomas's Hospital, London. He went to Granville, Burrard Inlet (now Vancouver), in 1884, and shortly afterwards to Australia; then back to England, where he joined his uncle George in practice at Stanmore. He married in 1887, and removed the following year with his wife to Vancouver, British Columbia, where he practiced his profession for some years, and subsequently joined his elder brother in business there. At Vancouver he organized the first Rifle Association, of which he was President for some years, took an active interest in and was President of the St. Andrew's and Caledonian Societies, and is now President of the Vancouver Club. Is a great reader and book collector. He married, March 9, 1887, Ethel Hulbert, daughter of John Henville Hulbert, of Stakes Hill Lodge, Hants. Their children are:

(1). Duncan Peter, born January 3, 1888.

(2). Robert, born July 31, 1893.

(3). Agnes, born January 26, 1889.

(4). Dorothy Ethel, born May 13, 1890.

3. WILLIAM went to Canada with his elder brother in 1882, and engaged in horse and cattle ranching near Calgary, Alberta. In 1900 he removed to Cuba and bought land in the Province of Santiago for ranching purposes, and is there now. He married, June 4, 1889, Mary Helen, daughter of Richard Hudson Beattie, of St. Michael's Torquay, and has children:

(1). Angus, born May 25, 1890.

(2). Kenneth, born September 11, 1892.

(3). Michael, born March 5, 1899.

(4). Heather, born June 25, 1891.

(5). Frances, born November 2, 1893, died 1896.

(6). Anna, born January 6, 1895.

(7). Ada, born March 15, 1896.

(8). Isa, born August 11, 1897.

5. MARGARETTA OGLE, married May 14, 1887, to Lieutenant-Colonel Edward A. Fraser, formerly 18th Hussars, afterwards
   Indian Staff Corps, and in Political department, Government of India. Their children are:
   (1). Lorna Agnes Helen, born May 26, 1888.
   (2). Hermia Edith Margaretta, born October 11, 1890.

6. ADRIANA married, January 27, 1885, to William Duncan Kerfoot of Calgary, Alberta, and their children are:
   (1). Duncan William, born October 14, 1885.
   (2). Ludovic, born 1887; died in infancy.
   (3). Adrian Ronald, born September 26, 1890.
   (4). Valentine McBean, born February 14, 1893.
   (5). Archibald Douglas, born July 29, 1898.
   (6). Percivale Caer, born October 12, 1900.
   (7). Olive Lee, born October 14, 1885.
   (8). Ludovica, born 1889; died in infancy.

ANDREW RAMAGE, the fifth son, was born in 1827. He was
also a merchant in the West Indies. As a sportsman, he was a
most enthusiastic salmon fisher and spent most of his leisure hours
on the banks of the Annan. His stock of salmon flies and feathers
for dressing them was something unique. He returned home
from Demarara in 1888, and finally came to reside at Bankside,
where he died unmarried in 1900. No more genial or kind-hearted
man ever lived.

SPORTING RECORD.

The present White Hill family appears to have inherited the
instinct of sport from their ancestors. John, when in the East,
owned and hunted a pack of Fox hounds in Shanghai from 1875
to 1880, and these hounds are still maintained as a subscription
pack. In the annual winter shooting trips in the Yangtse Valley
his party, which in later years included his brother James, made
the record bags in China from 1874 to 1889. The bag in 1877
amounted to 1711 head of game in eighteen days, and was com-
prised of 1495 pheasants, 90 deer, 113 wild fowl, etc. In racing he
was very successful, carrying off the Champion's race in Hongkong
for five years in succession, and winning 10 races at his last meeting
there in 1889. He has generally owned a steeple-chase horse in
Scotland, the most noteworthy of which was the well-known gray
"Champion," winner of thirty-seven cross country events, whilst
with "King of the Meadows" and "St. Boswells" he has thrice won

the Dumfriesshire Hunt Cup. As a salmon fisher, his best catch on the Annan was six fresh run fish, averaging 18½ lbs., one afternoon in 1894, on the Island Stream of Mount Annan. Hunting he still goes in for, and turns out with the Dumfriesshire hounds, throughout the winter months and with the Otter hounds during the summer. As a courser, he was associated with his Uncle George's greyhounds before going to the East, and his brothers, William Ogle and James, and he now possess a considerable kennel and have a Waterloo nomination. At the age of sixteen he won the mile race at school in four minutes forty-four seconds, and at the age of seventeen he walked from Edinburgh to Hoddom, a distance of eighty miles, in twenty hours.

David Jardine has been known as a keen curler and successful skip of a St. Mungo Rink for many years. As a game shot he was as good as most, though he lost part of his right hand through a gun accident when a young man, and in recent years he has also had the misfortune to lose his right eye through a gunshot. He was a keen man with hounds until this last accident occurred. As a Courser, though he does not own greyhounds, he has reared a Waterloo Cup winner, and there is no better judge of a course or a more regular attendant at local meetings. He has been Master of the Dumfriesshire Otter Hounds, the only pack in Scotland, since they were started in 1889. He is also a fair salmon fisher.

William Ogle was a well known big game shot in India, made record bags of snipe, and was a crack pigeon shot, carrying off various cups at the Calcutta Gun Club. He has always been a great salmon fisher, has had a river in Norway for a number of years, and spends several of the summer months salmon fishing in that country.

Andrew is fond of sports of all kinds, and did some big game shooting when with his battery in India. He is a keen salmon fisher, his heaviest fish on the Annan being a salmon of 41 lbs, a cast of which is to be seen at White Hill.

James Jardine is a good all round shot. In 1889 his party in the Yangtse Valley got a bag of 2049 head in twenty-one days' shooting, consisting of 1801 pheasants, 137 wild fowl, 68 woodcocks, etc., which is a record for China. His individual bag of autumn snipe in one day, 75½ couple, on the Canton River from Hongkong, was also a record. On the Tweed last autumn he landed 114 salmon in fifteen days, averaging 20 lbs. When in China he was also as successful in racing as his brother John; in this country

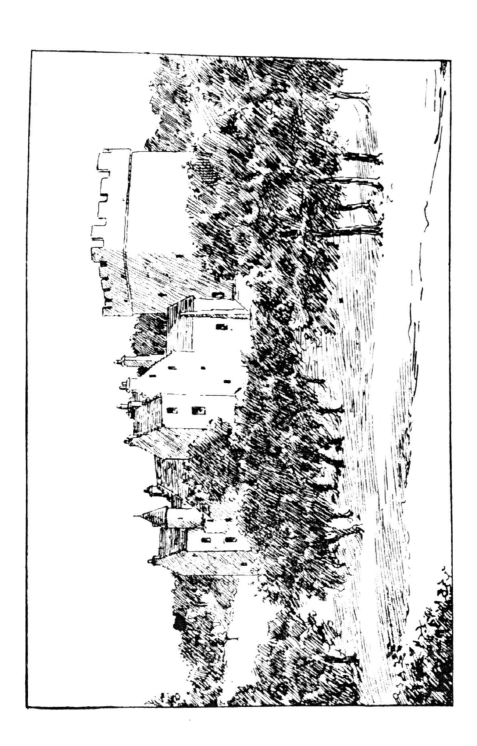

he has a flat racer or two and a steeplechase horse at the present time. He hunts with the Duke of Buccleugh's hounds — and he rears a big lot of pheasants at Minto.

THE LATE LAIRD JOHN BELL-IRVING OF WHITEHALL.

It is with deep regret that we are called upon to record to-day the death of Mr. John Bell-Irving, the venerable and respected laird of Whitehill, which took place at Whitehill at five o'clock on Wednesday morning. Mr. Bell-Irving had reached the great age of 93. He was blessed throughout his long life with rude and abundant health, and his remarkable vitality enabled him to protract his physical activities to an age to which few men are fortunate enough even to attain. Up to a few days ago, he was able to take his drive almost daily. In the end of last week he was seized with a slight indisposition, which was not attended with any organic trouble, and his death was due simply to the exhaustion of the natural forces.

Laird Bell-Irving belonged to a family which for centuries was animated by a robust and aggressive Border spirit, and was always typical of the tendencies of the place and the age. In 1549, Richard Irving — traditionally known as Duke Richard of Hoddom — received a charter of the lands of Knockhill and Whitehill from Lord Herries of Hoddom, as a reward for the services he had rendered in the Border feuds. Ever since, the Whitehill portion of the estate has remained in unbroken possession of the Irvings, who about a hundred and fifty years ago, through marriage with a Bell of Strands (Milkbank), assumed the surname of Bell-Irving. Mr. John Bell-Irving, the subject of this memoir, was born at Whitehill in the year 1813, the son of Mr. John Bell-Irving of Whitehill. As a lad he was for a time with Mr. John Farish, in Annan, who was town clerk and agent of the British Linen Co. Bank. In those days there was not the clear distinction in the scope of individual employments which the development of scientific and business methods have since evolved, and Mr. Bell-Irving received from Mr. Farish an all-round insight into the principles of banking as well as those of law. Professional men who have had to consult the deeds and registers of the time, speak of the beautiful penmanship which characterised the lad's clerical work. One of Mr. Bell-Irving's earliest recollections of Annan was the opening of the Annan Bridge in 1826, when he was thirteen years of age. In a letter which he wrote to an Annan gentleman about three years ago — one of the last which he penned — he recalled the fact with evident pride, and remarked that he was doubtless the only one alive of those who were present that day. On leaving Annan, Mr. Bell-Irving went to Edinburgh, with the purpose of qualifying for the law, but on the death of his father he came into possession of the property, and did not further pursue his intentions. This was about the year 1840, and from that time he was a leader and promoter of all forms of manly sport. He, with one of his first greyhounds, named Burke, won the Brampton Cups, in 1836. He was, in 1848, one of the founders of the Dumfriesshire Foxhunt. It is true that Dumfriesshire had been hunted as early as 1816, and at intervals in the thirties and forties, but for these opportunities local sportsmen were dependent on the good will of masters of hounds who were willing to bring their packs from other parts of the country. The taste which the Dumfriesshire gentlemen received of the joys of the chase, was so strong that the want of a regular pack of hounds impelled them to make a great effort for the establishment of an organization of their own. In 1848, Joe Graham was over hunting the district, and after the run a dinner was held in the Blue Bell Hotel at Lockerbie. The day's sport had been glorious, and when Joe made an offer to hunt two days a week for the sum of £240, a bargain was at once concluded. Thus the Dumfriesshire Hunt was established. Mr. Bell-Irving was one of its most ardent advocates, and continued to be one of the most regular attenders of the meets for many years. His death snaps the last living link with the earliest days of the hunt. He was a famous horseman. He rode to the hounds straight and fearless, and in spite of inevitable accidents, the fascination of the saddle never palled. He was expert with the rod and gun. He had passed his eightieth year when he landed his last salmon. He was a keen curler, and when the ice held he was there with his stones, and there was no mistaking his skill in the game. He was well-fitted by nature for outdoor activities, and he excelled because he studied to excel. He loved to exercise the abundant physical strength with which he was blessed. A strict and rigid etiquette governed his conduct and his thoughts in sport. He detested anything that was mean or unfair, and he loathed any element that was brutal or degrading. His nature was in sympathy with the joyousness and the manliness of life. He used to say that his hunting accidents had shortened his life by ten years. He certainly was not unduly modest in his patriarchal expectations of life, but the remark illustrates, at any rate, the soundness and the vigour of his mental and physical faculties. His personality impressed itself on all with whom he came in contact, and his comradeship was leal and true. For long Mr. Bell-Irving took an active part in agricultural pursuits. In conjunction with the late Mr. Chas. Stewart, of Hillside, Mr. Bell-Irving took a prominent part in the formation of the Lockerbie Farmers' Club, an institution which conferred great benefit upon the agricultural community. Later, this club merged into the Mid-Annandale Agricultural Society, and only last year this institution was combined with the similar body in Lower Annandale, the deceased gentlemen's second son (Mr. David J. Bell-Irving, of Bankside) being its president. Mr. Bell-Irving was also a highly successful breeder of sheep and cattle. Early in life, he founded a flock of Lincoln sheep, which were of great excellence, and secured a large number of awards all over the country. From this flock he annually sold drafts of about 200 shearling rams at the sales at Lockerbie, Castle-Douglas, Dumfries, and Edinburgh, where they always brought high prices. So well-known, indeed, did the flock become, that Colonial and foreign breeders were always anxious to secure drafts, for which high prices were readily given. His exhibits of fat cattle, especially at Christmas shows, were always in good demand, and on one occasion twenty of them were sold at an average price of £45 each. He preserved to the end the greatest interest in everything that was going on about him, and the recollections of his early days were remarkably vivid.

Mr. Bell-Irving married Miss Mary Jardine, sister of the late Sir Robert Jardine. He had a long and happy wedded life, and when his wife died about eighteen months ago, shortly after the celebration of their golden wedding, he received a shock from which he never thoroughly recovered. Along with Mrs. Bell-Irving, he took a keen interest in the social welfare of the parish in which he lived. He was generous and unselfish, and for many years he regularly invited the Sunday School children to Whitehill. He was for about fifty years a Justice of the Peace for Dumfriesshire. He had a family of ten — five boys and five girls — of whom four sons and three daughters are alive. These are: Mr. John Bell-Irving of Milkbank; Mr. David Bell-Irving, Bankside; Colonel Bell-Irving; and Mr. James Bell-Irving, Rokeby, York-shire; Miss Bell-Irving, who resides at Whitehill; Miss Cochrane, married to Capt. Cochrane, R. N., Banchory, Kincardineshire; and Mrs. Brook, married to Mr. E. J. Brook of Hoddom. Mr. Bell-Irving's sons inherit the sporting instincts of their father, and one of them, Mr. David Bell-Irving, is Master of the Dumfriesshire Otter-Hounds, which he was instrumental in establishing about seventeen years ago.

THE LATE MR. W. O. BELL-IRVING.

The "Indian News" has the following regarding the late Mr. W. O. Bell-Irving: We much regret to learn the news of the death of Mr. W. O. Bell-Irving, late a partner to Messrs Jardine, Skinner, and Co., Calcutta, which occurred on the 17th instant (November 17, 1904) at his residence, Milkbank, Dumfriesshire, N. B. Mr. Bell-Irving came out to India in 1874 to Messrs. Jardine, Skinner, and Co., and was admitted a partner in 1880, and finally retired after having risen to the leading position in the firm in 1895. He then went home, and was senior partner in the home branch up to the time of his death. He was a man who enjoyed a great popularity in India, and both for his sound business capacity and his social qualities, was universally esteemed. He certainly ranked as one of the most able directors of the great business house, with which his life-work was concerned. Mr. Bell-Irving has still a very large circle of friends left in India, who will sincerely deplore his loss; for although he belonged to a generation of Calcutta merchants, the ranks of which every year sees more and more depleted, he had comrades in the world of both business and sport all over the country. His death was quite sudden, as there was no previous intimation that he was ill. On the Indian Turf he was a well-known personality, and under the nom de course of "Mr. Annandale" he owned many a good horse, amongst the best known being Ernest, Dutchman, Florestan, and little Hopetown, who was no more than a pony, as ponies go to-day, and yet ran third in the Viceroy's Cup. Mr. Bell-Irving was also one of the best shots that has been known in India, and at the old Calcutta Gun Club he was an acknowledged champion. He also was a keen big game shot, and the number of tigers that fell to his rifle was very great. He was also a very expert fisherman, and of late years has had a river in Norway. Out of respect to Mr. Bell-Irving's memory, the firm's offices were closed yesterday immediately upon receipt of the unwelcome news.

PART III.

THE IRVINES OF DRUM.

(From a "Short Account of the Family of Irvine of Drum," BY CAPTAIN DOUGLAS WIMBERLY.)

The family of Irwin, Irvin or Irvine, or Erevine, is of very long standing in the south and southwest of Scotland, as well as in Aberdeenshire. According to Nisbet's Heraldry, the Erevines came with a colony of Gauls from the west coast of Spain, which settled in the east coast of Erin, and in the west of Albyn. Some of them acquired lands in the Cunningham district of Ayrshire, and gave their name to the river and town of Irvine; some of Dumfriesshire [1] and settled on the Esk, acquiring by marriage the lands of Bonshaw, which they still retain, and later, Robgill Tower; and some must have settled in the north of Ireland, where there are still many proprietors of the name, especially in the counties of Fermanagh, Tyrone, Sligo, and Roscommon.

The Irvines of Drum are descended from William [2] de Irvine, a son, probably the second son, of Irvine of Bonshaw, and a zealous adherent of King Robert Bruce.

1. WILLIAM DE IRVINE (1260–1333), the 1st laird of Drum was King Robert Bruce's armor-bearer, and accompanied him in prosperity and adversity during his endeavors to recover his kingdom from Edward I. of England, until the victory of Bannockburn.

He was rewarded for his fidelity and services with a grant, by Charter under the Great Seal, of a large portion of the Royal forest of Drum, in Aberdeenshire; the Park, which formed part of the chase, being reserved, and another portion having been recently granted to Alexander de Burnard.

This Charter [3] is still extant and is dated at Berwick-on-Tweed, 1st day of February in the "17th year of our reign" (1323). Another Charter by the same king, dated at Kynros, October 4th, in the eighteenth year of his reign, is also in the family archives, in which

---

[1] Nisbet's Heraldry.   [2] Sir Geo. Mackenzie.   [3] Charta in archiv. fam.

the lands are granted in free barony: in the former the name is spelled "de Irwin," in the latter "de Irwyn." King Robert also conferred upon him the device or arms which he had borne as Earl of Carrick, viz., three holly leaves.

According to a somewhat poetical legend, on one occasion, when Bruce with only three or four followers was closely pursued by his enemies, he was so overcome by fatigue that he required a few hours' rest, and lay down and slept under a holly bush, while Irvine kept watch: in allusion to this, it is said that holly forms part of the armorial bearings of the family, with the motto "Sub sole sab umbra virens," in testimony of his follower's unfailing fidelity and loyalty. There is also a Charter [1] by David Bruce, dated 10th February in the third year of his reign (1333), in favour of the same laird, of the lands of Whiteriggs and Redmires, on the resignation of Gilbert de Johnstone. William did not live long to enjoy his estate, and was succeeded by his son.

2. WILLIAM (otherwise Sir Thomas) the 2nd laird, son of the preceding (lived circa 1317–1380 or 1390). He married, according to Douglas' Peerage, ed. 1764, a daughter of Sir Robert Keith, Great Marischal, whom he had by Margaret, daughter of Sir Gilbert Hay, Lord High Constable. This Sir Robert was killed at the Battle of Durham, 1346. Her elder sister married Sir Robert Maitland of Thirlstane and Leithington, ancestor of the Earl of Lauderdale. But according to Douglas and Woods' Peerage, this Sir Robert Keith had no issue, and it was his sister who married Sir R. Maitland. According to Burke's Landed Gentry, this laird married, first, a daughter of Sir Robert Keith, and secondly, a daughter of Sir Thomas Montford of Lonmay: both these marriages seem doubtful. He was succeeded by his son.

3. ALEXANDER, the 3rd laird, son of the preceding, accompanied his cousin, the Earl of Mar, to Flanders: joined the army of the Duke of Burgundy 1409; was knighted on the morning of the Battle of Liege, and returned to Scotland 1410. He had a command in the Lowland Army, under the Earl of Mar, at the Battle of Harlaw, fought July 24, 1411, in which he [2] encountered Maclean of Dowart (or Duart), Lieut.-General under Donald of the Isles, and fought hand to hand with

---

[1] Charta in archiv. fam.   [2] Boethius.

him until both were killed. He had married Elizabeth, second daughter of his neighbor on the south side of the Dee, Sir Robert Keith, Great Marischal of Scotland, and had gone through the ceremony, but had never consummated the marriage. Tradition has it that there had been a feud of long standing between the Keiths and the Irvines, and that a fight had taken place at a spot on the north bank of the Dee, still called the Keiths' Muir, in which the latter were victorious, and drove their enemies across the river at the Keith Pot, and that the Estates of the Kingdom had interfered, and enjoined that a marriage should take place between the families, with a view to put an end to the feud. It is further stated that Drum, when on the march to Harlaw with his retainers, sat down on a stone on the hill of Auchronic in the parish of Skene, still called Drum's Stone, and urged his brother Robert, who accompanied him, to marry the lady, in case he should himself fall.[1] He was succeeded by his brother.

The two following stanzas are from the old ballad, "The Battle of Harlaw":

> " Gude Sir Alexander Irving,
> The much renounit laird o' Drum;
> Nane in his days were better sene,
> When they were semblit all and sum.
>
> To praise him we suld na be dumm
> For valour, wit, and worthiness;
> To end his days he there did cum
> Quhois ransom is remeidiless."

[1] I find that there is another version of this story, quite new to me, viz., that Alexander, the 3rd laird, who succeeded his father, probably about 1380, and was killed at Harlaw, was not the husband of Elizabeth Keith, but of a daughter of Montford of Lonmay; that he started from Drum for the battle, accompanied by his two sons, Alexander and Robert, and resting at Drum's Stone, exacted a promise from the elder to marry Elizabeth Keith, if he got back safe, and from the younger, that should his brother fall, and he survive, he would marry her; that the laird was killed, but Alexander his son returned to Drum and married the lady, being the 4th laird and progenitor of a long race.
I believe this version was adopted by Col. Forbes-Leslie, and am compelled to admit that there is good evidence of an Alex. Irvine of Drum and his brother Robert being both living in 1424. In a Charter of Confirmation by King James I. of the lands of Glassach, which had been granted by Wm. Fraser of Philorth to Wm. Forbes of Kinaldie, and his wife, Agnes Fraser, and signed at Aberdeen on August 12, 1424, among the witnesses are " Alexander de Irwine, miles dominus de Drum," and " Robertus de Irwine, frater suus." This Charter is quoted in Spald. Club Antiq. of shires of Aberdeen and Banff, as being from a collection of Scottish Charters M. S. in the Library at Panmure. In a note is quoted a Charter dated May 28, 1422, granted by Reginaldus de Irwyne, dominus de Maynes [near Dundee], to Patrick de Ogilvy and Christiane [de Keyth] his spouse, of all his lands of Maines, with the Mill, etc., in the county of Forfar, in excambion for the lands of Glencuthill [in the barony of Kinedward], with the Mill of the same in the county of Aberdeen. It is also mentioned that the "grantor's seal is appended, showing three holly leaves, with a mullet in the centre." This Charter was confirmed by the Regent Albany, June 19, 1422, to Patrick de Ogilvy de Grandown, son and heir of Alexander Ogilvy de Ochterhouse Patrick Ogilvy was Sheriff of Forfar. In 1466, Alex. Ogilvy of Auchterhouse was heir to his mother, Christian Keyth, in the lands of the lordship of Grandown and Fotherletter; and his daughter and heir, Margaret Ogilvy, married James Stewart, Earl of Buchan, bringing to him the barony of Auchterhouse. But who was Reginald de Irwyne? Evidently one of the Drum family, by his seal. I have hitherto failed to find out anything about the Montforts of Lonmay.

4. SIR ALEXANDER, the 4th laird, brother of the preceding, whose name he assumed instead of Robert. King Robert III. in like manner changed his name from John. He married, in compliance with the request above mentioned,[1] Elizabeth Keith, second daughter of Sir Robert, Great Marischal. This Sir Robert Keith had Charters dated 1375 and 1406, and gave a charter to his 2nd son, 1413 — vide Douglas and Wood's Peerage. His father, Sir William, built Dunottar Castle, and got with his wife, Margt. Fraser, only child and heiress of Sir John Fraser, the forest of Cowie, thanedom of Durris, the baronies of Strachan, Culperso, Johnston, and other lands in the county of Kincardine. Sir Alexander Irvine had issue by his wife, Elizabeth Keith:

(1). Alexander, younger, of Drum.

(2). A son —— who greatly distinguished himself at the Battle of Brechin (1452). He got from his father the lands of Whiteriggs and Redmires, and a Charter of the lands of Beltie from the Earl of Huntly. From this son are descended the Irvines of Lenturk and the Irvines in Germany.

This SIR ALEXANDER, on his marriage, got from Sir Robert Keith,[2] by Charter dated October 16, 1411, the lands of Strachan in Kincardineshire: and he also had a Charter,[2] under the Great Seal, of the lands of Learney, on the resignation of John Haliburton, dated 1446. He was one of the Commissioners[3] deputed by the Estates of Scotland in 1423 to treat concerning the ransom of King James I., and in the following year was knighted by that monarch for his services. In 1437, after King James's murder at Perth, and during the confusion that followed, the services of Sir Alexander were solicited by the inhabitants of Aberdeen for the defence of their town, and in 1440 he was, by consent of the burgesses, appointed Captain and Governor of the burgh, with an authority superior to that of the Chief Magistrate. This post he held for two years, and there is no other instance on record of a similar appointment in Aberdeen. When the Earl of Huntly, in the next century, became Chief Magistrate, it was by the title of Provost. In the east wall of Drum's aisle, the old family burying-place, adjoining the Church of St. Nicholas, above the recumbent effigies of a knight and his lady, there is a plate of brass with the following inscription:

[1] Douglas's Peerage, p. 452.   [2] Charte in archiv. fam.   [3] Hawthornden.

"Hic sub istâ sepulturâ jacet honorabilis et famosus miles dms Alexander de Irvyn secund, qda de drumn de achyndor et forglen qui obijt die mesis anno dui M°CCCC . Hic eciam jacet nobilis dna dna Elizabeth de Keth filia Qdam Roberti de Keth militis mareschalli Scociæ uxor Qda dci dni Alexandri de Irvyn que obijt die mesis ano dui M°CCCC ."

It will be observed that the month, day of the month, and year in each case are left blank or incomplete: dci is an abbreviation of dicti.

"The altar of Sancts Laurence and Ninian were of old founded and endowed by the Barones of Drum, in the Parish Church of Sanct Nicolas."— From an account of a "tenement" near St. Nicholas. St. Ninian was the patron saint of the Irvines.

He probably had a sister Agnes, daughter of the Baron of Drum, who married Wm. Leslie, 4th Baron of Balquhain, about 1430: their daughter, Elizabeth Leslie, married Norman Leith — vide Douglas' Baronage, under Leith of Leith-hall and Leslie of Wardes. Reginald de Irwyne mentioned above may have been a brother of the 4th laird. It is not known in what year he died: he was succeeded by his eldest son.

5. ALEXANDER, the 5th laird, son of the preceding, married ——
   Abernethy, daughter of the first Lord Abernethy of Saltoun, by whom he had, with other children, a son Alexander, the younger, of Drum. This laird was infeft [1] in his father's lifetime in the lands of Lonmay, Savoch, Corskellie, and Cairness in Buchan. He was succeeded by his son.

6. ALEXANDER, the 6th laird, son of the preceding, was twice married. His first wife was Elizabeth [2] (or Maroni), 3rd daughter of Alexander, first Lord Forbes, by whom he had 3 sons and 1 daughter.
   (1). Alexander, younger, of Drum.
   (2). Richard, of Craigton, from whom are descended the Irvines of Hiltown.
   (3). Henry, ancestor of the Irvines of Kingcaussie. One daughter, Elizabeth, married to Leslie of Wardhouse.
   His second wife was —— Lindsay, and by ,her he had issue eight daughters, of whom seven were married, viz.: 1. to Couts of Westercoul; 2, to Chalmers of Strichen; 3, to Skene

---

[1] Precept in archiv. fam.   [2] Douglas's Peerage, p. 265.

of that ilk; 4, to Ogston of Fettercairn; 5, to Ross of Auchlossan; 6, to Crawford of Fornet; 7, to Duguid of Auchenhove.

This laird was infeft [1] in 1457 in the lands and forestry of Drum and lands of Lonmay. He was succeeded by his eldest son.

7. SIR ALEXANDER, the 7th laird, son of the preceding, married Janet, daughter of Allardyce of that ilk, by whom he had a son and three daughters, viz.: Alexander, younger, of Drum; Daughters: 1. Janet, married to the laird of Balbegno; 2, a daughter, married to Fraser of Muchalls, ancestor of Lord Fraser; 3. Mary, married, as his [2] second wife, Sir Archibald Douglas of Glenbervie, knighted by King James V. — *Vide* Douglas Peerage.

This laird got a Charter from his father in 1499 of the lands of Forglen in favour of himself and his wife, Janet Allardyce. He got in 1506 a Charter [3] under the Great Seal of the lands of Drum, Lonmay, Auchindoir, and Tarland. He was succeeded by his grandson.

His eldest son and heir apparent, Alexander, had the lands of Forglen during his father's lifetime, to which he got a gift of non-entry dated December 4, 1527, bearing to be given [4] on account of Drum, his said son, and their friends, their good and thankful service done to the King in searching, taking, and bringing his rebels to justice. He married Elizabeth Ogilvy,[5] daughter of the laird of Findlater, by whom he had issue six sons and three daughters The sons:

(1). Alexander, who succeeded his grandfather.
(2). William of Ardlogie.
(3). Robert of Tillylair, of whom are the Irvines of Fortrie.
(4). Gilbert of Colairlie, predecessor of Murthill and Cults, whose great grandson succeeded to Drum in 1696.
(5). James, a Knight of Malta, ordained by the Grand Master Prior of the Order in Scotland, in succession to Sir James Sandilands, first Lord Forphichen, who died 1596. History of Knights of Malta, by Major Porter, R. E., and Douglas' Peerage under Torphichen.
(6). John, who died young.

Daughters —1, Janet, married to Gordon of Abergeldie; Eliza-

---

[1] Precept in archiv. fam.
[2] Charta in archiv. fam.
[3] Chart. in publ. arch.
[4] Writ. in arch fam.
[5] Contract penes Com. de Findlater 1526.
    Douglas's Peerage, p. 261.

beth, married to Seton of Meldrum; 3, Margaret,[1] married
to Cheyne of Arnage.

Elizabeth Ogilvy was, according to Douglas's Peerage, a daughter
of Alexander Ogilvy of Ogilvy, Deskford, and Findlater, by Janet
Abernethy, daughter of Alexander Lord Abernethy of Salton;
and apparently a sister of Margaret Ogilvy who married James
Gordon, 2nd laird of Lesmoir; both being granddaughters of Sir
James Ogilvy of Findlater and Deckford, who married Lady Agnes
Gordon, daughter of George, 2nd Earl of Huntly.

Alexander Gordon of Abergeldie, whose name appears in the
"bond for the Queen's service" in 1568, to co-operate with the
Earl of Huntly in aiding her, was probably Janet Irvine's husband;
and William Gordon of Abergeldie, who was one of those who got
a remission for the Battle of Glenlivat (1594), granted in 1603, was
probably her son.

Alexander, younger of Drum, took an active part in the stirring
events which occurred during the minority of the unfortunate Queen
Mary, and was killed at the Battle of Pinkie in 1547, during his
father's lifetime.

His brother, Gilbert of Colairlie, was ancestor, probably great-
grandfather, of Alexander, designed of Marthill, who succeeded to
Drum under an entail in 1696, as 13th laird, and married Jean,
daughter of Alexander, the 11th laird, by Lady Mary Gordon;
and also of John, who married Katharine, daughter of Fullarton of
Dudwick, and succeded his nephew as 15th laird in 1735, but
died without issue in 1737, when the estate went to the Artamford
branch.

The 7th laird was succeeded by his grandson.

8. ALEXANDER, the 8th laird, grandson of the preceding, married
   Lady Elizabeth Keith,[2] 2nd daughter of William, 4th Earl
   Marischal, and his wife Margaret, daughter and co-heiress
   of Sir William Keith of Inverugie, by whom he had five
   sons and four daughters. The sons:
   (1). Alexander, younger of Drum.
   (2). Robert, of Fornett and Moncoffer, extinct.
   (3). James, of Brucklaw, predecessor of Saphock, extinct.
   (4). William, of Beltie, extinct.
   (5). John of Artamford, whose descendant, Irvine of Crimond,
   succeeded to Drum in 1737.

[1] Discharge.   [2] Contr. in arch. fam., 1552. Douglas's Peerage, p. 454.

The daughters — (1), —— married to Hay of Ury, the eldest
cadet (failing heirs male of the 6th Earl), in 1541, of the
Errol family; (2),—— married to Keith of Inverugie (or
perhaps of Ludquhairn or of Ravenscraig; (3), Elizabeth,[1]
married to James Ogilvy of Boyne; (4), Margaret,[2] married
to Gilbert Menzies of Pitfodels.

It was in this laird's favour, but before he succeeded to the
estate, that a Charter[3] was granted, under the Great Seal of Scotland, on the resignation of his grandfather in favor of Alexander
Irvine, grandson and heir apparent of Alexander Irvine of Drum,
and the heirs male of his body, to the nearest and lawful heirs
male and assignees whatsomever, of the lands and barony of Drum,
with the lands and baronies thereto annexed, Lonmay, Learney,
Auchindoir, and particularly the lands of Tarland and Coul, dated
at Edinburgh, February, in the 12th year of the Queen's reign
(1554).

NOTE.— Alexander Irving of Beltie, and George, Earl of Huntly, signed
a Bond, July 26, 1560, by which the former bound himself to render leal and
true service to the latter, excepting the obedience, service, and homage due
to the Laird Drum.— Spald. Club Misc.

John Irving of Beltie, along with Robert Irving of Fedderat, and many
others, were appointed by the Convention of Estates to levy 1,300,000 merks
and 60,000 pounds as loan and tax for wants of the Scots army in Ireland:
the Lairds of Drum and Philorth appointed Conveners, August 15, 1643.

If the second daughter married Keith of Ravenscraig, her husband might
have been the son of John Keith of Ravenscraig, who got in 1543 a Charter
of part of the lands of Inverugie from his niece Margaret, who married William, 4th Earl Marischal. Sir James Gordon of Lesmoir married about same
time Rebecca, daughter of Keith of Ravenscraig, possibly sister of the Keith
who married Drum's daughter.

James Ogilvy, 5th baron of Boyne, got a Charter under the Great Seal,
during his father's life, of himself and Elizabeth Irvine, his spouse, of the
lands of Quhintee, Cavington, Kindrochit, and half the lands of Ardbragane,
dated February 22, 1597. They left issue, a son, Sir Walter, 6th Baron of
Boyne, who was a great loyalist, and suffered much on that account in the
reign of King Charles I.— *Vide* Douglas's Baronage.

Both the father and mother of Lady Elizabeth Keith, wife of Irvine of
Drum, were descended from George, 2nd Earl of Huntly, by the Princess
Annabella, daughter of King James I.: her father, Wm., 4th Earl Marischal,
was grandson of Wm., 3rd Earl Marischal, by Lady Elizabeth Gordon, daughter of 2nd Earl of Huntly; and her mother, Margt. Keith of Inverugie, was
granddaughter of Patrick, 4th Lord Gray, by Lady Janet Gordon, 2nd daugh-

[1] Discharge 1599.   [2] Discharges, 1597, 1598, and 1603 of Tocher, &c.
         [3] Chart. in publ. arch.

ter of 2nd Earl of Huntly. Lady Elizabeth's elder sister, Lady Anne, married first, in 1561, James, Earl of Moray, Regent of Scotland; secondly Colin, 6th Earl of Argyll, and had issue to both; her younger sister, Lady Alison, married, Alex., Lord Salton: another, Lady Mary, married Sir John Campbell of Calder; another, Lady Beatrix, married John Allardice of Allardice: another, Lady Janet, married James Crichton of Frendraught; and another married Sir John Kennedy of Blairquhan — all had issue. Her eldest brother, William, Lord Keith, predeceased his father by 14 months, dying in 1580, leaving 8 children; his 3rd daughter, Margt., married Sir William Keith of Ludquhairn, son of Gilbert Keith of Ludquhairn, by Margaret, daughter of James Gordon of Lesmoir.

There is extant in the family Charter chest a holograph bond, by King James VI. to Drum, for 500 marks, dated at Dalkeith, November 27, 1587, and payable at Whitsunday thereafter.

The 8th laird of Drum took part in the expedition sent under the young Earl of Argyll, in 1594, against the three Catholic lords, the Earls of Huntly, Angus, and Errol. Argyll, after failing to to take the Castle of Ruthven, in Badenoch, with the Campbells, Mackintoshes, Macleans and others, marched through Strathspey, and issued orders from Drummin on the Avon to the Forbeses, Frasers, Dunbars, Mackenzies, Irvings, Ogilvies, Leslies, and other clans or tribes in the north, to join him with all speed. But before they could join him, Huntly brought him to an engagement between Glenlivat and Glenrinnes, and defeated him in the battle of Glenlivat. Lord Forbes and the lairds of Balquhain and Drumminor, hearing of the defeat, resolved to unite with the Dunbars and others, and make an attack on the Gordons on their march homewards. Setting out from Drumminor, they had not gone far when one of the Irvines, while riding alongside of Lord Forbes, was unexpectedly shot dead by an unknown hand, and though all the firearms carried by the party were immediately examined, with the view of ascertaining who had committed the deed, every one was found to be loaded. This affair caused so much distrust and suspicion that the companies were broken up and returned home. Shortly afterwards, Huntly and his friends retired into Sutherland, and then went abroad during the King's pleasure, with the object of allaying the spirit of violence and discontent: sixteen months after, he was recalled, and he and the Earls of Angus and Errol were restored to their former honours and estates in 1597; within two years thereafter the King created Huntly a Marquis.

The 8th laird died in 1603, and was succeeded by his son.

9. ALEXANDER, 9th laird, son of the preceding, married Lady
    Marion Douglas,[1] daughter of Robert, 4th Earl of Buchan,
    and had by her 2 sons and 5 daughters. The sons:
    (1.) Alexander, younger of Drum.
    (2.) Robert of Fedderat, now extinct; he married Isobel,
        daughter of Sir Robert Campbell of Glenorchy, about
        1640, and had 2 daughters.— Douglas and Wood's
        Peerage.
    The Daughters: (1.) Margaret,[2] married to Sir Geo. Oglivie of
        Dunlugas, afterwards created Lord Banff, or Lord Oglivie
        of Banff, date of patent, 1642; their daughter Helen
        married 2nd Earl of Airlie;[3] (2.) Isabella,[4] married to
        Urquhart of Leathers; (3.) Janet,[5] married to Sir Will-
        iam Douglas of Glenbervie; (4.) Anne,[6] married to Sir
        John Ogilvie of Inverquharity; (5.) Mary,[7] married to
        Sir Robert Grahame of Morphie, 1628.

This laird got from his father in 1583 a Charter in favour of
himself and his heirs male, whom failing the nearest heirs male
whatsoever of himself, bearing the arms and surname of Irvine, or
his assignees, of the said lands and barony of Drum, the land of
Whiteriggs, Lonmay, &c. This Charter[8] is dated at Aberdeen,
April 4, 1583. He also got a Charter of confirmation from King
James VI. of the last named Charter, containing a new clause, of
new uniting the said lands into a barony and free forestry, to be
called in all time coming the barony of Drum, and a clause of *de
novo damus* thereof in favour of the said Alexander Irvine, younger
of Drum, and his heirs male and assignees aforesaid, dated at
Holyrood House, April 13, 1583.

His youngest brother, John Irvine of Artamford, married Beatrice Irvine of Pitmurchie, and had eight sons, who all died without
male issue, except James, the second son, who, by a transaction
with his elder brother, succeeded to Artamford, and married
Anne, daughter of Keith of Ravenscraig, who had been his father's
ward, by whom he had two sons, one, also named James, who suc-

---

[1] Douglas's Peerage, p. 25, where she is named Margaret. Contr. in arch fam. 1590.
[2] Discharge of Tocher: she is named Helen in Peerage, p. 68.
[3] Sir George Ogilvie of Dunlugas, younger of Banff and Dunlugas, got a Charter in favor
of himself and Margt. Irvine, his wife, of the Barony of Dunlugas, March 9, 1610–11:
he was created a Bart. of Nova Scotia, 1627: fought at the Bridge of Dee, 1639, and created
Lord Banff, 1642.— Douglas and Wood's Peerage.   The Ogilvies of Deskford were ancestors
of the Earls of Findlater: the first Ogilvie of Boyne was a brother of Deskford, and of
the same family as the Ogilvies of Dunlugas, as were also the Ogilvies of Carnousie.
[4] Contr. in arch. fam.   [5] Douglas's Baronage, p. 20.   [6] Contr. in arch. fam., 1622.
[7] Writ. in arch. fam.   [8] Writs in arch. fam. and in publ. arch.

ceeded him, and a son who died in infancy, and two daughters — Anne, who married Elphinstone of Glack, and Beatrice, who married Dalgarno of Millhill. Anne Keith's sister, Margaret, married Alexander Farquharson, younger of Finzean.— Spald. Cl. Misc.

The, James last mentioned, married Margaret, daughter of James Sutherland of Kinminity, in the parish of Keith, and had by her five sons and one daughter, viz:— (1.) Alexander, who sold Artamford to his brother William, bought Crimond, and then succeeded to Drum in 1737; (2.), William, who bought Artamford from his brother; (3), Robert; (4.), Thomas of Auchmunziel; (5.) Charles. And a daughter, Margaret, who married Hugh Rose of Clava.

The 9th laird restored the present mansion-house of Drum, attached to the old tower, which is of much earlier date; his initials, A. I., and those of his wife, M. D., and the date 1619, are on the pediments of the dormer windows, which were then either added or repaired. The two wings, "east and west jambs," are older than the centre part, as is the "fornet" which join it to the Tower, situate at the north, and helps to complete the courtyard. There is extant a discharge by the Earl of Morton to Drum for 10,000 merks out of the sum of 20,000 merks, payable by Drum to him in caes of his lady's succeeding to the Earldom of Buchan; in which case the said Earl of Morton makes the sum to be paid by him only 10,000 merks. This is dated November 14, 1605. He was named in 1610 a member of the Court of High Commission appointed that year.

The following letter to this laird is very interesting.

Copy of a letter from King James VI., superscribed by himself, and under the Privy Seal, to the Laird of Drum:—

" James R.,—

"Trusty and well beloved, we greet you well. Having understood by our Secretary, Sir Alexander Hay, of your ready forwardness, upon notice given unto you by him of our pleasure for some piece of service to have been done in the North parts of that our Kingdom, we have thought good to take special notice thereof, and to return unto you our very hearty thanks for the same, willing you to continue these your dutiful endeavors, and assuring you that we will be very mindful thereof, if any particular occasion, which may concern you, shall occur. And so we bid you very heartily farewell. At our Manor of Greenwich, the 29th of June, 1612."

Directed "To our trusty and well beloved the Laird of Drum."

His wife, Lady Marion Douglas, was daughter of Robert the 4th, and sister of James, the 5th Earl of Buchan. Her mother, Christina Stewart, was Countess of Buchan in her own right, having succeeded her grandfather, and married in 1569 Robert Douglas, 2nd son of Sir Robert Douglas of Lochleven, uterine brother of the Regent Murray; and her huband became Earl of Buchan in right of his wife. Lady Marion's only brother James, became the 5th Earl of Buchan, and married Margt. Oglivie, daughter of the 1st Lord Oglivie of Deskford, and died aged 21 in 1601, leaving an only daughter Mary, who, at the time of the curious transaction between Drum and the Earl of Morton, was only about four or five years old; and failing her, Drum's wife was heiress to the Earldom of Buchan. The little girl lived to grow up, and married John Erskine, son of John, 7th Earl of Mar, and as she was Countess of of Buchan in her own right, she carried the title into the Erskine family.

The Earl of Morton referred to was Lady Marion's uncle: he was, before succeeding to that title as 7th Earl, Sir William Douglas of Lochleven, the custodier of Queen Mary during her imprisonment in the Castle; elder brother of Robert Douglas, who became Earl of Buchan, and of George, who aided Queen Mary in her escape.

His father, Sir Robert Douglas, had been nominated as his heir by the 3rd Earl of Morton, and a Charter obtained in his favor in 1540; but the Earl, at a later date, altered the destination, and executed an entail, in favor of his daughter and *her* husband, James Douglas, afterwards the Regent, who became 4th Earl of Morton. The Regent left no lawful children, and was executed 1581, when his estates and titles were foreited to the Crown.

Upon this, John, 7th Lord Maxwell, whose mother was a daughter of the 3rd Earl, obtained in her right a new Charter of the Earldom, and became 5th Earl of Morton; but the attainder was reversed in 1585, and he had to relinquish the title, which then devolved on the next heir of entail, Archibald, 8th Earl of Angus, of the Douglas family, who became 6th Earl of Morton, and died without issue in 1588.

On his death, Sir Wm. Douglas of Lochleven succeeded as the next substitute under the second entail — and became 7th Earl. The date of his discharge to Drum is November 14, 1605, and he died in 1606.

Lady Marion Douglas, called in Douglas and Wood's Peerage,

Lady Janet, had been married to Richard Douglas, brother of Douglas of Whittinghame, before she married the laird of Drum.

In 1629 this laird of Drum mortified £10,000 Scots for the maintenance of four bursars of philosophy and two of divinity, at the Marischal College, Aberdeen, and of four bursars at the Grammar School of that place, vesting the right of presenting to them in the the family of Drum. His wife also, Lady Marion Douglas, bequeathed 3,000 merks in 1633 to endow an hospital for the widows and daughters of decayed burgesses, the patronage of which was to be in the Town Council.

The mortifier expected that his £10,000 would yield £400 per annum for the students of philosophy, £320 per annum for the bursars at school, and 400 merks for the divinity students; and he appointed the Magistrates of Aberdeen his trustees, who were to employ the capital in land or annual rent in all time coming. His son, Sir Alexander Irvine, offered to hand over the money, which was left *in gold* in his mother, Lady Marion's keeping, to the Magistrates, asking them to give security for payment of the annual rent for the purposes specified. The Magistrates declined, "as very hurtful and prejudicial to the town of Aberdeen," on the ground that "money could make no safe or constant rent (*i. e.*, interest) unless employed in heritable purchase of land, and that £10,000 was not likely to produce even about £500 per annum." Sir Alexander, consequently, had to take back that sum with him. This offer was made May 22, 1630. Its rejection caused much trouble and loss to the family more than two centuries afterwards.

In 1633, Sir Alexander obtained a decree of the Court of Session to retain the money, without payment of interest, till Whitsunday, 1640 (possibly with a view to increase the capital); after which term he was to provide sufficient land for employing the £10,000, worth in yearly rent the sum of £1,000, the lands to be bought and acquired by him, without reversion, to the use and behoof foresaid. (Date of decree, February 24, 1633). It is pretty certain that he could not purchase land, which even then was worth about 20 years' purchase, to yield £1,000 Scots per annum, with the money available; accordingly he virtually set aside the rents of a small detached property belonging to him, which subsequently for a long period did not yield that rent.

It happened that in 1596 the then laird of Drum had acquired from Patrick Forbes, merchant in Aberdeen, the lands of Kinmuck, and others in the parish of Kinkell, date of Charter, May 5, 1569;

and that in 1617 Alexander Irvine, with consent of Marion Douglas, his spouse, had granted a Charter[1] of these lands in favour of Sir Alexander Irvine, apparent heir of Drum, his son, and Magdalen Scrimgeour, his spouse, (date of Charter, July 22, 1617). It was these lands that were virtually burdened, by making the rents applicable to pay the bursaries. They appear to have been held by the successive lairds of Drum on this footing, viz.: that they were merely burdened with the payment of these bursaries; for in a letter from Alexander Thomson of Portlethen to the laird of Drum younger, in 1720, it is mentioned that each Grammar School bursar was getting only £67, and each College bursar £87, and that this this is a great reduction. The rents were insufficient to pay in full until about 1808.

Successsive lairds continued to nominate and pay the bursars up till about the year 1861, when the rental of Kinmuck, being then about £600 sterling per annum, thanks to the care bestowed upon the estate and the rise in the value of land, the University of Aberdeen raised an action, claiming the whole estate of Kinmuck, in which, after appeal to the House of Lords, they were successful. (See the 20th laird's time.)

Sir Alexander, the 9th laird, died in 1269 or 1630, and was succeeded by his eldest son.[2]

10. ALEXANDER, the 10th laird, eldest son of the preceding, married in 1617 Magdalen, eldest daughter of Sir John Scrimgeour of Dudhope, Constable of Dundee, by whom he had issue five sons and six daughters, viz.:—

(1). Alexander, younger of Drum.

(2). Robert.

(3). James.

(4). Charles.

(5). Francis.

All of whom, except Alexander, died without issue.

The daughters:— (1), Marion,[3] married James, first Viscount Frendraught, at the Church of Drumoak, November 8, 1642. (*Vide* Douglas's Peerage). Lord Frendraught was son of the laird whose name is connected with the burning of Frendraught;

(2),——; (3),——; (4), Jean, married George Crichton, brother

---

[1] Chart. in arch. fam.

[2] During the disputes between Gordon of Rothiemay and the laird of Frendraught, in the spring of 1630, which led to the burning of Frendraught, the Marquis of Huntly, when intending to try and compose the quarrel, was called away to Aberdeen to attend Drum's funeral.

[3] Disch. of Tocher, 1642. Douglas's Peerage, p. 167. Writs of the family.

of Lord Frendraught; (5),——; (6), Margaret, married Charles
1st Earl of Aboyne.

"Upon the aucht day of November, the Viscount of Convoy,
Lord Crichtoun, was mareit with [Marion] Irving, dochter to the
Laird Drum, at the Kirk of Dalmoak. His father was not at his
mareage, and wold not be callit lord nor viscount, but held him the
name of laird."— Spalding's Memorials.[1]

James Crichton, the eldest son of James Crichton of Frendraught, in Aberdeenshire, was seventh in descent from the celebrated
Lord Chancellor Crichton, and fifth from the Chancellor's grandson, the third Lord Crichton, in whom that title was forfeited February 24, 1484. The father of the first Viscount was involved in a
quarrel with Gordon of Rothiemay, in which the latter was killed on
January 1, 1630, which led to a further quarrel and feud, in connection with which the Castle of Frendraught was burned, and the
Marquis of Huntly's 2nd son, Lord Melgum, young Rothiemay, and
six of their attendants perished in the flames. This led to the
Gordons plundering Frendraught's lands, and one of his sons was
killed by Adam Gordon, August 23, 1642.

James, his eldest son, was created Viscount Frendraught by
patent dated August 29th in the same year. He accompanied
the Marquis of Montrose in his last unfortunate expedition, in
March, 1650, and was with him at Invercharron, in Ross shire,
when he was defeated by Colonel Strachan on April 27th following.
The Marquis's horse having been shot under him, he mounted the
horse of Lord Frendraught, which that young nobleman generously
offered him, and, galloping off the field, escaped for a few days.
His young friend, severely wounded, was taken prisoner, and
anticipated a public execution, by what Douglas, in his Peerage,
calls "a Roman death." He had two sons, James, the second,
and Lewis, the fourth Viscount.

Charles, 1st Earl of Aboyne, 4th son of George, 2nd Marquis of
Huntly, was first married to Margaret Irving, by whom he had a
daughter, Lady Anne Gordon, who was on June 17, 1665, served
heir of Lady Margaret Irving, wife of Charles, Earl of Aboyne,
her mother.— Inq. Ret. XXXII. 104. *Vide* Douglas and Wood's
Peerage, additions and corrections, p. 715.

Sir Alexander, besides getting from his father a Charter of the
lands of Kinmuck in 1617, got also in 1621[2] another of the lands of
Forglen. He was Sheriff-Principal of Aberdeenshire in 1634, and

---

[1] "The Laird" was a Covenanter.　　　　　　[2] Chart. in arch. fam.

in several subsequent years: he was held in high esteem by Charles
I., and a patent was made out creating him Earl of Aberdeen,
probably about 1638, which the breaking out of the great rebellion
prevented from passing the Great Seal.

The Drum family at that time possessed extensive estates in
the counties of Aberdeen, Forfar, Banff and Kincardine. The
lands in Cromar alone were situate in the parishes of Coul, Ruthven,
Logie Coldstone, Tarland, etc., and the barony of Drum in Drumoak,
Peterculter, Upper Banchory, and Echt: they had Fedderat,
Learney, Auchindoir, and Lonmay in Aberdeenshire; Forglen in
Banff; Kelly in Forfar, and Whiteriggs and Strachan in Kincardineshire. There is an old saying that the Laird of Drum could ride on
his own lands from Drum to Dundee.

A stanza of an old ballad probably refers to this time:

> "There are six great barons o' the North,
>   Fyvie, Findlater, and Philorth;
> An' if ye'd ken the other three,
>   Pitsligo, Drum, and Delgaty."

These barons were Seton, Ogilvie, Fraser, Forbes, Irvine and
Hay.[1]

In 1639 Sir Alexander continued to retain the office of Sheriff:
but, during his absence, 500 Highlanders under Argyll were quartered on his lands. On June 2, 1640, the Covenanter, General
Munro, accompanied by the Earl Marischal, marched to besiege
the Castle of Drum. Spalding states that the laird was from home,
but that his lady, with some "prettie men," were within the house,
which had been previously furnished with ammunition and provisions. When the Covenanters came within musket shot, they
were saluted by a discharge which killed two of their number, and
induced the assailants to try the effect of a parley. In answer to
the summons to surrender, the lady requested time for decision,
and twenty-four hours were granted that she might obtain her
husband's opinion. Previous to the expiry of this time the lady
determined to surrender, and deliver up the keys, on condition that
her garrison should be permitted to march out with their baggage,
and that herself, her children, and women servants should be

---

[1] Fedderat at this time belonged to Robert Irvine, Sir Alexander's brother, who
must have been a wealthy man: his name appears frequently in the Book of Annual
Renters and Wadsetters, 1633, as creditor for large sums, including 8250 merks due to him by
William Erle Merchell, and 33,000 merks due by the Erle of Errol. In the same book it
is shown that he owed his mother, Lady Marion Douglas, 5000 merks, of which he "sould
onlie pay aucht for ilk hundreth thairoff": and that her sons-in-law, Ogilvy of Inverquharty,
and Grahame of Morphie, each owed her 1000 merks.

allowed to remain and occupy an apartment in the place. These conditions being complied with, Munro left a garrison of an officer and forty men to live at free quarters, and enjoined the lady to send her husband to him on his arrival. He left Drum on June 5th, returning triumphantly to Aberdeen, where, accompanied by the Earl Marischal, he attended divine service and returned thanks for the capture of this stronghold without greater difficulty, delay, and loss. Sir Alexander's sufferings and losses in the Royal cause were very great: his house and lands were frequently occupied and plundered by the army of the Covenanters. He was imprisoned, fined 10,000 merks, and more than once obliged to flee for safety to England: he lost his second son, and his eldest son had a very narrow escape from being executed. His brother, Robert of Fedderat, was also imprisoned and fined 4000 merks. —*Vide* Castellated Architecture of Aberdeenshire, by Sir A. Leith-Hay, K. H.

The laird was re-appointed Sheriff of Aberdeen from time to time, and still held that office in 1644. Early in the year he "was chargit with letters in the King's name," though, as Spalding says, "God kenis if thay war with his Majestie's will," to raise troops and apprehend Sir John Gordon of Haddo. Joined by sundry barons, he set out and proceeded to the house, near Kelly, where Haddo was, but failed to find him.

When his two sons heartily joined Huntly in the month of March, "the old Laird Drum baid still at home, and miskenit all." He and Fedderat, when called upon to subscribe the Covenant in Aberdeen in 1643, had refused, urging that it was sufficient to do so at their own parish churches: it does not appear whether they did so or not. In spite of the laird's attempt to keep neutral, the Covenanters plundered the place of Drum.

The Marquis of Argyll, at the beginning of May, rode thither with about 400 horse from Dunottar, and was followed by the Earl Marischal with the Mearns' men: they were joined by the Earl of Lauthean [Lothian] and Laird of Lawers, with the Irish regiment of the latter, about 500 men.

"Sir Alexander Irving wes not at home when Argile and the rest came; bot his lady, and his gude dochter Ladie Marie Gordon, and sister dochter to Argile wes present. He and his company were all mad welcome according to the tyme." But as Spalding goes on, "the regiment leivit upon the Laird Drum's victuall and goodis. The Marquess schortlie removit the tua ladies and set thame out o yettis perforce (albeit the young ladie wes his awin sister dochter) with tua gray plaidis about thair heidis. Their haill servandis wes also put to the yet; bot the ladies cam in upone tua wark naiges in pitifull manner to New Abirdein, and took up thair lodging besyde the goodwyf of Auchluncart, then duelling in the toune.   Then thir runagat Irish soldiers fell to, and plunderit the place of Drum, quhairin wes stoir of insicht plenishing and riche furnitour, and all uther provisioun necessar. They left nothing which could be carrit, and brak doun the staitlie bedis, burdis and tymber work. They killit and destroyit the bestiall, nolt, scheip, ky, for their meit. They brak up girnellis, quhair they had plentie of meill and malt. They fand yirdit in the yaird of Drum ane trunk full of silver plait, goldsmith wark, jewellis, chaynes, ringes, and other ornamentis of gryte worth, and estimat about 20,000 pundis, quhairof pairt wes sein in Abirdene. Thus thir ladeis being removit with their servandis, and all thingis plunderit by thir Irish rogues, then the Marquis appointit ane capitane with 50 muskiteires of their people to keip this houss, and left tuo piece of ordinance also with them, quhair they leivit upone the lairdis girnellis and goodis quhill thay war removit."

He goes on to relate how there were following this Irish regiment 51 women with some young children, who were all quartered in Old Aberdeen, and that meal was brought for their support from the girnels at Drum, two pecks for each woman weekly: a captain was set over them to see that they got their allowance punctually and that they did no wrong.

"Thus," he continues, "is this auncient houss of Drum oppressit, spoilzeit, and pitifullie plunderit, without ony fault committit be the old laird thairof: bot onlie for his tua sones following of the hous of Huntlie, and as wes thocht soir against his will also. Aluaies this is to be nottit for the Marques of Argile's first peice of service in the play, without love or respect to his sister dochter or innocencie of the old Laird Drum, whair for a whyll I will leave him doubtless in greif and distress."

The old laird went to the Marquis of Argyll and Earl Marischal shortly after at Inverurie, "but fand littell comfort:" he then went to Frendraught. The young laird and his brother Robert were at this time with Huntly in Strathbogie.

The following old ballad relates to Margaret, Sir Alexander's youngest daughter:

THE EARL OF ABOYNE.

The Earl of Aboyne is to Lunin gane,
  An' a' his nobles are wi' him;
But he's left his bonnie ladie behin',
  An' she was a sorrowfu' woman.

But he's sent a letter back to her,
  To say that he was comin';
And when that she looked the letter o'er,
  She was a most joyfu' woman.

She has ta'en her up to her high tower head,
  To look if she saw him comin';
And there she saw ane o' his best grooms,
  Comin' straightway doun frae Lunin.

"Oh! far frae come ye my bonnie, bonnie boy?"
  "O ladie, I'm last frae Lunin."
"O gin this be true, that I hear ye say,
  Say when is my gude lord comin'."

"O here is a letter, my ladie fair,
  To tell you your gude lord's a comin';
An in less, I'm sure, than the space of an hour,
  He will be hame frae Lunin."

She said, "My grooms all, be ready on call,"
  "An' hae a' the stables shinin';
"Wi' embroider'd draigs trim ye weel the naigs,
  "For my gude lord's a comin'.

"My minstrels all, be ready on call,
  "Wi' harps weel tuned for singin';
"Wi' the best o' your springs, spare not the strings
  "When ye hear his bridle ringin.'

"My cookes all, be ready on call,
  "Your pots an' your spits weel rankin';
"Wi' the best o' roast, an' spare nae cost,
  "And see that naethin' be wantin'.

"My own cham'ermaids, be all on your guards,
  "Now hae ye the rooms weel shinin';
"Wi' herbs o' sweet air, sprinkle well the stair,
  "An' cover the floors wi' linen.

"My faithful man, John, wi' my butler Tom,
  "Hae ilka thing weel shinin';
"See the cups be clean, and the wine be clear,
  "To drink his health for his comin'."

She has called her servants one and a'
  And Marget her gentlewoman;
"Go, get my bodie some braw attire,
  "Sin' my gude lord is comin'."

O when the silk gown she had got on
  O' silver cypher the linin';
Then, as at the entrance wide she stood,
  She was a most beautifu' woman.

"Ye're welcome hame, my ain gude lord,
  "Ye're welcome hame frae Lunin;
"Ye're welcome to Aboyne, my ain dear Lord,
  "O, I've thocht lang for yer comin.'

"If I be as welcome," cried he, "as ye say,
  "Come kiss me now for my comin';
"For the morn should hae been my weddin' day,
  "Gin I had but stayed in Lunin.'

"Gin the morn should hae been your weddin' day,
  'Ye needna' hae fashed yoursel' comin';
"Cause saddle your horse, and ride back again,
  "An gae, kiss your quean in Lunin."

He turned him round to his merry men a',
  "Is na this a pretty scornin'?
"But I'll mak' a vow, an' keep it true,
  "She'll think lang for my returnin.'

"Come Thomas, my man, get my horse, an' that soon,
  "For we'll a' be awa instantlie;
"An' soon we'll alight at the bonnie Bog o' Gight,
  "An' meet wi' the Marquis o' Huntlie."

Her maidens fair were a' waitin' on her,
  An' the doctors were wi' her dealin';
But in a crack, her bonnie heart it brak',
  An' letters were sent to Lunin.

When he saw the letters were seal'd wi' black,
  O his heart was sairly heavin';
"I'd rather hae lost the lands o' Aboyne,
  "Than hae lost bonnie Peggy Irvine.

"Come mount ye, an' mount ye, my trusty men a',
  "I'm waefu' sorry for my journeyin';
"Frae our horse to our hat we shall a' gae in black,
  "An' mourn for bonnie Peggy Irvine.

"O wae for the day that I cam' away,
  "Sae foolishly back to Lunin;
"But I'll mak' a vow, and I'll keep it true,
  "Ne'er again sall I kiss a woman."

The 10th laird died in 1658, and was succeeded by his eldest son.

11. ALEXANDER, the 11th laird, eldest son of the preceding, was twice married.[1] 1st, December 7, 1643, to Lady Mary Gordon, 4th daughter of George, second Marquis of Huntly; and 2nd, to Margaret Couts or Coutts. By his first wife he had issue, 3 sons and 4 daughters, viz.:—

(1). Alexander, younger of Drum.

(2). Robert.

(3). Charles. Both died young.

Daughters.— (1), Mary,[2] married Patrick, Count Leslie of Balquhain; (2), Margaret,[3] married Gilbert Menzies of Pitfodels; (3), Jean,[4] married Alexander Irvine of Murthill, afterwards of Drum; (4), Henrietta, married Alexander Leslie of Pitcaple.

By his second wife he had one son and three daughters: (1), Charles, died young; daughters,— (1), Catherine, married to John Gray; (2), Anne; (3), Elizabeth or Elspet, who both died in minority, unmarried.

Spalding relates that "the Marquess was flittit to the Bog, making preparatioun for the mareage of his dochter, Ladie Mary, with Alexander Irving, the young Laird Drum, and in the meintyme wes furneshing the place of Achindoun with all necessares."

. . . "Upon Thuirsday, 7 December, the young laird Drum wes mareit to the foirsaid Lady Mary Gordoun, with gryte solempnitie, and mirth and myrriness aneuche in the Bog at thair brydell; but the Lord Gordoun wes not as his sisteris brydell, throw miscontentment betwixt his father and him."

Lord Gordon had just visited his aunt, Lady Strabane, who was staying at Lesmoir; had gone thence to Strathbogie, and back to Aberdeen.— Spalding.

He and his brother Robert, during the lifetime of their father, and as young men, joined the banner of Montrose in support of the Royal cause. He endeavored in vain to induce his father-in-law, Lord Huntly, to join them. No one can wonder at Lord Huntly's refusal. A few years before this, Montrose, when on the side of the Covenanters, had induced the Earl with his two sons to come to Aberdeen, and there arrested him and his eldest son, Lord Gordon, and sent them as prisoners to Edinburgh. Huntly never forgave this treatment, and after Montrose had heartily espoused

[1] Contract in fam. arch., 1634. [2] Contr. in arch. fam., 1679. [3] Contr. ibid, 1682. [4] Contr. ibid, 1694.

the King's cause, never could be induced to co-operate with him. In 1644, however, Huntly was appointed Lieut.-General in the North of Scotland, and levied troops for the King in Aberdeenshire and Banffshire, and again in 1646 he, with 1500 foot and 600 horse, took up arms, and made a strong effort on his behalf; but even then he refused to comply with Montrose's instruction to march to Inverness and aid him in an attempt to take it. Instead of this he marched upon Aberdeen, storming it in three places, defeated Colonel Montgomery, and recovered the town for the King. He allowed his Highlanders to pillage it, and they in large numbers returned with the booty to their own homes. Among those released from the tolbooth of Aberdeen at this time by Montrose were Alexander Irving of Lenturk, and John Gordon of Innermarkie.

Meantime Montrose was attacked in force by Middleton, who had left Aberdeen to relieve Inverness, and was obliged to retreat before him to Beauly, and thence by Strathglass and Stratherrick to the Spey. Middleton, however, remained in Ross-shire, and laid siege to the Earl of Seaforth's castle, in the Chanonry, and afterwards, on hearing of Huntly's advance on Aberdeen, retraced his steps, recrossed the Spey, and returned to Aberdeen. Later than this Huntly did what he could in the north; he levied troops, but was pursued by General David Leslie through Lochaber, and by General Middleton through Glenmoriston and Badenoch, and was at last taken prisoner by Lieut.-Colonel Menzies in Strathdon, and executed in Edinburgh on March 22, 1649.

The position of his sons during this civil war was very strange. Lord Gordon, the eldest, was for some time under the influence of Argyle, his uncle by the mother's side: Lord Lewis Gordon, the 3rd son, was fighting in the ranks of the Covenanters, having previously taken up arms for the King, and subsequently deserted the Covenanters and went over to Montrose: the 2nd son, Viscount Aboyne, and the 4th, Lord Charles, afterwards created Earl of Aboyne, both adhered firmly to the Royal cause. Lord Gordon, after the battle of Inverlochy, and the defeat of Argyle, joined Montrose, and commanded his horse at the battle of Auldearn; and, conjointly with Sir Nathaniel Gordon, had command of his right wing at the battle of Alford, where he was killed.

The connections by marriage between many of these combatants is interesting.

Archibald, the 7th Earl of Argyle, married Lady Agnes Douglas,

5th daughter of the 1st Earl of Morton, of the House of Lochleven, and 7th Earl. Archibald, their son, the 8th Earl and 1st Marquis of Argyle, married, as his first wife, Lady Margaret Douglas, 2nd daughter of William, 2nd Earl of Morton, of the House of Lochleven.

The 9th laird of Drum married Lady Marion Douglas, daughter of the 4th Earl of Buchan, who was 2nd brother of the 1st Earl of Morton, of the House of Lochleven.

The 7th Earl of Argyle's eldest daughter, Lady Anne Campbell, married, in 1607, George, 2nd Marquis of Huntly: consequently their children, Lord Gordon and his brothers and sisters, were nephews and nieces of the 8th Earl and 1st Marquis, their mother's brother; and first cousins of his son, the 9th Earl of Argyll.

The 11th laird of Drum married Lady Mary Gordon, 4th daughter of the 2nd Marquis of Huntly, and niece of the Marquis of Argyle, granddaughter of the Earl of Buchan, and grandniece of his brother, the Earl of Morton.

The three Marquises all met their deaths on the scaffold — Huntly in 1649, Montrose in 1650, and Argyle in 1661.

During Lord Huntly's first effort in the north, a party of 120 horse and 300 foot, commanded by the young Laird of Drum and his brother, young Gicht, Colonel Nathaniel Gordon and Colonel Donald Farquharson and others, proceeded, contrary to the opinion of the Marquis, from Aberdeen, which he had taken, to the town of Montrose, which they took, killed one of the bailies, made the Provost prisoner, and threw some cannon into the sea as they could not carry them away. But, on hearing that Earl of Kinghorn was advancing upon them with the forces of Angus, they made a speedy retreat, leaving thirty of their foot behind them prisoners. Somewhat later, after the young Laird of Drum and his brother were taken prisoners at Wick, a party of Montrose's horse took Forbes of Craigievar and Forbes of Boyndlie prisoners at Aberdeen, Some little time afterwards, Montrose, being then in Angus and preparing to cross the Grampians, and to march to Strathbogie and make another attempt to raise the Gordons, released Craigievar and Boyndlie on their parole, upon condition that Cragievar should procure the liberation of young Drum and his brother from the jail in Edinburgh, failing which, Cragievar and Boyndlie were both to deliver themselves up to him as prisoners before the first of November. This act of generosity on the part of Montrose was greatly admired, more particularly as Craigievar was one of the heads of the Covenanters, and had great influence among them. The effort, however, to effect an exchange of prisoners failed.

The brothers shared in Montrose's exploits, and also in his dangers, and distinguished themselves so highly in his service that they were excommunicated April 14, 1644, and had a price set upon their heads: 18,000 merks was offered for the young laird, dead or alive, and 9,000 for Robert. With the view of escaping to England, they sailed from Fraserburgh, accompanied by Lady Mary Gordon, Drum's wife, and Alexander Irvine, son of John Irvine of Artamford, but, being driven out of their course and obliged to land at Wick, where the Committee of Estates happened to be sitting, they were made prisoners, and warded in the Castle of Keiss. Thence they were conducted, under a strong escort, to Edinburgh, and lodged in the city jail. Robert died in prison six months afterwards: the young laird was then removed to the Castle under sentence of death. His execution, however, was stopped by the defeat of the Covenanters at Kilsyth in 1645, and, in compliance with the stipulations made by the Marquis of Montrose with the delegates from Edinburgh, he and the other prisoners there were set at liberty.

In 1646 he, with a troop of horse, and Farquharson of Inverey, with 200 infantry, beat up the quarters of the Covenanters on Deeside, within six miles of Aberdeen, taking 70 prisoners, with all their horses, baggage, and provisions.

After succeeding to Drum, and on the restoration and accession of King Charles II., the offer of the peerage which had been made to his father was renewed, but he declined it unless the patent bore the date of the one formerly granted. It is probable, however, that the great reduction which his estates and fortune had undergone during the civil war was the principal reason for his refusal. About this time he sold the estate of Kelly, in Forfarshire, to Lord Panmure. — *Vide* Cassillated Arch. of Abdnsh, by Sir Andrew Leith Hay, K. H.

About twenty years afterwards, King Charles II., in granting a Charter, dated at Windsor Castle, August 3, 1683, containing a novodamus of Drum's whole estates holding of the Crown, took occasion to express in it the deep sense which he had of the family's loyalty, and their services and sufferings in the Royal cause.

This Charter[1] proceeded on a Procuratory of Resignation dated

[1] Chart. in publ. arch.

April 4, 1683, for resigning in the King's hands the laird's lands and baronies of Drum, Fedderat, the tenandrie of Ruthven, the lands of Coull, Kinmucks, Kennerties, the barony of Auchtercoul, and others therein mentioned, for new infeftment thereof, to be granted to the said Alexander and his heirs; male which failing, to the heirs of entail to be contained in any nomination under his hand; and failing such a nomination, to his eldest heir female; which failing, to his nearest heir male whatsoever; which failing, to his nearest lawful heirs and assignees whatsoever.

The two following documents relate to this.

1. Copy Extract from the Books of Exchequer, 1684:—

"At Edinburgh the 8th day of February, 1684. His Majesty's letter underwritten directed to William Marquis of Queensberry, Lord High Treasurer, John Drummond of Lundie, Lord Treasurer Depute, and the remanent Lords of his Majesty's Exchequer, was presented and read, and ordained to be booked, whereof the tenor followeth: "Sic superscribitur. Charles R. Right trusty and right well beloved Cousine and Councillor: and Trusty and well beloved, we greet you well. Whereas in a signature (of the date of these presents) signed by us in favours of Alexander Irwing of Drum, we were graciously pleased in consideration of the eminent loyalty and good services of the family of Drum for several ages to change the holding of such of the lands as formerly held ward from simple ward to Taxt ward. We have also thought fit hereby to authorize and require you to pass the said signature in the ordinary form and method in such cases accustomed; and (in further consideration of the sufferings of several of that family upon the account of their adherence to the true interests of the Crown) to fill up the Taxt duties in the blanks that are left in the said signature for that effect, according to the old Retoured duties of those his ward lands, notwithstanding any orders or instructions formerly given by us to the contrary. For doing whereof this shall be your warrant. And so we bid you heartily farewell. Given at our Court at Windsor Castle the 3rd day of August 1683 years, and of our reign the 35th year. By his Majesty's command sic subscribitur Morray.

"Extractum de libris scaccarii per me.

"(Signed)   GEO. MACKENZIE, Cler. Reg."

2. Copy of Clause in the Charter of Resignation by Charles II. to Alexander Irvine of Drum, August 3, 1683:—

"Insafer nos pro bonis fidelibus et gratuitis servitiis nobis et progenitoribus nostris beatæ memoriæ nostris que successoribus per dictum Alexandrum Irvine de Drum ejus que progenitores et successores præstitis et præstandis: Præsertim vero ob magna et notanda servitia Willielmi Irvine de Drum unius ex ejus prædecessoribus, qui strenuo nostro antecessori Roberto Primo in omnibus suis bellis et extremitatibus inseparabiliter adhæserat, et quem nulla unquam Regis sui personam ant titulum declarare cogebant; ac prædecessoris sui non minus Domini Alexandri Irvine de Drum, qui ductu suo et valore ad Harlai prælium summa præstitit auxilia ad insolentem istam Insulanorum seditionem reprimendam, ubi eorum Ducem M'Lenum inter alios segregavit, oppugnavit, manuque propriâ in ipsa belli acie occidt, in associatorum terrorem et cladem, sed qui in eadem actione Principi suo vitæ pretio servivit, gloriam sibi repertans jus Regium propriamque fidem sanguine suo signari: nec non aliis Domini Alexandri Irvine de Drum ex ejus prædecessoribus, qui in publico Ducis Murdachi ministerio pro zelo, servito et magno suo erga Principem affectu, conspicuus apparuit in commissione illa, quæ, Illustrissimum progenitorem nostrum Jacobum Primum antiquo suo Regno et Regimini sretauravit, et hoc præter alia multa servitia fidelia, tam prænominatorum quam intergrorum aliorum antiquæ istius fidelis et inviolatæ familæ prædecessorum, diversis eorum sæculis peracta; sive pacis sive belli temporibus as in omnibus conditionibus quæ ipsos capaces redderent, vitis suis et fortunis sacris Regis sui personæ et prærogativæ sibi usquam caris, inservire et tueri: spectati vero in recentioribus instantiis fidelium et alacrium servitiorum et perpessionum tum patris Domini Alexandri Irvine de Drum, tum prænominati Alexandri nunc de Drum sui filii, qui nuperis calamitatum et rebellionis temporibus fidelium suorum antecessorum nomina meruerunt; idque fidissima eorum et tanacissima Illustrissimi nostri Patris Caroli Primi, sempiternæ memoriæ, nostris que rebus adhesione, in arctissimis nostris difficultatibus et angustiis, adeo ut non mulctæ, carceres, fortunarum minæ, excommunicatio, exilium, nec sententiæ id eorum vitam latæ, præsertim dicti Alexandri, in quem sententia lata fuit, et illico fuisset executa, si non providente Deo fidus noster tunc temporis Commissarius et Prafectus Montis rosarum Marchio eum in arce notra Edinburghina, ubi in arcta custodia jacebat, in libertatem assernisset; neque innumeræ aliæ crudelitates, oppressiones et devastationes per prævalentes tunc rebelles in ipsius et patris sui familias et fortunas late commissæ, nec ullæ aliæ severitates et difficultates, aut dura eorum temporum

pericula, eos unquam deterrebant, nec ullæ quæcunique suasiones
aut illecebræ eos unquam deviare fecerunt a sincera ista fide et zelo,
quibus erga peronam et prærogativam Regiam usquam claruerunt."

Such testimony to the continuous loyalty of the family, during
times when many illustrious families fought sometimes for and
sometimes against the Crown, is something worth inheriting.

An entail, subject to certain provisions and restrictions, including
power to heirs, who should succeed, to sell such lands as should be
necessary for paying the just debts of the entailer, was accordingly
executed, in form of a Procuratory of Resignation to the Crown,
and relative deeds, in 1683, two years before the Entail Act of 1685
was passed; and on September 4, 1687, Drum executed a Deed
of Nomination regulating the order of succession in favour of, first,
his son, Alexander; and failing him and the heirs of his body, and
failing other heirs of his own body, then of Alexander Irvine of
Murthill and his heirs male; and failing them, of James Irvine of
Artamford and his heirs male; and failing them, of Robert Irvine of
Cults and his heirs male; failing all of these, of the heirs female of
his own body without division. For some reason, Irvine of Saphock, who was the nearest heir male failing the entailer's own issue,
was entirely omitted. The entailer died about a month afterwards,
and (anticipating a little) the steps taken to make the entail valid
were as follows: Immediately after the grantor's death, Irvine of
Murthill petitioned the Court to record it, and as it was the very
first entail recorded under the Act of 1685, especial care was taken
that everything might be done in accordance with the requirements of the Act.

The Lords of Council ordained, "The Charter and Nomination
relative thereto, containing the said tailzie of the barony of Drum,
being produced and read, and collationed with the following record
of the same, in the presence of the Lords, that the said record thereof
be insert and registrate in the books appointed for the registration
of tailzie conform to 22nd Act of his Majesty's first Parliament,
concerning tailzies."

Then follow the Charter and Deed of Nomination, which were
recorded on July 31, 1688.

The question whether it was valid against creditors and singular
successors arose subsequently, as will be seen. The lands of Strachan over not included in the entail. Besides the entail and nomination, this laird executed, on the same day as he signed the latter,
a bond of provision in favor of his eldest son by his second mar-

riage, Charles Irvine, and his heirs, and to other heirs male
nominated to succeed to his estates, amounting to £80,000 Scots,
and another bond for 8,000 merks in favour of his daughter Elspet; and on the following day a disposition mainly in favor of
Margaret Coutts, his second wife, and their son Charles, securing
to them, and the heirs male of his son Charles, then of himself the
grantor, and his said wife, to the heirs specified in the entail
and nomination, ample provisions, under which Margaret Coutts
was to have the life-rent of the estate during widowhood, and
his son Charles, or any other heir succeeding to the estate, was
bound to pay to his other daughters, Catharine and Anna Irvine,
on their attaining the age of sixteen, a sum left blank in the deed.
Apparently his eldest son, Alexander, only lived till 1696, while his
widow, by 1690, had become the wife of Robert Irvine of Cults.
Much trouble resulted from these provisions. The timber in the
east and west woods of Drum, and that part called the Kitchen Bog,
was sold in 1685 for 18,000 merks, the purchaser, James Duncan,
being allowed ten years to cut and remove it.

There is an old ballad relative to this laird's second marriage,
which is entitled:

THE LAIRD O' DRUM.

The laird o' Drum's a huntin' gane
    Upon a mornin' early;
An' he has spied a weel faur'd May
    Was sheerin' at her barley.

O can ye fancy me, fair May,
    O can ye fancy me, O?
O can ye fancy me, fair May,
    An' let your sheerin' be, O?

I canna fancy ye, kind sir,
    I canna fancy ye, O;
For I'm nae fit to be your wife,
    Your miss I'd scorn to be, O.

Cast off, cast off the gown o' gray,
    Put on the silk and scarlet;
I'll mak' a vow, an' keep it true,
    Ye'll ne'er be miss nor harlot.

I canna wear your silken gown,
    They rattle at the heel, O;
But I can wear the linsey brown,
    And that sets me right weel, O.

My father is an old shepherd,
  Keeps sheep on yonder hill, O:
And ilka thing he bids me do,
  I work aye at his will, O.

He's ta'en him to her auld father,
  Keeps sheep on yonder hill, O;
Ye've a fair May to your daughter,
  Dear vow, I lo'e her weel, O.

She canna han'le china cups,
  Nor mak' your dish o' tea, O;
But she can milk baith cow and ewe,
  Wi' cogie on her knee, O.

She'll shak' i' the barn, and winnow corn,
  An' ca' your loads to mill, O;
In time o' need, she'll saddle your steed,
  An' draw your boots hersel', O.

O fa will bake my bridal bread?
  An' fa will brew my ale, O?
An' fa will welcome my bride hame?
  It's mair than I can tell, O.

O I will bake your bridal bread,
  An' I will brew your ale, O;
But fa will welcome your bride hame,
  It's mair than I can tell, O.

Fu' four and twenty lairds and lords
  Stood at the yetts o' Drum, O;
But ne'er a man did lift his hat,
  When the lady o' Drum was come, O.

But he has ta'en her by the hand,
  An' led her but and ben, O;
Says welcome hame, my lady Drum,
  For this is a' your ain, O.

Then out he spak' his brother dear,
  An angry man was he, O;
Says he, ye hae wedded this day a wife
  A shame to a' yer degree, O.
  [or That's far below your degree, O.]

Weel I hae wedded a wife to win,
  An' ye a wife to spen', O;
As long's my head my hat can bear,
  She'll be the lady Drum, O.

The first lady that I did wed
  She was o' high degree, O;
She could na gang out at the yetts o' Drum
  But the perlin abeen her een, O.

The first lady that I did wed.
  She was o' high degree, O;
I durst na come intil the rooms,
  But wi' hat below my knee, O.

When bells were rung, an' mass was sung,
  An' a' were boun' to bed, O;
The Laird o' Drum an' the shepherd's daughter
  In ae bed they were laid, O.

Gin' ye'd been come o' noble bluid,
  As ye're o' low degree, O;
We might hae walked into the street
  Amang gude companie, O.

I tauld ye lang ere we were wed,
  I was o' low degree, O;
An' now I am your wedded wife,
  I scorn this slight frae ye, O.

When you are dead, an' I am dead,
  An' baith laid i' the grave, O;
An' seven lang years are come and gane,
  Fu' justice I will hae, O.

She had nae been forty weeks his wife,
  Till she brought him a son, O;
She was as weel a loved lady
  As ever was in Drum, O.

This laird, the 11th, died in 1687, and was buried in Drum's
aisle, his funeral being attended by the magistrates and citizens
under arms. He was succeeded by his eldest son.

12. ALEXANDER, the 12th laird, born about 1646; died 1696. He
    married Marjory or May, daughter of Forbes of Auchreddie,
    but had no issue.

He does not appear to have had any enjoyment of his
paternal estates. These must have been considerably reduced
in extent and value. Kelly, and probably Forglen, had been
sold to pay fines and debts, contracted during the civil war,
and his father further burdened the estates with provisions
to his children or their husbands, and to his second wife, and
especially to his son by her. The late laird had also appointed
trustees and administrators for some reason or another for his
son, Alexander, and had nominated Alexander Irvine of Muthill as
his executor, as administrator for Alexander, his eldest son, and
as tutor for Charles, his second son.

It may be that the eldest had offended him by his marriage with Marjory Forbes, daughter of Forbes of Auchreddie, for I find a reference, in a discharge granted to Irvine of Murthill, dated January 6, 1688, to a claim made by Patrick, Count Leslie, for expenses going to Edinburgh with the Laird of Drum "in pursuit of the reduction of the marriage *alleged* to be made betwixt him and Marjory Forbes:" from which one may infer that he was married before his father's death. This marriage must have been recognized as valid, for his widow had a jointure paid to her for many years as the Dowager Lady Drum.

Or, again, he and his father may have quarrelled about the latter's second marriage. Perhaps the son was not thought competent to manage his affairs, or, more probably, advantage was taken of his father in his old age.

The old laird died, probably in October, 1687: Murthill was confirmed as his executor on November 10, 1687, and his accounts as executor and administrator were afterwards rendered, commencing in October of that year. He, too, seems to have had a hard time of it in consequence of claims made against the entailer's estate, and the burdens for jointures and provisions.

By February, 1690, Margaret Coutts had become the wife of Robert Irvine of Cults, one of the substitutes under the entail, and in February of that year, we find a process of suspension and multiplepoinding had been "raised at the instance of the tenants on the estate of Drum against Alexander Irvine of Murthill, one of the pretended administrators of the estate, and Margaret Coutts, relict of the late Laird of Drum, and then spouse to Robert Irvine of Cults," and an act and factory granted by the Court of Session, dated 28th February in that year, "nominating and appointing —— Irvine, younger of Kingcoussie, to be factor on the Highland estate of Drum, lying in Cromar, and within the parochines of Coul, Tarland, and Logie, or any other parish within the bounds of Cromar."

In 1691, Murthill, as Drum's executor, obtained a decree from the Commissary of Aberdeen against some debtors. In February of the following year the Lords of Council and Session gave a decision in his favor as administrator for Alexander Irvine, then of Drum, and as tutor nominate to Charles Irvine, second son of the late Drum, against the said Charles Irvine, Robert Irvine of Cults, James Irvine of Artamford (all substitutes in the entail), and Robert Irvine of Fedderat, for selling part of the estate of Drum.

In the same year and month, Patrick Leslie of Balquehain got a decree against the Laird of Drum and his tutors and curators, ordaining Alexander Irvine of Murthill, administrator for Drum, to pay him the by gone annual rents of the sum of 12,000 merks due to himself, and other sums therein specified.

The Laird of Balquhain seems to have got payment in full of the tocher of his wife, Mary Irvine, amounting to 12,000 merks, and to have granted a discharge dated November 24, 1685; but to have subsequently bargained with Murthill for 20,000 merks more, payable to him and Menzies of Pitfodels, equally between them, in augmentation of their wives' tochers, under date January 6, 1688, and further, on July 6th following, to have got a promise that Murthill would give them, or each of their ladies, one of the jewels that had been given him in custody by the Laird of Drum before his death. He granted a discharge of these obligations on November 28, 1693.

Early in 1692, Murthill, as assignee of the laird, made over to his own eldest son, Alexander Irvine, his heirs and assignees, all bonds, contracts, and sums of money due to the estate of the old laird, under "a translation" dated 14th April; and he died shortly after, in the same year. His son seems to have succeeded him in the administration of the estate, with all the attendant troubles and difficulties; and he married Jean Irvine, sister of the Laird of Drum, the date of the contract being July 12, 1693.

The laird's half-brother, Charles Irvine, died a minor early in the last mentioned year, as there is an account of the disbursements at his funeral, dated April, 1693. At the time of his death the bond of provision in his favour for £80,000 Scots was not paid; and later on an attempt was made by creditors to show that the then laird was his heir, in respect that this bond was granted in favor of Charles, and, failing him and the heirs male of his body, *of the heirs of entail;* and that, consequently, the then laird, their debtor, was bound to enter as heir to the said Charles in this bond of provision, with a view to making it a burden on the estate, and they succeeded.

In the first instance, it became necessary to sell part of the estate. Strachan, as already mentioned, was not included in the entail, and apparently an Act of the Scots Parliament was obtained for selling so much of the estate as would pay all the debts contracted before making the entail or by the entailer himself. There is extant a minute of agreement between Alexander Irvine of Murthill, administrator of the estate, and Sir Alex. Bannerman of Elsick, proceeding on the narrative that the parties had agreed upon a sale of the lands of Strachan, part of the estate of Drum, then purchased by Sir Alex. Bannerman for 28,800 merks Scots, and 10,000 merks for the timber, but that, owing to the incapacity of the then laird of Drum, there could be no alienation nor valid disposition granted by the administrator immediately. Provision was made for Sir A. Bannerman advancing the price, on terms therein specified, and for his entry at Whitsunday, 1695. This minute is dated February 6, 1695, but it is stated that it appears to have been cancelled, possibly owing to the death of the 12th laird; if so, a similar one was probably entered into for effecting the sale, on Murthill succeeding to Drum, as Sir A. Bannerman acquired Strachan about that time.

This laird died comparatively young in 1696, leaving a widow, but no issue, and in him failed the main line in direct descent. He was succeeded, under the entail, by his brother-in-law and fourth cousin.

13. ALEXANDER, the 13th laird, b. ——, died 1720, was a son of
    Alexander of Murthill, who died in 1692, and a descendant,
    probably great-grandson, of Gilbert of Colairlie, who was
    a younger son of Alexander who fell at Pinkie, and brother
    of the 8th laird, who married Lady Elizabeth Keith. He
    married, on July 12, 1693, Jean, daughter of Alexander, the
    11th laird, by Lady Mary Gordon, and had issue by her
    1 son and 2 daughters.
    (1). Alexander, younger of Drum.
    The daughters —(1), Helen, md. Gordon of Dorlathers; (2),
    Margaret.

He had also a brother, John, who, after his death, was tutor-at-law to his son, and, on the death of the latter, succeeded to Drum as heir of entail.

By their marriage contract, he became bound to infeft her in life-rent of the lands of Murthill, and should he succeed to the estate of Drum, to secure her in life-rent to 30 chalders of vitual and money rent out of said estate, counting 100 merks for the chalder of vitual, and to the manor-place of Drum with the offices, while the heir of the marriage should be minor or unmarried, and thereafter to £100 Scots yearly.

On this laird's succession in 1696, troubles gathered on him fast;

the nearest heirs of line threatened processes of reduction of the entail, and he had to undertake to pay considerable sums to Count Leslie of Balquhain, Menzies of Pitfodels, and others for securing his right.   He accordingly got a warrant or act of the Scots Parliament for selling so much of the estate of Drum as would pay off all the debts contracted either before making the tailzie or by the entailer himself: there can be no doubt that the debts of the entailer were considerable, besides a jointure to his widow, and an aliment to his son; but these proved the cause of further debts to the 13th laird.

He first carried out the sale of the lands of Strachan, which were not included in the entail, to Sir Alexander Bannerman: he then sold Auchtercoul, part of the estates in Cromar, for £48,000 Scots to Black of Haddo, but repurchased it in fee simple in 1702; and sold the lands of Hirn and Drumquhynie to Sir Thomas Burnett of Leys: he appears, a little before this time, to have sold his own property of Murthill to Robert Cuming, Master of the Mortifications of Aberdeen, with consent of his wife, who renounced her right under her marriage contract to the life-rent thereof, and he made provision for her by obligations dated 1697 and 1709, out of the manor-place of Drum and other lands, including Tarland, whereby she was to have the use of the manor-place until any heir male issue of their marriage should marry or become major; in which case she was, after her removal, to receive £100 yearly for mailling of a house.

The creditors, upon getting payment, disponed any rights they still had to a Mr. William Black, advocate, then Drum's trustee, who, sometime before his death, transferred them all in favor of Drum: at a later period Drum disponed all these rights, in 1719, in favor of Sir Alexander Cuming of Culter. This baronet had become bound as cautioner and co-principal for the 13th laird in several debts and sums of money as early as 1701; for between 1696 and 1701 Drum granted Sir Alexander bonds of relief, seven in number, amounting to 102,000 merks. There is also extant a memo. for the Laird of Drum, dated September 18, 1700, respecting the sale of part of his estate (possibly Auchtercoul) for paying off the debts and haill adjudications led therefor, which he had paid and purchased in upon his own and his friend's credit. Sir Alexander Cuming made great profession of his desire to assist Drum, and to maintain that ancient family, but, as will be seen below, his course of action was well calculated to ruin it. The

Laird of Drum then granted several heritable bonds over his estate of Auchtercoul, besides increasing his liabilities on bills and other bonds; and part of the provision for his wife, Jean Irvine, was secured on the lands of Tarland, in the barony of Auchtercoul.

His eldest son took part in the Earl of Mar's rising, in 1715, during which he was severely wounded, but escaped to the continent. There are extant letters from his father to him while he was abroad. In one, dated July 18, 1716, he writes that he has received his son's letter from Cambray, and describes his own embarrassments, and points out that he could not alter the entail, and saw no way of securing the estate to his son except by a remission. He concludes, "I doubt not, when the Government cannot get the estate, a remission will be easier got if this trial were once over;" probably referring to the trial at Carlisle of the prisoners taken at Sheriff-muir and elsewhere in Scotland; he refers to "the debts affecting his estate in spite of what had been paid off by the sale of lands. Estimating his estate to be then worth 16,260 merks a year, with superiorities yielding annually 9,000 merks, he desired to sell land to value of 7,200 merks a year and the superiorities; he reckoned that the proceeds would pay his debts, estimated at 135,000 merks, and that he would still have 9,000 merks a year, less an annuity payable to the Dowager Lady Drum."

In another letter, dated September 4, of same year, in reply to one from his son, and sent to care of Mr. Wm. Gordon, banquir at Paris, he says, "I am very desirous to have a remission for you in case I should die, and probably I cannot live long;" and again, "a remission will be much easier got now than if I were dead, because ye have presently nothing to lose."

His son was ultimately pardoned and must have returned to Scotland by the early part of 1719, for we find a letter from the laird to him, addressed to him in Edinburgh, and dated March 12th, and one from him to the Laird of Portlethen, enclosing a list of debts, dated Drum, June 10th, in the same year. This list purports to be "A List of Debts that People hath old Drum's bond for, by himself, viz., a nott of those who hath my own personal bond:" the amount of these is nearly £30,000 Scots, but it includes certain bonds marked "Payd" amounting to about £4,600, and others amounting to £2,500 "Transferred:" but he subjoines a further list of debts for which Culter was jointly bound with him, viz., to Lady Balquhain's children £4,333 6s 8d, and to Black of Haddo £26,661 13s. 4d.

A little earlier than this, Drum, having burdened his estate of Auchtercoul with several heritable bonds, with consent of his son, had by minute of sale dated 3rd and 18th September, 1718, sold and disponed to Sir Alexander Cuming the land and baronies of Auchtercoul and Tarland, for which the latter became bound to pay Drum 80,000 merks Scots, with liberty to apply the same towards purging the debts and incumbrances which affected his purchase. Sir Alexander then got a Charter and was infeft: a disposition with the further consent of Jean Irvine, Drum's spouse, followed, dated September 8, 1719; and there is an obligation or backbond of Sir Alexander's to Drum to hold compt of the same, dated March 13, 1722; and as he had by that time paid a considerable part of the price to Drum's creditors, and taken obligations to the debts, but had still a balance in his hands, he became bound to apply the residue in like mannner, in the event of his purchase being confirmed by the Court of Session in a process then depending against Drum and Sir Alexander at the instance of Irvine of Crimond, one of the substitute heirs of entail.

Shortly before his death, which took place in 1720, this Drum had a conversation with Captain Cuming, Sir Alexander's eldest son, and James Gordon of Barns, one of his creditors, relative to compounding and transacting his debts. Poor man, the more he paid the more the claims on him appear to have increased.

This was followed by a letter, dated October 29, 1719, from Sir Alexander Cuming to the young laird, referring to a proposal, which he says he had made to his father, to obtain an Act of Parliament to re-settle the lands and barony of Drum and others upon Alexander Irvine, younger of Drum, his heirs male, and the other heirs of entail, and for selling part (*i.e.* the remainder) of the Estate of Cromar, &c., for payment of the deceast Alexander Irvine of Drum's debts, and the other debts of the family, and raising children's provisions, &c. He continues, "Such an Act, even in the votes, will be far from being any prejudice to you, but people will see that there is a good old estate settled on you (how much nobody needs to know), and that is more than they can know of the estates of any of our countrymen." He then goes on to assure him that he has "no view in it but to serve the family, for his own purchase was perfectly secure, and, next to his own security, he wished young Drum's family better than any in the world." This letter was written at Bath; he urges him to come up with his charters, tailzie, and writings, and promises him every assistance, and in a P. S. assures him that "such Acts are common every year in settling great families, making jointures, paying debts, and raising provisions." Sir Alexander's scheme was now developed, viz., to force a judicial sale of the Drum estate, by making out that the incumbrances affecting them were so heavy that they could not be paid otherwise, and to resettle the land representing whatever residue might be over.

The young laird thus pressed, and led to believe that he would still have a moderate estate left, fell in with his proposals. He wrote to Alexander Thomson, of Portlethen, enclosing Sir Alexander's letter, and referring to his having already shown it to him, he thus reminds him, "I desired you to call to mind what debts you thought could be scraped together that could be said to be my grandfather's, who was the entailer, and so by adding them to the debts of his, still unpaid, which, with my sister's bonds of provision, would amount, by accumulating the annual rents from the date of the old bonds (which will be, I believe, very near 25 years back), to very near about 70,000 and odd pounds Scots, which, with any debts you could scrape together as aforesaid, might make up the sum demanded, which must be mentioned in the petition, and indeed must be made up to the value of (I mean the extracts from the registers of the bonds set up) 92,000, and as many pounds more as possibly you can find; it's no matter whether payed or not, being that's what will not be questioned." No wonder that he concludes the letter, "Pray keep all this as much a secret as possibly I can beg you, for reasons."

Such was the scheming going on between Sir Alex. Cuming and the young laird, the latter a foolish and unscrupulous tool, careless of the honour and interests of the family, provided a remnant of the estate was left free for him to enter on. They both wrote to Drum at this time; for the laird wrote to Sir Alexander referring to *both* letters in the same month, and mentioned a bond which played a very important part in enabling them to carry out the scheme referred to, and denuding the family of the greater part of their property. This bond was one for £80,000 Scots, with annual rent, granted by the entailer to his son by the second marriage, Charles, and to his heirs; whom failing, to his nearest heirs of tailzie. On the death of Charles, the 13th laird was the nearest male heir under the entail; and in this letter he wrote, "I think the production of it will make a clear demonstration of the necessitie of selling more land."

At this stage of the negotiations this laird died, at Whitsunday, 1720, and was succeeded by his son. He was survived by his widow, Jean, the entailer's daughter.

14. ALEXANDER, the 14th laird, born about 1695, died 1737. He does not seem to have been married.

Some acount has been already given of his younger days. Immediately on his accession as laird, Sir Alexander Cuming wrote to Thomson of Portlethen, on June 21, 1720, relative to Drum's health and affairs, and the letter shows his anxiety, lest he should die before the desired Act of Parliament could be obtained. He mentions that he had remitted some money to Edinburgh, and would send some small remittances to Aberdeen to meet pressing claims of Drum's creditors; and his readiness to venture a sum of £2,000, if it would satisfy the creditors, besides the entailer's debts; and that he "would with pleasure once more lend his helping hand to rescue that worthy family." But at the same time he desires to know what further security he could get till an Act of Parliament should be attempted, and refers to Drum's telling him that his mother would assign a considerable part of her jointure to him as a part of his security.

It is evident from documents that later on the Dowager Lady Drum also consented to restrict her jointure from 1950 merks to 1,500 merks, or £1,000 Scots, and that Sir Alexander wrote to her that the abatement was for the benefit of the laird of Drum, and should be applied accordingly.— *Vide* State of Process, &c., relative to judicial sale of the Drum estates, 1737, p. 176.

On the same day, June 2, 1720, a minute of sale between Alex. Irvine of Drum and Sir Alex. Cuming of Culter was signed, obliging the former to grant a disposition of the town and lands of Coul, &c., in Cromar, with entry at Whitsunday, 1720; the price to be applied in purchasing in the debts contracted by his grandfather, or any other debts contracted by the heirs of entail, affecting these lands; and the remainder, if any, for payment of debts for which Sir Alexander stood bound, either as co-principal or cautioner for Drum's father, or of Drum's debts to himself. Several debts are then specified, and there is a proviso that if it should be thought necessary to apply for an Act of Parliament, Sir Alexander was to advance the money to pay for it, and all other expenses, and that should the price of the estate not cover this, Drum and his heirs were to be liable in repayment to him. He then instructed Thomson of Portlethen, July 7, 1720, to pay off and compound with old Drum's creditors, as he must take assignations to their debts, "in order to lead to an adjudication to be a pretext for an Act of Parliament to confirm his articles of sale of the estate;" and further, "to muster up old debts and bonds, principals and annual rents, for those will be a pretext for an Act of Parliament; but it is not proper for you let any persons know more of this than what needs." Over and above this, the laird granted Sir Alexander a heritable bond over the whole of his estates, the lands and barony of Drum, Kinmuck, and all the lands in Cromar for his life-rent interest in them, but the latter disponed and transferred this to James Gordon of Barns for behoof of Drum's creditors in 1722.

Sir Alexander again wrote to Thomson of Portlethen, on July 16 and 21, 1720, referring to the proposed Act of Parliament, and says in the latter, "Meantime I will pay off old Drum, the entailer's debts, which will certainly affect the estate, and thereby I shall make up a title to the rest of the lands of Cromar, which I lately purchased, for as to the former my security is good enough."

By this time he had acquired right, in one form or another, to the whole of the Cromar estate; but he did not keep it long. His plans are further developed in his own letters. He wrote on July 30th following to Thomson of Portlethen, "If all old Drum's creditors will assign their debts and heritable bonds, &c., I will pay them when they please, and raise an adjudication against the estate, in order to be a pretence for a sale by Act of Parliament, without which, and mustering up debts sufficient to balance all the debts of the last and present Drum, none of their creditors can expect one groat: for the estate is liable for neither, and can only be affected during this Drum's life, and that, considering the jointure, will hardly relieve me, for he must still live, and you may be sure his rent will not maintain him here [viz., in London], and I am considerably in advance for him."

A letter of similar import followed of date August 4th; and in another dated 11th August, he refers to an old bond in favor of Irvine of Cults, thus, "I suppose if he assigns me to the heritable bond and all the annual rents since old Drum, the entailer's death, or these 39 years by past, if they be not discharged they will come to a large sum of money: and tho' he loses what was due by the last Drum, he wil have enough." This appears to refer to some old wadsets over the lands of Drum.

About this time Sir Alexander appears to have advanced the

£2,000 stg. to pay some of Drum's debts, and he held several bonds of relief in respect to obligations for which he had been Drum's cautioner; but he took very good care to protect himself. He had already got a heritable bond over the whole of the laird's estates for his life interest, but on 29th April, 1721, he got from him in addition a bond of £10,000 sterling, payable at Whitsunday following, with £2,000 of liquidate expenses and interest, with letters of special charge, raised thereupon at his instance against Drum, to enter heir in special to the deceast Charles Irvine, second son of the entailer, his uncle, in the bond for £80,000 Scots, granted as a provision for Charles. His object was, by getting this bond from Drum, as for money borrowed, or paid for him, to be in a position to get the said bond of provision (originally granted in favour of Charles) adjudged to be due to the present laird, as his heir, and afterwards to get the estate of Drum adjudged liable for the payment thereof. He succeeded on January 5, 1722, in getting a decree of adjudication against the estate for payment of the sum contained in the said bond, or at least so much of it as would pay off the £10,000.

It is true that he granted a back bond declaring this £10,000 stg. bond to be in trust for behoof of himself and Drum's other creditors, but by purchasing assignations of debts, he was the principal creditor. There was another decree relative to this same bond after Sir Alexander's death. Besides this, he got a decree of adjudication with respect to another bond, one for 8,000 merks, granted in favor of Charles' sister, Elspet: in both cases decree was granted with 30 years' annual rent, the Lords reserving certain objections raised by Irvine of Crimond, the next heir substitute in the entail. For about this time Crimond and his brother Artamford, interfered, seeing the risk of the family estates being sold and lost, and John Irvine, the next heir and uncle of the laird, was communicated with for his interest; he was then in Carolina. An attempt was then made to compromise with these prospective heirs; while the creditors on the estate assented to Sir Alexander Cuming's taking steps to effect a sale of it in order to obtain payment. A state of the circumstances of the family of Drum was drawn up and submitted to the creditors in 1723: there is also extant a memo. concerning Drum's creditors, and a memorial for John Irvine framed in the same year. These contain much interesting information.

The first of these documents runs as follows, viz.:

"Alexander Irvine, of Drum, entailed his estate with clauses de non alienando et non contrahendo debitum, and only allowed the heirs of tailzie to sell as much of the estate as would pay his own debts. This Drum's father succeeded as heir of t'ailzie, who, upon his entry, met not only with vast sums due by the entailer, but also with most litigious and expensive processes and law suits raised against him by the heirs male, heirs of line, and several other persons, which at last he was obliged to compound in the most prudent manner he could; and that obliged the last Drum to contract a vast many debts, and involved him in difficulties he could never yet extricate himself from.

The entailer's debts *yet unpaid* affecting the estate of Drum amount to......................................			£40,000 Scots	
The debts contracted by the last Drum will be about 100,000 merks...			66,666 13 4	
			£106,666 13 4	
The yearly amount whereof is 8000 merks....	£5333 6 8			
Jean Irvine, Lady Drum, her jointure is yearly (4000 merks)........................	2666 13 4			
Mey Forbes, Lady Drum, her annuity is (1950 merks)...............................	1300 0 0			
			9,300 0 0	
Rental of the estate of Drum, viz.:—The lands and barony of Drum, about 8000 merks	£5333 6 8			
The lands of Cromar yet unsold, about 3300 merks*........................	2866 13 4			
			8200 0 0	
Deficiency...........................			£ 1100 0 0	

* Should be 4300 merks.

So that during the ladies' life-rents this Drum had nothing to live upon, and there is a deficiency of £1100 yearly, so that will be wanting to pay the annual rents as long as they live."

"Seeing that the last Drum was bound up by the taimzie, none of the creditors will get a farthing unless Sir Alexander Cuming prevail in his adjudication upon a bond of £80,000 granted by the entailer to his son Charles, and a process of sale raised thereon (which is for the behoof of himself and all his other creditors); and even albeit Sir Alexander prevail, there will be a necessity for the creditors to give a considerable abatement of their respective debts, otherwise Drum will have nothing remaining for himself."

The memorandum concerning Drum's creditors is very interesting, but too long to be quoted here. Among other things, it is stated that, "The last Drum was far from being an ill manager; for, considering the great debts left by the entailer, the jointures and aliment payable out of the estate, there remained but a very small competency for himself to live upon, which he managed with great credit and frugality." This document is much to the same purport as the former, but the particulars are given more in detail.

The memorial for John Irvine gives a narrative of the state of matters, with his suggestions as to the course he should pursue for his own interest, as one of the heirs substitute under the entail, and with a view to his avoiding any step which might involve an irritancy of the entail, which Irvine of Crimond, the next substitute, might take advantage of.

To return now to Sir Alexander Cuming, the following extract from a letter from him to Drum, dated February 7, 1724, shows his mode of proceeding in the affair. After referring to the probability of his making terms with Drum's uncle, John Irvine, for £200 sterling, and an aliment of 500 merks per annum for life; to the negotiations with Crimond, and to Drum's own interest being met by selling the estate and securing for him any residue, he proceeds thus: "You must observe that, if we had met with opposition, tho' we should carry the principal sum, which is a great question, yet as to the annual rents, to which your father had right as apparent heir to Charles, yet if he possest the land which was liable therefor, no annual rent would be due; and tho' I have adjudged the £80,000 with annual rent, yet the annual rents due in your father's time is not a subject adjudgable; but altho' they had been due, they must be carried by confirmation: this is what none of them has yet discovered, but occurred to the President, my Lord Dun, and some others of our friends.

"There is another thing they have not yet discovered, to wit, that the bond is only payable by Drum's heirs male, which shows the intention was only to affect the lands which were not in the tailzie, that might have fallen to them.

"There is yet another difficulty which I will not mention till I see you, that would have been very hard upon you." He then urges him to sign the obligation to John Irvine at once, and assures him that he could not have done more for his service, and that of the Drum family, if he had been his own son.

What has been quoted shows that Sir Alexander knew the injustice of the course he was pursuing, but apparently he knew that he had means of getting his plans carried into execution through a perversion of justice. The unfortunate laird of Drum seems to have been like wax in his hands; and, convinced that unless he did as he was told, there would be nothing left for him, to have acquiesced and plotted along with him, to effect a sale of the estates.

The view taken of what was going on by a relative of the Drum family is seen by the following extract of a letter from John Elphinstone of Glack to Irvine of Crimond, dated July 7, 1723. In it he expresses "his fears that Mr. Irvine would go into Sir Alexander's measures for ruining that estate, notwithstanding his expressions that he would do nothing against the preservation of the family of Drum." He adds, "Its what I still feared, and, if you remember, I told you so (when I understood that Mr. Garrioch had so much the management of him), and I smelled by Mr. Garrioch his words that he was then much in Sir Alexander's interest, and I believe not without gold." In the same letter he speaks of Sir Alexander "having put his hand to the plough, and not being likely to look back until he build upon the destruction of that old family." He advises Crimond to enquire into the legality of their proceedings, but warns him that he "supposes what is done betwixt them will be so closely keeped that it will not be easily discovered;" and points out that no friend would advise him (Crimond) to venture his all upon such an uncertainty. Glack appears to have been a shrewd sensible man. John Irvine, Drum's uncle, apparently thought it best for his interest not to oppose the sale of the estate, in consideration of the offer, made to and accepted by him, of £200 sterling, and a yearly aliment of 500 merks for life.

Sir Alexander Cuming did not live to see the end of his plans. He died in 1725, and he died bankrupt! One may be pardoned for expressing some satisfaction in recording this. He must have died early in that year, for his son, Alexander, appears to have been confirmed as executor of his father on 5th May. The deceased baronet had granted a disposition, in favour of his son, of the lands of Culter in 1717; and had also, conjointly with Lady Cuming, granted one also in his favor, in 1720 (the son was then Captain Alexander Cuming): he had, besides this, granted a disposition of the lands of Glenbucket to Barns in 1723. On the other hand, his son had granted backbonds, more or less, in favour of his mother and her children. Sir Alexander granted a disposition of the bond for £10,000 sterling (granted him by Drum) on January 27, 1725, in favor of his son, Captain Alexander Cuming, Mr. John Ogilvie of Balbegno, James Gordon of Barns, Dr. John Gordon, and Alexander Thomson, the survivors and survivor, and their assignees, for the purposes therein mentioned.

The young Sir Alexander and the others, consequently, continued the steps already in progress for the sale of the Drum estates. His father's creditors brought the estate of Auchtercoul, as well as his own estate of Culter, to a judicial sale. Auchtercoul was purchased by the Earl of Aberdeen in 1729, as also Tarland and Culter; but Culter was, with part of the estate of Drum, purchased by Patrick Duff of Permnay in 1738.

The Trustees under Sir Alexander's disposition of January 27, 1725, then resolved to carry on the process of adjudication; and, with consent of Drum and his creditors, James Gordon of Barns was appointed factor on the estate: a deed of consent to this arrangement was signed by various parties between May 22d and July 23rd of the same year, in which it was provided, *inter alia*, that the factor was to uplift the rents of the whole estate of Drum, *except* the manor-place, gardens, woods, plantings, and enclosures, with the laird's croft and mains, including the Milltown, with pendicles, &c., computed to be about 800 merks Scots of yearly rent, but not in use to be rentalled: and reserving to Drum the superiorities, flying customs, leet peats, and services of the haill lands — all this was for the subsistence of the laird — next the factory was burdened with the payment of the preferable heritable creditors, who were in possession, and the yearly annuity of £1000 Scots to Marjory Forbes, Lady Drum; also with the payment of 500 merks yearly aliment to John Irvine, Drum's uncle; and of the annual rent of the provisions due to Mrs. Margaret and Helen Irvines, Drum's sisters; then with the expenses necessary for prosecuting the adjudication and sale of the estate of Drum in terms of the conveyance of the bond over the estate to the creditors: the residue of the rents to be applied towards payment of arrears of annuities due to Marjory Forbes, Lady Drum; then to the personal creditors of Drum.

The following year, November 16, 1726, the whole estate, excepting the manor place and others above specified, was sequestrated, and Alexander Thomson, writer in Aberdeen, appointed by the Court of Session factor on the estate, apparently with effect from 1725 inclusive, and Drum went to Brussels, whence he wrote a very business-like letter relative to his affairs to Dr. John Gordon, dated December 11, 1727, and a letter to Patrick Duff of Premnay, one of his principal creditors, complaining of the state of his health and of his want of means, under date February 13, 1728.

From Mr. Duff's reply it is evident that Drum had had recourse to drawing bills on him; and that he was trying to treat for better terms for himself the following year. By October, 1729, he had returned home and was at Drum, writing thence, and in March and April, 1730, in Edinburgh. In a letter written thence in April of that year, he says, "I am very much surprised what some people mean, except, because I have not had my health of late, they would have me renounce my reason, and do what they incline." A little later, June 22d, he writes from Edinburgh, complaining of ill-health, and says, "If added to that, disappointments, delays, and in short, struggling with all sorts of difficulties together, can create one trouble or make them uneasy, the case is mine."

By this time his mind, apparently never strong, had begun to give way; he was nearly penniless, but inclined, it was alleged, to live luxuriously — at any rate beyond his means; and his uncle, John Irvine, commenced to act as his tutor, on the ground that he was cognosced *incompos mentis, prodigus et furiosus*, from the month of December, 1730.

He must have been arrested for debt about this time, for his uncle writes, January 5, 1732, relative to getting a release of Drum's person, notwithstanding the several diligences against him, and mentions the prison dues as the principal bar to his deliverance: a lodging in the Canongate is suggested for him. The poor man only lived till 1735. I think he was more sinned against than sinning. The estate was much involved when he succeeded to it, and he appears so have fallen in with the schemes of an unscrupulous man, and became unscrupulous too, in order to get some small competency secured to himself; but for a long time in the belief that the succeeding heir of entail would continue to have the same. In the end, however, in 1729, under stress of poverty and worry, he tried to bargain for his own interest only, and to secure a remnant of the estate to be entirely at his own disposal.

Meantime, Irvine of Crimond and his brother, Artamford, had prosecuted their appeal against the interlocutors of the Lords of Session, 1726, 1727, and 1728, finding that the bond for £80,000, granted to Charles Irvine, was not extinguished in the person of Alex. Irvine of Drum, but was still a subsisting bond upon the estate, and then belonged of right to the creditors, and ought to be applied to their payment; but, as already stated, attempts were made to buy them off. Great expense must have been incurred, for the case was pending till 1733. A Mr. George Keith seems to have been employed to treat with Lord Aberdeen and Mr. Duff as to the terms of compromise, and to have held out for 20,000 merks against a lower offer. It appears that Crimond accepted this sum for his brother and himself; for his brother, Artamford, writes to another brother, Thomas, under date March 22, 1733; "How Crimond came to sign any paper without hearing from me is a thing he can never account for: and that they design to diminish the diversion is what I am fully certain of." He declares that he will never consent to dismiss the appeal without more favorable and more certain terms: and in this and another letter mentions that "D. Forbes [evidently of Culloden] had said the last interlocutor about the £80,000 bond was nonsense, and that we have all the justice on our side."

Artamford pressed hard for persisting in the appeal, unless they got satisfactory terms, viz., a larger sum of money, and good security for preserving part of the estate. It is evident that D. Forbes, then His Majesty's advocate, was engaged as their counsel, for he says that D. Forbes told him that he had obtained an oblige-ment from Mr. Dundas, who was counsel for the other side, that the compositions of debts should accrese to the estate of Drum, and the remainder, after payments of debts, should be secured to the heirs of entail; and on Artamford's demurring, he got a message sent by Colluden's servant, "that if I continued in that resolution, I behoved to engage another counsel, for he would not sign my case nor plead my cause." Artamford consequently had to give in; the terms were accepted, and judgment of the House of Peers given affirm-ing the same, dated May 4, 1733. Articles of agreement were drawn up but not signed, dated at Aberdeen, March 7, 1733, bearing that there were present the Earl of Aberdeen, Patrick Duff of Prem-nay, George Keith, advocate in Aberdeen, and James Irvine, advo-cate in Aberdeen, in which it was agreed to that Lord Aberdeen was to have the purchase of the Cromar estates at 20 years' pur-chase; that Duff was to get the purchase of so much of Drum's low country estate as should suffice to pay all his debts, real and per-sonal; Crimond to get 20,000 merks, and John Irvine £200 sterling, and expenses of law charges, so far as the price of the Cromar estate, also at 20 years' purchase, would not pay. On the other hand, Lord Aberdeen and Duff were to allow the compositions of the whole debts of Drum, already purchased by them, to go for behoof of John Irvine and the other heirs of entail, in the terms and under the conditions of the entail, under burden of the present Drum's aliment: the Earl and Duff to pay other creditors, asking nothing for themselves but the allowance of the principal sums paid out, and annual interest thereof, with law and other expenses, including those of obtaining the legal sale of the lands necessary to be sold. It seems quite evident from this, that Lord Aberdeen and Mr. Duff, by advancing money, compounded for and acquired right to a very large amount of debts affecting the estate of Drum and Cromar, and thus brought it about that they should be almost the only creditors ranked on the price of the estates when they were sold.

The 14th laird, poor man, died after a troubled life in 1735, and was succeeded by his uncle, John Irvine.

15 JOHN, the 15th laird, b. ——, d. 1737, married Katherine Fullerton, daughter of Fullerton of Dudwick, and had no issue. He seems to have been engaged in business in Carolina and Jamaica, probably as a planter, and to have come home about 1722 or 1723, on hearing what was going on upon his nephew's succeeding to Drum, to look after his own interests. The negotiations with him, and his taking upon himself the guardianship of his nephew, when *non compos*, have been already mentioned. During the two years he was laird, the troubles of the family came to a climax..

At his accession, the way had become clear for the creditors on the estate to obtain a decree in their action of ranking and sale of the Drum estates. A decree of sale of the lands and barony of Drum at the instance of the trustees for the creditors of the lately deceased Alexander, and John Irvine, then laird of Drum, was pronounced in 1736, and the estate was purchased by Alexander Tytler, writer in Edinburgh, for the trustees. The price fixed by the Lords as an upset was £159,554 3s. 10d. Scots, and Mr. Tytler was empowered to go up to £50,000 beyond in case of competition. The entail being now set aside, the trustees, in February, 1737, conveyed in favor of William, Earl of Aberdeen, and Patrick Duff of Premnay, who now had acquired sole right to rank as creditors, the whole rights, infeftments, and diligences affecting the whole lands and estate of Drum, and others mentioned.

In the following April the Earl and Mr. Duff, in terms of arrangements made, granted a disposition and *new entail* in favor of John Irvine and his heirs male, *and of the other heirs under the former entail* of a remnant of the estate, viz., of the Mains and Manor place of Drum, and other lands therein mentioned, without any payment therefor, and on the other hand, John Irvine granted *a deed of rati-fication, accepting for himself and future heirs of entail this provision,* and declaring that he had no claim against the grantors. Further decrees against John Irvine were obtained in June and July, 1737, at the instance of the Earl of Aberdeen and Patrick Duff of Prem-nay, adjudging the whole lands and estate of Drum in satisfaction of his own and his predecessors' debts, and in particular of the bond of provision to Charles Irvine, which, originally granted for £80,-000 Scots, amounted with interest to £275,000 Scots. — *Vide* State of Process, &c.

To secure their new possessions a Charter of resignation and sale in favor of Patrick Duff and Margaret, his spouse, of the lands and barony of Culter, and part of the lands of Drum, was obtained, dated November 29, 1738; and another Charter of adjudication and sale in favor of William, Earl of Aberdeen, of the lands of Ruthven, baronies of Fedderat and Auchtercoul, and others of the same date. These latter were the tailzied lands in Cromar: the unentailed part of Cromar, along with Culter, had been sold to Lord Aberdeen on Sir Alexander Cuming's death and bankruptcy in 1729. These two persons made over the small remnant of the estates, viz., the old Castle and Mansion-house, the Manor-place and Mains, and a small portion of the family estate, to John Irvine and his successors *ex gratia*. It has been shown that the bond of provision granted by the entailer to Charles, from which no member of the family got any benefit, was mainly used as a burden on the estate, against which debts were made chargeable, and by accumu-lations of interest this burden became so heavy that the creditors, represented by Lord Aberdeen and Duff of Premnay, who bought up their claims, forced a sale, and became proprietors of the greater part, in fact, of the whole of the estates, subject to their undertak-ing to re-settle a very small portion for the benefit of the family.

John Irvine was succeeded in the latter part of 1737 by ALEX-ANDER, of the Artamford branch, under the provisions of the entail.

16. ALEXANDER, the 16th laird, often designed "of Crimond," was the great-grandson of John Irvine of Artamford, who was youngest son of Alexander, the 8th laird, by Lady Eliza-beth Keith, and brother of Alexander the 9th laird (see under the 9th laird). This laird was b.——and died 1744. He married, August 18, 1698, Isobel, daughter of Thomas Thompson of Faichfield, by whom he had issue 3 sons and 6 daughters, viz.,—

(1). Thomas, b. at Faichfield June 1, 1699, d. —— January, 1701.

(2). James, b. at Crimond, December 22, 1709, d. unmarried.

(3). Alexander, b. at Crimond, June 24, 1711; afterwards of Drum.

The daughters, — (1). Margaret, b. at Faichfield, March 22, 1701; married James Rose of Clava; (2), Isobel or Isabella, b. at Fodelhills, on Faichfield, March 3, 1703; (3), Janet, b. at Crimond, March 1, 1705; (4), Ann, b. at Crimond, November 8, 1707; (5), Elizabeth, b. at Crimond February 25, 1715; (6), Mary, b. February 13, 1721.

He had succeeded his father, James Irvine, in the estate of Artamford, but sold that property to his brother William, and purchased Crimond in 1703. On succeeding as Laird of Drum, and finding what a poor and attenuated estate he had come into, he raised an action against the Earl of Aberdeen and Duff of Premnay, trying to set aside in part the recent arrangements, on the ground that the articles of agreement dated March 7, 1733, to which he had been a party, had not been duly implemented:' and in particular he claimed that other parts of the estate most contiguous to the House and Mains of Drum should have been preserved to the extent of 5000 or 6000 merks yearly to the family. The case was decided against him in 1741, the Lords holding that the agreement had been carried out. He became heir of line, as well as under the entail, by the death of Irvine of Saphock in 1744, and died himself the same year.

Artamford is near New Deer, and Crimond near Peterhead. This branch of the family had borne as a crest a bunch of arrows, and for some time after this laird's accession to Drum, the arrows were erroneously used. My grandfather, who was his grandson; had a bundle of arrows engraved on some plate early in this century: and the late Miss Christina Irvine told me how it came about some forty years ago.

He was succeeded by his eldest surviving son.

17. ALEXANDER,[1] the 17th laird, was b. 1711, and died 9th February, 1761. He married,[2] August 20, 1751, Mary, daughter of James Ogilvie of Auchiries, and had issue by her 3 sons and 3 daughters, viz.:—

(1). Alexander, younger of Drum, b. October 4, 1754.

[1] Charta in publ. arch.   [2] Charta in arch. fam.

(2). Charles, b. April 20, 1756, d. 1819. A Major-General in the army, of whom more afterwards.

(3). James, b. March 18, 1759, d. ——, married the widow of Manley, an artist, an Italian lady, by whom he had no issue.

The daughters, — (1), Margaret, b. May 14, 1752, o. s., d. unmarried; (2), Isbaella,[1] b. June 24, 1753, n. s., married Rev. Mr. Allan; (3), Rebecca,[2] b. December 27, 1757, married Geo. Ogilvie of Auchiries.

This laird joined Prince Charlie in his attempt to regain the crown in 1745. In that year, attended by two servants, James Adamson and James Buchan, he joined Lord Pitsligo's regiment of horse, which Sir Walter Scott tells us, in "Tales of a Grandfather," consisted of gentlemen and their servants. Lord Pitsligo's son, the Master of Pitsligo, married the daughter of James Ogilvie of Auchiries, and was consequently a brother-in-law of the laird of Drum. This regiment, about 100 strong, joined Prince Charlie after the battle of Preston, and was present at the Battle of Falkirk, January 17, 1746, where Drum received a wound or hurt on his leg. Upon the retreat of the Highland army towards Inverness, by Dunblane and Crieff, whence the Highlanders marched by the Highland road, and the Lowlanders and calvary by Montrose and Aberdeen, he was unable to keep up with the march, but followed by the nearest inland road, so that he escaped being seen in those parts where he was known. In this way he got to the north in time to be present at the Battle of Culloden: this his grandson, Mr. Forbes-Irvine, told me himself.

He was fortunate in escaping with his life, and was in hiding for some time; and he also escaped forfeiture — there was comparatively little left for him to lose — owing to the grand jury thrice throwing out bills of treason sent to them. When an Act of Indemnity was passed in June, 1747, granting a pardon to many of those who had been engaged in the rising, in addition to Lord Pitsligo — who was then a second time attainted, and had his estates confiscated, and was excepted, though he succeeded in concealing himself till his death, aged 85, in 1762 — upwards of 86 persons were specially excluded by name: among these were Irvine of Drum, Sir Alex. Bannerman, Farquharson of Balmoral, Gordon of Avochie, Hay younger of Rannes, Gilbert Menzies, younger of Pitfodels, Moir of Stoneywood, and Turner of Turnerhall, belonging to the

[1] Ibid.   [2] Ibid.

counties of Aberdeen, Banff, and Kincardine; and further of these previously attained, Lord Lewis Gordon, Sir William Gordon of Park, Gordon of Glenbucket, and Farquharson of Monaltrie. After a time the search for these excepted persons slackened, and Drum returned to and lived at his own home; but he died, aged 50, in 1761, when his eldest son was only 7 years old. His two faithful attendants, when with Pitsligo's Horse, lived to return and settle at Drum; Adamson got the farm of Mains of Drum, and Buchan that of Wardmill.

Drum's second son, Charles Irvine, my grandfather, like many others, sons of those who had fought for the Prince, served many years in the army of King George III. He got a commission in the 57th (which, after his time, got at Albuera the name of "the Die-hards") in 1779, and got his company in 1782: after serving about 15 years in it he went on half-pay. He had meantime married at Edinburgh, on August 18, 1790, Diana, second daughter of Sir Alexander Gordon, 6th Bart. of Lesmoir, by whom he had 3 sons and 5 daughters, viz.:

(1). Alexander b. about 1791, an officer H. E. I. C. S. in the Bengal European Regiment; died unmarried at Macassar in the Isles of Celebes, in 1816, after the capture of Java.

(2). Charles, b. about 1793. an officer R. N., lost at sea in command of a prize about 1812.

(3). George Nugent, b. October 26, 1801, an officer H. E. I. C. S. in 4th Local Horse, died 1827.

The daughters.— (1), Margaret, b. November 26, 1794, d. unmarried, 30th May, 1849; (2), Mary, b. July 31, 1796; married Rev. C. Wimberley, Chaplain H. E. I. C. S., in 1825, who was afterwards Rector of Scole, Norfolk; she died on her 91st birthday at Kensington, 1887; (3), Isabella, b. December 31, 1799, married in 1855 William Bland, Esq., of Hartlip Place, Kent; (4), Ann, b. about 1808, d. about 1810 at Montrose; (5), Diana, b. October 29 th, about 1810, married Mr. Mason, d. without issue in 1885.

Owing to the threatening state of matters in Ireland in 1795, a considerable number of fencible regiments were raised in Scotland, to which officers were appointed from half-pay; and Captain Irvine was appointed a Major in the Loyal Inverness Fencibles, his friend Gordon Cumming of Pitlurg getting the Lieut.-Colonelcy. The regiment was embodied at Inverness, 600 strong, of whom 350 were Highlanders from the adjoining counties, about 33 Welchmen, and

the remainder men enlisted at Aberdeen and Perth. It was at once
sent to Ireland, where it was actively employed during the Rebellion
of 1798, and on the death of Colonel Baillie of Dunain, near Inverness, in 1797, Lieut.-Colonel Gordon Cumming became Colonel,
and Major Irvine, Lieut.-Colonel.

In compliment to the good behavior of the corps, its designation
was changed to "the Duke of York's Royal Inverness-shire Highlanders." They had a sharp engagement with the rebels on June
18-19, 1798, of which the following account is given in "Musgrave's History of the Rebellions in Ireland," p. 286:

"Battle of Oviotstown near Kilcock [on the borders of Meath
and Kildare]. — Lieut.-Colonel Irvine, who commanded the Garrison of Trim, having received intelligence that a numerous body
of rebels were assembling near Kilcock on the 18th of June, marched
on that night with part of his garrison, consisting of the 4th Dragoons [this should be Dragoon Guards᷈ a troop of the Duke of
York's Fencible Cavalry, four companies of foot, and two batteries
guns, and the following yeomanry corps: — The Trim Cavalry,
one troop; the Navan and Murgallion Cavalry, one troop; the
Demifore, one troop. Soon after he passed through Kilcock, his
advanced guard was fired on by a large body of the rebels, of whom
the main body, supposed to consist of about 3000, was drawn up
in a line at the bottom of Oviotstown Hill, near Hortland House.

"As it was sometime before the Colonel could form, owing to
the unevenness of the ground, and the number of enclosures on it,
the rebels kept up a smart fire and made a desperate effort to seize
the cannon; but well-directed fire of the infantry made them abandon that enterprise. Soon after the troops formed, they routed the
rebels, who precipitately fled to a neighboring bog, where they
effected their escape, after two hundred of them had been slain.
The King's troops sustained the following loss:— 4th Dragoon
Guards, one sergeant killed; Captain Sir Richard Steele, one sergeant, two rank and file wounded; Murgallion Cavalry, one rank
and file wounded; Trim Cavalry, one rank and file wounded; Duke
of York's Highlanders, Ensign John Sutler, one sergeant, and five
rank and file killed; Lieut-Colonel Irvine, one sergeant, and seven
rank and file wounded, the first slightly."

On this occasion my grandfather had a narrow escape, his ear
being slightly wounded by a bullet which struck a button of his hat
on the side of his head, and then ran round and took off a small
piece of his ear. At the end of the rebellion, he went to Jamaica

and served under his friend General Sir George Nugent, first as Deputy Adjutant-General, 1801-2, and as Deputy Quartermaster-General from January 1, 1803, to January 22, 1805.

He rose by brevets to be a Major-General in the army, and died in Aberdeen, November 4, 1819, leaving a widow, 1 son, and 4 daughters surviving.

I got the following list from the War Office, May 8, 1889:

"Dates of Commissions of the late Major-General Charles Irvine:

Ensign 57th Foot	September 5, 1779
Lieutenant Do	November 12, 1781
Captain Do	May 3, 1782
Captain, Half-Pay, Do	1783
Captain 57th Foot	January 10, 1784
Captain Independent Co	October 23, 1793
Captain, Half-Pay, 30th Foot	November 12, 1794
Captain 68th Foot	March 1, 1800
Captain 62nd Foot	December 9, 1800
Captain, Half-Pay	June 25, 1802
Captain 85th Foot	November 20, 1802
Captain, Half-Pay, Indep. Co	February 19, 1807
Brevet Major	June 21, 1801
Brevet Lieut.-Colonel	March 9, 1803
Brevet Colonel	January 1, 1812
Major-General	June 4, 1814"[1]

The memo. from War Office further stated that he died June 4, 1819; but this is a mistake, for I have a certificate in my possession stating that he died on *November* 4, 1819, and that the Rev. George Glennie certified that he had attended his funeral on *November* 9th, and quoted an extract from the Register of Burials of St. Nicholas, Aberdeen. A tablet in memory of him and of his wife was erected in Drum's Aisle about 45 years afterwards.

[1] I got my nephew, Mr. Charles Herbert Gray, to compare and verify the War Office List with old Army Lists in the United Service Institution in August, 1892, when he found that Captain Charles Irvine's name was entered in Army List 1794 as Captain "New Independent Co. of Foot" with rank in Co. October, 23, 1793. He could find no entry in 1795; he found under "Majors," in 1796, Charles Irvine, September 21, 1794, Loyal Inverness Fencibles; in 1797 as in 1796; in 1798 under "Lieut.-Colonels," Charles Irvine, April 1, 1797, Loyal Inverness Fencible Infantry; in 1799 as in 1798, except that the Fencibles are called the "Duke of York's;" in 1800 the same as in 1799, under Lieut.-Colonels; but under 68th Regiment, Charles Irvine rank in company, March 1, 1800; in 1801 he found, under 62nd Regiment, Captain Charles Irvine; rank in regiment 9th December, 1800, rank in army March 1, 1800 [this is clearly an error]; in 1802 as in 1801, but also under Majors "Charles Irvine, 62nd Foot, D. A. Gen. in Jamaica June 21, 1801"; in 1803, under Majors, Charles Irvine with same details but omitted in 62nd [he had gone on half-pay June 25, 1802]; in 1804, under Lieut.-Colonels, "Charles Irvine, March 9, 1803, 85th Foot, D. Q. M. G. Jamaica;" and in same year, under 85th Foot, which was Colonel George Nugent's regiment, he is entered as Captain and Brevet Lieut.-Colonel.

It is very improbable that my grandfather ever did duty with
the 62nd or 68th; he may have exchanged to half pay, 30th, when
a Major in Inverness Fencibles, and I have often heard of his having
been in the 85th, of which General Nugent was for some time
Colonel, but he must have been at the same time on staff employ
in Jamaica.

There was another Charles Irvine in the army, who got a commission in the 4th Foot about the same time that he got one in the
57th, and who as years went on, was off and on on half pay; but
his career can be traced with care as quite distinct.   General Irvine's widow survived him many years, and died at Bromley, in
Kent, on January 27, 1853, aged 87.

Their eldest son, Alexander, got a cadetship in the service of
the Hon. East Ind. Co. in 1807, and went to their College at Great
Marlow, where he was cadet No. 80.   Proceding to India the
following year, he was gazetted Ensign, September 1, 1808, and
posted to the Bengal European Regiment, afterwards well known
as the 1st Bengal Fusiliers.   His promotion must have been very
slow, for in a statement of the strength of the regiment on August
12, 1812, his name occurs as fifth out of eight Ensigns, and he was
not gazetted Lieutenant till April 16, 1814.   His regiment was
part of the force employed in the reduction of Java and the Molucca
Islands, and subsequent occupation.   It left Dinapore and embarked at Calcutta in three detachments; the first in October, 1810,
the second in January, 1811, and the Head Quarters, under Lieut.-
Col. Eales, in February, 1812; the two first proceeded to Amboyna
to relieve the Madras Europeans, afterwards the 1st Madras Fusiliers, that had captured that island, February 19, 1810; and the
Head Quarters followed in the transports "Indiana," "Good Hope,"
and "Mussafa."

The attack on Batavia, in Java, in which the 78th Highlanders,
and H. M. S. 14th, 59th, 69th, and 89th were engaged under Sir
Samuel Ahmuty, commenced August 4, 1811, and the conquest was
not completed till 1814, but apparently the Bengal Europeans
were not present at any engagements.   They seem to have garrisoned the Moluccas with various detachments till the islands were
made over to the Dutch in 1817.   In the East Ind. Register, corrected to November 19, 1816, Lieut. Alex. Irvine's name appears
15th out of 22 Lieutenants, and again as Quartermaster, and stationed at Macassar, in the Isle of Celebes, and in the next vol. of
the Register, corrected to August 1, 1817, under casualties since

last publication, is recorded the death of Alex. Irvine, Lieut. European Regiment, on August 16, 1816, intimation of this evidently not having reached London in time for previous volume.

George Nugent, their third son, also got a cadetship, and went to India in 1820. He was a Lieutenant in the 11th Bengal Native Infantry in November, 1822, and served afterwards in the 4th Local Horse.

He was a Master Mason of the Masonic Lodge of True Friendship, No. 1 Bengal, at Calcutta, in March, 1822: a Knight Templar, November, 1822, and a Past Master, April, 1823, as his certificates show. An honorary member of Lodge Kilwinning in the East, as Nusseerabad, in November, 1826. He visited my father and mother in the Fort at Allahabad, in February, 1827, when he gave a horse to my aunt, his sister Isabella. He was afterwards quartered at Neemuch, where he was very ill, and started on sick leave for the hills, but died 3 marches from Neemuch, on December 3, 1827, attended by two brother officers of his regiment, who had his remains carried back to that place for burial.

I have in my possession a very small pocket Bible, printed in small, but clear type, in London, in 1658. It has been rebound long ago in calf with silver clasps, the hasps of which are missing, but the parts attached to the book have on one the initials I. I., and on the other I.G. I think I. I., must be for a James or John Irvine of the Artamford branch, and I. G., for his wife. The first name written in the book is "Rebecca Irvine," my grandfather's sister, born 1757, nearly 100 years after the book was printed; she married Geo. Oglivie of Auchiries; the next, my grandfather's name, apparently in his writing, "Charles Irvine"; the next, "Alex. Irvine," probably his eldest brother, the laird, because below it is written "Drum, September 14, 1839, to Margaret Irvine," my aunt, in her handwriting: below that is my own name.

The 17th laird died in 1761, and was succeeded by his eldest son.

18. ALEXANDER, the 18th laird, b. 1754, died 1844. He was only 7 years old at his accession; he married December 31, 1775, Jean, only daughter of Hugh Forbes of Schivas (she died March 12, 1786), and had issue by her four sons and one daughter.

    (1.) Alexander Forbes, younger of Drum, b. at Drum, January 10, 1777.

(2.) Charles, b. in Aberdeen, July 11, 1780; died——unmarried.

(3.) Hugh, b. in Aberdeen, August, 1782; died, unmarried, an artist.

(4.) Francis, b. at Drum, February 8, 1786, died——: Captain H. E. I. C. S., married Eliza Harrington, daughter of J. H. Harrington, Ind. Civil Service, and had issue one son, Francis, M. D., who married and went to New Zealand, and two daughters, Eliza, married her cousin, — Muston; and Mary, married — Keddie.

Daughters — Christian or Christina, b. at Drum, September 29, 1778, died unmarried.

During his minority his guardians thought proper to investigate the causes of the judicial sale of the estates. They considered it to have been fradulently conducted, fictitious debts having been raised up to give a color to the proceedings; accordingly an action of reduction was instituted in 1766 by the young laird and his curators against the Earl of Aberdeen, Mrs. Margaret Duff of Premnay, wife of Alexander Udny of Udny, Captain Robert Duff, R. N., and Alexander Thomson, advocate in Aberdeen, deceast. This involved a very long litigation and two appeals to the House of Lords, in the first of which Drum was successful; the second was dismissed April 16, 1777. The point of dispute in the first was whether the Defenders were bound to produce the writs and deeds called for. Failing in this, they raised a question whether they were obliged to produce the general and special charges and other warrants of the decrees in dispute, and got a decision of the Court of Session in their favor. But at the same time they raised a new plea and presented a petition accordingly, setting forth that the entail of of Drum had never been properly completed, under the Entail Act 1685, so as to be effectual against creditors and purchasers for a valuable consideration: for that the *original entail* itself, executed in 1683 [meaning the procuratory of resignation], had never been judicially produced before the Lords, as required by the statute, but only *the Charter and relative nomination of heirs.*

It was pleaded for the Pursuer that the entail of Drum, being the first that was recorded in consequence of the statute, the Court had been very careful in following its directions; that the Charter and relative Deed of Nomination, which contained the entail, had been produced, read, and compared with the record in presence of the Lords; that the Charter, following on the procuratory, together with the Deed of Nomination under the entailer's hand, was in every legal sense to be considered the entail; and, further, that the procuratory itself was *in manibus curiæ*, being recorded in the books of Session March, 16, 1684. The Charter and infeftment were ratified in Parliament in 1685.

It was contended for the Defenders that the Act expressly declared, *inter alia*, that the original tailzie must be produced before the Lords of Session judicially; that the Charter was not the original entail, nor was the Deed of Nomination, and that the record of tailzies could only be made up from original deeds presented to the Court and ordered by the Court to be recorded; and that in a similar case, "Kinnaird against Hunter," this plea had been sustained on appeal by the House of Lords in 1765.

The Court of Session found, July 3, 1772, "that the entail executed by Alexander Irvine of Drum in the year 1683, not being duly recorded, is not valid against creditors or other singular successors." This appears tantamount to finding that the Court of Session had made a mistake in 1688, and ordered a wrong document to be recorded as the entail on the application of Irvine of Murthill.

Drum reclaimed, and prayed the Court to postpone determining the validity of the entail until the proof (relative to alleged fraud, &c.) was advised, but the Lords pronounced the following interlocutor, July 24, 1772:— "In respect the interlocutor only finds that the entail executed by Alexander Irvine of Drum in the year 1687, not being duly recorded, is not valid against creditors, or other singular successors, but determines nothing as to the plea and defences, which may be competent to either party: the Lords in so far refuse the desire of the petition, and adhere to their former interlocutor."

The cause then proceeded: the facts relative to the alleged fraud were discussed, and the question was finally determined June 26, 1776, by the following interlocutor:— "The Lords having advised the state of the process, testimonies of the witnesses produced, memorials *hinc inde*, and whole papers and proceedings in the cause, and having heard parties' procurators thereon, sustain the defences, assoilzie the Defenders and decern."

The pursuer appealed. The House of Lords, on April 16, 1777, ordered and adjudged that the interlocutors of July 24 and 31, 1772, be affirmed; and it is further ordered and adjudged that the interlocutors of January 21, February 28, and July 24, 1771, and the interlocutor of June 26, 1776, be also affirmed; but without prejudice to any satisfaction in money that the appellant might be entitled to in respect of any claim he may have in virtue of the agreement 1733; and it is further ordered that the appeal be dismissed.

The expense must have been enormous. I suppose that Crimond must have been sold in consequence, and I believe no further attempt was made to claim anything under the agreement above referred to. The decision seems a strange one, both in respect to what document should have been recorded as the entail, the different dates ascribed to the entail in the interlocutors, and to the question of alleged fraudulent conduct of the transaction.

This laird married young, and was left a widower at 32. He was a J. P., an active Magistrate, and for some time Convener of the County of Aberdeen. He spent the greater part of the very long period, 83 years, during which he held the now small estate, at Drum, and as time wore on, led a very retired life. I spent some of my holidays at Drum in 1836, 1838, and 1843, and I think in in 1840, and remember him as a kindly old gentleman, but did not see much of him. He died in 1844, and was succeeded by his eldest son.

19. ALEXANDER FORBES, the 19th laird, b. 10th Jan.; 1777, d. 1861; married December 10, 1816, Margaret, daughter of James Hamilton, Esq., and had issue by her three sons and two daughters.

(1.) Alexander Forbes, younger of Drum, b. February 18, 1818.

(2.) James Hamilton, b. July 19, 1819, settled in Australia.

(3.) Charles, b. February 17, 1823. An officer H. E. I. C. S., long in 51st N. I., afterwards in 19th Punj. Infantry; a Major-General retired. Married, 1st, Georgina, daughter of Major John Doran of Ely House, Co. Wexford, and had issue, a son Hugh Alexander, b. August 26, 1864; 2nd, Juliet Isa, daughter of James Connell of Conheath, Dumfriesshire, and sister of J. W. F. Connell of Auchencheyne, in the same county.

Daughters — (1), Beatrice Wood, b. January 18, 1821; (2), Jane Christina, b. November 12, 1825, married Major Houchen; H. E. I. C. S., of the 55th N. I. and Bengal Staff Corps; d. March 20, 1880, without issue.

Major-General C. Irvine was gazetted from Addiscombe, December 10, 1842, and posted, on arrival in India, to the 51st Bengal Infantry; in 1843 he went through the Gwalior campaign, present

at Battle of Punniar (medal), and got six months batta; took part
in first Sutlej campaign 1845–46, his regiment being employed on
escort of siege train, got twelve months batta; present first and
second sieges of Mooltan, 1848–49 (medal); was, at time of outbreak
of Indian Mutiny, in command of Fort Michnie, and later second
in command of his regiment (which was subsequently numbered
the 19th and then the 27th Punjab Infantry) at Rawul Pindi;
went with same regiment on Expedition to China under Sir Hope
Grant 1860–61, and in command of one wing at Chusan; present
in Looshai Expedition 1865 (medal). Joined Bengal Staff Corps
on its formation, and retired with rank of Major-General January
23, 1875.

The 19th laird, having succeeded to the estate of Schivas, in right
of his mother, assumed the name of Forbes before Irvine. He was
admitted as an advocate at the Scottish bar in 1802, and lived for
many years partly in Edinburgh and partly at Schivas.

On succeeding to Drum he effected an excambion of land, by
which Schivas, near Methlic and Haddo House, passed into the
hands of Lord Aberdeen, and Kennerty, with other land, formerly
part of the barony of Drum, and latterly of Culter, was again acquired and called Schivas; these lands immediately adjoined what
had been left to the Drum family.

He made considerable improvements on the estate, and had a
home farm on his own hands, to which he devoted much attention.
Two stories of the old tower, which was probably built in the 14th
century, or earlier, were thrown into one with an arched roof, and
a large recess with a window of ample size cut out of the solid wall,
which was 12 feet thick. The ceiling is decorated with the arms
of the following families, connected with the Irvines by marriage,
viz.:— 1. Irvine of Drum. 2. Hamilton of Little Garnock.
3. Lord Forbes. 4. Ogilvie, Earl of Airlie. 5. Gordon Marquis
of Huntly. 6. Keith, Earl Marischal. 7. Fraser, Lord Saltoun.
8. Douglas, Earl of Buchan. 9. Barclay-Allardyce of Ury.
10. Scrimgeour of Dudhope, High Constable of Dundee. 11. Menzies of Pitfodels. 12. Douglas of Glenbervie. 13. Campbell of
Glenorchy. 14. Graham of Morphy. 15. This shield has 7 quar-
erings, viz.: Coutts of Westercourt; Chalmers of Strichen; Skene
of Skene; Ogston of Fettercairn; Ross of Auchlossan; Crawford of
Fornett; and Duguid of Auchinhove. 16. Ogilvie, Earl of Findlater. 17. Thomson of Faichfield. 18. Leslie of Balquhain.
19. Crichton of Frendraught. 20. Urquhart of Meldrum.

Mrs. Irvine, his wife, beloved by all who knew her, died suddenly in 1854; he survived a few years, and died in 1861.

20. ALEXANDER FORBES, the 20th laird, b. February 18, 1818; d. April 4, 1892; married, in December, 1848, Anna Margaretta, second daughter of Col. Jonathan Forbes-Leslie of Rothie Norman, formerly of the 78th Highlanders, by whom he had issue three sons.

    (1.) Alexander, b. February, 9 1850; d. August 7, 1856.

    (2.) Alexander Charles Quentin Hamilton, b. October 29, 1851; d. September 9, 1875.

    (3.) Francis Hugh, b. August 23, 1854.

The 20th laird was educated at Aberdeen University, and proceeded to Edinburgh to study law: he was called to the Scottish bar as an advocate in 1843. He was appointed Principal Clerk to the Court of Justiciary in 1867, and held that office till 1874, when he received the appointment of Sheriff of Argyll, which he only resigned in 1891. He was also Vice-Dean of the Faculty of Advocates from 1886, and for many years a Director of the Highland Agricultural Society: Chancellor of the Diocese of Brechin from 1858 until his death; Fellow of the Royal Society of Edinburgh, and Vice-President, and received the degree of LL. D., Edinburgh, in 1887. He also prepared several volumes of "Irvine's Reports of cases before the High Court and Circuit Courts of Justiciary," and was the author of a Treatise on the Game Laws, which has long been a standard work, and of which three editions have been published. He took a large share in the county work of Aberdeenshire, in which he was a Justice of the Peace, and Deputy Lieutenant; and held the important office of Convener of the county from 1862 till 1890, when County Councils were established under the Local Government Act (Scotland). His services were recognized on his retirement by the presentation to him of his portrait, painted by Sir George Reid, in 1891.

On his succession to the estates, it was his evil fortune to succeed to a law suit, raised against his father just before his death, and carried on against him by the University of Aberdeen, relative to the mortification of £10,000 Scots by the 9th laird, for founding bursaries, and the lands of Kinmuck. The Pursuers practically claimed that the lands of Kinmuck belonged to them for behoof of the bursars; see under the 9th laird. After obtaining decree, as there stated, Sir Alexander Irvine voluntarily executed a bond in 1656, which, however, was never delivered, but kept in his own repositories, and was not recorded till 1741, and then, probably, in consequence of the disentail and sale of the Drum estates. This bond contained an obligation on himself, his heirs and successors, "to deliver to the ten scholars and their successors in the said burses all contracts, dispositions, charters, procuratories of resignation, and other securities requisite with warrandice, at what time and how soon he and his foresaids might be desired."

The case was tried before the Lord Ordinary (Kinloch), who decided in favor of the University; and, on appeal, before the First Division, when the Lord President and three other judges concurred in reversing this decision, and gave judgment in favour of the Defenders with expenses; each of them giving his opinion, and Lord Deas laying stress on the fact that the 10th laird did not buy lands; nay, more, he did not even dispone them; that no formal deed followed upon the bond; and there were no words which, by the law of Scotland, would convey heritage; that they might imply an obligation to dispone, but did not dispone; that that essential word was not in the bond, and it was as open to repudiation as on the day it was granted.

It should be noted that the lands of Kinmuck were included in the procuratory of resignation by the entailer in 1683, but were not included in the disposition or entail of the diminished estate of Drum in 1737: apparently a judicial factor was appointed on Kinmuck in 1741 on petition of the Magistrates and others to uplift the rents and appoint bursars, and up to 1808 the rents were insufficient to pay the bursaries in full. In 1821, the then laird executed a deed of entail of Kinmuck.

The University appealed to the House of Lords against the finding of the First Division, and their judgment was reversed, March, 26, 1868. The Lords held that the right of the bursars was not limited to an annual rent of £1000 Scots, but that according to the legal effect and true meaning of the Deed of Mortification of 1656, the whole lands and the entirety of the rents were destinate to the use of the bursars, and remit was made to the Court of Session to prepare a scheme for the management and application of the revenue. The Lord Chancellor, Lords Cranworth and Westbury, took this view, Lord Colonsay dissenting. This was another instance of the uncertainty of the law. I should think the Scotch law lords were more fitted to interpret the bond of 1656 than the English lords, who here call it a Deed of Mortification. The lairds of

Drum retain right of presentation to the bursaries. They have been most unfortunate in their law suits.

The 20th laird spent a part of each year in Edinburgh, passing the remainder at his ancestral home. He devoted much time, energy, and ability, and also about £40,000 in money, to the improvement of his estates, the extent of which was now about 7000 acres, including some 3700 acres of Kennerty, etc., added about 1850 in lieu of Schivas.

Having been relieved of his more active public duties, owing to increasing age, and the substitution of County Councils for the Commissioners of Supply, he might have been expected to enjoy several years of comparative leisure, having had a good constitution and led an active life: but shortly after going to Drum to spend Easter, he was taken suddenly ill, and died within a few hours early in the morning of April 4, 1892, in the 75th year of his age, having been laird a little more than thirty years.

He was survived by his third son, Francis Hugh, and his widow, their eldest son having died in childhood, and the second in the 24th year of his age.

21. FRANCIS HUGH, the 21st laird, b. 1854; married, November 18, 1880, Mary Agnes, only child of John Ramsay of Barra and Straloch, Aberdeenshire, and has issue by her two sons.
    (1). Alexander, b. August 17, 1881.
    (2). Quentin, b. February 16, 1888.

This laird was educated at Winchester and Oxford, and called to the English bar: he is a member of the Inner Temple, and a J. P. for the County of Aberdeen. He was for some years attached to the staff of "The Times." He contested West Aberdeenshire in the Conservative interest in 1885 and 1886, against Dr. Farquharson of Finzean, who was returned as a supporter of Mr. Gladstone.

"THE IRVINES OF CAMLIN," BOYLE, COUNTY ROSCOMMON, IRELAND.

The line of descent of John V. and William F. Irwin, New York City, is as follows:

1. Thomas Irwin an officer in Cromwell's Army, b. 1631; m. Mary Jane Knott, d. (?).

2. Thomas Irwin (son of 1), b. 1673; m. Anne Walker, d. (?).

Camlin.

In parish of Eastersnow (near town of Boyle), county of Roscommon, Ireland.
Residence of IRWIN OF CAMLIN from 1716 to 1883. From a water-color taken
about 1850 by Mrs. Mira Duke, née Irwin, the original of which is in the possession
of John V. Irwin, 203 Broadway, New York City.

3.I

de
ent

AL
AI

H
W

3. John Irwin, J. P., of Camlin House (son of 2), b. 1716; m. Rebecca Phibbs, of Rockwood, Co. Sligo, 1757; d. 1791.

4. John Irwin, J. P., of Camlin House (son of 3), b. 1762; m. Elizabeth O'Malley, d. of George O'Malley, K. C. of Castlebar, General 68th Connaught Rangers, d. 1842.

5. John Irwin, J. P., of Camlin House (son of 4), b. 1800; m. Emily Bolton, d. of Richard Bolton, Esq., of Monkstown Castle, Co. Dublin, 1837; d. 1842.

6. John Irwin, Major 88th Connaught Rangers in Crimean War and Sepoy Rebellion (son of 5), b. Camlin House, 1838; d. New York City ,1891.

7. William Irwin Attorney, (son of 5); came to America in 1868, b. Camlin House, 1842; m. Elizabeth Vosburgh, of Albany, N. Y., U. S. A., 1873; d. New York City, 1902.

8. John V. Irwin, Attorney (son of 7), b. New York City 1874; m. Cornelia H. Merrill 1905. Address 203 Broadway, New York City. Ph. B. '94, L. L. B. '99 New York University. Member Society of Colonial Wars, Psi Upsilon and Phi Beta Kappa.

9. William F. Irwin (son of 7), b. Albany, N. Y., 1881. Address 1070 Lexington Ave. New York City. New York University 1903, Psi Upsilon.

ARMS. Arg.— Three holly leaves ppr. Crest.— A dexter arm in armor holding a thistle, all ppr. Motto: "*Sub sole, sub umbra, virens.*"

PEDIGREE OF THEODORE ROOSEVELT, PRESIDENT OF THE UNITED STATES.

History relates that the conquest of England by the Normans in 1066, brought a host of adventurers into the country, who were often rewarded for their part in the battle of Hastings by the sequestrated estates of the Saxon lords. Among others was Robert de Brus. Early in the eleventh century, Robert de Brus, or Bruce, held the title of Lord of the Valley of Annan or Annandale, besides large estates in Yorkshire, where he founded the Monastery of Gysburn. Says Johnstone, in his "Historical Families of Dumfriesshire":

"The pedigree of the Bruces goes back into the regions of fable. As Princes of Orkney and Caithness, they had a connection with

Scotland in the ninth century. Their chief, Crinus Erevine, married Beatrix, the eldest daughter of Malcolm II., King of Scotland. His son, Reginwald, a Sea King, roved through Europe in search of a bride, and found one in the daughter of Vladimir the Great, the first Christian Czar of Russia. Reginwald finally settled in Normandy, and his grandson, Robert de Brus, followed the Conqueror. Another branch of the family remained in England, where it still exists. The line of Robert I. became extinct in the male succession with David II., for his four brothers, all slaughtered during the long war with England, died childless. His daughter Marjory married Walter, son of James, High Steward of Scotland, and was ancestress of the Stuarts or Stewards, and of her gracious Majesty."

President Roosevelt is descended from this line of Stuarts, and from the Baillies or Balliols, of Hoprig and Leamington; from the Douglases of Dalkeith and Morton; and from Keith, Earl Marshall of Scotland, and from John Irvine of Cults (house of Drum), buried at Cults, with a monument, as follows:

Robert Stewart, Robert II., King of Scotland, had by his wife, Lady Annabelle, daughter of Sir John Drummond of Stobhall, a daughter, the Lady Elizabeth, who married Sir James Douglas, of Dalkeith and Morton. Their son, James Douglas of Dalkeith, had by his wife, Lady Agnes, daughter of the Earl Marshal of Scotland, a second son, named John (brother to James, created Earl of Morton), who was knighted, and married the heiress of Hawthorden of Abernathy, and became the founder of the house of Douglas of Tilquhille, or Tiliwhilly, about the year 1450. A lineal descendant of this house was another John Douglas, eighth in descent from the first Sir John Douglas, who was Sir John Douglas, of Tiliwhilly, who was born 1723 and died in 1749. By his wife, Agnes, daughter of Rev. James Home, minister at Elgin, he had a daughter, Euphemia Douglas, who died aged 55 years. In 1733 she married Charles Irvine of Cults, near Aberdeen, who died March 28, 1779, aged eighty-three. Their son, John Irvine, M. D., was born at Cults, September 15, 1742; came to Georgia, United States of America, in 1765, and became a prominent man in the colony, being a member of the last Royal Assembly in 1780. After this he went to London, and became so successful as a medical practitioner that he was appointed a Physician to the Admiralty, and assisted Dr. Mathew Baillie as Physician to King George III. Subsequently, Dr. Irvine returned to Georgia, and founded the

1. Andrew Jackson. 2. Washington Irving. 3. Benjamin Harrison.
4. Theodore Roosevelt.

Georgia Medical Society, which attended his funeral on October 18, 1809, at Savannah, Georgia. Dr. John Irvine, of Savannah, married his first wife at Sunbury, Ga., September 17, 1765. She was Elizabeth, daughter of Colonel Kenneth Baillie, ensign of the Darlin Rangers (1735), a colonial organization for exterminating the Indian race. Col. Kenneth Baillie was a lineal descendant of Hoprig and Leamington. While Ensign Baillie was serving in General Oglethorpe's expedition in 1740, against the Spaniards, he was taken prisoner and carried to Spain, but made his escape and returned to Georgia, where he commanded the Second Southern Colonial regiment.

Dr. John Irvine married, as his second wife, Anna Baillie. Their daughter, Anne Irvine, born January 14, 1770, married, April 13, 1786, Captain James Bulloch of the Georgia Line, in the Continental Army, the eldest son of Archibald Bulloch, President of Georgia in 1776, by his wife Mary, daughter of James de Veaux, Judge of the King's Court in Georgia, 1760; Commander of the First Regiment of Georgia Militia in 1775, by his wife Anne, granddaughter of Edmund Ballenger, first landgrave of his surname in South Carolina.

Captain James and Anne Irvine Bulloch's second son, James Stephen Bulloch, was major in Chatham's battalion. He married, first, a daughter of United States Senator John Elliot; and secondly, Martha, daughter of General Daniel Stewart, of the Georgia Line, in the Revolution, and by her he had a daughter, Martha, (sister to Irvine Bulloch, the sailing-master of the "Alabama" at the time of her fight with the "Keersarge"), who married Theodore Roosevelt, and became the mother of the President of the United States.

WASHINGTON IRVING

Washington Irving was born in the city of New York, April 3, 1783. He is descended from the House of Bonshaw, Drum branch, as follows:

William De Irwyn, or Sir William Irvine, as he is styled in "Nisbet's Heraldry," married Mariota, the daughter of Sir Robert Keith, Earl Marischal of Scotland, who led the horse at Bannockburn, and was killed at the battle of Dublin in 1332. Of this family, says Dr. Christopher Irvine, in an ancient document, quoted in Playfair's "British Families of Antiquity," are the Irvines of Orkney.

(Dr. Christopher Irvine, was Physician General and Historiographer of Scotland, and also Historiographer to King Charles II.)

A table was prepared with great accuracy by Mr. George Petrie, Clerk of the Records of Kirkwall, and corresponding member of the Society of Antiquaries of Scotland, from original deeds and other old manuscripts in the county archives; and it is a curious fact that he was enabled to do it without a break, from a facility afforded by the ancient "Udal" laws of the region, which required that lands, on the death of the owner, should be divided equally among the sons and daughters; a peculiarity which led, in partition, to the mention of the names, and definition of the relationship; of all the parties who were to draw a share.   A symmetrical and regularly attested table of descent carries his lineage through the senior representatives to Magnus, of 1608, the· first Shapinsha Irving, and passing thence to the neighboring island of Pomona, through James "the Lawmon," or Chief Judge of the Orkneys, of 1560, the father of Magnus and "John of Erwyne" of 1438.   Mention is made in Wilson's "Archæological and Prehistoric Annals of Scotland" of the first Orkney Irvine, and earliest cadet of Drum, William De Erevin, an inhabitant of Kirkwall in 1369, while the islands yet owned the sway of Magnus V., the last of the Norwegian Earls, and in which same year we find the name of his brother, Sir Thomas de Irwyn, the son and successor of the first Laird of Drum, among the barons in Parliament.   (See House of Drum.)

In 1809, Washington Irving wrote "A History of New York from the Beginning of the World to the End of the Dutch Dynasty," by Diedrich Knickerbocker.   He edited the "Analectic Magazine," in Philadelphia, 1813.   The "Sketch Book," portions of which had appeared in New York, was offered to Murray, and afterwards to Constable, but was refused by both these celebrated publishers. After unsuccessfully trying to publish it himself, Murray, on Sir Walter Scott's recommendation, took the "Sketch-Book," paying £200 for the copyright, which he afterwards increased to £400. In 1822 he wrote "Bracebridge Hall;" in 1824, "Tales of a Traveller;" 1828, "History of the Life and Voyages of Columbus," "Voyages of the Companions of Columbus," and "The Conquest of Granada;" 1832, "The Alhambra," a portion of which was written in the ancient palace of the Moorish Kings; 1835, "Legends of the Conquest of Spain," and "Mahomet and His Successors."   In 1829, he returned to England as Secretary to the American Legation.   In 1837 he received the honorary degree of LL.D. from

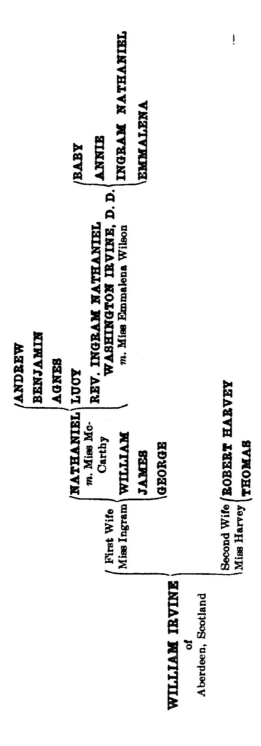

WILLIAM IRVINE
of
Aberdeen, Scotland

First Wife
Miss Ingram

NATHANIEL
m. Miss Mc-
Carthy

ANDREW
BENJAMIN
AGNES
LUCY
REV. INGRAM NATHANIEL
WASHINGTON IRVINE, D. D.
m. Miss Emmalena Wilson

BABY
ANNIE
INGRAM NATHANIEL
EMMALENA

WILLIAM
JAMES
GEORGE

Second Wife
Miss Harvey

ROBERT HARVEY
THOMAS

the University of Oxford, and next year returned to America. A visit to the Rocky Mountains produced his "Tour on the Prairies." In 1837 he wrote "Astoria." In 1842 he was appointed Minister to Spain. In 1846 he published the "Life of Goldsmith," and his great work, the "Life of Washington" was published 1855–1859. An edition of his works in 15 vols. reached a sale of 250,000 vols.

He died at Sunny Side on November 28, 1859, in his own "Sleepy Hollow," not far from the Catskill Mountains, on whose hazy summits his fame rests.

FAMILY OF WILLIAM IRVING.

Genealogy — From William Irvine to Annie Irvine, his great-granddaughter.

WILLIAM IRVINE:— Born in (or came from) Aberdeen, Scotland. Resided in Kenmare, Co. Kerry, Ireland, where he died; and was buried in the tomb erected for the Irvine family in the Old Protestant church yard. William Irvine was a member of the Episcopal Church of Scotland, and so both he and his household were all attendants at the services of the Established Church in Kenmare. He was married twice; on both occasions the service was performed in Scotland, his wife having come with him from Scotland, and after her death and burial in Kenmare, he visited Scotland and re-married. This second Mrs. Irvine was also, I believe, buried in Kenmare.

By his first wife, Miss Ingram (I think), the following sons were born: Nathaniel, William, James and George (4).

By his second wife, Miss Harvey (I think), the following sons were born: Robert Harvey and Thomas (2).

NATHANIEL IRVINE, being the eldest son, became heir to William Irvine's estates, etc. He married Miss Annie McCarthy (a second wife), by whom the following sons and daughters were born: Andrew Benjamin, Agnes, Lucy, and Ingram Nathaniel W. (2 sons, 2 daughters).

Nathaniel Irvine (my father) died and was buried in Dublin, Ireland. Lucy (my sister) also died and was buried in Dublin. My mother, brother Andrew Benjamin, sister Agnes and myself (Ingram N. W.), came to the United States of America in May, A. D. 1865. After some years, my brother Andrew, who married, traveled in the West, and it is thought by me that he is dead. My sister, now Mrs. Agnes Palmer, at this writing is residing in California. My mother died a few years after coming to the States and is buried in the church yard of St. James Protestant Episcopal Church, St. James, Suffolk County, N. Y., where I was rector for some years.

INGRAM NATHANIEL WASHINGTON IRVINE, youngest son of Nathaniel Irvine and Annie McCarthy, was born Sunday, July 8, 1849. Came from Ireland (as before given) in 1865; studied in the New York Nautical School; also in St. Stephen's Preparatory School, State of New York, and entered the General Theological Seminary of the Protestant Episcopal Church of the U. S., in 1871; graduated from there in 1874; was ordained Deacon by the Rt. Rev. Abraham Newkirk Littlejohn, D. D. LL. D., in the Church of the Redeemer, Brooklyn, Long Island, N. Y., the same year. On No-. vember 25, 1874, the Rev. Ingram N. W. Irvine married Miss Emmalena Wilson, daughter of Capt. George H. Wilson and Annie M. Burr, his wife. In the year 1875, he was ordained Priest by the same Bishop (Dr. Littlejohn) in St. Mark's Church, Williamsburgh, E. D. Brooklyn, Long Island. He has been successively Rector, Rural Dean, and Cathedral Dean. He received the Degree of Doctor of Divinity from Chaddock College, Quincy, Illinois. To him were born of Miss Wilson (his wife), four children, viz.: Baby, Annie, Ingram Nathaniel and Emmalena. All of these children died excepting Annie (now Mrs. James A. Roney).

NOTE.— I remember seeing my father's signet ring; my mother wore it in later years. It had engraved on a large precious stone, a Rose and Scotch Thistle, with a Cock in the act of crowing. It bore an inscription, in either Latin or French, I cannot now recall, the translation of which, I think, was "The Same Through (or in) Sunshine and Shadow." By an accident, the stone of the ring was broken — by the jamming of a door. I also saw my mother's marriage certificate. There is a strong remembrance on my part that my father told me that his mother was of British descent and was related to Oliver Cromwell, Lord Protector of England. My first name, "Ingram," was a family name on my father's mother's side. The church records in which were the dates, etc. of my father's life, our births, etc., were all burned during the partial destruction of the Rectory.

There are now *no* Irvines in that part of Ireland where my father and grandfather resided.

The facts which I give are very correct to the best of my memory. Respectfully,   INGRAM V. W. IRVINE,
Nov. 28, 1903.   437 N. 40th St., Philadelphia, Pa., U. S. A.

PART IV.

THE IRVINES OR IRWINS OR IRVINGS OF THE OLD COUNTRY AND THE NEW.

DRUM BRANCH OF THE HOUSE OF BONSHAW.

(Extracts from " The Irvines and Their Kin," First Edition.)

There were two and more branches of the Irvine family that belonged to the baronage — Bonshaw and Drum. The Lairds of Drum were descended from William de Irvine, who was armor-bearer to Robert Bruce, and was rewarded for his devoted services by a grant of the forest of Drum, Aberdeenshire, at that time part of a royal forest.

Sir Alexander Irvine, grandson of William de Irvine, was one of the chief commanders of the king's army at the battle of Harlaw. A. D. 1411. He was a valiant champion. In a hand-to-hand encounter with Eachin Ruadh mir Cath, of Clan McLean of Dowart, general of Donald of the Isles, "they fought like lions and killed one another dead on the spot." The prowess of this gude Sir Alexander Irvine is especially celebrated in the battle of Harlaw. Other heads of the family rendered important services to subsequent sovereigns, and in the seventeenth century the Lairds of Drum vied in wealth and power with many families of noble rank.

Sir Alexander Irvine, the Royalist, was eldest son of Alexander, ninth Laird of Drum, by Lady Marian, daughter of Robert Douglas, Earl of Buchan. He was born about 1598, and died May, 1658. He had a varied and stirring life. He was one of Charles II.'s most earnest Scottish supporters, and when Charles became king, in 1660, he offered Sir Alexander's son Alexander, tenth Laird of Drum, an earldom, which was refused. Sir Alexander, the Royalist, after the reverses his party suffered, was led to conform to the Covenant, though unwillingly, and was appointed Sheriff of Aberdeen in December, 1634. By his wife, Magdalen, daughter of Sir J. Scrymgeour, he had, besides other children, two sons: Alexander, who died 1687 (spoken of above), and Robert, who died February 6, 1645, in the tolbooth of Edinburgh (see "Memorials of the Trouble," Spalding Club; Gordon's "Scots Affairs," Spalding Club; "Miscellany of Spalding Club," Vol. 3; "Burk's Landed Gentry," and "Dictionary of National Biography," Stephens).

Christopher Irvine, M. D., who flourished between 1638 and 1685 — physician, philologist and antiquary — was a younger son of Christopher Irvine, of Robgill Tower, Annandale, and a barrister of the Temple, of the family of Irvine of Bonshaw, in Dumfriesshire. He calls himself on one of the title pages "Irwinus abs. Bon Bosco." He was a brother of Sir Gerard Irvine, Bart., of Castle Irvine, of Fermanaugh, who died at Dundalk, 1689. Christopher was a Royalist and an Episcopalian. He says that he was historiographer to Charles II. He married Margaret, daughter of James Wishard, Laird of Potterow, and had two sons: Christopher, M. D., and James. This Christopher died about 1685. He wrote many books, and his principal ones are: (1) "Bellum Grammaticale," Edin., 1650, 1658, and again 1698; (2) "Medicina Magnetica, or the Arts of Curing by Sympathy," London, 1656; (3) "Index Locorum Scotorum," Edin., 1664 ["An useful piece, and well deserves a new impression."— Bp. Nicholson's "Scot. Hist. Lib."]; (4) "Histori Scoticae, Nomenclature Latino-Vernacula," 1682, 1692, again 1719. (See Chambers' "Dictionary of Eminent Scotsmen," and "Burk's Landed Gentry.")

The following account of the Irvines is compiled from Robert Douglas's "Baronage of Scotland" and "Peerage of Scotland":

ELIZABETH, daughter of Sir Robert Keith (who was alive in 1421), heiress of Troup, married to Alexander Irvine, of Drum.

ELIZABETH, daughter of William, fourth Earl Marischal (who died October 7, 1581), by his wife, Margaret, married to Sir Alexander Irvine, of Drum.

ISABEL, daughter of Sir Robert Campbell, Glenurchy (who succeeded his brother 164–), by Isabel, daughter of Lachlan Macintosh, Captain Clanchattan, married to Robert Irvine, of Fedderat, son of Alexander Irvine, of Drum, and had two daughters.

MARGARET, daughter of John Johnston, of Johnston, Marquis of Annandale, married to Christopher, son and heir of Edmond Irvine, of Bonshaw, in the county of Dumfries — contract dated 1566.

ELIZABETH, third daughter of Sir Alexander, Lord Forbes (son of Sir John — died 1405), by Lady Elizabeth Douglas (daughter

Castle Irvine, Irvinestown, Ireland.

of George, Earl of Angus, and granddaughter of King
Robert II. — 1371-1390), married to Irvine, of Drum.

SIR ARCHIBALD DOUGLAS (son of Sir William who fell at Flodden,
1513), of Glenbowie, was knighted by James V. (1513-1542);
married (1) Agnes Keith, daughter of William, Earl
Marischal, and had one son and one daughter; married (2)
Mary, daughter of Sir Alexander Irvine, of Drum, and had
issue (see below).

LADY JANET, daughter of Robert Douglas, Earl of Buchan, by
Christina (daughter died 1580), widow of Richard Douglas,
married to Alexander Irvine, of Drum.

MARY, daughter of George Gordon, second Marquis Huntly (who
was beheaded at Market Cross, Edinburgh, March 22, 1649),
by Lady Jane Campbell, eldest daughter of Archibald,
seventh Earl Argyll (died June 14, 1638), married to Alexander Irvine, of Drum, December 7, 1643.

SIR ARCHIBALD DOUGLAS, by marriage with Mary Irvine, daughter
of the Laird of Drum, had two sons — James and John
— and six daughters — Isabel, Sarah, Margery, Eupham
and Grizel. Margery, fourth daughter, married to Irvine,
of Bailie.

SIR WILLIAM DOUGLAS (living in 1635), great-grandson of Sir Archibald, married a daughter of Alexander Irvine, of Drum,
by whom he had one son,— Sir William, his successor.

WILLIAM LESLIE, fourth Baron of Balquhair (who died in the reign
of James III., 1467), by Dame Agnes Irvine, his second wife,
a daughter of the Laird of Drum, had a son, Alexander, who
was the progenitor of the Leslies of Waldis.

JAMES CRICHTON, Viscount of Frendraught, married (2), at the
church of Drumoak, November 8, 1642, Margaret, daughter
of Sir Alexander Irvine, of Drum, and had two sons —
James, second Viscount of Frendraught, and Lewis, third
Viscount of Frendraught.

SIR GEORGE OGILVY married (1) Margaret, daughter of Sir Alexander Irvine, of Drum, and had one daughter — Helen,
who married Earl of Airlie. Sir George, of Dunlugus, had
a charter to himself and Margaret Irvine, his wife, of the
barony of Dunlugus (March 9, 1610-11), and another barony
of Inschedrour, wherein he is designated "younger Banff"
(February 14, 1628). Died August 11, 1663.

JAMES OGILVY (fifth Baron of Boyne, died 1619), had one son,

Walter, his successor. James' charter dated February 22, 1597: "Jacabo Ogilvy, apparenti de Boyne, et Elizabeth Irvine, ejus spousæ, terrarum de Quhinter, Cavintoun, Kindrocht, et diemdietet terraum de Ardbragane."

NORMAN LEITH, successor to Laurence Leith, his father (who died in the reign of James III., 1460–1488), married Elizabeth, daughter of William Leslie, fourth Baron Balquhair, by Agnes Irvine, his wife, daughter of a Baron of Drum. Norman died during the reign of James III.

SIR JOHN OGILVIE, of Innercarity (who was, by Charles I., created Baronet of Nova Scotia in 1626), married Anne, daughter of Sir Alexander Irvine, of Drum; issue, four sons and one daughter.

ALEXANDER SETON, of Meldrum, in his father's lifetime, got a charter under the great seal, dated 1578, for lands of Meldrum. He married (1) Elizabeth, daughter of Sir Alexander Irvine, of Drum — their only son, Alexander, died in 1590, during his father's lifetime; married (2) Jean, daughter of Alexander, Lord Abernethy.

JOHN URQUHART, who died November 8, 1631 (æt. 84), and was succeeded by his son, John (died December, 1631), got a charter, under the great seal, upon his father's resignation — Johannes Urquhart, Juniori, de Craigfintry, et Isabella Irvine, ejus spousæ — of the lands of Leathers and Craigfintry, in Aberdeenshire, dated July 28, 1612. By his first wife, Isabella, he had a son, John.

JEAN, first daughter of Sir John Johnston, sheriff of Aberdeen (1630), married to Irvine, of Brakely.

THOMAS JOHNSTON, eldest son of John Johnston, of that ilk, married (1) Mary, daughter of Irvine, of Kingouffie. They had four sons — Thomas (died in 1656), William, John and James — and three daughters.

A daughter of Patrick Forbes, of Carse, was married, in the sixteenth century, to Irvine, of Beltie.

GEORGE, second son of George Dundas, of that ilk, had a daughter Barbara to marry Alexander Irvine, of Supack, or Saphock, in the seventeenth century.

ELIZABETH, daughter of Alexander Seton, of Pitmedden (who died soon after, in 1630), married Patrick Irvine, of Beatty.

MARY, daughter of Janet and William Johnston, Esq., married to James Irvine, of Cove, in the latter part of the seventeenth century.

JANET, second daughter of Sir John Douglas, of Kelhead (son of
Sir William), married at Prestonfield, November 13, 1767,
to William Irvine, of Bonshaw; they had one son and one
daughter.

HON. EMILIA ROLLO, daughter of Andrew, third Lord Rollo (died
in March, 1700), by Margaret Balfour (died October 20,
1734)— Andrew and Margaret married November 1670
— married to William Irvine, of Bonshaw, in the county of
Dumfries, September 2, 1698, and died, his widow, at Bonshaw, March 20, 1747 (æt. 71).

HON. CLEMENT ROLLO (fourth son of Robert, fourth Lord Rollo,
who died April 16, 1765, aged eighty), who died at Dun-
crumb, January 14, 1762, married Mary Emilia, eldest
daughter of John Irvine, of Bonshaw, and had issue: Robert,
a captain in Forty-second Regiment Foot, who settled in
America 1784; John, barrackmaster at Perth; and Mary,
who died at Perth October 12, 1776.

MARGARET, daughter of Alexander Skene, of that ilk, who succeeded his father, James Skene, 1612, married to Robert
Irvine, of Fornet and Monteoffe.

JOHN CAMPBELL (son Hon. John Campbell), member of parliament
for the boroughs of Ayr, 1796, 1802 and 1806, married (1)
a daughter of Mr. Peter, merchant in London, widow of
—— Irvine, by whom he had a daughter, Caroline.

ALEXANDER IRVINE, of Coul, was a witness to a charter, dated
August 8, 1539, to John Keith, of Craig, who succeeded
John Keith, proprietor of barony of Craig.

HOUSE OF BONSHAW IN IRELAND.

I copy this passage from "The Scottish Nation," by William
Anderson, page 537:

"Irvine, a surname of ancient standing in Scotland, supposed
to have been originally Erevine, the latter word derived by some
antiquarians, from the Celtic-Scythic Erin vine or fein, that is, a
stout westland man; Erin, west (the native name of Ireland, as
lying west of Scotland), and vine, or fein, a strong, resolute man.
Nisbet (System of Heraldry, Vol. II., App. p. 69) says that when
the colonies of the Gauls came from the west coast of Spain and
seated themselves on the east coasts of Erin and in the west hills
and islands of Albyn, the Erevines came to both these islands.

In the latter country they had their seat in a part of Ayrshire, called Cunningham, and gave their name to the river and their own place of residence, now the town of Irvine.   One of them, Crine Erwine, was Abthane of Dull, and Seneschal and Collector of all the King's rents in the Western Isles.   He married the Princess Beatrix, eldest daughter of Malcolm II., and was father of Duncan I., King of Scotland.   Some of this family went to Dumfriesshire, and settled on the river Esk, where one of them obtained, by marriage, the lands of Bonshaw, in that county.   A descendant of his, in the seventeenth century, rendered his name obnoxious by his cruel persecutions of the Covenanters."

This passage confirms what Rev. Dr. Christopher Irvine, of Mountjoy, Omagh, Ireland, says in a recent letter to me about the Irvines.   Rev. Dr. Christopher Irvine wrote a history of the Irvines of Bonshaw, Irish branch, which has not been published.   It was placed in the hands of a publisher for publication, but the publisher failed in business and the manuscript history was lost.   The following is the entire letter of Rev. Dr. Christopher Irvine:

"The Irvines, Irvings, or Irwins, were one of the ancient original families, or clans, of Dumfriesshire, Scotland.   They were located in Annandale, Evisdale, Eskdale and Wauchopdale on the coast of this shire, close to the borders of England.   They developed into five separate divisions or sub-clans by the year 1500, or the sixteenth century, and from the year 1600 became widely spread through England and Ireland.   Between 1610 and 1660, the chief exodus to Ireland took place.   Members of the different sub-clans settled in Ulster, in the northern counties of that province.   The Irvings of Bonshaw were the first or chief sub-clan, and the Laird of Bonshaw was recognized as the chieftain of the whole Dumfriesshire clan or name.   King Robert Bruce made one of this family, Sir William Irvine, his secretary, and gave him the Forest of Drum, in Aberdeenshire, and thus were derived the various branches of the name in the north of Scotland.   The Irvines of Drum, the lineal descendants of Sir William, still retain the possessions granted them by Robert Bruce.

"The Irvines of Bonshaw suffered much in the wars with England, Bonshaw having been several times taken and burned to the ground by the English armies.   Edward Irving, of Bonshaw (1566 to 1605), was a turbulent chieftain, and carried on successful family feuds with rival clans — Maxwells, Kirkpatricks, Bells, etc., for which he was outlawed by the Scottish government.   He survived the government outlawries and confiscations, and strengthened himself by alliances with the Johnstons, the most powerful of the Dumfriesshire clans, his son Christopher having married Margaret, the daughter of Johnston, chieftain of that clan. By this alliance the Johnstons and Irvines, with their allies, were able to defeat the Lord Warden at the head of the government troops at the battle of Dryfersands, 1593, so that the King had to make peace with them, and appoint Johnston his head warden. The descendants of this Christopher Irving continued to reside at Bonshaw, and the present owner, Colonel John Beaufin Irving, is the present possessor. Among his predecessors who were distinguished as officers in the army was Sir Paulus Æmilius Irving, Baronet. The next brother of Edward of Bonshaw was Christopher of Robigilland Annan, known by the border name of Black Christie. He was also a turbulent chief, engaged in the cause of Queen Mary, 1567, etc. His son, John, married Mary, daughter of Johnston, of Newlie, and their son, Christopher, settled in County Fermanagh, Ireland, in 1613. From him are descended the Irvines, or Irvings, of Fermanagh, represented by Captain William D'Arcy Irvine, of Castle Irvine. One of the sons of Christopher Irvine, Sir Gerard Irvine, Baronet, was greatly distinguished in the Irish Rebellion of 1641. He was an officer in the Royal Army and fought on the side of the King against the Roundheads, both in Ireland and Scotland. He was also engaged on the side of King William III. in the wars of 1689, and died that year in Duke Schomberg's camp in Dundalk. Colonel William Irvine, of Castle Irvine, presided over the great meeting of volunteers at Dungannon in 1782. The several younger branches of the family included the Irvines of Killadees, Greenhill, St. Aidens, etc. Though it may be hard to trace the several families of Irvines who settled in Ireland, yet they mostly all belonged to the Dumfriesshire clan, though some may have come from Aberdeen and the north of Scotland."

COL. WILLIAM IRVINE, of Castle Irvine, born July 15, 1734; member for Ratoath in the Irish House of Commons, was High Sheriff County Fermanagh 1758, and of Tyrone 1768. He married, first, December 10, 1755, Hon. Flora Caroline Cole, daughter of John, first Lord Mount Florence; she died October 20, 1757, leaving a son, Christopher, died young He married, second, February 23, 1760, Sophia, daughter of Gorges Lowther, Esq., of Kilrue, County Meath (by Judith his wife, daughter of John Usher and Mary his wife, only daughter of George, first Lord St. George), and had eight sons and eight daughters:

1. GEORGE MARCUS, of whom presently.

2. WILLIAM HENRY, Rector of Tara and Dunshaughlin, County Meath, Justice of Peace for that county, born 1763; married Elizabeth, daughter of James Hamilton, Esq., of Sheephill, County Dublin, and died 1839, leaving by her (who died April 26, 1859,) issue:

    (1). Gorges Lowther, Rector of Rathregan, County Meath; married December, 1827, Henrietta Florence, daughter of Christopher Edmund John Nugent, Esq., of Bobsgrove, and by her (who died March, 1834,) had two daughters, Sophia, married John G. Holmes, Esq., of Rockwood, County Galway, and Henrietta, married Clement Hammerton, Esq., M. D.   Rev. G. Irvine died November, 1838.

    (2). James, Commander, Royal Navy, of Hardwick Place, Dublin, died unmarried, November, 1867.

    (3). Henry, of Rossclare, County Wexford, and Kilmore, County Tyrone, born 1802; married 1829, Elizabeth, daughter of Ebenezer Radford Rowe, Esq., of Ballyharty, County Wexford, and twin sister of Sophia, wife of Sir Thomas Esmonde, Bart., and has issue, John William Henry, born 1831; William Henry, late Captain Third Regiment (Buffs), married Maria Jane, daughter of Arthur Edward Knox, Esq., of Castlerea, by Lady Jane Parsons his wife, daughter of Lawrence, second Earl of Rosse, and has a daughter, Edith.

    (4). St.George Caulfeild, Rector of Kilmessan, County Meath, married Georgina, daughter of Nathaniel Preston, Esq., of Swanistown, County Meath, and had a daughter, Georgina, married Surgeon-Major McNalty.

    (5). Hans, M. D., died unmarried.

        a. Charlotte, died unmarried, 1874.

        b. Harriet, died unmarried.

        c. Caroline, married Rev. John Lowe, Rector of Dunshaughlin, County Meath.

3. CHRISTOPHER HENRY HAMILTON, Royal Navy, born 1776; died unmarried.

4. GEORGE ST. GEORGE, Major in the Army, of Ballinabown, County Wexford, High Sheriff, 1804, born 1771; married, first,

Bridget, daughter of Maurice Howlin D'Arcy, Esq., of Cooline, County Wexford; she died without issue. He married, second, Frances, daughter of Robert Doyne, Esq., of Wells, County of Wexford, and had issue:

(1). Edward Tottenham, of St. Aidans, County Wexford, Justice of the Peace and D. L., High Sheriff, County Wexford 1830, late Captain Sixteenth Lancers, born 1832; married, 1861, Elizabeth Beatrice, daughter of Edward Gonne Bell, Esq., of Streamstown, County Mayo, and has had issue, Edward St. George Tottenham, born February 12, 1883; Mary Sophia Georgiana, born February 13, 1863; died January 8, 1864.

    a. Frances Eleanor D'Arcy, married 1856, Rev. Charles Elrington.

    b. Sophia Maria, married, first, 1852, James Butler, Esq., of Castle Crine; second, 1860, Col. I. H. Graham, and died May 8, 1887.

5. HENRY WILLIAM, born 1772; married Rebecca Cooke, and had an only daughter, Rebecca, married David Onge, Esq.

6. AUDLEY MERVYN, born 1774; killed at Pondicherry.

7. JOHN CAULFEILD, Captain in the Army, Justice of Peace County Cork, born 1781; married Mary Broderick, daughter and co-heir of Henry Mitchell, Esq., of Mitchellsfort, County Cork, and relict of Grice Smyth, Esq., of Ballinatray; died without issue, 1850.

8. HUGH LOWTHER, born, 1783; killed at Montevideo.

Daughters—

1. SOPHIA MARIA, wife of Captain Carew Smith.

2. ELINOR JANE, wife of Henry Gonne Bell, Esq.

3. FLORENCE ELIZABETH ANN, wife of William Rathborne, Esq.

4. OLIVIA EMILY, wife of George Lennox Conyngham, Esq.

5. FRANCES MARY, wife of Jones Irwin, Esq., of County Sligo.

6. HARRIET, married John Carleton, Esq., of Mohill, County Leitrim.

7. LETITIA ST. PATRICIA MERVYN, wife of Colonel Alexander Stuart, only son of General James Stuart.

8. ELIZABETH EMILY, wife of Ebenezer Radford Rowe, Esq., Ballyharty, County Wexford; and second, of Samuel Green, Esq.

Col. Irvine died May ,1814. His eldest son, Major Gorges Marcus Irvine, of Castle Irvine, born November 26, 1760, married March 31, 1788, Elizabeth, daughter and heir of Judge D'Arcy, Esq., of

Dunmow Castle, County Meath (by Elizabeth his wife, daughter and heir of Richard Nugent, Esq., of Robbinstown). (The D'Arcys of Dunmow, of whom Mr. D'Arcy-Irvine is the heir general, were descended from the baronial house of D'Arcy, afterwards Earls of Holderness.) By the heiress of D'Arcy (who died 1829) Major Irvin had four sons and five daughters:

1. WILLIAM D'ARCY, of whom hereafter.
2. RICHARD, E. I., born 1794, died without issue.
3. GORGES MERVYN (Rev.), born 1798.
4. ST. GEORGE, born 1801; married Miss Catherine Fennell.
5. SOMERSET, R. N., born 1809; married a daughter of Abraham Hargrave, Esq., of Cove, County Cork; died without issue 1850.

Daughters—

1. LOUISA, born 1791.
2. ELIZABETH, born 1795; married Marquis Fernando Incontri, of Florence.
3. SUSANNA AMELIA, born 1797; died unmarried, 1870.
4. SOPHIA, born 1799; married Arthur, Viscount Dungannon, and died March 21, 1880.
5. LETITIA, born 1805; died unmarried April 5, 1884, aged 78.

Major Irvine died November 28, 1847, and was succeeded by his eldest son.

WILLIAM D'ARCY IRVINE, of Castle Irvine, of born January 22, 1793, adopted the surname of D'Arcy. He married in 1817, Maria, daughter of Sir Henry Crooke, first baronet of Cole Brooke, County Fermanagh, and by her (who died July 18, 1838) had issue:

1. HENRY MERVYN D'ARCY IRVINE, his heir.
2. RICHARD D'ARCY, Treasurer of County Fermanagh; died unmarried, 1857.
3. WILLIAM D'ARCY, heir to his nephew.
4. FRANCES D'ARCY, Major H. M. Indian Army, married 1854, Margaret, daughter of Col. Sewell, and has issue, William, Robert Judge, Somerset, Maria Elizabeth, and Henrietta.
5. ARTHUR D'ARCY, Captain in the Fermanagh Militia.
6. JOHN D'ARCY, Captain R. N., died 1885.

Daughters —

1. ELIZABETH, wife of John Caldwell Bloomfield, Esq., of Castle Caldwell, County Fermanagh.
2. MARIA.

Mr. Irvine died June 23, 1857, and was succeeded by his eldest son.

HENRY MERVYN D'ARCY IRVINE, Esq., of Castle Irvine, High Sheriff County Tyrone 1851, who by Royal license, April 27, 1861, assumed the additional surnames and arms of Mervyn and D'Arcy. He married, October 16, 1862, Huntly Mary, eldest daughter of Hon. Francis Prittie, and by her (who died March 2, 1864) left at his decease, July, 1870, a son —

HENRY HUNTLY D'ARCY IRVINE, Esq., of Castle Irvine, born August 14, 1863; died unmarried January 9, 1882, and was succeeded by his uncle, William D'Arcy Irvine, now of Castle Irvine.

Arms — Quarterly: First and fourth arg. a fess gu. between three holy-leaves vert, for Irvine; second, az. semée of cross-crosslets and three cinquefoils arg., for D'Arcy; third, or a chevron sa., for Mervyn. Crests — First, Irvine: A gauntlet fessways issuant out of a cloud and holding a thistle, all ppr.; Second, D'Arcy: On a chapeau gu. turned up erm. a bull passant sa., armed or; Third, A squirrel sejant ppr, cracking a nut gu. Motto — First, Irvine: *Dum memor ipse mei;* Second, D'Arcy: *Un Dieu, un roy;* Third, Mervyn: *De Dieu est tout.*

Seat: Castle Irvine, Irvinestown.

IRVINES OF CASTLE IRVINE.

IRVINE, WILLIAM D'ARCY, Esq., of Castle Irvine, County Fermanagh, formerly Captain Sixty- seventh Regiment, Justice of Peace and D. L., High Sheriff 1885; born 1823; married 1858, Louisa, daughter of Captain Cockburn, R. A., and has issue:

1. WILLIAM D'ARCY, Lieutenant Ninety-ninth Regiment, served in the Zulu War, and Captain Third Battalion Royal Inniskillen Fusileers; died unmarried September 25, 1879.

2. CHARLES COCKBURN D'ARCY, Captain Third Battalion Inniskillen Fusileers, High Sheriff 1886, born 1863; married March 13, 1884, Fanny Kathleen, daughter of Lieutenant-Colonel Jesse Lloyd, of Ballyleck, County Monaghan, and has issue:

    (1). Charles William, born 1885.
    (2). Henry Cockburn, born 1886.
    (1). Violet Kathleen, born 1888.

LINEAGE — The Irvines of Castle Irvine are of very ancient

Scottish ancestry. They are directly descended from the Irvings of Boneshaw, County Dumfries, the first on the name on record being Robert de Herewine, A. D. 1226 (see Irving of Bonshaw).

CHRISTOPHER IRVINE, a lawyer, bred at the Temple, London, was the first of the family who settled in Ireland, upon a grant, from King James VI. of Scotland and I. of England, of lands in Fermanagh. He built Castle Irvine, which was burnt by the rebels in 1641. He lived till after the Restoration, and died in 1666, at an advanced age. He married his cousin, Blanche, daughter of Edward Irvine, Laird of Stapleton (see Irving of Bonshaw), and had issue:

1. CHRISTOPHER, M. D., born 1618, Physician General to the State of Scotland, Historiographer to King Charles II., married Margaret, daughter of James Wishart, Laird of Pittarow, second son of Sir James Wishart and Lady Jean Douglas, third daughter of William, ninth Earl of Angus, and died 1693, leaving issue:

　(1). Christopher, M. D., of Castle Irvine, born 1642; succeeding to the Castle Irvine estates on the death of his uncle, Sir Gerard. He was High Sheriff County Fermanagh 1690, and Member of Parliament for the county from 1703 to 1713; married Phœbe, daughter of Sir George Hume, Baronet, of Castle Hume, and widow of Henry Blennerhassett, of Cavendish Castle, and died without issue May 9, 1714. She died 1710.

　(2). James, Surgeon-General, of Dumfries, married Miss Maxwell, and had one son, Christopher, who died young.

　(3). Thomas, married Sydney, daughter of Lancelot Carleton, of Rossfad, and died without issue 1694.

　(4). John, died unmarried, about 1698.

2. GERARD (Sir) of Ardscragh, County Tyrone, Lieutenant-Colonel in King Charles II.'s service before his Restoration, created a Baronet July 31, 1677; died at Dundalk Camp 1689, a Lieutenant Colonel in the Earl of Granard's regiment in King William's service; married, first, Catherine, daughter of Adam Cathcart, of Bandoragh, Scotland, and of Drumslager, County Tyrone (she died without issue); second, Mary, daughter of Major William Hamilton, and by her (who died 1865) had issue:

　(1). Christopher, born 1654; married Deborah, daughter and co-heiress of Henry Blennerhassett, Esq., of Castle Hassett, County Fermanagh, and died 1680 *v. p. s. p.*

(2). Charles, Lieutenant of horse, died unmarried 1684.

(3). Gerard, drowned at Enniskillen school.

(4). Margaret, wife of John Crichton, ancestor of the Earls of Erne.

3. LANCELOT, died unmarried.

4. WILLIAM.

Daughters —

1. MARGARET, married, first, Colonel Richard Bell, County Dumfries, and had issue; second, Captain Thomas Maxwell; and third, David Rhynd, of Derryvullen, County Fermanagh.

2. MARION, married, first, Andrew Johnston, second son of James Johnston, Laird of Beirholme, County Dumfries; second, her cousin, Lancelot Carleton, of Rossfad, and had issue; and third, Captain John Somerville.

The third son, William Irvine, of Ballindulla, was a Lieutenant of horse under King Charles II. at the Battle of Worcester, where he was wounded; and High Sheriff for County Fermanagh 1681. He married, first, Elizabeth, daughter of Herbert Gledstanes, a Colonel under Gustavus Adolphus, King of Sweden, and Governor of Walgast, and had issue:

1. CHRISTOPHER, of whom afterwards.

2. JOHN, ancestor of the Irvines of Killadeas (see Irvine of Killadeas).

3. CHARLES, Lieutenant-Colonel; married March 8, 1698, Margaret King, sister of William King, D. D., Archbishop of Dublin, and died without issue 1745.

4. LANCELOT, Lieutenant in Brigadier Wolseley's Regiment of Inniskillen Horse; died unmarried, 1701.

Daughters —

1. ELIZABETH, married, first, Samuel Eccles, Esq., and second,——Mayne, County Fermanagh.

2. MARGARET, married William Humphreys, Esq., of Dromard, who was attainted by James II. in 1689.

3. MARY, married James Johnston, Esq., High Sheriff, County Fermanagh, 1707.

4. KATHERINE, married Merrick Meige, Esq., of Greenhill, County Fermanagh.

5. MAGDALENE, married Robert Johnston, Esq.

Mr. Irvine married secondly, Anne Armstrong, and by her had further issue:

6. GERARD, Capt., of Greenhill, married Alice Forster, and died
   without issue March 21, 1755.

7. REBECCA, died young.

The eldest son, Christopher Irvine, commonly called Colonel
Irvine, succeeded (on failure of issue male of his uncles, Dr. Irvine
and Sir Gerard Irvine) to the Castle Irvine estates, in 1714, and was
High Sheriff, County Fermanagh, 1716.   He died 1723, having
married first, 1683, Mary, daughter of Rev. Mr. Bernard, and by
her had two daughters, Mary (Mrs. Hamilton), and Elizabeth;
and secondly, 1693, Dorothy Anne, daughter of Jeffry Brett, by
whom he left at his decease—

1. CHRISTOPHER.

2. CHARLES, married first, Susan Ferguson, by whom he had:
   John, died unmarried, and Elizabeth, Mrs. Humphreys;
   secondly, Anne Irvine, by whom he had John; and thirdly,
   Elizabeth Grant, who died without issue.

The eldest son, Christopher Irvine, Esq., of Castle Irvine, High
Sheriff for Fermanagh 1725, born April 15, 1697; married 1718,
first Dorcas, daughter of Col. Alexander Montgomery, but by her
had no issue.   He married, secondly, 1727, Elinor, daughter and
ultimately co-heir of Audley Mervyn, Esq., of Trillick, County
Tyrone (by Hon. Olivia Coote, daughter of Richard, first Lord
Colloony) and by her (who died July, 1767) had issue:

1. WILLIAM, his heir.

2. HENRY, married 1759, Harriett, daughter of Benjamin Bunbury,
   Esq., of Kilfeacle, and had a daughter, Mary, married Col.
   John Caulfeild, of Donamon.

1. OLIVIA, died unmarried.

2. MARY, died unmarried.

3. ELIZABETH, died unmarried.

4. ELINOR, married June, 1766, Oliver Nugent, Esq., of Farren-
   connel.

Mr. Irvine died 1755.

THE IRVINES AS MEN OF LETTERS.

Alexander Irvine: "De Jure Regni Diascepsis ad Regem Caro-
lum," Ludg., Bat., 1627.

Rev. Alexander Irvine: "Cause and Effect of Emigration from
the Highlands," 1802, noticed by Sidney Smith in "Edinburgh
Review."

Alexander Irvine: "London Flora," London, 1838 and 1846.

Alexander Forbes Irvine: "Prae-Treatise on the Game Laws of Scotland," 1850, Edin. ["The latest, fullest, and most complete collection of the forest laws, and the rules of game in bird and beast."— Perth Courier.]

Andrew Irvine: "Sermons," 1830. ["Good specimens of sound reasoning, pure theology and practical applications."— London Christian-Reerumb.]

William Irvine, M. D.: (1), "Essays on Chemical Subjects," edited by his son, W. J., M. D., London, 1805. (2), "Theories of Heat," Nic. Jour., 1803. See same in 1805.

William Irvine, M. D., son of preceding William: (1) "On Disease," 1802; (2) "Letters on Sicily," 1813; (3), "Latent Heat," Nic. Jour., 1804.

Patrick Irvine: (1) "Considerations on the Inexpediency of the Law of Entail in Scotland," second edition, Edin. 1826. ["A very short and very sensible book, on a subject of the utmost importance to Scotland."— Edin. Review, No. 36. "An ably written and philosophical tract in opposition to the practice of entail."— McCulloch Lit. of Polit. Econ.] (2) "Considerations on the Independency of the Law of Marriage in Scotland," 1828. ["Much valuable matter collected from many authentic sources."— Law Chronicle.]

Ralph Irvine: (1) "Peruvian Bark," Edin., 1785; (2) "Dispensations," 1786.

It may be seen, by referring to "Burk's General Armory," that Irvine (Arlingford, Scotland) has arms: Ar.— three holly branches, each consisting of as many leaves, ppr., bandled'gules, within a bordure, indented, vert. Crest — two holly leaves in saltire, vert. Motto — Sub sole viresco. Irvine (Drum, county Aberdeen), descended from William de Irwin, whom Robert Bruce, his armor bearer, etc., Ar.— three small shafts or bunches of holly, two and one vert, each consisting of as many leaves slipped of the last, banded gules. Crest — a sheaf of nine holly leaves. Supporters, two savages wreathed about the head and middle with holly, each carrying in his hand a baton ppr. Motto — *Sub sole, sub umbra virens.*

Irvine (Castle Irvine, county Fermanagh), Baronet, descended from the Irvines of Bonshaw. Of the Irish branch was Sir Gerard Irvine, created a baronet (29) by Charles II. His present representative is Sir Gorges Marcus d'Arcy-Irvine, of Castle Irvine,

Baronet, son and heir of William Mervyn Irvine, Esq., of Castle Irvine, by his wife, a daughter of Gorges Lowther, Esq., of Kilune, County Meath, member of parliament, and grandson of Christopher Irvine, Esq., of Castle Irvine, by Mary, his wife, second daughter and co-heir of Sir Audley Meryvn, of Trillick Castle, County Tyrone.   Arms. — A fess gules between three holly leaves, ppr. Crest — A dexter arm in armor fessways, issuant out of a cloud, a hand ppr. holding a thistle, also ppr.   Motto — *Dum memor ipse mei.*

In the coats of arms of the Irvines, Irvins, Irvings and Irwins holly leaves or the thistle are always to be found — one or both.

THE AMERICAN IRVINES.

The American Irvines, many of them, are of Scotch descent, being descended in a direct and unbroken line from the ancient houses of Bonshaw Drum, and Castle Irvine, Ireland.

Robert Irvine fled from Dumfriesshire, Scotland, to Glenoe, Ireland, in 1584.   He married Elizabeth Wylie, and they had one son, David, who married Sophia Gault, whose family were of the nobility of Scotland, and descended from the Shaws, who built Ballygally Castle on the shore of Larne in 1625.   Above the entrance door of this castle is this inscription: "God's Providence is my inheritance."   Previous to the time of their building Ballygally Castle on the shore of Larne, they had been Lairds of Greenock in Scotland. The Shaws intermarried with the Bissets.

The following was sent me from Larne, Ireland:

"The Ruins of Olderfleet Castle, near Larne Harbor. — The original size of this castle was considerably larger than it appears at present, and there is good reason for fixing the period of its erection at or about the year 1242, by a Scotch family by the name of Bisset, who were compelled to leave Scotland, owing to their implication the murder of Patrick Comyn, Earl of Athol.   The castle was at one time important as a defensive fortress against the predatory bands of Scots who infested the northeastern coast, and was once under direction of a governor.   The office was held in 1569 by Sir Moyses Hill, but in 1598 it was thought no longer necessary, and accordingly abolished.   The castle and adjoining territory were granted, in 1610, to Sir Arthur Chichester, the founder of the noble family of Donegal.   It was here that Edward Bruce, the last monarch of Ireland, landed with his band of Scots, when he endeavored to free Ireland from English rule in 1315."

Robert Irvine married Margaret Wylie, and had ten children born to him, viz.: Margaret, who married her cousin, Ephraim McDowell; Mary, who married her cousin, John Wylie (both Mary and Margaret died in Ireland, and lie buried in the old churchyard of Raloo); Thomas, who married —— and settled in Cushendal, Ireland, where he lived and died, and where his descendants now reside; Alexander, who married a kinswoman, a Miss Gault; George, David, William, Robert, James and Samuel. John and Robert Irvine were the sons of James, who was the son of Christopher, who fell at Flodden Field, 1513, and who was born after his death.

The seven last named Irvines all came to America between the years of 1725 and 1731. Alexander Irvine lived in Scotland, and he and his brother, Robert, were at a hunt in Argyleshire, where Alexander got into a difficulty with a man and gave him wounds from which he died. He and Robert fled from Scotland, in hunting dress, and came, by night, to Glenoe. Alexander was afterwards pardoned for his offense and returned to Scotland, and came from there to America; landed at Philadelphia, and went from there to Bedford county, Va.

This is the tradition that current in Glenoe to this day:

While Alexander Irvine was at Glenoe he fell in love with a beautiful Irish girl, of low degree, and she returned his love. They were in the habit of meeting at the Irvine and MacDowell mill at night-fall, beneath a tree which has ever since been called the "fatal trysting tree." The tree separated just where its immense bole came out of the ground, and formed two large trees.

The love affair of these two young people was destined to end in an awful tragedy. Some spy and informer, learning that they had plighted their troth, hastened to inform Alexander Irvine's family of the danger of his mesalliance with this beautiful girl, his first love, and he was called back to Edinburgh.

The night before he went away he and his sweetheart met, as was usual with them, beneath the trysting tree, and Alexander Irvine gave the girl a knife with a silver handle that had his name engraved, in full, upon it. They vowed eternal love and parted. In a short time after Irvine returned to Edinburgh he married a Miss Gault; removed to the north of Ireland, where his three sons, Andrew, William and Christopher, were born; and then came to America — some say from Scotland, some from Ireland. I am not able to say from which country he came, nor does it matter.

After he was married a short time, the young Irish girl to whom he had vowed to be true unto death, heard of his marriage, and one moonlight night she went to the trysting tree and stabbed herself in the heart and died, with the knife of her lover still in the wound. So her brother found her. He drew the knife from her pulseless breast, and holding it aloft, vowed "to never sleep until he plunged the knife, stained by his sister's blood, into Alexander Irvines's heart."

He started that night, in a boat that was to cross the North Channel, but which never landed, and went down with all on board, and rests to-day beneath the turbid waters that divide Ireland from Scotland.

It may be that Alexander Irvine removed from Scotland to the north of Ireland to be further away from the scenes of his early love, and perhaps he crossed the ocean to find ease for his troubled conscience. Certain it is that tradition has brought to me the story that he was a sad and silent man. He was my ancestor, and his son, Andrew, was my grandfather.

Andrew Irvine had many sons, but never named one for his father — "Alexander being considered an unlucky name"— so I have been told by my oldest kinswoman now alive. Miss Semple, of Larne, Ireland, in a letter to an Irvine descendant, says that it was Alexander Irvine I. who killed the man on the hunting field, and not the Alexander who came to Bedford county, Virginia; but she is mistaken, for the story of his misfortune was told by his son, Andrew, to an old lady, who was born in 1814, and who was alive a year ago.

He had three sons — Andrew, Christopher and William. Alexander Irvine and his wife died the same day. His wife's death grieved him deeply, but he went with some men into an orchard to have her grave made. He selected a suitable spot, under a spreading tree, and then returned to his house, lay down, and died without complaining of illness. He and his wife were buried in one grave. The Virginia Irvines reared Andrew, and the Pennsylvania Irvines brought up Christopher and William. Andrew Irvine was young when his father died, and, by the time he was grown, he had lost sight of his two brothers, both younger than himself, and never met them in this life.

Andrew Irvine married Elizabeth Mitchell. Elizabeth Mitchell was the daughter of William Mitchell and Elizabeth Innes, who were married in Edinburgh, Scotland, and came to Bedford county, Va.

Elizabeth Innes was the daughter of Hugh Innes, who came to Bedford county, Va., together with his two brothers, — James and Robert. The ship in which they sailed from Scotland to this country was wrecked, and the Innes brothers — James, Hugh, and perhaps, Robert — were all of the crew that were saved. For many years the descendants of these three Innes brothers vainly tried to obtain the fortune left by Miss Jane Innes.

The children of Andrew Irvine and Elizabeth Mitchell were: Robert, Stephen, John, Caleb, Joshua, William, Jane, Lucinda, Polly and Elizabeth.

It may be stated here that Andrew Irvine was a revolutionary soldier.

Robert Irvine died young and unmarried.

Stephen married, first, a Mrs. Whitside, widow; second, Betsey Barrier (maiden name, Janvier); John married Sarah Wilson; Joshua married a Miss Wilson; Caleb married Miss Mitchell, and was drowned in the Tennessee river, Tennessee. He was the grandfather of Wilbur Browder, of Russelville, Ky. William married Eliza Howe; Lucinda married Dr. Flavius Phillips; Jane and Mary married and died young; Elizabeth married Rev. Samuel Rogers, a pioneer preacher of Kentucky, and lineal descendant of John Rogers, Prebendary of St. Paul's, who was burned at the stake, 1555, and has his arms.

The seven Irvine brothers who came to America before and after the year 1729, were brothers to Margaret Irvine, who married Ephraim McDowell. Their names were: Alexander, George, David, William, Robert, James and Samuel. As has been stated before, their father and they fled from Scotland on account of political persecutions. They settled at Glenoe, where their ancestor, Robert Irvine, and his descendants, had owned land since 1584. The farm the Irvines occupied had been considered unlucky for generations; but they determined to cast aside all superstitious fears and occupy it. They made a bleaching green and built a mill, in partnership with the McDowells, their kinsmen.

A letter from Ireland to the author says:

"The Irvine and McDowell farm has a queer history. Altogether, you could not look on a more lovely or peaceful spot. It went from the first Irvine, to whom it belonged, to another, and so on, until it was sold to one Francis Lee, in 1731. The way he got the money to buy it was strange. He was up-rooting some small trees; below one of them he found a pot full of gold coins — with this he bought the farm. The Irvines had never had any luck on the farm as long as any member of the family lived on it. Lee enlarged the bleaching green and built new works, but he failed in everything he attempted to do, just as the Irvines had done, and was obliged to sell out. A man by the name of Agnew bought the place. Then it went to the present owner's grandfather, who killed himself drinking whiskey. The man who owns it to-day has what we call bad luck. His children have nearly all died, and he loses a number of his cattle every year. You will think we Irish are superstitious — nevertheless it is quite true, that at certain times around the old mill, built by the Irvines and McDowells, a bright light is seen that cannot be accounted for. It has been seen ever since Alexander Irvine's sweetheart killed herself beneath the trysting tree that overshadowed the mill."

There is the largest yew tree ever seen growing before the old home of the Irvines, which was planted by one of the Irvines.

From the parish church of Glenoe, that stands beside the water-fall, on the most romantic spot imaginable, overlooking the village, you could speak to one at the old home of the Irvines and McDowells.

As I have told you before, the Irvines and McDowells failed in business and went to America — some with Ephraim McDowell, and some of them afterwards. Seven brothers went, first and last.

William Irvine married Anne Craig, in Ireland; issue — Johannah, Christopher and David.

William Irvine buried his only daughter, Johannah, and his wife in the church yard of Raloo, and he and his sons, Christopher and David, came to America about 1729, and settled in Bedford county, Virginia.

Christopher Irvine, son of William Irvine and Anne Craig, went to Wilkes county, Georgia, and David Irvine married Jane Kyle, July 21, 1754, in Bedford county, Virginia, and came to Kentucky and settled in Madison county. He had thirteen children. Sophia, daughter of David Irvine and Jane Kyle, married William Fox. Sophia Irvine was a sister to Col. William Irvine (who died in 1819), and to Capt. Christopher, Robert, and Magdalen, who married Pittman. Sophia, who married William Fox, was grandmother of Mrs. Sophia Fox Sea, of Louisville, Ky. Sophia was born in 1779 and died in 1833. Amelia married a Hockaday and died in 1830. Mary married Adams and died in 1803. Elizabeth married Hale Talbot. Sally married Goggin. Margaret married Mr. Pace. Jane married Archibald Curle; she was born in 1769 and died 1833.

There was also a son, Henry. Frances married Rowland. Anne married Goggin.

Capt. Christopher Irvine, born about 1760, was killed while with General Logan in Ohio. Captain Christopher married Lydia Calloway, daughter of Col. Richard Calloway, who was killed at Boonesboro, Ky. Capt. Christopher Irvine and Lydia Calloway had two daughters, Fannie and Mary, and one son, David. Mary (born 1784, died 1869) married John Hart. Fannie married Robert Caldwell. The widow of Capt. Christopher Irvine married Gen. Richard Hickman.

Col. William Irvine was born in Campbell county, Virginia, in 1768; died near Richmond, Ky., January 18, 1819. Col. William Irvine married Elizabeth Hockaday. Issue: Christopher, who fell at Dudley's defeat; David, born 1796; Edmund, who married Sally Ann Clay 1823, but died soon after, and his widow married M. C. Johnston. Albert Irvine married Miss Coleman, and, after the death of his wife, removed to Texas. Adam married Minerva Stone, and had one son born to him, William McClannahan (born 1825, died 1891), who married his cousin, Elizabeth Irvine. Patsey married Ezekiel Field. Amelia married William McClannahan.

David, son of Col. William Irvine, married Susan McDowell, a grand-daughter to Gen. Isaac Shelby. They had four children: (1) Sarah, who married Gen. Addison White, and had six children — (a) Bettie, married Oliver Patton; (b) Alice, married Dr. Gilbert Greenway; (c) Susan, daughter of Sarah, married Judge Richard W. Walker, of the Alabama Supreme Court; (e) David Irvine, married Lucy Mathews; (f) Newton. (2) Isaac Shelby Irvine. (3) David W. Irvine. (4) Elizabeth S. Irvine, now of Richmond, Ky., who married William Irvine. The other Irvines to whom the Irvines mentioned are related are Abram Irvine, of Rockbridge county, Virginia, who was born in Ireland (some say Scotland) in 1725; married Mary Dean, born in Ireland in 1734; and had many children. John, one of the children (born 1755), came to Kentucky in 1786, and married Miss Armstrong, of Mercer county.

The Irvines immigrated to the east of Ireland and west of Scotland with the Gauls of Spain, and our immediate family moved to the North of Ireland during the protectorate of Cromwell. On May 9, 1729, some of the Irvines, McDowells, McElroys, Campbells and others sailed from Londonderry and landed the same year in Pennsylvania, where they remained until 1737, when they removed to Rockbridge and Bedford counties, Virginia, and were the first settlers on Burden's grant.

One of the immigrants in that party was John Irvine, a Presbyterian preacher. His children were probably all born in this country and consisted of one son, Abram, and four daughters, and probably other sons, but of this I am not certain.

IRVINES AND McDOWELLS.

Among the very earliest settlers in the valley of Virginia, were Scotch-Irish Presbyterian families, named Irvine, kinsmen of the McDowells, and probably descended from the brothers of Ephraim McDowell's wife, who immigrated with him to Pennsylvania and some of whom followed him to Burden's grant. Their names are found among the soldiers of the French and Indian War, as well as the War of the Revolution, from both Pennsylvania and Virginia. Members of the family were among the first settlers of Mercer county, neighbors to their McDowell kin. Among the magistrates who held the first county court in Mercer, in August, 1786, were John Irvine, Samuel McDowell, Sr., and Gabriel Madison. One of the family, Anna, daughter of Abram Irvine, became the wife of her kinsman, Samuel McDowell, of Mercer. The children born of this marriage were: John Adair, soldier in the War of 1812; married Lucy Todd Starling, daughter of William Starling and Susannah Lyne, of Mercer county, Ky. His daughter, Anne, married John Winston Price, of Hillsboro, Ohio.

Abram McDowell, born April 24, 1793, soldier in the War of 1812, fought at Missisenewa; was clerk of the Supreme Court, of the Court of Common Pleas, and of the Court in Banc, and was at one time mayor of Columbus, Ohio. He married Eliza Seldon, in 1817, daughter of Colonel Lord. Gen. Irvine McDowell, of the United States army, who attained the highest rank of any of his name, was his oldest son. Col. John McDowell, soldier in the Union army, was another son. Malcolm McDowell, also a soldier in the Union army, was another son; while his daughter, Eliza, married Major Bridgeman, of the regular army.

Col. Joseph McDowell married Sarah Irvine, sister to Anna Irvine, wife of Samuel McDowell. Samuel, son of Col. Joseph Irvine and Sarah Irvine McDowell, married first, Amanda Ball, granddaughter of John Reed, and cousin to James G. Birney. The sole issue of this marriage was a daughter, who married Dr. Meyer, of Boyle county, Ky.

CONCERNING THE IRVINES FROM SAN ANTONIO, TEXAS.

Abram Irvine, born in Scotland, May 1725, married Mary Dean, born in Ireland, February 22, 1733. They emigrated to Rockbridge county, Virginia. Mary Dean's mother was Jane McAlister, a Scotchwoman, who assisted at the siege of Londonderry. The Protestants were reduced to starvation, and Jane McAlister inverted the flour barrels and made the tops white with flour in order that the spies might think that article plentiful when they looked through the cracks of the weak walls.

The children of Abram Irvine and Mary Dean were: John, born February 25, 1755; married Prudence Armstrong, of Mercer county, Kentucky. (The children of John and Prudence Armstrong Irvine were: Samuel, Polly, Margaret, Sally, Abram, Priscilla and Robert).

Hans, born April 25, 1758, never married.

Margaret Irvine, born April 25, 1762; married, first, Samuel Lapsly; second, Rev. John Lyle.

Mary Irvine, married, first, William Adair; second, Issachar Paulding. (Her children were Alexander and William Adair).

Anne Irvine, born November 28, 1763, married Samuel Mc-Dowell. (Their children were John, Abram, William, Joseph, Sally, Reed and Alexander.)

Abram Irvine, born August 8, 1766; married, first, Sally Henry, and second, Margaret McAfee.

Robert Irvine, born in 1768, married Judith Glover. (Children: John, Polly, Judith, Abram D., Robert and Sarah.)

Nancy Irvine, born July 5, 1790; married Frank McMordie. (Children: Robert, Jane, Hans, Polly, Abram and Margaret.)

Elizabeth Irvine, born March 20, 1772; married George Caldwell, grandfather of Mrs. Mary Caldwell Crawford, of San Antonio, Texas. (The children of Elizabeth Irvine and George Caldwell were George, Polly, Abram, Isabella, John, William and Eliza.)

Sarah Irvine, born November 21, 1774; married Joseph Mc-Dowell. (Children: Sarah, Margaret, Lucy, Charles, Caleb and Magdalen, who is last living one of this generation, and is now Mrs. M. M. Wallace, and lives near Danville, Ky.)

William Dean Irvine, born August, 1775; never married. Was captain of volunteers in the War of 1812; died in Natchez, Miss.

WILLIAM IRVINE AND SOME OF HIS DESCENDANTS.

William Irvine married Anne Craig in Ireland. Issue: Johannah, who died, and lies buried in the old churchyard of Raloo, Ireland; Christopher and David. One writes from Ireland as follows: "I have found the old book of a stone-cutter, which is six hundred years old. He was in the habit of going to persons, who were entitled to coats of arms, and asking the privilege of copying their arms, in order to carve them on the tombstones of the dead. I send you the arms of William Irvine, given to this old stone cutter."

The writer then sends the arms of one branch of the Irvines of Bonshaw — motto: "*Sub sole, sub umbra, virens.*" These arms may have been chosen by William Irvine, but they are not the arms belonging to the Irish branch. Sir William D'Arcy Irvine was kind enough to send me the arms borne by the branch of the family of the house of Bonshaw that settled in Ireland, and they appear in the front of this book.

William Irvine's wife, Anne Craig, died and was buried at Raloo, and he and his two sons, David and Christopher, came to America; landed at Philadelphia, and from thence made their way to Bedford county, Virginia, and settled. Christopher Irvine, son of William Irvine and Anne Craig, removed from Bedford county, Virginia, to Wilkes county, Georgia, and David came to Kentucky, and was the progenitor of the Madison county Irvines.

The will of David Irvine, son of William and Anne Craig, was written in 1804 and recorded in 1805. Heirs: Mary, Elizabeth, Magdalen, Anna, William, Sarah, Jane, Robert, Frances, Margaret, Amelia, Sophia, Christopher (who died before the will was made). Sophia married William Fox; Amelia married Hockaday; Mary married Adams; Elizabeth married Hale Talbot; Sarah married Goggin; Margaret married Pace; Jane married Archibald Curle; Frances married Rowland; Anne married Goggin, and Captain Christopher was killed while with General Logan in Ohio.

William, son of David Irvine, married Elizabeth Hockaday. William came from Campbell county, Virginia; died in Richmond, Ky., in 1819, aged fifty-five years. His wife died in 1818. William Irvine was the first clerk of the court of Madison county, Kentucky. He was appointed clerk by the first court that was organized in that county, and held the office until his death.

His brother, Christopher, built the fort at Irvine's Lick. He was badly wounded at Little Mountain. Christopher was a delegate to the convention in Virginia in 1787-88, that ratified the Constitution of the United States; also delegate to the Danville, Ky., convention; elector of the United States Senate in 1792; district presidential elector in 1805 and 1817; elector at large in 1813; member of the Kentucky Society for Promoting Useful Knowledge. Christopher Irvine had eleven children. I am able to give the names of only seven — David, Christopher, Albert, Edwin, Adam. Mrs. Ezekiel Field and Mrs. Wm. McClannahan.

David, son of William Irvine, married a daughter of Dr. Ephraim McDowell and his wife — Shelby, daughter of first governor of Kentucky, Isaac Shelby. (The wife of Governor Shelby was a daughter of Nathaniel Hart, who was a distinguished member of the Transylvania Company and brother of Mrs. Henry Clay's father, and of United States Senator Archibald Dickson's grandfather).

David Irvine was born 1796, died 1872. Children: David, Irvine Shelby, Sarah and Elizabeth. The last, Elizabeth, married her cousin, W. M. Irvine, son of Adam Irvine. Sarah married Hon. Addison White. Christopher was a captain in the War of 1812; he was killed at Fort Meigs and there buried. Edwin, or Edmund, married Sarah Ann, daughter of Gen. Green Clay, sister of Gen. Cassius M. Clay; after the death of Edwin Irvine she married Mat. Johnson, distinguished financier of Lexington, Ky.

Albert, son of David Irvine, was a minister; his son, Adam, is a ranchman at Gainesville, Tex.

Christopher Irvine, brother of William, builder of Fort Irvine, and first clerk of Madison county, Ky., was a delegate to the Danville convention, in 1785, and deputy surveyor of Lincoln county, Ky., before the formation of Madison, together with Gen. Green Clay. He was also a member of the Lincoln county court in 1783; he was killed during an Indian raid in Ohio, in 1786. The wife of this Christopher was Lydia, daughter of Col. Richard Calloway; Lydia's second husband was Gen. Richard Hickman. The daughter of Gen. Richard Hickman and Lydia Calloway, married Samuel Hanson, and their son Roger Hanson, was the famous commander of the Orphan Brigade in the Confederate army. Richard Hanson, lawyer of Paris, Ky., was a son of Samuel Hanson, and the daughter of Gen. R. Hickman and Lydia Calloway, his wife; a daughter of Samuel Hanson married Captain Stern, soldier in the Mexican War.

Col. Christopher Irvine and his wife, Lydia Calloway, had three children: David C.; Fanny, who married Robert Caldwell; Mary, who married John Hart, of Fayette county, Ky. David C. married a Miss Howard, of Fayette county, Ky. To her is due the honor of founding the first temperance society in Madison county, Ky. She was a very talented woman.

Christopher Irvine, brother of David, son of William the widower, married, late in life, Jane, widow of Col. John Hardin, who was killed by Indians while on a peace mission under the government, beyond the Ohio river.

The children of Francis Irvine Caldwell, daughter of Col. Christopher Irvine and his wife, Lydia Calloway, were: James, a minister; David C., who moved to Missouri; Mary, who married Chief Justice Simpson, of Winchester, Ky., and Elizabeth, who married Orville Browning, of Illinois.

Mrs. Edmund Pendleton Shelby, of Lexington, Ky., is descended from Mary Irvine (daughter of Col. Christopher Irvine and his wife, Lydia Calloway), who married John Hart. The children of Mary Irvine and John Hart were David, who married Lucy Ann Goodloe; the children of this marriage were: Edwin, Christopher, Sophia, Isaac, Fanny, John, David, Lydia, Mary, Thomas, Sallie and Nathaniel. The children of David Hart, who married Lucy Ann Goodloe, are: Susan Goodloe, who married Edmund Pendleton Shelby. Their children are: Hart, William, Lucy, Lily F., Edmund, David, Isaac, Evan, Susan, Mary and Arthur. Lily Fontaine Shelby married George Sea Shanklin; issue — Shelby and George.

IRVINE–SEA CONNECTION.

Genealogy of Mrs. Sophia Fox Sea, of Louisville, Ky.— Mrs. Sea is well known in literary circles as a writer of great ability. She proves the saying that has been in the Irvine family for generations — "The Irvine women have ever been more brilliant and talented than the men."

DAVID IRVINE was born May 29, 1721; he died October 17, 1804.
> On July 21, 1754, in Bedford county, Virginia, he was married by the Rev. McKee, to Jane Kyle, who died February 15, 1809. Thirteen children:
> (1). Christopher, born September 11, 1755; killed by Indians in Ohio, about October 6, 1786. He married Lydia Calloway, daughter of Colonel Richard Calloway. He left three children, Mary, Fannie and David C. Mary was born in Madison county, Kentucky, March 4, 1784; married John Hart, and died in Fayette county, Ken-

tucky, September 14, 1869. Fannie married Robert
Caldwell.

(2). Mary, born September 15, 1757; married Christopher (?)
   Adams; died February 22, 1803.

(3). Elizabeth, born January 5, 1760; married Hale Talbot,
   and died.

(4). Anne, born May 18, 1761; married Richard Goggin
   September 28, 1791, and died.

(5). William, born in Campbell county, Virginia, June 2,
   1763; married Elizabeth Hockaday; died in Madison
   county, Kentucky, January 20, 1819.

(6). Magdalene, born July 6, 1765; married (1) Bourne Price
   December 26, 1787; (2) —— Pittman; died January
   25, 1830.

(7). Sarah, born January 9, 1767; married —— Goggin, and
   died about 1832.

(8). Jane, born July 2, 1769; married Archibald Curle, September 29, 1791; died July –, 1833.

(9). Robert, born March –, 1771; died October –, 1818.

(10). Frances, born —— 41st, 177 –; married —— Rowland,
   and died.

(11). Margaret, born April 6, 1774; married John Page
   December 18, 179–; died August 2, 1860.

(12). Amelia, born June 25, 1775; married Isaac Hockaday,
   March 31, 1796; died July 13, 1830.

(13). Sophie, born December 11, 1779; married William Fox,[1]
   May 13, 1802; died in Somerset, Ky., October 13, 1833.

The foregoing is taken from David Irvine's family Bible; the
record is now with Mrs. Sophie Boyd. This is a correct copy.

A. M. Sea, Jr., 1895.

THE FOX LINE.

The Fox family that settled in Virginia is of the same lineage as
Henry, Lord Holland, and retain to this day many strongly marked
racial characteristics. Of the latter family sprung William Fox,
son of Samuel Fox and Rhoda Pickering Fox. William Fox was
born in Hanover county, Va., March 1, 1779. He apprenticed
himself to his uncle, Peter Tinsley, clerk of the High Court of

[1] William Fox was my mother's grandfather. Her father was Judge
Fontaine F. Fox, of Danville, Ky.

Chancery, and it was to Mr. Tinsley that he was indebted for his fine penmanship and knowledge of jurisprudence. From 1799, until his resignation in 1846, he was clerk of the Pulaski County and Circuit Courts. His opinions, bearing upon knotty points of law, were accepted as incontrovertible authority by all the leading lawyers of his district. He was a man of inherited aristocratic social theories, but of exalted personal worth, high intellectual capacity, and of business finesse second to none. He married Sophia Irvine, youngest daughter of David Irvine and Jane Kyle, a worthy descendant of her ancient line of intellectual and virtuous gentlewomen. Sophia Irvine died October 15, 1833. William Fox married, second, Mary Irvine, daughter of Hale and Elizabeth (Irvine) Talbot, of Warren county, Mo. The children of William Fox and Sophie Irvine were:

1. FONTAINE TALBOT. (See 1. below).
2. Amanda Fitzalan, who married her cousin, Bourne Goggin, also a descendant of the Irvines. Campbell speaks of the Goggin family thus: The family of Gookin, or Goggin, is very ancient, and appears to have been originally found at Canterbury in Kent, England. The name has undergone successive changes — the early New England (Virginia) chronicles spelled it "Goggin." Daniel Goggin came to Virginia 1621, with fifty picked men of his own, and thirty passengers well furnished with all sorts of provisions, cattle, etc., and planted himself at Newport News. In the massacre of 1622 he held out against the savages, with a force of thirty men, and saved his plantation. It is possible that he affected to make a settlement independent of the civil power of the colony, and appears to have been styled by his son, "a lordship." It was above New Newport News, and called Mary's Mount. Their ancient crest is given by Campbell. Bourne Goggin and Amanda F. Goggin had four children:
   (1). William, banker, married to Katherine Higgins. They have children.
   (2). Ann, married to Timothy Pennington. They have five children: Bessie, Bourne, Ephraim, Amanda Fox, who married Philip Kemp (railroad official), and Timothy.
   (3). Richard, deceased, also married Katherine Higgins, and left two children: Bourne and Jeannie.
   (4). Amanda Fitzalan, unmarried.
3. Jane Pickering, who married, first, Dr. James Caldwell, and

second, Eben Milton, Esq. By Dr. Caldwell she had four children:

(1). Sophie Irvine, married to Dr. James Parker. They had four children: Samuel, Joseph, Zenice and Tea.

(2). Mary, who married Sy Richardson. No children.

(3). Isabella, unmarried.

(4). Amanda Fitzalan, deceased.

4. Elizabeth Fox, married to —— Fitzpatrick, and had three children:

(1)Sophie, married to Thompson Miller, of Missouri.

(2). Mary.

(3). James.

5. Sophie Irvine, married to Col. John S. Kendrick, a Virginian gentleman. She left one child.

(1.) Sophie, married to Judge Jas. W. Alcorn, of Stanford, Ky., a corporation lawyer of high standing. They have a number of children.

6. William Montgomery, married Sophronia Coffee. They had seven children:

(1). Jesse, married Jane Newell, and has five children.

(2). Fontaine, married Sallie Rout; one child.

(3). William, unmarried.

(4). Bourne, married Nannie Wood, and has two children.

(5). Frank, deceased.

(6). Montgomery, married Anne Baughman, and has two children.

1. FONTAINE TALBOT FOX (No. 1 above), late Judge of the Eighth Kentucky circuit, of Danville, Ky. Judge Fox spent a long life in public service, having filled many important offices of public trust, and in every capacity manifesting that incorruptible integrity, the inherited ruling principle of his nature. He made a large fortune at the legitimate practice of the law, having been retained at leading counsel in nearly all the most famous suits filed in the courts of Kentucky in his his day, his fine oratorical powers and keen wit rendering him invulnerable in argument. At his historic home near Danville, Ky., he entertained with almost princely lavishness. His name is a synonym throughout his native state for legal learning and acumen, and exalted personal worth. He married Eliza Hunton, daughter of Thomas and Ann (Bell) Hunton, of Charlottesville, Va. Mrs. Fox springs

from renowned English and American ancestry. Among the possessions of the Hunton family is a coat of arms granted the family by Queen Elizabeth, in consideration of a large money loan. She is a cousin of General Eppa Hunton, U. S. Senator from Virginia, and of electoral commission fame. Her three brothers, Felix, Logan and Thomas Hunton, form a coterie of legal lights rarely ever found in one family, Logan Hunton having been the author of the Allison letter, to which is accredited the election of Taylor to the presidency. In consideration of this fact he was offered a cabinet position, but declined the honor, unwilling to give up his large and lucrative practice at the New Orleans bar, but accepted the position of attorney for the district of Louisiana. Thomas Hunton was his law partner. In Missouri, during the stormy days preceding the civil war, Felix Hunton, although a cripple from rheumatism, by virtue of his splendid intellect and executive finesse, was the leader of the Democratic party, and could easily have had any office within the gift of the people. Mrs. Fox's maternal grandfather was John Bell, a Virginian, and a man of large wealth, who came to Kentucky at an early day. He married Frances Tunstall, a lineal descendant of the famous English family by that name. There is in possession of the Tunstall family a paper prepared by Froude, the English historian, whose mother was a Tunstall, tracing the Tunstall line through hundreds of years, down to the immigration to this country, a valuable document supplemented by the American branch. The children of Fontaine Talbot Fox and Eliza Hunton Fox are:

(1). Thomas Hunton, lawyer and brilliant writer. He married Henrietta Clay Wilson, a widow, née Gist, a descendant of the Gist family so famous in colonial and pioneer history. She died in 1889. He married, second, Mary Moberly, of a notable Kentucky family. By his first wife he had two children, Susan Gist, unmarried, and Eliza Hunton, who had married John Rogers, a farmer of Fayette county, Kentucky, and has two children, William and Thomas Hunton Rogers.

(2). William McKee Fox, deceased, a lawyer of distinguished ability and magnetic personality, invariably retained as counsel in every suit filed in his large and important judicial district. Unmarried.

1. Bonshaw Tower.
2. Col. John Beaufin Irving, owner of Bonshaw Tower.
3. Residence and Tower.
4. Room of Robert, The Bruce.

(3). Peter Camden Fox, deceased, lawyer, and Major of Scott's Louisiana Cavalry, on the Southern side during the war between the states; a man of strong mental endowments, and also of great magnetic personality. Unmarried.

(4). Fontaine Talbot Fox, lawyer, of Louisville, Ky., was assistant city attorney of Louisville, from 1870 to 1873. Appointed by Governor McCreary vice-chancellor. Ran for governor of Kentucky on the Prohibition ticket in 1887. Is author of two books, on the "The Warranty in the Fire Insurance Contract," and the "Woman Suffrage Movement in the United States." Is called a master of English language. He married Mary Bartonl daughter of Prof. Samuel Barton and Frances Pierce DuRelle, a widow, mother of Judge DuRelle, of the Supreme Court of Kentucky. Professor Barton was closely allied to the Key family of Maryland, and his wife is a member of the Pierce family of which President Pierce was the head. Judge and Mrs. Fox had five children: Fontaine, Frances, S. Barton, Mary Yandel, and Jessie St. John.

(5). Samuel Irvine Fox, a physician, residing in Montgomery county, Texas, who married Margaret Derrick, of a fine old South Carolina family. They had four children: Carrie Eliza, Margaret, Fontaine Talbot and Annie.

(6). Felix Goggin Fox, lawyer, and a man of scholarly attainments.

(7). Sophie Irvine Fox, married to Capt. Andrew McBrayer Sea. Mrs. Sea is a writer who has left her impress in poetry and prose on the literature of her time. Captain Sea is a descendant of pioneer families, and of the ancient Scotch-Irish race of McBrair or McBrayer. (See Anderson's "Scottish Nation.") He is a commission merchant of Louisville, and an elder in the Presbyterian Church, the church of his covenanting ancestry. Was a Confederate soldier, and won his spurs on hotly-contested fields. Captain and Mrs. Sea have four sons: Fontaine Fox, Robert Winston, Andrew McBrayer and Logan Hunton. Captain Sea's father, Robert W. Sea, was a wealthy merchant of Lawrenceburg, Ky., a man who stood very high in the community. It is said of him that he nearly put an end to litigation in his county, people going to him to settle their differences rather than to the courts.   He married Mary McBrayer, daughter of Andrew McBrayer and Martha (Blackwell) McBrayer, and died at the early age of thirty-five, in 1845.   In the Biographical Encyclopedia of Kentucky, is a statement to the effect that Wm. McBrayer, father of Andrew McBrayer, came, in 1775, to Kentucky from North Carolina, to which state he had immigrated from Ireland just prior to the Revolutionary War.   Leonard Sea, paternal grandfather of Captain Sea, was a soldier in General Wayne's army, and distinguished for bravery the battle of Fort Meigs and other bloody engagements.

(8). John Oliver Fox, a civil engineer, was employed in important work in several large European and American cities. He died in 1876, aged twenty-nine years.

(9). Ann Bell Fox, married to Jerry Clemens Caldwell, a successful stock-raiser and able financier, a man of large wealth.   He is a descendant of the Wickliffe, Caldwell and Clemens families of Kentucky.   They have five children: Charles Wickliffe, Eliza Hunton, Jerry Clemens, Fontaine Fox and Logan.

(10). Charles Crittenden Fox, lawyer, is city attorney at Danville, Ky., and master commissioner of the Boyle Circuit Court, and an elder in the Presbyterian Church.   His standing at the bar of Kentucky is second to none.   He married Mary Allen, daughter of Albert Allen and Mary (Offut) Allen, of Lexington, and niece of Madison C. Johnson, the celebrated jurist, nephew of Col. Richard M. Johnson, vice-president of the United States.   They have three living children: Allen, Anne Bell and Mary Hunton.   Samuel Fox, father of William Fox, married Rhoda Pickering, daughter of Richard and Lucy Pickering, at Richmond, Va., date unknown.   He came to Kentucky about 1783.   It is said he inherited a large tract of land under the Virginia law of primogeniture. He owned a large estate and many slaves in Madison county, Ky., where Foxtown is now located.   He died at Fox's, the name of his place, July 9, 1844, aged nearly ninety-nine years.

IRVINGS AND CABELLS.

(Copied from "Cabells and Their Kin," history written by the eminent historian and writer of Nelson county, Virginia, Mr. Alexander Brown.)

Clementia Cabell, born February 26, 1794, married at Union Hill, June 29, 1815, Jesse Irvine, of Bedford county, Va.; died at Otter, residence of her husband, near Peaks of Otter, June 12, 1841. Her husband, Jesse Irvine, was born in Bedford county, Va., 1792; educated at Washington Academy, 1810, and died February 2, 1876. He was the son of Wm. and Martha Burton Irvine. The father, Wm. Irvine, died in Bedford county, Va., in 1829. He was among the early settlers of that county. There were three brothers, David, Christopher, and William Irvine, who are said to have come originally from Ireland, i. e., to have been Scotch-Irish. Date of David's death unknown. Christopher died in 1769, and William in 1767. The widow of William Irvine married Robert Coman, of the same family as Wm. Coman, opposing lawyer to Patrick Henry in the beef case of Hook vs. Venable. Christopher's son, William, who is mentioned in his will, but William (died in 1829) is said to have been the son of first William, who died in 1767. Capt. Christopher and Col. William Irvine, who removed to Kentucky about 1779, were sons of one of the three emigrant brothers. Mrs. Clementia Cabell Irvine had issue by Jesse Irvine, her husband, as follows: Wm. Cabell (died in infancy), Martha (died in infancy), Ann C., Elvira Bruce (died young), Edward C., Sarah Cabell, Patrick Cabell, born in 1827, became a physician, died October 18, 1854, unmarried; Margaret, born 1829, died 1830; Mary Eliza, Jesse, Juliet M., Margaret Frances. Wm. Cabell Irvine, lawyer, married Mary Ann Lewis, daughter of Meriwether Lewis, of Milton, N. C.; died childless after being married three years. Wm. Cabell Irvine removed to California, where he died in 1851. Meriwether Lewis, of Milton, N. C., was a son of Robert Lewis and his wife, Ann Ragland. Robert Lewis was a son of Major James Lewis and his wife, Mildred Lewis. Major James Lewis was born October 8, 1720. Major James Lewis was the son of Col. Charles Lewis, born 1696; married in 1717, Mary Howell; settled "The Bird" plantation in Goochland county, April 17, 1733-1779. Anne C., a descendant of these, is still living. She married, first, March 26, 1845, David Flournoy, son of Dr. David Flournoy, of Prince Edward county, Va., a widower with six children. Dr. David Flourney died November 11, 1846, leaving one child by his wife, Anne C. Irvine, Sarah Irvine Flournoy, born 1846, died 1949. Mrs. Anne C. Irvine Flournoy married, second, March 12, 1848, J. Overby, Esq., a farmer of Prince Edward county, Va., a descendant of an old English family. Left seven children at his death.

Paul Carrington Cabell, born April 10, 1799, educated at "Union Hill" until 1813; lived with Dr. Geo. Calloway in Lynchburg, Va., and went to school to Holcombe and Jones in 1813-14, and to John Reid in 1814-15. Studied medicine under Dr. Calloway, a distinguished physician of Amherst county. Married June 12, 1823, Mary B. Irvine, daughter of Wm. Irvine of Bedford county, Va., vestryman of Lexington parish; died June 9, 1836; buried at "Mountain View." His wife died at Lynchburg, July, 1857, and was buried by her husband. The children of Paul Carrington Cabell and his wife, Mary B. Irvine, were: Wm. Irvine, Anne Carrington, Martha Elizabeth (who died young), Sallie Massie, Martha Burton (born 1833, died 1834), and Paul Clement.

HIGGINBOTHAM.

Margaret Washington Cabell, married first, December 7, 1815, at "Soldier's Joy," John Higginbotham, who died February 23, 1822. Issue: William, Thomas and Laura; born 1819, died 1827. Mrs. Margaret W. Higginbotham, married second, September 17, 1839, at Lynchburg, Va., Dr. Nathaniel West Payne, of Amherst county, Va., whose oldest daughter by his first marriage was the wife of Wm. A. S. Cabell, son of S. Cabell. Mrs. Payne died February 17, 1887, without issue by her second husband, who was the son of Col. Philip Payne and his wife, Eliza Danbridge, a descendant of Gov. John West, one of the founders of Virginia. Col. Philip Payne was a son of Col. John Payne, of Whitehall, frequently member of the House of Burgesses from Goochland, who died 1774. Col. John Payne was a son of George Payne, sheriff of Goochland, who died in 1874, and his wife, Mary Woodson, daughter of Robert Woodson and his wife, Elizabeth Ferris, of "Curls."

On October 6, 1783, Wm. Cabell, Jr., was appointed surveyor of Amherst county, by William and Mary College, and filled this office until December 1, 1788.

TUCKERS.

Sarah Cabell Irvine, born October 17, 1825; married November 25, 1846, by Rev. Jacob Mitchell, to Asa D. Dickinson, of Prince

Edward county, Va.   Asa D. Dickinson was born at "Inverness," Nottoway county, Va., March 31, 1816; prepared for college by David Comfort — was graduated from Hampden-Sidney College, September, 1836; attended lectures at William and Mary College, under Judge Beverly Tucker, in law; and under President Thos. R. Dew, in political economy, in 1837-38; located at Prince Edward Courthouse in 1838, to practice his profession, and soon attained a position of full practice at law.

Cornelia Rives, married first, in 1866, to Charles Harrison, son Prof. Gessner Harrison, of the University of Virginia, by his wife, Eliza Tucker, daughter of Prof. George Tucker and his wife, Maria Ball Carter.   Charles Harrison and his wife, Cornelia Rives, had no issue.   After the death of Charles Harrison, his widow, Cornelia Rives, married Mr. Wilborne, and has one child — Elizabeth Rives.

The first wife of George Rives was Mary Eliza, daughter of Robert Carter, of "Redlands," and his wife, Mary Coles, sister of Edward Coles, the first governor of Illionois, and a daughter of John Coles (1745-1808), and his wife, Rebecca E. Tucker (1750-1826).   Robert Carter, son of Edward Carter and Sarah Champe, his wife.   Edward C. was the son of second John Carter and Elizabeth Hill.   John Carter was the son of Robert Carter, alias King Carter, of Crotomon. The children of Mary Eliza Carter and George Rives were: Robert, who died unmarried; George Cabell, and James Henry.   George Rives married, second, at University of Virginia, March 31, 1806, Maria Farley Tucker, who survived him many years.   Maria Farley Tucker was the daughter of Prof. George Tucker, born 1775, in the Bermudas; came to Virginia and was a member of the Virginia Legislature and of the United States House of Representatives from Virginia, 1818-25; professor in University of Virginia, 1825-45, and author of numerous books; died April 10, 1861.   The wife of Prof. George Tucker was Maria Ball Carter, a daughter of the only daughter of General George Washington's only sister.   Thus, Maria Farley Rives was a great-grandniece to George Washington, and inherited many precious memorials.   She bore her husband four children, viz.: George Tucker, born ——, married 1843, at University of Virginia; in 1860 lieutenant in C. S. A.; taken prisoner at Roanoake Island; exchanged; unanimously elected captain of a company; fell while gallantly leading a charge made by Wise's brigade near Petersburg, March 29, 1865; never was married. Eleanor Rives, living, has Edward Rives, University of Virginia, 1863-67.   B. L., a lawyer, died May 22, 1877, in his twenty-seventh year; unmarried. Lawrence Alexander Rives, University of Virginia, 1868-69; died at little Rock, Ark., January 5, 1873, in his twenty-second year.

Mary Rives married William Eaton, vestryman of old Blandford church, near Petersburg; removed, with other members of his family, to North Carolina, in 1725, where he became a very prominent man. Their son, Thomas Eaton, married Anna Bland, sister to Frances Bland, who married, first, John Randolph, and became the mother of John Randolph of Roanoake. After the death of Hon. Thomas Eaton, his widow married Judge St. George Tucker; issue, Judge Henry St. George and Nathaniel Beverly. See "The Life, Influence, and Services of James Jones White," by Hon. John Randolph Tucker (only mention made).

From the diary of the late Major Cabell, of "Union Hill," February 7, 1856: "The interment of Joseph C. Cabell took place today at 12 o'clock; buried in his garden at Edgewood, by the side of Judge St. George Tucker and his wife, and Miss Parke Carter."

Mrs. Mary W. Cabell, widow of the late Joseph C. Cabell (no children) was the daughter of George Carter, Esq., of Lancaster, and his wife, Lelia, daughter of Sir Peyton Skipwith, Baronet. After the death of her first husband, Mrs. Lelia Skipwith married Judge St. George Tucker, October 8, 1791. Mr. Tucker was a widower, having lost his wife, Mrs. Frances Bland Randolph, mother of John Randolph, of Roanaoke.

HON. J. PROCTOR KNOTT.

The distinguished gentleman, whose name graces the head of this sketch, was descended from the Irvines as follows: Abram Irvine, a descendant of the house of Bonshaw and resident of the north of Ireland, came to this country some time before the war of the Revolution — the exact date his descendant have been unable to learn. He settled in Virginia and there married Mary Dean. He removed from Virginia to Kentucky some time between the years 1780 and 1790, and made his home in Boyle county, near Danville, Ky., within a few miles of Governor Shelby's residence. Abram Irvine and his wife Mary Dean, had nine children.

ABRAM IRVINE was the son of Rev. John Irvine. Mary Irvine, daughter of Abram Irvine and Mary Dean, his wife, married Samuel M'Elroy. Their son, William E. M'Elroy, married Keturah Cleland. Their daughter, Maria Irvine M'Elroy, married Joseph Percy Knott. Issue:

1. William T., who married Marian Briggs M'Elroy, and after
   her death married Mrs. Lydia M'Elroy (née Harrison),
   widow of Rev. Hugh Sneed M'Elroy.
2. Keturah Frances, married to Wells Rawlings (long since
   deceased).
3. Samuel Cleland, married Miss Sarah Gates, of Georgia.
4. Marian Margaret, married to Robert T. Nesbit.
5. Edward Whitfield, married Miss Mattie C. M'Koy (M'Coy).
6. Anne Maria, married to John Randolph Hudnell.
7. Joanne, married to Rev. Marcellus G. Gavin, of St. Louis,
   Missouri.
8. James Proctor, married Sarah Rosanna M'Elroy.

James Proctor Knott was born August 27, 1830; married June
14, 1858. Elected to the Missouri legislature the following August;
appointed attorney-general of the same state August, 1859, and
elected to that office August, 1860. Returned to Kentucky in 1862;
elected to the fortieth Congress in 1867; forty-first, 1868; forty-
fourth, 1874, and re-elected successively to the forty-fifth, forty-
sixth and forty-seventh. Elected Governor of Kentucky August
1883, and to the constitutional convention in August, 1890.

Governor Knott writes: "I know very little of my father's
ancestry of that name. The records were destroyed in the burning
of my grandmother's residence, when I was a small boy. All I
know is that my grandfather, my great-grandfather and my great-
great-grandfathers were all only sons, and all of them, except my
grandfather, were ministers of the Church of England; that they
were of Danish extraction, and lived in Northumberland, England,
— I mean their forebears, down to the immigration of my grandfather's grandfather, who was a curate on that estate (in Northumberland); and that I know by tradition only. There is a tradition,
also, that the last named married a daughter of Earl Percy, and in
that way the name Percy, which was borne by my father, grandfather and my great-grandfather came into the family, but I never
thought it worth while to ascertain.

"I was once assured by a painstaking antiquary that he had
traced my father's side of the house to Richard de Percy in a direct
line, one of the grim old barons appointed at Runnymede to see that
John Lackland should observe the Great Charta of English liberty
there extorted from him, and that my coat of arms is: Or, a lion
rampart, az. I am a Scotch-Irishman, however, and with many of
the traits of that race, I inherited the sentiment 'that blood is thicker

than water,' and, whether pleb. or patrician, I am always glad to recognize my kinsfolk."

In appearance, Governor Knott was of a very uncommon type of manhood. He was a little above the medium height; strongly and compactly built. At the first glance one was impressed by strength — mental and physical. He was not one with whom a stranger would attempt to converse uninvited, and yet those who knew him well say that he was the kindest and most gentle of men to women and children, and charitable almost to a fault. The speech of his, — known all over the world as "The Duluth Speech," — has been published again and again in this country, and has been translated into many languages. The school boys, by thousands, have recited it, and murdered its inimitable humor and fadeless and matchless fancies, ever since it first came before the public in 1871.

FAMILY OF ABRAM IRVINE.

"Abram Irvine was the son of Rev. John Irvine, Presbyterian minister of Coushindall, Ireland. John Irvine was brother to Robert Irvine, who married Margaret Wylie, and both were the sons of James Irvine, who was the son of Christopher, who fell at Flodden Field 1513."—*Old Chronicle*, Glenoe, Ireland.

On May 9, 1729, some of the Irvines, McDowells, McElroys, Campbells and others sailed from Londonderry, and landed the same year in Pennsylvania, where they remained until 1737, when they moved to Rockbridge county, Virginia, and were the first settlers on Burden's grant.

One of the immigrants in that party was John (or James?) Irvine, a Presbyterian preacher. Dr. McDowell says that his children were probably all born in this country, and consisted of one son, Abram, and four daughters, and probably other sons, but of this he is not certain. This is all the information, bearing directly on the Irvines, that I get from Dr. McDowell's letter. The remainder of it it devoted chiefly to the various marriages between the Irvines and McDowells.

I will now give the names of the descendants of Abram Irvine, the son of Rev. John (or James?) Irvine, the immigrant. But first, I would state that of the four sisters of this Abram Irvine, three married McElroys, and from them sprung the numerous families of that name in Marion and Washington counties, and in that part of the state, including the mother of ex-Governor Knott. The fourth

The Hon. R. T. Irvine, Big Stone Gap, Virginia.

sister never married. Abram Irvine was born in Scotland, May, 1725. He married Mary Dean, who was born in Ireland, February 22, 1733. Both had immigrated with their parents to Rockbridge county, Va.

(NOTE.— Another account I have says that Abram Irvine was born in Rockbridge county, Va., in 1731; and died June 1, 1814, and that Mary Dean was born in Rockbridge county, Va., January 1, 1733, and died in 1801. I think the account I have adopted above is correct as to the times and places of their births. Certainly, neither of them was born in Virginia, as the McDowells and Irvines did not go from western Pennsylvania to "Burden's grant" in Rockbridge county, Va., until 1737.)

The maiden name of Mary Dean's mother was Jane McAllister, who was one of the heroic women who aided in the successful defense of Londonderry, in the great siege by James II., in 1690. At the close of the War of the Revolution, Abram Irvine removed with his family from Rockbridge county, Va., to Kentucky, and settled in what afterwards became first the county of Mercer, and subsequently and now, the county of Boyle, on the waters of Salt river, about five miles southwest of the present town of Danville. A few miles to the east, Isaac Shelby, who afterwards became the first governor of Kentucky, settled, and the places of Abram Irvine and Shelby are both noted on the first map of Kentucky, made, I think, in 1786, by John Filson.

Abram Irvine and Mary Dean had eleven children, nine of whom married and reared families of children. These children and their descendants are as follows:

1. JOHN IRVINE, born February 25, 1755; married Prudence Armstrong, of Mercer county, Kentucky. He is one of the magistrates who held the first county court in Mercer county while it was still a part of Virginia. This was in August, 1786, and associated with him were Samuel McDowell and Gabriel Madison. The children of John and Prudence Armstrong Irvine were:

    (1). Samuel, who married, first, Cassy Briscoe, and by her had three children: (a) Rev. John, who married Matilda Smith; ((b) Jeremiah Briscoe, and (c) William, who married Eliza Mann; and second, Elizabeth Adams, by whom he had two children, Mary, who married James Forsythe, and David.

    (2). Mary, who married Dr. James McElroy, and by him had

three children: (a) Alice, who married a Norton in
Marion county, Mo.; (b) Dr. Irvine, who married, also
in Marion county, Mo.; and (c) Milton, who never married.   They all lived in Missouri.

(3). Margaret, who married Dr. David Clarke, who, with their
family, also lived in Missouri, chiefly in Marion county.
Their children were: (a) Robert, who died unmarried;
(b) Margaret, who married a Dr. Gore; and (c) Josephine,
who married a Hatcher.

(4). Sarah who married Horace Clelland, of Lebanon.   Their
children were: (a) Elizabeth, who married a Dr. Walker;
(b) John, who died unmarried; and (c) Rev. Thomas
H., who was married three times; his third wife was
Sally Ray.

(5). Abram, who married Amelia Templeton.   Their children
were: (a) Leonidas, who married Belle Burton; (b) Lucy,
who married Rev. Robert Caldwell; (c) Ellen P., who
married Joseph McDowell, a grandson of Col. Joseph
McDowell and Sarah Irvine, daughter of Abram and
Mary Dean Irvine; (d) Joseph W., who married, first,
Mariah Brumfield, and second, Mary Davis, of Bloomfield, Ky.; (e) Margaret C., who married Anthony Mc-
Elroy, of Springfield; (f) Gabriel C., who was married
three times, his first wife being Elizabeth Gregory, and
his second being her sister; his third wife was a Miss
Hughes; (g) Abram P., who married Elizabeth Fleece.

(6). Priscilla, who married Dr. M. S. Shuck, of Lebanon.   Their
children were: (a) Mary, who married Charles R. Mc-
Elroy, of Springfield; (b) John Irvine, who married
Mary Young, and (c) Solomon S.

(7). Robert.   I do not know the names of his wife and children.

2. HANS, born April 25, 1758.   He was never married.

3. MARY, married, first, William Adair, by whom she had two
children: (1)Alexander who married Elizabeth Monroe, by
whom he had six children; (a) Anna, who married Dr. Lewis
of Greensburg, Ky.; (b) Mary, who married Thomas Wagner,
of Greensburg; (c) Kate, who married Gen. E. H. Hobson,
of Greensburg; (d) Monroe; (e) John, and (f) William.   Her
second husband was Dr. Issachar Paulding, by whom she
had no children.

4. MARGARET, born April 25, 1762; married, first, Samuel Lapsley, and second, Rev. John Lyle, the first Presbyterian preacher in Kentucky, by whom she had the following children:

(1). Sarah, whose first husband was Rev. Joseph B. Lapsley, by whom she had two children: (*a*) Samuel, who married Mary Jane Bronaugh, and resided at Lincoln, Mo., and (*b*) Margaret, who married John Taylor, of Missouri. Her second husband was a Witherspoon, of Missouri. I do not know their children. This family all lived in Missouri.

(2). John R., who married his cousin, Sarah Irvine, daughter of Robert and Judith Glover Irvine. Their children were: (*a*) William J., who married his cousin, Ellen Lyle, of Paris; (*b*) Robert B., who married Mary McElroy, of Lebanon; and (*c*) Edwin, who died unmarried after reaching maturity. There were other children, but they died early.

(3). Abram Irvine, who married Frances Hunly, by whom he had two children: (*a*) John Andrew, who married Belle Russell; (*b*) Joel Irvine, who married, first, Emma Railey; and second, Cornelia Railey.

5. ANNE, born November 28, 1763, who married her cousin, Samuel McDowell (born March 8, 1764), who was a youthful soldier of the Revolutionary War. They had the following children:

(1). Mary, who married William Starling. Their children were: (*a*) General Lyne, of the Union army, who married Marie Antoinette Hensley; (*b*) Colonel Samuel, also of the Union army, who married Elizabeth Lewis; and (*c*) Col. Edmund Alexander, also of the Union army, who married Anna L. McCarroll, of Hopkinsville.

(2). John Adair, who married Lucy Todd Starling, and removed to Columbus, Ohio, where he afterwards became a judge, but died at thirty-four years of age. Their children were: (*a*) Anna Irvine, who married Judge John Winston Price, of Hillsboro, Ohio; (*b*) Starling, who died young; (*c*) Jane, who married John A. Smith, of Hillsboro; and (*d*) William, who never married.

(3). Abram Irvine, who married Eliza Selden Lord. He resided at Columbus, and was clerk of the Supreme Court of Ohio for many years. Their children were: (*a*) Gen. Irvine McDowell, who commanded the United States Army at Bull Run. He married a Miss Burden, of Troy, N. Y.; (*b*) Anna, who married a Massey, formerly of

Virginia, but afterwards of Memphis, Tenn.; (c) John, who was a colonel in the Union army; (d) Eloise, who married a Colonel Bridgeman, of the United States army; and (e) Malcolm, who married Jane Gordon, and resided in Cincinnati.

(4). Wm. Adair, who married Mariah Hawkins Harvey, of Virginia. He was a physician, and resided in Louisville. Their children were: (a) Sarah Shelby, who married Judge Bland Ballard, of Louisville; (b) Henry Clay, who married Annette Clay, granddaughter of Henry Clay, and daughter of Lieut.-Col. Henry Clay, who was killed at Buena Vista (they reside at "Ashland," the old Clay homestead, near Lexington); (c) Anna; (d) Magdalen; (e) William Preston, who married Katherine Wright, and resides in Louisville; and (f) Edward Irvine, who was a soldier in the Union army and was killed at Resaca. He was never married.

(5). Joseph, who married Anne Bush, and settled in Alabama. Their children were: (a) Mary, who married Judge Clarke of Mississippi; and (b) Elizabeth, who married Dr. Welch, and settled in Galveston, Texas.

(6). Sarah, who married Jeremiah Minter, of Columbus. Their children were: (a) Ann, who married Alonzo Slayback, of Missouri; (b) McDowell, who never married; (c) Magdaline, who married a Kidd, of Illinois; (d) Mariah, who married a Colorado man, whose name I do not know; (e) Bertrude, who died in the Union army during the war, unmarried; (f) Ellen; and (g) Susan. I do not know whom they married. Nearly all of this family and their descendants live in Missouri.

(7). Reed.

(8). Alexander, who married, first, Priscilla McAfee, daughter of Gen. Robert McAfee, who had removed from Mercer county to Missouri. She, with her only child, perished in the burning of a steamboat on the Mississippi river. His second wife was Anna Haupt, of Mississippi. Their children were: (a) Louise Irvine, who married her cousin, Dr. Hervey McDowell, of Cynthiana; and (b) Anna, who never married.

1. ABRAM, born August 8, 1766; married, first, Sally Henry, a relative of Patrick Henry, and second, Margaret McAfee.

By his first wife he had only one child, Jane, who married
Lee M. Speak. Their children were: (*a*) Frank, who
married Mary Hunter; (*b*) Magdalen, who married James
McKee, and removed to Texas; (*c*) Sarah, who married
Rev. J. L. McKee, D. D., vice-president of Centre College;
(*d*) Jane, who married Dr. William Mourning, of Springfield;
(*e*) Julia, who married Castello Barfield, of Tennessee;
(*f*) Ermine, who married John Mitchell, of Missouri; and
(*g*) Irvine, who died unmarried. The children of Abram
Irvine and Margaret McAfee were:

(1). James H., who married Elizabeth Williamson. Their
children were: (*a*) John Williamson, who married
Anna Simpson, of Indiana; he resides in Missouri;
(*b*) Anna Bella, who never married; (*c*) Elizabeth, who
never married; and (*d*) Cornelia Crittenden, who married
her cousin, Joseph McDowell Wallace, and resides at
Danville.

(2). Abram Lyle, who married Sarah Hughes. Their only
child was Letitia Reed, who married Capt. A. M. Bur-
bank. They reside in Atlanta.

(3). Issachar Paulding, who married Margaret Muldrough.
Their only children, Hugh and Letitia, died unmarried.

(4). Elizabeth, who married Anselm D. Meyer. Their children
were: (*a*) Ardis Rebecca, who married Thomas R.
Browne, of Washington county; (*b*) Margaret C., who
married Stephen E. Browne, and removed to Missouri;
(*c*) James, who died unmarried; (*d*) John Miller, who
married Fanny English; (*e*) Edward Hopkins, who
married Alice Mann, of Mercer; and (*f*) Mary Irvine, who
never married.

(5). Mary Paulding, who married her cousin, Abram Dean
Irvine, son of Robert Irvine and Judith Glover. Their
children were: (*a*) Abram Walter, who married Sophia
Tate, of Taylor county (these were my parents); (*b*)
Elizabeth M., who married Rev. L. H. Blanton, D. D.,
chancellor of Central University; (*c*) Robert Lyle, who
married Anna Seymour, of Chillicothe, Ohio, to which
place he removed; (*d*) Mary Paulding, who was never
married; and (*e*) Rev. William, who married Elizabeth
Lacy Hoge, of Richmond, Va. There were several
other children, who died young and unmarried; their

names were: Margaret Sarah, Judith Glover, John, and Sally Lyle.

7. ROBERT, born 1768, married Judith Glover. Their children were:

(1). John Glover, who married Emiline Drake. Their children were: (*a*) William Drake, who married Corilla Parker, of Fayette county; and (*b*) Emeline, who died unmarried.

(2). Abram Dean, who married his cousin, Mary Paulding Irvine, whose children I have enumerated above.

(3). Robert, who married Ann Armstrong. Their children were: (*a*) Robert Andrew, who married Mattie Logan, of Shelby county; (*b*) Judith Emma, who married Rev. William Cooper.

(4). Mary, who married, first, Walter Prather. Their children were: (*a*) Martha, who married, first, a Caps, and second, a Cunningham; (*b*) Mary, who married, first, Nineon Prather; second, Thomas Rickets, and third, Samuel Varble; (*c*) William, who married Susan Blackwell; (*d*) Robert, who married Martha Johnson; (*e*) Walter, who married Mary Prather; (*f*) Irvine, who married Sarah Peyton; and (*g*) Sarah, who married Benjamin Baker. The second husband of Mary Irvine was a Shrock, by whom she had one child, Edward, who married Laura Taylor.

(5). Judith, who married a Brink. They had no children.

(6). Celia, who married William Davenport. They had only one child, Judith, who married, first, George St. Clair, and second, John Sparks.

(7). Sarah, who married her cousin, John R. Lyle, whose children I have already given.

8. NANCY, born July 5, 1770, married Francis McMordie. Their children were:

(1). Abram Irvine, who married, first, Jane Armstrong, and by her had one child, Francis, who died, a Confederate soldier, during the war, and unmarried; second, Jane Hurt, by whom he had the following children: (*a*) Nancy, who married Samuel Lackey and removed to Texas; (*b*) Mary, who died without issue; (*c*) Magdalen, who married Elijah Vanarsdale, of Mercer; (*d*) Abram Irvine, who married Nancy Harris, of Mercer.

(2). Mary, who married William Cowan. Their children were:

(*a*) John, who never married, he died in Cuba; (*b*) Nancy, who married Rev. John Bogle; (*c*) Sarah, who married William Harrison; (*d*) Robert, who was a Confederate officer, and was killed in the battle of Green River Bridge, unmarried; (*e*) Jane, who married Rev. Geo. O. Barnes; (*f*) Dr. Francis, who died in the City of Mexico, unmarried; (*g*) James, a Confederate soldier; and (*h*) Abram Irvine. The last two went to Colorado; I do not know about their descendants.

(3). Margaret, married, I think, James Crawford, of South Carolina. I do not know about their children, if any.

Nancy Irvine and Francis McMurdie had three other children — Robert, Jane and Hans, but I think they all died unmarried and without issue.

9. ELIZABETH, born March 20, 1772; married George Caldwell. Their children were:

(1). Abram Irvine, who married his cousin, Anne McDowell. Their children were: (*a*) Belle, who died unmarried; (*b*) William, who married Callie Adams; (*c*) Elizabeth, who married Preston Talbott; (*d*) Anne, who married John Yeiser; (*e*) Irvine, who died unmarried; (*f*) Caleb, who married Lou Woolfork; and (*g*) Cowan, who married John C. Crawford, of Texas.

(2). Isabella, who married Benjamin Perkins. Their children were: (*a*) Mary, who married Nicholas Bowman; and (*b*) George, who never married.

(3). Dr. John, who married Jane Fox. Their children were: (*a*) Mary, who married Cyrus Richardson; (*b*) Amanda, (*c*) Belle, neither of whom was ever married; and (*d*) Sophia, who married Dr. Parker, of Somerset, Ky.

There were three other children of Elizabeth Irvine and George Caldwell — George, Mary, and Eliza, but I think none of them married, or left descendants.

10. SARAH, born November 21, 1774; married her cousin, Col. Joseph McDowell, a brother of Judge Samuel McDowell, who married Anna Irvine, the elder sister of Sarah. Their children were:

(1). Samuel, who married, first, Mariah Ball; they had only one child, Mary, who married Dr. J. M. Meyer. His second wife was Martha Hawkins, and their children were: (*a*) Joseph, who married his cousin, Ellen Irvine, whom

I have mentioned before; (*b*) Charles; (*c*) Nicholas, who married Elizabeth McElroy, of Springfield; (*d*) Samuel, who married Mattie McElroy, sister of Elizabeth; (*e*) William, who died unmarried.

(2). Anne, who married her cousin, Abram I. Caldwell, and whose children have already been given.

(3). Sarah, who married Michael Sullivan, of Columbus, Ohio, afterwards Illinois. Their children were: (*a*) Anna, who married E. L. Davidson, of Springfield, Ky.; (*b*) Sallie; (*c*) Joseph McDowell, of Illinois; (*d*) Lou, who married William Hopkins, of Henderson, Ky.

(4). Margaret, who married Joseph Sullivant, brother of Michael; their only child was Margaret Irvine, who married Gen. Henry B. Carrington, of the United States army.

(5). Lucy, who died unmarried.

(6). Charles, who died unmarried.

(7). Caleb, who died unmarried.

(8). Magdalen, who married Caleb Wallace, of Danville. She survives him, with two sons: (*a*) Joseph McDowell, who married his cousin, Cornelia C. Irvine, before mentioned; and (*b*) Woodord.

11. WILLIAM DEAN, born August 1775 (?); never married. He was an officer in the War of 1812, and subsequently died at Natchez, Miss.

In this I have attempted merely to give you a list of the descendants of Abram Irvine and Mary Dean to the third generation. It is a mere skeleton. To fill in, to give life and flesh, dates of birth and death, collateral marriage connections, the occupations, the achievements, and leading characteristics of all who are worthy of special mention, would require a volume. It is a noble line — pure Scotch-Irish, the blood that has done more than any other to turn the American wilderness into the strongest and most enlightened nation the world has yet known. We shall search history in vain, I think, for a family that combines, in a higher degree, love of God, of kindred and country, with the highest personal integrity, dauntless will, energy of purpose, and a burning devotion to liberty in all its forms, that could have been nourished nowhere else than among the intrepid clans that followed Wallace and Bruce to battle.

My chief objection to our great composite national life is, that members of our best families are too prone to become absorbed in

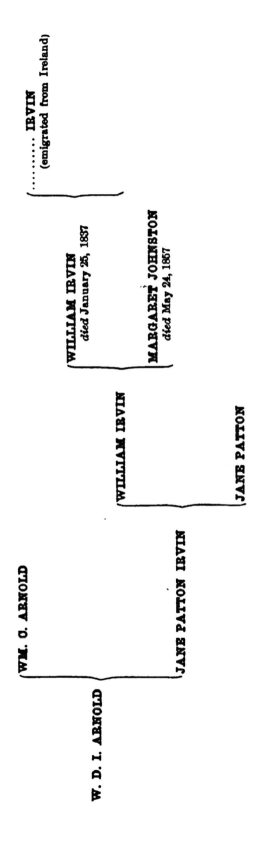

W. D. I. ARNOLD

WM. O. ARNOLD

JANE PATTON IRVIN

WILLIAM IRVIN

JANE PATTON

WILLIAM IRVIN
died January 25, 1837

MARGARET JOHNSTON
died May 24, 1857

.... IRVIN
(emigrated from Ireland)

the general hurlyburly, and to forget their past. This is to lose the greatest of all stimulants to lofty purpose and unceasing exertion. The noble work you are doing will do much, very much, to recall us of the present, and the generations yet unborn, to realize the debt we owe to heredity, and to incite us to new resolves to meet that responsibility.

ELIZABETH IRVINE.

Since this story was told me, an immeasurable desert of buried years, haunted by the ghosts of departed hopes, stretches between me and the distant time I listened to it, and I can hardly realize that I and the child who wept over the fate of fair Elizabeth Irvine are one and the same person. The name of Elizabeth Irvine's father — other than Irvine — I know not, but this I heard: that he was a Scotch-Irishman, of a noble family, and that he came to this country and married a beautiful French woman, who could not speak English well, and who brought great wealth to her husband on her marriage day. Elizabeth Irvine was born in the South. Why I have always thought that she was born near New Orleans, I do not know, but such an impression has been borne in on my mind ever since I heard her story, now more years ago than I care to count. Elizabeth inherited her mother's beauty and her father's intellect, which was said to have been considerable; and to these rare possessions had been added, by the time Elizabeth had reached her eighteenth birthday, a good education. She had been graduated in some large city in the East, but, if I ever heard the name of it, it does not dwell in my memory.

In the town — or city, as I think it was — where Elizabeth Irvine was born, there lived a certain wealthy and distinguished judge, whom I shall call Judge S., for fear, if I should be more particular, I might offend some one now living who might be nearly related to him — his direct descendant he could not be, for, although the judge married, he drew a blank in the infant lottery, and no child ever called him father. Judge S., was forty years old the first time he and Elizabeth met, after her return from school; but he was not bald nor gray, and was eminently handsome and attractive. Judge S. had been the schoolmate and friend of Mr. Irvine, although Mr. Irvine was a few years his senior. He was often invited to Mr Irvine's house, and often took the liberty of a life-long friend to call when he was not invited. In this way he saw a great deal of Elizabeth, and no one was surprised when he asked her to be his wife — not even Elizabeth, although she promptly, but kindly, refused to marry him. She took the sting from her refusal by saying that she intended to see the world before she entered into so solemn and responsible a compact as marriage, and that the judge must give her time to look about her. The judge did not feel hopeless about finally winning Elizabeth, because there was no rival in view, even if Elizabeth did have a vast deal of attention from the young men of her acquaintance. But there was a rival coming from an obscure corner of a distant State, and one whom the judge, if he had only known, might have dreaded through his whole life.

One morning, as the judge sat in the morning room of his stately mansion, there came a ring at the door-bell, and a young man just from a long journey stood before him. At the first glance the judge, who was well versed in human nature, knew that the youth before him was no ordinary character; for, besides being handsome, his bearing was that of an educated gentleman; and the judge arose, gave his name, and offered the young man a chair. The young man gave his own name, thanked the judge, and seated himself. I shall call this young man James Allen, although that was not his name, nor anything like it; but it will serve my purpose in this story as well as another name, and much better than the one he afterwards made famous, and which he had legally inherited from his father. Judge S. took this young man to board in his house, and gave him the use of his law books and his office, and in a year after Mr. Allen's first appearance in Judge S.'s presence, he was admitted to the bar, and had won golden opinions from many of the older lawyers, and had stolen the heart of Elizabeth Irvine, who, it seemed, had had time to take a look about her and to see the world, for she was willing to enter into the solemn and responsible compact of marriage with Mr. Allen, if he would wait a year before it should be solemnized by law and the church. Elizabeth's mother was a Catholic of the Roman persuasion, and her father was a Presbyterian; but neither of them was of the strictest sect, for they never had discussions on their different faiths, but went their several ways in quietness and peace, and often went to the Presbyterian church together; and as often, sat side by side while the old priest held forth, before the altar, of the only way to Heaven. Thus Elizabeth, hearing much doctrinal truth, and having as much love for and faith in one parent as she had in the other, sought out a way to save her own soul, as also a means in so doing of offending neither parent, and she became an Episcopalian. She had been baptized when she was a few weeks old, so it only remained that she be confirmed in the church of her choice. Her father and mother both attended her at her confirmation, and afterwards they went with their only and beloved child to her church, and she went to theirs; and still there were no religious disputes, nor were any fears expressed that any member of that family of three souls was in danger of — shall I say hell-fire? Preachers used to rap out that expression in my youth, and although I shuddered at it, it made me afraid to do wrong, so I shall let it stand.

Mr. Allen besought Elizabeth more than once to shorten his probation and name an earlier day for their wedding, but she held firmly to the first arrangement, and Mr. Allen was forced to wait for the blessings in store for him, and the time when he should call Elizabeth his wife, and be enabled to bask, from day to day, in the light of her gracious presence. Those two, Elizabeth and James Allen, were betrothed one June evening, in what year I am sorry I can not tell, and Mr. Allen said, as he placed the ring on Elizabeth's finger, "This day one year I shall replace this ring with another, and then you will be mine, Elizabeth, through time and eternity."

How much sorrow and misfortune can gather and fall in twelve months! Six months after this date Elizabeth's mother sickened and died, and before the year was out her father slept beside her. At his death it was learned that security debts would sweep away his whole estate. Elizabeth was left not only alone, but almost penniless. She begged Mr. Allen to postpone their marriage; and he, in his sorrow for his beloved, did so, and Elizabeth went East to the school in which she had been educated, and remained there until within a few weeks of the time appointed for her marriage to take place. An old friend, who had loved her father and mother, and who had loved Elizabeth from her infancy, had written Elizabeth to beg that she should be married from her house. This friend lived in sight of Mr. Irvine's old home, now in the possession of strangers, and when Elizabeth came to stay with her, to wait for the appointed time that was to make her and Mr. Allen one, she thought that the change she saw in Elizabeth was due to grief and sorrow at beholding the pleasant home that was hers no longer. When Judge S. called to see Elizabeth, he could not understand the manner of the woman he still loved, but he made no comments, and the day came on for which Mr. Allen had waited so impatiently, and he and Elizabeth stood before the altar to be made man and wife.

Judge S. was to give the bride away. Just as the clergyman had opened his lips to begin the service, Elizabeth fainted, or, they said, pretended to faint, and a second time the wedding was postponed, this time indefinitely.

Mr. Allen had an interview with Elizabeth on the evening of the day on which he had hoped to have claimed her for his own. What passed between them was never known, but it must have had a stormy termination, for he left town that night. When Elizabeth arose from her bed of illness, her friends noticed that she no longer wore her engagement ring; but on this subject she was silent as the grave, and none dared question her. Months went by — six of them — and still Mr. Allen did not return. Judge S. again renewed his attentions to Elizabeth, and with greater success than formerly, for she not only agreed to marry him, but appointed an early day for their nuptials. Just before her wedding day Mr. Allen returned. He was present and heard her promise, in a clear, distinct voice, to honor and obey Judge S., but he and others noticed that, if she promised to love him, she must have done so in an undertone, for she could not be heard. Judge S. entered into partnership with Mr. Allen, and the latter boarded with the judge, as he had done before the marriage, but Mrs. Grundy noticed that he never went to his meals nor near Judge S.'s house in the judge's absence. Another thing Mrs. Grundy took note of: Elizabeth was growing thin and pale. She was always most gentle and considerate in her manner to Judge S., and acted as if she had done him a great wrong and wished, in some way, to make atonement for it.

She had not been married very long, when her husband was elected to Congress. As he was elected some time during President Jackson's administration, I come to the only date I have yet been able to furnish. He removed to Washington, with his wife, some time beteween the years 1829 and 1837. Elizabeth seemed to regain her wonted appearance and spirits in the capital, which was said to have been very gay at that time. Elizabeth was very much admired and was entertained by, and she and her husband entertained, all the dignitaries who were assembled at Washington from this country and abroad. There never was a whisper against Elizabeth's fair fame, although Andrew Jackson was President of the United States, and held his court to please himself, and made and unmade his cabinet without regard to the murmurs and complaints that came from all over the country. I never heard that Judge S.'s wife did or did not meet Andrew Jackson, but this I have heard, which I shall never forget, Elizabeth became a consummate politician and wrote learned articles on the vexed issues of the day and made herself famous by being the author of the "Jackson Letters," so-called, because they were written during General Jackson's administration.

Although magazines and newspapers are the evangels of civilization and progress, nothing is so evanescent as the fame of those who write for them. "The Jackson Letters" are lost. I may be the only one now living who ever heard of them, and the only soul on earth who knows the story of fair Elizabeth Irvine. She died in Washington, D. C., and her broken-hearted husband took her body to the place of her nativity.

> "Among familiar scenes to rest,
> And in the place of her youth."

On her death-bed she said to one, who told me her story, "If 'the wages of sin is death,' the wages of ambition are ash and dust. Bury me in my wedding gown. I have kept it for that purpose, but I did not think to need it so soon. Comfort my husband when I am gone. I have tried to be faithful to him, but when I am in the grave, none will ever know how sad a heart death has stilled." One must have suspected, for, at nightfall on the day Elizabeth was laid to rest by her mother and father, a man who lived near the graveyard saw James Allen climb the crumbling stone wall that enclosed the churchyard and make his way to Elizabeth's grave, and he saw him leave it the next morning before sunrise. Mr. Allen lived to the verge of extreme old age, but he never married. His name is well known to American people, for he became famous. Thus endeth a lesson that will not teach.

THRENODY.

Along the far horizon's verge the smoldering sundown burns;
The sky, above its dying light, to opal softness turns.
Now, ghostly, by each vale and stream the mists and shadows creep,
While, in the faded autumn trees, birds hush their young to sleep,
And whispering winds, from other lands, pass softly on their way,
As twilight weaves a purple shroud for the departed day;
While on the hilltop's line of light, etched on the fading sky,
The gentle kine are standing, mute, to watch the daylight die.

How many years before I lived the sun shone down yon vale,
And on this path, where lovers walked, to tell that endless tale!
Then other birds, in other trees, sang out their tuneful lay,
And other hearts, as sad as mine, beat out their little day.
Here, long ago, some gentle maid has watched the evening star
Lead all the hosts of heaven to light the deeps of night afar;
Then turned to watch the harvest moon climb o'er the eastern hill,
While the twin phantoms, Love and Hope, her heart with rapture fill.
Alas! why did she come to earth, so short a time to stay,
And where now is her gentle soul among the stars to-day?

I call to where the millions sleep, within their moldy beds,
And where, beneath a starless sky, eternal darkness spreads.
The sages turn within the dust, and murmur in their sleep:
"The keys of life and death are hid in mystery's dungeon deep.
Man lives and loves; he toils and weeps; then lies so cold and still,
Forgetting, in his narrow bed, how once his heart could thrill;
And he who followed duty's path, and he who won renown,
Have somewhere in the narrow vale laid all their burdens down:
And she who drained dark sorrow's grail is calm and peaceful now,
Since death's impartial touch has smoothed care's lines from cheek and brow.
The wherefore is forever hid till suns shall cease to set —
Then murmur not that life should mean to love and to forget!"

CYNTHIANA, KY., September 29, 1897. — *L. Boyd.*

THE FAMILY OF CHRISTOPHER IRVINE.

1. ISAIAH TUCKER IRVINE, married, 1840, Miss Elizabeth Joyner, daughter of William Howlett Joyner, of Beaufort county, South Carolina. Their children are five sons and three daughters, viz.:

(1). Sarah Joyner, married, 1863, James Hillhouse Alexander, son of Adam L. Alexander, who was a prominent and honored citizen of Washington, Ga., and who reared a family of ten children, widely known and respected throughout Georgia. Their children are two sons and one daughter, viz.: (*a*) Irvin, attorney at law, Atlanta, Ga., unmarried; (*b*) Hugh H. married, 1891, Miss Mary Burton, daughter of Thos. J. Burton, a large planter, of Burke county, Georgia. They have one daughter, Louisa Porter, born 1893; (*c*) Elizabeth, married, 1894, Llewellyn G. Doughty, son of Dr. Wm. H. Doughty, a distinguished physician of Augusta, Ga. They have one daughter, Jean Irvine, born 1896.

(2). William Howlett, married, 1867, Miss Hattie Callaway, daughter of Wm. R. Callaway, of Wilkes county, Georgia, and granddaughter of the celebrated pioneer Baptist preacher of Middle Georgia, Enoch Callaway. They have ten living children, five sons and five daughters: (a) Claude, unmarried, went to the West about 1890; (b) William Howlett, Jr., married in 1894, and has two children; (c) Elizabeth J., married, 1896, William Martin, a farmer of Oglethorpe county, Georgia; (d) Sarah Alexander; (e) Charles Edgar; (f) Annie May; (g) Isaiah Tucker; (h) Everett; (i) Willie Rosa; (j) Hattie.

(3). Charles Edgar, married Miss Mary Fortson, daughter of Benjamin W. Fortson, a prominent citizen of Wilkes county, Ga. Their children are: (a) Isaiah Tucker; (b) Reba; (c) Alexander; (d) Mary; (e) Emma.

(4). Jean Isabella, married Major Norman W. Smith, of Augusta, Ga., a well-known business man, and a prominent officer in the Quartermaster's Department of the Confederate Army. They have no children.

(5). Benjamin Screven, married, first, Miss Sallie Hill, of the large and distinguished family of that name in Wilkes county, Georgia, by whom he has one son, Paul; and, secondly, Miss Brownie Brewer, of a prominent and cultured family, of Hayneville, Ala., by whom he has one infant daughter, Mildred.

(6). Isaiah Tucker, married (1874), Miss Elizabeth Willis, daughter of James H. Willis, a distinguished public-spirited citizen of Wilkes county, Georgia. Their children are four, viz.: (a) Sarah Elizabeth; (b) Leila; (c) Benjamin S.; (d) Willis.

(7). Barnett, married (1892), Miss Ruth Foreman, daughter of Rufus L. Foreman, merchant and farmer, of Washington, Wilkes county, Georgia.

(8). Mary Bowdie, married George Twiggs Bryan, son of Gen. Goode Bryan, who was distinguished in the Florida War, and a Brigadier-General in the Confederate Army. She died in 1892, leaving one daughter, Anna Twiggs Bryan.

Isaiah T. Irvine, the father of this family of eight children, was prominent as a lawyer and an official, being Speaker of the Georgia

House of Representatives at the period of his untimely death. He lost his life in a steamboat explosion, in 1860, while traveling in Texas, on the Buffalo Bayou, near Houston. His wife, Mrs. Elizabeth Joyner Irvin, died in Augusta, Georgia, in 1891, at the home of her daughter, Mrs. Alexander.

One of the finest military companies that entered the Confederate service from Georgia was the Irvin Guard, organized by Isaiah T. Irvin, in 1860, of which he had been commissioned captain just prior to his death. His son, Charles E. Irvin, aged then about sixteen, entered the service in this company, as a private, and before the close of the war had become its captain, serving with marked efficiency and gallantry throughout the Confederate War. All the males of the family and connections over fifteen years of age served with the Confederate Army.

My grandfather (James Callaway's grandfather), Christopher Irvine, enlisted in the Fifth Virginia Regiment, February 15, 1776. He married Louisa Tucker, by whom he had two sons, Charles and Isaiah Tucker. He moved to Georgia when these boys were small (I do not know what year); settled in Wilkes county, and married a second time. By his second wife he had two children — one son, Judge David Irvine, of Marietta, Ga., and one daughter, Lucinda, dead.

My father, Isaiah Tucker, son of Christopher Irvine, married Isabelle Barkston and settled in Wilkes county, Georgia. They lived together in the same place fifty-three years. Father died at the age of seventy-three, mother ninety-one. He succeeded well, had a large plantation, country store, blacksmith, shop, and public gin. Carried his cotton to Augusta, Ga., the nearest market, 100 miles away, on wagons. They had eight children — two sons, Charles and Isaiah Tucker, and six daughters, Louisa, Nancy, Lucinda, Prudence, Mary, and Martha. All were Christian people and joined the Baptist church, except Isaiah Tucker, who joined the Methodist; were baptized at Sardis, by Enoch Callaway and Jesse Mercer.

Charles Irvine, son of Isaiah Tucker, son of Christopher Irvine, married Harriet Battle, and had two children, Charles B. Irvine, of Atlanta, Ga., and Mary Bell (Mrs. M. B. Wharton, of Norfolk, Va.).

Isaiah Tucker, son of Isaiah Tucker, son of Christopher Irvine, married Elizabeth Joyner, and had eight children — five sons, Howlett, Charles, Benjamin, Isaiah Tucker, Barnett; and three daughters, Sallie (Mrs. James H. Alexander, of Augusta, Ga.); Janie (Mrs. Norman W. Smith, of Agusta, Ga.); and Mamie (Mrs. Geo. T. Bryan, dead).

Louisa, daughter of Isaiah Tucker, son of Christopher Irvine, married, first, Lewis Davis, and had six children; second, Baylis Crosby, and had five children.

Nancy, daughter of Isaiah Tucker, son of Christopher Irvine, married Thomas Favor, and had seven children.

Prudence, daughter of Isaiah Tucker, son of Christopher Irvine, married, first, John P. Johnson, and had one child; second, Iverson L. Brooks, and had two children.

Mary, daughter of Isaiah Tucker, son of Christopher Irvine, married John Walton; three children. Afterwards married Merrell Calloway; four children.

Martha, daughter of Isaiah Tucker, son of Christopher Irvine, married Oliver L. Battle. They had five children — two sons, Charles and John Tucker, and three daughters, Eliza, Mary Belle and Annie Porter.

Charles Battle, son of Martha (great-grandson of Christopher Irvine), married Lou Walker.

John T., son of Martha (great-grandson of Christopher Irvine), married Rosalie Waddey. They had three children, Oliver I., Waddey W. and Mary Belle.

Eliza, daughter of Martha, and great-granddaughter of Christopher Irvine, married John F. Ficklen. They had two children, John Fielding and Irvine.

Mary Belle, daughter of Martha, and great-granddaughter of Christopher Irvine, married John F. Ficklen.

Anna Porter, daughter of Martha and great-granddaughter of Christopher Irvine, married Wm. Howell Wood, and had one child, Mary Belle.   MARTHA IRVINE BATTLE.

———

I am requested by my cousin, Mrs. M. B. Wharton, of Norfolk, Va., to send you a few items of the history of my father and his family. My father, David Irwin, or Irvin or Irvine, I don't know exactly which, as some of them spell it the two last-named ways, and some as my father did, Irwin, though we know we are closely related. The two first of the name that I have any history of were William and John, who came, I think, to Philadelphia from Ireland. William Irwin had a son named Christopher, who went to Virginia and from there to Wilkes county, Georgia, where he married a

Miss Tucker, by whom he had two sons, Isaiah Tucker and Charles. His wife died, and he married Prudence Echols, by whom he had Christopher, Jr., William, John, Smith, Heflin, and a daughter, Catherine, and the youngest child was a son, David, who was my father; he married Sarah Royston, from which union the following children were born: Marcus J., died, aged twenty-three years; Mary Elizabeth, died, aged seven years; Margaret Isabella, who married George N. Lester, who was Attorney-General at his death, in 1892, and his wife, Margaret, died the same year, leaving five sons and two daughters, viz.: Mary I. Lester, David P. Lester, Joseph H. Lester, Geo. N. Lester, Jr., Sarah Lester, Irwin Lester and Robert T. Lester. Next was Julia Irwin, who married Greenlee Butler, who died in 1864, leaving her a widow; next is Maria E., who is unmarried; next, Robert C., who is an attache of the Comptroller-General's office of Georgia (I should have said insurance clerk); next, David, Jr., who died in 1856, aged ten years; next, Thomas B., who is a lawyer in Marietta, Ga.

My wife was Miss Mary Lane, and Thomas B. married Miss Lilla Atkinson, granddaughter of ex-Governor Chas. J. McDonald, deceased. My father, David Irwin, obtained, by his own untiring effort, a fine education, by energy succeeding in getting sufficient education to study the legal profession, and was for a number of years a judge of the Superior Court. He was elected by the Legislature, with two others, to compile the first Code of Georgia, and appointed to revise it, alone. During the days of Reconstruction he was nominated by the Democratic party for Governor, but, Georgia being under military rule, he was informed by General Meade, who was in command of this department, that he would not be allowed to take his seat, if elected, which his friends thought was a foregone conclusion, as all the leading Republicans were supporting him, as well as the Democrats. His opponent was Rufus E. Bullock. My father declined the race, and General Gordon was put up and defeated by Governor Bullock. The reason General Meade gave was that my father had been an elector for Jefferson Davis when he was a candidate for President, but the true reason was that a faction got the General to give this opinion to get my father out of the race, because he had been an old Whig, and was carrying the Republican party for that reason, and they thought he might be too good a friend to those of that party who supported him. He was a self-made man, as his father died when he was a few years old, leaving his mother but little of this world's goods, and though he was the youngest child, she had to depend on him more than on any of the others.

The first named John, I think, is the founder of the western branch of the family, many of whom are in Mississippi, Tennessee, and Illinois. My father was related to the Adamses of Virginia, and also the McDowells, I think, of Pennsylvania, but I don't know the relationship. He died in 1885, at the age of seventy-eight.

R. C. IRWIN.

P. S.— I forgot to give names of children of R. C. The children of Robt. C. Irwin and Mary W. Lane are: Julia Greenlee, Mark A., Sarah, Hope (a boy), Lucy Mary and Margaret I. Sarah and Margaret I. died when young. The children of Thos. B. Irwin and Lilla Atkinson are: David, Mary Ann, Alexander A. and George L.

DESCENDANTS OF GEN. ROBERT IRVINE.

General Robert Irvine, who married Mary Alexander, was on of the signers of the Mecklenburg "Declaration of Independence." General Robert Irvine lived in Charlotte, N. C.

Margaret Irvine, daughter of General Robert Irvine, was married to Hugh McDowell, of Mecklenburg county, North Carolina. Hugh McDowell was the son of John McDowell, of Revolutionary fame. Margaret McDowell, daughter of Hugh McDowell and Margaret Irvine his wife, married Andrew Lawson Barry, of South Carolina, son of John Barry and grandson of Capt. Andrew Barry, celebrated at the battle of Cowpens.

The issue of the marriage between Margaret McDowell and Andrew Lawson Barry was as follows: Euphemia Elizabeth, Robert Lindsay, Mary Jane and Sarah Ann.

Euphemia Elizabeth married William Adolphus Moore; issue: Emma Eliza; Sallie Irvine, who died in 1875; Susan Margaret, who died in childhood; Mary Lou, who died in 1881; William Andrew, who died in childhood; Anna Euphemia, John McDowell, Jessie and Wilmer Lee.

Emma Eliza married William Wood Draper of Alabama; issue: William Moore, Robert Daniel, Mary Emma, Bessie, Jesse H., and Wallace Wood.

Anna Euphemia married Seaborne Wright, of Rome, Ga.; issue: Thomas Barry, Louis Moore, Max, Seaborne, who died in infancy, and Graham.

John McDowell Moore married Hattie Grace Wharton; issue: Wharton Adolphus, Elizabeth Irvine, May Bell, Emma; who died in infancy, and Bertha Hardon.

Jessie Moore married Hugh L. McKee; issue: Jessie Moore and Margaret Moore.

Wilmer Lee Moore married Cornelia Jackson; issue: Cornelia Jackson.

THE HOUSE OF BONSHAW — IRISH BRANCH.

Hugh McDowell, of Mecklenburg, N. C., son of John McDowell of Revolutionary fame, married Margaret Irvine daughter of Gen. Robert Irvine, one of the signers of the Mecklenburg Declaration of Independence.

Sarah Salina, daughter of Hugh and Margaret McDowell, married Andrew Moore Sloan, of South Carolina; issue: John Hugh, Charles Andrew, Oscar Adam and Robert Eugene.

John Hugh married Mary C. Winn, of Thomasville, Ga.; issue: Johnnie Hugh.

Johnnie Hugh married Edward Burckley, of Manistee, Mich.; issue, Virginia.

Charles Andrew married Mollie L. Morris, of Monticello, Fla.; issue, Emma.

Oscar Adam married Elizabeth Irwin Sloan, of McDonough, Ga.; issue: Sarah Eva, Annie May and Andrew Moore.

Robert Eugene married Ida Turnbull, of Monticello, Fla.; issue: Richard Turnbull, Robert Eugene and Sarah Salina. Second wife, Virginia Turnbull, of Monticello, Fla.

Robert Linsey Barry, son of Dr. Andrew Lawson Barry and Margaret Irvine [McDowell, married Laura Augusta Hackett, of Georgia; issue: Robert Edwin and Margaret.

Robert Edwin Barry married Mary Bryan Thiot, of Savannah, Ga.; issue: Ruth, Mary Bryan and Robert Andrew. Second marriage, Anna Henderson Green, of Atlanta, Ga.; issue, Edwin Joseph.

Margaret Barry married Edwin P. Ansley of Atlanta, Ga. issue: Laura Barry Ansely and Mamie Ansley.

Mary Jane Barry, daughter of Andrew Lawson Barry and Margaret Irvine McDowell, married Dr. Adolphus Sherard Fowler, of Georgia; issue: Eugene Moore, Minnie Lee, Mary Jane, Hugh Barry and Jessie Euphemia.

Eugene Moore married Minnie Riggs, of Forney, Tex.; issue, Hugh Chilton.

Minnie Lee married Melvin Gardner, of Norfolk, Va.; issue: Dorothy and John Nicklin.

Mary Jane married Roy Nall Cole, of Newman, Ga.

Sarah Ann Barry, daughter of Andrew Lawson Barry and Margaret Irvine McDowell, married William C. Sloan, of Georgia; issue: Elizabeth Irvin, Willie Emma, Julia Scott, Thomas Adam, Annie Gertrude, Euphemia, Laura Barry and Robert Andrew.

Elizabeth Irvin married Oscar Adam Sloan, of Florida; issue: Sarah Eva, Anna May, Andrew Moore and Willie Emma.

Willie Emma married Oscar Emerson Hám, of Georgia; issue: Alton Sloan, Emma Estelle, Rosa Irene and Emerson Barry.

Julia Scott married Edgar Leslie McDonald, of Georgia; issue: Eddie Claude and Julia Irvin.

Thomas Adam married Annie Iola Tye, of Georgia; issue: Thomas Adam, Carl and Wyman.

Annie Gertrude married Herbert Greenberry Bryan, of Georgia.

Euphemia married William P. Bellinger, of Florida.

Laura Barry married Joel Echols Smith, Florida.

Another descendant of the Irvines of Bonshaw is Rev. Dr. L. W. Irvine Porter, of the Radford Presbyterian Church, Radford, Va.

Rev. David C. Irwin married Martha Lucretia Pryor, daughter of George E. Pryor, M. D., of Frederick county, Md.; issue: James Elizabeth, George, Julia, Mary Virginia, William, Leonidas, H. David and Lucretia (twins), Mary W. and James Emory Irvine (died in infancy).

Elizabeth Willson Irvine married Pryor Boyd, of Wheeling West Virginia.

George Pryor Irwin married Signora J. Wilson, daughter of Robert Wilson, of Rockbridge county, Va.; issue: Essie L., George Pryor, Elizabeth W. (died in infancy).

Julia Sweeney Irvine died in infancy.

Mary Virginia Irvine died in infancy.

William Pryor Irwin married Julia Rush Junkin, daughter of Rev. E. D. Junkin, D. D.; issue: Wilfred P., John Preston, Agnes J., Leonidas W. (died in infancy), George J.

Rev. Leonidas Willson Irwin.

Lucretia Irwin.

Harry David Irwin married Anna White, daughter of Wm. S. White, Esq., of Lexington, Va ; issue, Frances W.

Mary W. Irwin.

THE WHARTON-IRVINE CONNECTION.

Mrs. Belle Irvine Wharton is descended from William Irvine, one of the seven brothers who came from Larne, Ireland, about 1729–30. William Irvine married Anne Craig, who died and was buried in Ireland in the churchyard of Raloo, by the side of her daughter Johanna, who had fallen asleep before her.

William Irvine and his two sons, David and Christopher, came to America and settled in Bedford county, Va. David Irvine came to Kentucky, and was the progenitor of the Madison county Irvines. Christopher went to Wilkes county, Ga., in 1794.

Christopher Irvine married Louisa Tucker, of Amherst, Va., and they had two sons, Charles and Isaiah Tucker. Charles Irvine removed to Richmond, Va., and died there in the early part of the present century. Isaiah Tucker Irvine, at the age of ten years, was taken by his father, Christopher Irvine, to Wilkes county, Ga., in 1794, as before stated.

Before leaving Virginia, Christopher Irvine was married the second time, to Miss Echols. They had six sons and one daughter born to them. I have been able to learn the names of but four of these children — Christopher, William, David and Catherine. Mrs. Wharton, great-granddaughter of Christopher Irvine, writes: "I think, indeed I know, that Christopher Irvine had, by his marriage with Miss Echols, a son John, and I think he had a son Robert, and an Andrew." These are family names among the Irvines of Bonshaw, from whom Christopher Irvine was descended.

Isaiah Tucker Irvine, son of Christopher Irvine and his wife Louisa Tucker, married Isabella Lee Barkston, issue: Louisa, Nancy Herndon, Prudence, Charles Mercia, Mary, Isaiah Tucker, Martha, Lucinda and Stephen. (Stephen died in infancy.)

Charles Mercia Irvine, son of Isaiah Tucker and his wife, Isabella Lee Barkston, married Harriette Andrews Battle (sometimes spelled Battaile), had two sons born to him, Reuben and Charles Battle, and one daughter, Mary Isabella, who married Rev. Dr. M. B. Wharton, and is the subject of this sketch.

The children of Rev. Dr. Morton Bryan Wharton and his wife are Charles Irvine (who died in infancy), Harriette Grace and Morton Bryan. Harriette Grace Wharton married John McDowell Moore; issue: Wharton Adolphus, Elizabeth Irvine, May Belle, Emma, and Bertha Herndon.

Morton Bryan Wharton, Jr., married Kitty Holt; issue, one daughter, Mary Catherine.

Charles Battle, son of Charles Mercia Irvine and his wife, Harriette Battle, married Mary Speer. His brother, Reuben Battle Irvine, died in infancy. The children of Charles Battle Irvine and his wife, Mary Speer, are two sons, who died in infancy, and three daughters whose names are May Speer, Ruby Lillian and Harriette Battle. May Speer Irvine married Logan Crichton, M. D.; Charles Barskton Irvine died in infancy; Ruby Lillian Irvine, married Herbert Willis Post.

Rev. Dr. M. B. Wharton, husband of Belle Irvine, was born April 5, 1839. He is the son of Malcolm H. and Susan R. Wharton. He was educated at Richmond College and at the University of Virginia; ordained pastor of the Baptist Church at Bristol, Tenn., in 1862; married Belle Irvine in 1864; elected pastor of the First Baptist Church of Eufaula, Ala., in 1867, and remained there five years; elected pastor of the Walnut Street Baptist Church, Louisville, Ky., in 1872, and remained there three years; elected pastor of the First Baptist Church, Augusta, Ga., in 1876, remaining there one year; elected corresponding secretary of the Southern Baptist Theological Seminary for a time. In 1881, Dr. Wharton was made United States Consul to Germany by President Garfield. After his return to this country from abroad, Dr. Wharton became editor of the *Christian Index*, and held that position one year, when he was called to the pastorate of the First Baptist Church of Montgomery, Ala. He remained at Montgomery as pastor of the church above mentioned for six years, and in 1897 was called to the Freemason Street Baptist Church of Norfolk, Va., where he now resides.

Dr. Wharton is a man of wide and varied learning. He is a patriot, author, poet, and a Christian gentleman whom the South loves to honor. He is author of "European Notes: or, What I Saw in the Old World," "Famous Women of the Old Testament," and "Famous Women of the New Testament," and poems many of which will live and move the world long after the hand that penned them is ashes and dust. Dr. Wharton was made Doctor of Divinity by Washington and Lee University in the year 1876, and the title could have been bestowed on no more worthy follower of the meek and lowly Jesus.

He is descended from the younger brother of Sir George Wharton — Lord Thomas Wharton — as follows: First Sir George Wharton had sons — George, Thomas, Jesse, John and Joseph; second George had sons — John, Joseph and William; third George had sons — Zachary and Samuel; Samuel Wharton had sons — Wil-

liam, John, Joseph, Samuel and Malcolm; Malcolm Wharton had
sons — William, Joseph, John, Samuel Morton Bryan, Malcom
Frederick and Henry Marion. Morton Bryan Wharton married
Belle Irvine, and had a son, Morton Bryan Wharton, who married
Kitty Holt.

The arms of the Whartons (as borne by Philip Wharton, the
celebrated Duke of Wharton,) are: Sa. a mauch ar. within a bordure
or, charged with eight pairs of lion's paws saltireways, erased gu.;
the bordure being an augmentation granted by Edward VI. Crest,
a Moor, kneeling, in coat of mail, all ppr. ducally crowned or, stab-
bing himself with a sword of the first, hilt and pommel of the
second. Another crest, and the one used by Rev. Dr. M. B. Wharton, is: A bull's head erased ar., attired or, gorged with a ducal
coronet, per pale of the second and gu. The arms of the Irvines of
Bonshaw (Irish branch), from whom his wife is descended, are thus
described: Ar. a fesse gu. betw. three holly leaves, ppr. Crest, a
dexter arm in armor, fesseways, issuant out of a cloud, hand ppr.
holding a thistle, also ppr.; motto: "*Dum memor ipse mei.*"

Mrs. Martha Irvine Battle, daughter of Isaiah Tucker Irvine
was described by Richard Malcolm Johnson as "a girl that was
simply glorious." In a recent letter from Baltimore, to a kinsman of Mrs. Battle, he says: "I should rather see Mat Battle than
any one now alive." How I should like to see a woman who receives praise from such a man as Georgia's most gifted son, whose
pen pictures are like the paintings of Hogarth, easy to understand,
but never to be imitated or surpassed in this world.

HON. WILBUR F. BROWDER.

Wilbur F. Browder is descended from the Irvines of Bonshaw, in
the following line: Alexander Irvine, married Sophia Gault;
issue: Andrew, William and Christopher, born in the North of Ireland. Alexander, his wife and sons came to Bedford county, Va.
Alexander Irvine and his wife died the same day. William Irvine,
brother of Alexander, reared Andrew Irvine, who was eight years
old at the time of his father's death. The Irvines of Pennsylvania
reared Christopher and William, and I have never been able to rely
upon any information that has been given me concerning them.
Some say that William was a General in the Revolution, but I have
never been able to prove it to my satisfaction. There was one

William Irvine, a General in the Revolution, but, if he was Andrew's brother, it has not been made plain to me.

Andrew Irvine married Elizabeth Mitchell, daughter of Elizabeth Innes and William Mitchell, of Edinburgh, Scotland. Caleb Irvine, son of Elizabeth Mitchell and Andrew Irvine, married Elizabeth Ewing Mitchell; issue: Norval, Thomas, Caleb Ewing, Robert Green and Elizabeth Eleanor. Elizabeth Eleanor Irvine married Rev. David Browder, November 18, 1842; issue: Bettie Green, James Thomas, Robert Irvine, Wilbur Fisk (born December 12, 1848), Helen Mary, David, Caleb Ewing, Richard, Edward McClure and Fannie Irvine. The children of David Browder and his wife are all dead except three sons, Hon. Wilbur F. Browder, of Russellville, Ky., Edward McClure, now living in Arizona, and Richard, now living with his wife and five children, in Montgomery, Alabama.

Wilbur F. Browder was graduated from the University of Virginia in 1868, and from the Law Department of the Kentucky University in November, 1869, and has since that time been distinguished in his profession in this and other states.

On January 18, 1872, Mr. Browder married Bettie Bernard Wills, a great-niece of Geo. M. Bibb. The children of this marriage are: Wilbur Fisk, Marion Castner, John Caleb, Lucien McClure and Eugene Irvine.

Wilbur Fisk Browder, born November 23, 1872, married Hattie Martin Frayer, November 23, 1893, and has a son, Wilbur Fisk Browder (third), born February 19, 1895.

Marion Castner Browder graduated from Bethel College, June, 1892, and from University of Virginia, June, 1894, and from University of Berlin, Germany, in 1895.

John Caleb Browder is now a student at the University of Virginia.

Lucy McClure Browder is a student at Bethel College, and the youngest son, Eugene Irvine Browder, is at a private school at Russellville, Ky.

Caleb Irvine, son of Andrew and Elizabeth Irvine, was drowned in Mayfield creek in 1825. He was an excellent swimmer, but in attempting to cross Mayfield creek, swollen by recent rains, his horse threw him. He must have been hurt in the fall, for he never came to the surface of the stream. His wife walked the shore of the stream, day and night, until the water subsided and her husband's body was found. He was clinging to the roots of a tree that overhung the water. His wife lived until 1868, and died at the house of her son-in-law, Mr. Browder, in Montgomery, Ala., at the advanced age of eighty-five years.

Caleb Ewing Irvine, son of Caleb above mentioned, was born a few weeks after his father's death. He was educated at West Point, became Lieutenant in the United States Army and served with great distinction in the war with Mexico. After the war was over he was ordered to the far West to quell an outbreak of certain turbulent tribe of Iandians. In the fight with these savages he was, in some way, cut off from his command, and his soldiers, fearing the worst, after the skirmish was over, crept back to learn his fate. Lieutenant Irvine's command was outnumbered, ten to one, by the Indians. They saw Irvine bound to a stake and faggots piled around him. Not being able to rescue their commander, and determined not to witness his suffering, they fled. When they rallied a sufficient number of troops to attempt his rescue they returned to the spot where they had seen him tied to the stake. There had been a fire, but no charred remains of a body could be found. Nevertheless, Lieutenant Irvine was reported dead.

How he escaped being burned by the Indians my informant did not know, but some time after Lieutenant Irvine resigned his commission in the army. If his resignation was published his relatives did not see it, and they mourned him as dead for many years. He went to the wilds of Oregon and made himself a home, and his existence was not known to his relatives and friends until 1885, when he was discovered by his great-nephew, Judge Robert Green Irvine, son of Lieutenant Irvine's nephew of the same name. Judge Robert Green Irvine was Circuit Judge of Butte City Judicial District and Montana Territory, and was, for many years, a very influential and popular Democrat of that part of the country.

Why Lieutenant Irvine acted in this manner toward his relatives and friends he never made known to any one. He was one of the most handsome and soldierly-looking men of his time, and his record in the army, whether in active service or in camp, was without blemish.

Judge Robert Green Irvine died in 1892 at Deer Lodge, Montana.

Rev. Robert Green Irvine, son of Caleb Irvine and Elizabeth Ewing Mitchell, his wife, was a minister of great eloquence and prominence in the M. E. Church, South, and died at Columbia, Tenn., in 1892, beloved and mourned by a host of friends.

Robert Ewing Irvine is unmarried and lives in the old homestead at Columbia, Tenn.

THE McELROYS.

The arms of the McElroys, from whom the McElroys of this country are descended, are described as follows: Or on a bend azure, a star of six points between two crescents argent, and in base a bow and arrow of the second. Crest — A hand, erect, holding a battle axe, ppr. Motto — Trusty and true.

I subjoin a letter from a friend in Ireland, and make no apologies for copying it word for word:

MOUNTHILL, LARNE, IRELAND, October 12, 1897.

MY DEAR MRS. BOYD: * * * The McElroys, some of them, live about a mile from here. The first of the name who came here was Charles McElroy. He was a soldier, stationed at Carrickfergus Castle, and came in the army of Gen. Robert Monroe, who was sent here in the wars of 1641. That was a fearful time. There was a great battle fought near Larne, on a hill that was called Shiner-roe, where General Monroe was slain, and the hill takes its name (in part) from General Monroe.

This McElroy distinguished himself at that battle, as did many others. McElroy was of the party who chased Phelim Roe O'Neill, of Shane's Castle, near Antrim Town, off the battlefield. He was rewarded for his gallant services with some fine land near Ballyclare, where some of his descendants now reside. Others of his descendants live at Ballymena.

Charles McElroy was a native of Inverness-shire, Scotland, and the fierce highland blood that ran in his veins fires some of his descendants to this day. I knew one of them, William McElroy, and like his ancestor, Charles, he was an old soldier and had five medals. He was the first man to place his foot on the heights of Alma.

*   *   *   *   *   *   *

The churchyard of Raloo covers about a half acre of ground. The walls of an old church are still standing, although the church was burned by the Catholics in 1641. In this old church were all the records of the Scottish families who had settled here. They were all destroyed by the fire that burned the church. But every family handed down its own records and arms. The arms are contained in an old book, hundreds of years old. If a neighbor knew the ancestry of one who was not versed in his own lineage, he gave it to him that it might be preserved.

The dear old churchyard of Raloo holds the dust of many of your ancestors — the Fords, Gaults, and at the eastern corner, on which the first beams of the rising sun rest, sleep the Irvines, among their kinsmen, the Wylies.

I do not think you quite understood what I wrote you concerning Alexander Irvine, who killed the man in Scotland, on the hunting field. He was a brother to Robert, who was the founder of the Irvine family here, in the early part of the sixteenth century, and great-uncle to Alexander (one of the seven brothers who came to America in 1729-30), from whom you are descended. Alexander, your immediate ancestor, was the son of James Irvine and Sophia Gault, his wife, and Alexander married his kinswoman, a Miss Gault.

*   *   *   *   *   *   *

I think this a mistake. The tradition has been handed down in my mother's family, from generation to generation.

The following pages were sent to me by Mr. William T. Knott, of Lebanon, Ky.

I send you the following notes from my manuscript sketches of the McElroys, of Kentucky, who married with the Irvine family. The McElroys are a numerous family, widely distributed throughout the United States, from the Atlantic to the Pacific, and from the Lakes to the Gulf. First immigration — the original families were from North Ireland, County Down, and adjacent localities; were not only all Protestants, but Presbyterians of no uncertain type. Some of them were members of the Old Covenanters and some of the Associate Church or Seceders.

About the year 1730, James McElroy, with his young bride, Sarah McHugh (or McCune), sailed on the vessel "George and Anne," in company with the Irvines, McDowells, McCunes (or McHughs) and others. They first settled, on the borders of Pennsylvania, in New Jersey or Delaware, thence farther west in Pennsylvania; and later the family of James McElroy and John Irvine, a Presbyterian minister, moved South and settled in Campbell county, Va. James McElroy had five sons: John, Archibald, Hugh, Samuel and James. John and Archy were married (the names of their wives not known) and moved to South Carolina. Their descendants are scattered over the southern states from the Carolinas to Texas. The third, fourth and fifth sons, Hugh, Samuel and James, married three sisters, Esther, Mary and Margaret Irvine, daughters of John Irvine, mentioned above. John Irvine's children were: John, Esther, Nancy, Mary, Elizabeth and Margaret. While in Pennsylvania, during the French and Indian wars, Nancy was captured by the Indians and held prisoner for a few days, when she was rescued by her friends.

In the year 1786 or '87, Hugh McElroy and his brother-in-law, John Irvine, moved from Compbell county, Va., to Kentucky, Irvine settling near where is now the city of Danville, Boyle county; Hugh McElroy settled near where is now Springfield, Washington county.

In the autumn of 1789, Samuel and James McElroy followed, Samuel settling about four miles east, and James one mile south-west, of where is now the city of Lebanon, Marion county. Hugh McElroy and Esther Irvine, his wife, had ten children; six sons and four daughters. Samuel McElroy and Mary Irvine, his wife, had thirteen children; eight sons and five daughters. James McElroy and Margaret Irvine, and wife, had eleven children; three sons and eight daughters. The descendants of the three McElroy boys and their Irvine wives, may be found in almost every state of the Union.

The children of Hugh McElroy and Esther Irvine were as follows:

1. James married Rosa Hardin and (second) a widow, Mrs. Pickett.
2. Margaret, married William Muldraugh, whose father gave his name to Muldraugh Hill.
3. Sarah, married —— Sandusky, a son of an old pioneer.
4. Mary, married John Simpson (first) and John McElroy (second husband).
5. John, married Miss Hundley; his descendants are the Springfield McElroys.
6. Hugh, married Miss Dorsey; some of his descendants lived in Hardin county, Ky.
7. Samuel, married Mary Wilson; many of his descendants moved to Missouri.
8. Robert married Miss Hudney; his descendants live in Washington and Marion counties, Ky.
9. William, married Miss Crawford, and left two children; lived Marion county, Ky.
10. Elizabeth, never married; lived to a good old age, in Springfield, Ky.

The children of Samuel McElroy and Mary Irvine were as follows:

1. Sarah, born in 1767, married Alexander Handley; their descendants live in southern Kentucky.
2. John, born 1769, married Miss Copeland (first) and Mrs. Mary Simpson, his cousin (second wife).

3. James, born 1770, died young.
4. Hugh, born 1772, married Miss Gilkie; had only one son, Hiram, a noted lawyer in his day. The McElroys of Union county, Ky., are his descendants.
5. Margaret, born 1773, married James Wilson; their descendants live in Mississippi and Arkansas.
6. Abram, born 1774, died young.
7. William, born 1776, married twice—first, Miss Keturah Cleland, sister to Rev. Dr. Thomas Cleland, of Providence Church, Mercer county; second wife was Miss Mary Kirk. Ex-Governor J. Proctor Knott is his grandson by his first wife, Miss Cleland.
8. Samuel, born in 1777, married twice: First wife, Miss Minnie Briggs; second wife, Miss Jane B. Grundy.
9. Mary, born in 1778, married William McColgan; had no children.
10. James, born in 1780, married Esther Simpson; moved to Missouri.
11. Abram, born in 1780, married Miss Radford; moved to Christian county, Ky. (James and Abram were twins.)
12. Elizabeth, born in 1782, married George Wilson, and moved to Indiana.
13. Nancy, born in 1785, married Mr. Robbins; moved to Indiana.

The children of James McElroy and Margaret Irvine were as follows:
1. John, died in young manhood, not married.
2. Sarah, died young.
3. Elizaheth, married General Allen.
4. Margaret, married Dr. Blythe.
5. Mary, married (first) Allen, and (second) Speed.
6. Sarah died young.
7. Nancy, died young.
8. Esther, married Felix B. Grundy.
9. James A., married Mary Irvine, and moved to Missouri.
10. William I., married Jane Muldrow, and moved to Missouri.

The ancestors of this trio of McElroy boys who married the three Irvine girls were originally from Scotland. Tradition says that during the religious persecution in Scotland three brothers, McElroys, went from Argyle and Lanark counties, Scotland, one from each county, and one from Glasgow, and settled in the county Down, Ireland, purchasing large landed estates, and from those three brothers, the McElroys in North Ireland and immigrants to America had their origin.

IRVINE ANCESTORS OF JAMES CALLAWAY.

James Callaway, is descended from William Irvine, one of the seven brothers who came to America between 1721 and 1730. William Irvine married Ann Craig, who was of noble blood, in Ireland. Three children were born to them — Johanna, Christopher, and David. William Irvine's wife died and was buried in the churchyard of Raloo, near Mounthill, Larne, Ireland, beside her daughter, Johanna, who had died a short time before. William and his two sons, Christopher and David, came to America. They landed at Philadelphia, Pa., and afterwards removed to Bedford county, Va. David Irvine came to Kentucky, and Christopher Irvine went to Wilkes county, Ga. I quote from a letter written by James Callaway, for a Southern periodical: "Christopher Irvine settled the old Irvine plantation, in 1796. It is yet in the Irvine family, owned by Luther Cason, whose wife is a lineal descendant, a great-granddaughter of Christopher's son, Isaiah Tucker Irvine. Christopher Irvine's wife was Louisa Tucker, of Virginia. This Christopher Irvine, a far-off descendant of Christopher Irvine who commanded the light horse for King James IV. at the battle of Flodden Hill, or, as Sir Walter Scott, in "Marmion," has it, "Flodden Field," was a captain of a Virginia company in the Revolutionary War, and, for service in the army, impressed a yoke of steers belonging to John Hook, a Tory, for which Hook sued him after the war. He was defended by Patrick Henry. Old-time schoolboys, like Bill Arp, Robert J. Bacon or Richard Malcolm Johnston, remember Henry's speech. In impassioned rhetoric he presented the hardships of the war, the great struggle for independence, pictured the general rejoicing of the people, and while all America was shouting for joy, for victory won, here comes one Hook, crying "Beef, beef!"

Christopher, son of William Irvine and Annie Craig, married Louisa Tucker. Issue: Charles and Isaiah Tucker.

Isaiah Tucker Irvine married Isabella Lee Barkston. Issue: Charles Mercia, Isaiah Tucker, Stephen (who died in infancy), Nancy Henderson, Prudence, Caroline Carter, Mary Anne, Martha, and Louisa.

Mary Anne Irvine, married first, John Walton. Issue: Belle, who married Robert Bacon (and who reared A. O. Bacon, U. S. Senator from Georgia), John and Stokes. After the death of John Walton, Mary Anne Irvine married Merrel Price Callaway. Issue: Merrel, Henry Irvine, James and Isaiah Tucker.

James Callaway married the accomplished and beautiful Vieva Flewellyn Furlow, daughter of Col. T. M. Furlow and Margaret Holt. Margaret Holt was the daughter of Tarplay Holt, son of Simon Holt, who had eight sons and one daughter. This only daughter married a Mr. Colquitt, and was the mother of the celebrated Walter T. Colquitt, and grandmother of General Alfred H. Colquitt.

The children of James Callaway and his wife, Vieva F. Furlow, are; Merrel, James Woodfin, Margaret Holt, Mary Irvin, Henry Irvin, Kate and Holt.

Mr. Callaway was a Confederate soldier. He responded to the call of his country at the early age of sixteen, and was quartermaster and commissary sergeant of his regiment, the Third Georgia Reserves. In South Carolina, where his regiment held Fort Coosawhatchee, the exposure to shot and shell was great. Mr. Callaway's duties required him to daily cross the bridge over the Tulafinee river and the long trestle across the swamp in shooting distance of the Federal sharpshooters. A solitary plank ran across this trestle and bridge, and each trip was fraught with danger. Though running the gauntlet of shot and shell and whizzing bullets safely, he was not proof against swamp miasma, and for weeks he lay prostrate with typho-malarial fever. Medicines there were none — not even a lemon, and nothing but pluck and the hope of meeting his mother again inspired strength to pull through that terrible ordeal.

Mr. Callaway graduated from Mercer University in 1868. After marriage he lived the quiet life of a farmer in Mitchell county, Georgia. His wife's health required a change, and in 1885 he became editor of the Albany "News and Advertiser." In the fall of 1886 he took work with the Macon "Telegraph," and is yet a member of its staff. As a writer, he is easy and graceful, and his contributions to his paper are perused with pleasure by its readers.

Mr. Callaway's mother was a glorious type of the old Southern matron. She had intellect enough to rule an empire and love enough to save the world. Her father was Isaiah Tucker Irvin, a man whose very appearance bespoke the nobleman. He was a king among men, yet so thoroughly democratic in nature and manners that the humblest approached him with ease and confidence. Indeed, his grand old home was Liberty Hall to all comers. Writing of his grandfather, Mr. Callaway says: "My grandfather was not so tall of stature, but his magnificent presence produced the impression of Louis XIV., whom people thought over six feet, but who in reality was only five feet eight inches. He

amassed a large fortune and entertained royally.   His beverage was
'cherry bounce,' and it put to shame any mint julep brewed by
the Virginians.   His home was twelve miles from Washington, Ga.
Before reaching his house you ascended a hill, on the brow of which
were large and venerable chestnut trees, with wide-spreading shades,
in front of which was his country store, from which a broad drive-
way led to the hospitable home.   Near by was the spring and that
celebrated spring-house where melons and apple cider and 'good
things' were stored."   More remarkable was Mrs. Irvin, a granddaughter of Joseph Henderson.   Of Mrs. Irvin General Robert
Toombs was especially fond, and while hiding out from the Federal
soldiery after the war, he sought on a dark night Mrs. Irvine's room
in Washington, Ga., and spent hours in conversing with her about
his own father and mother and "old times" in Wilkes county.

"It seems to my childish recollections," continues Mr. Callaway,
"that my grandfather's blacksmith shop was a half a mile from the
house, but it must not have been, for grandfather, when he wished
to give orders to 'Sol,' the blacksmith, would step to the edge of
his porch and call out, 'S-o-l, you, S-o-l-o-m-o-n!' and the response
always came, 'S-i-r!'"

In starting life, Isaiah Tucker Irvin was sometimes in need of
money.   His neighbor, Beasley, was rich, dressed in purple and
fine linen, wore a hat that told of pride of purse, on his hands were
big gloves, and he drove fine horses.   One day Major Irvin approached Beasley seated in his buggy and requested a loan of $100.
Beasley treated him rather haughtily and drove on, but not before
Major Irvin could say to him: "Beasley, I'll have my revenge."
Beasley, the fast young man, by high living and fast driving, and
careless habits came to want, and all his houses and lands and
negroes and mules and horses were put up for sale.   Everything
was knocked down to I. T. Irvin, who bought all Beasley possessed.
The sale over, Beasley approached Major Irvin and said: "Major,
you have had your revenge; allow me to redeem my family pictures."   Major Irvin turned to Beasley and said: "Yes; be a man,
Beasley, and redeem all," and Beasley turned over a new leaf.   He
became a man and redeemed his property.

This story illustrates the man, Isaiah T. Irvin.   He hurt no man
when down, but extended the hand of generosity.   His grandchildren
children love his very name, which hangs, like a memory keepsake,
around the neck of each of them.

Isaiah Tucker Irvin, son of Isaiah T. Irvin and Isabella Henderson Bankston, was born May 25, 1819, in Wilkes county, Ga. He was aboard the steamer Bayou City, plying between Galveston and Houston, along with O. L. Battle and M. P. Callaway, his brothers-in-law, going to his farm in Texas, when the steamer exploded her boiler on the night of September 27, 1860. He was seen rushing aft, and it was thought he fell overboard.

Mr. Irvin was a graduate of the State University at Athens and divided the first honors with Professor S. P. Sanford, who became the distinguished professor of mathematics of Mercer University. Mr. Irvin chose the law as his life profession, in which he became distinguished. He ranked with the first statesmen of Georgia.

His friend and neighbor, Gen. Robt. Toombs, then United States senator from Georgia, was at Hancock Superior Court when came to him the news of Irvin's death. This distinguished Senator, in subdued and saddened tone, remarked: "In Washington (Ga.), to-day, every man, woman and child, white and black, will be in mourning and in tears; and more than all, their sorrow is sincere. He was the friend of everyone, and everyone was his friend."

At the time of his death I. T. Irvin was speaker of the Georgia House of Representatives, and the Committee on Resolutions, reporting, say: "Resolved, That in his death the state has sustained incalculable loss in her public councils; this House has been deprived of a presiding officer rarely equaled and never surpassed in efficiency, fairness and courtesy; society has lost one of its most useful members, and the cause of morality and religion a faithful defender."

Mr. Irvin had served for years also in the Georgia Senate, and Gen. A R. Lawton, of Chatham, said: "I. T. Irvin was a true son of Georgia. All his heart and talents were devoted to her interest and prosperity. . . . It is a sad thing, Mr. President, to lose him in this hour of Georgia's peril. It is a sad thing that heaven can not spare those whom earth so much needs."

Mr. Turner, of Putnam, among other things so eulogistic of Speaker Irvin, said: "The highest honors of the land were clustering around his head, and the graces scarcely crowned his temples with one wreath ere the hand of patriotic friendship twined another for his blushing brow. The people of Georgia desired to have his hand at the helm. We wanted for our state executive Isaiah Tucker Irvin. We wanted our friend, but God wanted him too, and He said to His servant, Come up higher."

THE McDOWELL KINSHIP

"McDowall, McDougall, McDugall or McOul (Lord of Lorn), quarterly, first and fourth, arms: Az. a lion ramp. or; second and third or a lymphad sa., with a beacon on the topmast ppr. Crest: An arm in armour embowed fesseways, couped ppr. holding a cross crosslet fitchée. Motto: *Vincam vel mori.* — Burke.

When Mrs. Elizabeth McDowell Welch was traveling in Europe she secured and brought home with her to the United States the arms above described, from the Herald's College, London, England, as the arms belonging to the M'Dowells of this country. The motto differs from that above in that it has Vincere in place of Vincam.

The McDowells of this country and the old have intermarried with the Irvines so often that the Irvine pedigrees would hardly be complete without a short sketch of the McDowells.

"Of all the fierce and warlike septs that ranged themselves beside the Campbells, under the leadership of the chiefs of the name, in the struggles so replete with deeds of crime and heroism, of oppression and stubborn resistance, which had their fruit in the overthrow of the right line of the Stuarts, there was none more respectable, nor one which more perfectly illustrated the best qualities of their race than the sons of Dowall. Sprung from Dougall, the son of Ronald, the son of the great and famous Somerland, they had, from the misty ages, marched and fought under the cloudberry bush, as the badge of their clan, and had marshalled under the banner of the ancient Lords of Lorn, the chiefs of their race. The form of McDowell was adopted by those of the McDougal clan who held lands in Galloway, to which they, the Black Gaels, had given its name. The latter branch became allied by blood and intermarriages with the Campbells, Presbyterians of the strictest sect, and, deeply imbued with the love of civil and religious freedom which had ever characterized the followers of John Knox, they found their natural leaders in the house of Argyle. In what degree related to the chiefs of the name was the McDowell who left behind him the hills of his native Argyleshire, to settle with others of his name and kindred and religion in the north of Ireland, during the protectorate of Cromwell, can not be accurately stated; he was, so far as can be gleaned from vague traditions, one of the most reputable of the colonists who there founded the race known as the 'Scotch Irish,' the characteristics of which have since been so splendidly attested by its heroes, scholars, orators, theologians and statesmen all over the world. This Scotch colonist, McDowell, had, among other children, a son Ephraim: which of itself, indicates that he was a child of the covenant. It was fitting that Ephraim McDowell should become, at the age of sixteen years, one of the Scotch-Irish Presbyterians who flew to the defense of heroic Londonderry on the approach of McDonald of Antrim, on the 9th of December, 1688, and that he should be one of the band who closed the gates against the native Irishry, intent on blood and rapine. During the long siege that followed, the memory of which will ever bid defiance to the effacing hand of time, and in which the devoted preacher, George Walker, and the brave Murray, at the head of their undisciplined fellow-citizens — farmers, shopkeepers, mechanics and apprentices, but Protestants and Presbyterians — successfully repelled the assaults of Rosen, Marmont, Persignan and Hamilton, the McDowell was conspicuous for endurance and bravery in a band where all were brave as the most heroic Greek who fell at Thermopylæ.

"The maiden name of the woman who became the worthy helpmeet of the Londonderry soldier boy was Margaret Irvine, his own full first cousin. She was a member of an honorable Scotch family who settled in Ireland at the same time as their kinspeople — the McDowells. The names Irvin, Irvine, Irving, Irwin, and Erwin are identical — those bearing the name thus variously spelled being branches from the same tree. This name was, and is, one of note in Scotland, where those who bore it had intermarried with the most prominent families of the kingdom, breeding races of soldiers, statesmen, orators and divines."

"Ephraim McDowell, who fought at Boyne river, as well as at Londonderry, was already an elderly man when, with his two sons, John and James, his two daughters, Mary and Margaret, and numerous kinsmen and co-religionists, he emigrated to America to build for himself and his a new home. . . . The exact date of his arrival in Pennsylvania is not known. Certain it is that, about 1729, Ephraim and his family, and numerous other McDowells, Irvines, Campbells, McElroys and Mitchells, came over and settled in the same Pennsylvania county.   T. M. GREEN."

The strong traits of character that marked the personality of the first McDowells and Irvines, distinguishes them still, and the love of warfare, that seems to lie at the very root of their nature, has made their names famous in all the wars of this country.

MAJOR HENRY CLAY McDOWELL.

Prominent among the distinguished McDowells of Kentucky, and of the United States, is Major Henry C. McDowell of Lexington.

Major McDowell is a direct descendant of John Irvine, the immigrant, who came to America together with the seven Irvine brothers who arrived in this country in 1729. Ephraim McDowell, who married his cousin, Margaret Irvine, and who fought at Boyne River, or "Boyne Water," as the Irish say, and at Londonderry, came to America with the Campbells, McElroys, Mitchells and Irvines, all related to one another.

Abram Irvine was the son of John Irvine, the immigrant. The daughter of Abram Irvine and Mary Dean, Anna, married Samuel McDowell. Major Henry C. McDowell is a grandson of Samuel McDowell and Anna Irvine. I copy a short notice of Major McDowell which appeared in a volume of "Kentucky Biographies:"

"Henry Clay McDowell, son of William Adair McDowell and Maria Hawkins Harvey, born in Fincastle county, Virginia, in 1832, coming to Kentucky in 1839, when his father returned to his native State. He graduated at the Louisville Law School, and won his way to a successful practice in his profession, being for some years a partner of his brother-in-law, Judge Bland Ballard. He was among the earliest in Kentucky to take up arms for the Union on breaking out of the Civil War, and was commissioned by Mr. Lincoln as assistant Adjutant General, and served on the staff of Gen. Rousseau and Gen. Boyle. He was afterwards commissioned by Mr. Lincoln as United States Marshal for Kentucky, being the same office held by his grandfather, Samuel McDowell, under commission of General Washington.

"He married Anna Clay, daughter of Lieutenant-Colonel Henry Clay, who was killed at the battle of Buena Vista, and was a son of the matchless orator, Henry Clay.

"Major McDowell purchased Ashland, the home of his wife's grandfather, and lives at ease, devoting himself to agricultural pursuits, and giving some attention to the Lexington & Eastern Railway Company, of which he is president. In politics he was first a Whig, later a Republican.

"Major McDowell appears yet in his prime. The time to do him justice is far distant, it is to be hoped, as no man's history can be rightly written until his biographer may look from the beginning of his life to its close."

Another descendant of the same line as Major H. C. McDowell, was the late Judge Alexander Keith Marshall McDowell, who lies buried at Cynthiana, Ky. He was born in Mercer county, Kentucky, in 1806. He was a soldier in the Black Hawk War and a soldier in the Confederate army in time of the late Civil War. Judge McDowell was as near perfect manhood as a human being could be. He was a scholar, a soldier, and a true Christian. At the time of his death it was said of him: Judge McDowell has bequeathed to his descendants a legacy of far more worth than the long line of ancestry from which he came, or the armorial bearing that would have been carved above his place of repose had he died in Scotland, the father of his people — a spotless name. Carve above his tomb, "*Resurgam.*" He was a true Christian.

MAJOR AND DOCTOR HERVEY McDOWELL.

Dr. Hervey McDowell is the son of Capt. John Lyle McDowell and his wife, Nancy Vance. Major McDowell combines in a remarkable degree the traits of his family. About his manner there is a quiet reserve and a bearing that impress thoughtful observers with a certain knowledge that he is a thorough gentleman, incapable of falsehood, without fear, and full of all the amenities of life.

He graduated, in 1856, at a military school at Frankfort, Ky., and later at a celebrated medical college in St. Louis, Mo.

He was, in the late Civil War, commissioned Major in the Confederate Army and fought from its beginning to its close with the most dauntless courage. So much for the man in whose veins runs the blood of Dougall the son of Ranald. Macdougall or Macdugall, a clan who derive their name from Ranald the son of the famous Somerled. The name Dhu Gall, means dark complexioned stranger. The chiefs were generally styled De Ergadia, or Lords of Lorn. The Clan badge was the cloudberry bush. The Macdougalls are not mentioned in history till 1284. In the list of those who attended the convention of that year we find the name of Alexander de Ergadia, and it is supposed that his presence was the consequence of his holding his lands by crown charter. Another form of the name is MacDowall — used especially by those of the race who held lands in Galloway, to which district the Dhu Galls, or black Gaels, are said to have given its name.

At the time that Robert Bruce asserted his claim to the throne of Scotland, the name of the Chief was Alexander. He had married the third daughter of the Red Comyn, whom Bruce slew in the Dominican church at Dumfries. In consequence, he became the mortal enemy of the King. After his defeat at Methvin on June 19, 1306, when Bruce with only 300 followers, approached the borders of Argyleshire, he was attacked by Macdougall of Lorn, at the head of 1,000 men, part of whom were MacNabs, who had joined the party of John Balliol, and after a severe conflict, was compelled to abandon the field. The battle was fought at a place called Dalree, and in retreat, one of the Macdougalls having come up with the King, seized hold of his plaid, which was fixed across his breast by a large brooch. In the struggle which ensued the man was killed, but the plaid and brooch were left in his dying grasp. The latter, under the title of "The Brooch of Lorn," was long preserved by chiefs of the Macdougalls, and after having been carried off in the civil war has been restored to the family. In the " Life of Bruce" (vol. I. pages 18-18) will be found other instances of the unrelenting enmity of the Macdougalls to the King.

To punish the hostile clan, Bruce, in 1308, proceeded into Argyleshire, but found John of Lorn, son of Alexander, with a band of followers posted at the narrow pass Cruachan Ben, between Loch Awe and Loch Etine. Having sent a party to threaten them in front and he succeeded in putting them to flight. The chief of the Macdougalls, who was, during the action, on board a small vessel on Loch Etine, took refuge in his castle of Dunstaffnage. After laying waste the territory of Lorn, Bruce laid siege to the castle, which he soon surrounded, and the Lord of Lorn was compelled to swear homage to the King. John, his son, however, refused to submit, and took refuge in England. Being appointed by King Edward II. to the command of the English fleet, John, after the battle of Bannockburn, sailed with it to the Western Isles. Thither Bruce, on his return from Ireland, directed his course, and to avoid the necessity of doubling the Mull of Kintyre, he sailed up Loch Fyne to Tarbet with his own galleys, which he caused to be dragged across the narrow isthmus which connects Kintyre with Knapdale, by means of a slide of smooth planks of trees laid parallel to each other. It is said he was induced to do so by a superstitious belief, that had long been entertained amongst the inhabitants of the Western Islands, that they should never be subdued till their invaders sailed across this narrow neck of land. The islanders were quickly subdued, the English fleet dispersed, and John of Lorn captured and imprisoned in Dumbarton Castle, and afterwards in the Castle of

Lochleven, where he died. His son, John of Ervin, the last Macdougall of Lorn, married a niece of David II., and was restored to the ancient possessions of his family, which had been forfeited. He died without male issue. He had two daughters. One of them married Robert Stewart, founder of the Rosyth family, who obtained through her the district of Lorn, which he sold to his brother, the husband of the other daughter, John Stewart of Innermeath, ancestor of the Stewarts, Lords of Lorn.

Chieftainship now passed to Macdougall of Dunolly, brother to Ewen, the last Lord. The Macdougalls adhered to the cause of Charles I., and suffered much for their loyalty. In 1715, they took part in the insurrection of the Earl of Mar, and in consequence the Chief was attainted. Just previous to the rebellion of 1745, the estate was restored to the family, which prevented them from joining in the rebellion of that year. The force of the Macdougalls of that period was estimated at 200 men.

The Macdougalls of Raray, represented by Macdougall of Ardincaple, were a branch house of Lorn. The principal cadets of the family of Donolly were those of Gallanach and Soroba. The line of the Macdougalls of Markerston, Roxburgshire, terminated in an heiress, who married General Sir Thomas Brisbane, baronet, who in her right, assumed the name of Makdougall.

*   *   *   *   *   *   *

Sir Thomas Makdougall Brisbane, a general in the army, succeeded his father on his death in 1812, and in 1819 he married Anna Maria, only daughter of Sir Henry Hay Makdougall, baronet, of Markerstoun and Roxburghshire, a kinsman of Sir Walter Scott, and representative of one of the most ancient families in Scotland, and on his death, he succeeded, in right of his wife, to his extensive and valuable domains, when he assumed the name of Makdougall, before his own, being authorized by sign manual, dated August 14, 1826.

CARLISLE OR CARLYLE.

The first of this name in Scotland was one of the English colonists brought by Robert de Brus into Annandale, when he obtained a grant of that district from King David II. In the reign of William the Lion, one Endo de Carlyle was witness to a charter of mortification, by Eustace de Vesey, of twenty shillings per annum out of the will of Sprouston to the monastery of Kelso, about 1207. Adam de Carleolo had a charter of several land properties in Annan-

Hon. John G. Carlisle

dale from William de Brus, who died 1215. Gilbert de Carlyle was was one of the Scottish Barons who swore fealty to King Edward I., 1296. Sir William de Carlyle obtained in marriage the Lady Margaret Bruce, one of the daughters of Robert, Earl of Carrick, and sister of King Robert the Bruce, as appears by charter of that monarch to them of the lands of Crumanston, in which she is designated "our dearest sister." Their son, William Carlyle, received a charter from Robert the First, under the name of William Karlo, the King's sister's son, of the lands of Culyn, now Callin, in the County of Dumfries. He also possessed the lands of Rouean in the vicinity. There are now two villages bearing these names in the vicinity of Dumfries.

William Cairleil was one of the numerous train of knights and esquires who attended Princess Margaret of Scotland, daughter of James I., into France, on her marriage to Louis the Dauphin, in 1436.

Sir John Carlyle of Torthorwald, the first Lord Carlyle, was active in repelling the invasion of the banished Douglases in 1455, when James, Earl of Douglas, entered Scotland with a considerable force, by the West Marches, and being met in Annandale by the Earl of Angus, the lord Carlyle of Torthorwald, Sir Adam Johnston of Johnston, and other barons, sustained a complete loss. Archibald, Earl of Moray, one of his brothers, was killed, and Hugh, Earl of Drumond, another of them, was taken prisoner by Lord Carlyle and the Laird of Johnston, for which service King James II. granted them the land of Pettinain in Lanarkshire. He sat as Lord Carlyle in the parliament of November and December, 1475. He was subsequently sent on an embassy to France, and in recompense for the great expense attending it, he had several grants from the crown in 1477. Among others, he received a charter of the lands of Drumcall, forfeited by Alexander Boyd. On the accession of James IV., these lands were claimed by the King, as pertaining to his eldest son and his successors, by letters of annexation made of Drumcoll — perpetually to remain with the Kings of Scotland, and princes, their sons, — previous to the grant of the same to Lord Carlyle, and on January 19, 1488, the Lords auditors decreed that the said lands of Drumcoll were the king's property. His Lordship died before December, 22, 1509. He was twice married. By his first wife, Janet, he had two sons John and Robert, and a daughter, Margaret, married to Simon Carruthers of Monswald. His second wife, Margaret Douglas, widow of Sir Edward Maxwell of Monreith, had also two sons to him, namely John and George. John, Master of Carlyle, the eldest son, died before his father, leaving a son, William, second Lord Carlyle, who was one of three persons invested with the honor of knighthood, January 29, 1488, when Alexander, second son of King James the Third, was created Duke of Ross. By Janet Maxwell, his wife, daughter of Lord Maxwell, he had two sons, James, third Lord, and Michael, fourth Lord Carlyle. Michael Carlyle joined the association for the support of the authority of King James VI., in 1567. Soon after, he joined Queen Mary's party and entered into the association on her behalf, at Hamilton, May 8, 1568.

He had three sons, namely : William, Master of Carlyle, Michael, and Peter. His eldest son, William, died in 1572, in the lifetime of his father, leaving an only child, Elizabeth Carlyle, who married Sir James Douglas of Parkhead, slain by James Stewart on High street, Edinburgh, July 31, 1608. On the death of his eldest son, Lord Carlyle granted a charter of alienation of the barony of Carlyle, etc., in favor of Michael, his second son, dated at Torthorwald, March, 14, 1573, to which Adam Carlyle of Bridekirk, Alexander, his son, John Carlyle of Brakenquhat, and Peter Carlyle, the third son, were witnesses. Of the family of Bridekirk, here mentioned, the late Dr. Alexander Carlyle, of Inveresk, a notice of whom follows, was the male representative. The above settlement of the estate was effected only after a long litigation, at a ruinous expense, and the barony of Carlyle was, on the death of the fourth Lord in 1580, found to belong to his granddaughter, Elizabeth, already mentioned, who thus succeeded to the peerage in her own right. A charter was granted to George Douglas, second legitimate son of George Douglas of Parkhead, of the Barony of Carlyle, etc., in the Counties of Dumfries and Lanark, dated on the last day of February, 1594. It is supposed that he acquired the estate from his brother, Sir James, who, as above stated, married the heiress of the title and estates, and had three sons, Sir James, Archibald, and John, the two latter of whom died without issue.

Sir James Douglas, the eldest son, was, in right of his mother, created Lord Carlyle of Torthorwald, in 1609. He married, first, Grizel, youngest daughter of Sir John Gordon, of Lochinvar, by whom, it is said, he had a son, William, who sold his estate and died abroad without issue; secondly, Anne Saltonstall, and by her he had a son, James, baptized in Edinburgh, January 2, 1621. According to Crawford, James, Lord Carlyle, resigned his title in 1638 to William, Earl of Queensberry, who had acquired his estate.

The Hon. Henry J. Furber, Jr., Chicago.

In 1730, William Carlyle of Lochantur, in the stewartry of Kirk-cudbright, was served heir to Michael, fourth Lord of Carlyle, as descended from Michael, his second lawful son. This William Carlyle died about 1757, and was succeeded by his brother, Michael Carlyle of Lochantur, who on his death, left his estate to the heir male of the family. By a decree of the House of Lords, in 1770, the heir male was found to be George Carlyle, whose ancestor lived in Wales. In him also, it was thought, lay the right of the peerage; but after dissipating his estate in Dumfries, in a few years, he returned to Wales. The Rev. Joseph D. Carlyle, professor of Arabic in Cambridge University, and who died in 1831, was understood to be the next heir.

This surname has acquired considerable literary luster from its being borne by Thomas Carlyle, a celebrated contemporary author, a native of Dumfriesshire.

McDougall's History of Dumfries says: "The Carleils, or Carlyles trace their descent from Crinus Erevine (see ante). A fresh luster has been cast upon this old Annandale family by Thomas Carlyle, the distinguished author."

And this historian may add that Hon. John G. Carlisle, of New York City, proved that blood, like water, can rise as high as its source. John G. Carlisle was Governor of Kentucky, Senator, in Congress of the United States, and many years United States Treasurer under President Cleveland, and was, in his day, the most eloquent man in America and second to none, in his country, as advocate.

IRVINES IN WISCONSIN.

ROBERT IRWIN was the son of John, youngest brother of Robert, who married Elizabeth Wylie, and belonged to the House of Bonshaw, Irish Branch. He was the son of Rev. John, of Coushindal.

ROBERT IRWIN married Sarah Miller in Ireland. Emigrated from Dublin in 1776 with son Robert, 6 months of age. Their children were Robert and Mary. Robert, b. in Ireland, Nov. 15, 1775; died July 19, 1852; m. in Carlisle, Pa., 1796, to Catherine Singer, b. Sept. 5, 1781; died April 9, 1843 in Green Bay, Wis. They had issue:

Robert, b. December 24, 1797, in Carlisle, Pa., died July 9, 1833, at U. S. Indian Agency, Ft. Winnebago, Mich. Ter. (Now Wisconsin); m. in Erie, Pa., Hannah Reese, 1820, born

Erie, Pa., July 29, 1802, died April 17, 1886, at Muskegon, Mich. Children:

Mary, b. Green Bay, June ——; (an historic character, being the first white child of resident parents in Wisconsin); died August, 1903; m. Wm. Mitchell. They had children:

  a. Jessie, b. Green Bay; m. Theodore E. Harris, in Green Bay.

    (a.) Emily, b. Green Bay; m. Frank Murphy in Green Bay; died ——, Green Bay.

    (b.) A son, born and died young in Green Bay; Emily b. Green Bay.

  b. William, b. Green Bay.

  c. Adeline, b. Green Bay; m. Frederick Babcock in Green Bay, Wisconsin. Had children:

    (a). Adeline, b. Green Bay, died in Kenosha, Wis.; m. first, Bavid Blish, drowned in Lake Michigan. Children:

      a. Mary Augusta, b. Kenosha, Wis.

      b. Irwin, b. Kenosha, Wis., died ——

    Adeline, married, second, W. S. Strong in Kenosha, Wis. Children:

      a. William E. Strong, m. Minnie Martin; resides in Kenosha.

  d. Rebecca Jane, b. Green Bay; died in Muskegon, Mich.; m. Luther Whitney. Had children:

    (a). Grace, died in infancy in Green Bay.

    (b). George, b. ——; died in Chicago about 1900.

    (c). Dyche, b. ——; m. Julia Hill; resides in Chicago.

  e. Louis Cass, b. Green Bay, died ——; m. Nellie Walker.

2. Alexander J., second son of Catherine and Robert Irwin, b. Greensburgh, Pa., March 1, 1799; died in Green Bay, June 14, 1847; m. Francis Pamilia Smith in Ft. Howard (now Green Bay), December 2, 1827. She b. Ballston Spring, N. Y., November 8, 1809; died in Kenosha, Wis.; interred in Green Bay. They had issue:

(1.) Maria Jane, b. Green Bay, m. Charles L. Wheelock, b. Ogdensburg, N. Y., died in Milwaukee, Wis. They had children:

  a. Francis Irwin, b. Green Bay, died in infancy.

  b. Charles Alexander, b. Green Bay, m. Kate Irwin.

1. Marie J. Wheelock.
2. Dwight Irwin Fallett.
3. Catherine Frances Robinson.
4. Kate Irwin Wheelock.
5. Catherine Irwin Fallett.
6. Mary Irwin Mitchell.*
7. Elizabeth Frances Whitney.
8. Jessie Ann Mitchell Harris.
9. Emilie Virginia Irwin.
*First white child born in Wisconsin.

Their children were: Charles Alexander, b. Green
Bay; m. Kate Irwin. Their children were Frances
Irwin, Guy Matson and Kate.

(2.) Kate Irwin, b. Green Bay, resides in New York. Unmarried.

(3.) Elizabeth Frances, b. Green Bay; m. Joshua Whitney,
resides in Green Bay. Their children:

a. Alexander Irwin, died in infancy.

b. Emmeline Henshaw; b. Green Bay, m. Walter C. Calhoun in Green Bay, resides in Buffalo. Issue:

(a.) George Whitney, b. Green Bay, ——

c. Robert Alexander, b. Green Bay, died in Belle Plaine,
Minn.; m. Celia A. Chatfield in Belle Plaine, Minn.
Had issue:

(a). Frank Irwin, b. Belle Plaine, m. Lizzie —— in Belle
Plaine. Children:

(a). Frances Chatfield, b. Belle Plaine.

(b). Henry, b. Belle Plaine.

b. Andrew Gould, b. in Belle Plaine; m.; have eight
children.

c. Elvira Furber, b. Belle Plaine; m. Wilson Martin in
Belle Plaine. They have children:

(a.) Frances, b. Belle Plaine ——

(b.) Florence, b. Belle Plaine. ——

d. Charles Wheelock, b. Belle Plaine, m. ——

e. Alexander J., b. Belle Plaine, m. ——; children:

(a.) Mary, 6th, died in infancy.

(b.) Oscar, 7th, died in infancy.

(4.) Cynthia Elvira, b. Green Bay; m. Henry J. Furber, b.
Rochester, N. H., in Green Bay, Wisconsin. Children:

a. William Elbert, b. Green Bay.

b. Henry Jewett, b. Green Bay, Lawyer.

c. Frank Irwin, b. Tenafly, N. J.; m. Clara Proby, in
Chicago, Ill. All residing in Chicago.

(5.) Harriete Brown, b. Green Bay; resides Green Bay, unmarried.

(6.) Horace Smith, b. Green Bay, died in infancy.

(7.) Emilie Virginia, b. Green Bay, resides there; unmarried.

3. James, third son of Robert and Catherine Irwin, died in infancy.

4. Samuel, fourth son, b. Erie, Pa., March 17, 1803; unmarried,

died at Ft. Winnebago, February 14, 1845; buried in Green
Bay.

1. Mary, first daughter of Robert and Catherine Irwin, b. Erie,
Pa., June 29, 1805; m. Captain John Burnham in Green
Bay, 1826. Had children:

(1). Ellen, died in infancy.

(2.) Ann, died in infancy.

(3.) Harriet, died young in Green Bay.

2. Elizabeth, second daughter, b. in Erie, Pa., September 3, 1807;
died February 20, 1891, at DePere, Wis.; m. William Dickinson, in Green Bay, June 23, 1825. He died in 1848. They
had children:

(1.) Catherine, died young.

(2.) Mary Jane, b. De Pere; m. Col. Maurice Maloney, U. S. A.,
in Green Bay.

(3.) William, b. De Pere, drowned in Fox River when young.

(4.) Charles, b. De Pere, died ——; m. Marcena Newton in
Green Bay.

(5.) Robert, b. De Pere, m., —— Lawton.

(6.) Zachary Taylor, b. De Pere ——; died —— m. ——

3. Jane, third daughter of Robert and Catherine Irwin, b. Erie, Pa.,
December 4, 1810; died October 2, 1894; m. John V. Suydam, January 2, 1833, in Green Bay; died November 14,
1885. Had children:

(1.) Robert Irwin, b. Green Bay, died in infancy.

(2.) Catherine Frances, b. Green Bay, died 1901; m. Albert
C. Robertson in Green Bay. They had children:

a. Jennie, b. Green Bay ——   m. Henry Weare in Green
Bay.

b. Abblie, b. Green Bay —— resides there; unmarried.

c. Emily, b. Green Gay,; resides there; unmarried.

d. Virginie, b. Green Bay — m. —Holbrook in Green
Bay. Children: John Suydam, b.——.

(3.) Charles David, b. Green Bay; m. Susan Scott; had
children:

a. Marie, b. Green Bay. ——

b. Blanche, b. Green Bay; m. Henry Strong; resides in
La Grange, Illinois.

c. Letha, b. Green Bay; m. Fredriche Allan, resides in
La Grange, Illinois. Their children: Edith and
Helen.

1. Robert Irwin, Sr. 1775–1852. 3. Henry J. Furber, Sr.
2. Mrs. Elvira Irwin Furber. 4. Alexander Johnson Irwin, 1799–1847

4. Catherine, fourth daughter of Robert and Catherine Irvin, b. Detroit, Michigan Ter., October 19, 1817; d. October 14, 14, 1894, in Green Bay, Wis.; m. Emmons W. Follett, November 8, 1838.   Their children:

(1.) Dwight Irwin, b. Green Bay; died there; m. Rosamunde Brown; d. Green Bay. Had issue:

a. John, b. Green Bay.

1. MARY IRWIN, daughter of Robert and Sarah (Miller) Irwin, was born in Carlisle, Pa., January 20, 1782; died in Erie, Pa., November 21, 1869, aged 87 years, 10 mos. 1 day. She married John Clemens, who was born in Armagh, Ireland, and died in Waterford, Erie Co., Pa., October 7, aged 60 years. Their children:

(1.) Letitia, b. Dec. 16, 1799; m. February, 1823 to Wm. Boyd; died April 8, 1837.

(2.) William J., b. June 11, 1802; died July 9, 1875.

(3.) Sarah, b. September 16, 1864; m. Archibald Thompson, November, 21, 1827; died April 14, 1889.

(4.) Mary Ann., b. April 8, 1807; died May 14, 1875.

(5.) Robert Irwin, b. August 16, 1809; died November 24, 1814.

(6.) Amelia, b. January 23, 1812; m. Moses Curtis, died December 1, 1886. Had children: Myra, b. Waterford; unmarried; a son, who died February, 1904.

2. Elizabeth Irwin, b. April 23, 1814, died 1903, in Erie, Pa.; m. William W. Eaton, May 25, 1841. Had children:

(1.) Emma, b. Erie, Pa.; m. — Hay.

(2.) daughter, —— b. Erie, Pa.

(3.) son, —— b. Erie, Pa.

3. Sophia Reed, b. July 27, 1816; m. in Erie, William M. Caughey, March 3, 1842; died, April 9, 1892. Had issue:

(1.) Agnes, b. Erie, Pa.; m. Thomas Walker.

(2.) Josephine, b. Erie, Pa.; —— died —— m. —— Witters.

(3.) Clemens, b. Erie, Pa. His children:

a. Elenore, b. Erie, Pa.; resides in New York.

b. John, b. Aug. 18, 1818; died July 24, 1892; m. Lydia Hutchinson; had issue:

(a.) Rinaldo E., b. Erie, Pa.

From "Who's Who In America."

Furber, Henry Jewett, Jr., lawyer, born Green Bay, Wis., 1866; s. Henry Jewett and Elvira (Irwin)F.; grad. Univ. of Chicago, B. S., 1886; studied Univs. of Berlin, 1886-7, Vienna, 1887-8, Leipsic, 1888-9, Halle, 1889-90 (A. M., Bowdoin Coll.; A. M., and Ph.D. magna cum laude, Halle); studied law Northwestern Univ. Law Sch. and office of Geo. S. Steers; unmarried. Prof. Economics, Northwestern Univ., 1892-4; in France and Italy, 1894-6; was instrumental in opening univs. of France to foreigners on same basis as those of Germany; 1st vice-pres. Nat. Life Ins. Co. of Washington, 1897-1900; admitted to bar, 1897; since member of law firm of Steere & Furber (now of law firm Furber & Wakelee). Elected 1901 pres. Internat. Olympian Games of 1904. Chevalier of Legion of Honor, France; mem. Chicago Academy of Sciences, Chicago Literary Society, Am. Economic Assn., Chicago Yacht Club, Columbia Yacht Club. Write: Geschichte der Oekonomischen Theorien in Amerika, 1891 (Doctor's thesis, Halle); also many contributions to econom. jours. Residence: 816 Pullman Building. Office, 1001 New York Life Bldg., Chicago.

THE FAMILY OF MATHEW IRWIN.

MATHEW IRWIN, Sr., was a native of Ireland who came to America before the Revolution (1775-1783), and made his home at Philadelphia, Pa., and although quite young, he took a prominent part in that war, that founded a great Republic, that now stretches from sea to sea. He loaned money to the Government, then barely existing, and in the struggle for independence he was as brave as any, and no soldier appealed to him for aid in vain. He was appointed to offices of trust, but not profit, as the records tell. He was Quartermaster General of the State of Pennsylvania, in 1777-1781; he was Port Warden of Philadelphia, in 1785, and served for several years, as Master of the Rolls and Recorder of Deeds in Philadelphia. He married a sister of Thomas Mifflin, who was a General in the Revolution, and later was Governor of Pennsylvania.

THOMAS IRWIN, the eldest son of Mathew Irwin, was U. S. District Judge of West Pennsylvania. Another son was a merchant in Philadelphia. His third son, Mathew, Jr., was born, reared educated in that city, and afterwards held a Government position in Chicago, Ill. In 1813, he was appointed Assistant Commissary of Purchases for the Army in the War of 1812, serving in that capacity until the war closed in 1815. In 1816 he was stationed at Green Bay, it being a Military Post. He was commissioned by Gov. Cass, in 1818, as first Chief Justice and Judge of Probate, and held the position until 1820. In 1816 he married Miss Mary Walker of Uniontown, Pa. He died in Unionton, Pa., aged 75 years. He left three sons and two daughters. One daughter married Judge Hogan and settled in Quincy, California. One son went to Missouri; another, Col. M. W. Irvin, was editor of a periodical in Uniontown, Pa. and later, editor of the St. Louis *Union*. He died at St. Paul, Minn, November 23, 1858, at the early age of 38 years. Rilands, the youngest son, lived in California, and was a member of the Legislature of that State. Judge David Irvine held the first court in the county at Portage in 1841.

IRVINES OF PENNSYLVANIA.

WILLIAM IRWIN came from Dublin, Ireland, in the time of the American Revolution (1775–1783), and made his home either at Philadelphia, or in New Jersey. William Irwin married a Miss Perry, first cousin to Commodore O. H. Perry. He was living in Eastern Pennsylvania when his three sons and one daughter were born, namely: William H., John, James and Mary, who married a Jordon. James Perry Irwin, of Erie, Pa., is the son of William H. Irwin.

The great grandfather of Dr. F. H. Erwin, of Bethlehem, Penn., was Col. Arthur Erwin, who, for services under Gen. Putnam in time of the Revolution, received from the government extensive land grants, in Bucks county, Pennsylvania (at which place he made his home), and in Luzerne county, Pa., and greater still in the county of Steuben, N. Y., where he has many descendants at the towns of Bath, Erwin Centre and Painted Post. Dr. F. H. Erwin mentions a Col. Harper Erwin, who is on the staff of the Governor of North Carolina, who is of the Scotch-Irish Branch of the Erwins, or Irvines.

In a letter from Miss Edith Irvin, Royal House, Kingstown, Ireland, the facts following are to be gleaned: William Irvin was the eldest of ten children; his brothers were Robert, Henry, Hastings, and Crommelin; his sisters, Eliza, Maria, Alice, Fanny and Harriet. (Wm. Irvin was Miss Edith Irvin's great-great-grandfather.) William Irvin's arms are same as those of Drum. Crommelin, my great-grandfather, of Carrowdose Castle, County Down, Ireland, married Mrs. S. Dalachnoes, who was of a fine old French family. My great-great-grandfather, William, and perhaps his brother, Robert, lived at an old family seat called Mt. Irvin, County Armagh,

Ireland (where Miss Edith was born). "My first cousin, Henry Irvin, is a Judge, just home from India; his brother George holds a place, under government, in the Secret Service of India. Rev. Blaney Irvin was my grandfather's brother. He had three sons and three daughters. Rev. Robert and Major Henry in Dublin, Ireland, and William in Galway. Elizabeth Irvin did not marry. — (name of second daughter not given); the third daughter of Rev. Blaney Irvin married Col. Browne, brother to Felicia Dorothea Browne, the celebrated poetess.

John Irwin, Jr., P. A. Paymaster, U. S. N., writes from U. S. S. Essex, Navy Yard, N. J.:

"My great-grandfather was John Irwin, one of the founders of Pittsburg, Pa.; his son William Wallace Irvin, my grandfather, was Mayor of Pittsburg, member of Congress, and U. S. Minister to Denmark. His son, John Irwin, my father (lately passed away), entered the U. S. Navy and retired in 1894 with the rank of Rear Admiral. My father's half-brother is now living in Japan, where he is one of the foremost of foreign-born citizens, he being very wealthy. He married a Japanese lady. My ancestors were Scotch, as our crest will show — a hand holding a thistle. Motto: "*Nemo me impune lascessit.*"

Descended from the House of Bonshaw, Irish Branch, is Col. J. B. D. Irvin of Chicago, Ill. He writes, among other things relating to the American Irvines: "My notes show that 200 Irvines have served as commissioned officers in the Army and Navy of the U. S. since 1775.

U. S. Recruiting Office, 75 West Fort Street.

DETROIT MICHIGAN, June 14, 1904.

MY DEAR MADAM: I am in receipt of your kind letter of May 23rd ult., and desire to thank you for same. Your letter having been addressed to the Army and Navy Club, New York, was duly forwarded to me here, where I have been stationed since last November, and where I hope to remain till sometime in the fall of next year. I was much interested in the circular and prospectus of the book on the Irvine family, and I shall subscribe for same when published. In regard to pedigree, I may say I know but little of my father's people. He was born in the County Down, Ireland, about 1816 or 1817. He studied under Dr. Chalmers in Edinburgh, after going through Queen's College in Belfast. He was sent to New Brunswick by the Irish Presbyterian Church. From there he went to other Churches in Canada and the United States, and finally settled in Augusta, Georgia, where he died in 1881. He married in 1845, a Miss Orr, daughter of Robert Orr, a barrister of the Four Courts, in Dublin, and a son, I believe, of Archdeacon Orr. One of my names is Crombie, who was grandfather of my mother, Rev. D. Crombie, who, I understand, was from Perthshire in Scotland, but of whose history I know little. I have heard he was connected with a family named Dalrymple. Perhaps you could give me some data in connection with these people.

I am a Major in the 9th United States Infantry, a Regiment having had service in the Philippines, Cuba and China, where it was associated with many of the foreign armies, English, French, Russian, German and Japanese, in the Boxer days, in 1900 and 1901. I was not present with it on that occasion, but went through with it the Samar Campaign of 1901 and 1902, in the Southern Philippines. At present I am detached on recruiting duty in this city. By addressing me, care of the Military Secretary, U. S. Army, Washington, D. C., I can always be found, as all our movements are controlled from his office. I showed the circular to Mr. William H. Irvine, a lawyer in this city, and he intends to get up some data also. His address is, No. 6, Moffat Building, this city. With many thanks for your courtesy, I remain, very sincerely yours,

R. J. C. IRVINE.

IRISH BRANCH OF THE HOUSE OF BONSHAW.

"Of these Irvines of Bonshaw are the most part of the Scotch Irvines descended, and those of Ireland in a very near line, especially Sir Gerard Irvine's family, his father being Christopher Irvine, who was bred a lawyer, or advocate, at the Temple, in London, and was the first of the family that settled in Ireland, upon a grant of some lands given him in the northwest parts of Ulster (near the great lakes of Erne), by King James, Sixth of Scotland and First of England, soon after his coming to the English crown. There he built Castle Irvine, which was destroyed by the Irish in the Rebellion of 1641, but was since rebuilt by his son, Sir Gerard Irvine, Bart. Sir Gerard's mother was Blanche Irvine, eldest daughter of Edward Irvine, that was Laird, and built the House of Stapletown. Edward was second son to Edward of Bonshaw, and grandchild to Christopher Irvine, the Laird of Bonshaw who commanded the Light Horse at Solway Moss, 1542, against the English, and was there killed.

"Sir Gerard's grandfather was John Irvine, who married a daughter of the Laird of Johnston, the chief of that ancient family (now Earls of Annandale). He died young ; he was son to Christopher Irvine, commonly called "Black Christy" of Robgill and Annan, which land belonged to him, a man of considerable repute in those days. He was son to Christopher Irvine, Laird of Bonshaw, who commanded the Light Horse at Solway Moss (as aforesaid) where he, with most of his sons, brothers, and friends, were killed by the treachery of some of the Scotch nobility against their King, James V. (who outlived his defeat but a few days, and died from grief over it), and his General, Oliver Sinclaire. At the said battle, Irvine and his Light Horse defeated the English advance party, and gallantly charged into the main body, thinking the Scots Army was following him; but, through the treachery of the Maxwells, and others, he was left to himself and cut off with his whole party. He was buried in the church of Gretna, with divers friends who were killed with him, and under his command, and his monument and epitaph are still to be seen. This Christopher was son to Christopher, and grandson to Christopher of Bonshaw, who had the same command at the fields of Flodden in 1513, against the English (where King James IV. was slain, with many of the Scotch nobility). Here he and all the male Irvines of the House of Bonshaw that were able to carry arms, were killed and few left to preserve the name but those children unborn."— (Dr. Christopher Irvine, Historiographer to King Charles II. and Historian of Scotland 1678.

In 1610 King James appointed Gerard Lowther to be Judge of the Court of Common Pleas in Ireland. And this circumstance led to the settlement in that country, not only of Gerard Lowther himself, but also of his relatives, Lancelot Carleton and Christopher Irvine, thus changing the destiny which the latter had intended for himself. For, at this period, the plantation of Ulster was in operation; extensive tracts of land forfeited, in the rebellion of O'Neil of Tyrone, were disposed by the Crown to British undertakers to whom they were conveyed, and transferred from one to another. These conveyances and transfers were confirmed by Royal Letters Patent, and by the Lords Justices and Council of Ireland, through the Commissioners appointed for the Plantation. Accordingly, in this manner, Gerard Lowther, Christopher Irvine and Lancelot Carleton, obtained property in Ireland in the year 1613. Their lands adjoined each other and were situated near the Lower lake Erne, in the Barony of Coolemakernon or Lurg, County Fermanagh.

Christopher Irvine settled finally at Portage, or Lowtherstown, lately founded by Gerard Lowther, its previous owner, who sold it to Christopher Irvine for a term of years; afterwards purchased this property in perpetuity. Christopher died in 1666 and was buried with his wife, Blanche, daughter of Edward Irvine, Laird of Bonshaw, in the family burying place in this churchyard at Irvinestown. He left three sons, Christopher of Edinburgh, Gerard of Ardstron, County Tyrone, who succeeded him, and William of Ballindullagh, County Fermanagh.

General Irvine, second son of Christopher Irvine, was distinguished for his services against the rebels during the Irish Rebellion of 1641.

PRESIDENT BENJAMIN HARRISION'S IRVINE DESCENT.

(From the Library of Newberg, Pa,)

James Irwin, of the Peters township, Cumberland, now in Franklin county, made his will May 24, 1776. It was probated April 28, 1778. In it he mentions his wife Jean and children as follows:

1, Joseph; 2, James; 3, Archibald, who married Jean M'Dowell; 4, Elizabeth, twice married — first, William McConnell, second, Aaron Torrence; 5, Mary, married William Nesbitt; 6, John, married Martha Maclay; 7, Jean married John Baggs; 8, Lydia married Moses, Porter (had children, Phineas and Jean), 9; Margaret, married Thomas Patton; 10, Martha, married John Paull. The executors of the estate were one son, James Irwin, and son-in-law, William Nesbitt.

ARCHIBALD IRWIN, son of James Irwin, great-grandfather of President Harrison, was born in the north of Ireland about the year 1734; died 1799. He served in the French and Indian wars as ensign in 1756, and during the war of the Revolution. He was quartermaster of Col. Culbertson's battalion of Cumberland Co. Militia, in active service. He married, about 1757, Jean M'Dowall. He had issue:

(1). James, born April 14, 1758.

(2). Mary, born February 14, 1760.

(3). Margaret, born September 15, 1761.

(4). Nancy, born April 27, 1763, married William Findlay; died July 27, 1824.

(5). William, born February 5, 1766.

(6). Elizabeth, born August 24, 1767.

(7). Jane, born June 22, 1769, or 8; m. Grubb, parents of William Findlay Irwin of Cincinnati.

Elizabeth Irwin married John Scott Harrison and was the mother of Benjamin Harrison, President of the United States.

Of this family is descended Wm. Torrence Handy, of Cynthiana, Ky., who married Mamie Welch, to whom were born William (who died in infancy), Nancy, Priscilla, and Hattie.

Also descended from the same line, is William Torrence — united in marriage with Jessie Peckover, to whom two sons, Findley and Joseph, were born. William Torrence died at Colorado Springs, Col., a few years since.

Descended from Archibald Irwin, whose father was Archibald, whose father was James, born in Ireland, is T. D. Irwin of Indianapolis, Ind.

WILLIAM MANNING IRWIN, Commander in the U. S. N., at Washington, D. C., was the son of William Irwin of Mt. Irwin, Ireland, who was churchwarden of Tyrone. He lived at Mt. Irwin, although he owned Camagh.

LEWIS FRANCIS IRWIN, born 1728, in 1766 married Elizabeth, only sister of John Harrison, Morton Place, Co. Lincoln, England. He died in 1815, aged 82 years. The children: John Lewis; Crinus, in Holy Orders, Archdeacon of Ossory, who married in 1807, Anne, eldest daughter of the late Justice Chamberlain of the King's Bench in Ireland.

JOHN LEWIS IRVINE, of Tanago, County Sligo, was born in April, 1770; served as High Sheriff, and died aged 80 years.

Arms — Arg., three holly leaves ppr. Crest: a hand issuing out of a cloud, grasping a thistle. Motto — "*Nemo uno impune lascessit.*" Seat — Tanago Colony. His son, Lewis Irwin Sr., was born August 1830, married a daughter of Alanson Woodruff, in 1854, in Ogdensburg, N. Y. He has one son, John Lewis Irwin, M. D.

(Copied from Family Records and notes from Gen. A. G. Ellis' Recollections, now in the Historical Collection of Wisconsin.)

(Supplied by Mrs. Henry J. Furber.)

Robert Irvin married Sarah Miller in Ireland, and came from Dublin in 1776 to Carlisle, Pa., when his son Robert was about six months old. Their daughter, Mary, was born January 20, 1789. Robert was reared in Baltimore, Maryland. He returned to Carlisle, Pa., and married in 1796, Catherine Singer, who was born September 5, 1781, died April 19, 1842, and is buried in Green Bay, Wisconsin.   Robert Irvin and his wife lived in Carlisle, Pa., until their eldest child, Robert, was born and then removed to Greensburg.   On the breaking out of the War of 1812, he entered the U. S. Army as Lieutenant and was Adjutant of his regiment. He was also appointed Assistant of the Commissary department in May, 1812.   He served until the Army disbanded in 1821.   He served, principally between Buffalo and Erie, and finally at Detroit, Michigan, where he later made his home for a time, afterwards settling permanently in Green Bay, Wis., where he died, July 19, 1852, aged 77.   He outlived his four sons, and of his four daughters, three still survive: Mrs. Wm. Dickerson, aged 80; Mrs. J. D. Suydam, 67, and Mrs. E. W. Follett, 61; also, the widows of his two sons, Alexander and Robert Irvin, aged respectively, 74 and 67 years.   They all reside near the old homestead at Green Bay, and are among the most honored and respected citizens of that country.

ᶜ⁄ AGNEW–IRWIN DESCENDANTS.

Probably there exists no fuller or more comprehensive biographical record of any American family, than that of the Agnew lineage.   Imbued with a clannish love of race, they have kept, religiously, the history of their family.   In the various phases and separations to which American families are subjected, which render any lineage of an American family so difficult to complete, no traces of the different ramifications have been lost.   There are few families which exhibit, to such a marked degree, the same physical, moral, and mental characteristics.   The members of the Agnew family have always been remarkable for their great height and splendid physical development.   No finer example exists of this trait of height and physique than in the father and uncles of John Park Agnew, the subject of this sketch, who was the son of John Agnew and Elizabeth (Park) Agnew, grandson of David Agnew and Mary (Irwin) Agnew, and great-grandson of James Agnew and Rebecca (Scott) Agnew, and great-great-grandson of James Agnew, the founder of this branch of the family in America, who was descended from the Agnews of Lochnaw, Scotland, for 400 years hereditary sheriffs of Galloway, which family, through the marriage of Margaret Kennedy, daughter of the Honorable Sir Thomas Kennedy, of Culzean, with Sir Andrew Agnew, Sheriff of Galloway, claim a double royal descent, from King James II., of Scotland, and from King Henry VII., of England. Another marked characteristic of the ancestors of the American family of Agnews was their extraordinary mental activity, and their keen perceptions of the duties and requirements of their life-work. In whatever branch of life-work they are found, they stand pre-eminent. The founders of the Agnew family in America were always prominent in religious matters. They were ever active in all the observances of religion, both in church work, and in their daily life. The three original heads of the Agnew family in this country were all elders of the same church — the Seceder, or Associate Presbyterian. It was their Protestant principles which impelled them to seek a home in the then British Colonies. They were of the people who had made famous the glens and moors of Ireland and Scotland, and, who, rather than yield their convictions of faith and duty, suffered the sharpest persecutions, coming, eventually, to this side of the Atlantic Ocean to find homes more congenial to their taste. Men of strong intellect, independent thinkers, intolerant of oppression, gentle in peace, but terrible in war, they have left their impress upon all the institutions of the country of their adoption. James Agnew, founder of the American family of Agnews, made settlements, about 1737, in the north-western part of York, now Adams County, on Tom's and Marsh Creeks. In the quaint, old, deserted burying-ground at Gettysburg lie a number of the earlier members of the Agnew family in this country. On one stone was a rude carving of weights and measures, with the further inscription: "The Weights and Measures of Scotland." On another was a carving of the coat of arms of the Agnews of Lochnaw, Scotland. It is with the fourth child of James Agnew and Rebecca (Scott) Agnew that the Agnew-Irwin intermarriage begins. The name of this son was David Agnew, and he was born July 17, 1743. On attaining his maturity he was married, in Franklin County, Pennsylvania, April 2, 1772, to Mary Irwin, daughter of John Irwin, who was a brother of Archibald Irwin, ancestor of President Benjamin Harrison. Mary Irwin, who married David Agnew, was a step-sister of Mary Ramsey, who married James Agnew, a colonel in the Revolutionary Army, and Mary Ramsey was a sister of Col. James Ramsey, whose daughter Mary married Archibald Irwin, the Irwin ancestor of the Harrisons. After the death of David Agnew, and after four years of widowhood, Mary (Irwin) Agnew became the wife of Rev. Alexan-

der Dobbin, of Gettysburg, Pennsylvania; and the Old Dobbin
house, a fine stone mansion in Gettysburg, possessing vast historic interest, has, by option, become the property of the Gettysburg Chapter of the American Revolution, which purposes its
restoration for use as a museum and library. David Agnew and
Mary (Irwin) Agnew had twelve children; and their son, John,
married Elizabeth Park, daughter of Dr. Robert Park, and Jane
Bailey, his wife. John Park Agnew, son of John Agnew and Elizabeth (Park) Agnew, was born at Ebensburg, Penn., December
25, 1819 or 1820, and died June 7, 1892. He was an elder in the
Presbyterian Church 1839–92; Member of the Board of Aldermen,
Alexandria, 1870; married, September 10, 1846, Matilda Elizabeth,
daughter of John Lewis Thomas, of Cumberland, Maryland, and
Matilda Louisa (Seeley Thomas, his wife. John Park Agnew was
for many years one of Alexandria's most prominent citizens, and
was a successful business man of three cities, Georgetown, Washington and Alexandria. He was descended from Captain James Agnew,
who was born in Scotland in 1701, from the Agnews of Lochnaw.
John Park Agnew was the father of ten children; Park, David Smith
Edward Lewis, Augustus Harrison, Leonora Matilda, Ann Rebecca,
Mary Virginia, Lily, Minnehaha, and Margaretta Linton.

Honorable Park Agnew, of Alexandria, Virginia, born July
3, 1847, eldest son of John Park Agnew and Matilda Elizabeth
(Thomas) Agnew, is a lineal descendant of Captain Robert Seeley,
New Haven, Conn., 1630, and of other distinguished New England
ancestors: William Phelps, Edward Griswold, Captain John Bissell,
John Wilcox, John Hand, John Pettibone, Bagot Eggleston,
Thomas Holcombe, John Moulthrop and Lieutenant Andrew Moore,
ancestors of his maternal grandmother, and is descended, through
his grandfather, John Lewis Thomas, from Christopher Bartholo-
mew Mayer, born at Carlsruhe, Germany, 1702, and of Melchior
Mayer, who was Stadthauptmann of the Free Imperial City of
Ulm, Germany, in 1550. Honorable Park Agnew has been
Collector of Internal Revenue for 6th District; Chairman State
of Virginia Republican Committee for several years; President
and Director of several Corporations; married, October 26, 1871,
Laura Richards, daughter Robert Bell, of Alexandria, Virginia.
Leonora Matilda, daughter of John Park Agnew, and Matild, Elizabeth (Thomas) Agnew, married Archibald Greenlees. The family
of Greenlees originated in the Parish of Cambleton, County Argyle,
and belongs to the "Clan Campbells," of Argyleshire. Augustus

Harrison Agnew, son of John Park Agnew and Matilda Elizabeth (Thomas) Agnew, married Mabel Anderson. He is President of the Cheeseman Chemical Company, of Scranton, Penn. The other children of John Park Agnew are still unmarried. John Park Agnew was a most worthy descendant of David Agnew and Mary Irwin. His whole life gave evidence of the genuineness of his Christian character. He was distinguished for superior intellectuality, and for his universal kindness and gentleness. But with all his gentleness he possessed great decision of character. His death was a great loss to the city in which he lived, for he was one of its most enterprising and distinguished citizens. After a long and useful life, he died in the full possession of his faculties, and in the enjoyment of perfect peace, and with a bright hope of a happy immortality through faith in Jesus Christ. John Park Agnew was an own cousin of Dr. D. Hayes Agnew, the noted physician, of Philadelphia, Pennsylvania, and resembled the latter in the loveliness and strength of his character.

ꝗ RECORD OF THE AGNEW FAMILY IN AMERICA.

The record begins with the following note from the memoirs of Sir Andrew Agnew of Scotland:

"The name Agnew or Agneau is of Norman origin, and the family tradition is that its founder came over to England with 'William the Conqueror.' Ancient records point to a very early connection with the De Courceys."

The following is an extract from "The Origin and Signification of Scottish Names," by Clifford Stanley Simms, Albany, N. Y., 1862: "The name Agneau in Norman, as also in French, means a lamb. A branch of the family came into England at a very early date, and some of them accompanied 'Strongbow' to Ireland. Others settled in Scotland, where Sir Andrew Agnew was hereditary sheriff of Wigtonshire in 1452, which office the family retained about four hundred years."

It has been handed down as tradition that three brothers of the name of Agnew, emigrated from Great Britain to the colonies (now the United States) in America, early in the eighteenth century, and that one of them settled in New Jersey, one in Pennsylvania, and the other in South Carolina, but the South Carolina has been proved to be an off-shoot of the Pennsylvania family. So we will only follow the fortunes of James, who settled in Pennsylvania, and whose descendants are the principal subjects of the following records.

Sir Andrew Agnew of Scotland (the present baronet), thinks that our ancestor, James, was a direct descendant of the "Locknaw Agnews" as Andrew, a younger son of the last "laird of Galdenoch," was a merchant in Belfast in the early years of the seventeenth century.

James Agnew, the first of the line in America, was born in Great Britain in 1671, and emigrated to America early in the eighteenth century, 1717. The date of his death in unknown. He settled in Pennsylvania, in what was then known as Lancaster county, but which was afterward divided into quite a number of small counties, and the place of his residence, or date of his death, cannot now be ascertained. He had a son James, our great-great-grandfather, who was born in 1701, in Scotland, and in 1741 he was one of the first settlers on "Mark Manor," a tract of land near the present town of Gettysburg, Pa. In 1756, he was captain of a military company for defense against the Indians. In 1765, he was granted a land warrant of five hundred acres of land in Lancaster, now Adams County, in Hamiltonban township, which includes the present Drais, Winthrode and Scott farms. The mansion house was probably on the Winthrode farm.

James Agnew died on October 2, 1770. He had two wives: Martha, who left two children, and Rebecca Scott, who was our ancestor. She left nine children; the third, James Agnew, our great-grandfather, was born May 1, 1742. Col. James Agnew, Jr., was granted a land warrant for 250 acres of land in 1765, in Hamiltonban township. He owned what is known as the Dubbs farm. The Tapper farm, as now known, belonged to his brother John, born March 4, 1732, only son of the first wife, Martha. John Agnew, Judge, died June 6, 1814. Col. James Agnew, Jr., married Mary Ramsey and both died in Gettysburg in the summer of 1825. The above is taken from town records, deeds, tombstones, etc., in and near Gettysburg, Pa.

The following is copied by the writer, Martha R. Robinson, from an old family Bible belonging to the second James, and which was printed in Edinburgh in 1734. It gives his family record, and throws light on the family history.

JAMES AGNEW, second, was married to Martha in 1732, who gave birth to two children: John, born March 4, 1733 and James, born August 22, 1735. John, afterward Judge, left no children. Janet

Agnew married Hugh Scott (youngest brother of Rebecca Scott, her step-mother). She left several children, two of whom died in Adams County, Pa. One was the father of Margaret, Hugh and Dr. Scott of Pittsburg, Pa. Martha, the first wife of James, died in 1735, and in 1737 he married Rebecca Scott, who had nine children, as follows:

1. SAMUEL, the eldest son of James and Rebecca Agnew, born January 27, 1738; removed from Marsh Creek, near Gettysburg, Pa., to South Carolina, about the time of his father's death in 1770. There he married Miss Searight, a native of Ireland, and settled about six miles from where the present town of the Due West now stands. During the War of the Revolution, he was a "whig" and suffered many losses and privations. He raised a family of three sons and some daughters. The names of his sons were James, Andrew and Samuel. His grandson, Rev. Samuel A. Agnew, is now (1891) living at Bethany, Lee Co., Mississippi.

2. MARTHA, eldest daughter of James and Rebecca Agnew, born September 9, 1740, married Samuel Patterson of Lancaster Co., Pa.

3. JAMES, born May 1, 1724; married Mary Ramsey; died April 10, 1825.

4. DAVID, born January 17, 1744, married Mary Irwin; died January 17, 1797.

5. MARGARET, born August 27, 1745, married James Patterson also of Lancaster Co., Pa.

6. REBECCA, born May 3, 1747; married John McClanahan of Franklin Co., Pa.

7. SARAH, born May 15, 1749; married Archibald Douglass of York Co., Pa.

8. ABRAM, born December 25, 1750, died at three years old, March 11, 1753.

9. ANNA, born October 3, 1753; married Rev. John Smith.

The following, taken from the family Bible of Dr. Samuel Agnew, son of third James and Mary Ramsey, will be of interest to their descendants. "I never saw my grandfather,— James second,— he having died eight years before my birth. I saw and remember my grandmother, being eleven years old when she died. I remember my uncles and aunts, with the exception of Aunt Martha and Uncle Abram. They were all of large stature, especially Uncle

David, and my aunts were distinguished for personal beauty. All married well and left a good record."

Mary Ramsey lived with her brother, Col. James Ramsey, near the present town of Mercersburg, Pa. (The Heister farm.) James Agnew saw her first as she walked down the aisle of the church, and fell in love with her at sight. He was twenty-six and she fifteen when they were married in 1768. He was a Colonel in the war of the Revolution. They spent their married life on a farm a few miles from Gettysburg, removing to the town in their later years, where they died in 1825 — James on April 10, and Mary July 16. The old stone homestead on the farm, as well as the town house — a large brick building,—still stand (1891), the latter in good repair. The following children were the fruit of this happy marriage: James, born July 31, 1769; died September 9, 1855; Rebecca, born October 17, 1771; died October 26, 1817; John, born October 18, 1773; died 1801; Mary Ann, born October 9, 1775; died January 26, 1849; Samuel, born August 10, 1778; died November 25, 1849; David, born September 14, 1780; died October 14, 1851; Martha, born February, 17, 1787; died January 20, 1823; Elizabeth Ramsey, born May 6, 1789; died 1842. Of these children the following record has been gathered from various sources:

1. COL. JAMES AGNEW, the eldest son (a colonel in the war of 1812), married Elizabeth Findley, September 22, 1801. She died March 9, 1816. They had children:

    (1). James Findley, born November 6, 1802; died January 5, 1824.

    (2). Mary Ramsey, born December 6, 1803; died March 11, 1815.

    (3). William Findley, born March 15, 1805.

    (4). Sarah, born June 17, 1806.

    (5). Elizabeth, born June 21, 1808.

    (6). John Robinson, born June 8, 1810.

    (7). David, born November 9, 1811.

    (8). Samuel, born November, 18, 1814.

Col. James Agnew married a second wife, named Rebecca Scott, formerly Rebecca Patterson, who died January 28, 1827, without children.

2. JOHN AGNEW, a second son of James and Mary Ramsey, born October 18, 1773; married Rebecca Smith in 1792; she died March 3, 1818. Their children:

    (1). James, drowned in a tan vat at two years of age.

(2). John, married Mary White.

(3). Anna Maria, born January 7, 1799; married Benjamin
Junkin. She was still living in the full possession of all
her faculties, December, 1890, aged 92.

1. MARY ANN AGNEW, daughter of James and Mary Ramsey Agnew,
married Alexander Caldwell, date unknown. They died
the same year, 1849. Their children were:

(1). Hugh Ramsey.

(2). James Agnew, died in Texas, 1842.

(3). Samuel.

(4). Jane Maria.

(5). Alexander.

(6). William.

(7). Martha.

(8). Mary.

3. SAMUEL AGNEW, M.D., surgeon in war of 1812, son of James and
Mary Ramsey Agnew, married Jane Grier and settled in
Harrisburg, Pa., where he died in 1849. She died at the
home of her daughter in Pittsburg on July 21, 1859. Their
children:

(1). John Holmes (Rev.), born May 9, 1804.

(2). Mary Ann, born December 28, 1806; died August 16,
1830.

(3). James Caldwell, born December 25, 1808.

(4). Harriet Jane, born May 2, 1810; died October 6, 1811.

(5). Harriet Jane Holmes, born June 14, 1812; still living,
1891.

(6). Samuel David, born May 11, 1816; died August 26, 1819.

4. DAVID AGNEW, son of James and Mary Ramsey Agnew, married
Elizabeth Dickey March 4, 1818, and she died on September
15, 1873, leaving no children.

2. MARTHA AGNEW, third daughter of James and Mary Ramsey
Agnew married David Wilson on March 25, 1890. She was
born in 1775, and died January 1822. They had seven
children:

(1). Jane Rowan, born January 3, 1810; married Christian
Herr.

(2). James Agnew, born July 6, 1811; died 1822.

(3). Mary Eliza, born 1813; died 1822.

(4). Harriet Martha, born December 23, 1815; married Robert
Paxton.

(5). Rebecca, born March 15, 1818; married Hamilton Long-
well.

(6). Florence McLean, born January 6, 1820; married Matthew
Irwin.

(7). David Agnew, born December 5, 1821; married Emeline
McConaughey.

3. ELIZABETH RAMSEY, youngest daughter of James and Mary
Ramsey Agnew, married Rev. John Pettit, and left no
children.

4. REBECCA AGNEW, the eldest daughter of James and Mary Ram-
sey Agnew, married, on July 17, 1793, Rev. Wm. Baldridge
who was the son of Alexander Baldridge, whose ancestor
— Rev. John Baldridge — had married Lady Jane Holmes,
only sister of Lord John Holmes of Ireland, who died in Dublin, leaving a large portion to his sister's heirs in America.
Alexander Baldridge removed from Pennsylvania to North
Carolina the middle of the eighteenth century. There
William was born in March, 1760. After the close of the
War of the Revolution, he began the study of Latin to
prepare himself for college, and studied afterward at Dickinson College, Carlisle, Pa., and graduated with the honors
of that institution. He was a student of theology under
the Rev. Alexander Dobbin of the Associate Reformed
Church. He was licensed to preach by the Marsh Creek
Presbytery of the Associate Reformed Presbyterian Church
about the year 1791. It was while studying for the ministry
with Rev. Alexander Dobbin of Gettysburg, that he met
Rebecca Agnew, whom he married in 1793. In the year
1794, he became pastor of two respectable congregations in
Rockbridge Co., Virginia. For fifteen years, he served as
their pastor with great acceptance. Although born in
the South, and his father having held slaves, he became
convinced of the evils of it, and so imbued his people with
his own principles, that in the Spring of 1809, he, with forty
families of the Virginia congregation, took his wife and
children, with all needed household goods, over the mountains, in wagons, to the then free State of Ohio, bringing their
negroes with them. They took farms in Adams Co., on the
west fork of Brush Creek, called "Cherry Fork." A stone
church was built one mile from his own farm and here he
labored with good success, his sons attending to the farm

work, until his death from heart disease on October 26, 1830. He was interred in the burial ground of Cherry Fork congregation. His wife, Rebecca Agnew, died an hour after the birth of her daughter, Mary Jane Ramsey. They had thirteen children as follows:

(1). James Ramsey, born May 22, 1793; died July 25, 1868.

(2). Alexander Holmes, born June 13, 1795; died July 25, 1874.

(3). John Young, born December 20, 1796.

(4). William Steele, born May 1, 1799; died October 3, 1812.

(5). Samuel Caldwell, died August 4, 1857.

(6). Rebecca Gibson, born February, 18, 1801; died April 2, 1862.

(7). David Agnew, born May 25, 1903.

(8). Wade, born August 6, 1805.

(9). Agnew, born December 5, 1807; died October 26, 1850.

(10). Joseph Gilmore, born June 16, 1810, born October 26, 1811.

(11). Ebenezer W., born August 1, 1812; still living, 1891.

(12). William, born August 17, 1814; died June 1, 1893.

(13). Mary Jane Ramsey, born October 26, 1817.

Rev. William Baldridge, above mentioned, married a second wife, Mary, daughter of Samuel Logan, born in Cumberland Co., Pa. August 22, 1782. She was the widow of James Anderson and had two children at the time of her marriage, May 16, 1820. Of this marriage the following children were born: Benjamin Logan, born February 9, 1821; Nancy Ann, born October 18, 1822; died March 17, 1843.

CINCINNATI IRVINES
(Another family not connected with Agnews).

JOHN IRVINE, born Newton Limivady, County Derry, Ireland, and his wife Ann Ramsey went to Carnmoon, County Antrim, Ireland, about 1812.

1. JOHN IRVINE, oldest son of John and Ann Irvine, was born February 21, 1809, Parish of Billey, County Antrim, Ireland, and died July 3, 1887, Pueblo, Col. U. S. A.

2. NANCY AGNES IRVINE, first daughter of John and Ann Irvine was born, 1804, County Antrim, Ireland, and died January 25, 1868, near Lennoxville, Township of Ascot, Province of Quebec, Canada.

3. REBECCA IRVINE, second daughter of John and Ann Irvine, born
———; died in Ireland, December, 1876.

4. JOSEPH IRVINE, second son of John and Ann Irvine, was born
———; died in Ireland.

5. DAVID IRVINE, third son of John and Ann Irvine, was born October 3, 1812, in Ireland, and died in Litchfield, Mass.

6. ROBERT IRVINE, fourth son of John and Ann Irvine, was born
———; died in Ireland.

7. SAMUEL R. IRVINE, fifth son of John and Ann Irvine, was born
September 29, 1822, County Antrim, Ireland, died March
14, 1903, at Toledo, Ohio.

1. JOHN IRVINE, oldest son of John and Ann Irvine, was born February 21, 1809, Parish of Billey, County Antrim, Ireland;
married Mary Boyd August 11, 1833; died July 3, 1887,
Pueblo, Col. Mary Irvine, his wife, oldest daughter of
Samuel and Nancy Boyd, was born July 15, 1810, Parish
of Billey, County Antrim, Ireland. Their children:

(1). Samuel Irvine, oldest son of John and Mary Irvine, was
born May 28, 1834, in Philadelphia, Pa.

(2). John Irvine, second son of John and Mary Irvine, was born
May 2, 1838, in Philadelphia, Pa.

(3). Wm. Jas. Irvine, third son of John and Mary Irvine, was
born August 9, 1838, in East Liberty, Pa.

(4). David Irvine, fourth son of John and Mary Irvine, was
born October 14, 1840, in Allgheny, Pa. Died July 8,
1841 at Allegheny, Pa.

(5). Elizabeth Irvine, first daughter of John and Mary Irvine,
was born November 30, 1842, in Allegheny, Pa. Died
October 9, 1899, Tempe, Ariz.

(6). David Alexander Irvine, fifth son of John and Mary Irvine,
was born January 17, 1844, in Pittsburg, Pa.

(7). Washington Irvine, sixth son of John and Mary Irvine,
was born March 22, 1846, in Pittsburg, Pa. Died
October 19, 1848, at Sandusky Ohio,

(8). Washington Irvine, seventh son of John and Mary Irvine,
was born April 15, 1849, at Sandusky, Ohio. Died
January 1852 at Sandusky, Ohio.

(9). Milton Boyd and Franklin Fleming, eighth and ninth
sons of John and Mary Irvine, born March 9, at Sandusky, Ohio. Franklin Fleming, ninth son, died August
5, 1851, at Sandusky, Ohio.

(10). Anna Irvine, second daughter of John and Mary Irvine, was born February 7, 1853, at Sandusky, Ohio; died August 5, 1853, at Sandusky, Ohio.

(1). Samuel Irvine, oldest son of John and Mary Irvine, born May, 28, 1834, in Philadelphia, Pa. U. S. A.; married Daphne Rody Foster, near Sandusky, January 1, 1866. Daphne Rody Irvine, his wife, second daughter of William and Caroline Charlotte Foster, was born October 6, 1839, about five miles from Sandusky, Ohio. Their children :

a. Carrie May Irvine, first daughter of Samuel and Daphne R. Irvine was born November 14, 1866, at Wathena, Kans.   Died January 10, 1894.

b. Helen Luella Irvine, second daughter of Samuel and Daphne R. Irvine, was born October 16, 1868, at Sandusky, Ohio.   Died May 7, 1884.

c. John William Irvine, first son of Samuel and Daphne R. Irvine, was born July 19, 1870, at Sandusky, Ohio.

d. Justin Samuel Irvine, second son of Samuel and Daphne R. Irvine, was born December 18, 1873, at Sandusky, Ohio.

c. John William Irvine, oldest son and third child of Samuel and Daphen Irvine was born July 19, 1870, at Sandusky, Ohio; married Rose Lillian Kirkpatrick June 29, 1898, at Cincinnati, Ohio. Rose Lillian Irvine, his wife, second daughter of William and Sara Ann Kirkpatrick, was born at Hillsboro, Ohio, July 20, 1871. Their children:

(a). Daphne Ann Irvine, oldest daughter of above born December 11, 1899, at Cincinnati, Ohio.

(b). Carrie Luella Irvine, second daughter, born February 28, 1902, at Cincinnati, Ohio.

(c). Helen Lucille Irvine, third daughter, born December 30, 1903, at Cincinnati, Ohio.

(2). JOHN IRVINE, second son of John and Mary Irvine, was May 3, 1836 in Philadelphia, Pa..; married Mrs. Louie Wilson Austin, née Louis W. Wilson, May 5, 1873. Mrs. Louie W. A. Irvine, his wife, was born at Cullensberg, Pa., August 4, 1843, and died at Chicago, June 10, 1891 Their children:

a. Edgar Wilson Irvine, first son of John and Louie W. Irvine, was born April 24, 1874, at Pueblo, Col.

b. Frank Boyd Irvine, second son of John and Louie W. Irvine, was born June 18, 1877 at Pueblo, Col.

c. Albert Huntly Irvine, third son of John and Louie W. Irvine, was born January 20, 1880, at Highland Ranch, Col.

d. Earl Ramsey Irvine, fourth son of John and Louie W. Irvine, was born March 24, 1883, at Highland Ranch, Col.

e. Elsie Grace Irvine, first daughter of John and Louie W. Irvine, was born October 14, 1884, at Highland Ranch, Col.

John Irvine married, second, Miss Alice Isabella Petrie, daughter of Frederick and Phebe Petrie, who was born at Volney, Oswego Co., New York; married on the 7th of February, 1893, at Kenosha, Wisconsin.

5). WILLIAM JAMES IRVINE, third son of John and Mary Irvine, was born August 9, 1838, in East Liberty, Pa; married Jennie Frost, May 1, 1878, at Pueblo, Col. Jennie Frost, his wife, was born December 11, 1848, at Marcellus, New York. Their children:

a. Florence Maie Irvine, first daughter of William J. and Jennie Irvine, was born February 16, 1879, at Green Horn, Col.

b. Allan Boyd Irvine, first son of William J. and Jennie Irvine, was born November 21, 1881, at Green Horn, Col.

c. Ralph Bloomer Irvine, second son of William J. and Jennie Irvine, was born March 29, 1889, at Rocky Ford, Col., and died August 1, 1890.

6). Elizabeth Irvine, fifth child and first daughter of John and Mary Irvine was born November 30, 1842, at Pittsburg, Pa., and died October 9, 1899, Tempe, Arizona; married Archibald Craig, September 3, 1863, at Elwood, Kans. Archibald Craig, her husband, was born October 31, 1838, at Franklin, Ohio; died October 3, 1865, at Elwood, Kans. Had Issue:

a. Dudley Irvine Craig, only son of Archibald and Elizabeth Craig, was born March 10, 1865, at Elwood, Kans.

Elizabeth Irvine married, second, Robert Anderson Iron, March 7, 1868, at Denver, Col., who was born June 18, 1840, at Stanton, Ohio.

a. Dudley Irvine Craig, only son of Elizabeth and Archibald Craig born March 10, 1865, at Ellwood, Kans., married Geraldine Estella Gerald, March 5, 1902, at Globe, Arizona. Geraldine Estella Gerald, his wife, born June 12, 1877, at Cambridge Springs, Pa. Their children:

(a). Robert Gerald Craig, first son of above, born December 22, 1902, at Tempe, Arizona.

(b). Gerald Irvine Craig, second son, born August 15, 1904, at Tempe, Arizona.

(6). David Alexander Irvine, fifth son of John and Mary Irvine, born January 17, 1844 in Pittsburg, Pa; married Mina Boltze, October 18, 1899, at Colorado Springs, Col. Mina Boltze, his wife, born October 25, 1860, at Fort Madison, Ia. Their children:

a. David McKinley Irvine, first son of above, born October 14, 1900, at Colorado Springs, Col.

b. Theodore Roosevelt Irvine, second son, born February 20, 1903, at Fort Madison, Iowa.

(7). Milton Boyd Irvine, eighth son of John and Mary Irvine, was born March 9, 1851, at Sandusky, Ohio; married Clara Elizabeth Holcomb December 21, 1882, at Lansing, Michigan. Clara Elizabeth Holcomb, his wife, was born November 17, 1860, at Lansing, Michigan. Their children:

a. Ruby May Irvine, first daughter of above, born November 4, 1883, on Cheyenne Creek, three miles from Colorado Springs, Col.

b. Norman Lee Irvine, first son of above, born November 18, 1886, at Colorado Springs, Col.

c. Milton Holcomb Irvine, second son, born October 3, 1887, on farm five miles west of Rocky Ford, Col.

2. NANCY AGNES IRVINE, first daughter of John and Ann Irvine was born —— 1804, in the County Antrim, Ireland; died January 25, 1868 near Lennoxville, Township of Ascot, Province of Quebec, Canada; Robert McFadden, her husband, was born in the County Antrim, Ireland, 1812, and died March 25, 1871, at Lennoxville, Quebec, Canada. Their children:

(1). John McFadden, oldest son of Nancy Agnes, (Irvine) and Robert McFadden, was born August 14, 1833, in the County Antrim, Ireland, and died November 5, 1893, at

Bishop Crossing, in the township of Dudswell, Quebec, Canada.

(2). Eliza Ann McFadden, first daughter of Nancy and Robert McFadden, was born May 17, 1835, in the County of Antrim, Ireland, and died January 20, 1841, at Lennoxville, Quebec, Canada.

(3). Hugh McFadden, second son of Robert and Nancy McFadden, was born January 17, 1838, township of Ascot, Quebec, Canada, and died September 17, 1875, at township of Ascot, Quebec, Canada.

(4). Robert McFadden, third son of Robert and Nancy A. McFadden, was born March 25, 1840, at Lennoxville, Quebec, Canada.

(5). Samuel McFadden, fourth son of Robert and Nancy A. McFadden, was born May 2, 1342, at Lennoxville, Quebec Canada.

(6). David McFadden, fifth son of Robert and Nancy A. McFadden, was born June 3, 1844, at Lennoxville, Quebec, Canada.

(1). John McFadden, oldest son of Nancy and Robert McFadden, was born August 14, 1833, in County Antrim, Ireland; married Ann E. Westman April 12, 1871, in Province of Quebec, Canada; died November 5, 1893, Bishop Crossing in the township of Dudswell, Province of Quebec, Canada.   Their children:

a. Maria S. and Mary N. McFadden, twins, born November 16, 1872, at Dudswell, Quebec.

a. Maria S. McFadden, married M. S. McDonald, M. D., August 2, 1900, in the township of Dudswell, Province of Quebec, Canada.

a. Mary N. McFadden, was married September 27, 1899, to L. F. McKenzie, in the township of Dudswell, Province of Quebec, Canada.

a. John Robert McFadden, oldest son of John and Ann E. McFadden, was born January 7, 1875 in the township of Dudswell, Province of Quebec, Canada; married J. Harriet Little, of Quebec, June 16, 1902.

(3). Hugh McFadden, second son of Robert and Mary A. McFadden born January 17, 1838, township of Ascot, Quebec, Canada; married Nancy McCurdy in January, 1871, in the township of Ascot, Quebec, Canada; died September 12, 1875, in township of Ascot, Quebec, Canada. Their children:

a. Jennnie Elizabeth McFadden, oldest daughter of Hugh and Nancy McFadden, was born February 19, 1872, in township of Ascot, Quebec, Canada.

b. Archibald Robert McFadden, oldest son of Hugh and Nancy McFadden, was born August 19, 1873, in the township of Ascot, Quebec, Canada, and married Mary Louise Taylor, of the city of Montreal, February 23, 1904.

c. Hugh Irvine McFadden, second son of Hugh and Nancy McFadden, was born July 12, 1875, in the township of Ascot, Quebec, Canada.

(4). Robert McFadden, third son of Robert and Nancy McFadden, was born March 25, 1840, at Lennoxville, Province of Quebec, Canada; married Elizabeth Berry, July 14, 1874, at Sawyersville, Quebec, Canada. Elizabeth Berry his wife was born at Sawyersville, Quebec. Their children:

a. Ella Agnes McFadden, oldest daughter of Robert and Elizabeth McFadden, was born December 24, 1878, in Township of Ascot, near Lennoxville, Quebec, Canada.

b. George Samuel McFadden, oldest son of Robert and Elizabeth McFaddden, was born August 9, 1881, in Township of Ascot, near Lennoxville, Quebec, Canada.

c. Alice Wesley McFadden, second daughter of Robert and Elizabeth McFadden, was born July 29, 1888, at township of Ascot, near Lennoxville, Quebec, Canada.

(5). Samuel Robert McFadden, fourth son of Robert and Nancy A. McFadden was born May 2, 1842 at Lennoxville. Quebec, Canada; married Margaret Keyes, January 24, 1872, at Stoke, Quebec, Canada. Their children:

a. Ellen Agnes McFadden, oldest daughter of Samuel and Margaret McFadden, was born July 8, 1873, at Township of Ascot, near Lennoxville, Quebec, Canada, and married Albert E. Wiggett of the city of Sherbrooke, Quebec, August 4, 1898.

b. Caroline Phœbe McFadden, second daughter of Samuel and Margaret McFadden, was born May 14, 1875, at Township of Ascot, near Lennoxville, Quebec, Canada, and married Daniel J. Hay, of the city of Montreal, September 10, 1902.

c. Robert Thomas Campbell McFadden, first son of Samuel and Margaret McFadden, was born December 19, 1879, at Township of Ascot, near Lennoxville, Quebec, Canada.

d. David McFadden, married and living in Chicago, Ill., but impossible to secure further information.

REBECCA IRVINE, second daughter of John and Ann Ramsey Irvine, was born ——— in Ireland and died in December, 1876, in Ireland. John McKay, her husband, oldest son of Daniel McKay (whose Fife name in Scotland was Clark), was born ——— in Ireland and died in November, 1870 in Ireland. They had children:

1. DANIEL McKAY, oldest son of John and Rebecca Irvine McKay, was born ———, in Ireland and died there.

2. SAMUEL McKAY, second son of John and Rebecca Irvine McKay, was born ——— in Ireland; lives (1904) at Bushmill, County of Antrim.

3. JOHN McKAY, third son of John and Rebecca Irvine McKay, was born ——— in Ireland and died ——— in New York.

4. ANN McKAY, first daughter of John and Rebecca Irvine McKay, was born ——— in Ireland and died there.

5. MARGARET McKAY, second daughter of John and Rebecca Irvine McKay, was born ——— in Ireland and died there.

6. MARY McKAY, third daughter of John and Rebecca Irvine McKay, was born ——— in Ireland and died there.

7. DAVID McKAY, fourth son of John and Rebecca Irvine McKay, was born ——— in Ireland and lives (1904) in Waitsfield, Vermont.

(1). David McKay, fourth son of John and Rebecca Irvine McKay, was born August 14, 1848, Carnmoon, County Antrim, Ireland; married Eliza Steele, April 5, 1870, in New York City, lives in Waitsfield, Vermont; Eliza Steele, his wife, was born June 2, 1846, Toberkeig, County Antrim, Ireland. Their children:

a. Eliza McKay, oldest daughter of David and Eliza Mc-McKay was born November 25, 1870, Toberkeigh, County Antrim, Ireland.

b. John McKay, first son of David and Eliza McKay,

was born March 14, 1874, in Jersey City, New
Jersey.

    c. Adam McKay, second son of David and Eliza McKay,
was born January 6, 1876, at Carnmoon, County
Antrim, Ireland.

    d. Mary I. McKay, second daughter of David and Eliza
McKay, was born March 22, 1878, at Carnmoon,
County Antrim, Ireland.

    e. Clara B. McKay, third daughter of David and Eliza
McKay, was born November 25, 1889, in Fayston,
Vermont.

DAVID IRVINE, third son of John and Ann Irvine was born October 3, 1812, in Ireland and died in Holyoke, Mass., July 7, 1898. Margaret A. Sharp, his wife, was born October 15, 1836, in Ireland, and died May 11, 1896, at Boston, Mass.   Their children:

1. Robert J. Irving, first son of David and Margaret Irvine, was born January 4, 1855, in Ireland; died ——— .

2. Annie Irving, first daughter of David and Margaret Irvine, was born April 3, 1837 in Ireland, and died ———.

3. Joseph S. Irving, second son, was born December 12, 1858, in Ireland, and died ———.

4. James Irving, third son, born December 15, 1860, in Ireland, died August 20, 1894, at Fitchburg, Mass.

5. Hugh O. Irving, fourth son, was born July 2, 1862, at Huntingsville, Quebec, Canada.

6. Samuel R. Irving, fifth son, was born April 28, 1865, at Sherbrooke, Quebec, Canada.

7. Nancy Jane Irving, second daughter, was born October 30, 1866, at Sherbrooke, Quebec, Canada.

8. Mary Irving daughter, third was born November 18, 1868, at Sherbrooke, Quebec, Canada.

9. Sarah L. Irving, fourth daughter, was born June 2, 1873, at Fitchburg, Mass.

1. ANNIE IRVING, first daughter of John and Ann Irvine, was born April 3, 1857, in Ireland; married Samuel Campbell at Fitchburg, Mass.   Samuel Campbell, her husband, was born January 28, 1850, at Greenfield, Mass., and died March 10, 1900. Their children:

    (1). Arland Campbell first son of Samuel and Annie Campbell was born November 29, 1886 at Brattleboro, Vt.

    (2). Almon Campbell, first daughter, was born October 4, 1898, at Bernardston, Mass.

2. JOSEPH IRVING, second son of John and Ann Irvine, was born December 12, 1858 in Ireland; married Lillian Barnes at Bridgeport, Conn.

3. Hugh O. Irving, fourth son of John and Ann Irvine, was born July 2, 1862, at Huntingsville, Quebec, Canada; married Annie B. Craig, at Fitchburg, Mass.; Annie B. Craig, his wife, was born November 1, 1868 at Pascoag, R. I. Had issue:

(1). Cluster C. Irving, oldest son of Hugh and Annie B. Irving was born April 26, 1895, at Fitchburg, Mass.

4. SAMUEL R. IRVING, fifth son of John and Ann Irvine, was born April 28, 1865, at Sherbrooke, Quebec, Canada. Lena Craig, his wife, was born October 12, 1874.

5. NANCY JANE IRVING, second daughter of John and Ann Irvine was born October 30, 1866 at Sherbrooke, Quebec, Canada; married Oscar F. Moriarty at Fitchburg, Mass. Oscar F. Moriarty, her husband, was born January 18, 1861, at Putnam, Conn. Their children:

(1). Alfred I. Moriarty, first son of Oscar and Nancy Moriarty, was born February 14, 1888, at Fitchburg, Mass.

(2). Ruth Moriarty, first daughter of Oscar and Nancy Moriarty, was born August 18, 1892, at Fitchburg, Mass.

(3). Oscar F. Moriarty, Jr., second son of Oscar and Nancy Moriarty, was born January 26, 1898, at Boston, Mass.

6. MARY IRVING, third daughter of John and Ann Irvine, was born November 12, 1868 at Sherbrooke, Quebec, Canada; married Henry C. Willmott at Fitchburg, Mass; her husband was born April 4, 1858, at Fitchburg, Mass. Their children:

(1). Florence E. Willmott, first daughter of Henry and Mary Willmott, was born March 4, 1891, at Fitchburg, Mass.

(2). Henry I. Willmott, first son of Henry and Mary Willmott, was born June 25, 1894, at Fitchburg, Mass.

7. SAMUEL RAMSEY IRVINE, fifth son and seventh child of John and Ann Irvine, was born September 29, 1822, in County Antrim, Ireland; married Margaret Elinor Sinclair, December 30, 1857, at Sandusky, Ohio. Margaret Elinor Sinclair, his wife, was born August 12, 1830, at Isle of Isla, Scotland, and died April 11, 1893, at Toledo, Ohio. Their children:

(1). Anna Victoria Irvine, first daughter of Samuel R. and Margaret E. Irvine, was born October 4, 1858, at Sandusky, Ohio.

(2). Florence Nightingale Irvine, second daughter, born September 22, 1860, at Sandusky, Ohio.

(3). Arthur Wellesley Sinclair Irvine, first son, born November 4, 1862, at Sandusky, Ohio.

(4). Jessie Benton Fremont Irvine, third daughter, born September 21, 1865, at Sandusky, Ohio.

(5). Clair Irvine Coghlin, fourth daughter, born July 29, 1868, at Sandusky, Ohio.

    a. Florence Nightingale Irvine, second daughter of Samuel R. and Margaret E. Irvine, was born September 22, 1860, at Sandusky, Ohio; married John Ames, Jr., July 28, 1880, at Toledo, Ohio. John Ames, Jr., her husband, was born at Lansingburg, New York, April 18, 1845. Their children:

        (a). Edna Florence Ames, oldest daughter of Florenec N. and John Ames, was born August 18, 1884, at Toledo, Ohio.

    b. Arthur Wellesley Sinclair Irvine, first son of Samuel and Margaret E. Irvine, was born November 4, 1862 at Sandusky, Ohio; married Mary Tracy Austin, November 23, 1887, at Toledo, Ohio. Mary Tracy Austin, his wife, was born in Ohio, March 25, 1866. Their children:

        (a). Austin Sinclair Irvine, oldest son of Arthur W. and Mary T. Irvine, was born December 21, 1890, at Toledo, Ohio.

        (b). Edwin Victor Irvine, second son of Arthur W. and Mary T. Irvine, was born October 19, 1896, at Toledo, Ohio.

    c. Jessie Benton Fremont Irvine, third daughter of Samuel R. and Margaret E. Irvine, was born September 21, 1865, at Sandusky, Ohio; married Joseph Burtzman Birdsell Hutchison, December 12, 1888, at Toledo, Ohio. Joseph Burtzman Birdsell Hutchison, her husband, was born May 19, 1863, at Mt. Vernon, Ohio.

    d. Clair Irvine, fourth daughter of Samuel R. and Margaret E. Irvine, was born July 29, 1868, at Sandusky, Ohio; married Amadens Martin Coghlin, November 8, 1892, at Toledo, Ohio. Amadens Martin Coghlin, her husband, was born October 29, 1865 at Toledo, Ohio. Their children:

(a). Florence Sinclair Coghlin, oldest daughter of
Amadens and Clair I. Coghlin, was born December 11, 1893, at Toledo, Ohio, and died December 11, 1893.

(b). Alice Sinclair Coghlin, second daughter of Amadens M. and Clair I. Coghlin, was born November 24, 1894, at Toledo, Ohio.

THE PENNSYLVANIA ERWINS.

COL. ARTHUR ERWIN, born in 1726, a Scotch-Irish immigrant
of considerable means, came from County Antrim, Ireland, and
settled at Erwinna, Bucks County, Pennsylvania, in 1768. The
family, consisting of his wife, Mary Scott Erwin, and seven children,
sailed from Newry on a ship called the Newry Assistance about May
1st, and landed at Philadelphia, Pa., August 18, 1768. The wife
and an infant born at sea, had died and been buried at sea about
the tenth of July. In 1776–77 Arthur Erwin was Colonel respectively of the Fourth and Second Battalions of the Bucks County
Militia, in which rank several letters and orders, which are still in
existence, were addressed to him by General Washington, just
previous to the Battle of Trenton. The Christmas Eve before the
battle, Col. Erwin carried many of our soldiers across the river in
his own boats, from his estate on the banks of the Delaware. He
was shot and killed at Tioga Point, supposedly by a squatter, June
9, 1791. Col. Erwin possessed large tracts of land also in Luzerne
county, Pennsylvania, and Steuben county, New York. Before his
arrival in 1768, Col. Arthur and his brother, William Erwin, had
not only visited this country, but had purchased large tracts of land
in Tinicum township, Bucks county, Pennsylvania, and the Colonel
brought his family for permanent residence on his possessions. The
children of Col. Arthur Erwin and Mary Scott, his first wife, were:

1. LIEUTENANT JOHN ERWIN, born in Ireland, November 12, 1756,
died February 17, 1782, from disease contracted in prison
ships, New York Harbor, where he was held prisoner over
four years, having been captured at the destruction of Fort
Washington. Unmarried.

2. JOSEPH ERWIN, born July 24, 1758, in the Parish of Gromlin,
County Antrim, Ireland. He never married, but lived as
a country gentleman, spending the winters in Philadelphia,
and the summers at Erwinna. Joseph Erwin did effective

service in his country's defense, both at home and in France. He held several important offices, and died February 9, 1807.

3. WILLIAM LIVINGSTON ERWIN, born in Ireland February 12, 1760; was commissioned Captain in the First Regiment of Foot in the Continental service May 14, 1781. Thirty years later he represented Bucks county for several terms in the State senate. He married, in 1782, Achsah, daughter of Dr. John and Rachel (Robinson) Rockhill, of Hunterdon county, New Jersey.

4. SARAH ERWIN, born in Ireland September 16, 1762; married Judge John Mulhollen; died May 5, 1809.

5. FRANCIS ERWIN, born and died in 1764.

6. ARTHUR ERWIN, born in Ireland 1765; drowned in the Delaware River, May, 1769.

7. HUGH SCOTT ERWIN, born in Ireland February 8, 1767; died May 31, 1846, leaving no family, though married.

1.   Descendants of Col. Arthur Erwin and

2.   Mary Scott, first wife, who died at sea.

3. Sarah Erwin, fourth child, was born in Ireland September

4.   16, 1762; married Judge Mulhollen, who was born in Ireland November 11, 1754; and died April 5, 1815. Sarah, his wife, died May 5, 1809.

THEIR CHILDREN — SECOND GENERATION.

5. Mary Mulhollen, born March 27, 1779; died October 30, 1813;

6.   married Judge Thomas McBurney.

7. William Mulhollen, born January 20, 1781.

8.

9. John Mulhollen, born November 3, 1782; married

10.   Miss Ives of Philadelphia, Pa.

11. Arthur Mulhollen, born May 18, 1785.

12. Hugh Mulhollen, born May 5, 1787; married South, and died, leaving one daughter.

13. Christian Mulhollen, born March 13, 1789; died October 4, 1790.

14. Joseph Mulhollen, born May 23, 1791; died February 4, 1815.

15. Elizabeth Mulhollen, born May 3, 1794; married

16.   David Wolcott.

17. Daniel Mulhollen, born November 30, 1796; married

18.   Electa Trowbridge.

19. Thomas Mulhollen, born December 12, 1800; died January 20, 1801.

20. Sarah Mulhollen, born July 1, 1804; married
21. Matthew McHenry.

THIRD GENERATION.

Mary Mulhollen and Thomas McBurney (5 and 6).

22. (1). John McBurney; married.
23. (2). Sarah McBurney; married John Magee.
24. (3). Eliza McBurney; married — Bacon.
25. (4). Maria McBurney; married — Cotton.
26. (5). Caroline McBurney; married.
27. (6). Thomas McBurney; married.

David Wolcott and Elizabeth Mulhollen Wolcott.
(15 and 16).

28. Erwin and others.

Matthew McHenry and Sarah Mulhollen McHenry.
(20 and 21).

29. James and others.

Daniel Mulhollen and Electra Trowbridge Mulhollen.
(17 and 18).

30. (1). Sarah Mulhollen, born February 12, 1825; married
31. Clark Ballard of Dryden, N. Y.; died without issue.
32. (2). William Mulhollen, married Mrs. Anna —; he served
33. nearly five years in Civil War.
34. (3). Frances Mulhollen; married J. Burnham Sargent; one
35. daughter.
36. (4). Louise Mulhollen; died unmarried.
37. (5). Jane Mulhollen; died unmarried.
38. (6). Lizzie Mulhollen; died unmarried.
39. (7). James Mulhollen; died young.
40. (8). Henry Clay Mulhollen, born June 16, 1854; married
41. Luna Maria Taylor in 1870; he died in Jasper, Steuben County, N. Y., June 14, 1896.

FOURTH GENERATION.

William Mulhollen and Mrs Anna. (32 and 33).

42. (1). Frank Mulhollen, married Anna Dennis; two children.
43.
44. (2). Albert Mulhollen, married Amy Lamson; two children.
45.
46. (3). May Mulhollen, married Archie Hardy; one child.
48. (4). Jessie Mulhollen, married George Dennis; four children.
49.

J. Burnham Sargent and Frances Mulhollen Sargent.
(34 and 35).

50. Daughter Louise M. Sargent, married John B. Edgett, who
51.   died May 25, 1906; no children.

Henry Clay Mulhollen and Luna Maria Taylor.
(40 and 41).

52. (1). Lyman Frank Mulhollen, married Olive Grace Knapp
53.   of Canisteo, N. Y., December 16, 1896. He was
        born in Jasper, N. Y., May 3, 1871; pastor of Metho-
        dist Church, Hornell, N. Y., 1906. Born to them two
        sons, Lyman F., born September 21, 1898; died
        January 11, 1899; and Harold Stephen Mulhollen,
        born February 2, 1900.

54. (2). Josephine Southwick Mulhollen, born February 2, 1875;
55.   married Stephen E. Potter. Children, Luna, Arthur,
        Howard, and Sylva.

Children of William Livingston Erwin and Achsah
Rockhill Erwin.

(1). Mary, born 1783; married Phillip Howell; died 1836.

(2). Rachel, born 1787; married Thomas Kennedy as his
     second wife; died 1858.

(3). Scott R. Erwin, born 1789; died unmarried in 1823.

(4). Julianna, born 1791; married Thomas Kennedy, as his
     first wife; died 1823.

(5). Charlotte Erwin, born 1797; married John P. Robinson;
     died 1845.

     In 1769 Col. Erwin married his second wife, Miss
     Mary Kennedy of Easton, Pa. She died at Easton
     on Tuesday morning, July 29, 1817, at twenty min-
     utes after four o'clock.

(1).   Children of Colonel Arthur Erwin and his second wife,
        Mary Kennedy Erwin, of Erwinna, Pennsylvania.

3. (1). Samuel Erwin, born at Erwinna, Pa., May 4, 1770;
4.   married, 1800, Miss Rachel Heckman of Easton, Pa.,
        and had issue, seven sons and three daughters. He
        died at Painted Post, N. Y., November 10, 1836,
        aged 66 years, 6 months, and 6 days. She died August
        26, 1860, aged 77 years.

5. (2). Mary Erwin, born May 12, 1773; married, May 22, 1798,
        Dr. John Cooper of Easton, Pa. Had issue, one son
        and four daughters. She died in Easton, November
        19, 1854. The doctor died.

7. (3) Rebecka Erwin, born June 1, 1775. married, 1805,
8.   Dr. William McKeen of Easton; issue, one daughter.
     She died at Painted Post, N. Y., April 19, 1848.

9. (4). Major Arthur Erwin, born October 15, 1777; married
10.   three times — first, M. N. Erie; second, Lamphere;
     third, Sarah Clark of Erwin, born August 4, 1800;
     had issue four daughters and two sons. He died
     April 7, 1842; she died May 19, 1863.

11. (5). Francis Erwin, born at Erwinna, February 29, 1780;
     unmarried; died at Painted Post, September 6, 1839.

12. (6). John Erwin, born at Erwinna, 1786; unmarried; died
     in Easton, Pa., June 4, 1820.

GRANDCHILDREN.— THIRD GENERATION.

First.— The Family of Capt. Samuel and Rachel
Heckman Erwin of Painted Post. (3 and 4).

13. (1). Eliza Erwin, born at Easton, Pa., October 15, 1801;
14.   married Edward Townsend of Bath, November
     22, 1821; had issue, one daughter and one son.
     Mr. T. died.

15. (2). Arthur H. Erwin, born in Painted Post, November
16.   26, 1803; married Miss Frances Maria McKeen at
     Painted Post, February 21, 1828; had issue, seven
     daughters and five sons. He died August 1, 1863.
     She died February 17, 1882.

17. (3). Francis E. Erwin, born in Painted Post May 3, 1806.
18.   married Miss Sophia McCall, January 23, 1827; had
     issue, five sons and two daughters. His wife died in
     Painted Post, May 16, 1856. He died July 6, 1887,
     aged 81 years, 2 months, and 3 days.

19. (4). John Erwin, born in Painted Post, March 21, 1808;
20.   married Miss Nancy Pease of Warren, Trumbull
     county, Ohio, June 29, 1836; had issue, two sons
     and eight daughters. She died.

21. (5). Mary Erwin, born in Painted Post, October 17, 1810;
     died January 5, 1828.

22. (6). William Erwin, born in Painted Post, June 11, 1813;
23.   married Miss Mary Evans of Philadelphia, Pa., May
     2, 1839; had issue, four sons and four daughters.
     He died 1894. She died April 9, 1899.

24. (7). Rachel A. Erwin, born in Painted Post, November 20,
     1815; married William J. Gilbert of Painted Post,

October 30, 1839; had issue, six sons and three daughters. He died in Erwin in 1863. She died August 26, 1890, at Painted Post.

26. (8). Samuel Erwin, born and died March 20, 1817.

27. (9). Samuel Kennedy Erwin, born in Painted Post, August
28.   11, 1819; married Miss Mary Eliza Kern at Erwin, June 11, 1845; had issue two sons. He died at his residence near Calvert, Robertson county, Texas, July 28, 1874.

29. (10). Charles Heckman Erwin, born in Painted Post, April
30.   30, 1822; married Miss Antoinette Curtis of Campbell, N. Y., January 15, 1850; no issue. She died January 8, 1884. He died September 6, 1890, at Painted Post.

31.   Hugh Erwin, son of Capt. Samuel Erwin; born in Easton;
32.   married Miss Mary Powers (sister of the distinguished sculptor Hiram Powers of Cincinnati, Ohio); issue, one daughter. Died.

Births copied from the family bible of Capt. Samuel Erwin. Second.— The family of Dr. John and Mary Erwin Cooper of Easton, Pa. (5 and 6.)

33. (1). John Cooper, Jr., born in Easton, Pa., May 25, 1779;
34.   married Miss Elizabeth M. Evans of Philadelphia, January 6, 1828; had issue, seven sons and two daughters. He died October 23, 1863.

35.   Charlotte Cooper, born in Easton, August 15, 1801;
36.   married Rev. Dr. John Vandervere of Easton, July 31, 1824; no issue.

37.   Elizabeth Cooper, born in Easton, December 13, 1810;
38.   married Theodore Sedgwick Paul, October 28, 1830; had issue, eight sons and three daughters. She died January 13, 1879.

39.   Mary Cooper, born in Easton, August 1, 1812; died August 28, 1812.

40.   Sarah Ann Cooper, born in Easton, June 18, 1815;
41.   married Joseph F. Randolph of Belvidere, N. J., September 8, 1840; had issue, two daughters and two sons.

Third.— The Family of William and Rebecka Erwin McKeen. (Nos. 7 and 8).

[16.] (1). Frances Maria McKeen, born in Easton, Pa.; married Arthur H. Erwin of Painted Post, N. Y. (See Nos. 15 and 16, ante).

Fourth.— The Family of Arthur and Sarah Clark
Erwin. (Nos. 9 and 10).

42. (1). Rachel Erwin, born in Erwin, N. Y., March 8, 1821;
43.   married Henry Huntington Birdsall of Addison, N. Y.,
          June 14, 1843; had issue, three daughters and two sons.
44. (2). Mary E. Erwin, born in Erwin, Feb. 27, 1824; unmarried;
          died June 28, 1884.
45. (3). Samuel C. Erwin, born in Erwin, August 11, 1827;
46.   married Miss Mary Elizabeth Thompson of Erwin,
          December 24, 1856; had issue, three sons and three
          daughters. He died in October, 1896.
47. (4). Charles Erwin, born in Erwin, February 26, 1829; mar-
48.   ried Miss Kate Willard of Carlisle, Pa.; had issue,
          five children.
49. (5). Sarah Elizabeth Erwin, born in Erwin, October 1, 1833;
50.   married George H. Weatherby of Addison, November
          2, 1853; had issue, three sons. He died April 30, 1861.
51. (6). Annie E. Erwin, born in Erwin, June 22, 1837; married
52.   Amaziah S. KcKay of Addison, December 20, 1859;
          had issue, one son and one daughter.
53.   John Francis Erwin, son of Major Arthur Erwin and
54.   M. N. Erie Erwin, born in Bethelem, Pa., married
          Miss Johanette Louise Schneider; had issue, four sons
          and one daughter; died February 8, 1883.
55.   Arthur Erwin, Jr., son of Major Erwin and — Lamphere
56.   Erwin, born December 1, 1807; married a daughter
          of James Thompson, Isabella, for his first wife. She
          died. Married daughter of Bascom Jones of Addison,
          Miss Martha, second wife; had issue, six sons and
          four daughters.

GREAT-GRANDCHILDREN, OR FOURTH GENERATION

First.— The Family of Edward and Eliza Erwin
Townsend of Erwin. (13 and 14).

58. (1). An infant daughter, died December 15, 1823.
59. (2). Edward Erwin Townsend, born near Tioga Point, Pa.,
60.   January 23, 1825; married Miss Nancy Lawrence
          Jerome of Long Island, N. Y.; had issue, four sons and
          four daughters.

Second.— The Family of Arthur H. and Frances
Mariah McKeen Erwin, Painted Post, N. Y.
(15 and 16).

61. (1). Mary Kennedy Erwin, born at Painted Post, April 2, 1831;
62.   married Marcus Stevens of Detroit, Mich., Decem-
           ber 26, 1855; had issue, one daughter. He died.
63. (2). Eugene Hamilton Erwin, born in Painted Post, August
64.   14, 1832; married Miss Elizabeth H. Cook of Painted
           Post, November 13, 1861. Had issue, one daughter.
           Died in 1893.
65. (3). Emily Rebecca Erwin, born June 27, 1834, in Painted
           Post; died unmarried.
66. (4). Frances Virginia Erwin, born in Painted Post, April
           15, 1836.
67. (5). Elizabeth Erwin, born in Painted Post, July 15, 1838;
68.   married Dr. J. B. Dudley of Painted Post, February
           16, 1881; died in 1905.
69. (6). Dewitt Clinton Erwin, born March 10, 1840; died Decem-
           ber 11, 1873.
70. (7). Annie Maria Erwin, born in Painted Post, May 2, 1842;
71.   married Charles Iredell of Painted Post, April 8,
           1869; had issue, one son. She died.
72. (8). Arthur H. Irwin, Jr., born in Painted Post, May 10, 1844;
73.   married Miss Gertrude Maria Brown of Addison,
           October 19, 1870; had issue, two daughters, Agnes
           M. Erwin, married —; second, Gertrude Frances Erwin,
           married Van Willard Tyler, has daughter Agnes.
           Arthur H. Erwin, Jr., married, second, Mrs. Mary —,
           in Oklahoma; one son, Arthur H. Irwin.
74. (9). Harriet Louise Erwin, born in Painted Post, July 9, 1846;
75.   married John Lutman of Detroit, Mich., July 16,
           1873; have issue, one son and two daughters.
76. (10). Winfield Scott Erwin, born in Painted Post, December
           18, 1848; died 1905, unmarried.
77. (11). Helen Erwin, born June 14, 1851; died September
           5, 1855.
78. (12). John Jay Erwin, born May 1, 1854; died August 30,
           1855.
        Third.— The Family of Gen. Francis E. and Sophia
        McCall Erwin, Painted Post. (17 and 18).
        (Copied from Francis Erwin's Bible Record.)
79. (1). Samuel Stanbury Erwin, born in Painted Post, October
80.   28, 1827; married first wife, Miss Amelia Shaw,
           August 7, 1850; had issue, four sons and one daughter.

First wife died. Married Susan Williams of Lyons,
81   second wife; had issue, one son.

82. (2). Edward E. Erwin, born in Painted Post, November
83.   22, 1829; married Miss Susan Gamble, November
            22, 1852; had issue, one son.

84. (3). Mary Elizabeth Erwin, born in Painted Post, June
85.   20, 1831; married Cephas F. Platt of Campbell, May
            26, 1852; had issue, two daughters and one son.
            Mr. Platt died November 28, 1883.

86. (4). Francis Erwin, born in Painted Post, January, 5, 1834;
87.   married Miss Helen Campbell, October 27, 1853;
            had issue, one daughter and one son.

88. (5). John Erwin, born July 16, 1838; died August 28, 1838.

89. (6). Harriet Maris Erwin, born in Painted Post, January
90.   4, 1836; married Robert B. Wilkes of Bath, N. Y.,
            March 27, 1860; had issue, four daughters and four
            sons. Mr. Wilkes died November 23, 1876.

91. (7). John Ansel Erwin, born January 18, 1840; died April
            13, 1841.

        Fourth.— The Family of John and Nancy Pease
        Erwin, Cleveland, Ohio. (19 and 20).

(Copied from John Erwin's Family Bible by C. H. Erwin, in
        March, 1882, in the city of Cleveland, Ohio.)

92. (1). Calvin Pease Erwin, born in Warren, O., May 12, 1837;
            died December 26, 1854.

93. (2). Cornelia Pease Erwin, born in Cleveland, O., August
94.   9, 1839; married Dr. William H. Beaumont, March
            24, 1863. Had issue, three daughters and four sons.
            Mr. B. died.

95. (3). Laura Grant Erwin, born in Warren, O., September
96.   10, 1841; married Charles Edward Pease of Dayton,
            O., October 3, 1865; issue, two sons.

97. (4). William H. Erwin, born in Warren, O., August 26,
            1843.

98. (5). Arthur John Erwin, born in Cleveland, O., October
            10, 1845.

99. (6). Florence Heckman Erwin, born in Cleveland, O., Novem-
100.   ber 17, 1847; married Henry L. Page, December 20,
            1865; had issue, two daughters and two sons.

101. (7). Mary Pease Erwin, born in Cleveland, O., January

29, 1850; married Cyrus E. Johnston November 30, 1870. No issue.

103. (8). Kate Granger Erwin, born in Cleveland, O., April 8, 1852.

104. (9). Grace Erwin, born in Cleveland, O., August 9, 1854; died December 24, 1854.

(Copied from their Bible Record, March 1882, by C. H. Erwin.)

105. (10). Leonora Erwin, born in Cleveland, O., April 26, 1857;
106.   married Lieut. Henry H. Wright, U. S. A., February 19, 1879; have issue, one son.

Fifth.— The Family of William and Mary Evans Erwin, Cleveland, O. (22 and 23).

107. (1). Elizabeth Wallis Erwin, born in Painted Post, March
108.   14, 1840; married J. Ralph Ward of Elmira, N. Y., June 17, 1864; had issue, three sons. · Mr. Ward
109.   died December, 1880. Married Robert A. Craig at St. Paul, Minn., December 16, 1882.

110. (2). Mary Evans Erwin, born June 4, 1841, at Painted Post; died September 15, 1842.

111. (3). William Wilberforce Erwin, born in Painted Post, July
112.   12, 1843; married two times. Miss Mary J. King of Ravenna, Minn., September 27, 1881.

113. (4). John Evans Erwin, born in Painted Post, May 8, 1844; married in 1884.

114. (5). Alice Murray Erwin, born October 14, 1845, in Painted Post; died July 5, 1848.

115. (6). Albert Erwin, born in Painted Post, November 10, 1846; died November 26, 1863.

116. (7). Thomas Wallis Erwin, born in Painted Post, April 22, 1849; died September 10, 1849.

117. (8). Mary Alice Erwin, born in Painted Post, March 15,
118.   1852; married Charles H. Potter of Hartford, Conn., November 28, 1876, at Painted Post, N. Y.; have issue, one son and one daughter; died July 19, 1890.

Sixth.— The Family of William J. and Rachel A. Erwin Gilbert, Painted Post, N. Y. (24 and 25).

119. (1). Helen Gilbert, born in Painted Post, August 15, 1840;
120.   married Charles M. Fay of Prattsburg, N. Y.; had issue, one son; died in infancy.

121. (2). Henry Erwin Gilbert, born August 26, 1843; died in Union Army, December 1, 1861.

122. (3). William Gilbert, born in Painted Post, August 25, 1845; died July 28, 1846.

123. (4). Samuel Erwin Gilbert, born in Painted Post, May 1,
124.   1847; married December 17, 1866, Miss Sarah E. Adams; had issue, four daughters.

125. (5). William J. Gilbert, born in Erwin, August 21, 1849;
126.   married Miss Anna Badger of Painted Post, November 15, 1871.

127. (6). Nora N. Gilbert, born August 17, 1851.

128. (7). Sidney L. Gilbert, born in Erwin, March 18, 1854; mar-
129.   ried Miss Sarah Kelley of Detroit, Mich., December 21, 1881.

130. (8). Mary Erwin Gilbert, born in Erwin, June 16, 1856;
131.   married Frank W. Douglass of Corning, N. Y., December 29, 1880. She died in the city of Chicago, Ill., November 21, 1881.

132. (9). Charles B. Gilbert, born in Erwin, January 10, 1859.

Seventh.— The Family of Samuel Kennedy and Mary Eliza Kern Erwin, late of Calvert, Texas.

(27 and 28).

133. (1). Franklin Kern Erwin, born August 13, 1849, in Erwin; died in Milan, Milan County, Texas, January 24, 1879.

134. (2). Eugene Erwin, born in Erwin, February 3, 1858.

Eighth.— The Family of Dr. John and Elizabeth M. Evans Cooper of Cooper's Plains, N. Y.

(32 and 34).

135. (1). Francis Erwin Cooper, born in Erwin, September 1, 1829; unmarried.

136. (2). Mary Erwin Cooper, born in Erwin, June 6, 1831;
137.   married Willard C. Morse of Painted Post, April 6, 1853; had issue, one son and one daughter.

138. (3). John Cooper, born in Erwin, October 24, 1833; married
139.   Miss Ophelia Bronson of Erwin, December 19, 1867; have issue, four daughters and four sons.

140. (4). Thomas Wallis Cooper, born February 10, 1835; died October 31, 1862; Lieut. U. S. V. A.

141. (5). Theodore Cooper, born January 12, 1837.

142. (6). Samuel Erwin Cooper, born February 6, 1841; died August 3, 1864.

143. (7). Frederick Stephen Cooper, born in Cooper's Plain,

144.   October 24, 1842; married Miss Frances Josephine Merrill of Plainsville, O., November 27, 1872. Have issue, two sons and one daughter.

145. (8). Charlotte Elizabeth Cooper, born October 24, 1844;
146.   married William Bryson of Mechanicsburg, Pa.; have issue, three sons.

147. (9). Arthur Erwin Cooper, born April 12, 1848; married
148.   Miss Eliza Burch; have issue, four daughters and one son.

149. (10). Charles John Cooper, son of Dr. John Cooper, born in
150.   Easton, Pa., May 13, 1823; married September 15, 1846, Miss Martha A. Pierce of Campbell; issue, four sons and one daughter.

Ninth.— The Family of Theodore Sedgwick and
Elizabeth Cooper Paul, Belvidere, N. J.
(37 and 38).

151. (1). John Cooper Paul, born October 1831; died 1833.

152. (2). Elizabeth S. Paul, born 1833; married, November 5,
153.   1857, Henry Neil Paul of Philadelphia, Pa.; had issue, two daughters and two sons.

154. (3). Thomas Paul, born February, 1833; died 1859.

155. (4). Mary Erwin Paul, born 1837.

156. (5). Theodore Paul, born 1840; died in infancy.

157. (6). Arthur Erwin Paul, born —; died in infancy.

158. (7). Charlotte Vandevere Paul, born September 1843; mar-
159.   ried John C. Welling of Chicago, Ill., November 5, 1874; have issue, one daughter and one son. She died in 1906.

160. (8). Francis Erwin Paul, born —; died in infancy.

161. (9). Coneggs Paul, born August, 1846.

162. (10). Frank Ellinwood Paul, born —; married Miss Minnie
163.   Pope of Boston, Mass., March, 1877; have issue, one son and one daughter.

Tenth.— The Family of Joseph F. and Sarah Ann
Cooper Randolph of —, N. J. (40 and 41).

165. (1). Charlotte Vandervere Randolph, born April 12, 1842; unmarried.

166. (2). Joseph F. Randolph, Jr., born December 4, 1843;
167.   married Miss Harriet W. Talcott; no issue.

168. (3). John Cooper Randolph, born December 20, 1847.

169. (4). Mary Erwin Randolph, born March 11, 1850.

Eleventh.— The Family of Henry Huntington and
Rachel Erwin Birdsall, Addison, N. Y.

(42 and 43).

170. (1). Adelaide Frances Birdsall, born in Addison, March 30,
171.   1844; married Horace D. Baldwin of Addison, N. Y.,
           April 18, 1882; one son, died in infancy.
172. (2). Henry James Birdsall, born in Addison, September 12,
           1847; died in the Navy, October 31, 1863.
173. (3). Frank Erwin Birdsall, born in Erwin, N. Y., September
           12, 1850; died February 17, 1859.
174. (4). Mary Erwin Birdsall, born in Erwin, November 25,
175.   1852; married William S. Landers of Afton, N. Y.;
           have issue, two sons.
176. (5). Rachel Elizabeth Birdsall, born in Erwin, October 24,
           1857; married Dr. Charles W. Spencer of Sidney,
           N. Y.; no children.

Twelfth.— The Family of Samuel C. and Mary
Elizabeth Thompson Erwin of Hornby, N. Y.

(45 and 46).

177. (1). Helen E. Erwin, born August 20, 1857; died October
           14, 1862.
178. (2). Carrie M. Erwin, born June 15, 1859; married Fred L.
           Rogers; issue, one son and three daughters.
179. (3). Samuel C. Erwin, born April 21, 1861; married Minnie
           Crane.
180. (4). Arthur Erwin, born October 18, 1864.
181. (5). James Thompson Erwin, born December 1, 1867;
           married Lillian —; have issue, four children.
182. (6). Elizabeth Thompson Erwin, born May 28, 1869; married
           Rev. H. F. Cope.

Thirteenth.— The Family of Charles and Kate
Willard Erwin of Washington, D. C.

(47 and 48).

183. (1). Mary Erwin, died in infancy.
184. (2). Annie Erwin, born August 5, 1867; married; children.
185. (3). Sarah Elizabeth Erwin, born November 11, 1871;
           married; one son, Charles.
     (4). Arthur Erwin, born August 23, 1877.
     (5). Katie Erwin, born August 25, 1885.
     (6). Nora Erwin, born August 14, 1888.

Fourteenth.— The Family of George H. and Sarah
Elizabeth Erwin Weatherby of Addison, N. Y.
(49 and 50).

186. (1). George H. Weatherby, born —; died June 26, 1859.

187. (2). Albert Erwin Weatherby, born August 7, 1854; in
U. S. Signal Service; died —; one son, George H.

188. (3). George H. Weatherby, born August 27, 1861.

Fifteenth.— The Family of Amaziah S. and Anna
E. Erwin McKay of Addison, N. Y.
(51 and 52).

189. (1). Helen S. McKay, born April 3, 1861; married H. S.
Rose.

190. (2). Arthur P. McKay, born May 19, 1864; died unmarried.

Sixteenth.— The Family of John Francis and
Johanette Louise Schneider Erwin, who were
married May 7, 1829.
(53 and 54).

191. (1). Ambrose John Erwin, born March 9, 1830; married
192. March 17, 1857, Mary A. Clauder. He was Mayor of
Bethlehem three years; in City Council nine years;
Member of Assembly at Harrisburg, term of 1876
and 1877; Volunteer in Fifth Pennsylvania Regiment.
Their children are: Francis H. Erwin, born January
29, 1859; Martha L. Erwin, born February 7, 1861;
Annie C. Erwin, born January 11, 1863; Charles A.
Erwin; Carrie M. Erwin, born September 16, 1866;
William C. Erwin, born June 30, 1870.

193. (2). Mary K. Erwin, born March 15, 1832; married Horace
B. Jones of Philadelphia, who joined 46th Regiment
Pennsylvania Volunteers; served as First Lieutenant
and Adjutant in forty engagements. One daughter,
Florence L. Jones, born May 20, 1857.

194. (3). William Arthur Erwin, born June 27, 1838; married,
April 7, 1864, Ella Kast of Weisport, Pa.; Corporal
in 129th Regiment Pennsylvania Volunteers. Also
served in 34th Regiment. Their children were: Lulu
Erwin, born July 10, 1866; died February 3, 1867;
Edith N. Erwin, born February 4, 187–; Harold K.
Erwin, born January 7, 1879; died September 2,
1881.

(4). Edward Francis Erwin, born October 13, 1841; unmarried.

    (5.) Bertine S. Erwin, M. D., born May 30, 1845; married
        Mrs. M. Dimmick of Mauchchunk, October 7, 1878.
  Seventeenth.— The Family of Arthur, Jr., and his
      two wives, Miss Isabella Thompson Erwin and
      Miss Martha Jones Erwin of Erwin.
              (55, 56 and 57).

195. (1). James T. Erwin, born in Erwin, May 19, 1833; married
196.   Miss Densey Knapp; no issue.
197. (2). Arthur Erwin, born in Erwin, May 8, 1835.
198. (3). Edward Erwin, born in Erwin, October 22, 1837: mar-
199.   ried Miss Ella Dodge, Indiana; he died December 24,
          1875; no issue.
200. (4). Mary E. Erwin, born in Erwin, August 10, 1840; mar-
201.   ried Llewellyn M. Jones of Addison; have issue, two
          sons and one daughter.
202. (5). John Erwin, born in Erwin, April 12, 1843; died un-
          married.
203. (6). Scott Erwin, born in Erwin, April 10, 1845.
          (By second wife, née Miss Jones.)
204. (7). Henry S. Erwin, born in Erwin, March 7, 1848; married
205.   Miss Sarah Webster of Michigan; have issue three
          sons and one daughter, Harry, Hugh, Guy, and Martha.
206. (8). William Erwin, born in Erwin, October 22, 1850.
207. (9). Kate Erwin, born in Erwin, May 18, 1853.
208. (10). Cora Erwin, born in Erwin, July 15, 1855.
    Eighteenth.— The Family of Hugh, son of Capt.
    Samuel Erwin and Mary Powers Erwin of
    Cincinnati, O. (31 and 32).
209. (1). Mary Jane Erwin, died unmarried 1906.

    GREAT-GREAT-GRANDCHILDREN, OR FIFTH GENERATION.

    First.— The Family of Edward Erwin and Nancy
    Lawrence Jerome Townsend of Erwin.
            (59 and 60).
210. (1). Fanny Jerome Townsend, born in Erwin, July 1, 1849;
          died August 7, 1869.
211. (2). Frederick Jerome Townsend, born in Erwin, October
212.   6, 1850; married Mrs. Viola Tibbot of Tulare, Cal.;
          have issue, two daughters and three sons.
213. (3). Mary Townsend, born in Erwin, February 15, 1852;
          died September 13, 1853.

214. (4). Arthur E. Townsend, born in Erwin, December 20, 1854; assassinated near Tulare, Cal., July 7, 1879, by son of Indian chief.

215. (5). Jerome Townsend, born in Erwin, May 2, 1858; died October 25, 1876.

216. (6). Eliza E. Townsend, born in Erwin, February 15, 1860; died September 16, 1869.

217. (7). Edward E. Townsend, born in Erwin, April 14, 1863; died October 12, 1876.

218. (8). Annie L. Townsend, born in Erwin, March 7, 1856; married H. C. Hermans of Corning, N. Y.

Second.— The Family of Marcus and Mary Erwin Stevens of Detroit, Mich.   (61 and 62).

219. (1). Helen E. Stevens, born in the City of Detroit, November 17, 1859.

Third.— The Family of Eugene H. and Elizabeth H. Cook Erwin, of Painted Post, N. Y.
(63 and 64).

220. (1). Alice A. Erwin, born September, 30, 1862.

Fourth.— The Family of Charles and Annie Erwin Iredell.   (70 and 71).

221. (1). Arthur Erwin Iredell, born in Painted Post, January 31, 1870.

Fifth.— The Family of Arthur H. and Gertrude Maria Brown Erwin of Addison, N. Y.
(72 and 73).

222. (1). Agnes Maria Erwin, born in Erwin July 26, 1871.

223. (2). Frances Gertrude Erwin, born September 2, 1872.

Sixth.— The Family of John and Harriet Louise Erwin Lutman of Detroit, Mich.
(74 and 75).

224. (1). Arthur Erwin Lutman, born in Detroit, October 17, 1874.

225. (2). Francis Erwin Lutman, born in Detroit, September 18, 1876.

226. (3). Harriet Louise Lutman, born in Detroit.

Seventh.— The Family of Samuel S. and his two wives, Amelia Shaw and Susan Williams of Corning, N. Y.   (79, 80 and 81).

227.
228. (1). Harriet Sophia Erwin, born May 29, 1851; married Wesley Darrin of Corning, N. Y.; had issue, one son. She died August 26, 1878.

229. (2). Frank Erwin, born in Corning, March 27, 1853; mar-
230.   ried Miss Hattie D. Clute of Corning, October 10, 1878.
231. (3). Samuel Erwin, born October 13, 1857; married Miss
232.   Emma Tupper.
233. (4). Edward Erwin, born in Corning, November 27, 1860.
234. (5). Robert Erwin, born September 20, 1865; died Septem-
       ber 11, 1866.
235. (6). Harry Erwin.

Eighth.— The Family of Edward E. and Susan
Gamble Erwin of Painted Post. (82 and 83).

236. (1). William Gamble Erwin, born December 5, 1855; died
       October 11, 1871.

Ninth.— The Family of Cephas F. and Mary
Erwin Platt of Painted Post. (84 and 85).

237. (1). Sophia Erwin Platt, born in Painted Post, November
238.   4, 1854; married Chester A. Tousey, December
       15, 1875.
239. (2). Elizabeth Platt, born December 18, 1857.
240. (3). Frank Platt, born January 25, 1866.

Tenth.— The Family of Francis and Helen Campbell
Erwin of Erwin. (86 and 87).

241. (1). Sophia H. Erwin, born September 7, 1859.
242. (2). Arthur B. Erwin, born June 29, 1863.

Eleventh.— The Family of Robert B. and Harriet
Erwin Wilkes of Bath, N. Y. (89 and 90).

243. (1). Sophia Wilkes, born in Bath, N. Y., February 16, 1861.
244. (2). Annie Wilkes, born in Bath, June 13, 1862.
245. (3). Robert Wilkes, born in Bath, January 18, 1864.
246. (4). Harriet Jane Wilkes, born in Bath, August 5, 1865.
247. (5). Francis Erwin Wilkes, born in Bath, March 2, 1867.
248. (6). James Shannon Wilkes, born in Bath, October 20, 1868.
249. (7). Mary Elizabeth Wilkes, born in Bath, October 13, 1871.
250. (8). Samuel Erwin Wilkes, born in Bath, June 3, 1873.

Twelfth.— The Family of Dr. William H. and Cornelia Pease Erwin Beaumont of Cleveland,
Ohio. (92 and 93).

251. (1). George Henry Beaumont, born June 16, 1865.
252. (2). Martha Bowles Beaumont, born March 29, 1868.
253. (3). Arthur Erwin Beaumont, born December 18, 1872.
254. (4). Laura E. Beaumont, born October 17, 1875.
255. (5). John Erwin Beaumont, born November 17, 1879.

Thirteenth.— The Family of Charles Edward and Laura Grant Erwin Pease of Dayton, Ohio. (94 and 95).

256.   (1). Calvin E. Pease, born May 1, 1867.

257.   (2). Ned Pease, born December 3, 1871.

Fourteenth.— The Family of Henry L. and Florence Heckman Erwin Paige of St. Louis. (98 and 99).

258.   (1). Annie Erwin Paige, born March 26, 1867.

259.   (2). Erwin Paige, born September 23, 1870.

260.   (3). Albert Paige, born July 13, 1872.

261.   (4). Florence Paige, born August 13, 1873.

Fifteenth.— The Family of Lieut. in U. S. A. Henry H. and Leonora Erwin Wright, New Mexico.   (104 and 105).

262.   (1). Arthur John Wright.

263.   (2). Harry Haviland Wright.

Sixteenth.— The Family of J. Ralph and Elizabeth Wallis Erwin Ward of Elmira, N. Y. (106 and 107).

264.   (1). William Ward.

265.   (2). Ralph Ward.

266.   (3). Daughter.

Seventeenth.— The Family of Charles H. and Mary Alice Erwin Potter of Cleveland, Ohio. (116 and 117).

267.   (1). Mary Antoinette Potter, born in Cleveland, September 27, 1879.

268.   (2). Charles Mason Potter, born in Cleveland, November 1, 1881.

Eighteenth.— The Family of Charles M. and Helen Gilbert Fay of Chicago, Ill. (118 and 119).

269.   (1). A son, Gilbert, born in Painted Post.

Nineteenth.— The Family of Samuel Erwin and Sarah E. Adams Gilbert of Painted Post. (122 and 123).

270.   (1). Alice F. Gilbert, born in Painted Post, August 29, 1868.

271.   (2). Celia E. Gilbert, born in Painted Post, April 16, 1872.

272.   (3). Lulu M. Gilbert, born in Painted Post, October 28, 1873.

273. (4). Edna J. Gilbert, born in Painted Post, May 4, 1879.
    (5). Hazel.
       Twentieth.— The Family of William J. and Anna
        Badger Gilbert of St. Louis, Mo.
            (124 and 125).
274. (1). Louise Badger Gilbert, born January 20, 1873.
       Twenty-first.— The Family of Willard C. and
        Mary Cooper Morse of Erwin, N. Y.
            (135 and 136).
275. (1). John Cooper Morse, born September 22, 1854.
276. (2). Elizabeth Evans Morse, born February 19, 1857;
      died October 21, 1864.
       Twenty-second.— The Family of Dr. John and
        Ophelia Bronson Cooper of Painted Post, N. Y.
            (137 and 138).
277. (1). Alice Cooper, born August 19, 1869.
278. (2). John Cooper, born January 7, 1871; died April 22, 1872.
279. (3). John Vandervere Cooper, born October 19, 1873.
280. (4). Louise Cooper, born April 27, 1875; died April 27,
      1876.
281. (5). Randolph Cooper, born March 3, 1877.
282. (6). Mary Cooper, born August 25, 1879.
283. (7). Harley Bronson Cooper, born October 9, 1880.
       Twenty-third.— The Family of Frederick Stephen
        and Frances Josephine Merill Cooper of White
         Rock, Kansas. (142 and 143).
284. (1). Frederick Merrill Cooper.
285. (2). Nellie Ervans Cooper.
286. (3). Eddie Merrill Cooper, born 1881.
       Twenty-fourth.— The Family of William and
        Charlotte Elizabeth Cooper Bryson of Mechanics-
         burg Pa. (144 and 145).
287. (1). Thomas B. Bryson, born April 9, 1872.
288. (2). John Cooper Bryson.
289. (3). Fred Struthers Bryson.
       Twenty-fifth.— The Family of Arthur Erwin and
        Eliza Burch Cooper of Cooper's Plains, N. Y.
            (146 and 147).
290. (1). Lizzie May Cooper, born at Cooper's Plains, February
      5, 1873.
291. (2). Charlotte J. Cooper, born February 6, 1874.

292. (3). Kathleen Cooper, born December 15, 1876.
293. (4). Thomas W. Cooper, born February 10, 1879.
294. (5). Bessie Evans Cooper, born April 29, 1881.

Twenty-sixth.— The Family of Charles John and
Martha Pierce Cooper of Erwin, N. Y.
(148 and 149).

295. (1). Charles J. Cooper, Jr., born July 9, 1847; died September 25, 1872.
296. (2). Benjamin Pierce Cooper, born in Erwin, January 14,
297. 1849; married Miss Callie Owens of Jackson, Miss.; issue, one son and one daughter.
298. (3). Mary Erwin Cooper, born December 12, 1850; married
299. Dr. A. E. Overhiser of Campbell, N. Y., May 10, 1876; had issue, two daughters and one son; she died January, 10, 1882.
300. (4). John Ernest Cooper, born September 27, 1852; married Mrs. Mary Freslaider of Bavaria, Germany, June 1872; have issue, two sons and one daughter.
302. (5). Frank B. Cooper, born December 11, 1854.

Twenty-seventh.— The Family of Henry Neil and
Elizabeth S. Paul of Philadelphia, Pa.
(151 and 152).

303. (1). Meta Neil Paul, born September 26, 1860; died in infancy.
304. (2). Henry Neil Paul, Jr., born September 25, 1863.
305. (3). Elizabeth Duffield Paul, born October 1, 1867; died in infancy.
306. (4). Theodore Sedgwick Paul, born November 13, 1873; died in infancy.

Twenty-eighth.— The Family of John C. and
Charlotte Vandevere Paul Welling of Chicago,
Ill. (157 and 158).

307. (1). Bessie Paul Welling, born August, 1875; died in infancy.
308. (2). John Paul Welling, born September 6, 1881.

Twenty-ninth.— The Family of Frank Ellinwood
and Minnie Pope Paul of Belvidere, N. J.
(161 and 162).

309. (1). Edith Vandevere Paul, born December, 1877.
310. (2). Russell A. Paul, born March, 1880.

Thirtieth.— The Family of William S. and Mary
Erwin Birdsall Landers of Afton, N. Y.
(173 and 174).

311. (1). Maurice Birdsall Landers, born April 3, 1882.

(2). Roland Henry Birdsall Landers, born November 25, 1883.

Thirty-first.— The Family of Ambrose and Mary C. Erwin of Bethlehem, Pa. (190 and 191).

312. (1). Francis H. Erwin, married Mary E. Spahr, York, Pa.; one daughter, Lydia.

313. (2). Carrie M. Erwin, married Harry Wilbur, Bethlehem; children, Helena, John, Warren, Martha, Louise.

314. (3). Charles, died 1901; married Louise; children, Annie, William C., unmarried.

Thirty-second.— The Family of James and Denise

315. (1). Knapp Erwin of Erwin, N. Y. (194 and 195).

316. (2).

Thirty-third.— The Family of Llewellyn and Mary Erwin Jones of ——. (199 and 200).

317. (1). Arthur Erwin Jones, born November, 1871.

318. (2). Janis M. Jones; died.

319. (3). Walter Weston Jones, born May 5, 1880.

Thirty-fourth.— The Family of Henry and Sarah Webster Erwin of Erwin. (203 and 204).

320. (1). Harry Edward Erwin, born May 10, 1872; married Miss Elizabeth May Crawford of Rathbone, N. Y., June 4, 1902; issue, one daughter, Hazel Elizabeth Erwin, born December 4, 1903.

321. (2). Hugh Llewellyn Erwin, born June 19, 1874; married Frances Cecilia O'Connell of Hornell, N. Y., February, 1895. Issue, two children, Arthur Raymond Erwin, born October 6, 1895; Katharine Sarah Erwin, born August 22, 1903.

322. (3). Guy Asaph Erwin, born May 26, 1876.

223. (4). Martha Marie Erwin, born September 26, 1881; married Ray Benedict Murray of Addison, N. Y., June 19, 1906.

(5). James Ray Erwin, born April 10, 1884; died in Mishawaka, Indiana, in 1886.

SIXTH GENERATION

The great-great-great grandchildren of Col. Arthur and Mary Kennedy Erwin of Erwinna, Bucks Co., Pa.

First.— The Family of Frederick Jerome and
Viola Talbot Townsend of Erwin, N. Y.
(210 and 211).

324.   (1). Fanny Jerome Townsend, born October 30, 1878.
325.   (2). Mary Townsend, born October 3, 1880.
326.   (3). Clarence Ellsworth Townsend, born April 7, 1882.

Second. — The Family of Wesley and Hattie Sophia
Erwin Darrin of Corning, N. Y.
(226 and 227).

327.   (1). Samuel Wesley Darrin, born August 23, 1878.

Third.— The Family of Benjamin Pierce and
Callie T. Owens Cooper of ——.
(294 and 295).

328.   (1). Maud C. Cooper, born March, 1875.
329.   (2). Charles J. Cooper, Jr., born September, 1881.

Fourth.— The Family of Dr. E. A. and Mary
Erwin Cooper Overhiser of Campbell, N. Y.
(296 and 297).

330.   (1). Helen C. Overhiser, born July 10, 1877.
331.   (2). Mary L. Overhiser, born June 8, 1879.
332.   (3). Charles J. Overhiser, born July 4, 1881.

Fifth.— The Family of John Ernest and Mary
Freslaider Cooper of Painted Post.
(298 and 299).

333.   (1). John Cooper, born October, 1873.
334.   (2). Mary Cooper, born February, 1882.

THE IRISH BRANCH OF THE HOUSE OF BONSHAW.

GENEALOGY OF THE DESCENDANTS OF COL. ARTHUR ERWIN.

Col. Arthur Erwin, born in 1726, a Scotch-Irish immigrant of considerable means, came with his brother William to America before the Revolution, about 1765, remaining about one year, when he returned for his family, who were living in Parish Crumlin, Co. Antrim, Ireland. He spent some time settling his business, and early in May, 1768, he embarked his family and many relatives and servants on the ship Newry Assistance, of Newry, then anchored in Carlingford Bay, and commanded by William Cheevers. They landed at Philadelphia about August 18, 1768. His family consisted of his wife, Mary Scott Erwin, five sons and one daughter. Mary Scott Erwin died July 10, 1768, while at sea, and was buried there. Col. Arthur Erwin married for his second wife Miss Mary Kennedy of Easton, Pa., on July 28, 1771. She died on Tuesday morning, July 29, 1817.

Joseph, Col. Arthur Erwin's second son, wrote: "We resided for the autumn and winter at Dyerstown, in a house belonging to my Uncle William. The first property my father bought in America was two plantations in Tinicum township, Bucks Co., Pa., one of which was known as the 'Red house farm,' containing 416 acres, conveyed to him by William Pidgeon, Esq., and to this farm we moved and settled on about May 1, 1769." Later, besides large holdings in Bucks Co., he purchased large tracts of land in Luzerne Co., Pa., and Steuben Co., New York.

In 1776–77, Arthur Erwin was Colonel of the 4th and 2nd Battalions, respectively, of Bucks County Militia, in which rank several letters and orders, which are still in existence, were addressed to him by General Washington just previous to the battle of Trenton. The Christmas Eve before the battle Col. Erwin carried many of our soldiers across the river in his own boats from his estates on the banks of the Delaware. He was shot and killed by a squatter named Thomas on July 9, 1791, while at the house of one Daniel McDuffey, a tenant, at Tioga Point, Luzerne Co., Pa. He was buried at Erwinna, Pa., July 17th, in the Erwin family lot on the banks of the Delaware river.

CHILDREN OF ARTHUR AND MARY SCOTT ERWIN.

1. JOHN ERWIN, born in Ireland November 12, 1756; died February 17, 1788. He was a 1st Lieutenant in the Flying Camp of the Continental Army; was taken prisoner at the fall of Ft. Washington and held for four years, dying a few months after his release. Unmarried.

2. JOSEPH ERWIN, born July 24, 1758, in Parish Crumlin, County Antrim, Ireland; died February 9, 1807. He served a term in Congress about 1790, and held several important governmental positions. He did effective service for his country both at home and in France. He lived as a country gentleman and never married.

3. WILLIAM LIVINGSTON ERWIN, born in Ireland, February 12, 1760; died June 16, 1836. He was commissioned a Captain in the 1st Regt. of Foot in the Continental Army May 14, 1781. Thirty years later he represented Bucks County for several terms in the Pennsylvania State Senate. He

married Achsah, daughter of Dr. John and Rachel (Robesen) Rockhill of Hunterdon, N. J., in 1782.

4. SARAH ERWIN, born in Ireland, September 16, 1762; married Judge John Mulhollen; she died May 5, 1809; he died April 5, 1815; they had issue, three daughters and eight sons.

5. FRANCIS ERWIN, born and died in 1764.

6. ARTHUR ERWIN, born in Ireland 1765; drowned in the Delaware river May 17, 1769.

7. HUGH SCOTT ERWIN, born in Ireland, February 8, 1767; died May 31, 1846; married, but left no family.

DESCENDANTS OF COL. ARTHUR AND MARY KENNEDY IRWIN.

An authentic record of the lineal descendants of Col. Arthur Erwin and Mary Kennedy, his second wife, of Erwinna, Pa., including all the husbands and wives marrying into the family, as far as possible to ascertain, to the present date, 1907. They had issue:

1. SAMUEL ERWIN, born May 4, 1772; died November 10, 1836; married, first, 1800; married second, Miss Rachel Heckman of Easton, Pa.; she died August 26, 1860, aged 77 years. On January 10, 1799, he was commissioned by President Adams 1st Lieutenant in the 11th Regt. U. S. Infantry. His commission expired with the President's term of office. On February 16, 1802, President Jefferson commissioned him 1st Lieut. of the 2nd Regt. U. S. Inft., and he was subsequently promoted to the rank of Captain. He died in Painted Post, N. Y. First wife's name not known. One son.

2. MARY ERWIN, born May 12, 1773; married May 22, 1798, Dr. John Cooper of Easton, Pa., who died February 2, 1851. She died November 19, 1864. They had issue, one son and four daughters.

3. REBECCA ERWIN, born June 1, 1785; married Dr. William McKeen of Easton, Pa., in 1805; died April 19, 1848; had issue, one daughter.

4. ARTHUR ERWIN, born October 15, 1777; died April 7, 1842; married three times: first, M. N. Erie, issue, one son; second, Miss Lamphear, issue, one son; third, Sarah Clark of Erwin, N. Y., who died May 19, 1863; they had issue, two sons and four daughters.

5. FRANCIS ERWIN, born February 29, 1780; unmarried; died September 6, 1839.

6. JOHN ERWIN, born December, 1786; unmarried; died June 4, 1820.

GRANDCHILDREN — THIRD GENERATION.

1. HUGH ERWIN, son of Captain Samuel Irwin by his first wife, married Miss Mary Powers, sister of the distinguished sculptor, Hiram Powers, of Cincinnati, Ohio; had issue, one daughter.

(Children of Capt. Samuel Erwin and 2nd wife, Rachel Heckman.)

2. ELIZA ERWIN, born October 15, 1801; died December 28, 1883; married, November 22, 1821, Edward Townsend, who died November 25, 1825; had issue, one son and one daughter. On a pillow across the saddle in front of her father, she came from Easton, Pa., to Painted Post, N. Y., in the spring of 1803.

3. ARTHUR H. ERWIN, born November 25, 1803; died August 1, 1863; married, February 21, 1828, at Painted Post, Miss Frances Mariah McKeen, his cousin, who died February 17, 1882; they had issue, five sons and seven daughters.

4. FRANCIS E. ERWIN, born May 3, 1806; died July 6, 1887; married, January 23, 1837, Miss Sophia McCall of Bath, N. Y., who died May 16, 1856; they had issue, five sons and two daughters. While in the New York legislature he was a member of the Military Committee. General Erwin held all of the military offices in the State Militia from the rank of Corporal to that of General, save that of Captain.

5. JOHN ERWIN, born March 21, 1808; died January 15, 1888; married, June 29, 1836, Miss Nancy Pease of Warren, Ohio; they had issue, two sons and eight daughters.

6. MARY ERWIN, born October 17, 1810; unmarried; died January 5, 1825.

7. WILLIAM ERWIN, born June 11, 1813; died June 23, 1894; married, May 2, 1839, Miss Mary Evans of Philadelphia, Pa., who died April 23, 1899; had issue, four sons and four daughters.

8. RACHEL A. ERWIN, born November 20, 1815; died August 26, 1890; married, October 30, 1839, William J. Gilbert of Painted Post, N. Y., who died November 21, 1863; had issue, six sons and three daughters.

9. SAMUEL ERWIN, born and died March 20, 1817.

10. SAMUEL KENNEDY ERWIN, born August 11, 1819; died July 28, 1874; married, June 11, 1845, his cousin, Miss Mary Eliza Kern of Erwin, N. Y.; had issue, two sons and one daughter.

11. CHARLES HECKMAN ERWIN, born April 30, 1822; died September 6, 1890; married, January 15, 1850, Miss Antoinette Curtis of Campbell, N. Y.; she died January 28, 1884; no issue.

Children of Mary Erwin and Dr. John Cooper, Easton, Pa.

1. John Cooper, Jr., born May 26, 1799; died October 23, 1863; married, second, January 6, 1828, Miss Elizabeth Evans of Wilksbarre, Pa., who died December 9, 1889; they had issue, seven sons and two daughters. Name and date of first marriage unknown; one son.

2. Charlotte M. E. Cooper, born August 15, 1801; died May 9, 1889; married, July 31, 1824, Rev. Dr. John Vandeveer of Easton, Pa., who died April 28, 1878; no issue.

3. Elizabeth Cooper, born December 13, 1810; died January 13, 1879; married, October 20, 1830, Theodore Sedgwick Paul, who died October 7, 1887; they had issue, eight sons and three daughters.

4. Mary Cooper, born August 18, 1812; died August 28, 1812.

5. Sarah Ann Cooper, born June 18, 1815; died October 15, 1905; married, September 8, 1840, Joseph F. Randolph of Belvidere, N. J., who died March 19, 1872; they had issue, two sons and two daughters.

Family of Rebecca Erwin, and William McKeen, Easton, Pa.

1. Frances Mariah McKeen, born 1808; died February 17, 1882; married, February 21, 1828, Arthur H. Erwin of Painted Post, N. Y., who died August 1, 1863; they had issue, five sons and seven daughters.

Family of Maj. Arthur Erwin and his first wife, M. N. Erie.

1. John Francis Erwin, born February 18, 1803; died February 8, 1883; married, May 7, 1829, Miss Johnnette Louise Schneider; had issue, four sons and one daughter.

Family of Maj. Arthur Erwin and second wife, Miss Lamphere.

2. Arthur Erwin, Jr., born December 1, 1807; died February 4, 1892; married, first, Miss Isabelle Thompson, January 13, 1831; she died January 15, 1845; second, Miss Martha

Jones, May 19, 1847; she died January 30, 1892; had issue by first wife, five sons and one daughter; by second wife, two sons and two daughters.

Family of Maj. Arthur Erwin and third wife, Sarah Clark, Addison, N. Y.

3. Rachel Erwin, born March 8, 1821; married, June 14, 1843, Henry Huntington Birdsall, Addison, N. Y., who died June 23, 1894; had issue, two sons and three daughters.

4. Mary Erwin, born February 27, 1824; unmarried; died June 28, 1889.

5. Samuel C. Erwin, born August 12, 1827; died October, 1896; married, December 24, 1856, Miss Mary Elizabeth Thompson, Erwin, N. Y.; issue, three sons and three daughters.

6. Charles Erwin, born February 26, 1829; married Miss Kate Willard; had issue, one son and six daughters.

7. Sarah Elizabeth Erwin, born October 1, 1833; married, November 2, 1853, George H. Weatherby of Addison, N. Y., who died April 30, 1861; had issue, three sons.

8. Annie E. Erwin, born June 22, 1838; married, December 20, 1859, Amaziah S. McKay of Addison, N. Y.; had issue, one son and one daughter.

GREAT-GRANDCHILDREN — FOURTH GENERATION.

Col. Arthur Erwin	Mary Kennedy	1st.
1 Capt. Samuel Erwin	First wife	2nd.
1 Hugh Erwin	Mary Powers	3rd.
Cincinnati, Ohio.		

Mary Jane Erwin, born July 23, 1833; unmarried; died July 25, 1906.

Col. Arthur Erwin	Mary Kennedy	1st.
1 Capt. Samuel Erwin	Rachel Heckman	2nd.
2 Eliza Erwin	Edward Townsend	3rd.
Erwin, N. Y.		

Edward Erwin Townsend, born January 23, 1825; died September 25, 1898; married, September 7, 1848, Miss Nancy Lawrence Jerome of Plum Island, N. Y., who died December 1, 1904; had issue, four sons and four daughters.

Col. Arthur Erwin	Mary Kennedy	1st.
1 Capt. Samuel Erwin	Rachel Heckman	2nd.
3 Arthur H. Erwin	Frances Mariah McKeen	3rd.
Painted Post, N. Y.		

1. Mary Kennedy Erwin, born April 2, 1831; died June 13, 1903; married, December 26, 1855, Marcus Stevens of Detroit, Mich.; issue, one daughter.

2. Eugene Hamilton Erwin, born August 14, 1832; married, November 13, 1861, Miss Elizabeth H. Cook of Presho, N. Y.; issue, one daughter.

3. Emily Rebecca Erwin, born June 27, 1834; died October 27, 1891; unmarried.

4. Frances Virginia Erwin, born April 15, 1836; unmarried.

5. Elizabeth Erwin, born July 15, 1838; died October 26, 1905; married February 16, 1881, Dr. John B. Dudley of Bath, N. Y.; no issue.

6. DeWitt Clinton Erwin, born March 10, 1840; died December 11, 1873; unmarried. He was Second Sergt. of Co. F, 50th N. Y. Engrs., Union Army.

7. Anna Maria Erwin, born May 2, 1842; died June 17, 1898; married, April 8, 1869, Charles Iredell of Painted Post, N. Y.; had issue, one son.

8. Arthur H. Erwin, Jr., born May 10, 1844; married, first, October 19, 1870, Miss Gertrude Brown of Addison, N. Y.; issue, two daughters; married, second, August 15, 1899, Mrs. Mary Gay Bressie; issue, one son.

9. Harriet Louise Erwin, born July 9, 1846; married, July 16, 1873, John Lutman of Detroit, Mich.; issue, one son and two daughters.

10. Winfield Scott Erwin, born December 18, 1848; unmarried; died October 30, 1905.

11. Helen Erwin, born June 14, 1851; died September 5, 1855.

12. John Jay Erwin, born May 1, 1854; died August 30, 1855.

Col. Arthur Erwin	Mary Kennedy	1st.
1 Capt. Samuel Erwin	Rachel Heckman	2nd.
4 Francis E. Erwin	Sophia McCall	3rd.

Painted Post, N. Y.

1. Samuel Stanbury Erwin, born October 28, 1827; married, first, Amelia Shaw, August 7, 1850; she died August 22, 1870; issue, four sons and one daughter; married, second, Susan Williams of Tyrone, N. Y., November 11, 1876; issue, one son.

2. Edward E. Erwin, born November 22, 1829; died November 18, 1899; married, November 22, 1852, Miss Susan Gamble of Auburn, N. Y.; issue, one son.

3. Mary Elizabeth Erwin, born June 20, 1831; married, May 26,

1852, Cephas F. Platt of Campbell, N. Y.; he died November 28, 1833; issue, one son and two daughters.

4. Francis Erwin, born January 5, 1834; married, October 27, 1858, Miss Helen Campbell, Painted Post, N. Y.; she died December 25, 1900; had issue, one son and one daughter.

5. Harriet Maria Erwin, born, January 4, 1836; married, March 27, 1860, Robert B. Wilks of Bath, N. Y.; died November 23, 1876; had issue, four sons, four daughters.

6. John Ansel Erwin, born July 16, 1838; died August 28, 1838.

7. John Ansel Erwin, born January 18, 1840; died April 13, 1841.

Col. Arthur Erwin	Mary Kennedy	1st.
1. Capt. Samuel Erwin	Rachel Heckman	2nd.
3. John Erwin	Nancy Pease	3rd.

Cleveland, Ohio.

1. Calvin Pease Erwin, born May 12, 1837; unmarried; died December 26, 1854.

2. Cornelia Pease Erwin, born August 9, 1839; married, March 24, 1863, Dr. William H. Beaumont, Cleveland, Ohio; had issue, four sons and three daughters.

3. Laura Grant Erwin, born September 10, 1841; married, October 3, 1865, Charles Edward Pease of Dayton, Ohio; have issue, two sons.

4. Lillian H. Erwin, born August 26, 1843; unmarried; dead.

5. Arthur John Erwin, born October 10, 1845.

6. Florence Heckman Erwin, born November 17, 1847; married, December 20, 1865, Henry L. Paige of St. Louis, Mo.; have issue, two sons and two daughters.

7. Mary Pease Erwin, born July 29, 1850; married, November 30, 1870, Cyrus E. Johnston of Painesville, Ohio.

8. Kate Granger Erwin, born April 9, 1852; married ——— McCrea.

9. Grace Erwin, born August 9, 1854; died December 24, 1854.

10. Leonore Erwin, born April 26, 1857; married, February 19, 1879, Lieut. Henry H. Wright, U. S. A.; have issue, two sons.

Col. Arthur Erwin	Mary Kennedy	1st.
1. Capt. Samuel Erwin	Racher Heckman	2nd.
7. William Erwin	Mary Evans	3rd.

Painted Post, N. Y.

1. Elizabeth Wallis Erwin, born March 14, 1840; married, first, J. Ralph Ward of Elmira, N. Y., June 17, 1864; he died

December 2, 1880; had issue, three sons; married, second, Robert A. Craig of New York, December 16, 1882; no issue.

2. Mary Evans Erwin, born June 4, 1841; died September 15, 1842.

3. William Wilberforce Erwin, born July 12, 1843; married, first, Carmelita Freida Van Buskin, 1874; second, Mary J. King, Ravona, Minn., September 7, 1881; third, Ann Olive, 1898; no issue. He is First Lieut. Co. K, 74th Regt. Inft. N. Y. Vols.

4. John Evans Erwin, born May 8, 1844; married, 1889, Miss Julia Gazley of Cleveland, Ohio; issue, one daughter.

5. Alice Murry Erwin, born October 14, 1845; died July 5, 1848.

6. Albert Erwin, born November 10, 1846; died November 26, 1863.

7. Thomas Wallis Erwin, born April 22, 1849; died September 10, 1849.

8. Mary Alice Erwin, born March 15, 1852; died July 19, 1890; married, November 28, 1876, Charles H. Potter of Hartford, Conn.; issue, one daughter and one son.

Col. Arthur Erwin	Mary Kennedy	1st.
1. Capt. Samuel Erwin	Rachel Heckman	2nd.
8. Rachel A. Erwin	William J. Gilbert	3rd.

Painted Post, N. Y.

1. Helen Gilbert, born August 15, 1840; died July 24, 1886; married, December 13, 1864, Charles M. Fay of Prattsburg, N. Y.; died 1902; issue, one son.

2. Henry Erwin Gilbert, born August 26, 1843; died December 1, 1861. Soldier Co. D, 23rd Regt. Inft., N. Y. Vols.

3. William Gilbert, born August 25, 1845; died July 28, 1846.

4. Samuel Erwin Gilbert, born May 1, 1847; married, December 17, 1867, Miss Sarah E. Adams of Painted Post, N. Y.; issue, seven daughters.

5. William Jewett Gilbert, born August 21, 1849; married, November 15, 1871, Miss Anna Louise Badger, Painted Post, N. Y.; issue, one daughter.

6. Nora Neil Gilbert, born August 7, 1851; unmarried.

7. Sidney Lawrence Gilbert, born March 18, 1854; married, December 21, 1881, Miss Sadie Kelly, Detroit, Mich.; issue, none.

8. Mary Erwin Gilbert, born June 16, 1856; died November 21, 1881; married, December 29, 1880, Frank W. Douglas of Corning, N. Y.; issue, none.

9. Charles B. Gilbert, born January 10, 1859; died March 27, 1889; unmarried.

Col. Arthur Erwin   Mary Kennedy   1st.
   1. Capt. Samuel Erwin   Rachel Heckman   2nd.
  10. Samuel Kennedy Erwin Mary Elica Kern   3rd.
              Painted Post, N. Y.

1. Mary E. Erwin, born December 27, 1847; died December 28, 1847.

2. Franklin Kern Erwin, born August 13, 1849; died January 24, 1879; unmarried.

3. Eugene Erwin, born February 3, 1858; died October 23, 1897; married, December 19, 1892, Miss Susan Anderson of Galveston, Tex.; issue, two sons and one daughter.

Col. Arthur Erwin   Mary Kennedy   1st.
   2. Mary Irwin   Dr. John Cooper   2nd.
   1. Dr. John Cooper, Jr. 1st wife   3rd.

1. Charles John Cooper, born May 13, 1823; died November 4, 1883; married, September 15, 1846, Miss Martha Pierce of Campbell, N.Y.; issue, four sons and one daughter.

By second wife, Elizabeth M. Evans, Cooper's Plains, N. Y.

2. Francis Erwin Cooper, born September 1, 1829; died February 14, 1893; unmarried.

3. Mary Erwin Cooper, born June 6, 1831; died July 1, 1892; married, April 6, 1853, Willard C. Morse of Painted Post, N. Y.; died October 9, 1898; issue, one son and one daughter.

4. John Cooper, born October 24, 1833; died July 11, 1904; married, December 19, 1867, Miss Ophelia Bronson, Painted Post, N. Y.; they had issue, four sons and three daughters. He was Surgeon Fremont's Staff, 1861; S. A. Surg. U. S. A., 1862.

5. Thomas Wallis Cooper, born February 10, 1837; died October 31, 1862; unmarried. 1st Lieut. Co. B, 7th U. V. Vol. Inft.

6. Theodore Cooper, born January 12, 1839; unmarried. He was 2nd Asst. Eng. U. S. N., and was Consulting Engineer Eads Bridge, St. Louis.

7. Samuel Erwin Cooper, born February 6, 1841; died August 3, 1864; unmarried.

8. Fredrick Stephen Cooper, born October 24, 1842; married, November 27, 1872, Miss Frances Josephine Merrill of Painesville, Ohio; issue, three sons and one daughter. He was 2nd Lieut. Co. F, 4th Mo. Cav.

9. Charlotte Elizabeth Cooper, born October 2, 1844; married, June 22, 1871, William Bryson of Mechanicsburg, Pa., who died; issue, three sons.

10. Arthur Erwin Cooper, born April 12, 1848; she died September, 1906; married, September 13, 1871, Miss Eliza Burch; issue, three sons and five daughters.

Col. Arthur Erwin	Mary Kennedy	1st.
2. Mary Erwin	Dr. John Cooper	2nd.
3. Elizabeth Cooper	Theodore Sedgwick Paul	3rd.

Belvidere, N. J.

1. John Cooper Paul, born October 6, 1831; died December 26, 1855.
2. Elizabeth S. Paul, born October 29, 1833; married, November 5, 1857, Henry Neil Paul of Philadelphia, Pa., a second cousin; he died April 9, 1899; issue, two sons and two daughters.
3. Thomas Paul, born July 14, 1835; died January 31, 1861.
4. Mary Erwin Paul, born April 19, 1857.
5. Theodore Sedgwick Paul, born June 25, 1839; died June 13, 1840.
6. Arthur Erwin Paul, born April 7, 1841; died April 8, 1843.
7. Charlotte Vandeveer Paul, born August 9, 1844; married, November 5, 1874, John C. Welling, Chicago, Ill.; he died November 9, 1906; issue, one son and two daughters.
8. Francis Erwin Paul, born December 5, 1848; died October 27, 1850.
9. Comegys Paul, born July 19, 1846; died June 29, 1906.
10. Frank Ellinwood Paul, born February 7, 1852; married, March 15, 1877, Miss Minnie Pope of Boston, Mass.; issue, one son and one daughter.
11. Theodore Sedgwick Paul, born April 2, 1855; died December 21, 1880.

Col. Arthur Erwin	Mary Kennedy	1st.
2. Mary Erwin	Dr. John Cooper	2nd.
5. Sarah Ann Cooper	Joseph F. Randolph	3rd.

Red Bank, N. J.

1. Charlotte V. Randolph, born April 12, 1842; died December 27, 1870. Unmarried.
2. Joseph F. Randolph, Jr., born December, 4, 1843; married, October 17, 1872, Miss Harriet W. Talcot of Morristown, N. J.; she died March, 1891; issue, one child.
3. John Cooper Randolph, born December 20, 1847.
4. Mary Erwin, born March 11, 1850.

Col. Arthur Erwin	Mary Kennedy	1st.
4. Maj. Arthur Erwin	M. N. Erie	2nd.
1. John Francis Erwin	Johnnette L. Schneider	3rd.

Bethlehem, Pa.

1. Ambrose John Erwin, born March 9, 1830; married, March 17, 1857, Miss Mary Clanders; issue, three sons and three daughters. He was mayor of Bethlehem, Pa., three years; in city council nine years. A member of the Assembly 1876–77. A volunteer in 5th Pa. Regt.

2. Mary K. Erwin, born March 15, 1832; married Horace B. Jones of Philadelphia, Pa.; issue, one daughter. He was successively first lieutenant and adjutant of Forty-sixth Regiment, Pennsylvania Volunteers, and was in forty engagements.

3. William Arthur Erwin, born June 27, 1838; married, April 17, 1864, Miss Ella Hart of Weissport, Pa.; issue, one son and three daughters. He was corporal in the 129th Regiment, Pennsylvania Volunteers; also in Thirty-fourth Regiment.

4. Edward Francis Erwin, born October 31, 1841; unmarried.

5. Bertine S. Erwin, born May 30, 1845; married, October 7, 1878, Mrs. M. Dimmick of Mauchchunk, Pa.; issue, one daughter.

Col. Arthur Erwin	Mary Kennedy	1st.
4. Maj. Arthur Erwin	Miss Lamphere	2nd.
3. Arthur Erwin	Isabelle Thompson	3rd.

Addison, N. Y.

1. James T. Erwin, born May 19, 1833; married Miss Densey Knapp; no issue.

2. Arthur Erwin, born May 8, 1835; died in California.

3. Edward Erwin, born October, 22, 1837; died December 24, 1875; married Miss Ella Dodge of Indiana; no issue.

4. Mary E. Erwin, born August 12, 1840; married Llewellyn M. Jones of Addison, N. Y.; issue, two sons and one daughter.

5. John Erwin, born April 12, 1843; died January 26, 1903; unmarried.

6. Scott Erwin, born April 15, 1845; unmarried.

Children of Arthur Erwin and 2d wife, Martha Jones.

7. Henry S. Erwin, born March 7, 1848; married, first, Miss Sarah Webster; she died October 9, 1888; married, second, Miss Carpenter; issue, four sons and one daughter

8. William Erwin, born October 22, 1850; unmarried.

9. Katherine Erwin, born May 18, 1853; unmarried.

10. Cora Erwin, born July 15, 1855; unmarried.

Col. Arthur Erwin	Mary Kennedy	1st.
4. Maj. Arthur Erwin	Sarah Clark	2nd.
3. Rachel Erwin	Henry H. Birdsall	3rd.

Addison, N. Y.

1. Adelaide Frances Birdsall, born March 30, 1844; married, April 18, 1882, Horace D. Baldwin, Addison, N. Y.; no issue.
2. Henry James Birdsall, born September 12, 1847; died October 31, 1863; unmarried. Served in United States Navy. Buried at Fortress Monroe, Va.
3. Frank Erwin Birdsall, born September 12, 1850; died February 17, 1859.
4. Mary Erwin Birdsall, born November 25, 1852; married, October 6, 1880, William S. Landers of Afton, N. Y.; he died July 24, 1896; issue, two sons.
5. Rachel Elizabeth Birdsall, born October 24, 1857; married, May 26, 1886, Chas. W. Spencer of Afton, N. Y.; issue, none.

Col. Arthur Erwin	Mary Kennedy	1st.
4. Maj. Arthur Erwin	Sarah Clark	2nd.
5. Samuel C. Erwin	M. Elizabeth Thompson	3rd.

Hornby, N. Y.

1. Helen E. Erwin, born August 20, 1857; died October 15, 1862.
2. Carrie M. Erwin, born June 15, 1859; married, October 8, 1885, Frederick Rogers of Hornby, N. Y.; issue, one son and three daughters.
3. Samuel C. Erwin, born April 21, 1861; married, January 17, 1895, Miss Minnie Crane, Addison, N. Y.; issue, one daughter.
4. Arthur A. Erwin, born October 23, 1863.
5. James T. Erwin, born December 1, 1865; married, 1894, Miss Lillian Bly; issue, three sons and one daughter.
6. Elizabeth T. Erwin, born May 28, 1868; married, August 9, 1893, Rev. Henry Frederick Cope of England; issue, three sons and two daughters.

Col. Arthur Erwin	Mary Kennedy,	1st.
4. Maj. Arthur Erwin	Sarah Clark	2nd.
6. Charles Erwin	Kate Willard	3rd.

Washington, D. C.

1. Mary Erwin, died in infancy.
2. Annie Erwin, born, August 5, 1867; married twice: first, —Cathall; issue, one son; second, —Turley.

3. Sarah Elizabeth Erwin, born November 11, 1871; married; issue, one son.
4. Henrietta Rachel Erwin, born —.
5. Arthur Erwin, born August 23, 1877.
6. Kathleen Erwin, born August 25, 1885.
7. Nora Erwin, born August 14, 1888.

Col. Arthur Erwin	Mary Kennedy	1st.
4. Maj. Arthur Erwin	Sarah Clark	2nd.
7. Sarah E. Erwin	George H. Weatherby	3rd.

Addison, N. Y.

1. Albert Weatherby, born August 7, 1854; died of small pox in New Orleans, La.; was in United States Signal Service.
2. George H. Weatherby, born November 23, 1858; died June 26, 1859.
3. George H. Weatherby, born August 27, 1861; married, June 26, 1895, Miss Fannie Shufeldt Robinson; issue, one son.

Col. Arthur Erwin	Mary Kennedy	1st.
4. Maj. Arthur Erwin	Sarah Clark	2nd.
8. Ann E. Erwin	Amaziah S. McKay	3rd.

Addison, N. Y.

1. Helen S. McKay, born April 3, 1861; married, 1889, Herman S. Rose, Addison, N. Y.; no issue.
2. Arthur P. McKay, born March 19, 1864; unmarried; died February, 1889.

GREAT-GREAT-GRANDCHILDREN — FIFTH GENERATION.

Col. Arthur Erwin	Mary Kennedy	1st.
1. Capt. Samuel Erwin	Rachel Heckman	2nd.
2. Eliza Erwin	Edward Townsend	3rd.
2. Edward E. Townsend	Nancy L. Jerome	4th.

Painted Post, N. Y.

NOTE.— These are of the fifth generation, children of Edward E. Townsend, second son of Eliza Erwin, second daughter of Capt. Samuel Erwin, eldest son of Col. Arthur Erwin of the first generation. The same reading applies to each family table.

1. Fanny Jerome Townsend, born July 1, 1849; died August 7, 1869; unmarried.
2. Frederick Jerome Townsend, born October 6, 1850; married, May 23, 1876, Mrs. Viola Rodman Tibbot of Plano, Cal.; she died May 2, 1907, at Bridge, Cal., and buried at Fresno, Cal.; had issue, four sons and two daughters.
3. Mary Townsend, born February 15, 1852; died September 13, 1853.

4. Arthur E. Townsend, born December 20, 1854; unmarried; died July 7, 1879; was assassinated near Plano, Cal., by son of an Indian chief.

5. Richard Jerome Townsend, born May 2, 1858; died October 25, 1876.

6. Eliza E. Townsend, born February 15, 1860; died September 16, 1869.

7. Edward E. Townsend, born April 14, 1863; died October 12, 1876.

8. Annie Lawrence Townsend, born March 7, 1865; married, March 17, 1886, Harry Clay Heermans of Corning, N. Y.; issue, three sons and two daughters.

Col. Arthur Erwin	Mary Kennedy	1st.
1 Capt. Samuel Erwin	Rachel Heckman	2nd.
3 Arthur H. Erwin	Frances McKeen	3rd.
1 Mary Kennedy Erwin	Marcus Stevens	4th.
Detroit, Mich.		

1. Helen Erwin Stevens, born November 17, 1859; married, April 20, 1885, Drury Leseuer Gaulden of Georgia; issue, one son and one daughter.

Col. Arthur Erwin	Mary Kennedy	1st.
1 Capt. Samuel Erwin	Rachel Heckman	2nd.
3 Arthur H. Erwin	Frances M. McKeen	3rd.
2 Eugene H. Erwin	Elizabeth H. Cook	4th.
Painted Post, N. Y.		

1. Alice A. Erwin, born September 30, 1862; died 1901; unmarried.

Col. Arthur Erwin	Mary Kennedy	1st.
1 Capt. Samuel Erwin	Rachel Heckman	2nd.
3 Arthur H. Erwin	Frances M. McKeen	3rd.
7 Anna M. Erwin	Charles Iredell	4th.
Painted Post, N. Y.		

1. Arthur E. Iredell, born January 31, 1870; married, December 26, 1895, Miss Isabelle Paxton Rogers of Bristol, Pa.; issue, one son and two daughters.

Col. Arthur Erwin	Mary Kennedy	1st.
1 Capt. Samuel Erwin	Rachel Heckman	2nd.
3 Arthur H. Erwin	Frances M. KcKeen	3rd.
8 Arthur H. Erwin Jr. 1st	Gertrude M. Brown	4th.
Addison, N. Y.		

1. Agnes Mariah Erwin, born July 26, 1871; married twice: first, Allan Monroe of Buffalo, N. Y.; second, Hazzard of Buffalo, N. Y.; no issue.

2. Frances Gertrude Erwin, born September 2, 1872; married
Van Willard Tyler; issue, one daughter.

Arthur H. Erwin, Jr. 2nd.	Mary Gay Bressie	4th.

Ponca City, Okla.

3. Arthur H. Erwin (3rd), born September 1, 1900.

Col. Arthur Erwin	Mary Kennedy	1st.
1 Capt. Samuel Erwin	Rachel Heckman	2nd.
3 Arthur H. Erwin	Frances M. McKeen	3rd.
9 Harriet Louise Erwin	John Lutman	4th.

Painted Post, N. Y.

1. Athur Erwin Lutman, born October 17, 1874; died.
2. Frances Erwin Lutman, born September 18, 1876; died.
3. Harriet Louise Lutman, born —.

Col. Arthur Erwin	Mary Kennedy	1st.
1 Capt. Samuel Erwin	Rachel Heckman	2nd.
4 Genl. Francis E. Erwin	Sophia McCall	3rd.
1 Samuel S. Erwin, 1st.	Amelia Shaw	4th.

Corning, N. Y.

1. Harriet Sophia Erwin, born May 29, 1851; died August 26, 1878;
married, September 22, 1875, John Wesley Darrin of Corning,
N. Y.; issue, one son.
2. Frank A. Erwin, born March 27, 1853; died October 15, 1906;
married, October 10, 1878, Miss Hattie D. Clute of Corning,
N. Y.; issue, none.
3. Samuel Erwin, born October 13, 1857; married, October 15, 1878,
Miss Emma Tupper, Corning, N. Y.; no issue.
4. Edward Erwin, born November 27, 1860; married, May 5, 1901,
Miss Lena Haischer of Corning, N. Y.; no issue.
5. Robert Erwin, born September 20, 1865; died September 11, 1866.

1 Samuel S. Erwin, 2nd.	Susan William,	4th.

6. Henry A. Erwin, born May 28, 1881.

Col. Arthur Erwin	Mary Kennedy	1st.
1 Capt. Samuel Erwin	Rachel Heckman	2nd.
4 Genl. Francis E. Erwin	Sophia McCall	3rd.
2 Edward E. Erwin	Susan Gamble	4th.

Painted Post, N. Y.

1. William Gamble Erwin, born December 5, 1855; died December
11, 1871.

Col. Arthur Erwin	Mary Kennedy	1st.
1 Capt. Samuel Erwin	Rachel Heckman	2nd.
4 Genl. Francis E. Erwin	Sophia McCall	3rd.
3 Mary E. Erwin	Cephas F. Platt	4th.

Painted Post, N. Y.

1. Sophia Erwin Platt, born November 4, 1854; married, December 15, 1875, Chester A. Tousey of Painted Post, N. Y.; no issue.
2. Mary Elizabeth Platt, born December 18, 1857; married, October 10, 1883, Willis H. Hamilton of Campbell, N. Y.; issue, one daughter.
3. Frank C. Platt, born January 25, 1866; married, January 7, 1895, Miss Jennie Faulkner of Corning, N. Y.; issue, two sons.

Col. Arthur Erwin	Mary Kennedy	1st.
1 Capt. Samuel Erwin	Rachel Heckman	2nd.
4 Genl. Francis E. Erwin	Sophia McCall	3rd.
4 Francis Erwin,	Helen Campbell,	4th.

Painted Post, N. Y.

1. Sophia H. Erwin, born September 7, 1859.
2. Arthur Bradford Erwin, born June 29, 1863; married, October 9, 1884. Miss Anna Githler of Painted Post, N. Y.; issue, one son and one daughter.

Col. Arthur Erwin	Mary Kennedy	1st.
1 Capt. Samuel Erwin	Rachel Heckman	2nd.
4 Genl. Francis E. Erwin	Sophia McCall	3rd.
6 Harriet M. Erwin	Robert B. Wilks	4th.

Bath, N. Y.

1. Sophia Wilks, born February 16, 1861; married Andrew Patten, Brackney, Pa.; issue, one son and two daughters.
2. Annie Wilks, born June 13, 1862; married Giles Hunter of Rockford, Ill.; issue, two sons and three daughters.
3. Robert B. Wilks, Jr., born January 18, 1864; married Miss Harriet Peck of Addison, N. Y.; issue, one daughter.
4. Harriet Jane Wilks, born August 5, 1865.
5. Francis Erwin Wilks, born March 2, 1867.
6. James Shannon Wilks, born October 20, 1868; married Miss Annis Patton of Stevensville, Pa.; issue, two sons and one daughter.
7. Mary Elizabeth Wilks, born October 13, 1871.
8. Samuel Erwin Wilks, born June 2, 1873.

Col. Arthur Erwin	Mary Kennedy	1st.
1 Capt. Samuel Erwin	Rachel Heckman	2nd.
5 John Erwin	Nancy Pease	3rd.
8 Cornelia Pease Erwin	Dr. Wm. H. Beaumont	4th.

Cleveland, Ohio.

1. George Henry Beaumont, born June 16, 1865.
2. Martha Bowles Beaumont, born March 29, 1868.
3. Arthur Erwin Beaumont, born December 18, 1872.

4. Laura Erwin Beaumont, born October 17, 1875.
5. John Erwin Beaumont, born November 17, 1879.

Col. Arthur Erwin	Mary Kennedy	1st.
1 Capt. Samuel Erwin	Rachel Heckman	2nd.
5 John Erwin	Nancy Pease	3rd.
3 Laura Grant Erwin	Chas. Edw. Pease	4th.

Dayton, Ohio.

1. Calvin E. Pease, born May 1, 1867.
2. Edward Pease, born December 3, 1871.

Col. Arthur Erwin	Mary Kennedy	1st.
1 Capt. Samuel Erwin	Rachel Heckman	2nd.
5 John Erwin	Nancy Pease	3rd.
6 Florence H. Erwin	Henry L. Paige	4th.

St. Louis, Mo.

1. Anna Erwin Paige, born March 26, 1867; married.
2. Erwin Paige, born September 23, 1870.
3. Albert Paige, born July 13, 1872.
4. Florence Paige, born August 13, 1873.

Col. Arthur Erwin	Mary Kennedy	1st.
1 Capt. Samuel Erwin	Rachel Heckman	2nd.
5 John Erwin	Nancy Pease	3rd.
10 Leonore Erwin	Lieut. Henry H. Wright	4th.

New Mexico.

1. Arthur John Wright, born —.
2. Harry Haviland Wright, born —.

Col. Arthur Erwin	Mary Kennedy	1st.
1 Capt. Samuel Erwin	Rachel Heckman	2nd.
7 William Erwin	Mary Evans	3rd.
1 Elizabeth W. Erwin	J. Ralph Ward	4th.

Elmira, N. Y.

1. William Ward, born May 7, 1865.
2. Ralph Howard Ward, born May 7, 1868; died in infancy.
3. Ralph Howard Ward, born May 11, 1870; died September, 19, 1881.

Col. Arthur Erwin	Mary Kennedy	1st.
1 Capt. Samuel Erwin	Rachel Heckman	2nd.
7 William Erwin	Mary Evans	3rd.
4 John Evans Erwin	Julia Gazeley	4th.

Cleveland, Ohio.

1. Julia Gazeley Erwin, born 1890.

Col. Arthur Erwin	Mary Kennedy	1st.
1 Capt. Samuel Erwin	Rachel Heckman	2nd.
7 William Erwin	Mary Evans	3rd.
8 Mary Alice Erwin	Charles H. Potter	4th.

Cleveland, Ohio.

1. Mary Antoinette Potter, born September 27, 1879; married, November 26, 1903, William Hopkins of Cleveland, Ohio.

2. Charles Mason Potter, born November 1, 1881; married, June 1904, Nadine Christy of Cleveland, Ohio; issue, one son.

Col. Arthur Erwin	Mary Kennedy	1st.
1 Capt. Samuel Erwin	Rachel Heckman	2nd.
8 Rachel A. Erwin	William J. Gilbert	3rd.
1 Helen Gilbert	Charles M. Fay	4th.

Painted Post, N. Y.

1. Gilbert William Fay, born September 24, 1876; married May 24, 1877.

Col. Arthur Erwin	Mary Kennedy	1st.
1 Capt. Samuel Erwin	Rachel Heckman	2nd.
8 Rachel A. Erwin	William J. Gilbert	3rd.
4 Samuel E. Gilbert	Sarah E. Adams	4th.

Painted Post, N. Y.

1. Alice Fay Gilbert, born August 29, 1868; married, October 15, 1895, Edward Balcom Hodgman, Painted Post, N. Y.; issue, two sons and one daughter.

2. Amy Gilbert, born September 2, 1870; died September 2, 1870.

3. Celia Eloise Gilbert, born April 16, 1872.

4. Mary Lulu Gilbert, born October 28, 1873; married, June 7, 1899, Frank Elmer Waite of Corning, N. Y.; issue, three sons.

5. Elsie Gilbert, born September 5, 1875; died September 5, 1875.

6. Edna Ione Gilbert, born May 4, 1879; married, September 26, 1900, Ferrel de Loss Smith, Bath, N. Y.; issue, two daughters.

7. Hazel Gilbert, born April 23, 1890.

Col. Arthur Erwin	Mary Kennedy	1st.
1 Capt. Samuel Erwin	Rachel Heckman	2nd.
8 Rachel A. Erwin	William J. Gilbert	3rd.
5 William Jewett Gilbert	Anna L. Badger	4th.

Painted Post, N. Y.

1. Louise Badger Gilbert, born January 20, 1873; married, January 15, 1895, William Gregg Dunham of St. Louis, Mo.; issue, two sons and one daughter.

Col. Arthur Erwin	Mary Kennedy	1st.
1 Capt. Samuel Erwin	Rachel Heckman	2nd.
10 Samuel K. Erwin	Mary Eliza Kern	3rd.
3 Eugene Erwin .	Susan Anderson	4th.

Cleburne, Texas.

1. Robert Eugene Erwin, born October 18, 1893.

2. Franklin Kern Erwin, born December 16, 1894.

3. Mary Elizabeth Erwin, born August 21, 1897.

Col. Arthur Erwin	Mary Kennedy	1st.
2 Mary Erwin	Dr. John Cooper	2nd.
1 Dr. John Cooper, Jr.		3rd.
1 Charles John Cooper	Martha Pierce	4th.

Cooper's Plains, N. Y.

1. Charles J. Cooper, born July 9, 1874; died April 25, 1872.

2. Benjamin Pierce Cooper, born January 14, 1849; married Miss Callie Owens of Jackson, Miss.; issue, one son and one daughter.

3. Mary Erwin Cooper, born December 12, 1850; died January 10, 1882; married, May 10, 1876, Dr. A. E. Overhiser of Campbell, N. Y.; issue, one son and two daughters.

4. John Ernest Cooper, born September 27, 1852; married, June, 1872, Mrs. Mary Freslaider of Bavaria, Germany; issue, one son and one daughter.

5. Frank B. Cooper, born December 11, 1854.

Col. Arthur Erwin	Mary Kennedy	1st.
2 Mary Erwin	Dr. John Cooper	2nd.
1 Dr. John Cooper, Jr.	Elizabeth Evans.	3rd.
3 Mary Erwin Cooper	Willard C. Morse	4th.

Painted Post, N. Y.

1. John C. Morse, born September 22, 1854; married, December 28, 1898, Miss Minnie Bassett of Painted Post, N. Y.

2. Elizabeth Evans Morse, born February 19, 1857; died October 21, 1864.

Col. Arthur Erwin	Mary Kennedy	1st.
2. Mary Erwin	Dr. John Cooper	2nd.
1. Dr. John Cooper, Jr.	Elizabeth Evans	3rd.
4. Dr. John Cooper	Ophelia Bronson	4th.

Painted Post, N. Y.

Alice Cooper, born August 19, 1869.

John Cooper, born June 7, 1871; died April 22, 1872.

John Vandeveer Cooper, born October 19, 1873; married, December 20, 1898, Miss Mary Cornelia Tomer; issue, one son and one daughter.

Louise Cooper, born April 27, 1875; died April 27, 1877.

Randolph Cooper, born March 3, 1877.

Mary Cooper, born August 25, 1878.

Harley Bronson Cooper, born October 9, 1880.

Col. Arthur Erwin	Mary Kennedy	1st.
2. Mary Erwin	Dr. John Cooper	2nd.

1. Dr. John Cooper, Jr.	Elizabeth Evans	3rd.
8. Fredrick S. Cooper	Frances J. Merrill	4th.
White Rock, Kan.		

Fredrick Merrill Cooper, born December 12, 1873; died July 28, 1879.

Nellie Evans Cooper, born February 20, 1875; died July 6, 1875.

Edward Merrill Cooper, born May 24, 1881.

Theodore Cooper, born May 10, 1883.

Col. Arthur Erwin	Mary Kennedy	1st.
2. Mary Erwin	Dr. John Cooper	2nd.
1. Dr. John Cooper, Jr.	Elizabeth Evans	3rd.
9. Charlotte E. Cooper	William Bryson	4th.
Mechanicsburgh, Pa.		

Thomas B. Bryson, born April 9, 1872.

John Cooper Bryson, born February 7, 1875; married, November 30, 1898, —— Welch; issue.

Fred Carothers Bryson, born November 30, 1877; died March 22, 1880.

Col. Arthur Erwin .	Mary Kennedy	1st.
2. Mary Erwin	Dr. John Cooper	2nd.
1. Dr. John Cooper, Jr.	Elizabeth Evans	3rd.
10. Arthur Erwin Cooper	Elisa Burch	4th.
Cooper's Plains, N. Y.		

Elizabeth Cooper, born February 5, 1873; died February 9, 1873.

Charlotte I. Cooper, born February 6, 1874; married, July 10, 1901, Clifton C. Walker, Colora, Md.; issue, two sons, one daughter.

Kathleen Cooper, born December 15, 1876.

Thomas W. Cooper, born February 10, 1879; married, December 8, 1906, Miss Caroline Elizabeth Reiger of Philadelphia, Pa.

Elizabeth Evans Cooper, born April 29, 1881; married, June 26, 1906, Edgar W. Burchfield, Lewistown, Pa.

Theodore Arthur Cooper, born February 18, 1884.

Louise Cooper, born May 1, 1886.

Francis F. Cooper, born September 14, 1890.

Col. Arthur Erwin	Mary Kennedy	1st.
2. Mary Erwin	Dr. John Cooper	2nd.
3. Elizabeth Cooper	Theodore S. Paul	3rd.
2. Elizabeth C. Paul	Henry N. Paul	4th.
Philadelphia, Pa.		

Meta Neil Paul, born September 26, 1860; died in infancy.

Henry Neil Paul, Jr., born September 25, 1863; married, January 30, 1889, Miss Margaret Crosby Butler.

Elizabeth Duffield Paul, born October 1, 1867; died in infancy.

Theodore Sedgwick Paul, born November 13, 1873; died in infancy.

Col. Arthur Erwin	Mary Kennedy	1st.
2. Mary Erwin	Dr. John Cooper	2nd.
3. Elizabeth Cooper	Theodore S. Paul	3rd.
7. Charlotte V. Paul	John C. Welling	4th.

Chicago, Ill.

Bessie Paul Welling, born August 3, 1875; died November 16, 1879.

John Paul Welling, born September 6, 1880.

Robert Kennedy Welling, born March, 1882; died in infancy.

Mary Erwin Welling, born January 25, 1885; died in infancy.

Col. Arthur Erwin	Mary Kennedy	1st.
2. Mary Erwin	Dr. John Cooper	2nd.
3. Elizabeth Cooper	Theodore S. Paul	3rd.
10. Frank E. Paul	Minnie Pope	4th.

Belvidere, N. J.

Edith Vandeveer Paul, born December 30, 1877.

Augustus Russell Paul, born March 25, 1880.

Col. Arthur Erwin	Mary Kennedy	1st.
4. Maj. Arthur Erwin	M. N. Erie	2nd.
1. John Francis Erwin	Johnnette L. Schneider	3rd.
1. Ambrose Erwin	Mary A. Clanders	4th.

Bethlehem, Pa.

Francis H. Erwin, born January 29, 1859.

Martha Louise Erwin, born February 7, 1861.

Annie C. Erwin, born January 11, 1863.

Twins -{ Charles A Erwin, born September 16, 1866; died.
{ Carrie M. Erwin, born September 16, 1866.

William C. Erwin, born June 30, 1870.

Col. Arthur Erwin	Mary Kennedy	1st.
4. Maj. Arthur Erwin	M. N. Erie	2nd.
1. John Francis Erwin	Johnnette L. Schneider	3rd.
2. Mary K. Erwin	Horace B. Jones	4th.

Philadelphia, Pa.

Florence L. Jones, born May 20, 1857.

Col. Arthur Erwin	Mary Kennedy	1st.
4. Maj. Arthur Erwin	M. N. Erie	2nd.
1. John Francis Erwin	Johnnette L. Schneider	3rd.
3. William Arthur Erwin	Ella Hart	4th.

Bethlehem, Pa.

Lulu Erwin, born March 29, 1865.

Kate Erwin, born July 10, 1866; died February 2, 1881.

Edith M. Erwin, born February 4, 187–.

Harold K. Erwin, born January 7, 1879; died September 2, 1881.

Col. Arthur Erwin	Mary Kennedy	1st.
4. Maj. Arthur Erwin	M. N. Erie	2nd.
1. John Francis Erwin	Johnette L. Schneider	3rd.
5. Bertine S. Erwin	Mrs. M. Dimmick	4th.

Bethlehem, Pa.

Johnette L. Erwin.

Col. Arthur Erwin	Mary Kennedy	1st.
4. Maj. Arthur Erwin	Miss Lamphear	2nd.
2. Arthur Erwin, Jr.	Martha Jones	3rd.
4. Mary E. Erwin	Llewellyn Jones	4th.

Elkland, Pa.

Arthur Erwin Jones, born November, 1871; married Miss Rose
Campbell of Pennsylvania.

Janis N. Jones, born 1874.

Walter Weston Jones, born May 5, 1880; married, January 12, 1906,
Miss Emma Rose Beck of Hammondsport, N. Y.

Col. Arthur Erwin	Mary Kennedy	1st.
4. Maj. Arthur Erwin	Miss Lamphear	2nd.
2. Arthur Erwin, Jr.	Martha Jones	3rd.
7. Henry S. Erwin	Sarah Webster	4th.

Addison, N. Y.

Harry E. Erwin, born May 10, 1872, married, June 4, 1902, Miss
Elizabeth M. Crawford, Rathboneville, N. Y; had issue,
one daughter.

Hugh L. Erwin, born June 19, 1874; married, February, 1895, Miss
Frances C. O'Connell of Hornell, N. Y.; had issue, three sons
and two daughters.

Guy A. Erwin, born May 26, 1878; married.

Martha M. Erwin, born September 26, 1881; married, June 19, 1906,
Ray B. Murray of Addison, N. Y.

James Ray Erwin, born April 10, 1884; died July, 1888.

Col. Arthur Erwin	Mary Kennedy	1st.
4. Maj. Arthur Erwin	Sarah Clark	2nd.
3. Rachel Erwin	Henry H. Birdsall	3rd.
4. Mary E. Birdsall	Wm. S. Landers	4th.

Addison, N. Y.

Maurice B. Landers, born April 3, 1882.

Roland Henry Birdsall Landers, born November 25, 1883.

Col. Arthur Erwin	Mary Kennedy	1st.
4. Maj. Arthur Erwin	Sarah Clark	2nd.
5. Samuel C. Erwin	M. Elizabeth Thompson	3rd.
2. Carrie M. Erwin	Frederick Rogers	4th.

Hornby, N. Y.

Elizabeth Rogers, born June 24, 1886.

Frederick Lain Rogers, born January 8, 1888.

Carolyn Rogers, born June 12, 1893.

Helen Rogers, born April 6, 1895.

Col. Arthur Erwin	Mary Kennedy	1st.
4. Maj. Arthur Erwin	Sarah Clark	2nd.
5. Samuel C. Erwin	M. Elizabeth Thompson	3rd.
3. Samuel C. Erwin, Jr.	Minnie Crane	4th.

Addison, N. Y.

Irene Crane Erwin, died in infancy.

Col. Arthur Erwin	Mary Kennedy	1st.
4. Maj. Arthur Erwin	Sarah Clark	2nd.
5. Samuel C. Erwin	M. Elizabeth Thompson	3rd.
5. James T. Erwin	Lillian Bly	4th.

Addison, N. Y.

Nellie Irene Erwin, born April 18, 1895.

James Thompson Erwin, born February 18, 1897.

Kenneth McKay Erwin, born June 22, 1902.

Robert Erwin, born September 17, 1906.

Col. Arthur Erwin	Mary Kennedy	1st.
4. Maj. Arthur Erwin	Sarah Clark	2nd.
5. Samuel C. Erwin	M. Elizabeth Thompson	3rd.
6. Elizabeth T. Erwin	Rev. Fred'k Cope	4th.

Hornby N.Y.

Henry Erwin, Cope, born August 25, 1894.

Elizabeth Jessica Cope, born May 14, 1898.

Franklin Doane Cope, born January 24, 1900; died October 15, 1900.

Maurice Albert Cope, born February 5, 1902.

Dorothy Thompson Cope, born March 27, 1904.

Col. Arthur Erwin	Mary Kennedy	1st.
4. Maj. Arthur Erwin	Sarah Clark	2nd.
6. Charles Erwin	Kate Willard	3rd.
2. Annie Erwin	—— Cathell	4th.

Washington, D. C.

Ralph Cathell.

Col. Arthur Erwin	Mary Kennedy	1st.
4. Maj. Arthur Erwin	Sarah Clark	2nd.
6. Charles Erwin	Kate Willard	3rd.
3. Sarah Elizabeth Erwin	——	4th.

Washington, D. C.

Charles.

Col. Arthur Erwin	Mary Kennedy	1st.
4. Maj. Arthur Erwin	Sarah Clark	2nd.
7. Sarah Elizabeth Erwin	George H. Weatherby	3rd.

3. George H. Weatherby   Fanny S. Robinson   4th.
              Addison, N. Y.

George Bliss Weatherby, born January 26, 1896.

GREAT-GREAT-GREAT-GRANDCHILDREN — SIXTH GENERATION.

Col. Arthur Erwin	Mary Kennedy	1st.
1. Capt. Samuel Erwin	Rachel Heckman	2nd.
2. Eliza Erwin	Edward Townsend	3rd.
2. Edward E. Townsend	Nancy L. Jerome	4th.
2. Fred'k J. Townsend	Viola R. Tibbets	5th.
	Painted Post, N. Y.	

Fanny Jerome Townsend, born October 30, 1878; married, June
    27, 1900, William E. Bryan of Corning, N. Y.; had issue,
    two daughters.

Mary Lawrence Townsend, born October 3, 1880.

Clarence Ellsworth Townsend, born April 7, 1882.

Frederick Augustus Townsend, born October 20, 1883.

Arthur Townsend, born July 17, 1885; died August 25, 1886.

Roy Rodman Townsend, born August 1, 1889.

Col. Arthur Erwin	Mary Kennedy	1st.
1. Capt. Samuel Erwin	Rachel Heckman	2nd.
2. Eliza Erwin	Edward Townsend	3rd.
2. Edward E. Townsend	Nancy L. Jerome	4th.
8. Annie L. Townsend	Harry C. Heermans	5th.
	Corning, N. Y.	

Ruth Heermans, born June 3, 1888.

Joseph Fellows Heermans, born November 28, 1891.

Jerome Townsend Heermans, born July 6, 1893.

Helen de Kay Heermans, born January 6, 1895; died August 31,
    1896.

Donald Heermans, born September 11, 1896.

Col. Arthur Erwin	Mary Kennedy	1st.
1. Capt. Samuel Erwin	Rachel Heckman	2nd.
3. Arthur H. Erwin	Frances M. McKeen	3rd.
1. Mary Kennedy Erwin	Marcus Stevens	4th.
1. Helen Erwin Stevens	Drury Leseuer Gaulden	5th.
	DeLand, Fla.	

Leseuer Gaulden, born July 14, 1686.

Erwinna Gaulden, born June 22, 1889.

Col. Arthur Erwin	Mary Kennedy	1st.
1. Capt. Samuel Erwin	Rachel Heckman	2nd.
3. Arthur H. Erwin	Frances M. McKeen	3rd.
7. Anna M. Erwin	Charles Iredell	4th.
1. Arthur Erwin Iredell	Isabell Paxton Rogers	5th.
	Painted Post, N. Y.	

Charles Vernon Iredell, born December 27, 1896.

Frances Barrett Iredell, born September 16, 1902.

Anna Patricia Erwin Iredell, born July 12, 1905.

Col. Arthur Erwin	Mary Kennedy	1st.
1. Capt. Samuel Erwin	Rachel Heckman	2nd.
3. Arthur H. Erwin	Frances M. McKeen	3rd.
8. Arthur H. Erwin, Jr.	Gertrude Brown	4th.
2. Frances G. Erwin	VanWillard Tyler	5th.

Buffalo, N. Y.

Agnes.

Col. Arthur Erwin	Mary Kennedy	1st.
1. Capt. Samuel Erwin	Rachel Heckman	2nd.
4. Gen. Francis E. Erwin	Sophia McCall	3rd.
1. Samuel S. Erwin	Amelia Shaw	4th.
1. Harriet Sophia Erwin	John Wesley Darrin	5th.

Corning, N. Y.

Samuel Wesley Darrin, born August 23, 1878.

Col. Arthur Erwin	Mary Kennedy	1st.
1. Capt. Samuel Erwin	Rachel Heckman	2nd.
4. Genl. Francis E. Erwin	Sophia McCall	3rd.
3. Mary E. Erwin	Cephas F. Platt	4th.
2. Mary Elizabeth Platt	Willis H. Hamilton	5th.

Campbell, N. Y.

Harriet Elizabeth Hamilton, born September 22, 1884; married, April 30, 1907, Henry Edward Joint of Savona, N. Y.

Col. Arthur Erwin	Mary Kennedy	1st.
1. Capt. Samuel Erwin	Rachel Heckman	2nd.
4. Genl. Francis E. Erwin	Sophia McCall	3rd.
3. Mary E. Erwin	Cephas F. Platt	4th.
3. Frank C. Platt	Jennie Faulkner	5th.

Painted Post, N. Y.

Gerald Platt, born October 2, 1895.

Chester Platt, born October 21, 1898.

Col. Arthur Erwin	Mary Kennedy	1st.
1. Capt. Samuel Erwin	Rachel Heckman	2nd.
4. Genl. Francis E. Erwin	Sophia McCall	3rd.
4. Francis Erwin	Helen Campbell	4th.
2. Arthur Bradford Erwin	Anna Githler	5th.

Corning, N. Y.

Kittie Erwin, born August 3, 1885; died January 3, 1886.

Francis Jacob Erwin, born October 19, 1886.

Col. Arthur Erwin	Mary Kennedy	1st.
1. Capt. Samuel Erwin	Rachel Heckman	2nd.
4. Genl. Francis E. Erwin	Sophia McCall	3rd.
6. Harriet Maria Erwin	Robert B. Wilks	4th.
1. Sophia Erwin Wilks	Andrew Jacob Paston	5th.

Brackney, Pa.

Mary Harriet Patton, born May, 1889.

Jane Wilks Patton, born October, 1900.

Thomas Patton, born January, 1902.

Col. Arthur Erwin	Mary Kennedy	1st.
1. Capt. Samuel Erwin	Rachel Heckman	2nd.
4. Genl. Francis E. Erwin	Sophia McCall	3rd.
6. Harriet Maria Erwin	Robert B. Wilks	4th.
2. Anna Wilks	Giles F. Hunter	5th.
	Rockford, Ill.	

Robert James Hunter, born April, 1887.

Bertha Hunter, born September 1, 1889.

Jane Wilks Hunter, born June, 1892.

Sophia Hunter, born December, 1893.

Giles Hunter, born July, 1895.

Col. Arthur Erwin	Mary Kennedy	1st.
1. Capt. Samuel Erwin	Rachel Heckman	2nd.
4. Genl. Francis E. Erwin	Sophia McCall	3rd.
6. Harriet Maria Erwin	Robert B. Wilks	4th.
3. Robert B. Wilks, Jr.	Harriet Peck	5th.
	Bath, N. Y.	

Lena Elizabeth Wilks, born September 11, 1896.

Col. Arthur Erwin	Mary Kennedy	1st.
1. Capt. Samuel Erwin	Rachel Heckman	2nd.
4. Genl. Francis E. Erwin	Sophia McCall	3rd.
6. Harriet Maria Erwin	Robert B. Wilks	4th.
6. Rev. James S. Wilks	Annie Patton	5th.

Harriet Erwin Wilks, born May, 1898.

William Crockett Wilks, born April, 1899.

Robert Thomas Wilks, born October, 1905.

Col. Arthur Erwin	Mary Kennedy	1st.
1. Capt. Samuel Erwin	Rachel Heckman	2nd.
7. William Erwin	Mary Evans	3rd.
8. Mary Alice Erwin	Charles H. Potter	4th.
2. Charles M. Potter	Nadine Christey	5th.
	Pittsburg, Pa.	

William Erwin Potter, born January 18, 1907.

Col. Arthur Erwin	Mary Kennedy		1st.
1. Capt. Samuel Erwin	Rachel Heckman	2nd.	
8. Rachel A. Erwin	William J. Gilbert		3rd.
4. Samuel Erwin Gilbert	Sarah E. Adams		4th.
1. Alice F. Gilbert	Edward B. Hodgman		5th.
	Seattle, Wash.		

Gilbert Lawrence Hodgman, born October 3, 1898.

Helen Hodgman, born April 16, 1900.

Stanford Balcom Hodgman, born October 25, 1904.

Col. Arthur Erwin	Mary Kennedy	1st.
1. Capt. Samuel Erwin	Rachel Heckman	2nd.
8. Rachel A. Erwin	William J. Gilbert	3rd.
4. Samuel Erwin Gilbert	Sarah E. Adams	4th.
4. Mary Lulu Gilbert	Frank E. Waite	5th.

Corning, N. Y

Neville Elmer Waite, born July 25, 1900.

Samuel Gilbert Waite, born February 5, 1902.

Bayard Wyman Waite, born April 30, 1906.

Col. Arthur Erwin	Mary Kennedy	1st.
1. Capt. Samuel Erwin	Rachel Heckman	2nd.
8. Rachel A. Erwin	William J. Gilbert	3rd.
4. Samuel Erwin Gilbert	Sarah E. Adams	4th.
6. Edna Ione Gilbert	Ferrel D. Smith	5th.

Bath, N. Y.

Frances Ione Smith, born July 12, 1901.

Rachel Gilbert Smith, born April 4, 1905.

Col. Arthur Erwin	Mary Kennedy	1st.
1. Capt. Samuel Erwin	Rachel Heckman	2nd.
8. Rachel A. Erwin	William J. Gilbert	3rd.
5. William J. Gilbert	Anna L. Badger	4th.
1. Louise B. Gilbert	William G. Dunham	5th.

Spring Valley, N. Y.

John Samuel Dunham, born September 29, 1896.

William Gilbert Dunham, born November 13, 1899.

Anne Dunham, born January 1, 1904; died June 8, 1906.

Col. Arthur Erwin	Mary Kennedy	1st.
2. Mary Erwin	Dr. John Cooper	2nd.
1. Dr. John Cooper, Jr.	1st wife	3rd.
1. Charles J. Cooper	Martha Pierce	4th.
2. Benj. Pierce Cooper	Callie Owen	5th.

Jackson, Miss.

Maud C. Cooper, born March, 1875.

Charles J. Cooper, born September, 1881.

Col. Arthur Erwin	Mary Kennedy	1st.
2. Mary Erwin	Dr. John Cooper	2nd.
1. Dr. John Cooper, Jr.	1st wife	3rd.
1. Charles J. Cooper	Martha Pierce	4th.
3. Mary E. Cooper	Dr. A. E. Overhiser	5th.

Campbell, N. Y.

Helen C. Overhiser, born July 10, 1877; died June 24, 1904; married, October 12, 1898, Benjamin G. Balcom, Curtis, N. Y.; had issue, one daughter.

Mary L. Overhiser, born June 8, 1879.

Charles J. Overhiser, born July 4, 1881.

Col. Arthur Erwin	Mary Kennedy	1st.
2. Mary Erwin	Dr. John Cooper	2nd.
1. Dr. John Cooper, Jr.	1st wife	3rd.
1. Charles J. Cooper	Martha Pierce	4th.
4. John Ernest Cooper	Mary Freslaider	5th.

Painted Post, N. Y.

John C. Cooper, born October 7, 1873; married, June 9, 1894, Miss Jennie Mills of Campbell, N. Y.; had issue, two sons.

Mary A. Cooper, born March 12, 1882.

Col. Arthur Erwin	Mary Kennedy	1st.
2. Mary Erwin	Dr. John Cooper	2nd.
1. Dr. John Cooper, Jr.	Elizabeth M. Evans	3rd.
4. Dr. John Cooper, 3rd	Ophelia Bronson	4th.
3. Rev. John V. Cooper	Mary C. Tomer	5th.

Sodus, N. Y.

John Vandeveer Cooper, Jr., born November 9, 1899.

Marion Elizabeth Cooper, born August 11, 1901.

Col. Arthur Erwin	Mary Kennedy	1st.
2. Mary Erwin	Dr. John Cooper	2nd.
1. Dr. John Cooper, Jr.	Elizabeth M. Evans	3rd.
10. Arthur E. Cooper	Eliza Burch	4th.
2. Charlotte J. Cooper	Clifton C. Walker	5th.

Colora, Md.

Arthur Cooper Walker.

Kathleen Walker, died in infancy.

Robert Walker.

Col. Arthur Erwin	Mary Kennedy	1st.
2. Mary Erwin	Dr. John Cooper	2nd.
3. Elizabeth Cooper	Theodore S. Paul	3rd.
2. Elizabeth Cooper Paul	Henry Neil Paul	4th.
2. Henry Neil Paul, Jr.	Margaret C. Butler	5th.

Philadelphia, Pa.

Theodore Sedgwick Paul, Jr., born February 9, 1890.

Mary Russell Paul, born July 29, 1891.

John Rodman Paul, born April 18, 1893.

William Allen Butler Paul, born February, 24, 1895.

Samuel Hollingsworth Paul, born July 5, 1896.

Arthur Paul, born August 28, 1898.

Henry Neil Paul, born April 6, 1900.

Margaret Neil Paul, born June 4, 1904.

Col. Arthur Erwin	Mary Kennedy	1st.
4. Maj. Arthur Erwin	Miss Lamphear	2nd.

2. Arthur Erwin, Jr.	Marsha Jones	3rd.
7. Henry S. Erwin	Sarah Webster	4th.
1. Henry E. Erwin	Elizabeth M. Crawford	5th.

Addison, N. Y.

Hazil Elizabeth Erwin, born December 4, 1904.

Col. Arthur Erwin	Mary Kennedy	1st.
4. Maj. Arthur Erwin	Miss Lamphear	2nd.
2. Arthur Erwin, Jr.	Martha Jones	3rd.
7. Henry S. Erwin	Sarah Webster	4th.
2. Hugh L. Erwin	Frances Cecilia O'Connell	5th.

Addison, N. Y.

Arthur Raymond Erwin, born October 6, 1895.
Katharine Sarah Erwin, born August 22, 1903.
Francis Cyril Erwin, born September 15, 1906.

GREAT-GREAT-GREAT-GREAT-GRANDCHILDREN — SEVENTH GENERATION.

Col. Arthur Erwin	Mary Kennedy	1st.
1. Capt. Samuel Erwin	Rachel Heckman	2nd.
2. Eliza Erwin	Edward Townsend	3rd.
2. Edward E. Townsend	Nancy L. Jerome	4th.
2. Frederick J. Townsend	Viola Rodman Tibbot	5th.
1. Fanny J. Townsend	William E. Bryan	6th.

Painted Post, N. Y.

Adelaide May Bryan, born May 1, 1901.
Kathryn Townsend Bryan, born August 26, 1902.

Col. Arthur Erwin	Mary Kennedy	1st.
2. Mary Erwin	Dr. John Cooper	2nd.
1. Dr. John Cooper, Jr.	1st wife	3rd.
1. Charles J. Cooper	Martha Pierce	4th.
3. Mary E. Cooper	Dr. A. E. Overhiser	5th.
1. Helen C. Overhiser	Benjamin G. Balcom	6th.

Corning, N. Y.

Ruth Balcom, born March 17, 1901.

Col. Arthur Erwin	Mary Kennedy	1st.
2. Mary Erwin	Dr. John Cooper	2nd.
1. Dr. John Cooper, Jr.	1st wife	3rd.
1. Charles J. Cooper	Martha Pierce	4th.
4. John E. Cooper	Mary Freslaider	5th.
1. John C. Cooper	Jennie Mills	6th.

Campbell, N. Y.

Hypolite John Cooper, born May 23, 1895.
Frederick Charles Cooper, born September 5, 1896; died November 13, 1896.

DESCENDANTS OF COL. ARTHUR ERWIN AND HIS FIRST WIFE,
MARY SCOTT.

John Erwin, born November 12, 1756; unmarried; died February
    17, 1782.

Joseph Erwin, born July 24, 1758; unmarried; died February 9,
    1807.

William Livingston Erwin, born February 12, 1760; died June 6,
    1836; married, 1783, Achsah Rockhill, Hunterdon county,
    N. J.; had issue, one son and four daughters.

Sarah Erwin, born September 16, 1762; died May 5, 1809; married
    Judge John Mulhollen; he died April 5, 1815; they had issue,
    eight sons and three daughters.

Francis Erwin, born and died in 1764.

Arthur Erwin, born, 1765; drowned in Delaware River, May 17,
    1769.

Hugh Scott Erwin, born February 8, 1767; died May 31, 1846;
    married; no issue.

GRANDCHILDREN — THIRD GENERATION.

	Col. Arthur Erwin	Mary Scott	1st.
3.	Wm. Livingston Erwin	Achsah Rockhill	2nd.

Mary Erwin, born, 1783; died, 1836; married Philip Howell.

Rachel Erwin, born, 1787; died, 1858; married Thomas Kennedy
    as second wife.

Scott R. Erwin, born, 1789; died, 1823; unmarried.

Julianna Erwin, born, 1791; died, 1825; married Thomas Kennedy
    as first wife.

Charlotte Erwin, born, 1797; died, 1845; married John P. Robeson.

	Col. Arthur Erwin	Mary Scott	1st.
4.	Sarah Erwin	Judge John Mulhollen	2nd.

Mary Mulhollen, born March 27, 1779; died October 30, 1813;
    married Judge Thomas McBurney; he died August 30, 1828;
    they had issue, two sons and four daughters.

William Mulhollen, born January 20, 1781; married Jane———.

John Mulhollen, born November 3, 1782; married Miss Ives of
    Philadelphia, Pa.

Arthur Mulhollen, born May 18, 1785.

Hugh Mulhollen, born May 5, 1787; married and died in the South,
    leaving one daughter.

Christian Mulhollen, born March 13, 1789; died October 4, 1790.

Joseph Mulhollen, born May 23, 1791; died February 4, 1815.

Elizabeth Mulhollen, born May 3, 1794; died December 25, 1847; married David Wolcott, who died November 16, 1858.

Daniel Mulhollen, born November 30, 1796; died August 19, 1871; married Electa Trowbridge; she died June 30, 1842; had issue, four sons and four daughters.

Thomas Mulhollen, born December 12, 1800; died January 20, 1801.

Sarah S. Mulhollen, born July 1, 1804; died June 19, 1851; married Mathew McHenry, who died February 26, 1854; had issue, five sons and two daughters.

GREAT-GRANDCHILDREN — FOURTH GENERATION.

Col. Arthur Erwin	Mary Scott	1st.
4. Sarah Erwin	Judge John Mulhollen	2nd.
1. Mary Mulhollen	Judge Thomas McBurney	3rd.

Corning, N. Y.

John McBurney, born August 29, 1796; died August 10, 1867; married, first, Jemima Patterson, 1817; she died 1831; had issue, one son and two daughters; married, second, Almariah Knox, 1832; she died, leaving one son; married, third, wife unknown; married, fourth, Mrs. Edwards, Hammondsport, N. Y., a daughter of Cornelius Younglove.

Sarah McBurney, born, 1799; died May 5, 1828; married, January 6, 1820, John Magee of Watkins, N. Y., Pres. of Fall Brook R. R. & Coal Mines; he died April 5, 1868; no issue.

Eliza McBurney, born, 180-; married — Bacon.

Mariah McBurney, born May 8, 1805; died January 30, 1832; married Henry G. Cotton.

Caroline McBurney.

Thomas McBurney, born, 1814; died March 31, 1870; married Jane Ann ——, who died October 8, 1851.

(Data of the families of William Mulhollen and Jane ——, John Mulhollen and Miss Ives, Hugh Mulhollen, and Elizabeth Mulhollen and David Wolcott, not known.)

Col. Arthur Erwin	Mary Scott	1st.
4. Sarah Erwin	Judge John Mulhollen	2nd.
9. Daniel Mulhollen	Electa Trowbridge	3rd.

Addison, N. Y.

Sarah Mulhollen, born February 12, 1825; married Clark Ballard of Dryden, N. Y.; no issue.

William Mulhollen, married Mrs. Anna (?); had issue, two sons and
two daughters.

Frances Mulhollen, married J. Burnham Sargent; issue, one
daughter.

M. Louise Mulhollen, born, 1834; died October 2, 1855.

Jane E. Mulhollen, born, 1836; unmarried; died February 19, 1880.

M. Elizabeth Mulhollen, born 1840; died November 19, 1856.

James T. Mulhollen, born, 1838; died June 10, 1860.

Henry Clay Mulhollen, born June 16, 1854; died June 14, 1896;
married, 1870, Luna Maria Taylor; had issue, one son and
one daughter.

Col. Arthur Erwin	Mary Scott	1st.
4. Sarah Erwin	Judge John Mulhollen	2nd.
11. Sarah S. Mulhollen	Mathew McHenry	3rd.

Painted Post, N. Y.

Hugh E. McHenry, born December 23, 1827; died January 20, 1851.

Frances M. McHenry, born August 8, 1833; died September 14,
1849.

Edward McHenry, born August 13, 1834; died November 15, 1855.

John H. McHenry, born April 7, 1836; died September 12, 1849.

James McHenry.

Sylvester McHenry, born June 29, 1842; died April 1, 1856.

Sarah P. McHenry, born April 23, 1845; died August 23, 1845.

GREAT-GREAT-GRANDCHILDREN — FIFTH GENERATION.

Col. Arthur Erwin	Mary Scott	1st.
4. Sarah Erwin	Judge John Mulhollen	2nd.
1. Mary Mulhollen	Judge Thomas McBurney	3rd.
1. John McBurney	{ 1st wife Jemima Patterson	4th.
	2nd wife Almariah Knox	4th.

Mary Patterson, married C. K. Miller of Corning, N. Y.

James Patterson.

Jemima Patterson, married John Dodge of Corning, N. Y.

John Knox McBurney (by second wife).

(Data of the families of Eliza McBurney and — Bacon's; Mariah
McBurney and Henry G. Cotton; Thomas McBurney and Jane Ann
—, not known.)

Col. Arthur Erwin	Mary Scott	1st.
4. Sarah Erwin	Judge John Mulhollen	2nd.
9. Daniel Mulhollen	Electa Trowbridge	3rd.
2. William Mulhollen	Mrs. Anna(?)	4th.

Frank Mulhollen, married Anna Dennis; had issue, two children.

Albert Mulhollen, married Amy Lamson; issue, two children.

May Mulhollen, married Archie Hardy; issue, one child.

Jessie Mulhollen, married George Dennis; had issue, four children.

Col. Arthur Erwin	Mary Scott	1st.
4. Sarah Erwin	Judge John Mulhollen	2nd.
9. Daniel Mulhollen	Electa Trowbridge	3rd.
3. Frances Mulhollen	J. Burnham Sargent	4th.

Louise M. Sargent, married John B. Edgett; he died May 25, 1906.
No issue.

Col. Arthur Erwin	Mary Scott	1st.
4. Sarah Erwin	Judge John Mulhollen	2nd.
9. Daniel Mulhollen	Electa Trowbridge	3rd.
8. Henry Clay Mulhollen	Luna M. Taylor	4th.

Lyman Frank Mulhollen, born May 3, 1871; married, December
16, 1896, Olive Grace Knapp of Canisteo, N. Y.; had issue,
two sons. He is pastor of M. E. Church at Hornell, N. Y.

Josephine Southwick Mulhollen, born February 2, 1875; married
Stephen E. Potter; had issue, two sons and two daughters.

(Data of the families of Mary Patterson and C. K. Miller,
Jemima Patterson and John Dodge, Frank Mulhollen and Anna
Dennis, Albert Mulhollen and Any Lamson, May Mulhollen and
Archie Hardy, Jessie Mulhollen and George Dennis, not known.)

GREAT-GREAT-GREAT-GRANDCHILDREN — SIXTH GENERATION.

Col. Arthur Erwin	Mary Scott,	1st.
4. Sarah Erwin	Judge John Mulhollen	2nd.
9. Daniel Mulhollen	Electa Trowbridge	3rd.
8. Henry Clay Mulhollen	Luna M. Taylor	4th.
1. Lyman Frank Mulhollen	Olive Grace Knapp	5th.
	Hornell, N. Y.	

Lyman F. Mulhollen, Jr., born September 21, 1898; died January
11, 1899.

Harold Stephen Mulhollen, born February 2, 1900.

Col. Arthur Erwin	Mary Scott	1st.
4. Sarah Erwin	Judge John Mulhollen	2nd.
9. Daniel Mulhollen	Electa Trowbridge	3rd.
8. Henry Clay Mulhollen	Luna M. Taylor	4th.
2. Josephine S. Mulhollen	Stephen E. Potter	5th.
	Jasper, N. Y.	

Laura Potter.

Arthur Potter.

Howard Potter.

Sylva Potter.

GENEALOGY OF JAMES JAY ERWIN.

CHRISTOPHER ERWIN was born in the north of Ireland in 1741. In the third century of the Christian era, when the Norsemen took possession of the islands which lie west and north of the British Isles, and hordes of their number overran the northern and western parts of Scotland, pressed back the native tribes and became masters of the soil, they found a clan of the Gallic Nations from the west coast of Spain who had settled in the most northern portion of the island. Tradition informs us that the antecedents of the branch of the Erwin family from which Christopher sprang were represented in these two races. He was left an orphan, and according to the custom of the times, was apprenticed to a blacksmith. The kind of work was distasteful, and his master cruelly severe. At the age of fifteen he took ungranted leave and secretly embarked on board a transport bearing a portion of Abercrombie's troops which "sailed for New York in the last of April 1756." Later he was enrolled and entered the ranks. When hostilities closed he remained in the colonies and eventually settled in New Jersey, where he married Mary Folk, a lady of German parentage. He was next known as a resident of Loudoun County, Va. About the year 1808 he moved with his family to Youngstown, Ohio, where he lived until his death in February, 1836.

Christopher and Mary Erwin became the parents of seven children who grew to maturity and became the heads of families. They were John, who married Louisa Kincade; Jacob, who married Elizabeth Osborn; Thomas, who married Katie Watrose; William, who married Johanna Lanterman; Margaret, who married Robert Kincade; Elizabeth, who married James White, and Joseph; who married Mary Osborn.

JACOB ERWIN was born in Loudoun County, Virginia, December 3, 1785. In 1807 he moved to Youngstown, Ohio, purchased one hundred and sixty acres of land and commenced a struggle for life in the primitive forest. In 1810 he married Elizabeth Osborn. He was a typical physical representative of his branch of the Erwin family. His was an enviable physique; six feet two inches in height, large bones, powerful muscles and no superfluous fat; strong, courageous, with an indomitable will and a man of good judgment, he became a power of influence in the community in which he lived. A devout Methodist, he gave freely to charities and no destitute person went uncomforted from his door. The pleasure of his declining years was enhanced from the results of a life of industry and a creditable frugality. He died on June 3, 1862. To Jacob and Elizabeth Erwin were born seven daughters and three sons, namely: James, who married Nancy Hull; Mary, who married Samuel Henderson; Elizabeth, who married James Eckman; Sarah, who married James McCartney; Jane, who married Jonathan Henderson; Ann, who married Samuel Gibson; Henry, who married Eliza Jane Squier; Elanor, who married Miles Marshall; Rachael, who died unmarried, and John, who died in infancy.

HENRY ERWIN was born in Youngstown, Ohio, June 9, 1825, married Eliza Jane Squier, February 4, 1847, and died at Newton Falls, Ohio, January 31, 1905. During his life he first followed farming; then the milling business, from which he retired on a competency. He was ingenious, eminently practical, and a good teacher. A student of nature, he was quick to see, and quick to profit by his observations. He was a leader among men, and was ambitious to be worthy of his following. In affairs of public trust he bore his part among his fellow-townsmen. It was said of him by his biographer that "his advice was often sought by his neighbors and acquaintances." His children were Phebe, who married Hon. James Kennedy; James J., who married Nellie Spencer, and Amanda, who married L. Frank Merrill.

JAMES JAY ERWIN was born near Newton Falls, Ohio, January 30, 1850, and spent the life of his youth on a farm. He became a student of medicine under a preceptor, September 1, 1866, though continuing his studies in the high school during school years, which curriculum he finished in the spring of 1868. Owing to business reverses, which deprived his parents of means to assist him in his study of medicine, he accepted dentistry as an avocation, and commenced work under instructions on September 1, 1869. Here his struggle for success or failure began. After practicing in different states, — Ohio, Pennsylvania, and Michigan, — in December, 1871, he passed a satisfactory examination before the board of examiners provided by law for the practice of dentistry in Ohio, and was regularly registered and licensed to practice in that state. During his leisure hours he continued the study of medicine, and with it that of pharmacy and pharmacology. In July, 1883, he sold his office equipment and quit dentistry to enter pharmacy, hoping for a more speedy elevation to the profession of his choice. He was graduated from the medical department of the University of Wooster, July 27, 1887, and in Pharmacy, Chicago, Illinois, 1888. He began his regular professional career in Youngstown, Ohio, whence he moved to Cleveland, Ohio, in 1891. In his professional work he has been successful, both in medicine and surgery. He was graduated president of his class, and has since served as president of his alumni association. Ingenious and inventive, when circumstances arose in any of his work where an instrument or appliance seemed to have been called for that could not be procured in the market, he prepared a model, and had the thing made according to his own liking, so as to have it conveniently accessible should necessity again arise.

He has been a conspicuous figure in society work, and his contributions to medical literature have been interesting and instructive. He retired from practice when discharged from military service, June 30, 1901, and has since lived most of the time at his winter home in Eustis, Florida.

During the nine months he served in the war with Spain, and the two years service with the Army of the Philippines, he kept a journal of items of general interest which, when mustered out, he closed with this significant entry:

"During my terms of service, included within the time covered by this record, I have not had a report returned for correction, nor has a patient died of disease while intrusted in my professional care; and my accounts, when audited, were always found to be correct. My final settlements with the different departments verify this statement."

He inherited his military enthusiasm from a long line of descent through both parents. His great-grandfather, Christopher Erwin, came to America with Abercrombie's troops to serve in the war between England and France, fought mostly on American soil. His great-great-grandfather, on his mother's side, Zopher Squier, served in the same war, and in many campaigns against the Indians. In the former he was wounded in the knee. By these two ancestors he became eligible to membership in the Military Order of Colonial Wars. His great-grandfather, Christopher Erwin, served in the war of the American Revolution. His great-grandfather, James Squier, also did service in the same. By the patriotism of these two he became a member of the Military Order of the Sons of the American Revolution. His great-grandfather, Anthony Osborn, and his grandfather, Jacob Erwin, served in the war of 1812. His great-grandfather, William Morrow, on his mother's side, also did service in the same. By the acts of these he became a member of the Military Order of the War of 1812. By the service of his father, Henry

Erwin, in the Civil War, he became a member of Camp No. 1, Sons of Veterans of Ohio. By the service of these, and by his own service in the War with Spain, he became eligible to membership in, and organized the Ohio Commandery, Military Order of Foreign Wars, and became its first Commander. He was also elected Vice-Commander-General of the National Commandery. His service under two commissions in the insurrection in the Philippines rendered him eligible to membership in the Military Order, Veteran Army of the Philippines.

His military career began May 18, 1893, when he was commissioned Captain and Assistant Surgeon, Fifth Infantry, O. N. G. From this he was transferred, without change of grade or loss of rank, to the First Light Artillery O. V. N. G.; thence to the Naval Reserves of Ohio, which he assisted in organizing, and with which he went into the Tenth O. V. I., — when the Naval Reserves formed the Second Battalion of that regiment in the War with Spain. After nine months service with that regiment, he was commissioned Captain and Asst. Surgeon, U. S. V., and assigned to duty with the 30th Infantry, U. S. V., for foreign service. When service closed with that command, he was re-commissioned Captain and Asst. Surgeon to serve two years longer in the Philippines, but was discharged because of physical disability contracted in line of duty.

The 30th Infantry formed a part of the Schwan's Expeditionary brigade which did such valiant work on the Island of Luzon, South of Manila. He considered it his good fortune to have been actively engaged on every field in which any part of his regiment had become a factor during this campaign. It was his practice on each occasion to attend the injured on the firing line, and at the skirmish near Magallanes, January 10, 1900, he received special mention in the report of the commanding Officer, Major T. L. Hartigan. On January 21, 1900, General Schwan, with a part of his brigade, met General Kaieles, strongly entrenched, with two thousand insurgents, on San Diegos Hill, about two and a half miles easterly from San Pablo. The topography of the country was such that, to reach a point where they could attack, the Americans must advance across a level valley about four hundreds yards, then ascend the hill—about five hundred yards — by a dug road along its side, to a position affording partial cover, all in full view and in excellent range of the insurgent sharpshooters. That day it was the duty of the Second Battalion of the 30th, to which Dr. Erwin was attached, to guard the wagon train at the rear. When firing began in front, he asked permission of Major M. F. Steele, commanding the battalion, to go onto the firing line, which was granted. He "rode the gauntlet" safely, and took position with Lieut. C. S. Tarlton's sharpshooters of the 30th, who were supporting a battery in action. After about an hour an orderly arrived bearing orders from the regimental surgeon, ordering him to return to his battalion. Without hesitation he returned over the road by which he had come, the mauser shots of the enemy pattering around him like hailstones in a storm, and reported to the Colonel of the regiment, Col. C. Gardener, stated his case and obtained permission to return. Then again the dangerous passage was safely made.

It has been a characteristic with the Doctor to aim not to fail in anything he has considered worthy of his undertaking; as an illustration: In 1896, the Association of Military Surgeons of the United States had become insolvent and very much in debt. The proceedings of the meeting of the previous year were in the house of the publisher, who declined to finish his work until evidence of remuneration was forthcoming. At the annual meeting in May, in Philadelphia, Dr. Erwin was chosen Treasurer, with a hope that he might be able to finance the institution onto a sounder financial basis. He began the duties of his office by becoming personally responsible for the indebtedness which barred the issuing of the previous year's report: secured and distributed the publication, then set to work to find a way for publishing and distributing the proceedings of the last meeting. Seemingly but little interest had been manifested by others who had been chosen to officially conduct the different parts of the work. After much correspondence the records were located in possession of the stenographer, whom he advised to send them to the Chairman of the Publication Committee. This gentleman sent them to the editor, and he without disturbing the seal put on by the stenographer sent them to the Treasurer. By this time the President had become afflicted with a lingering illness which practically relieved him from official duties the remainder of the year. The Secretary had become displeased with some act of the President and declined to answer any further correspondence. The First Vice-President had died on his return trip from the meeting at which he had been elected. But the Treasurer remained steadily at work, and assuming all responsibilities, he audited, compiled and classified the work; read the proof, did all the work not strictly belonging to the publishing house, paid for, received and distributed the publication; then with the help of a few enthusiastic members who unfor-

Hon. James Jay Erwin, M. D.

tunately had not secured offices, set to work to pave the way for a successful meeting in 1897. The effort was gratifying in its result. This meeting was undoubtedly the most potent of the series, and fresh inspiration was infused by the report of the Treasurer, which showed all indebtedness canceled and five hundred dollars ($500.00) in the treasury. For his zeal and success in the performance of his duties he was made an Honorary Member, May, 1903.

The association now stands eminent among its peers, has become international, and is one of the first of its kind in the world.

Dr. Erwin is also a lover of high class literature. He has not only familiarized himself with the writings of standard authors but has memorized many of their finest productions. Goldsmith's Traveler has been one of his favorite recitations, requiring forty-five minutes for the declamation. He is, himself, an author of verse quite commendable.

His regard for sociability, and an appreciation of the principles involved, led him into fraternal society work, in which he has been quite active. He was raised to the sublime degree of Master Mason November 17, 1875. The meeting following he was elected Senior Deacon. The next office he filled was that of the Senior Warden. Then he served his lodge as Master. He passed through all the grades of the York Rite, and became a Noble of the Mystic Shrine. In the Scottish Rite he was known as an able ritualist, and was crowned a Sovereign Grand Inspector-General, 33d and last degree.

At the next meeting following that at which he had been knighted a Knight of Pythias he was elected Vice-Chancellor. Six months later he became Chancellor Commander. Later he represented his lodge four years in the Grand Lodge, then declined a re-election. He is also an Odd Fellow and a member of other fraternities.

On October 15, 1877, he married Nellie Spencer. To their family were born three children — Nellie, who married Dr. Francis A. Reed; Jessie, who married Harrie D. Cram; and Edith, who died in babyhood.

FAMILY OF JAMES IRWIN.

James Irwin, married Agnes Irwin, in Cumberland county, Pennsylvania, February 2, 1786. To them were born Ann Irwin, November 1, 1786; John Irwin, February 18, 1788; Mary Irwin, April 9, 1789; Jane Irwin, May 19, 1791; James Irwin, March 12, 1793; Robert Irwin, March 19, 1795; William Irwin, October 19, 1797;

Nancy Irwin, November 25, 1799; David Irwin, January 7, 1802, and George Irwin, October 11, 1805.

Robert Irwin was my grandfather. He removed to Butler county, Ohio, with his father in 1798. Robert Irwin married Lydia Cox, March 28, 1816. To them were born the following:

William C. Irwin, February 2, 1817; died February 3, 1896; Nancy Irwin, born December 9, 1818; died August 19, 1858; James Irwin, born May 1, 1821; died November 16, 1841; Richard M. Irwin, born August 26, 1823; died May 22, 1849; Mary Jane Irwin, born August 22, 1830; died December 13, 1857; David Irwin, born July 24, 1825; died March 29, 1850; Robert M. Irwin, born January 5, 1828; died March 18, 1841; Margaret Ann Irwin, born March 22, 1833; died September 26, 1898; George E. Irwin, born October 2, 1835; died July 3, 1858; John Irwin, born November 11, 1840; died March 27, 1874.

Robert Irwin, died June 10, 1875. Lydia Cox, his wife, died June 25, 1844. All the children were born near Mason, Warren county, Ohio. John Irwin was my father. He married, December 14, 1864, Ruth A. Moore, who was born in Butler county, Ohio, March 31, 1846. To them were born, in Warren county, Ohio:

Minnie Irwin, December 19, 1868. George Moore Irwin, November 22, 1870, which is myself.

Minnie Irwin, married Edgar A. Bowyer, October 7, 1889, and to them were born three daughters: La Verne Bowyer, October 4, 1894; Miriam Bowyer, April 6, 1902; Georgia Bowyer, August 31, 1904.

George Moore Irwin, married Myrtle Wood Caldwell, at Warrensburg, Missouri, October 18, 1899. To them has been born a daughter, Virginia Irwin, May 6, 1906.

FAMILY OF ROBERT B. IRWIN.

Robert B. Irwin married Celia A. Chatfield, January 16, 1856. Their children were:

Frank Chatfield Irwin, born April 15, 1857. Alexander J. Irwin, born June 18, 1858; died February 11, 1859. Mary Smith Irwin, born November 4, 1860; died April 6, 1861. Andrew Gould Irwin, born February 8, 1862. Charles Wheelock Irwin, born January 7, 1866. Alexander Johnson Irwin, born April 3, 1868.

Elvira Furber Irwin, born March 10, 1870. Oscar Craig Irwin, born December 5, 1880; died February 10, 1884.

CHILDREN AND GRANDCHILDREN.

Frank C. Irwin, married Lizzie C. Bay, October 2, 1878, and had issue:

Charles Francis Irwin, born August 26, 1880; died February 5, 1884. William Chatfield Irwin, born March 31, 1882; died February 13, 1884. Frances Chatfield Irwin, born July 1, 1885. Harry Alexander Irwin, born September 27, 1887. Frank Clarence Irwin, born May 28, 1891; died August 21, 1893.

Andrew Gould Irwin, married Katherine Costello, June 8, 1889, and had issue:

Andrew Gould Irwin, born March 18, 1890; died August, 1890. Andrew Chatfield Irwin, born March 17, 1891. Irene Irwin, born July 16, 1892. Rosalie Irwin, born March 14, 1894. Robert Irwin, born May, 1895. Marcus Irwin, born December 23, 1896. May Irwin, born May 6, 1898. Eunice Irwin, born May, 1900. Andrew Gould Irwin, born October 2, 1902.

Charles W. Irwin, married Emma L. Klanke, June 12, 1889. His children:

Lillian H. Irwin, born May 26, 1890. Elvira Irwin, born October 8, 1894.

Alex. J. Irwin, married Nellie E. Rosenberg, June 10, 1903, and has issue:

Harriette Alexandria Irwin, born April 30, 1904. Baby Irwin (infant daughter), born March 30, 1906.

Wilson M. Martin, married Elvira Furber Irwin, July 9, 1889, to whom were born:

Florence Irwin Martin, born January 21, 1892. Frances Chatfield Martin, born September 5, 1893.

MISSISSIPPI ERVINS.

HINDS, MISS., May 7, 1853.

MY DEAR BOB: — This is the third letter I've attempted to write after receiving your kind favors, the last dated February 4th. I will say it is not for want of a due regard, I assure you, for ofttimes your name is held in kind remembrance. I will charge it to pure laziness or you may, and with this ask your forgiveness, and promise for the

future to be more punctual.   In answer to the last, I claim a small
share or claim somewhat of an apology, having waited some time
to see Mary Cooper, hoping to gratify your request by sending you
an account of marriages, ages, etc., but on examining I only find
your grandfather Ervin's marriage with your grandmother, Jane
Witherspoon; this was in 1775.   I have mislaid the memorandum
of date, but in my next will send date, with the age of your old aunt
Ford, who was born in 1782.   Their increase who lived to maturity
were your father, your aunt Elizabeth, and James.   Your grandfather Ervin's second marriage was to my mother, Margaret Ervin.
Their issue was your Uncle Hugh, from whom one of your names
springs — that of Hugh — and myself.   Hugh was born July 9,
1792; myself, December 2, 1796.

Your great-grandfather Ervin was from Ireland, and your great-
grandmother also.   A great grand uncle, Hugh Ervin, came from
Ireland.   The two brothers settled in Williamsburg district.   Your
great-grandfather, whose name was John, settled on Black River,
near a little place called King's Tree.   He had three sons, your
grandfather John, Robert, and James; the daughters were Jane,
Sarah, and Elizabeth.   Jane married a James; a brother or a son
of the James who gave the British officer such a cold-handed
reception.   (See Marion's life.)   Sarah married a Mathews, and
Elizabeth, a Fulton.

Your grand uncle Robert married a sister of my mother, Jane
Ervin.   James also married, but I am not aware who, and left two
sons who died young.   Your great grand uncle Hugh had two wives.
The first family were Hugh, and two daughters, Mrs. McColure, Mrs.
Cannon — whose daughter married a Connally, and I have been told
her daughter is wife of your I. Clemens.   My grandmother was a
James, sister of the noted James whom I mentioned above.   Their
issue were James, William, Jane, and Margaret.   You may readily
judge that I am an Irishman, and yourself not far from it.   Your
father was married thrice, the first was a Mrs. Sarah James, daughter
of Capt. Dewites; they had a little son who died quite young.   His
second marriage was to Harriet Keith, of Darlington district, and
their issue that lived to mature age were Amelia, Harriet, and James.
The third was your mother.   I have given you as correctly as I well
can, and for a more correct statement will refer you to your cousin
Samuel, of Sops, who can be addressed at Darlington Court House,
South Carolina.   I will make some inquiries of some relatives for
your benefit as well as myself.   You wished to know if Hugh moved

west of Missouri. He merely went to look at the country, but came back disappointed and located in old Hinds again, three miles from where he formerly lived. He has some 1,100 acres of tolerably good upland. Can you get him a good wife? I rather think he is a candidate or soon will be; his children are scattered. He has his little boys with him. His eldest daughter is with Thomas going to school; his youngest is with me; a daughter lives about six miles from me; Henry, three miles; Margaret is living in Claiborne, twenty-seven miles. They are all steady and hope will do well. You requested me to say something of Burch. The last I knew he was teaching school between Raymond and Clinton — and at that time was doing well — but you are well aware of his weak points. My crop this last season was good, some nine bales to the hand, making some $275.00 to the hand, — plenty of provisions, corn, meat, etc. You wrote me your plan of farming, which I think is good. Had I the facilities should adopt it, let cotton go ahead or not. It gives room for great improvements to the farm. Where we have a full cotton crop it is out of the question. I will come to a close, and reserve for next. Give my best respects to your Sarah, and tell her I should be much pleased to become acquainted with her, if she could stand my roughness. I should write more, but am about starting to church. Your affectionate Uncle,

JOHN ERVIN.

ALABAMA ERVINS.

Samuel Ervin, was born on the Big Pe De River, in Marion District, South Carolina, and married in Wilcox county, Alabama, to Mary Ann Gullett, a widow, daughter of John Eades and Jane Fee Eades.

Robert Hugh Ervin, the issue of this marriage, was born September 11, 1822, at Coal Bluff, Wilcox county, Alabama, and died January 11, 1875. He married January 5, 1848, at Dry Fork, Wilcox county, Alabama, Sarah Ashbury Rives, a widow, daughter of James Asbury Tait and Elizabeth Goode Tait; Sarah A. Ervin died March 13, 1905. The issue of this marriage was Albert Goode Ervin, born September 20, 1848; Walter Eades Ervin, born November 25, 1849; died February 11, 1851; Jennie Fee Ervin, born March 24, 1851; Aurora Roberta Ervin, born March 18, 1853; Caroline Ervin, born November 23, 1854; Lilia Grayson Ervin, born December 23, 1856; Martha Beck Irvin, born December 3, 1858; Samuel James

Ervin, born November 27, 1860; and Robert Tait Ervin, born May 27, 1863.

Albert Goode Ervin, married Elizabeth Cumming, September 28, 1875, and had children, Hugh Cumming Ervin, born March 8, 1877; Daniel Ervin, born May 13, 1879; Ethel Ervin, born December 31, 1881; Gertrude Ervin, born July 1, 1884; Margaret Ervin, and Albert Goode Ervin, Jr.

Jennie Fee Ervin, married, August 17, 1888, W. C. Larkin, of Athens, Texas, and had issue, Faith Larkin, born September 10, 1889.

Aurora R. Ervin, married, December 23, 1873, Hurieosco Austill, of Mobile, Ala., and had issue: Margaret Austill, born October 26, 1874; Robert Ervin Austill, born January 20, 1878; Jennie Fee Austill, born October 30, 1882 (married Ellis Day Gates); Hurieosco Austill, born May 15, 1884; Aileen Austill, born September 20, 1888; Jere Austill, born October 17, 1890.

Caroline Ervin, married, August 30, 1875, Anderson J. Phillips; issue, George A. Phillips, born August 2, 1880; Adelle Phillips, born February 9, 1883, (married Hugh Will Hoon); Emma Phillips, born March 9, 1885, (married Sanford Milliken).

Leila G. Ervin, married, December 12, 1883, Arthur S. McDaniel, of San Antonio, Texas, and had issue: Arthur Bee McDaniel, born August 31, 1895.

Martha B. Ervin, married, March 12, 1889, John W. Pharr, of Catherine, Alabama; issue, Austill Pharr, Bessie Pharr, Katherine Pharr, and Adelle Pharr.

Samuel J. Ervin, married Madison McWilliams of Camden, Ala., and had issue: Leila G. Ervin, Amelie Ervin, Robert Hugh Ervin, Sarah Ervin, and Samuel James Ervin.

Robert Tait Ervin, married, June 8, 1897, Francis Patterson Pybas, of Jackson, Tenn., and had issue: Francis Patterson Ervin, June 10, 1898, Robert Tait Ervin, March 25, 1902, and Marina Ervin, April 19, 1906.

"PLEASANT GARDENS" BRANCH.

HUNTING JOHN MCDOWELL of "Pleasant Gardens," North Carolina, was one of the pioneers of Western Carolina; came first from Pennsylvania to Virginia and from the valley of Virginia to Pleasant Gardens in 1743. He entered large tracts of land in 1750. He was

too old for active service and was not in the Revolution of 1775, and
he refused to ask protection from the British and preferred to drive
his cattle off to the cove, for hiding.   His county was then Rowan,
and he attended court at Salisbury one hundred miles away.   Afterwards, his county was Burke, 1777, and later on it was McDowell, in
honor of his illustrious son Joseph.

Hunting John was of Scotch-Irish descent, and is said to have
been related to Ephraim McDowell of Virginia, probably a nephew.
John McDowell married Annie Edmisten, of Virginia, and by her
he had three children, — Joseph, Rachel, and Annie.   The latter
married a Whitson and their descendants are to be found in Buncombe county, North Carolina, and in California.   Rachel married
Col. John Carson, and after her death he married Joseph McDowell's
widow, Mary Moffett.

JOSEPH McDOWELL, of "Pleasant Gardens," the only son of
"Hunting John" McDowell, was married to Mary Moffett (a
daughter of Col. George Moffett and Sarah McDowell) in Augusta
county, Virginia, Staunton being the post-office.   The writer has
a letter, written by Col. George Moffett to his daughter Mary, and it
was written from Augusta county, Virginia, July 2, 1807, and posted
at Staunton, Virginia.

When a boy of eighteen, Joseph of Pleasant Gardens was in
Rutherford's campaign against the Indians, in 1776 — and killed an
Indian with his own sword.   Two or three years ago his sword was
found in the garret at Pleasant Gardens and sent to the Museum at
Raleigh, North Carolina.   He was a man of delicate constitution,
and in addition to being "A fervent patriot, had considerable taste
for military affairs."   He was a man of "great dignity and modesty
of character, and was regarded as possessing the brightest intellect
of his day."   I have in my possession a manuscript from Silas Mc-
Dowell of Macon county, North Carolina, who endeavored to correct
all errors, and give the people historical facts.   He was born in 1795,
four years before the death of Joseph of Pleasant Gardens, and was
a man of remarkable memory, and gathered facts.   He says of
Joseph McDowell: — "If there was any man in this part of the
State that distinguished himself in mind, as ranking far above his
fellows, except Joseph McDowell of Pleasant Gardens, Burke county,
tradition has not transmitted the fact; though there were scores of
strong-minded, honorable, and patriotic men in this division of the
State, who figured in the Revolutionary war.   McDowell's light
went out when he was in his noon-day prime, and in the last decade

of the 18th century, 1799, and from that time till 1820 there has arisen no bright and particular star." Joseph McDowell of Pleasant Gardens was born February 25, 1758, and died, as I said, in 1799, at the age of forty-one.   Young as he was, he soon went into the Patriot army, and was soon promoted to Major under his cousin Charles, who was Colonel, afterwards General.   Joseph met Colonel Furgerson at Gilbert Town, and drove him back and prevented his crossing the mountain.   I have it from my father, Dr. John McDowell, who had been told by his father, the Hon. James McDowell, and his Aunt Annie, the son and daughter of Joseph, of Pleasant Gardens, and Mary Moffett, that while Joseph was stationed at Gilbert Town (now this is a fact), his wife, Mary Moffett, molded bullets and carried them tied under her skirts to her husband.   She went from Pleasant Gardens to Gilbert Town on horseback, a distance of twenty-six miles through a rough country, and on the way she was encountered by rough Tories who took her horse by the bridle and tried to prevent her going further; but with the courage of the women of that day, she managed to get out of the ruffians' way, and made a safe trip.   Joseph was engaged in the battles of Cowpens and Ramsaurs Mills, and was the McDowell who commanded his own and General Charles McDowell's troops at Kings' Mountain.   Robbing Joseph of Pleasant Gardens of command of the troops at that battle, has been a mistake on the part of some historian; and because of the mistake, in saying that "Joseph of Quaker Meadows was the Superior Officer," and commanded his brother Charles' troops — the name McDowell does not appear on the Kings' Mountain monument.   The two Josephs were cousins and married sisters, Mary and Margaret Moffett, and both fought at Kings' Mountain, one commanded the right and one the left wing of the regiment, and both were brave and honorable in all things, but having the same name, and both being soldiers, then statesmen, a great deal of confusion has arisen.

Joseph of Pleasant Gardens was undoubtedly the commander at Kings' Mountain; all of my family, from my grandfather James, Joseph's son, and Annie, his daughter, down to my father and mother, have said so, and I think the china, which is in the possession of the writer, is proof conclusive.   The china was given to Annie McDowell by her mother, Mary Moffett McDowell, telling her that the set of china was given to her father, Joseph, from Furgerson's belongings after the battle of Kings' Mountain.

Annie married her cousin, Capt. Charles McDowell, of Quaker

Meadows, Burke Co., N. C., and she gave the china to her daughters. Both the Woodfin ladies, Annie and Capt. Charles' daughters, have pieces of this china, and Miss Anna Woodfin still has a piece, a cup and saucer; and when she showed it to me a year ago, she said, "My mother told me this was given to my great-grandfather, Joseph, of Pleasant Gardens, after the battle of Kings' Mountain." Mrs. Bynum, another daughter of Annie and Capt. Charles, and granddaughter of "Joseph of Pleasant Gardens," gave a plate from the same set of china, to her son Judge Gray Bynum, of Morganton, making the same statement to the writer that the Woodfin sisters had made. I believe that plate is the only thing I ever coveted. Judge Bynum and his wife died without children and there was no one to inherit the china. The Judge gave the same to his much beloved brother-in-law, George Green, of Wilson, N. C., who married my cousin. I wrote to Mr. Green and asked him if he would give me the china and allow it to remain in the family, and not pass out of the name. Being a big-hearted and honorable man, he brought the china plate to me, saying he had rather give it to me than send it to the Museum at Raleigh. So I have the china and send you a photo of same. Getting it was an answer to prayer.

Joseph was a lawyer and his law books are in the family; and from them I send his autograph, "J. McDowell, P. G." "If Joseph of P. G. was the rightful commander, posterity should know it," says Judge Locke McCorkle, and to that just man I am indebted for a great deal of data, that corresponds with all my family have said. "Again," he says, "no man had more distinguished descendants than 'Joseph of Pleasant Gardens,' according to their number." Joseph was major before the battle of Kings' Mountain, and Colonel after that. He served in the North Carolina Legislature from 1785 to 1792. "He was a member of the North Carolina convention in 1788, for the purpose of adopting or rejecting the Constitution of the U. S., in which he made a statesmanlike speech, opposing its adoption on the ground that it did not guarantee the rights of the states, trial by jury, and the great writ of habeas corpus,"— so said the Hon. Locke McCorkle, who made a big effort to do justice to both Joseph of Pleasant Gardens, and Joseph of Quaker Meadows.

Joseph, as I said, died in 1799, and was buried at Round Hill, the family burying ground at Pleasant Gardens, and his grave is unmarked.

As I said, John, James, and Annie were the children of Joseph and Mary Moffett,— two others having died young. Hon. John McDowell of Rutherford was a most estimable man, several times served his county honorably in the Legislature, as did his brother James, of Burke Co., and while James was in the Legislature the new county taken off of Burke was named through compliment to him, for his father, Joseph of Pleasant Gardens, 1820, and was called McDowell county.

John married a Miss Lewis and his descendants are scattered over North Carolina, and to his daughter Miss Sarah McDowell, and his grandson, John Michael, and to Dr. Michael and Major Ben Burgin, who was 95 years old fifty years ago, when he gave my father, Dr. Michael, and others, a great deal of information concerning "Joseph of Pleasant Gardens," I am indebted for much that I've written.

James McDowell married Margaret Erwin of "Belvidere," Burke county, N. C., and lived until after her death at Pleasant Gardens, and from there he removed to Yancey Co., leaving three sons and two daughters to the care, mostly, of his wife's relatives at Belvidere, the oldest being ten and the youngest one year old. James McDowell, like many of the name, was celebrated for his hospitality, and the sister-in-law, who brought up his infant and did a great deal for all the children, has often said to the writer (she was my great aunt, Miss Cecelia Erwin): "Brother James McDowell was the kindest and best brother-in-law I ever knew." James McDowell, it seems, never refused to go security for his friends and kin; and through the latter, he lost his Pleasant Gardens home,— same being sold for security debts, and then he moved to Yancey county, where he died in 1854.

James McDowell and Margaret Erwin had, as I stated, three sons and two daughters, besides two children who died when a few months old. The brothers were Joseph Alburto, William Wallace, and John Calhoun McDowell. Owing to these three men being left, when very young, without a mother, and their father being, in a measure, broken up, and having to leave his home and go to Yancey county, which was almost out of civilization, these three brothers were thrown considerably on their own resources — though they had the kindest of fathers. However, they were fairly well educated.

Joseph, the eldest, read medicine with Dr. Hardy of Asheville, and from there went to the Medical College at Charleston, from

which he graduated and settled at Hot Springs, N. C., and afterwards at Asheville, N. C. He was considered an excellent physician, and was a man of the finest personal appearance; was called
a "Chesterfield" in manner. He married Julia Patton of Asheville (daughter of John C. Patton), and their children are living in
North Carolina, South Carolina, Georgia, and Florida. Mrs.
James Walton, his eldest daughter, lives in Morganton, N. C.

William Wallace McDowell married Sarah Smith, of Asheville,
who was a daughter of James Smith (he who was the first white
child born west of the Blue Ridge), and lived and died there, as did
his brother Dr., or Col., Joseph, of whom I have just made mention.
These two brothers were officers during the Civil War. Joseph
was Colonel, and William, Major. William was Captain of the first
volunteer company that left Asheville in 1861. The flag with which
the Captain was presented was made from an old U. S. flag (recon-
structed) by the ladies of Asheville. "This flag was adopted as
the regimental flag by the First Regiment, commanded by Gen.
D. H. Hill, and was dedicated at Big Bethel Church battle, June
10, 1861."

W. W. McDowell's courage at that battle was highly spoken of
by D. H. Hill and others, the first battle between the North and the
South. Captain W. W. McDowell of the Buncombe Rifles, of 1861,
became Major in the 60th North Carolina Regiment, his brother,
Joseph, being Colonel of the regiment. They were both at Mur-
freesboro, Tenn. Col. Joseph was born December 22, 1821, and
died March 10, 1875, at Asheville. Major William was born February, 1824, and died June, 1893, at Asheville. Major William
Wallace McDowell "was the grandest old man I ever knew."
This was said of him, or rather, written of him, by a friend and a
Northerner, who had lived in the Major's home for years. Surely
he ought to have known the "Maj." as every one called him. The
writer knew him thirty years, or even longer, and can say he was
the best man she had ever known. After the death of my father,
his brother, Dr. John C. McDowell, I was a great deal in his family,
and agree with the writer who said of him, "He was as brave as
a lion and as gentle as a lamb." I never heard him speak harshly
to any one; always gentle and loving in his family. 'Twas hard
for him to say "No," but when it was said, no one would dream
of his saying "Yes." He was truly a Christian; was an Elder
in the Presbyterian church — a real Scotch Presbyterian in many
things,— had inherited that bravery and religion of the Clan. He

was of Scotch-Irish descent. W. W. McDowell's children are living in North Carolina and Seattle, Washington. Two daughters, Annie and Mary, are at the old home in Asheville.

Dr. John Calhoun McDowell, the third son of James McDowell, and brother to Col. Joseph and Major William, was born at Pleasant Gardens, July 7, 1825, and died at his home on John's River, near Morganton, August 2, 1876. He married Sarah Erwin of Bellevue, daughter of James Erwin, and settled first in Morganton, where he began the practice of medicine. He read medicine in Morganton with Dr. McRee, and from there he went to the Medical College at Charleston, South Carolina. He was said to be a very handsome man, a man with a great big heart and quick intellect. He did not care for office or honors, and never allowed his name to go before the public but once — then he was elected to the Convention of '61 from Burke; and, at the same time, his brother Joseph was elected from Buncombe. He was a Democrat, as were his brothers, and during every campaign worked for his party, as few men did, only when working for self. The McDowell's were Democrats, while nearly all their kin were Whigs.

Col. Walton, one of Burke's historians, said "Dr. John C. McDowell died without an enemy." W. W. Avery, another writer, said, "He did not care for office; he only cared to shine in social life, and was a prince of entertainers," and "Always thinking and planning for the advancement of his family." "He was a kind and indulgent husband and father." It was said by others, and I know it to be a fact, that he was the kindest of neighbors,— and his slaves loved him with a peculiar devotion. His sons say, "He was the biggest man they ever knew." He died greatly beloved, at his home at the old home of Gen. Joseph McDowell, of Quaker Meadows, and was buried at Morganton. Gen. Joseph sold said home to Albert Corpening, and from Albert it descended to his son, David, and David sold same to Dr. J. C. McDowell and wife, Sarah Erwin, and the part of the old plantation on which Joseph of Quaker Meadows lived, and the home of Dr. John Calhoun McDowell belongs to the writer.

Dr. Jno. C. McDowell was not in the army during the Civil War, but was in active home service, fighting the Tories and protecting the homes. He loved his church; was a Presbyterian. His descendants are living in North Carolina. Most of them are at Morganton, Burke county, North Carolina, the county of the McDowells of old.

Kathrine Ann and Margaret Erwin McDowell were the daughters of Col. James McDowell and Margaret Caroline Erwin. "Kate" was born November, 1826, and died at Asheville, June, 1898. She married Montreville Patton of Asheville, N. C. She was a remarkably handsome woman; was called "queenly." She was a devoted wife, step-mother, sister and aunt; and was far above the average woman for common sense and judgment. Left no children. Margaret married Marcus Erwin of Asheville, one of North Carolina's most prominent lawyers. She was a remarkably sweet and amiable woman. Was born about 1828, and died in 1859, leaving two little sons. One, Hamilton Erwin, is now living in Morganton, N. C. The other died young.

The children of Dr. John C. McDowell and Sarah Erwin are: James Erwin McDowell, married and lived at Durham, N. C.; Margaret Erwin McDowell, not married, lived at Morganton; William B. McDowell, married and died, leaving 4 children; John C. McDowell, married and lived in Morganton, had two children; Elizabeth C. McDowell, not married, lived at Morganton; Frank McDowell, married, lived at Morganton, 4 children; Kate McDowell, married H. T. Newland, dead, one child, who lived at Morganton with her aunts.

MRS. E. M. TABER'S LINE.

IRISH BRANCH.

WILLIAM IRVINE came from Ireland to America in the beginning of the 18th century aged 14 years. A brother two years older than he accompanied him, but when of age, returned to Ireland and received his inheritance. He returned in a ship which landed at Baltimore, and there he settled. They came from County Antrim, and were related to the Earl of Antrim.

William Irvine (first emigrant) married Elizabeth McClane and had a son named Joseph.

After the death of Elizabeth McClane, his wife, William Irvine married, second, Jane Hoffman. He was 75 years old when the American Revolution began. He was a whig and a great friend of George Washington. He was obliged to leave Dutchess county, N. Y., where he had settled, and go to Orange county, across the Hudson river. He afterwards made his home five miles west of Newbury, where he died aged 86.

William Irvine and Jane Hoffman his (second wife) had issue:

Robert who married Mary Pell.

James who married Margaret Patten.

William who married Jane Ennis.

Allen who married Esther Townsend.

Mary who married Samuel Wickham.

Margaret who married Jacobs Ockmoody.

Elizabeth who married Joseph Simmons.

James Irvine, son of William and Elizabeth, his first wife, married Margaret P. Childers, and had issue:

William P. Irwin who married M. Hayward.

Robert, who married Elizabeth Salt.

Israel.

James.

Jane, who married Timothy Thompson.

Ann.

Elizabeth, who married Stanard.

William P. Irvin, married M. Hayward, and had issue:

Theodore who married Louisa Branan.

Dudley M. who married Mary Miller.

David M. who married Harriet L. Nash.

Daniel P. who married Elizabeth Nash.

William P. twice married; first to A. M. Andrew; second to A. M. Teller.

His children:

Frances M. who married A. G. Morey.

E. M. Irvine who married O. A. Taber.

Theresa M. who married H. C. Rew.

Harriet, married J. C. Williams.

Theodore Irvine, son of William P. Irwin and M. Hayward, had one son, Theodore.   Dudley Irvine had one son, Dudley M.   David had two children, Charles D. and Harriet E.   William had five daughters and one son, Theodore D.

DESCENDANTS OF JOHN IRVINE.

JOHN IRVINE born February 25, 1755, married Prudence Armstrong of Mercer county, Kentucky. Among children of John Irvine was:

1. Robert Irvine, son of John Irvine, married Joanna Ryland, in Kentucky, in 1825; came to Missouri late in 1825, or early in 1826.   To Robert Irvine and Joanna (Ryland) Irvine were born the following children:

1. Glenoe Village.
2. Larne Harbor.
3. Ballygally Castle.

4. Given to Col. Joseph McDowell of
   Pleasant Gardens, N. C., after
   battle of King's Mountain.

(1). James Ryland Irvine, born November 29, 1826; married Susan Melissa Bridgeford (born April 7, 1839); she was daughter of Richard Bridgeford and Melissa (Thomason); Bridgeford's father was also named Richard, and his mother's maiden name was Nancy Guthrie; Melissa Thomason was daughter of William and Susan (McQuiddy) Thomason. Three sons were born to James Ryland Irvine and wife, and grew to manhood:

a. Robert Leonidas Irvine, born in August, 1866; died in March, 1893.

James Milton Irvine (born January 17, 1871, at Hannibal, Mo.). Married, January 2, 1895, at St. Joseph, Mo., to Mildred Patterson, daughter of Richard Patterson and Mildred (Faulconer) Patterson. Two children have been born to James and Milton Irvine and wife, Robert and Helen, who, with their parents, live at St. Joseph, Mo.

b. George Wolfe Irvine, born September 26, 1872; unmarried, and living at Fort Smith, Ark.

(2). Katherine Irvine; died at New London, Mo., in 1881 unmarried.

(3). Rose Irvine; married Thomas Greaves of Ralls county, Mo.

(4). Sarah Milton Irvin; married Charles Overman; now dead.

(5). Henrietta Paulina Irvine; married —— Kersting.

(6). George Robert Irvine; married Frazer Deckard; now living at Neodesha, Kans.

EVANSTON IRVINES.

David W. Irwin, married Harriet L. Nash; their children were: Charles David Irwin, and one daughter (Mrs. Root).

Charles David Irwin born at Albany, N. Y., April 19, 1859; married Hettie Frances Duryea at Nyack-on-Hudson, October 26, 1881; their children are:

Jessie Nash Irwin, born in Chicago, October 27, 1883.

David Duryea Irwin, born Chicago, May 4, 1887. (Yale Scientific 1908.)

The present home of the family is in Evanston, Ill.

A statement of Ancestry and Tradition relative to his family made by Rev. Samuel Irvine, D. D., of Fredericksburg, Wayne Co., Ohio, reduced to writing by his son, John E. Irvine, in his presence and at his dictation, at his home on Thursday, April 4, 1861.

THE PENNSYLVANIA IRVINES.

I was born at or near Derg Bridge, County Tyrone, Ireland, on the 22nd day of June, 1786. My parents emigrated to the United States the next year, leaving Ireland in May and arriving in Philadelphia in August, a month or six weeks before the rising of the Convention that formed the present Constitution of the United States. My father lived, until the next spring, about nine miles west of Lancaster, in Lancaster Co., Pa., and then moved to Kishocoquillas Valley, in Mifflin Co., Pa., where he lived until 1796, when he moved to the farm where he lived and died in Shaver's Creek Valley, Huntington Co., Pa. I entered Jefferson College at Gannonsburgh, Pa., in 1810. In November, 1810, I began the study of theology under the instruction of John Anderson, D. D., of Service, Beaver Co., Pa. I was licensed to preach the gospel by the Associate Presbytery of Philadelphia, which met at Carlisle, Pa., for that purpose on the 12th day of August, 1819. After spending a term of some eight or nine months preaching in the Carolinas and Tennessee, I visited this part of Ohio and received a call from Salt Creek, Newman's Creek, Wooster and Mohican churches, which I accepted and was ordained as their pastor by the Presbytery of Chartiers, which met at the Court House in Wooster, Ohio, for that purpose in March 1821. I had spent the fall and winter among those churches. I have ever since been pastor of the Church of Salt Creek, and of the branches, from time to time, united with it.

I had four brothers: John, born in Kishocoquillas Valley, in March, 1789; Christopher, born at same place in 1793; James S., born at Shaver's Creek, June 22, 1799; David, born at Shaver's Creek, September 11, 1802. I had one sister, Elizabeth, born in October, 1795 at Kishocoquillas Valley, Pa. She married Alexander Campbell and left two daughters, Sarah and Elizabeth, the first, the wife of John Henderson, of Shaver's Creek, Pa., and the other, of Hugh Lee of Linn Co., Oregon.

My father, James Irvine, born, 1761, near Derg Bridge, Tyrone Co., Ireland, was the youngest son of his father by a second marriage — there were fifteen children of his father in all. My father was brought up (his father having died during his own infancy) by his older full brother, John Irvine, who followed the trade of blacksmith near Derg Bridge. I only remember the name of one other of my father's brothers — Christopher Irvine — who emigrated to America and settled on the Yadkin in the southwest part of Rowan Co., North Carolina. He was a young man, unmarried, I think, when he emigrated. His oldest children were as old as my father. He was there long before the beginning of the Revolution. Uncle Christopher left a large family of sons and daughters — in 1819 they were very old. I saw a grandson of Uncle Christopher, named Graham, proprietor of a hat establishment in Statesville, North Carolina — a fine man, — he gave me the best hat I ever owned. My Uncle John Irvin, of Derg Bridge, had three sons, Christopher, William and John. Cousin Christopher was a farmer, William was a scholar — he built a hotel at Derg Bridge (or Castle Derg). William's son John once visited me at Fredericksburg and returned to Ireland. He had traveled and peddled in America. I don't know what became of Uncle John's son John. My grandfather, John Irvine, was twice married, and had a family of fifteen children. He was a blacksmith. His father, my great-grandfather, was likewise called John Irvine and was a blacksmith. He (my great-grandfather) was renowned for his great strength. I have heard father say that he could straighten out a horseshoe — he received the freedom of the City of Londonderry, for what he did in the siege,— the exact nature of which I do not now recollect. He served throughout the siege in the Derg garrison. Where father was born and bred the people were all Scotch-Presbyterians. My mother, Sarah, was the third youngest daughter of Samuel Semple. He had a large family and came and settled with them in Kishocoquillas — Margaret, wife of Hugh Braham, and Elizabeth, wife of James Flemming. My father had a full cousin, General James Irvine, of Carlisle, Pa., who was an old man at the time of the Revolution. Before father left Kishocoquillas Valley I remember that two young brothers, William and John Irvine, came from Ireland and spent a winter in Kishocoquillas. They were fine looking men and I used to admire them for their appearance. My father called them cousins, but I do not know what was the degree of relationship between them. They both married and settled in Center Co. Gen. James Irvine of Center county is the son of that John Irvine. I know of many other branches of Irvine in this country, but none of whose relationship to us I am clearly informed.

JOHN IRVINE, renowned for his great strength — given the freedom of Londonderry for services rendered during the siege of 1689. He was a blacksmith.

JOHN IRVINE, son of above, resided near Derg Bridge, County Tyrone, Ireland. Father of fifteen children by two marriages.

1. Christopher, supposed to be issue by first wife; emigrated to America long before the Revolution and settled on the Yadkin, in the southwest part of Rowan county, North Carolina.
2. John, also a blacksmith, who brought up James; had issue:
    (1.) Christopher,
    (2). William,
    (3). John.
3. James, born 1761, near Derg Bridge, Ireland; married Sarah, youngest daughter of Samuel Semple; emigrated to America; May, 1787, arriving in Philadelphia, August, 1787. He had issue:
    (1) Rev. Samuel Irvine, D.D., born at or near Derg Bridge, Ireland, June 22, 1786; came to America with his parents, arriving at Philadelphia in August, 1787, being at that time a little more than one year old. Entered Jefferson College at Cannonsburgh, Pa., in 1810, as a student of theology. Licensed to preach by the Associated Presbytery of Philadelphia at Carlisle, Pa., August 12, 1819; spent a term of eight or nine months in travelling and preaching in the Carolinas and Tennessee, going thence to Wooster, Ohio; received a call from Saltcreek, Newman's creek, Wooster and Mohican churches, (all near Fredericksburg, Ohio, Saltcreek being in that town) which he accepted and was ordained their pastor by the Presbytery of Chartiers at the Court House in Wooster, Ohio, March, 1821. He was the pastor of the church of Saltcreek from this date until his death, at Fredericksburg, Ohio, April 28, 1861, an uninterrupted ministry of nearly forty-two years. The degree of Doctor of Divinity was conferred on him, date and college unknown to the writer. He married Maria, daughter of Samuel and Hannah (Kirkpatrick) Glasgow, January 24, 1822, and had by her (who died February 26, 1871) the following issue:
    (a) James Irvine, who was born at Wooster, Wayne County, Ohio, December 24, 1822, where he remained until he was ten years old, when with his parents he went to Fredericksburg, Wayne Co., Ohio; on finishing his education he began teaching school. He taught in Ashland County, Ohio, and the schools of Fredericks-

burg. At the age of twenty-four he entered as a student, the law office of Sapp & Welker, Millersburg, Holmes County, Ohio, and was admitted to practice about the time war was declared between the United States and Mexico. In May, 1847, he assisted in recruiting and organizing a company for service in this war, the company marching from Millersburg to Zanesville, Ohio, and being received with great enthusiasm all along the route. From Zanesville they took steamboat to Cincinnati, Ohio. This company was afterward known as Company G, Fourth Ohio Volunteer Infantry. He was elected second lieutenant of this company on its organization in May, 1847, and in September of the same year, at the city of Matamoras, Mexico, was elected its Captain, which position he retained until discharged in 1848, at Cincinnati, Ohio. On receiving his discharge he went to Coshocton, Ohio, and taught school for one year; then began the practice of his profession, the law. He was mayor of the town of Coshocton from 1852 to 1854, the only political office he ever held, although he always labored zealously in the interests of the Republican party of which he was a member, making political addresses, both in his home county and other portions of the state. In 1861, he assisted in recruiting and organizing the first company of volunteers from Coshocton County, called, "The Union Guards" and was elected its captain. This company was mustered into service of the United States at Camp Jackson, Ohio, April 27, 1861, and was assigned to the Sixteenth Ohio Infantry, three months service, becoming Company A of that Regiment. On the organization of the regiment he was appointed its colonel and served in that capacity until the regiment was mustered out August 18, 1861, at Columbus, Ohio. In 1863, he recruited a company of cavalry which rendevouzed at Camp Dennison, Ohio, and became Company N of the Ninth Ohio Cavalry. On the organization of this company he was elected its captain, and on the organization of the regiment was commissioned its major, afterward becoming its lieutenant-colonel, which position he held until mustered out at the close of the war at Lexington,

North Carolina, July 20, 1865. He then resumed the practice of law at his home, Coshocton, Ohio, where he died June 23, 1882. On June 26, 1852, he was married to Annie Isabelle Humrickhouse of Coshocton, Ohio, sixth daughter of Peter Humrickhouse, junior (born August 26, 1783, at Germantown, Pa., and died at Coshocton, Ohio, August 23, 1839), and Sarah (Schuman) Humrickhouse (born July 10, 1788, at Hagerstown, Md.; died at Coshocton, Ohio, August 13, 1854), born March 12, 1828, and now living at Coshocton, Ohio, and by her had the following issue:

(a.) Sarah, born October 18, 1855, married L. S. Staver. Issue:
    (a.) Alice, married Virgil Loos.
    (b.) Belle, married Robert Crawford.
    (c.) Harry.

(b.) Samuel Irvine, born October 23, 1857, at Coshocton, Ohio, married October 19, 1887, to Annie (Anderson) Irvine, who was born at Keene, Ohio, December 12, 1865, by whom he has the following issue:
    a. Mary Agnes, born July 16, 1888, at Coshocton, Ohio.
    b. James, born December 7, 1893, at Pittsburgh, Pa.

(c.) Mary, born October 12, 1861; married C. E. Anderson, and had issue:
    a. Annie, born 1888.
    b. S. Irvine, born 1894.
    c. Sarah M., born 1903.

(2) Matilda, born at Wooster, Ohio, July 7, 1824; died at Monmouth, Ill., ——; married Rev. James H. Peacock, August 26, 1845. He died at Coulberville, Ill., February 1, 1875; issue:

    a. Theophilus Glasgow, attorney and judge, born at Mt. Vernon, Ohio, July 5, 1846; married Emma Schiller August 23, 1881; resides in Monmouth, Ill.
    b. Maria, born 1847; died 1849.
    c. Elizabeth, born 1849; married Wm. Pinkerton.
    d. Sarah, born 1851.
    e. Anna, born 1853.
    f. Catherine F., born 1854; married Samuel McMillan.

g. Jessie, born 1856.

h. Maria C., born 1858; died 1880.

j. Matilda H., born 1860.

k. Samuel I., born 1862; died 1862.

l. James H., born 1864; died 1865.

(3) Rev. Samuel G., born August 14, 1826; died October 31, 1895; pastor Albany, Oregon, U. P. Church; married March 27, 1851, to Mary Rainey, who was born June 14, 1830, and died April 13, 1869; issue:

a. Maria G., married W. H. Gaston.

b. Cora J., married C. H. Stewart.

c. Elizabeth, born 1857.

d. Oliver H., born 1860. On December 6, 1871, he married Margaret Martin, 2d wife; and by her had the following issue:

e. Rev. Samuel Elliott, born 1875, now pastor of Etna, Pa., United Presbyterian Church.

f. James C., born 1877.

(4) Sarah, born February 29, 1828; married December 28, 1848; died June 7, 1900. Married Rev. Wm. Wishart, now living in Allegheny, Pa. Issue:

a. Maria L., born 1849; married Jno. A. Gray.

b. Martha, born 1851.

c. Samuel I., born 1852; died 1853.

d. Elizabeth, born 1853.

e. Janette, born 1856.

f. Matilda, born 1858.

g. Agnes, born 1860.

h. James, born 1862; died in 1863.

j. William I., born, 1864; pastor 8th U. P. Church, Allegheny, Pa.

k. John E., born 1866; pastor Ingram, Pa., U. P. Church.

l. Margaret M., born 1868.

m. Charles F., born 1870; pastor 11th U. P. Church, Allegheny, Pa.

(5) John E., born January 18, 1830; died May 17, 1869; married Emma Shelly February 20, 1862, who was born 1842, and had the following issue:

a. Shelly, born 1865.

b. James, born 1865.

(6) Eliza, born February 28, 1833; died August 24, 1885.

(7). Oliver, born February 18, 1835; died August 10, 1836.

(8). Maria, born November 9, 1840; married Dr. S. K. Crawford, born 1835, November 2, 1865; issue:

    a. Ada Louise, born 1866; died 1874.

    b. Charles, born 1868.

    c. Mary I., born 1869.

    d. Samuel K., born 1874.

    e. Hugh, born 1875; died 1876.

    f. Fannie C., born 1877.

    g. G. May, born 1878.

    h. Jno. Jay, born 1880.

2. John, born at Kishocoquillas Valley, Pa., March, 1789; married Eliza Elliott.

3. Christopher, born at Kishocoquillas Valley, Pa., 1793; married Martha (?) Wilson.   Had issue:

    (1). Jane.

    (2). Dr. James M. Irvine.

4. Elizabeth, born 1795; married Alexander Campbell, and had issue:

    (1). Sarah, married John Henderson.

    (2). Elizabeth, married Hugh Lee.

5. James S., born at Shaver's Creek, Pa., June 22, 1799; married Louise Armour; issue:

    (1). Sarah, married Rolland Aukney.

    (2). John A.

    (3). William H.

    (4). Maria Louisa.

    (5). Thomas.

    (6). Jessie, married J. R. Hammond.

6. David, born at Shaver's Creek, Pa., September 11, 1802 (his son gives this date as 1801); he lived to be over 90 years of age; died at Kirkwood, Ill.; married October 9, 1833, to Jane Wilson Davidson, who was born September 1, 1808, and by her had the following issue:

    (1). James Power, born in Huntingdon Co., Pa., May 15, 1835; married Hattie M. Ely, November 13, 1861; by whom he had the following issue:

        a. Elizabeth Ely, born September 3, 1862; died August 22, 1869.

        b. Annabelle, born November 5, 1783.

    (2). Robert Davidson, born in Huntingdon Co., Pa., July 20, 1837.

(3). John Monroe, born in Huntingdon Co., Pa., April 21, 1838;
    married Mattie A. Beatty November 22, 1866; died
    February 7, 1877; had issue:
    a. David Sample, born September 13, 1867.
    b. Ransom Dunbar, born January 1, 1870.
(4). David Sample, born in Huntingdon Co., Pa., June 11,
    1839; killed at battle of Nashville, Tenn., December 16,
    1864.
(5). Alexander Bruce, born in Huntingdon Co., Pa., September
    7, 1840; died September 15, 1840.
(6). Edwin Easton, born in Huntingdon Co., March 29, 1842.
(7). Isabelle Ellenore, born in Warren Co., Ill., July 31, 1844.
(8). Sarah Jane, born in Warren County, Ill., January 2, 1847.

ROBERT IRWIN, JR., son of Robert Irwin, was born December
23, 17—.

ALEXANDER JOHNSON IRWIN was born March 1, 1799.

If the above named were brothers there must be an error in
dating. I do not understand it, but give it just as I find it written
on a sheet of paper as a copy of something my uncle, Wm. Clemens,
found in a book that was marked as the property of Robert Irwin,
who, I think, must have been Mary Irwin's brother.

Mary Irwin (my grandmother), was born in Carlisle, Pa., January
20, 1782. I do not know the date of her marriage, but her first
child, Letitia Clemens, was born December 16, 1799. John Clemens
died in Waterford, Erie County, Pa., October 7, 1822, aged 60
years. Mary Irwin Clemens died in Erie, Pa., November 21, 1869;
aged 87 years, 10 months and 1 day.

Children of John and Mary Clemens:

Letitia Clemens was born December, 1799; married to Wm. Boyd
    in February 1823; died April 8, 1837.
William J. Clemens was born June 11, 1802; married Sarah Cul-
    bertson; died July 9, 1875.
Sarah Clemens was born September 16, 1804; married, November
    21, 1827, to Archibald Thompson; died April 14, 1889.
Mary Ann Clemens was born April 8, 1807; died May 14, 1875.
Robert Irwin Clemens was born August 16, 1809; died November
    24, 1814.
Amelia Martin Clemens was born January 23, 1812; married to
    Moses Curtis; died December 1, 1886.
Elizabeth Irwin Clemens was born April 23, 1814; married to Wm.
    W. Caughey March 3, 1842; died April 9, 1892.

John Clemens was born August 16, 1818; died July 24, 1892; married Lydia ———; had 3 children.

(1). Wilberforce Clay, died February, 1898.
(2). Emma Irwin.
(3). Retta Elizabeth.

FAMILY OF JOHN ERWIN.

Family Records copied from an old Bible, the first page of which bears the following inscription:

JOHN ERWIN'S FAMILY BIBLE
My father purchased this bible about the year 1814.
JOHN W. ERWIN.

John Platt, son of John Platt and Alice Stevenson, daughter of William Stevenson and Mary Stevenson, all of New Jersey, were married. Samuel Irwin, son of JOHN ERWIN and Mary, his wife, and Naomi Jones, daughter of Jeremiah Jones, were married in New Jersey.

JOHN ERWIN, son of Samuel and Naomi Erwin, and Elizabeth Platt were married at Wilmington, Delaware. She died July 5, 1846, at Richmond, Ind. They had issue:

BIRTHS.

1. JOHN ERWIN, born June 25, 1781.
Elizabeth Erwin, born July 9, 1785.
Mary Ann Erwin, born September 22, 1803.
Lydia Erwin, born September 22, 1805.
Elizabeth Erwin, born April 5, 1807.
John Wardell Erwin, born September 9, 1808.
George Washington Erwin, born September 25, 1810, in the state of Delaware.
Alice P. Erwin, was born March 4, 1813.
Susan B. Erwin, was born May 22, 1815.
Maria Erwin, born November 24, 1817.
——— Erwin was born September 3, 1819; died September 4, 1819.
Samuel Erwin, born October 19, 1820.
Edwin P. Erwin, born August 11, 1823.
William Platt Erwin, born October 21, 1829, in the state of Indiana.
G. W. Barnes, born 1814; died 1843.

DEATHS.

Elizabeth, wife of John Erwin, died July 5, 1846, at Richmond, Indiana.

John Erwin died November 29, 1849, three miles northwest of Richmond, Indiana.

Copy of the family record taken from a Bible, the first page of which bears the following inscription, "John W. Erwin, Camden, Ohio, October 29, 1840."

MARRIAGES.

John W. Erwin and Ann Eliza Chadwick were married on the 12th day of May, 1833, at the town of New Paris, Preble County, Ohio.

BIRTHS.

Henry Turpin Erwin, son of John W. and Ann Eliza Erwin, was born at New Paris, Ohio, on the 18th day of August, 1834.

Charles Rulon Erwin, son of John W. and Ann Eliza Erwin, was born at Camden, Ohio, on the 13th day of October, 1836.

Mary Erwin, daughter of John W. and Ann Eliza Erwin, was born at Camden, Preble County, Ohio, on the 30th of August, 1840.

Elizabeth Jerusha, daughter of John W. and Ann Eliza Erwin, was born at Hamilton, Butler County, Ohio, on the 15th day of March, 1843.

Frank Chadwick Erwin, son of John W. and Ann Eliza Erwin, was born on the 2nd day of March, 1846, in the town of Hamilton, Ohio.

BIRTHS.

John W. Erwin, son of John and Elizabeth Erwin, was born in New Castle County, State of Delaware, on the 9th day of September, 1808.

Ann Eliza Chadwick, daughter of Samuel R. and Jerusha Chadwick, was born in the Township of Chatham, County of Morris, and State of New Jersey, on the 22nd day of March, 1812.

DEATHS.

Henry Turpin Erwin, son of John W. and Ann Eliza Erwin, died at Hamilton, Ohio, on the 8th day of July, 1847.

Charles Rulon, son of John W. and Ann Eliza Erwin, died at Hamilton, Ohio, on the 5th day of November, 1856.

Frank Chadwick, son of John W. and Ann Eliza Erwin, died at Hamilton, Ohio, on the 22nd day of July, 1863.

Elizabeth Jerusha Erwin, daughter of John W. and Ann Eliza Erwin, died February 23, 1867.

FAMILY RECORD.

Copied from a Bible, the inscription on one of the first pages being: A Sacred Token from John W. Erwin to Ann Eliza Erwin.

MARRIAGES.

John W. Erwin, son of John and Elizabeth Erwin, and Ann Eliza Chadwick, daughter of Samuel R. and Jerusha Chadwick, were married on the 12th day of May, 1833, at New Paris, Ohio.

Thorwald Eugene Bernadotte DeLopez Brandt, son of Christian and Caroline Brandt, and Mary Erwin, daughter of John W. and Ann Eliza Erwin, were married at Hamilton, Ohio, November 5th, 1868.

Frank Erwin Bernadotte Brandt, son of Eugene and Mary E. Brandt, and Anna Margaret Spoerl, daughter of Frederick and Christina Spoerl, were married at Hamilton, Ohio, August 15, 1889.

BIRTHS.

John W. Erwin, son of John and Elizabeth Erwin, was born in New Castle County, State of Delaware, on the 9th day of September, 1808.

Ann Eliza Chadwick, daughter of Samuel R. and Jerusha Chadwick, in the Township of Chatham, County of Morris, State of New Jersey, on the 22nd day of March, 1812.

Henry Turpin, son of John W. and Ann Eliza Erwin, was born in New Paris, County of Preble, and State of Ohio, August 18, 1834.

Charles Rulon, son of John W. and Ann Eliza Erwin, was born in Camden, Preble County, and State of Ohio, on the 13th day of October, 1836.

Mary Erwin, daughter of John W. and Ann Eliza Erwin, was born in Camden, Preble County, and State of Ohio, on the 30th day of August, 1840.

Elizabeth Jerusha, daughter of John W. and Ann Eliza Erwin, was born in Hamilton, Butler County, and State of Ohio, March 15, 1843.

Frank Chadwick, son of John W. and Ann Eliza Erwin, was born in Hamilton, Butler County, and State of Ohio, on the 2nd day of March, 1846.

Frank Erwin Bernadotte Brandt, son of Eugene and Mary E.

Brandt, was born at Hamilton, Butler County, Ohio, on the tenth day of August, 1869.

Lutie Caroline Brandt, daughter of Eugene and Mary E. Brandt, was born at same place as above on the 21st day of September, 1870.

Thorwald Eugene Bernadotte DeLopez Brandt was born in Copenhagen, Denmark, on the 30th of December, 1838 — son of Christian and Caroline Brandt.

Died at Santa Barbara, California, July 5, 1877.

Mary Erwin Spoerl Brandt, daughter of Frank Erwin Bernadotte Brandt and Anna Margaret Brandt was born at 6:15 p. m., on Saturday, July the nineteenth, in the year 1890, in Hamilton, Ohio.

Erwin Chadwick Brandt, son of Frank Erwin Bernadotte Brandt and Anna Margaret Brandt, was born at 6 a. m., on Sunday morning, November 1, 1891, in Hamilton, Ohio.

Anna Margaret Brandt, daughter of Frederick and Christina Spoerl, and wife of Frank Erwin Bernadotte Brandt, was born on February 24, 1866, in Hamilton, Ohio.

DEATHS.

Henry Turpin Erwin died July 8, 1847, at Hamilton, Butler County, Ohio.

Charles Rulon Erwin died November 5, 1856, at Hamilton, Ohio.

Frank Chadwick Erwin died July 22, 1863, at Hamilton, Ohio.

Elizabeth Jerusha, always called Lutie Erwin, died Saturday morning, February 23, 1867, at Hamilton, Ohio.

Lutie Caroline Brandt died April 20, 1871, at her grandparents' residence, Hamilton, Ohio.

Ann Eliza Erwin, wife of John W. Erwin, died on Sunday, January 10, 1886, and was buried on Tuesday, January 12th, at Greenwood Cemetery.

John W. Erwin died at Hamilton, Ohio, Wednesday evening, April 17, 1889, and was buried on Saturday, April 20th, at Greenwood Cemetery.

Mary Erwin Brandt, wife of Thorwald Eugene DeLopez Brandt, died March 12, 1890, from the old homestead in Hamilton, Ohio. Forever blessed is her memory.

The above was compiled from family Bibles in my possession, on April 10, 1895.

FRANK ERWIN BERNADOTTE BRANDT.

NORTH CAROLINA ERWINS.

Joseph Ernest Erwin, secretary-treasurer of the Alpine Cotton Mills, Morganton, N. C., of which W. A. Erwin is president, writes Mrs. L. Boyd:

MY DEAR COUSIN:— Please accept thanks for your esteemed favor.

Nathaniel Erwin came to Bucks Co., Penn., from Belfast, or thereabouts, and his sons William, Alexander, and Arthur, came south with their sister Susan; Alexander and Arthur settled here in Burke Co., and William in York Co., S. C., and these three sons have an innumerable number of descendants in this state and South Carolina, as well as Tennessee, etc. The great Zeb Vance, our war governor, and for many years senator, was a relation of ours (my third cousin); Bishop Galloway, of Georgia, is a cousin also.

My great-great-aunt, "Pretty Polly Erwin," married a celebrated Presbyterian minister, Macamy Wilson, whose grandson went to South Africa and educated and converted Paul Kruger.

I live on the farm settled by Alexander Erwin, who was the father of James, the father of Joseph, who was my father. The old brick house was built by James Erwin.

I will take pleasure in helping you to get up a list of names of the different branches of the family, which inhabit this section. Please let me know when you want them and I will get them up.

I can give you our genealogy whenever you want it, and if you are not in a great hurry for the names I will make them out at leisure and send them to you.

Mr. John Hugh McDowell, of Union City, Tenn., is getting up a family tree of our family, and could give you considerable information, as could Gen. John B. Erwin, of Wisconsin Ave., Washington City. Mr. Bulow Erwin of Asheville could help you, too.

JOSEPH ERNEST ERWIN.

JOHN WARDELL ERWIN.

Although no attempt has been made to establish his direct genealogical connection with the clan Irvine, it is believed that the late John Wardell Erwin, for many years closely identified with the history of Hamilton, Butler County, Ohio, and with his adopted state, was a representative of one branch of the family.

The following data has been secured from his grandson, Rev.

1. Joseph Boyd   2 Hal M Boyd.   3. M. W. Boyd.   4. S. R. Boyd.

Frank Erwin Brandt, a clergyman of the Episcopal Church, residing at Dundee, Illinois:

John Wardell Erwin was born in New Castle county, state of Delaware, on September 9, 1808, being the son of John and Elizabeth Platt Erwin, the grandson of Samuel and Naomi Jones Erwin, and the great-grandson of John and Mary Erwin. His parents and grandparents were natives of New Jersey. His mother, Elizabeth Platt Erwin, was the daughter of John Platt 2nd, who was born in New Hanover township, Burlington county, New Jersey, and who, in 1777, received his commission in the Delaware regiment of Foot, on the Continental Establishment (Col. Hall), and served until 1783, when he became one of the original members of the Delaware Society of Cincinnati. He died at his place, "Chatham," in 1823, near Wilmington, Delaware. (See Notes upon the ancestry of John Platt, printed for private distribution by David Pepper of Philadelphia.)

In the summer of 1828, John Wardell Erwin crossed the Allegheny mountains on foot and located at Richmond, Indiana, where, having previously prepared himself for the profession, he received and filled for five years, an appointment as assistant civil engineer on the eastern division of the Cumberland or National road, extending from Indianapolis to the state line east, the work being in charge of Capt. Brewster of the U. S. Engineer Corps. In 1833, at New Paris, Preble county, Ohio, he was married to Ann Eliza Chadwick, daughter of Samuel R. and Jerusha Chadwick of Chatham township, Morris county, New Jersey. Shortly after his marriage he located at Hamilton, Ohio, where he lived until his death, April 17, 1889. His wife was connected with the Hopping, Richards, and Crane families of New Jersey, and was a descendant of Robert Treat, the colonial governor of Connecticut.

In 1835–6 Mr. Erwin located the Hamilton, Rossville, Newcomb and Eaton turnpike, which was the first public work of the kind, built with gravel, west of the mountains. In 1837–8 he located the Dayton and Eaton; the Hamilton and Darrtown; the Venice and Scipio, and the Greenville and New Paris turnpikes, all in Ohio. The hydraulic works at Hamilton, Middletown, Franklin, and Troy, in Ohio; at Goshen, Elkhart, and Bristol in Indiana; and at Constantine, Michigan, were located by him, and he also made the preliminary surveys for the Cincinnati, Hamilton & Dayton, the Eaton & Richmond, and the Richmond & Chicago railroads. In 1847–48, he was a party to the erection of the first paper mill in Hamilton, and he built the first flouring mill, run by water furnished by the Hamilton Hydraulic Company. For a long period of years Mr. Erwin was resident engineer on the Miami and Erie canal, extending from the Ohio river at Cincinnati, to Toledo, a distance of nearly three hundred miles and was identified with many of the public works of Ohio and with private enterprises of the city of Hamilton. Socially, he was a Knight Templar and Odd Fellow. His knowledge of the Indian tribes of North America was most extensive, and he was an authority on the history of the western country and its pioneer traditions, and on geology. Up to the time of the civil war he was an ardent Democrat of the old Jacksonian type, but at the outbreak of the war he became a "war Democrat" and was one of the editors of the "Free Soil Banner," a Hamilton publication, later becoming a Republican in politics. Of his union with Ann Eliza Chadwick, five children resulted, Henry, Charles, Frank, Lutie and Mary — all deceased.

Further particulars of Mr. Erwin's life are given in the "Biographical Cyclopædia and Portrait Gallery of Distinguished Men, with an historical sketch of Ohio," and in Vol. I. of the History of Hamilton by Stephen D. Cone. From the latter work we extract the following: "William Dean Howells in his book 'A Boy's Town,' refers to a visit he made, when but a youth, to the Erwin home. The name of the family is not given, but Mr. Howells has since stated that the residence mentioned was the Erwin homestead. It seems that the youthful Howells came to spend the night with one of Mr. Erwin's sons, but grew homesick during the night and wanted to get back to his father's house. Mr. Erwin arose, lighted a lantern, and, although it was late at night, took the little fellow to the Howells residence. One of the illustrations in 'A Boy's Town,' pictures a man leading a little boy through the darkened streets of the town, carrying a lantern to guide them on their way."

From the same volume we take the following: "No man in Hamilton was more respected than John W. Erwin. He belonged to the 'old regimé' and was a gentleman of the old school. He died as he had lived, an honest, Christian gentleman, with a high sense of honor, and an exalted idea of his duty as a citizen. He was never, in the course of a long and useful life, known to break his word when given to another. His purse was ever open to the cry of the needy and he often relieved the necessities of the poor. He needs no epitaph, as his virtues are engraved on memory's tab-

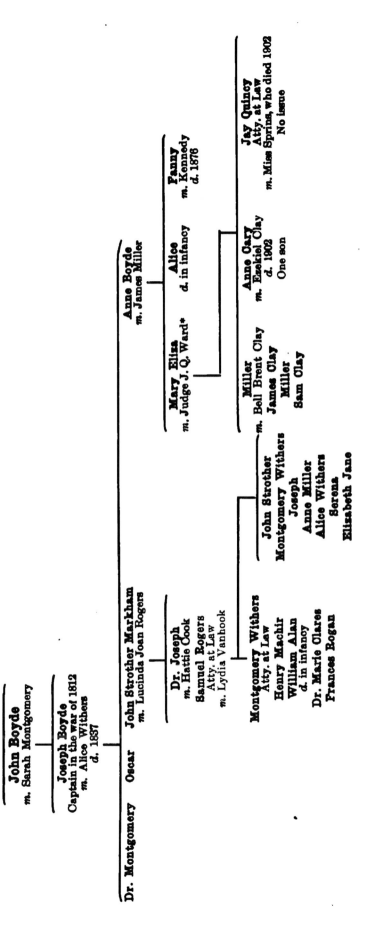

John Boyde
m. Sarah Montgomery

Joseph Boyde
Captain in the war of 1812
m. Alice Withers
d. 1837

Dr. Montgomery   Oscar   John Strother Markham
m. Lucinda Joan Rogers

Anne Boyde
m. James Miller

Dr. Joseph
m. Hattie Cook
Samuel Rogers
Atty. at Law
m. Lydia Vanhook

Montgomery Withers
Atty. at Law
Henry Machir
William Alan
d. in infancy
Dr. Marie Clares
Frances Bogan

John Strother
Montgomery Withers
Joseph
Anne Miller
Alice Withers
Serena
Elizabeth Jane

Mary Eliza
m. Judge J. Q. Ward*

Alice
d. in infancy

Fanny
m. Kennedy
d. 1876

Miller
Bell Brent Clay
James Clay
Miller
Sam Clay
m.

Anne Clay
m. Ezekiel Clay
d. 1902
One son

Jay Quincy
Atty. at Law
m. Miss Spring, who died 1902
No issue

*John Quincy Ward, Judge of Superior Court of Kentucky, died 1899

lets, and the records of his good deeds are transcribed in the Book of Life, which is read and approved by the Almighty God."

Mr. Erwin was not a member of any church. His parents and grandparents were members of the Society of Friends, and he adhered throughout his life to the religious faith of his ancestors.

His grandson, Rev. Frank Erwin Brandt of Dundee, Illinois, is married and has two children, Mary Erwin Brandt and Erwin Chadwick Brandt.

1. John Erwin and Mary, his wife.
2. Samuel Erwin and Naomi (Jones) his wife.
3. John Erwin and Elizabeth (Platt) his wife.
4. John Wardell Erwin and Ann Eliza Chadwick.
5. Mary Erwin, daughter of John W. and Ann Eliza Erwin, and wife of Eugene Brandt.
6. Frank Erwin Brandt, son of Eugene and Mary Erwin Brandt.
7. Mary Erwin Spoerl Brandt and Erwin Chadwick Brandt, children of Frank Erwin Brandt and Anna Margaret (Spoerl) Brandt.

(Copied from the Family Bible of Samuel and Naomi Erwin.)

Sarah Erwin, daughter of Samuel and Naomi Erwin, born the 7th of ye 12th month, 1783.

Mary Erwin, daughter of Samuel and Naomi Erwin, born 18th of ye 8th month, 1786.

Naomi Erwin, daughter of Sam'l and Naomi Erwin, born 16th of ye 3rd month, 1789. Departed this life first of 3rd month, 1872.

Jeremiah Erwin, son of Sam'l and Naomi Erwin, born 1st of ye 8th month, 1792 — died 8th of 5th mo., 1825.

Hannah Erwin, daughter of Sam'l and Naomi Erwin, born 19th day of ye 11th mo., 1794.— died 27th of 4th mo., 1871.

Samuel Erwin — son of Samuel and Naomi Erwin, born 11th of ye 6th mo., 1797 — died 16th of 1st mo., 1798.

Samuel Erwin — son of Sam'l and Naomi Erwin — born 11th of ye 4th mo., 1799 — died 6th mo., 1827.

Elma Penn Erwin — daughter of Samuel and Naomi Erwin — born 12th of 11th mo., 1801 — died 11th mo., 21st day, 1884.

The Erwins of Hamilton, Ohio, as well as family connections bearing the name of Robinson, in Richmond, Indiana, are descended from one of four Erwin brothers, members of the Society of Friends, who came to America with William Penn. Their emigrant ancestor, in spite of his principles of non-resistance, was engaged with the colonies in their battle for freedom, and a punch bowl, which he found among the effects of some Hessian soldiers whom he captured, is still preserved by a member of this family. The Erwins of Hamilton, as well as the Richmond (Ind.) connections, are descended in this same line from a John Erwin (born May 25, 1781, died November 29, 1849), of Wilmington, Delaware, who was a member of the Delaware state senate, and a son of Samuel and Naomi Erwin. The Erwins are very desirous of securing information as to the English (or Scotch(?)) ancestry of the four Erwin brothers, who accompanied William Penn to this country, and any information of this character would be received very thankfully by Rev. Frank Erwin Brandt, of Dundee, Kane County, Illinois.

BOYDS, OR BOYDES, OR BOYTS.

"This is a surname of very considerable antiquity in Scotland, according to our genealogical writers. The first recorded ancestor of the Boyds, Earls of Kilmarnock, was Simon, brother to Walter, the first High Steward of Scotland, and youngest son of Alan, the son of Flathald (the fabulous Fleance of Shakespeare), who, following his brother into Scotland, witnessed his foundation charter of the Monastery of Paisley in 1160, and is therein designated "*frater Walteri filii Alani, clapiferi.*" He is said to have been the father of Robert, called Boyt, or Boyd, from his fair complexion, the Celtic word *boidh*, signifying fair or yellow. He died before the year 1240, and from him are descended the various families of that name in Scotland."

The lands of Kilmarnock, Bondington, and Hertschaw, which belonged to John de Balliol, and other lands in Ayrshire, were granted by Robert the Bruce to his gallant adherent, Sir Robert Boyd, the ancestor of the Earls of Kilmarnock.

The Boyds of Pinkhill and Trochrig were descended from Adam Boyd, third son of Alexander, the second son of Robert, Lord Boyd, the famous Chamberlain of Scotland in the minority of James the Third. Space forbids that full history of the Boyds be written in this, the Irvine Book, but, as one married a descendant of the Irvines of Bonshaw, I shall add the following, copied from Chronicles of Cynthiana, Ky., which was gathered from Boyd descendants, who hold the records, and Green's "Short History of the English People": "Descended from the Earls of Kilmarnock, was John, son of Robert Boyde, who married Sarah Montgomery, daughter of John Montgomery, descended from the same line as Gen. Richard Montgomery, who fell at Quebec. John Boyde was of the clan Boyd, in Scotland, which had the feud with the Hamiltons. Both clans, Hamilton and Boyde, were banished to Ireland."

The Boydes assisted at the siege of Londonderry. One John Boyde, whose wife was Sarah Montgomery, as stated above, came to America from Ireland in time of the Revolution, or a short time before, and took shelter in Bledsoe's Fort, Tennessee, where were gathered for mutual defense and safety nearly all the progenitors of the distinguished people of the Southwest. Among others was Isaac Bledsoe, who married Katherine Montgomery, sister to Sarah, wife of John Boyde, before mentioned.

From Isaac Bledsoe and Katherine Montgomery, his wife, are descended the Deshas of Kentucky, and those further south, to which branch Consuelo Vanderbilt, Duchess of Marlborough, belongs.

ARMS OF LORDS BOYDS AND EARLS OF KILMARNOCK: Az.— a fesse chequy, argent and gules: Crest.— A hand issuing out of a wreath pointing with the thumb and two fingers. Motto: *"Confido."* In more than one instance members of the family had for crest three feathers, sable.

BOYDE ARMS.— Az.— A fesse chequy or and gu. in chief; three mullets of the second in base a crescent or. Crest.— Three ostrich feathers, sable. Motto: *"Confido."*

The only descendants of John Boyde and Sarah Montgomery, his wife, now alive are: the children of the late John Strother Boyd, who for twenty years was Judge of the 12th Judicial District of Kentucky, and the descendants of his only sister Anne, who married James Miller.

Captain Joseph Desha, son of General Lucius Desha, and grandson of Gov. Joseph Desha, brother to Robert Desha, ancestor of Consuelo Vanderbilt, who married the Duke of Marlborough, was a brave Confederate soldier and a Christian gentleman. He died May 15, 1902.

A LAMENT.

An unseen hand beat taps at eventide,
An angel stood beside an open door
And, in an unknown tongue, he called the roll
Of soldiers marching to the Better Land.

Our hero heard; and straightway answered: *Here!*
Shook off the mortal dust that clothed his soul
And joined the comrades he had loved erewhile,
And led to fields whereon they slept and sleep.

His deeds of valour glow on history's page,
To fire the heart of youth in time to come;
But those who loved him tell another tale
Here where he lived and toiled, and sleeps at last.

They tell of widows' tears he wiped away,
And orphans who have been his constant care;
Of words of comfort whispered in the sinner's ear,
And outcasts sheltered when the storms were near.

So let the turf, that wraps his glorious clay,
Keep green by tears of those who loved him well;
His brave, but modest soul, scorned earthly fame,
But found that hidden way and sought the stars.

L. Boyd, Historian, U. C. D.

BONSHAW TOWER.

'Tis sung on harps of high acclaim
That here the Irvings, mighty name,
Erst held, in all the pride of yore,
Their wide domain from fells to shore;
That glory starred their battle crown,
That honor wove their high renown;
For oft across the Solway flood
When ran its tide waves red with blood,
The bold moss-trooper fled afar
Before the rush of feudal war,
And to their wilds and fastness hie,
From Irvings' warriors turned to fly.

W. S. Irving, 1814.

This tower was built A. D. 900 (date doubtful) by the chieftain of what Irvin clan unknown. It came into the possession of the Irvines in about the year A.D. 1285, and has ever since been the seat of the clan; its Baron or Chieftain residing in it, and his clansmen living in clachans, or huts, within sound of the great bell which still hangs in the tower, where it has hung for centuries. This tower, having come down in a direct line of descent, through a thousand years, to Irvine chieftains who have inhabited it, the clan will pardon one who gives a minute description of it.

This tower is square, and rises to a height of about seventy feet from foundation stones to battlements. The walls are eight feet thick, in places, and six in others. It stands on an eminence that rises a hundred feet above the "Kirtle Water." Its only door of entrance is on the east, and is built of oak and barred with imitation iron bars and is fashioned after the ancient iron "yetts" destroyed by order of James VI. This door admits you to the vestibule, which is six by four feet and ten feet from floor to roof. Coming down from the center of this roof, shaped like a great seal, is the "Crusaders' Stone," brought home from the Holy Wars by Edward Irving. On it is carved in Hebrew characters "I. H. S." This stone is said to bring a blessing on every Irvine who stands under it.

Through another door, just such as has been described above, you enter the Retainers' Kitchen. It is a long chamber, with stone floor and stone vaulted roof, and from this frowning stone roof hangs an immense hook, which is securely fixed in the stones and which was used by the Barons Irving, in ye good old days "when might made right," to hang prisoners upon, if they gave promise of being too troublesome. There is an embrasure in each of the four walls, just above the heavy foundation, which is eight inches wide and five high, within, but flaring, fanlike, as it passes through the thick wall, it stretches to four feet on the outside of the tower. Thus constructed, these openings gave every advantage to the defenders of the tower over their enemies without. On the south side of the Retainers' Kitchen is the Dungeon. As the heavy door clanks open, one shudders to behold the black, damp cell, in which, ages ago languished prisoners, many of whom met "Jedwood justice" on the tower hook.

Perhaps some young Borderer was confined there, who had gone into battle for the first time, on a sunny morning, and baptized his unstained sword in the blood of his enemies. Doubtless, around its hilt was twined a tress of long fair hair. Night found him a captive, his sword broken, his high hopes failed of fruition, the tress of hair stained blood-red and blown about on the field of his defeat, and at midnight he heard Charon's boat touch the sands along the boundary of mortal life and soon after he set sail on the river Styx. By his side may have stood a hoary-headed chieftain, "in whose veins coursed the blood of kings." He knew how to die. Defeat gave death its only sting to him. Long since these prisoners slept, and sleep, and their dust nourishes

"The violets of their native land."

From the left of the vestibule, as you enter it from the Retainers' Kitchen, is the first step of the stone wheel Stairway leading to the battlements. Thousands and thousands of feet have worn away the solid stones of this masterpiece of ancient workmanship. Kings have trodden its winding way, and chieftains, long since forgotten, have ascended it to view their possessions, spread far and wide beneath them. There stood Robert the Bruce, to watch for his enemies, and there a warder walked day and night, with slow and measured step, ever pausing to watch the signal mound, outlined against the Southern sky.

Hundreds of years ago the chieftain who stood on the battlements of Bonshaw tower knew that his over-lordship extended from the south side of the Clyde; in the north side of Grangebarge he had the lands of Dule, the chieftains residing in the Castle Garth. These lands lie on the north side of the river Tay, from its rise to where it joins the Timmel, and are called the Strath Tay. He knew what law was in force as he gazed afar:

> "The good old law the simple plan,
>   That they should take who have the will
> And they should keep who can."

Birrenswark is to be seen from the battlements of the tower. It is an oval-shaped, irregular hill, rising to a height of 600 feet; it is 900 feet long and 450 wide. From its summit the view is wide and beautiful. It is bounded on the north by a range of mountains that encloses the valleys of the rivers Esk and Annan, but in every other direction, one may see as far as the eye can reach. Says an ancient chronicle:

"Here the Selgovae Gael had his place of strength in the days of independence and international quarrels, when, as yet, their swords were the only umpires of their disputes, and Roman interference was unknown." But in the beginning of the Christian era Cæsar and the Roman legions stood on this height and surveyed the land, spread out beneath them, which was afterwards to be conquered and made a part of the Roman Empire.

Tacitus says: "These districts were surrounded by castles and forts, disposed with so much attention to judgment that no part of Britain, hitherto unknown to the Roman arms, escaped unmolested, and the Roman camps, in fact, are but a small part of the multiform labors of that people in Britain during nearly four hundred years."

There are three rooms in the Tower, built one above another. The first, above the Retainers' Kitchen and the Dungeon, is called Robert the Bruce's room. In this room he lived, and was protected by an Irving chieftain and his clan, while he was pursued by the emissaries of Edward Longshanks, King of England. This room has three small windows, to admit light, and a narrow loophole to the north. Built in the east wall is a "Wumbray," an altar, at which the Bruce was wont to kneel and pray, he being a Catholic, as all the Irvines were at that time. He knelt before it to receive communion, together with Chieftain Irving and all his clan. Before it the children of many successive chieftains were baptized, and many Irvines, men and maids, were married.

It seems a Holy Shrine still; filled, as it is, with relics brought from foreign lands and considered sacred by those who used them. A string of blue glass beads is there, having a brass crucifix attached, tarnished by time or stained with blood. The present owner of Bonshaw took it from the neck of a soldier, a follower of King Theodore, who lay dead at the gates of Magdala after its fall. A small sacred jar, taken from a Buddhist Temple, in China, stands side by side with a communion cup once belonging to those who believed in the "Real Presence." If these worshippers did not all believe alike, they placed their faith in The Unseen Power, which is all merciful.

The room above, "The Bruce's Room," is where many of the Chieftains were born, and where at last they laid down their honors and their arms at the feet of that Black Sergeant whom none can fight. But whether an Irvine Chief met death on couch or field, he faced it

"Like one that wraps the drapery of his couch
About him, and lies down to pleasant dreams."

The third room, just beneath the battlements, belonged, perhaps, to the Irving maiden whose sad fate I am about to recount.

As long ago as before "Flodden Field" the Maxwells and Irvings were at bitter feud. The Chieftain at Bonshaw Tower, at the time I mention, had an only daughter, who, in times of peace, strolled at evening by the side of Kirtle Water. There, by the light of the full moon one evening, she met young Maxwell. They had never met before, but Maxwell saw that the Irving maiden was fair to look upon, and loved her at first sight and she knew that she had found the lover of her dreams. Love needs not words to make itself understood. A single glance, in passing, may communicate to one's affinity that love pervades his soul. After this, the full moon always found these lovers beside the Kirtle Water, screened, as they thought, from the warder of the Tower.

But Baron Irving learned that his only daughter had promised to wed the son of his enemy, and he called his sons to meet with him in council. They decided that, if the maiden refused to give up young Maxwell, she should die.

One summer evening Chieftain Irving and his sons took the only daughter of the house to the battlements of the Tower. The soft, gray twilight of this northern climate fell on the beautiful scene, spread beneath their gaze, like a benediction. The murmur of the memory-haunted "Kirtle Water" fell on the maiden's ear, sweet as a love song. By the contending lights of sunset and moonrise she looked about her. Across the Kirtle was the spreading hawthorn, beneath which she and her lover were wont to sit, and as she looked, a band of daring moss-troopers passed swiftly along the Borderers' road. When the tallest among them came opposite the thorn he waved a white pennon for an instant and stopped his horse. The maiden took a long white scarf and let its folds float over the battlements, and whispered: "O! my love, my love, farewell forever!" A certain prescience told her that she must die that night. She folded the scarf across her heart and faced her judges — fair as Eve, just fashioned of God. She was timid as a fawn before the hunter in all save love, but fired by that master passion of the human soul, she defied even death. She was hurled from the battlements and died on the cruel stones below. And here, on the time-stained battlements of this ancient Tower, she is said to "walk" whenever the summer moon salutes the sinking sun.

Who shall say that she does not "walk"? Who shall prove it?

All men are not born with equal strength of body and mind. May not a few men be born with attributes of mind so fine and far-reaching that those who have them not cannot even believe that they exist. We know that a very few have been possessed of a spiritual vision which has enabled them to annihilate space and to reach across and touch all coming time. Their souls did not seem to depend on the five senses, that imprisoned them, for all the cognitions that come to them. Their vision seemed to pierce the veil of shadows that hides another life, and to look face to face on immortal souls.

Has any man ever stood face to face with the Immortals? I know not; but this I believe: memory and imagination are the house not made with hands, in which the soul dwells while on earth.

The pictures on its walls are painted in fadeless and faultless colors, and are seen by a light

"That never shone on land or sea."

This house not made with hands is but the vestibule to the house of many mansions which we shall inhabit when we have passed the portals of the Great Unseen and Unknown.

"Alas the lovers, pair by pair,
    The wind has blown them all away;
The young and yare, the fond and fair
    Where are the snows of yesterday!"

BONSHAW.

The Bonshaw Towers are stout and strong
    Their high walls frown o'er wood and wave,
The tempest whirls their leaves along,
    Or 'round their heavy turrets rave;
Of Irvine's race, the stay, the pride,
    Their boast in war, their prop of glory,
Gone like the foam upon the tide,
    Their being but in story;
But every rock and tower and tree
Bear witness of their ancestry.
                        W. S. IRVING, 1814.
                (In Fair Helen, A Tale of the Border).

MAJOR-GENERAL JAMES IRVINE

Major-General James Irvine was born in Philadelphia, Penn., August 4, 1735. He was a son of George Irvine, a native of the North of Ireland, who emigrated to America and settled in Philadelphia. In time of the war joined Capt. Atleir's company in 1760. He was first made Ensign, then Captain, and saw actual service against the Indians under Col. Bouguet, 1764, in the Northwest Territory. He was made delegate to the Provincial conference at Philadelphia, January 23, 1775, and Captain in the First Penn. Batt.; promoted Lieut.-Colonel November 25, 1775, and in 1776 he was made Colonel of the 9th Regiment of the Pennsylvania Line. He served in the Canada Campaign and was transferred to the 2d Regiment. He resigned June 1, 1777, when a question of rank arose. He was made Brigadier-General of Militia August 26, 1777, commanding the 2d Brigade; which occupied extreme right of the American line at the Battle of Germantown, and was wounded and made prisoner at the battle of Chestnut Hill, December 5, 1777. He was exchanged June 1, 1781; was appointed Commander of Fort Pitt by Congress, October 11, 1781. He was commissioned Major-General, May 27, 1782. He commanded the Pennsylvania Militia in 1782 and 1793. He was a member of the Supreme Executive Council 1782–1785; was Vice President of the State, 1784–1785; a member of the General Assembly 1785–1786; State Senator 1795–1799, and was an original trustee of Dickinson College. He died in Pennsylvania, April 28, 1819.

BRIGADIER–GENERAL WM. IRVINE.

Brigadier-General Wm. Irvine was descended from the Irvines of Rockfield, Fermanagh, Ireland. His present representatives in Ireland (in 1830) are: Gen. Irvine, surgeon, and Wm. Irvine, merchant. His grandfather was an officer in the corps of Grenadiers who fought so desperately at the battle of the Boyne, July 1, 1690. The grandfather of Gen. Wayne was at the same battle under the same command. The descendants of both were together in the Revolution.

Brigadier-General Wm. Irvine was born in Ireland, November 3, 1741; graduated from Trinity College, Dublin; studied medicine and surgery; was appointed surgeon on board ships of war and served during part of the war (1756–63) between Great Britain and France. He emigrated to America in 1764 and settled in Carlisle, Penn. The present village of Irvine in that State is named for him. He married Anne Callender, daughter of Robert Callender of Middlesex near Carlisle, Penn. In the Revolution he took part with the Colonies. He was a member of the Provincial Convention July 15, 1774, and remained a member until he was appointed, by Congress, January 10, 1776, Col. of the 6th Battalion, afterwards named the 7th Regiment of the Pennsylvania Line. He was ordered to join the Army in Canada. He was taken prisoner at the battle of the Three Rivers in June, 1776; released in parole August 3rd of that year, but was not exchanged until April, 1778. In July, 1778, he was a member of the Court Martial that tried Gen. Charles Lee.

May 12, 1779, he was promoted to the rank of Brigadier-General, and assigned to command of the 2d Brigade of the Pennsylvania Line. In the successful attack of Gen. Wayne at Bull's Ferry, July 21–22, 1780, he commanded his Brigade. In the Autumn of

1781 he was ordered to Fort Pitt to take command of the troops on the Western frontier, where he remained until October, 1783.

In 1785 he was appointed agent for the State of Pennsylvania, under an "Act for the Distribution of Lands donated, or promised the soldiers of the Commonwealth." He was member of Congress in 1787. He, Gilman and Kain were selected as commissioners to settle the accounts between the United States and the several States. From 1793 to 1795, he was a member of Congress. In 1794 he was assigned to the command of the Pennsylvania troops to quell the whiskey insurrection. In 1801, he was appointed Superintendent of the Military Stores in Philadelphia, and was President of the Society of Cincinnati at his death, which took place July 30, 1804.

A brother of Gen. William was Captain Andrew, who served in the war of the Revolution from its beginning to its close. Another brother, Mathew Irvine, was a surgeon in Gen. Lee's Division of Light Dragoons from 1775 to the close of the Revolution.

Of Gen. Irvine's sons, Callender was Captain of Artillery and Engineer, 1798–1807. He succeeded his father, August 8, 1812, as Superintendent of Military Stores at Philadelphia. He died August 9, 1841.

Another son, William Neil, was born 1778 in Carlisle, Penn.; died September 25, 1854, at Harrisburg, Penn. He was member of the U. S. Army from 1803 to 1815, and retired with the rank of Colonel. He married Juliana Galbraith, and had a son, Andrew, a physician of Warren Co., Penn.

A third son of Gen. William Irvine, Armstrong, who was graduated at U. S. Military Academy in 1812, served through the war of 1812; was Captain in the 4th Rifles, 1813, and served in his brother, W. N. Irvine's regiment. He was aide to Gen. Ripley in 1816; died at Fort Warren, Mass., January 15, 1817.

Charles Irvine of Maryland, was Ensign of the 4th Maryland, December 10, 1776; died September, 1777.

John Irwin, of North Carolina, was appointed Ensign of the 1st North Carolina, March 28, 1777; 2d Lieutenant, April 4, 1777; resigned August 28, 1777. He was Colonel of the North Carolina Militia 1780–1781.

John Irwin, of Pennsylvania was Ensign of the 1st Continental Infantry January 1, 1776; 2d Lieutenant, August, 1776; Captain, May 16, 1779. He retired January, 1781, and died May 11, 1808.

Henry Irwin, of North Carolina, was Lieutenant-Colonel of the

5th North Carolina, May 7, 1776. He was killed at the battle of Germantown, October 4, 1777.

Capt. Mathew Irwin, of Philadelphia, Penn., was Capt. of Malcolm's additional Continental Regiment, May 12, 1777, and resigned January 20, 1778. He was Lieutenant of the 2d Cavalry, "Pulaski Legion," May, 1779, and served until the close of the war. He died March 10, 1800.

William Irvine, of Virginia, was 2d Lieutenant, June 15, 1812; 1st Lieutenant 7th Infantry, May 17, 1813; resigned September 25, 1816.

Gerard Irvine, of Pennsylvania, was 1st Lieutenant of the 9th Pennsylvania, December 18, 1776. (Omitted from the records January, 1777.)

FAMILY OF JOSEPH ERWIN.

JOSEPH ERWIN, born at Rowan County, N. C., about 1760; died in Mississippi 1846; married in Rowan County, N. C., in 1782, to Catharine Cowan. The children of above were: Thomas B., Joseph, James P., John J., Eli, Cowan, William, Frank, Abel Alexander, M. L., Nancy, Mary, Catharine, and Margaret.

ABEL ALEXANDER ERWIN, son of Joseph Irwin, was born in Rowan County, N. C., October 5, 1815; died at West Point, Ga., December 5, 1898; married at La Grange, Ga., September 12, 1850, to Eliza Frances Ashford, who was born in Fairfield District, S. C., August 3, 1827. He died at West Point, Ga., August 7, 1897. The children of above were:

1. Georgia Belle Erwin, born at LaGrange, Ga., September 14, 1853.
2. Chas. Henry Erwin, born at West Point, Ga., March 1, 1855; died November 29, 1881.
3. Thomas Cowan Erwin, born at West Point, Ga., April 29, 1858.
4. Harriet Ashford Erwin, born at West Point, Ga., August 5, 1861.
5. Sarah Lee Erwin, born at West Point, Ga., September 14, 1863.
6. Mary Elizabeth Erwin, born at La Grange, Ga., December 7, 1866.
7. Abel Alexander Erwin, Jr., born at West Point, Ga., in 1870, and died November 6, 1876.

Georgia Belle Erwin was married to E. J. Collins, at West Point, Ga., January 21, 1872. Their children were:

(1). Erwin Collins, born at West Point, Ga., January 17, 1873; died February 23, 1902.

(2). Charlie Belle Collins, born at West Point, Ga., June 10, 1881.

Thomas Cowan Erwin was married to Elsie Schuyler Campbell at Millburn, N. J., October 12, 1898, and had issue:

(1). Catherine Campbell Erwin, born at Marietta, Ga., November 6, 1899.

(2). Thomas Cowan Erwin, Jr., born at Marietta, Ga., September 9, 1901.

Harriet Ashford Erwin was married to William J. Campbell of Atlanta, Ga., December 6, 1882. Their children were:

(1). Willie Belle Campbell, born at West Point, Ga., February 12, 1884.

(2). Charles Erwin Campbell, born at Atlanta, Ga., January 12, 1889; died September 3, 1899.

Sarah Lee Erwin was married to Phillip Trammell Shutze at Altanta, Ga., October 16, 1884. Their children were:

(1). Mary Frances Shutze, born at West Point, Ga., June 29, 1887.

(2). Harriet Erwin Shutze, born at West Point, Ga., April 12, 1889; died February 29, 1890.

(3). Philip Trammell Shutze, Jr., born at Columbus, Ga., August 18, 1890.

(4). Thomas Erwin Shutze, born at Columbus, Ga., June 8, 1896.

Mary Elizabeth Erwin was married to Hubert N. Merck at West Point, Ga., October 27, 1887, and had issue:

(1). Herbert Nathaniel Merck, Jr., born at Gainesville, Ga., July 30, 1888.

(2). Abel Erwin Merck was born at Gainesville, Ga., August 28, 1891.

(3). William Campbell Merck was born at Gainsville, Ga., July 30, 1895.

(4). Philip Schutze Merck was born at Gainesville, Ga., August 23, 1901.

SOUTH CAROLINA IRVINES.

The legatees and witnesses to the wills of James Erwin, February 27, 1770; Christopher Erwin, January 22, 1791; Joseph Erwin, June 20, 1793; Agnes Erwin, August 3, 1803; William Erwin, September 22, 1815, all of Rowan County, N. C., as compiled from the records in Salisbury, N. C., by J. F. McCubbins, C. S. C., February 7, 1903, are given following:

Under the will of James Erwin (February 27, 1770) the legatees were: his wife, Agnes; sons, Alexander, William, James, Joseph and Isaac; and daughters, Agnes, Mary, Isabella, Jane, and Elizabeth. The witnesses to the will were: Alexander McCorkle, Richard King, and Agnes McCorkle.

Under the will of Christopher Irwin (January 22, 1791), the legatees were: his wife, Mary; and children, Jane Grahams, John Irwin, Margaret McEwen, Wm. Erwin, Sarah Brown, Andrew Erwin, Christopher, Mary, George, Thomas, and Robert Irwin. The witnesses were: Robt. Love, Stephen Kerr, and John Corrigan.

Under the will of Joseph Ervin, June 20, 1793, the legatees were: his wife, Agnes; daughters, Mary, Gracie, Agnes, and Peggy; and sons, William and Joseph. The witnesses were, Hugh Dobbins, and Patrick Barr.

Under the will of Agnes Ervin (August 3, 1803), the legatees were: his son, Joseph, and daughters, Isabel Johnson, Nancy Dobins, Mary Ervin, Nancy Walker, Gracey Dobbins, and Margaret. The witness was George Glatfelder.

Under the will of Wm. Erwin, September 22, 1815, the legatees were: his wife, Elizabeth; sons, Joseph and John; and daughters, Jane, Agnes, Sally, and Elizabeth. The witnesses were, Alexander Dobbins and John Barr; and the executors: Wm. Dancey, Wm. Kirkpatrick, and Samuel McNeely.

THE FAMILY OF NATHANIEL ERWIN.

The following is a copy of the last will and testament of Nathaniel Erwin, who was the father of Alexander, who was the father of James, who was the father of Joseph J. Erwin, which is in the records of the Superior Court of York County, S. C. (One son, Arthur, is not mentioned in this instrument.)

His name is spelled "Irwin" in this, but his sons spelled it "Erwin."

"In the name of God, Amen. December the thirteenth, Anno Dom. 1793, I, Nathaniel Irwin, of the County of York, and State of South Carolina, being weak of body but sensible and of perfect mind and memory, thanks to God, calling to mind Mortality, I recommend my soul to God and my body to the earth; as touching my worldly estate, I give, devise and bequeath in the following manner, that is to say:

I give and bequeath to my beloved son by law and daughter, Abram and Mary Roach, Thirty Pounds sterling money, three cows, four sheep, to be levy'd out of my estate.

Likewise, I give and bequeath to my beloved daughter, Abigail Irwin, one hundred pounds, North Currency, to be levy'd out of my personal estate.

I give and bequeath to my beloved son, Alexander Irwin, one-fourth part of my real estate; that is, 'my lands, messuages and tenements, according to quantity and quality of same.

I give and devise to my beloved son, William Irwin, one-fourth part of my real estate, that is, my messuages and tenements.

I likewise give and devise to my beloved son, Nathaniel Irwin, one-fourth part of my real estate, my lands, messuages and tenements, according to quanity and quality.

I likewise give and devise to my beloved son, James Irwin, one fourth part of my real estate, to be divided according to quantity and quality.

I give and bequeath to my beloved daughter, Susana Irwin, fifty pounds, to be levy'd out of my personal estate.

I give and bequeath to my beloved daughter, Sofia Irwin, fifty pounds, to be levy'd out of my personal estate.

My beloved wife, Leah Irwin, to enjoy the manshion house during her life, or widow-hood.

Likewise constitute and appoint my beloved wife, Leah Irwin, and my brother-in-law, Jacob Julian, my sole executrix and executor of this my last will and testament and no ——— to be made the rest of my estate, not mentioned, to be ordered according to their will as they shall think best with their schooling and clothing the children, and revoke all other wills and wills, legacies and bequeathes, and acknowledge this as my last will and testament, the day and year above, Witness my hand and Seal.

NATHANIEL IRWIN. (SEAL)

Sealed, signed, published and pronounced, by I, Nathaniel Irwin, as his last Will and Testament, in the presence of us.

William Kerr   John F. Garrison

William Elliott   Mark Garrison

GENEALOGY OF BENJAMIN IRVING OF WASHINGTON, D.C.

——— Irving or Irwin married ——— Wigham.

Robert, son of above, married Elizabeth Foster.

Robert, son of preceding, married Isabella Johnston.

Benjamin, son of preceding, married Jane Penny.

Benjamin, son of Benjamin, married Lois A. Stout, and had issue: Benjamin Barton, 1891; Iona Margarèt, 1893; Robert Lewis, 1900; Jane Catherine, 1905.

Benjamin Irving, son of Benjamin Barton Irving, was born near Edinburgh, in 1860; educated at Muckhart parish school, Perthshire; pupil-teacher at Sauchie public school, Clackmannan-shire, 1874-1876; assistant teacher deaf-mute department, Donald-son's Hospital, Edinburgh, 1876-1881; in civil service of Queen Victoria as Island Revenue Officer, 1881-1888; clerk, Humboldt warehouses, San Francisco, 1888; teacher at Oregon school for deaf-mutes, 1888-1899; in civil service of United States as clerk, General Land Office since 1900; degree of bachelor of laws, George Washington University, 1904; admitted to bar of District of Columbia, 1904; father's family held lands on the Cumberland side of the Border; quaker stock.

NATHANIEL ERWIN.

Nathaniel Erwin came to Bucks County, Pennsylvania, from Ireland about the year 1730. His sons were: Alexander, Arthur, William, Nathaniel and James Erwin; and daughters, Mary, Susana, Abigail and Sophia Erwin. It seems that Nathaniel Erwin, having left two sons Alexander and Arthur, located in Burke County, North Carolina, went to York County, South Carolina, and settled; from that place his will was written and dated December 13, A. D. 1793. His name was written "Irwin," but on the records it is spelled with "*Erwin;*" as the descendants in North Carolina have always written it. Nathaniel speaks of his wife Leah, and his brother-in-law, Jacob Julian, so it is to be supposed she was born Leah Julian. Their son, Alexander Erwin, was a man of integrity and energy, and accumulated a fine property in Burke County, North Carolina. He was quite hostile to Tories, and had proclamations made from the Court House that all Tories should leave town before 6 P. M., and those who failed to obey his mandate he drove out by force.

Alexander Erwin was first C. S. Clerk of Burke, which office he filled honorably for many years. He was a brave soldier during the Revolution, and bore the title of Colonel. Tradition tells us that it was largely by his wit and bravery that our forces won the battle of King's Mountain. Alexander Erwin first married Sarah Robinson, daughter of James and Catherine Robinson, and was (I think) sister of Martha Robinson Bratton, a brave heroine in South Carolina during the Revolution. Hannah Erwin, daughter of Alexander and Sarah Erwin, married Zebulon Baird, was the grandmother of North Carolina's beloved and brilliant sons Zebulon B. and Robert Vance; also grandmother to Miss Baird, who became Mrs. Bob Taylor of Tennessee, a most gifted and charming woman. Another daughter, Mary, married the distinguished Rev. John Mac-Kannie Wilson, of the Presbyterian Church. Their son, Alexander E. Wilson, was a missionary to Africa and had the honor of having converted "Oom" Paul Kruger. Margaret, a woman of strong mind and great energy, married Hugh Tate, and was mother of Drs. Wm. C. and Samuel Tate of Morganton, noted physicians and men of high character and social position. Through Alexander's second marriage to Margaret Crawford came the Bren and Fox families of Charlotte, Cynthia Erwin having married Dr. Stephen Fox. Alexander's daughter Harriet married Lewis Dinkens of Mecklenburg, North Carolina, and from them is descended Bishop Chas. B. Galloway, the gifted orator and the bright light of the Methodist Church. Alexander Erwin had only one son, who married and left children, his oldest son by his first marriage, James, a man of mark and influence in his day; of bright mind, untiring energy, and great business tact. He married Margaret Phifer, daughter of Colonel Martin Phifer and wife Elizabeth Locke, daughter of Colonel Matthew Locke of Rowan and wife, who was a daughter of Richard Brandon. James Erwin had six children who married. William C. married Miss Walton and left several daughters. Joseph J. married Miss Elvira Holt, a woman of fine intellect and great strength of character, who survived him many years. They left ten children, four sons who honorably bear the name in the financial, religious, and social world of North Carolina. These are the only males who bear the name in Alexander Erwin's family. Arthur Erwin (son of Nathaniel) was a brave soldier of the Revolution. He married a Miss Brandon. Their son, William W., was a most excellent man and married Matilda Sharpe, daughter of the soldier of that name, of the Revolution. They had a large family, but there are but few descendants left.—Justice A. C. Avery and Capt. Geo. Phifer Erwin and Miss M. Matilda Erwin, the only living grandchildren. Nathaniel Erwin's son William was also a Colonel of the Revolution. He lived in York county, South Carolina, and married Sarah Ross, sister of Major Frank Ross, of Revolutionary fame. Their son, Arthur, married the daughter of Thomas Spratt. William married Elizabeth Bratton. Dorcas married Alexander Moore. Dr. Maurice Moore was an excellent man and wrote the history of York County, South Carolina. Susie married John Graham, brother of Gen. Joseph Graham of the Revolution, who, after a few months, was killed by the Indians. Nathaniel Erwin's son, Nathaniel, I feel sure was the Rev. Nathaniel Irwin of Neshaminy Presbyterian Church, Doylestown, Pennsylvania, a man of much piety, force, and influence. Jas. Erwin, the other son of Nathaniel, was the father of the late Major Robert Erwin, of Savannah, Georgia. Nathaniel's daughter Mary married Abram Roach of York, South Carolina. The Brandons mentioned were descended from Sir William Brandon, Prime Minister of Henry VIII., of England.

SOME SCOTTISH TRADITIONS.

Extracts from Macfarlane's Genealogies of Scottish Families.

"Lauchlan Lubanich (MacLean) had by Mac Donald's daughter a son called Eachin ruoidh na Cath or Hector Rufus bellicosus. He commanded as Lieutenant General under the Earl of Ross at the battle of Harlaw in the year 1411, where he and Irvin of Drum, seeking out one another by the Armorial Bearings on their Shields, met and killed each other. His body was carried from the Field of Battle by the Clan Innes and Clan vic vilvory of Morvern and buried at I Collumkill. . . . After the Battle of Harlaw, there was a mutual Agreement 'twixt the Lairds of Drum and Maclean to exchange swords, which was kept up for a long Time by both Familys to cancell all Enmity for the future that might happen on Account of the above narrated Slaughter. Such another Agreement there was 'twixt the Families of Grant and Maclean."

"28 Mar. 1639. Patent. King Charles 1st to James Lord Kintyre, brother to the Earl of Argyle, Creating him Earl of Irvine, Sibi Suisque heredibus Masculis. (p. 386.)

" Patent. King Charles 2d to Sir Arthur Ingram, Creating him Viscount of Irvine, and the heirs male of his body. (p. 391.)

"Earl of Ross from Kilravock's Book says 'Archibald, Earl of Argyle, Collonell in Flanders for the King of Spain under Spinola and his Son, the Earl of Irvine, Collonell in France under King Lewis the 13th.'" (p. 115.)

(Daughters of Irvine of Drum, of several generations, intermarried with the Leslie family of Earl of Leven.)

Macfarlane also mentions the following:

Daughters of Patrick Forbes of Corss "one married to Kinstairs, the 2d to Irving of Beltic." (p. 258.)

"Alexander Forbes of Achredie Married Irvine of Brachlaw, his Daughter — Who bear to him 2 Daughters, One Lady Drum, the other Unmarried." (p. 234.)

"Alexander Forbes being cheated out of his estate by his Uncle Thomas married Irvine of Savok his daughter; he bought Blakhouse in the parish of Bourtie." (p. 241.)

"The Laurus Leslie. Janet 2d Daughter married 3d Robert Irwine of Tyllilyrie, brother to the Laird of Drum."

(The Irvines who were rewarded with the lands of Drum, naturally enough intermarried with northern Scottish families, acquired local color and traditions, and except the name, seem to have had nothing in common with the red-handed roughriders of Eskdale and Liddesdale. — B. I.)

Extract from "The Historical Families of Dumfriesshire and the Border Wars" by C. L. Johnstone, (Miss), whose address is Clarendon Place, Leamington, England:

"The Irvines of Robgill and Bonshaw at this time (1552) occupied the Scottish territory nearest to the mouth of the Esk. William Johnstone of Gretna and Newbie mortgaged Sarkbrig and Conheath to Richard Irving, and leased Stapleton to Christopher Irving of Bonshaw, whose son married Margaret, a daughter of Johnstone of that Ilk. There were one or two more marriages between the Irvings and Johnstones of Newbie and of Johnstone, so that the Irvings acquired a "kyndlie," i. e., a kinsman's right to live in the barony of Newbie without title-deeds. Their name early appears among the followers of Robert Bruce; and Dick Irving, a notorious freebooter, was captured by the English in 1527. His relatives retaliated by seizing Geoffrey Middleton, a connection of Lord Dacre, the English Warden, on his return from a pilgrimage to St. Ninian's in Galloway; and in spite of the object of his journey which, by the rules and regulations of warfare, ought to have protected him, they kept him in prison till Lord Dacre should ransom him by releasing Dick Irving. Christie Irving of Bonshaw, Cuthbert Irving of Robgill, the Irvings of Pennersach, Wat Irving, and Jeffrey Irving surrendered to the English in 1547 with 290 retainers. They have direct male descendants."

Extracts from Armstrong's History of Liddesdale and the debatable land.

"The Numbre of Most Able horsemen within Annerdale to defend their cuntry, the hedesmen particularly nominate" (Johnstones, Bells, etc., and then)

Irrewings:

Cuthbert Irruwyng and Watt Irrewing	xiij	horsemen
Herbert Irrewing of the Kyrk	iij	horsemen
The Procteur of Luce	ij	horsemen
Dukes Richie	x	horsemen
William Irrewing of Southwode	x	horsemen
Cristei Irrewing, Mathoe's sone	iij	horsemen
Cristie's sone of Bonneschaw	v	horsemen
Hebbe Irrewing of Trailtrowe	iiij	horsemen
Jefferay Irrewing	viij	horsemen
Dawe Irrewing	— Appendix No. LXX.	

"Abstract of Gentlemen and Princepall Headsmen of the West Marches of Scotland taken in assurance by Lord Wharton, who made oath and delivered pledges to serve the King's Majestie with such numbers of persons as followeth:

Christopher Vrwen of Boneshawe	102	Annerdal
Cuthbert Vrwen of Robbgill	34	Annerdal
Richie Vrwen, Dick's Richie	142	Annerdal
Christofer Vrwen of Ponnersauges	40	Annerdal
Wattie Vrwen	20	Annerdal
Jeffrey Vrwen	93	Annerdal
	Appendix No. XXXIX	

"In Lower Eskdale on the borders of the Debatable Land, a place called Stakeheugh, on the Irving burn, was occupied by a branch of the Irvings.[1] The head of this clan resided at Bonshaw, on the Kirtle Water, in Annandale, where the clan was powerful and at one time numbered upwards of 500 men." — (Armstrong.)

[1] "Eirryn, Erwing, Erwyn, Hurven, Irewing, Irrewing, Irruwing, Irwin, Irrwing, Irveyn, Irvin, Irving, Irvinn, Irwan, Irwen, Irwin, Irwing, Irwyn, Irwyne, Irwynn, Urwen, Vrwin, Yrwen, Yrwin, Eurwings, Irrewings, Irrwingis, Irvyerins, Irwaynes, Irwenis, Irwingis, Irwynnis, Urwens, Yrwens, Yrwins. The arms illustrated are described in Stodart's Scottish Arms, Vol. II, p. 378. In 1504 David Irwin was called at the justice court of Dumfries for his lands of Irwen and Hegeland. Books of Adjournal, MS. Justiciary Office, Edinburgh, Vol. 1493-1504, f. 95, p. 2."

(After the battle of Flodden, Lord Dacre overran the West and Middle Marches, spreading dool and wae among the strongholds of the Border mosstroopers. Here is an o'er true tale that even yet may make the red blood pulse quick in the veins of the far flung Irvine clan. — B. I.)

"On Weddinsday Sir Christopher (Dacre) assembled divers of the King's subgjects beyng under my reull, and roade all that night into Scotland and on Thurisday, in the moryning, they begane upon the said Middell Marchies and brynt the Stakehughe (the Manor place of Irewyn) with the hamlets belonging to them, down Irewyn burne, beyng the Chambrelain of Scotland owne lands and undre his reull, continewally birnyng from the brake of days to oone of the clok after noon, and then wan, tooke and brought away CCCCma hede of cattell; CCCma shepe, certain horses and very miche insight, and siew two men, hurte and wounded diverse other persons and horses and then entred Ingland grounde again at vij of the clok that night."

(But our ancestors could wipe out a score with greater ease perhaps than some of their modern descendants, as witness the following from a long per contra account.— B. I.)

"Appendix No. XX: The Injuries committed by the Scotts upon the Inhabitants of the West March of England, 1528.

" Item the xxiij day of Apriell last past, on Sande Armstrong, with the Irwense of Stakhugh, Scottis and other Scottismen, cam by nyght unto blak Edward Story housez, and there brent and toke his goodes, and the same tyme brent vj housez of Hik Graymes.

* * * *

"Item the ixth day of May, about ix of the cloke before none, the Irwenes of Stackhugh, to the nombr of vj, did enter Englond ground, and lyght upon Sir John Aruhureth and Jame Grayme, called Jame Fern, Englyshemen, and chasyd them to the housez of Long Will Graymes of Stuble, and brent the said Lang Will best howse with xxx other howsez standyng next to the same, and toke and had away the said Inglyshemen and ther horsses.

"Item the xvijth day of May last past Sande Armsrtang with the said Irwens cam to Brakanhill, and tok and had away certain goods and cattles, and slewe William Waugh, and Thomas Stavert, Inglyshemen, in foloying the same.

"Item the xxxday of May, tymelie in the mornyng, th Armstrangis with the Irwens of Hoddom, Scottismen, com to the groundis betwixt Eske and Leven, and there brent all the howsez hereafter named (here are enumerated in the Warden's report forty houses and several barns, the names of the English owners being mentioned in detail; and in addition there is the following:) "At Stuble, where lang Wyll Grame dwelt xix howsez which were left unbrent when the Irwins brent the residue. (On the same day the same band apparently) "to the number of lx persons with open day forreye, ran betwixt Eske and Levyn and ther tooke and had away lxxvj hed of cattaill, ij nags and viij sleyn."

Armstrong gives the armorial bearings of all the Border clans, and that of the Irvings as a shield, showing three green holly leaves on a silver ground.

OLD BALLAD

I ha' heard a lilting at the ewes' milking —
A' the lasses lilting before break of day:
But now there's a moaning in ilka green loning
Since the flowers o' the forest are a' wed awa.

At brights in the morning nae blythe lads are scorning,
Our lasses are lonely and dowie and wae:
Nae doffing, nae gabbing, but sighing, and sabbing
Each lass lifts her leglin and hies her awa.

Will ha' nae mair lilting at the ewes' milking,
Our women and bairns now sit dowie and wae;
There's naught heard but moaning in ilka green loning
Since the flowers o' the forest are a' wed awa.

THE LOST WARDER OF BONSHAW TOWER

At night a restless disembodied soul
Around the Tower of Bonshaw used to stroll;
A warder he had been, an Irving strong,
Who walked the battlements to guard from wrong.

For ages he had prayed to Life and Fate
His wandering soul again to incarnate;
But years and years dragged their slow length along,
His grave was lost; he did not live in song.

One night he stood beneath the solemn stars,
And watched till dawnlight spread its rosy bars,
Then prayed: "O! God in Heaven, hear my cry!
Let my soul be embodied or I die!"

Then from some silent, mystic, far-off land
An Angel came and took him by the hand,
And passed with him to Egypt's distant shore,
Where men of might had dwelt in days of yore.

There rose the sphinx, in the pale morning light,
The hand that wrought it wrapped in darkest night.
The pyramids gave token, here and there,
That fame on Earth is fleet as evening air.

The lazy Nile was murmuring on the shore,
That Antony and his love strolled by no more;
While in the mummy-pits lay fast asleep,
A xxxxxx form amidst the shadows deep.

"Take thou this form and wear it for a time
From xxx to xxxxx thou shalt surely climb.
And in far ages reach to man's estate.
Pray thou to God! Pray thou no more to Fate!"
Thus spake the Angel, and then fled away —
Lost in the splendors of the coming day.

Now on the battlements of Bonshaw Tower
Walks a grim Warder — black as midnight hour —
But still the soul looks to the coming years
As restless, as of yore, with hopes and fears.　　— L. B.

BONSHAW BURN.

By Bonshaw Burn the springtime ran
　And touched the sleeping flowers;
The snowdrops woke and led the van
　In field and garden-bowers.

Then violets in blue and white,
　Those flower nuns so fair,
Slow swing their censers while the light
　Fades from the evening air.

The tulips, clad in garments gay,
　Refuse to go to mass;
The nuns then close their eyes and say;
　They are not chaste, alas!

And glad to see their early friends,
　The robins now rejoice,
While clear and sweet as evening ends
　You hear their piping voice.

What wakes, in spring, the sleeping flower
　And makes the robin sing?
Immortal Love! Death hath no power
　O'er it a change to bring.

The ploughman turns the fallow land
　For grain that is to be,
While on yon hill lie fast asleep
　The chiefs I may not see.

The Burn runs on, in careless haste,
  Nor pauses tales to tell
Of Border chieftains who have fought
  And by its waters fell.

But to my home of Dreams they come,
  Where all my heroes dwell,
And gather in the twilight hour
  Their Border tales to tell.

O! land of Dreams, where love abides,
  Eternal in its youth,
Where warriors fight their battles o'er
  Then sit in solemn ruth.

Abide with me till I shall pass
  Beyond the bounds of time;
Then shall my soul be as a thought
  And pass from clime to clime.   — L. B.

THE BORDERER'S ROAD.

This road running by Kirtle Water which passes Bonshaw Tower
is considered holy ground by the Irvines. It runs past Peele Towers
and castles — some of them in ruins now, but once strong and im-
pregnable, and all in their possession, to the Solway on the south,
and ending on the north among the hills of Roxburghshire. It is
sheltered by cliffs or rising grounds to right and left, and passes
through as beautiful a green country as ever the sun shone on.

Along this grass-grown way once walked the Druids, whose
history is obscured by the mists of oblivion. They reared mounds,
built temples, and set tall stone obelisks, which still tower in the
air, and upon these shafts, made of a single stone, they carved inscriptions, recording the honors and glories of their race, in the vain
hope of perpetuating them for all time. But their temples have
long since been razed to the ground; the hieroglyphics on obelisk
and fallen stone cannot be deciphered, and their places of sepulture
are unknown. At a later time the Salgovian chiefs led their followers along this way; and later still the early Briton there marshalled his hosts and led them by the murmuring Kirtle to meet the
invading Romans. Great Cæsar scanned it with his far-seeing eyes,
weighed it in a balance, found it wanting and ordered another road
to be constructed, such as the Romans only knew how to fashion. A
thousand years before Christ the Phœnicians trod its winding way
in traffic with the early inhabitants of Caledonia.

1. Bruce's Castle, Lochmaben. 3. The Moat, Bruce's Castle, Lochmaben.
2. Bruce's Statue, Lochmaben. 4. Castle Loch, Lochmaben.

At a much later time, as late as the 13th century, Robert the Bruce came, in hot haste along this Borderer's road, to take shelter in Bonshaw Tower, the footsteps of the emissaries of Edward Longshanks echoing behind him.

This road passes the Cave in which Bruce was concealed from his pursuers. It is supposed to have been excavated by the Druids and was hollowed out in the smooth, sheer face of the red limestone that rises to the height of a hundred feet above the Kirtle at that point. Its door of entrance is covered today, as it must have been when Bruce took shelter there, by trailing vines, and is high on the rock and could only have been found by the initiated. This cave is about ten or twelve feet high in the middle of the dome-shaped roof, and 12 by 12 feet from wall to wall. A crazy, rotten bridge makes its whereabouts known to-day, and a stout person risks his life who determines to walk across it to enter "Bruce's Cave." Still, in default of ladders, the risk is often made.

Near the Kirkconnel churchyard is the cross of "Fair Helen" Irving. It stands on the spot where she fell by the shot that was meant for her lover. The cross is of stone, and its base is surrounded by flowers. The place, on the bank of the Kirtle Water, where it rises, grey and lichen covered, is solemn and beautiful. She was murdered in Mary, Queen of Scots' time.

> "Here let the fern grass grow,
>   With its green drooping.
> Let the Narcissus blow
>   O'er the wave stooping!
> Let the brook wander by.
>   Mournfully singing!
> Let the wind murmur nigh,
>   Sad echoes bringing."

Near the Kirtle is also to be seen the funeral cross at Marklands, for whom, and by whom, erected, none will ever know.

THE SOLWAY.

This estuary is a projection of the Irish Sea, northeastward between England and Scotland, and has the most remarkable tides of any body of water in the world. When they begin to sweep up the sandy plain they have ebbed from, they rush at the startling speed of ten miles an hour, and are preceded by a mist, and a roar that may be heard twenty miles away. A long cloud of spray is seen as if whirling on an axis, zoned with mimic rainbows, sweeping onward with the force of a strong or steady breeze, and with the speed of the fleetest cavalry. Then follows a long, curved, white flowing surf, and then appears the majestic run of the tide, a deeply dimpled body of waters, from 3 to 6 feet high abreast, rolling impetuously forward, and bringing closely in its rear a tumbling mass of sea, glittering and gorgeous all over with the most fitful play of prismatic colors.

I have been told that the Irvines have loved the Solway from generation to generation. They knew its fearful tides and its equally terrible quicksands. Not so, the invaders from England, who were ignorant that: "He that dreams on the bed of the Solway, may wake in the next world." But the despairing cries of those who have perished there have been carried out to sea, and lost, hundreds of years ago, and the Solway, like the past eternity, keeps its own secrets.

On the Scottish shores of the Solway, just above Annan on one may see Criffel, on the right, and Skiddaw on the left, and will surely think of the local rhyme:

"If Criffel's got on its cap
And Skiddaw on its hood,
All the little hills about
May expect but little good.

Another is:

"If Skiddaw wears a cap
Criffel wots full well of that."

ANNAN.

Annan is the capital of Annandale, and was founded before the time of Robert the Bruce. It was frequently plundered, and burned in the hottest periods of Border forays, in 1298, by English invaders. In 1300, Robert Bruce built a castle at Annan, for its defense, in which he occasionally resided.

In 1332 Edward Balliol, soon after being crowned at Scone, summoned the nobility to the castle of Annan to do him homage, and here Archibald Douglas, as the herd of 1,000 horsemen, came upon him by surprise at night, slew his guards and many of his chief adherents, and frightened him, half-naked, on a horse without a saddle or bridle, to take flight to Carlisle. The castle

1. Annan. 2. Annan. 3. Fair Helen's Bower.
4. Victim of tight stays. 5. Kirkconnell Kirkyard.

1. Robert Irvine's House, 1585.   3. Springkell, once Kirkconnell.
2. Thomas Carlisle's House.   4. Old burying place of Irvings of Luce.

has long disappeared, but the little Royal burgh is still a stronghold of the Irvines.

CARLISLE.

Sixteen miles from Bonshaw Tower is Carlisle, which was founded by a British King 1,000 years before Christ. It was once a walled town, and to this day is called the "Border City." The survival of the British names shows that it was a place of importance in early times. Caer-Lywelydd (whether this was a tribal, or local, or a personal name, it would be hazardous to say) still bore its old name, through Roman and English occupation, and Luguvalio, Lugubalia, Caerluel, Carliel, Carlile, Carlisle are the only phonetic variations of the earliest forms. Its castle was built by William Rufus in 1092. He set up the walls of that town and garrisoned them; then Lugubalia became Caerluel.

Among the distinguished Lord Wardens and kings who dwelt in this castle was Richard, Duke of Gloucester, afterwards Richard III. (brother to Edward IV.). How often, when he was Lord Warden of the Marches, did he heart he cry: "A horse! A horse!" before he, himself, cried so earnestly: "A horse! A horse! My kingdom for a horse!"

In this castle of Carlisle, Mary, Queen of Scots, took refuge after the battle of Langside, 1568. She arrived with no clothes except those she wore. She asked Queen Elizabeth to supply her with a few suitable garments, and the royal lady sent her "two torn shifts, two pieces of velvet, and two pairs of shoes." One may still see the lonely walk by the castle walls where the beautiful, but unfortunate queen whiled away the many hours of a captivity that was to end in death. It is called "The Lady's Walk."

The Cathedral was begun by Norman Walter in 1092. Of this cathedral Paley was archdeacon. Its choir is one of the finest in England; it is 138 feet long, and consists of 8 pointed arches. The east window of nine lights is considered the finest decorated window in all England. This cathedral was frequented by the Irvines.

DUMFRIES.

Twenty-two miles from the Tower is Dumfries. Historians are not agreed upon the date of its foundation. McDowall, in his history of Dumfries, says: "It is not unlikely that the Selgovæ, who inhabited Nithsdale and neighboring districts at that time, and who, by means of their rude, but strong forts, long resisted the legions of Agricola, may have raised some military works of a defensive nature on or near the site of Dumfries."

There are many places of interest in this municipal burgh, which space forbids me to notice. But the antiquary looks longest at a church called "Grey Friars," which stands on the site of the monastery founded in 1200, in the chapel of which Robert Bruce stabbed the Red Comyn in 1305. Comyn gave Bruce the lie. Bruce then ran his sword through him, and rushed without and told one Kirkpatrick that he feared he had killed Comyn. "Fear!" said Kirkpatrick "I'll make siccar!" Then, entering the chapel, he made sure of his death.

In this generation the point of interest is Burns' mausoleum. Burns wasn't an Irving (more's the pity), nor a descendant of one, but the clan will forgive one who says that he was, and is, enshrined in the heart of every Scotsman that has lived since his time, and that none ever stands near the holy ground where his body rests, except with uncovered head. His big, warm heart, that moved him to love nature and humanity better than any man that ever lived; his poverty, which he bore without repining; his transcendent genius, the light of which was so soon withdrawn, make one believe that God is Love, and that when he looked on the clay of Robert Burns, He breathed a double portion of Himself into it along with the breath of life, when this poet seer became a living soul.

EMINENT SCOTTISH IRVINGS.

Extracts from the Book of Eminent Scotsmen, compiled and arranged by Joseph Irving:

IRVINE, SIR ALEXANDER, born ——, died 1411; grandson of Sir William the First of Drum; commands the Lowland army at Harlaw, and fell there, fighting hand to hand against Donald of the Isles. The old ballad on the event praises him for "valor, wit and worthiness." His dominions almost touched the field of battle where this great Lowland deliverance was secured against Celtic disorder and oppression.

IRVINE, ALEXANDER, of Drum, — Born ——, died 1687; supports the cause of King Charles; excommunicated, fined and imprisoned 1644; liberated after Kilsyth; receives a peerage, but on receiving a new charter of estates is thanked by Charles II. for his services to the royal cause. Buried in Drum's aisle, St. Nicholas, Aberdeen.

IRVINE, CHRISTOPHER, M. D.— 1620, - 1690.— Son of Christopher of Robgill, Annandale; entered Edinburgh University, but is expelled for resisting the Covenant, 1639; joining in the Irish trouble, he is deprived of his estate, and takes to teaching,— first at Leith, then at Preston; returns to Edinburgh, where he practices as a physician; appointed chirurgeon to the army by Monk, 1650; published "Bellum Grammaticale," same year; writes also a curious work on Animal Magnetism, "Medicina Magnetica, or the Rare and Wonderful Art of Curing by Sympathy," 1656; best known book, "Historiæ Scoticæ Nomenclatura Latino-Vernacula," 1682; historiographer to Charles II.; permitted to practice in Edinburgh free of interference by College of Physicians.

IRVING, ALEXANDER.— Lord Newton, 1760–1832. Senator of the College of Justice, son of George, of Newton. Passed advocate, 1788, and holds for a number of years the office of Treasurer to that body; joint Professor of Civil Law with John Wild, 1800; takes his seat on the bench as Lord Newton, December, 1826.

IRVING, DAVID, LL. D.— 1972–1834.— Biographer and librarian; born in Langholm, Dumfriesshire, and educated at Grammar School there; entered Edinburgh University, 1796; writes lives of various Scottish poets 1799–1801; devotes himself to literature instead of the church, as at first designed; publishes "Lives of Scottish Poets," 1804, and "Life of George Buchanan," 1867; an LL. D., of Marischal College, Aberdeen, 1808; librarian to Faculty of Advocates 1820; edited various remains of ancient national literature for Bannatyne and Maitland clubs; and contributed largely to seventh edition Encyclopœdia Britannica; resigned librarianship 1849. Died in Edinburgh, aged 82.

IRVING, REV. EDWARD.— 1792–1834.— Son of a farmer in the burgh of Annan, where the great preacher was born. Educated there and at Edinburgh University, distinguishing himself in mathematical studies; teacher in Haddington and Kirkcaldy; licensed to preach by Presbytery of Annan, 1819, and removes afterwards to Edinburgh, and then to Glasgow, where he enters on his duties as assistant to Dr. Chalmers in St. John's parish; accepts a call from a small congregation of Scots Presbyterians, meeting in Hatton Garden, London, 1822; rises to great fame as a preacher, his church being always crowded by a fashionable and educated audience; preaches sermon for London Missionary Society, May, 1824, and another on Prophecy for Continental Society, 1825; noticed to be departing from doctrinal standards of

Church of Scotland, concerning Christ's human nature about 1827; new church in Regent Square, London, opened 1829; carried away by his views concerning unfulfilled prophecy, miraculous gifts, and, above all, by "unknown tongues," practiced among a few crazy disciples; the matter was taken up by the Scottish Church in London and sent down to Annan Presbytery, which solemnly deposed him from the office of the ministry, after an animated defense by himself, March 13, 1833. Edward Irving then spoke frequently in the open air in his native district, but his exertions brought on consumption, of which he died in Glasgow, aged only 42. Irvingite or Apostolic Catholic body follow Irving's teachings. Life of Edward Irving was published by Mrs. Oliphant in 1862, and obituary notice by Thomas Carlyle in Fraser's Magazine, No. 61, 1835.

Example of Rev. Edward Irving's style, taken from his Orations on the Oracles of God. In cold type his words read well, but glowing from the eloquent lips of a man of striking personality, vivid imagination and rapt enthusiasm, it is no wonder that such words swayed the minds and hearts of men:

"There was a time when each revelation of the word of God had an introduction into this earth which neither permitted men to doubt whence it came, nor wherefore it was sent. If, at the giving of each several truth, a star was not lighted up in heaven, as at the birth of the Prince of Truth, there was done upon the earth a wonder, to make her children listen to the message of their Maker. The Almighty made bare his arm; and, through mighty acts shown by his holy servants, gave demonstration of his truth and found for it a sure place among the other matters of human knowledge and belief.

But now the miracles of God have ceased, and Nature, secure and unmolested, is no longer called on for testimonies to her Creator's voice. No burning bush draws the footsteps to his presence chamber; no invisible voice holds the ear awake; no hand cometh forth from the obscure to write his purposes in letters of flame. The vision is shut up, and the testimony is sealed, and the word of the Lord is ended, and this solitary volume, with its chapters and verses, is the sum total of all for which the chariot of heaven made so many visits to the earth, and the Son of God, himself, tabernacled and dwelt among us."

IRVING, FRANCIS.— 1565-1633.— Descended from the Annandale house of Bonshaw, a prominent merchant and magistrate of the burgh of Dumfries; three times Provost; and representative in Parliament 1617; son, also, Provost and member of Parliament. Died, aged 68.

IRVING, GEORGE VERE, of Newton, Lanarkshire.— Antiquarian and historian; son of George, of Newton. Vice-president of British Archæological Association; author of the archæological and historical section of "Upper Ward of Lanarkshire," described and delineated in conjunction with Alexander Murray, 3 vols. 8vo., 1864; Captain of Carnwath troop of volunteers.

IRVING, JOSEPH.— 1830.— Historian and annalist. Born in Dumfries and educated at adjoining parish school of Traqueer; wrote "History of Dumbartonshire," and book of "Dumbartonshire," 1879; "Annals of Our Time," 1837–1878; "Dictionary of Scotsmen," 1880; and some contributions to newspaper and periodical literature.

IRVING, LIEUTENANT-GENERAL SIR PAULUS ÆMILIUS.— 1751–1828.— Of the Bonshaw house; commander-in-chief in the West Indies, and received thanks from George III. for the victory achieved at La Vigie, 1795; created a baronet, September, 1809. A son of Sir Paulus succeeded, and also Sir Thomas St. Lawrence, with whom the title became extinct in 1859.

IRVING WITH SIR JOHN FRANKLIN.

LIEUTENANT JOHN IRVING, R. N., was born in Edinburgh in 1815, fourth son of John Irving, a much respected member of the Society of Writers to the Signet, who, in his youth and at Edinburgh High School was the intimate friend of Sir Walter Scott; educated at Edinburgh Academy; entered Royal Naval College at Portsmouth, 1828; appointed third lieutenant, H. M. S. Terror, one of the ships of Sir John Franklin's expedition to the polar region; evidence that he was in command of the crew of his vessel after they had abandoned the ship, and at the time of his death near Point Victory; his grave was discovered by Lieutenant Schwatka, the American explorer, in 1879, and Irving's remains identified by a silver medal which he had gained at the Naval College in 1830. Lieutenant Irving's remains were taken home and buried with full naval and military honors in the Dean Cemetery, Edinburgh. An imposing funeral cortege wended to the burial place, the funeral hymn by the band being relieved at intervals by the melancholy plaint of "The Flowers of the Forest" from the bagpipes. Major-General Irving was one of the pall-bearers, and the service at the grave was conducted by the Rev. John Irvine, a nephew of the honored dead.

IRVING IN THE ACT OF UNION.

Extract from the proceedings of the Parliament of Scotland, 19th March, 1647.

"To delict out of the first exception of the propositions (for Union with the English Parliament) the Lord Hereis, Lord Ogilbie, Earl of Forth, Lord Ythan, and . . . Irwing of Down and Alexander, Leslie and intimate the same to the Parliament of England."

Extract from "The Orygynale Cronykil of Scotland," by Androw of Wynton·

"Of sqwieris that thiddyre wyth hym rad
Sex knychts in his ward were made:
John of Suthirland, his nievew,
A lord apperand of vertew
Heritabill Erle of that countré
Knycht was made at that journé
Alexander of Keth knycht made syne
Wes, and *Alexander of Erewyn*;
Andrew Stewart his bruthire, foure,
And John the Menyeis his banneoure;
The Lord of Nachtane Schir Williame
The Hay, a knycht than of gud fame
Maid, and Schir Gilbert the Hay, kyncht,
Thir sex knychts stout and wycht,
Wyth foure knychts before than maid,
Of his nation than ten he had,
Manfull, hardy, stout and wycht
In al the hale force of that ficht."

Extract from an old poem, "The Battle of Harlaw," reciting the losses of the Lowlanders in their hard-won victory:

"Gude Sir Alexander Irvine,
   The much renownit Laird of Drum,
Nane in his days was bettir sene,
   Quhen they ware semblit all and sum,
   To praise him we sould not be dumm,
For valour, witt, and worthyness,
   To end his days he ther did cum,
Quhois ransom is remeidyless."

PART V.

CLAN CONTEMPORARIES IN SCOTLAND.

List of some modern Scottish Irvines or Irvings, holding or occupying lands in Scotland, being an extract from the County Directory of Scotland, 20th century edition, 1902.

Irvin, David, Bloomfield, Cove, Dumbartonshire.

Irvine, Captain, Abbey Ville, Newburgh, Fife.

Irvine Bros., Kirkasettar, Scalloway, Shetland.

Irvine, David, Gateside, Belhelvie, Aberdeen.

Irvine, David, Soulisquoy House, Kirkwall.

Irvine, George, Quoyloo, Stromness, Orkney.

Irvine, Herbert, Murraythwaite Mains, Ecclefechan, Dumfriesshire.

Irvine, J., Stove, Sanday, Kirkwall.

Irvine, J. W., Starkigarth, Cunningsburgh, Lerwick.

Irvine, James, Breachacha Farm, Coll, Oban.

Irvine, James, Cherry Valley, Whithorn, Wigtownshire.

Irvine, James, Cowden, Drumlithie, Kincardineshire.

Irvine, James, Montgomerie Lodge, Ayr.

Irvine, John, Millsteads, Canonbie, Dumfriesshire.

Irvine, W., Woodland, Udny, Aberdeenshire.

Irvine, William, Ardlarich, Rannoch, Perthshire.

Irvine, William, Boreland, Dunscore, Auldgirth, Dumfriesshire.

Irvine, William, Drum, New Deer, Aberdeenshire.

Irvine, William, Lochspouts, Maybole, Ayrshire.

Irvine, William, Upper Tack, Brucklay, Aberdeenshire.

Irvine, Mrs., Mountpleasant, Kirkmahoe, Dumfriesshire.

Irvine, Mrs. M. A. Forbes, of Drum, Drum Castle, Drumoak, Aberdeenshire.

Irving, Col. B., Bonshaw, Ecclefechan, Dumfriesshire.

Irving, A. Bell, Bankside, Lockerbie, Dumfriesshire.

Irving, Andrew, Seafield, Annan, Dumfriesshire.

Irving, C., Blackearn, Castle Douglas, Stewartry of Kirkcudbright.

Irving, C., Langdyke, Ecclefechan, Dumfriesshire.

Irving, C., Longfords, Annan, Dumfriesshire.

Irving, Charles Forsyth, Muir House, Juniper Green, Midlothian.
Irving, D. B., Knockhill, Ecclefechan, Dumfriesshire.
Irving, David, Nouthill; Ecclefechan, Dumfriesshire.
Irving, Donald, Gareloch Lodge, Roseneath, Dumbartonshire.
Irving, G., Heathfield, Lockerbie, Dumfriesshire.
Irving, G., Townfoot, Mouswald, Ruthwell, Dumfriesshire.
Irving, G., Tulliesfield, Annan, Dumfriesshire.
Irving, Herbert C., of Burnfoot, Ecclefechan, Dumfriesshire.
Irving, J., Aimsfield Mains, Haddington.
Irving, J., Harelawhole, Canonbie, Dumfriesshire.
Irving, J. B., Whitehill, Lockerbie, Dumfriesshire.
Irving, J. Y., Burnswark, Ecclefechan, Dumfriesshire.
Irving, J. Bell, Mount Annan, Annan, Dumfriesshire.
Irving, James, Becton Hall, Ecclefechan, Dumfriesshire.
Irving, James, Broomhouses, Lockerbie, Dumfriesshire.
Irving, James, Glenharvey, New Abbey, Dumfriesshire.
Irving, James, Woodhead, Canonbie, Dumfriesshire.
Irving, John, Cowthat, Ecclefechan, Dumfriesshire.
Irving, John, Drumillan, New Abbey, Dumfriesshire.
Irving, John, Langdyke, Ruthwell, Dumfriesshire.
Irving, John, Pearsby Hall, Lockerbie, Dumfriesshire.
Irving, John, Pennersaughs, Ecclefechan, Dumfriesshire.
Irving, John, Stubbyknowe, Gretna, Carlisle.
Irving, John, Whitehill, Kirtlebridge, Ecclefechan, Dumfriesshire.
Irving, N., Annfield, Woodside, Coupar Angus, Forfarshire.
Irving, R., East Gill, Annan, Dumfriesshire.
Irving, T., Paddockhole, Lockerbie, Dumfriesshire.
Irving, T., Shillinghill, Lochfoot, Dumfries.
Irving, T., Tulliesfield, Annan, Dumfriesshire.
Irving, Thomas, Grange, Lockerbie, Dumfriesshire.
Irving, Thomas C., Altimeg, Ballantræ, Ayrshire.
Irving, Thomas Caven, Birkshaw, Dunscore, Auldgirth, Dumfries-
    shire.
Irving, W., Glencartholm, Langholm, Dumfriesshire.
Irving, W., Jockstown, Kirtlebridge, Ecclefechan, Dumfriesshire.
Irving, W., Whitestonehill, Lockerbie, Dumfriesshire.
Irving, W. O. Bell, Bankside Yett, Lockerbie, Dumfriesshire and
    Millbank Ho., Lockerbie, Dumfriesshire.
Irving, William, Cowburn, Lockerbie, Dumfriesshire.
Irving, William, Stormont Cottage, Gretna, Carlisle.
Irving, Mrs., Gullielands, Annan, Dumfriesshire.

Irving, Mrs., Plumdon, Annan.
Erwin, Major, Dowie Vale, Gasstown, Dumfriesshire.

Extract from the drama "Partium," wherein Sir David Lindsay of the Mount represents Common Theft, a Borderer, brought to the gallows, as taking farewell of his companions thus:

"Adieu, my brother Annan thieves,
That helpit me in my mischieves!
Adieu, Crossars, Niksons and Bells,
Oft have we fared through the fells,
Adieu Robsons, Hanslies and Pyles
That in our craft have mony wiles,
Littles, Trimbulls, and Armstrongs,
Taylors, Eurwings [1] and Elwands,[2]
Speedy of foot and light of hands,
The Scots of Ewesdail and the Græmes
I have no time to tell your names;
With King Correction be ye fangit,
Believe right sure ye will be hangit."

CONTEMPORARIES IN AMERICA.

BALTIMORE, MARYLAND.

Irvin, Arthur B., 1506 North Bethel Street.
Irvin, Bertha H., 2109 West Pratt Street.
Irvin, David, 1524 East Preston Street.
Irvin, Emily V., 747 Linden Avenue.
Irvin, Geo. L., 1702 Park Avenue.
Irvin, Geo. W., 947 Linden Avenue.
Irvin, Harry J., 540 East Clement Street.
Irvin, Herbert V., 1508 North Bethel Street.
Irvin, J. Harry, 220 North Liberty Street.
Irvin, James, 1109 North Monroe Street.
Irvin, James B., 1810 North Charles Street.
Irvin, James H., 707 North Calvert Street.
Irvin, John, 947 Linden Avenue.
Irvin, John H., 1903 West Baltimore Street.
Irvin, John H., 1508 North Bethel Street.
Irvin, John R., 1508 North Bethel Street.
Irvin, Laurence, 1524 East Preston Street.
Irvin, Robert, 1524 East Preston Street.
Irvin, Roger, 1810 West Charles Street.
Irvin, Thomas J., 540 East Clement Street.

[1] Erwins.   [2] Elliotts.

Irvin, William J., 1702 Wilkins Avenue.
Irvin, William P., 400 Forrest Avenue.
Irving, Ambrose M., 712 Linwood Avenue.
Irving, Carroll M., 1723 West North Avenue.
Irving, Edward A., 1742 East North Avenue.
Irving, George W., 1505 East Fayette Street.
Irving, L. G., 1505 East Fayette Street.
Irving, Lewis J., 1018 Wilcox Street.
Irving, Thomas H., 1247 North Broadway.
Irving, William, A., 409 North Ann Street.
Irving, Adam, 235 North Monford Avenue.
Irwin, Charles A., 1649 Milliman Street.
Irwin, Charles B., 727 West Fayette Street.
Irwin, Charles H., 1208 South Charles Street.
Irwin, Edward W., 109 East Lafayette Street.
Irwin, Ellen T., 1430 Park Avenue.
Irwin, Frank, 2103 Clifton Avenue.
Irwin, Harry C., 109 East Lafayette Street.
Irwin, Harry C., 298 Roland Avenue.
Irwin, Harry J., 1095 Lafayette Avenue.
Irwin, J. Stewart, 412 East LanVale Street.
Irwin, James B., 407 North Greene Street.
Irwin, James L., 2543 West North Avenue.
Irwin, John, 323 Warren Avenue.
Irwin, John, 1144 York Road.
Irwin, John A., 412 East LanVale Street.
Irwin, John W., 343 East Twenty-second Street.
Irwin, John W., 1012 Riverside Avenue.
Irwin, Milton C., 17 East Fayette Street.
Irwin, Patrick H., 1801 North Charles Street.
Irwin, Richard E., 2543 West North Avenue.
Irwir, Robert, 407 North Greene Street.
Irwin, Samuel S., 3035 Elliott Street.
Irwin, Thomas J., 1012 Riverside Avenue.
Irwin, William, 1511 West Mt. Royal Avenue.
Irwin, William F., 1012 Riverside Avenue.
Irwin, William R. G., 933 North Stricker Street.

BOSTON, MASSACHUSETTS.

Irvin, Annie S., 43 West Newton Street.
Irvin, George A., 52 Purchase Street.

Irvin, Joseph J., 1530 Dorchester Street.
Irvine, John E., 70 Francis, Roxbury.
Irvine, Percy S., 45 Congress Street.
Irvine, Thomas, 60 Union Street.
Irvine, William, 184 West Eighth Street.
Irvine, William, 184 West Eighth Street.
Irvine, William, 211 Bolton, South Boston.
Irving, Albert S., 2 Ivanhoe Street.
Irving, Arthur P., 150 Boylston Street.
Irving, A. S., 39 Clarendon Street.
Irving, Charles R., 150 Boylston Street.
Irving, Charles S., Blue Hill Avenue, Corner River, Mattapan.
Irving, Charles, M. D., 125 Broad Street.
Irving, Edith, 162 Corey, West Roxbury.
Irving, Edward H., 86 Phillips Street.
Irving, Edward O., 713 East Fourth Street, South Boston.
Irving, Emma J., Emerson School, East Boston.
Irving, George, 17 Gladstone, East Boston.
Irving, George, 43 Utica Street.
Irving, Harry A., 124 Dorchester Street.
Irving, Herbert E., 212 Borden, East Boston.
Irving, John, 383 Washington Street.
Irving, John B., 439 Albany Street.
Irving, Lewis M., 343 Norfolk, Dorchester.
Irving, L. Dudley, 63 Mascot, Dorchester.
Irving, Milton H., 64 Rookville, Mattapan.
Irving, Walter F., 103 Bedford Street.
Irving, William, 64 Rookville, Mattapan.
Irving, William H., 341 Meridian, East Boston.
Irving, William J., 106 Court Street.
Irving, William M., 178 Devonshire Street.
Irving, William N., 30 Tremont Street.
Irving, William T., 43 Utica Street.
Irving, Winthrop F., 53 State Street.
Irwin, Arthur, 6 Street, Margaret, Dorchester.
Irwin, Charles, H., 43 Franklin Street.
Irwin, Charles R., 22 Ellet, Dorchester.
Irwin, Daniel E., 409 Sears Building.
Irwin, George C., 61 Tuttle, Dorchester.
Irwin, George E., 14 Rutland Square.
Irwin, George H., 46 Fairview, Roslindale.

Irwin, Harold M., 137 Pearl Street.
Irwin, James J., 409 Sears Building.
Irwin, Joseph M., 18 Reading, Roxbury.
Irwin, Mary E., Roger Clap School, South Boston.
Irwin, Patrick J., 168 West Ninth Street, South Boston.
Irwin, Richard F., 9 Dore, Roxbury.
Irwin, Richard J., American Express Company.
Irwin, Robert W., 60 Clarkson, Dorchester.
Irwin, Thomas S., 30 Winter Street.
Irwin, William, 40 Harvard, Dorchester.
Irwin, William F., 174 Maverick Street.
Irwin, William G., 53 State Street.
Irwin, William J., 14 Rutland Square.

BROOKLYN, NEW YORK.

Irvin, Charles H., 244 Warren Street.
Irvin, Isaiah, 89 Fifth Avenue.
Irvin, Will A., 757 Sterling Place.
Irvine, Alexander, 2251 Eighty-third Street.
Irvine, Charles W., 207 Division Avenue.
Irvine, Edward, 284 Clinton Street.
Irvine, Fannie A., 183 Pulaski Street.
Irvine, Frank, M., 124 North Elliott Place.
Irvine, George A., 259 Penn.
Irvine, George E., 124 North Elliott Place.
Irvine, George W.
Irvine, Isabella T., 289 Myrtle Avenue.
Irvine, John, 918 Lafayette Avenue.
Irvine, J. Leslie, 745 Union Street.
Irvine, Lawrence, 325 Humbolt.
Irvine, Lewis, 115 Park Place.
Irvine, Percy, 229 Twelfth Street.
Irvine, Robert R., 232 St. Marks Avenue.
Irvine, Samuel, 918 Lafayette Avenue.
Irvine, Samuel, 382 Fifth Street.
Irvine, William, 166 Union Avenue.
Irvine, William, 814 Carroll Street.
Irvine, William, 37 East Third Street.
Irvine, William, 297 Humboldt.
Irving, Charles, 44 Powers.
Irving, George, 97 Gold Street.

Irving, George, 23 Adelphi Street.
Irving, Harry, 8 VanVoorhis.
Irving, Richard, 102 Fleet Street.
Irving, Robert, 222 Nassau Street.
Irving, Robert L., 1246 Fulton Street.
Irving, Samuel, 1996 Bergen Street.
Irving, William H., 1005 Putnam.
Irving, William J., 332 Hart Street.
Irwin, Abraham, 220 Eleventh Street.
Irwin, Arthur, 63 St. Felix Street.
Irwin, Alfred, 34 Harrison Street.
Irwin, Daniel, W., 310 Thirteenth Street.
Irwin, Edward J., 238 Baltic Street.
Irwin, Edward W., 284 Clinton Street.
Irwin, Elfretta L., 314 Prospect Park, West.
Irwin, George, 389 Park Place.
Irwin, George LeR., Fort Hamilton.
Irwin, George W., 318 Jefferson Avenue.
Irwin, George W., 316 Fifteenth Street.
Irwin, George W., 310 Fulton Street.
Irwin, Harry, 797 Carroll Street.
Irwin, Harry, 305 Park Place.
Irwin, James, 9 Ocean Place.
Irwin, James L., 746 Decatur.
Irwin, James W., 111 Washington.
Irwin, John, 35 Cheever Street.
Irwin, John, 72 Waverly Avenue.
Irwin, John, 124 Eckford Street.
Irwin, John E., 88 Kingston Avenue.
Irwin, John H., 152 Bay — Sixteenth.
Irwin, John S., 235 Fifty-second Street.
Irwin, John W., 196 State Street.
Irwin, Joseph, 102 Concord Street.
Irwin, Joseph, Huntington, Long Island.
Irwin, Joseph, 235 Fifty-second Street.
Irwin, Joseph W., 132 York Street.
Irwin, Louis H., 115 Park Place.
Irwin, Luke P., 235 Fifty-second Street.
Irwin, Major, 245 Fifty-third Street.
Irwin, Mina, 350 Bedford Avenue.
Irwin, Robert, 35 Cheever Place.

Irwin, Samuel T., 329 Fifty-first Street.
Irwin, Samuel W., 56 South Tenth Street.
Irwin, Sarah A., 504 Greene Street.
Irwin, Stafford, Fort Hamilton.
Irwin, Thomas, 475 Eleventh Street.
Irwin, Thomas C., 565 Monroe Street.
Irwin, Thomas E., Huntington, Long Island.
Irwin, Thomas J., 318 Jefferson Avenue.
Irwin, Thomas W., 318 Jefferson Avenue.
Irwin, Wesesly, 144 Grove Street.
Irwin, William, 347 South Fourth Street.
Irwin, William, 264 Keap Street.
Irwin, William, 618 Tenth Street.
Irwin, William, 814 Bedford Avenue.
Irwin, William H., 925 Greene Street.

CHICAGO, ILLINOIS.

Irving, Martin, 3147 Wentworth Avenue.
Irving, G., 207 Evergreen Avenue.
Irving, Mrs. Mary, Room 305, 159 La Salle Street.
Irving, Mrs Mary, 3323 Archer Avenue.
Irving, Robert, 6601 South Peoria Street.
Irving, Robert, 241 West Taylor Street.
Irving, Robert, 3150 Archer Avenue.
Irving, S. C., 311 Belden Avenue.
Irving, William, 391 West Taylor Street.
Irving, Mrs. William, 26 Forty-sixth Street.
Irving, W. E., 11 Gurley Street.
Irving, W. J., 3810 West Sixty-fourth Street.
Irving, W. M., 399 West Van Buren Street.
Irving, W. R., 5621 Lafayette Avenue.
Irwin, Miss Ada, 105 Seminary Avenue.
Irwin, Alexander, 5805 Michigan Avenue.
Irwin, A. T., 197 North Morgan Street.
Irwin, Anthony, 5269 Dearborn Street.
Irwin, Arthur, 524 Flournoy Street.
Irwin, Arthur, Jr., 524 Flournoy Street.
Irwin, A. B., 28 Walton Place.
Irwin, A. J., 73 North State Street.
Irwin, Arthur, 4800 St. Lawrence Avenue.
Irwin, Austin, 180 Seventy-ninth Street.

Irwin, B. F., 645 West Sixty-third Street.
Irwin, Miss C. F., 326 Warren Avenue.
Irwin, Col. B. J. D., 575 Division Street.
Irwin, J. C., 334 Clark Street
Irwin, Miss Kate, 334 Clark Street.
Irwin, C. D., Room 130, 145 Van Buren Street.
Irwin, C. E., 348 West Erie Street.
Irwin, C. E., 884 North Maplewood Avenue.
Irwin, Mrs. C., 1120 North Western Avenue.
Irwin, C., 3815, Indiana Avenue.
Irwin, D., 929 Elston Avenue.
Irwin, D. A., 6511 Ellis Avenue.
Irwin, D. I., 5739 Drexel Avenue.
Irwin, William P., Lakota Hotel.
Irwin, William T., 754 Lunt Avenue.
Irwin, Wilmer H., 2 Forty-fourth Place.
Irwin, Joseph W., 225 South Fifty-second Avenue.
Irwin, Miss J., 10513 Torrence Avenue.
Irwin, J. P., 2768 Winchester Avenue.
Irwin, Mrs. K., 3000 Michigan Avenue.
Irwin, L. N., 1st floor Federal Building.
Irwin, Miss Mae V., 225 South Fifty-second Avenue.
Irwin, Miss M., 154 South Desplaines Street.
Irwin, Mrs. M., 655 West Thirteenth Street.
Irwin, Mrs. M., 3024 South Park Avenue.
Irwin, Mrs. M., 76 Ruble Street.
Irwin, Miss M. J., 10513 Torrence Avenue.
Irwin, Miss M. R., 326 Warren Avenue.
Irwin, Maurice, 3405 Auburn Street.
Irwin, Miss May, 434 Thirty-sixth Street.
Irwin, Milo, 11913 Butler Street.
Irwin, Miss M. I., 6025 Lexington Avenue.
Irwin, Mrs. M. S., 273 Park Avenue.
Irwin, N. B., 516 West Adams Street.
Irwin, Miss Nellie J., 6025 Lexington Avenue.
Irwin, Patrick, 655 West Thirteenth Street.
Irwin, Patrick, 12 Cass Street.
Irwin, R. L., 102 Stephenson Avenue.
Irwin, Richard, 232 South Fifty-second Avenue.
Irwin, Robert, 638 West Forty-first Street.
Irwin, Robert, 334 West Fourteenth Place.

Irwin, R. A., 1612 West Sixty-seventh Street.
Irwin, R. A., 1765 Eighty-seventh Place.
Irwin, R. C., 6022 Calumet Avenue.
Irwin, R. H., 334 West Fourteenth Place.
Irwin, R. W., 146 Fifty-fourth Street.
Irwin, Russell, 28 Sixteenth Street.
Irwin, S. W., 8538 South Green Street.
Irwin, Thomas, 125 Erie Street.
Irwin, T. C., 607 West Sixty-first Street.
Irwin, F. J., 5166 Wabash Avenue.
Irwin, Miss Lenona, 1591 Lill Avenue.
Irwin, W. B., 754 Lunt Avenue.
Irwin, W. W., 202 North State Street.
Irwin, W. V., 2nd floor, 178 Market Street.
Irwin, William.
Irwin, William, 196 Seventy-sixth Street.
Irwin, William, 621 West Twenty-first Place.
Irwin, William, 412 Forty-second Street.
Irwin, William, 1474, Eighty-first Place.
Irwin, William C., 3242 Calumet Avenue.
Irwin, William E., 1874 Humboldt Boulevard.
Irwin, William E., 514 West Adams Street.
Irwin, William J., 1409 W. Harrison Street.
Irwin, William L., 1978 Thirty-sixth Street.
Irwin, William N., 3747 South Maplewood Avenue.
Irwin, Edward, 1751 Wrightwood Avenue.
Irwin, E. A., 4214 Calumet Avenue.
Irwin, E. G., 988½ North Leavitt Street.
Irwin, E. M., 283 West Monroe Street.
Irwin, E. H., 3644 Lake Avenue.
Irwin, Miss E. A., 6025 Lexington Avenue.
Irwin, F. C., 601 Armitage Avenue.
Irwin, F. G., 54 West Chicago Avenue.
Irwin, F. J., 516 West Adams Street.
Irwin, Garrett, 1209 Lexington Street.
Irwin, George, 62 Arbor Street Place.
Irwin, G. A., 3823 Archer Avenue.
Irwin, G. A., 5437 Armour Avenue.
Irwin, C. D., 330 and 145 Van Buren Street.
Irwin, G. L., 4316 Langley Avenue.
Irwin, H. M., 326 Warren Avenue.

Irwin, Harry, 49 Sixteenth Street.
Irwin, H. A., 268 South Lincoln Street.
Irwin, H. D., 937 Chase Avenue.
Irwin, H. E., 3157 Forest Avenue.
Irwin, H. J., 6517, Jackson Avenue.
Irwin, H. L., 733 Fiftieth Street.
Irwin, Henry, 147 South Canal Street.
Irwin, Miss I., 6025 Lexington Avenue.
Irwin, J. C., 5819 Michigan Avenue.
Irwin, James, 3756 S. Lincoln Street.
Irwin, J. D., 102 Stephenson Avenue.
Irwin, J. H., 1510 North Troy Street.
Irwin, J. J., 5437 Amour Avenue.
Irwin, Miss Jane, 498 South Wood Street.
Irwin, Miss J. A., 3024 South Park Avenue.
Irwin, Miss J. B., 1120 North Western Avenue.
Irwin, J. W., 510 North Troy Street.
Irwin, John, 6317 Jackson Avenue.
Irwin, John, 157 North Union Street.
Irwin, John, 5808 Michigan Avenue.
Irwin, J. B., 158 Locust Street.
Irwin, J. C., 1064 Fifty-sixth Street.
Irwin, J. J., Room 670, 324 Dearborn Street.
Irwin, J. L., 244 Erie Street.
Irwin, J. R., 130 North State Street.
Irwin, J. T., 607 West Sixty-first Street.
Irwin, J. S., 7330 Stewart Avenue.
Irwin, J. B., 2400 West Forty-ninth Street.
Irwin, J. H., 161 South Halsted Street.
Irwin, Adelbert, 3656 Indiana Avenue.
Irwin, Alfred, Corn Exchange Bank.
Irwin, Arba, 2566 North Ashland Avenue.
Irwin, Bernard, 3727 Armour Avenue.
Irwin, Miss Carrie, 2017 Clark Street.
Irwin, Miss Carrie B., 3029 La Salle Street.
Irwin, Charles J., 2010 West Sixteenth Street.
Irwin, Clarence H., 290 West Jackson Boulevard.
Irwin, Earl E., 6357 Champlain Avenue.
Irwin, Edwin V., 1145 West Garfield Boulevard.
Irwin, Mrs. Emma C., 3255 Prairie Avenue.
Irwin, George, 3257 State Street.

Irwin, G. W., 3029 La Salle Street.

Irwin, Miss Ida, 4456 Lowe Avenue.

Irwin, John, 613 Fulton Street.

Irwin, John, 6552 Justine Street.

Irwin, John P., 5743 Calumet Avenue.

Irwin, Jonas, 3128 Dearborn Street.

Irwin, Joseph M., 2061 Kenmore Avenue.

Irwin, Mrs. Laura, 414 Twenty-seventh Street.

Irwin, Mark C., 2949 Armour Avenue.

Irwin, Miss Mary, 4920 State Street.

Irvin, Miss Mary M., 5342 Cornell Avenue.

Irvin, Maurice, 3405 Auburn Street.

Irvin, Miss Minnie I., 6025 Lexington Avenue.

Irvin, Denil, 1942 Lexington Avenue.

Irvin, Patrick, 3415 Dubost Street.

Irvin, Busse J., 2061 Kenmore Avenue.

Irvin, Patrick, 3730 Lowe Avenue.

Irvin, Samuel, 498 South Wood Street.

Irvin, Thomas, 1612 West Sixty-seventh Street.

Irvin, Thomas, Jr., 1605 West Sixty-seventh Street.

Irvin, Thomas, 210 Thirty-first Street.

Irvin, Washington J., 2566 North Ashland Avenue.

Irvin, William, Room 722, 185 Dearborn Street.

Irvin, William, 499 North Winchester Avenue.

Irvin, William T., 4456 Lowe Avenue.

Irvin, William Ray, 4456 Lowe Avenue.

Irvine, Albert E., 7018 Wallace Street.

Irvine, Miss Alberta, 5937 Calumet Avenue.

Irvine, Alexander S., 7108 Vernon Avenue.

Irvine, Charles E., 4321 Emerald Avenue.

Irvine, Edward E., 587 South Forty-first Avenue.

Irvine, Ephraim D., 5722 Prairie Avenue.

Irvine, Frederick C., 2755 Kenmore Avenue.

Irvine, Frederick H., 5829 Wabash Avenue.

Irvine, George C., 7146 Lexington Avenue.

Irvine, George F., 5937 Calumet Avenue.

Irvine, George J., 6900 Madison Avenue.

Irvine, George D., 164 Clark Street.

Irvine, Gerald, 140 Illinois Street.

Irvine, Hugh, 6420 Monroe Avenue.

Irvine, James A., 6900 Madison Avenue.

Irvine, James W., 4639 Evans Avenue.
Irvine, John, 6900 Madison Avenue.
Irvine, John H., 1326 Seventieth Place.
Irvine, John, 6356 South Marshfield Avenue.
Irvine, John J., 1422 Thirty-fifth Street.
Irvine, Joseph, 71 Van Buren Street.
Irvine, Joseph C., 5829 Wabash Avenue.
Irvine, Mrs. Los Angeles, 1422 Thirty-fifth Street.
Irvine, Mrs. Mary, 1710 Wallace Street.
Irvine, Miss Mary D., 808 Morse Avenue.
Irvine, Mrs. Matilda, 833 West Sixty-seventh Street.
Irvine, Mrs. Rebecca E., 2229 Prairie Avenue.
Irvine, Richard, 71 Van Buren Street.
Irvine, Robert, 162 North Curtis Street.
Irvine, Robert A., 2469 Lexington Avenue.
Irvine, Robert E., 1975 Carroll Avenue.
Irvine, Robert L., 870 Forty-eighth Street.
Irvine, Mrs Sophronia A., 1030 Fulton Street.
Irvine, Thomas A., 1975 Carroll Avenue.
Irvine, Thomas J., 4525 Prairie Avenue.
Irvine, Thomas W., 452 Diversey Boulevard.
Irvine, William., Jr., 361 The Rookery Building.
Irvine, William A., 2755 Kenmore Avenue.
Irvine, William C., 3072 North Ashland Avenue.
Irvine, Wilson H., 639 West Sixty-ninth Street.
Irving, Albert, 6939 Throop Street.
Irving, Alexander, 3323 Archer Avenue.
Irving, B. R., 6521 Union Avenue.
Irving, Mrs. Catherine, 2442 Dearborn Street.
Irving, C. E., 95 South Centre Avenue.
Irving, David, 5409 Indiana Avenue.
Irving, Mrs. Emily, 1251 Michigan Avenue.
Irving, Forrest, 148 Dearborn Avenue.
Irving, Frank, 3033 Indiana Avenue.
Irving, George, 2597 Winchester Avenue.
Irving, George, 6626 South Sangamon Street.
Irving, G. F., 260 Twenty-eighth Street.
Irving, Miss Georgia, 998 West Madison Street.
Irving, James, Rear 221 Johnson Street.
Irving, James, 26 Forty-sixth Street.
Irving, J. D., 282 Flournoy Street.

Irving, Joshua, 7111 Greenwood Avenue.
Irving, Mrs. J. W., 6601 South Peoria Street.
Irving, La Fayette, 812 West Eighty-second Street. ·
Irving, L. J., 3857 Cottage Grove Avenue.
Irving, Miss Maggie, 917 Thirty-eighth Street.
Erwin, Harry, 267 Clark Street.
Erwin, Miss H. U., 7132 Parnell Avenue.
Erwin, H. C., 1635 North Spaulding Avenue.
Erwin, H. O., 394 West Congress Street.
Erwin, James, 74 Twenty-second Place.
Erwin, James, 5349 Indiana Avenue.
Erwin, J. A., 394 West Congress Street.
Erwin, Jeremiah, 6420 Parnell Avenue.
Erwin, John, 3016 Wentworth Avenue.
Erwin, J. D., 5349 Indiana Avenue.
Erwin, J. M. F., Room 1024, 153 La Salle Street.
Erwin, J. E., 7132 Parnell Avenue.
Erwin, Miss K., 971 West Division Street.
Erwin, Miss L. A., 11924 Lowe Avenue.
Erwin, Miss L. M., 11924 Lowe Avenue.
Erwin, L. B., 6008 Jefferson Avenue.
Erwin, Marion, 6016 South Peoria Street.
Erwin, O. R., 394 West Congress Street.
Erwin, Robert, 497 South Wood Street.
Erwin, Thomas, 324 West Jackson Boulevard.
Erwin, Thomas, 160 South Desplaines Street.
Erwin, Walter L., 55 St. James Place.
Erwin, William, 688 West Twenty-first Place.
Erwin, William, 942 West Fifty-third Place.
Erwin, E. H., 6039 Calumet Avenue.
Erwin, Frank, 28 Forty-third Street.
Erwin, Harry, 6120 South Peoria Street.
Erwin, Mrs. H. B., 501 Byron Street.
Erwin, Miss L. A., 984 Garfield Boulevard.
Erwin, Mrs. H. J. H., 6039 Calumet Avenue.
Erwin, Hugh, 1500 Newport Avenue.
Erwin, Mrs. Mary, 19 Thirty-ninth Street.
Erwin, Peter, 94 Law Avenue.
Erwin, Thomas, 713 South May Street.
Erwin, William C., 3100 Groveland Avenue.
Erwin, William E., 3031 Calumet Avenue.

Erwin, William L., 332 North Homan Avenue.
Erwin, Allen N., 293 South May Street.
Erwin, A. G., 55 St. James Place.
Erwin, Mrs. Augusta, 55 St. James Place.
Erwin, Charles, 1412 Wabash Avenue.
Erwin, Charles, 374 Park Avenue.
Erwin, C. R., 1300, and 67 Wabash Avenue.
Erwin, C. W., 66 South Hamilton Avenue.
Erwin, Mrs. Christine, 242 Erie Street.
Erwin, C. F., 495 Fullerton Avenue.
Erwin, Miss Emma, 2223 Wabash Avenue.
Erwin, Frank, 28 Forty-third Street.
Erwin, F. B., 6722 Wabash Avenue.
Erwin, G. G., 2 floor, Wells Street Depot.
Erwin, G. L., 384 South Western Avenue.
Irwin, Maurice, 3405 Auburn Street.
Irwin, Miss May, 434 Thirty-sixth street.
Irwin, Milo, 11913 Butler Street.
Irwin, Miss M. I., 6025 Lexington Avenue.
Irwin, Mrs. M. S., 273 Park Avenue.
Irwin, N. B., 516 West Adams Street.
Irwin, Miss Nellie J., 6025 Lexington Avenue.
Irwin, Patrick, 655 West Thirteenth Street.
Irwin, Patrick, 12 Cass Street.
Irwin, R. L., 102 Stevenson Avenue.
Irwin, Richard, 232 South Fifty-second Avenue.
Irwin, Robert, 635 West Forty-first Street.
Irwin, Robert, 334 West Fourteenth Place.
Irwin, R. W., 146 Fifty-fourth Street.
Irwin, R. A., 1612 West Sixty-seventh Street.
Irwin, R. A., 1765 Eighty-seventh Place.
Irwin, R. C., 6022 Calumet Avenue.
Irwin, R. H., 334 West Fourteenth Street.
Irwin, Russel, 28 Sixteenth Street.
Irwin, S. W., 8538 South Green Street.
Irwin, Thomas, 125 Erie Street.
Irwin, T. C., 607 West Sixty-first Street.
Irwin, F. J., 5166 Wabash Avenue.
Irwin, Miss Leona, 1591 Lill Avenue.
Irwin, W. B., 754 Lunt Avenue.
Irwin, Robert C., 6022 Calumet Avenue.

Irwin, Robert A., 1765 Eighty-seventh Place.
Irvine, George J., 6900 Madison Avenue.
Irvine, Gerald, 248 Erie Street.
Irvine, Hugh, 6420 Monroe Avenue.
Irvine, James, 4719 Evans Avenue.
Irvine, Miss Jane M., 1975 Carroll Avenue.
Irvine, John, 6900 Madison Avenue.
Irvine, John, 6536 South Marshfield Avenue.
Irvine, John H., 6810 South Peoria Street.
Irvine, John K., 823 Morse Avenue.
Irvine, Joseph C., 5829 Wabash Avenue.
Irvine, Mrs. L. M., 242 Thirtieth Street.
Irvine, Lore S., 2586 North Forty-second Street.
Irvine, Mary D., 823 Morse Avenue.
Irvine, Robert E., 1975 Carroll Avenue.
Irvine, Robert N., 7737 Stewart Avenue.
Irvine, Sherman G., 833 West Sixty-seventh.
Irvine, Thomas, 1330 Wabash Avenue.
Irvine, Thomas A., 1975 Carroll Avenue.
Irvine, Thomas J., 4525 Prairie Avenue.
Irvine, Thomas W., 228 Abbott Court.
Irvine, William, Jr., 55 Fifty-third Street.
Irvine, William, 2755 Kenmore Avenue.
Irvine, William, 201 Sixty-fourth Street.
Irvine, William A., 2887 North Hermitage Avenue.
Irwin, Andrew, 3302 Parnell Avenue.
Irwin, Arthur, 524 Flournoy Street.
Irwin, Arthur, Jr., 524 Flournoy Street.
Irwin, Arthur, 4800 St. Lawrence Avenue.
Irwin, Arthur B., 195 South Canal.
Irwin, Arthur W., 5430 Lexington Avenue.
Irwin, Benjamin F., 654 West Sixty-third Street.
Irwin, Bernard J. D., 575 Division Street.
Irwin, Bernel, 4731 Evans Avenue.
Irwin Bros. Co., 334 Clark Street.
Irwin, Miss C. F., 326 Warren Avenue.
Irwin, Charles D., Evanston, Illinois.
Irwin, Charles E., 348 West Erie Street.
Irwin, Charles E., 884 North Maplewood Avenue.
Irwin, Daniel R., 163 South Winchester Avenue.
Irwin, David A., 6511 Ellis Avenue.

Irwin, David Q., 5739 Drexel Avenue.
Irwin, Edward, 342 Austin Avenue.
Irwin, Edward, 1751 Wrightwood Avenue.
Irwin, Edward A., 181 Bowen Avenue.
Irwin, Edward G., 140 Walnut Street.
Irwin, Edward H., 3024 South Park Avenue.
Irwin, Eldor, 283 West Monroe Street.
Irwin, Emmitt H., 1109, 239 Dearborn Street.
Irwin, John C., 4800 St. Lawrence Avenue.
Irwin, John H., 6235 Cottage Grove Avenue.
Irwin, Dr. John L., 244 Erie Street.
Irwin, John R., 662 West VanBuren Street.
Irwin, John T., 617 West Sixty-third Street.
Irwin, Johnston S., 5034 Princeton Avenue.
Irwin, J. Paul, 2768 North Winchester Avenue.
Irwin, Kate, 5825 State Street.
Irwin, Miss Lillie, 3434 Rhodes Avenue.
Irwin, Luther W., 174 Adams Street.
Irwin, Miss Margaret, 154 South Desplaines Street.
Irwin, Miss Mary R., 326 Warren Avenue.
Irwin, Milo S., 5223 South Halsted Street.
Irwin, Miss Minnie I., 6025 Lexington Avenue.
Irwin, Nathaniel B., 516 West Adams Street.
Irwin, Miss Nettie, 1735 Racine Street.
Irwin, Patrick, 655 West Thirteenth Street.
Irwin, Patrick, 270 Illinois.
Irwin, Paul F., 7134 Union Avenue.
Irwin, Richard, 313 South Fifty-second Avenue.
Irwin, Robert, 334 West Fourteenth Street.
Irwin, Robert A., 406 Sixtieth Street.
Irwin, Thomas J., 6038 Washington Avenue.
Irwin, Miss Verona, 1591 Lill Avenue.
Irwin, Walter B., 754 Lunt Avenue.
Irwin, Walter W., 1467 Michigan Avenue.
Irwin, Walter W., 216 North State Street.
Irwin, William, 196 Seventy-sixth Street.
Irwin, William, 691 West Twenty-first Street.
Irwin, William, 4437 Langley Avenue.
Irwin, William E., 1874 Humboldt Boulevard.
Irwin, William E., 516 West Adams Street.
Irwin, William H., 7823 Woodlawn Avenue.

Irwin, William J., 1409 West Harrison Street.
Irwin, William L., 1978 Thirty-sixth Street.
Irwin, William P., care of Lakota Hotel.
Irwin, William T., 4798 North Clark Street.
Irwin, William V., 237 Franklin Street.
Irwin, Wilmer H., 4 Forty-fourth Place.
Irvin, William, 4050 Indiana Avenue.
Irvin, William T., 4454 Wallace.
Irvin, William T., 4606 Union Avenue.
Irvin, W, W., 216 State Street.
Irvine, Alexander S., 7108 Vernon Avenue.
Irvine, Miss Edna J., 1975 Canal Avenue.
Irvine, Ephraim D., 5820 Indiana Avenue.
Irvine, Frederick C., 2755 Kenmore Avenue.
Irvine, George C., 6749 Evans Avenue.
Irvine, George F., 5937 Calumet Avenue.
Irvine, William C., 7018 Wallace.
Irvine, Wilson H., 542 South Richmond.
Irving, Miss Florence, 3810 West Sixty-fourth Street.
Irving, Frank S., 3033 Indiana Avenue.
Irving, George, 2597 North Winchester Avenue.
Irving, James, 3614 Ellis Avenue.
Irving, James D., 692 Walnut Street.
Irving, John J., 1775 South Sangamon.
Irving, John W., 7111 Greenwood Avenue.
Irving, Joshua, 816 West Sixtieth Place.
Irving, Louie J., 3857 Cottage Grove Avenue.
Irving, Robert, 6400 Parnell Avenue.
Irving, Robert, 3164 Archer Avenue.
Irving, Robert J., 435 West Taylor Street.
Irving, Samuel C., 311 Belden Avenue.
Irving, William, 94 Lytle Street.
Irving, William, 221 Ohio Street.
Irving, William E., 227 West Sangamon Street.
Irving, William J., 3810 West Sixty-fourth Street.
Irving, William M., 399 West Van Buren Street.
Irving, William R., 5621 Lafayette Avenue.
Irwin, Albert, 42 South Ada.
Irwin, Albert J., 2566 North Ashland Avenue.
Irwin, Alexander, 5808 Michigan Avenue.
Irwin, Miss Ernestine A., 6025 Lexington Avenue.

Irwin, Fred C., 1581 Milwaukee Avenue.
Irwin, Fred G., 54 West Chicago Avenue.
Irwin, Frederick J., 516 West Adams.
Irwin, Garett, 1209 Lexington.
Irwin, Guy, 4333 Langley Avenue.
Irwin, Harlam M., 326 Warren Avenue.
Irwin, Harry A., 268 South Lincoln Avenue.
Irwin, Harry D., 937 Chase Avenue.
Irwin, Harry L., 733 Fiftieth Street.
Irwin, Henry E., 3106 Wentworth Avenue
Irwin, Henry J., 6532 Cottage Grove Avenue.
Irwin, Iphigenia (Miss), 6025 Lexington Avenue.
Irwin, James, 3756 South Lincoln Avenue.
Irwin, James, 262 West Randolph Street.
Irwin, James C., 5819 Michigan Avenue.
Irwin, James H., 348 West Erie Street.
Irwin, James P., 2115 South Canal Street.
Irwin, Miss Jane A., 3024 South Park Avenue.
Irwin, Miss Janet B., 1120 North Western Avenue.
Irwin, Jene W., 260 North Carpenter.
Irwin, John, 157 North Union.
Irwin, John, 123 West Fifty-eighth Street.
Irwin, John, 505 Dearborn Avenue.
Irwin, John B., 54 West Chicago Avenue.
Irwin, John B., 159 Locust Street.
Irwin, Robert H., 334 West Fourteenth Place.
Irwin, Royal W., 4800 St. Lawrence Avenue.
Irwin, R. J., 1720 Arlington Place.
Irwin, Samuel W., 8536 South Green Street.
Irwin, Miss Susannah, 524 Flournoy Street.
Irwin, Thomas C., 617 West Sixty-third Street.

CINCINNATI, OHIO.

Irvin, Carter, Omaha Street (C. L. & N.)
Irvin, David, 3740 Derr Street.
Irvin, George W., 3526 Columbia Avenue.
Irvin, Gertrude M., 525 West Eighth Street.
Irvin, Rebecca, 674 West Fifth Street.
Irvin, Thomas, 232 McFarland Street.
Irvine, Arzilia, 466 East Sixth Street.
Irvine, Charles D., 1726 Hewett Avenue.

Irvine, Charles W., 1726 Hewett Avenue.
Irvine, J. S., 2126 Alpine Place.
Irvine, J. W., 2126 Alpine Place.
Irving, Fannie, 915 Race Street.
Irving, Henry S., 2518 Ingleside Avenue.
Irving, Joseph, Rockdale and Burnett Avenue.
Irving, Mark E., 2518 Ingleside Avenue.
Irving, William D., 914 John Street.
Irwin, A. E., 918 East McMillan Street.
Irwin, A. M., 3200 Woodburn Avenue.
Irwin, C. E., 315 Sycamore Street.
Irwin, Charles A., 2826 May Street.
Irwin, Edwin U., 37 East Third Street.
Irwin, Ellis J., 1519 Providence Street.
Irwin, Frank G., Care of Ballman & Company.
Irwin, Henry J., 873 Rockdale Avenue.
Irwin, John K., Dayton, Ky.
Irwin, Howard, 634 West Fourth Street.
Irwin, James, 340 West Fifth Street.
Irwin, Dr. James T., 37 East Third Street.
Irwin, Jane, 2667 Highland Avenue.
Irwin, Jennie, 580 West Sixth Street.
Irwin, Lewis W., 310 Lincoln Inn, Street.
Irwin, Matel, 128 Garfield Place.
Irwin, Maria A., 578 West Sixth Street.
Irwin, Mary, 1086 Gilbert Avenue.
Irwin, Patrick J., 1086 Gilbert Avenue.
Irwin, Sarah, 578 West Sixth Street.
Irwin, M. G., Hartwell, Ohio.
Irwin, William, 578 West Sixth Street.
Irwin, William J., 501 Woodward.
Irwin, William T., 423 East Fourth Street.
Irwin, Willis, 211 West Ninth Street.

COVINGTON, KENTUCKY

Irvine, Ada, 710 Main Street.
Irvine, Arthur, 194 West Sixth Street.
Irvine, Charles A., 83 West Second Street.
Irvine, Clara, 710 Main Street.
Irvine, Jane, 194 West Sixth Street.
Irvine, Robert W., 83 West Second Street.

Irvine, Raymond W., 83 West Second Street.
Irvine, William N., 710 Main Street.
Irving, Ira W., 1536 Madison Avenue.
Irving, James B., 1536 Madison Avenue.
Irwin, A. H., 1011 Greenup Street.
Irwin, Ellen J., 430 Bakewell Street.
Irwin, George, 71 West Eighth Street.
Irwin, Mary F., 1011 Greenup Street.

CLEVELAND, OHIO.

Irvin, Charles T., 193 Wellington Avenue.
Irvin, George H., 236 Huron.
Irvin, George W., 193 Wellington Avenue.
Irvin, Clifford, 193 Wellington Avenue.
Irvin, Harry R., 193 Wellington Avenue.
Irvin, John K., 47 Perkins Avenue.
Irvine, Andrew, 177 Aetna Street.
Irvine, Andrew, Jr., 177 Aetna Street.
Irvine, Andrew J. F., 32 Mabie Street.
Irvine, Francis M., 4 Pearl Place.
Irvine, Hood H., 32 Mabie Street.
Irvine, John, 1588 St. Clair Street.
Irvine, Joseph, 39 Cedar Avenue.
Irvine, Oliver S., 1097 East Madison Avenue.
Irvine, Robert W., 32 Mabie Street.
Irvine, Robert P., 32 Mabie Street.
Irvine, Samuel, 69 Coutant (Lake Wood).
Irvine, Thomas M., 1097 East Madison Avenue.
Irving, Esther G., 222 Vanek Street.
Irving, William, 171 Edwards Avenue.
Irving, William R., 222 Vanek Street.
Irwin, Alexander, 21 West Trenton.
Irwin, Charles A., 135 Bolton Avenue.
Irwin, Della, 327 Prospect Avenue.
Irwin, Emma W., 1641 Harvard.
Irwin, George, 24 Oregon Street.
Irwin, George E., 19 Miller Avenue.
Irwin, Harold G., 70 Fairview Avenue.
Irwin, Harry C., 475 East Madison Avenue.
Irwin, Hattie, 160 Dodge Street.
Irwin, Ida M., 78 Buckwood St.

Irwin, James G., 128 Broadway.
Irwin, James R., 256 Buckner Avenue.
Irwin, James R., Jr., 256 Buckner Avenue.
Irwin, James T., 1688 Pearl Street.
Irwin, John B., 481 East Madison Avenue.
Irwin, John C., 154 East Madison Avenue.
Irwin, Myra, 121 Alabama Street.
Irwin, Rodney, 90 River Street.
Irwin, Sarah E., 26 Hurlburt Street.
Irwin, Thomas, 57 West Trenton Street.
Irwin, William, 26 Hurlburt Street.
Irwin, William M., 82 Eldridge Avenue.

COLUMBUS, OHIO.

Irvin, Edward, 163 East Runnell Street.
Irvin, Harry T., 200 Wilson Avenue.
Irvin, John A., 958 Neil Avenue.
Irvin, Lemuel B., 524 East Third Avenue.
Irvine, Ellsworth C., 869 Franklin Avenue.
Irvine, Henry H., Care of Emerson Hotel.
Irwin, Abraham, 416 West Seventh Avenue.
Irwin, Agnes, 197 North Washington Avenue.
Irwin, Angie M., 35 South Sixth Avenue.
Irwin, Arthur F., 197 North Washington Avenue.
Irwin, Charles, 790 Summet Avenue.
Irwin, Charles A., 297 West Second Avenue.
Irwin, Charles G., 302 Tappan Street.
Irwin, Edna A., 550 East Spring Street.
Irwin, Edward, 163 East Runnell Street.
Irwin, Ella, 197 North Washington Avenue.
Irwin, Frank A., 349 East Naghten Street.
Irwin, Howard, 312 East Blenkner Street.
Irwin, James E., 593 Edward Street.
Irwin, John A., 958 Neil Avenue.
Irwin, John J., 343 East Naghten Street.
Irwin, Joseph A., 197 North Washington Avenue.
Irwin, Katherine, 312 East Long Street.
Irwin, Lawrence, 197 North Washington Avenue.
Irwin, Lawrence, Jr., 385 East Naghten Street.
Irwin, Lewis, 99 North Garfield Avenue.
Irwin, Michael A., 345 Lexington Avenue.

Irwin, Nellie M., 219 Hamilton Avenue.
Irwin, Samuel, 283 East Fifth Avenue.
Irwin, Samuel, 244 King Avenue.
Irwin, Sylvester A., 343 East Naghten.
Irwin, William J., 336 Mosette Avenue.
Irwin, William S., 283 East Fifth Avenue.
Irwin, William T., 197 North Washington Avenue.

DAYTON, OHIO.

Irvin, Horace A., 122 East Third Street.
Irvin, James M., 224 North Salem Avenue.
Irvin, John, Care of Dayton Spice Mills Company.
Irvin, Obed. W., 395 West First Street.
Irvin, William, 241 South Baxter Street.
Irving, Tamas E., 24 East Hayes Street.
Irwin, James C., 324 East Fourth Street.
Irwin, John C., 324 East Fourth Street.
Irwin, Joseph, 323 North Taylor Street.
Irwin, Otto J., 14 South Morton Avenue.
Irwin, Thomas H., 621 West North Avenue.
Irwin, Washington, 49 West Fluhart Avenue.
Irwin, William, 208 East Ohio Street.
Irwin, William H., 49 West Fluhart Avenue.

DENVER, COLORADO.

Irvin, Elizabeth F., 364 Sherman Avenue.
Irvin, Thomas A., 2088 Ogden.
Irvine, Ethel A., 141 Irvington Place.
Irvine, Fred, 2825 West Thirty-second Avenue.
Irvine, James, Eighth Avenue and Platte River.
Irvine, Dr. J. C., 2800 William Street.
Irvine, Chris, 2248 Clarkson Street.
Irvine, George W., 2130 Arapahoe Street.
Irving, John, 254 Columbine.
Irving, Walter P., 2825 West Thirty-second Street.
Irving, William H., 2351 Pennsylvania Avenue.
Irwin, Alexander E., 434 West Colfax Avenue.
Irwin, Breck, 525 South Lincoln Avenue.
Irwin, Charles W., 1406 Champan
Irwin, David S., Care of M. J. Micklin.
Irwin, Fred D., 2900 West Twenty-fifth Avenue.

Irwin, Harry, 419 Clark Street.

Irwin Harry P., 2433 West Thirty-third Avenue.

Irwin, James H., 2433 West Thirty-third Avenue.

Irwin, Nicholas, 2258 Curtis.

Irwin, P. H., Care of Flint Lomax Company.

Irwin, William A., 1022 Broadway Street.

Irwin, William T., 401 Sixteenth Street.

Irwin, William W., 1373 South Fourteenth Street.

DETROIT, MICHIGAN.

Irvin, Alice, 126 East Congress Street.

Irvin, Richard, Vice-Pres. Brisco Mfg. Co. (Res. New York City).

Irvine, Alice, 578 East Congress Street.

Irvine, Alice, 14 Willis Avenue North.

Irvine, George W., Washington Arcade.

Irvine, Jennie, Wid. Ford J. 312 Cherry Street.

Irvine, John, 512 Mullet Street.

Irvine, John S., 284 Meldrum Avenue.

Irvine, Lawrence L., 578 Congress Street E.

Irvine, Margaret A., 1750 Jefferson Avenue.

Irvine, Matilda, Wid. J. D., 43 Garfield.

Irvine, Richard, 60 Columbia, West.

Irvine, Richard J., 60 Columbia, West.

Irvine, Maj. Robert J. C., 75 Fort Street West.

Irvine, Sinclair, 947 Champlain Street.

Irvine, Sinclair and Son Wm. M., 970 Champlain Street.

Irvine, Thomas, 578 Congress Street East.

Irvine, William, 578 East Congress Street.

Irvine, William A., 45 Greenwood Avenue.

Irvine, William G., 530 Monroe Avenue.

Irvine, William H., 43 Garfield Avenue.

Irvine, William J. Jr., 280 Third Avenue.

Irvine, William H., 947 Champlain Street.

Irvine and Waltensperger, 1167, 1169 Jefferson Avenue.

Irvine and Wise, 6 Moffat Bldg.

Irving, Mrs. Adelaid, 74 Sherman Street.

Irving, Alice A., Wid. David N., 66 Washington Avenue.

Irving, Mrs. Blanch, 430 Fifth Street.

Irwin, Alfred, 1514 West Grand Boulevard.

Irwin, Annie, Hotel Cadillac.

Irwin, Bernard L., 195 Chene Street.

, Bernice, 3 North Wabash.
, Charlotte, Wid. George, 230 Third.
, Charlotte, 36 Philadelphia.
, Edward, 146 Porter Street.
, Edward C., 146 Porter Street.
, Florence, 140 Congress
, Frank, 522 Vinewood.
, Frank J., 346 High West.
, Frank W., Oliver D. Cromwell, Woodmere.
, Frederick, 65 Russell.
, Frederick C., 1255 Second.
, George B., Lincoln Avenue.
, George H., 713 Wabash.
, Helen, 522 Vinewood.
, H. G., 43 Church Street.
, James, 36 Philadelphia.
, James, 230 Sidney.
, John, 165 Congress East.
, John, 13 Herkimer Avenue.
, John, 630 West Grand Boulevard.
, John O., 393 Trumbull.
, Katheryne M., 166 Second.
, Margaret, Wid. Samuel, 5 Vinewood.
, May N., 1365 Sixteenth Street.
, Mrs. Oliver A., 626 One Hundred and Forty-fifth Avenue.
, Oliver M., 626 Fourteenth Avenue.
, Orville, Thirteenth and Herkimer Avenue.
, Philip, 1365 Sixteenth Street.
, Rebecca, Wid. William B., 372 Wabash Avenue.
, ——, 364 West High.
, Robert J., 141 Milwaukee Avenue East.
, Robert L., 863 Humbolt Avenue.
, Robert O., 463 McKinley Avenue.
, Samuel T., William H. Irwin.
, Thomas, 1364 Sixteenth Street.
, Thomas B., 626 Fourteenth Avenue.
, Thomas, 863 Humbolt Avenue.
, Thomas, J., 393 Trumbull.
, T. J. and Son, 542 Michigan Avenue.
, Viola, 364 High Street West.
, Walter, 520 East Fort Street.

Irwin, William H., Jefferson Avenue C.

Irwin, William H., 3 Magnolia.

Irving, Rev. Charles H., 73 North Grand Boulevard.

Irving, Mrs. Elizabeth, Solvay Lodge.

Irving, George S., 152 Macomb Street.

Irving, Henry G., 303 Nineteenth Street.

Irving, John H., Solvey Lodge D.

Irving, Samuel J., 382 Dragoon Avenue.

Irving, Richard J. S., 382 Dragoon Avenue.

Irving, Rubey M., Grace Hospital.

Irving, Stuart, (bds. 945 Fourteenth Avenue), 430 Fifth Street.

Irving, The, 36-38 Clifford Street.

Irving, Thomas D., 954 Fourteenth Avenue.

Irving, William E., 189 Kirby Avenue East.

Erving, Andrie V., 896 Meldrum Avenue.

Erving, Caroline L., 3 Hancock Avenue West.

Erwin, George, 80 Harrison.

Erwin, George B., 763½ Twenty-sixth Street.

Erwin, Jennie E., 397 Hancock Avenue West.

Erwin, Louise C., 80 Harrison Street.

Erwin, George, 39 National Avenue.

Erwin, Harry 754 Bagley Avenue.

Erwin, James F., 309 National Avenue.

INDIANAPOLIS, INDIANA.

Irven, Henry, 422 North Senate Avenue.

Irvin, Benjamin, 927 West Maryland.

Irvin, Charles, 1753 North West Avenue.

Irvin, Davis H., 308 Trowbridge.

Irvin, James B., 1183 River Avenue.

Irvin, Joseph, 725 South East.

Irvin, Melissa, 826 West Eleventh Street.

Irvin, Richard, 862 West North.

Irvin, William, 2206 Ashland Avenue.

Irvine, Garrett W., 920 East Washington.

Irvine, Hamilton, 1031 West Michigan.

Irving, Ellis L., 31 East Maryland.

Irving, Jacob R., 1022 Central Avenue.

Irving, Jesse, 19 South West.

Irving, Joseph, 1034 Reynolds Avenue.

Irving, Joseph L., 222 East Sixteenth Street.

Irving, Rilly, 1519 Nevada.
Irwin, Alfred, 1039 Bellefontaine.
Irwin, Amory T., 1304 N. Delaware.
Irwin, Bernice J., 740 West Washington.
Irwin, Helen M., 1533 Broadway.
Irwin, Hugh C., 1533 Broadway.
Irwin, John D., 602 East Walnut.
Irwin, Margaret, 603 Eddy.
Irwin, Mark T., 1120 Bellefontaine.
Irwin, Robert M., 1115 West Thirtieth Street.
Irwin, Robert T., 114 South Pennsylvania.
Irwin, Rollin C., 1130 Hoyt Avenue.
Irwin, Sherman W., 2518 East Washington.
Irwin, Thomas, 1520 Garfield Place.
Irwin, Thomas H., 1008½ East Washington.
Irwin, Vorhees T., 307 East Vermont.
Irwin, Millard, 409 East South.

KANSAS CITY, MISSOURI.

Irvin, Alice, 409 East Thirteenth Street.
Irvin, Emma, 933 Genesee Street.
Irvin, Frank, 1515 Steptoe Street.
Irvin, Frank W., 1331 A. Troost.
Irvin, F. J., 1012 Locust Street.
Irvin, George W., 1315 Park Street.
Irvin, Henry H., Care of Jones & Irvin.
Irvin, James F., 3950 East Fourteenth Street.
Irvin, Walter, 2410 East Ninth Street.
Irvin, Webb T., Care of Meter Gas Engine Company.
Irving, Charles, 1311 Locust Street.
Irving, James H., 435 West Fourteenth Street.
Irving, Junius B., 927 Holmes Street.
Irwin, Arthur D., 3107 Park Street.
Irwin, Arthur J., 1012 Locust Street.
Irwin, Arthur W., 523 Chestnut Street.
Irwin, Charles E., 2209 Elma Street.
Irwin, Charles H., 3885 East Ninth Street.
Irwin, Cyrus C., 4108 Michigan.
Irwin, Edward, 1822 East Ninth Street.
Irwin, Elva, 1300 East Sixteenth Street.
Irwin, George W., 1508 West Fourteenth Street.

Irwin, Harvey, 550 Cherry Street.
Irwin, Homer N., 1014 Harrison Street.
Irwin, Jared, 1722 Allen Street.
Irwin, John, 1300 East Sixteenth Street.
Irwin, Joseph C., 2331 Prospect Avenue.
Irwin, Joseph R., 3006 Euclid Avenue.
Irwin, Lorne A., 2327 Park Avenue.
Irwin, Margaret A., 2661 East Ninth Street.
Irwin, William A., 523 Chestnut Street.
Irwin, William C., 2013 East Ninth Street.
Irwin, William L., 3724 Baltimore Avenue.

LOUISVILLE, KENTUCKY.

Irvan, Oscar B., 627 First Street.
Irvin, Rev. James, Zion M. E. Church.
Irvin, Lucian, 717 Fourth Street.
Irvin, Mary, 2624 Eighteenth Street.
Irvine, Frederick K., care of Franklin Printing Company.
Irvine, George E., 212 Clay Street.
Irvine, Hugh J., 825 Franklin Street.
Irvine, James, 513 East Broadway.
Irvine, James F., 825 Franklin Street.
Irvine, John M., 208 Clay Street.
Irvine, Josiah J., 3427 Rudd Avenue.
Irvine, Armand H., 3428 Rudd Avenue.
Irvine, Robert H., 3428 Rudd Avenue.
Irvine, William Hoge, 821 Second Street.
Irving, George L., 2624 Eighteenth Street.
Irving, George W., 3728 Rudd Avenue.
Irving, Harry B., 3728 Rudd Avenue.
Irving, Howard U., 2815 Montgomery Street.
Irving, I. Mack., 3728 Rudd Avenue.
Irving, Lee D., 3728 Rudd Avenue.
Irving, William H., 3108 Bank Street.
Irwin, Alfred, 1408 Twentieth Street.
Irwin, Benoni, 904 Second Street.
Irwin, B. C., 211 West Hill Street.
Irwin, Daniel L., 904 Second Street.
Irwin, Edward T. (Dr.), 430 Twenty-sixth Street.
Irwin, Miss Fannie, 914 Fifth Street.
Irwin, Harvey, 2233 West Walnut Street.

Irwin, James T., Care of Carter Dry Goods Company.
Irwin, John F., 3526 Bank Street.
Irwin, John F., Jr., 3526 Bank Street.
Irwin, Dr. Joseph W., 421 West Chestnut Street.
Irwin, Lucian J., 717 Fourth Street.
Irwin, Millard F., 422 Twenty-sixth Street.
Irwin, Stephen H. S., 430 Twenty-sixth Street.
Irwing, J. T., 3011 Alford Avenue.
Irwin, George B.
Irwin, Harvey S., 710 Columbia Building.
Irwin, Howard C.
Irwin, James L.
Irwin, James T.
Irwin, John.
Irwin, John A.
Irwin, John F.
Irwin, Dr. Joseph W. 1344 Second.
Irwin, Julia C., widow W. H.
Irwin, Lucian J., 714 Fourth.
Irwin, Mary E., widow D. L.
Irwin, M. F., 422 Twenty-sixth.
Irwin, Stephen S.
Irwin, William.
Irwin, William C.
Irwin, William R.
Erwin, John.
Erwin, Ada.
Erwin, Elsie.
Erwin, Hartwell B.
Erwin, Horace.
Erwin, Mabel.
Erwin, Robert B.
Erwin, Samuel B., 507 Twenty-fifth.
Irvin, Margaret H., widow of James.
Irvine, Edward, 249 West Jefferson.
Irvine, George E., 212 Clay.
Irvine, Hugh J.
Irvine, James.
Irvine, James F.
Irvine, Jessie W.
Irvine, J. Wiley.

Irvine, Lottie.
Irvine, Mamie.
Irvine, Ormond H., 3428 Rudd.
Irvine, Robert H.
Irvine, Roselle, widow J. B.
Irvine, Samuel A.
Irvine, William.
Irving, Frances A., widow G. W.
Irving, George L., 2624 Eighteenth Street.
Irving, Harry B.
Irving, Harry B.
Irving, Howard W.
Irving, Lee D., 3728 Rudd.
Irving, Mary C.
Irving, William H.
Irwin, Alfred J.
Irwin, Anne.
Irwin, Anne H.
Irwin, Bessie.
Irwin, Brown C., 202 West Hill.
Irwin, Charles.
Irwin, Edwin T., 430 Twenty-sixth.
Irwin, Edwin T., Jr.
Irwin, Elizabeth, widow Thomas.
Irwin, Emily E.
Irwin, Fannie.
Irwin, Frank.

MINNEAPOLIS, MINNESOTA.

Ervin, Genevieve, 612 Jefferson Street.
Ervin, H. C., Jr., 1515 University Avenue, Southeast.
Ervin, J. H., 612 Jefferson Street.
Ervin, J. F., 426 Second Avenue, South.
Ervin, Robert, 612 Jefferson Street.
Irvin, G. U., 1418 Northeast Third Street.
Irvin, G. W., Jr., 1418 Northeast Third Street.
Irvine, C. G., Jr., Flat 460 North Twelfth Street.
Irvine, Dr. H. G., 2200 Grand Avenue.
Irvine, Mrs. Matilda, 3128 Portland Avenue.
Irvine, Mrs. R. M., 3128 Pleasant Avenue.
Irvine, Thomas, 2014 Third Avenue, North.
Irvine, T. H., 511 Eighth Avenue, Northeast.

Irving, Miss Agnes M., 2312 Sixteenth Avenue, South.
Irving, Miss A. M., 833 Summer Street.
Irving, A. A., 1525 Northeast Washington Street.
Irving, Mrs. Anna, 1524 Monroe Street.
Boyd, Anna E., 813 Eighth Avenue, South.
Boyd, C. G., 1421 North Fifth Street.
Boyd, C. P., West 56 Street, cor. France Avenue.
Boyd, D. C., 123 West Fifteenth Street.
Boyd, Mrs. Florence, 217 Nicollet Avenue.
Boyd, Frank, 335 East Nineteenth Street.
Boyd, F. M., 3336 Irving Avenue.
Boyd, G. E., 3114 Southeast Fourth Street.
Boyd, G. S., 3115 Fifteenth Avenue, South.
Boyd, Mrs. G. B., 316 South Tenth Street.
Boyd, Miss Helen W., 3336 Irving Avenue, South.
Boyd, James, 326 Second Avenue, South.
Boyd, J. C., 1115 Second Avenue, South.
Boyd, J. J., St. James, Minn.
Boyd, J. M., 316 South Tenth Street.
Boyd, J. W., 1200 South Second Street.
Boyd, Leonn, 516 Fifteenth Avenue, Southeast.
Boyd, Mrs. Mary, 6 South Thirteenth Street.
Boyd, R. R., 1717 Southeast Fourth Street.
Boyd, Mrs. R. H., 928 Nicollet Ave.
Boyd, Miss Sarah, 1507 South Fifth Street.
Boyd, William H., 317 South, Eighth Street.
Boyd, William M., 1113 Second Avenue, South.
Irving, Miss A. E., 402 Southeast Sixth Street.
Irving, Arthur, 2029 Willow Avenue.
Irving, Mrs. Catherine, 759 Northeast Washington Street.
Irving, Ernest, B. W. S., Lydale Avenue, West, 3 n. of Limits.
Irving, Frances, 570 Northeast Fifth Street.
Irving, Frank, 250 First Avenue, South.
Irving, Harry, 723 Northeast Washington Street.
Irving, J. P., 612 Jefferson Street.
Irving, John, 709 Jackson Street.
Irving, J. J., 723 Northeast Washington Street.
Irving, J. J., 2312 Sixteenth Avenue, South.
Irving, J. T., 833 Summer Street.
Irving, Miss Mary, 2312 Sixteenth Avenue, South.
Irving, Miss M. A., 2306 Fourth Avenue, South.

Irving, Mrs. N. A., Flat 2, 1516 Elliot Avenue.
Irving, S. S., Flat B., 221 Eighth Avenue, Southeast.
Irving, S. S., Jr., Flat B., 221 Eighth Avenue, Southeast.
Irving, Thomas, 641 Northeast Fifth Street.
Irving, F. F., 607 Quincy Street.
Irving, T. P., 2001 Polk Street.
Irving, William, 2312 Sixteenth Avenue, South.
Irwin, Dr. A. F., 2429 Colfax Avenue, South.
Irwin, Miss A, C., 300 Union Street.
Irwin, Arthur, 631 Aldrich Avenue, North.
Irwin, D. S., 317 Delaware Street.
Irwin, G. M., 631 Aldrich Avenue, North.
Irwin, H. D., 5 West Thirty-third Street.
Irwin, Miss Jennie, 2429 Colfax Avenue, North.
Irwin, John, 833 Third Avenue, Northeast.
Irwin, J. B., Richfield, Minn.
Irwin, J. F., 2445 Humboldt Avenue, South.
Irwin, J. L., 300 Union Street.
Irwin, Miss M. A., 833 Third Avenue, Northeast.
Irwin, Miss May, 631 Aldrich Avenue, North.
Irwin, Robert, 833 Third Avenue, Northeast.
Irwin, Robert, 1047 First Avenue, North.
Irwin, Thomas, 833 Third Avenue, Northeast.
Irwin, Thomas, 300 Seventh Avenue, North.
Irwin, William J., 631 Aldrich Avenue, North.

NEWPORT, KENTUCKY.

Irwin, Laura, 419 East Fourth Street.
Irwin, W. R., 572 East Fourth Street.
Irwin, W. T., 605 Lexington Avenue.

NEW YORK CITY.

Irvin, Charles, 1272 Third Avenue.
Irvin, Effingham T., 120 Fifth Avenue.
Irvin, George C., 116 Nassau Street.
Irvin, John J., 311 E. 73rd. Street.
Irvin, Ralph V., 174 East Seventy-fourth.
Irvin, Richard, 25 Broad Street.
Irvin, Thomas S., 25 Broad Street.
Irvin, Rev. William, 345 Lexington Avenue.
Irvine, Alexander G., Arlington, N. J.

Irvine, Allen A., 317 West One Hundred and Twenty-first Street.
Irvine, Harry F., 25 Broad Street.
Irvine, James, 18 Broadway.
Irvine, John, 151 West Sixty-second Street.
Irvine, John, 1672 First Avenue.
Irvine, John M., 315 Eighth Street.
Irvine, Mary, 310 West Fifteenth Street.
Irvine, Robert, 227 Alexander Avenue.
Irvine, Thomas B., 454 Mott Avenue.
Irvine, Thomas W., 75 West Ninety-seventh Street.
Irvine, William, 332 East Twenty-third Street.
Irvine & Co., 217 West One Hundred and Twenty-fifth Street.
Irving, A. Bues., 152 Madison Avenue.
Irving, A. McR., 77 Pine Street.
Irving, Alexander B., 47 Cedar Street.
Irving, Alexander D., Jr., 47 Cedar Street.
Irving, Andrew, 329 East Twenty-second Street.
Irving, Benjamin H., 32 Broadway.
Irving, Charles, 51 West Twenty-eighth Street.
Irving, Charles S., 424 West Twentieth Street.
Irving, Clarence J., 6 West One Hundred and Sixteenth Street.
Irving, Clarence J., 25 West One Hundred Twenty-ninth Street.
Irving, Cortlant, 55 Liberty Street.
Irving, David, 150 Amsterdam Avenue.
Irving, Garnet, 215 West Eightieth Street.
Irving, George, 157 East Eighty-first Street.
Irving, George, 476 Cherry Street.
Irving, George, 209 West Eighteenth Street.
Irving, George C., 116 Nassau Street.
Irving, George H., 403 West Twenty-fourth Street.
Irving, Guy A. E., 90 Front Street.
Irving, H. Sutherland, 18 Wall Street.
Irving, Henry, 338 West Twenty-first Street.
Irving, Henry, Jr., 10 West One Hundred Thirty-Fourth Street.
Irving, Haywood H., 55 East Ninety-third Street.
Irving, James A., 1106 Home Street.
Irving, John, 96 Fifth Avenue.
Irving, John, 256 Church Street.
Irving, John, Jr., 431 Amsterdam Avenue.
Irving, John D., 45 Broadway.
Irving, John H., 548 North Forty-seventh Street.

Irving, John W., 1091 Third Avenue.
Irving, John T., 121 East Thirty-seventh Street.
Irving, Joseph, 637 Eighth Street.
Irving, Leonard, 141 West Twenty-fourth Street.
Irving, Martin, 149 West Sixty-sixth Street.
Irving, Philip H., 316 West Thirtieth Street.
Irving, Richard A., 71 Broadway.
Irving, Robert A., "The Ansonia."
Irving, Robert W., 271 Broadway.
Irving, Shannon, 228 East Twenty-first Street.
Irving, Sidney F., 1078 Fairmount Place.
Irving, Thomas, 201 Varick Street.
Irving, Thomas C., 337 East Forty-second Street.
Irving, Thomas J., 348 St. Nicholas Avenue.
Irving, Walter E., 207 West One Hundred Fortieth Street.
Irving, Washington, 47 Cedar Street.
Irving, William, 99 Franklin Street.
Irving, William, 57 East One Hundred Thirtieth Street.
Irving, William E., 57 West Sixty-second Street.
Irving, William F., 342 West One Hundred Nineteenth Street.
Irving, William J., 1350 Amsterdam Avenue.
Irving & Green, 51 West Twenty-eighth Street.
Irwin, A. R., 60 West Tenth Street.
Irwin, Albert S., 226 West One Hundred Sixteenth Street.
Irwin, Alexander, 857 East One Hundred Thirty-ninth Street.
Irwin, Andrew P., 96 Wall Street.
Irwin, Charles H., 436 Manhattan Avenue.
Irwin, Charles O'C., 77 West Eleventh Street.
Irwin, E. W., 114 Liberty Street.
Irwin, Etes W., 22 West Nineteenth Street.
Irwin, Edward, 206 West Sixty-seventh Street.
Irwin, Edward W., 114 Liberty Street.
Irwin, Elizabeth, (M. D.)., 153 East Forty-seventh Street.
Irwin, Emma L., 390 Canal Street.
Irwin, Ernest L., 66 Pine Street.
Irwin, Francis, 216 West Sixty-seventh Street.
Irwin, Frank H., 3184 Broadway.
Irwin, Dr. F. N., 10 West Thirty-ninth Street.
Irwin, George M., 52 Broadway.
Irwin, Harry B., 18 Broadway.
Irwin, Harry, 48 Wall Street.

Irwin, Harry, 506 West Twenty-fourth Street.
Irwin, James, 75 Barclay Street.
Irwin, James D., 48 Wall Street.
Irwin, James F., 1077 Ogden Avenue.
Irwin, James H., 16 Harrison.
Irwin, James H., 456 East One Hundred Sixteenth Street.
Irwin, James R., 907 East One Hundred Forty-ninth Street.
Irwin, James W., 154 East Twenty-third Street.
Irwin, Dr. John A., 14 West Twenty-ninth Street.
Irwin, John F., 456 West Forty-first Street.
Irwin, John H., 235 Front Street.
Irwin, John P., 2102 Amsterdam Avenue.
Irwin, John V., 203 Broadway.
Irwin, Joseph E., 140 West One Hundred Third Street.
Irwin, K. L., "White Plains," New York.
Irwin, Richard, 242 West One Hundred Twelfth Street.
Irwin, Richard T., 472 West One Hundred Sixty-fifth Street.
Irwin, Robert, 343 West Forty-ninth Street.
Irwin, Robert E., 413 A. Produce Exchange.
Irwin, Robert F., 96 Wall Street.
Irwin, Robert N., 118 East One Hundred Fifteenth Street.
Irwin, Roman, 14 Barclay Street.
Irwin, Russell M., 112 Chambers Street.
Irwin, Theodore, 10 West Thirty-third Street.
Irwin, Thomas, 438 West Nineteenth Street.
Irwin, Thomas & Sons, 48 Wall Street.
Irwin, Thomas A., 226 West One Hundred Sixteenth Street.
Irwin, Thomas C., 390 Canal Street.
Irwin, Thomas H., 744 East One Hundred Forty-fifth Street.
Irwin, Thomas H., 81 Centre Street.
Irwin, Thomas H., 269 West Fifty-fourth Street.
Irwin, W. W., 210 East Twenty-third Street.
Irwin, Walter, 326 West Twenty-first Street.
Irwin, Walter W., 76 Williams Street.
Irwin, Washington, 1006 Second Avenue.
Irwin, Will J., 32 Chambers Street.
Irwin, Dr., W. J., 146 East Fifty-fifth Street.
Irwin, Will J., 155 Avenue D.
Irwin, Will T., 71 Hudson Street.
Irwin, Philips & Co., 72 Leonard Street.

PHILADELPHIA, PENNSYLVANIA.

Irvin, Albert, 5739 Ludlow Street.

Irvin, Andrew, 674 North Thirty-third Street.

Irvin, Annie, 424 North Eleventh Street.

Irvin, Benjamin B., 4639 Paschall Street.

Irvin, Cal. C., 1900 North Thirteenth Street.

Irvin, Charles, 674 North Thirty-third Street.

Irvin, Charles, 1840 Wylie Street.

Irvin, Charles, 1817 Ginnode Street.

Irvin, Charles F., Lawnton Avenue, near Sixty-sixth Avenue.

Irvin, Charles L., 920 North Thirteenth Street.

Irvin, Charles W., Lawnton Avenue, near Sixty-sixth Avenue.

Irvin, Chester, 430 North Thirty-eighth Street.

Irvin, Clarence, 1331 Miffin Street.

Irvin, David, 6124 Naudain Street.

Irvin, Edward, 1230 Potts Street.

Irvin, Edward, 2707 East Somerset Street.

Irvin, Edward, 516 East Thompson Street.

Irvin, Edwin, 914 Lombard Street.

Irvin, Elihu C., 407 Walnut Street.

Irvin, Frank, 824 North Forty-second Street.

Irvin, Frank, 1243 Belmont Avenue.

Irvin, Frank, 2546 Dover Street.

Irvin, George, 256 North Sixteenth Street.

Irvin, Gerard H., 7250 Gray's Avenue.

Irvin, Harry, 774 Martin Street.

Irvin, Harry, 1045 Daily Street.

Irvin, Isaac J., 2131 Dover Street.

Irvin, James, 2327 North Twenty-ninth Street.

Irvin, James B., 3927 Market Street.

Irvin, James C., 4223 Pechin, Roxboro.

Irvin, James H., 3634 Sansom Street.

Irvin, James L., 318 North Holly Street.

Irvin, Jared, 528 South Taney Street.

Irvin, John, 1227 Hamilton Street.

Irvin, John, 705 North Forty-third Street.

Irvin, John H., 410 Wilder Street.

Irvin, Joseph, 1718 Meadow, Frankford.

Irvin, Manus, 824 North Forty-second Street.

Irvin, Rebecca V., 1524 Arch Street.

Irvin, Richard, 4634 Chester Avenue.

Irvin, Robert, 2409 North Nappa Street.
Irvin, Samuel, 4505 Paul, Frankford.
Irvin, Spencer P., 1157 South Nineteenth Street.
Irvin, John A., 2116 East Orleans Street.
Irvin, Spencer P., Jr., 1157 South Nineteenth Street.
Irvin, Thomas, 2562 North Thirtieth Street.
Irvin, Thomas W., 2125 Natrona Street.
Irvin, Walter, 1045 Daly Street.
Irvin, Wesley, 3071 Edgemont Street.
Irvin, William, 837 North Marshall Street.
Irvin, William, 1220 Cambria Street.
Irvin, William, 524 Natrona Street.
Irvin, William, 3131 French Street.
Irvin, Will J., 2562 North Thirtieth Street.
Irvin, Will J., 7017 Tulip Street, Tacony.
Irvin, Wylie, 3242 North Front Street.
Irvine, Alexander, 2428 Carpenter Street.
Irvine, Alexander, 1420 South Twenty-second Street.
Irvine, Andrew, 2010 South Tenth Street.
Irvine, Herbert W., 3945 Baring Street.
Irvine, Edward, 223 South Thirty-third Street.
Irvine, Edwin A., 223 South Thirty-third Street.
Irvine, Edwin C., 3945 Baring Street.
Irvine, Edwin G., 1716 North Banbrey Street.
Irvine, Francis, 2007 East Sergeant Street.
Irvine, Frank, 223 Vine Street.
Irvine, George B., 4220 Otter Street.
Irvine, George B., 2428 Carpenter Street.
Irvine, Homer, 2643 North Thirtieth Street.
Irvine, Hugh, 2763 Helen Street.
Irvine, Rev. Ingram N. W., 437 North Fortieth Street.
Irvine, James, 5224 Westminster Avenue.
Irvine, James, 2025 Brainbridge Street.
Irvine, James, 1604 South Eleventh Street.
Irvine, James P., 958 Shackamaxon Street.
Irvine, John, 1009 South Twenty-first Street.
Irvine, John, 2428 Carpenter Street.
Irvine, John J., 3033 Janney Street.
Irvine, Louis, 1138 Wilder Street.
Irvine, Robert, 2763 Hilen Street.
Irvine, Robert, 1138 Wilder Street.

Irvine, Samuel, 3401 Westmoreland Street.
Irvine, Thomas, 1904 East Fifth Street.
Irvine, Walter, 1604 South Eleventh Street.
Irvine, William, 2008 Titan Street.
Irvine, William, 2007 East Sergeant Street.
Irvine, William, 3030 North Laurence Street.
Irvine, William B., 2239 Spring Garden.
Irving, A., 2127 Stewart Street.
Irving, David J., 3112 East. X.
Irving, D. Edward, 110 Chestnut Street.
Irving, George, 2324 Collins Street.
Irving, James A., 3270 Chancellor Street.
Irving, Joseph, 4365 Germantown Avenue.
Irving, Lloyd, 3533 Locust Street.
Irving, Lucas, 2325 St. Albans.
Irving, Morris, 3144 York Street.
Irving, Thomas, 4749 Pennsylvania, Frankford.
Irving, Thomas, 1022 Foulkrod, Frankford.
Irving, Vance, 245 West Chilton Avenue, Germantown.
Irving, Willard L., 3215 Sansom Street.
Irving, William H., 3110 North Carlisle Street.
Irving, William W., 3110 North Carlisle Street.
Irwin, Albert, 2237 Page Street.
Irwin, Albert H., 2446 Jefferson Street.
Irwin, Alexander D., 1623 Oxford Street.
Irwin, Andrew, 636 North Marshall Street.
Irwin, Andrew P., 830 North Forty-eighth Street.
Irwin, Andrew S., 2329 Germantown Avenue.
Irwin, Anna, 70 North Thirty-fourth Street.
Irwin, Arthur A., 23 South Thirty-fourth Street.
Irwin, Asbury E., 4737 Cedar Avenue.
Irwin, A. Wallace, 911 Farragut Terrace.
Irwin, Barton, 3328 Rhawn Bldg.
Irwin, Benjamin A., 1202 Locust Street.
Irwin, Benjamin G., 2617 North Colorado Street.
Irwin, Boyle, 70 North Thirty-fourth Street.
Irwin, Charles, 162 A "City Hall."
Irwin, Charles, 1907 Ellsworth Street.
Irwin, Charles A., 429 Chestnut Street.
Irwin, Charles J., 674 North Thirty-third Street.
Irwin, Charles M., 911 Farragut Terrace.

Irwin, Chester G., 430 North Thirty-eight Street.
Irwin, Clarence W., 2750 North Fifteenth Street.
Irwin, C. L., 1840 Wylie Street.
Irwin, David, 2072 East Rush Street.
Irwin, Dennis, 416 West Pennsylvania, Germantown.
Irwin, Edward, 806 East Allegheny Avenue.
Irwin, Edward, 1618 South Fifteenth Street.
Irwin, Edward, 217 Chestnut Street.
Irwin, Edward, 1618 South Fifteenth Street.
Irwin, Edward, 2850 North Front Street.
Irwin, Edward J., 1618 South Fifteenth Street.
Irwin, Frank, 2968 Melvale Street.
Irwin, Frank B., 5433 Master Street.
Irwin, F. H., 911 Farragut Terrace.
Irwin, George D., 2244 North Seventeenth Street.
Irwin, George G., "Broad Street Station."
Irwin, George L., 2606 North Twenty-ninth Street.
Irwin, George W., 706 North Thirty-fourth Street.
Irwin, Hallowell, 70 North Thirty-fourth Street.
Irwin, Harold D., Care L. G. Graff & Son.
Irwin, Harris E., 1509 Venango Street.
Irwin, Harry, 4312 Wayne Street.
Irwin, Harry C., 2556 North Bancroft Street.
Irwin, Harry G., 2021 North Thirtieth Street.
Irwin, Harry M., 139 North Sixty-third Street.
Irwin, Harry W., 328 North Fortieth Street.
Irwin, Henry B., 3619 Wallace Street.
Irwin, Harry M., 1613 Ranstead Street.
Irwin, Horace D., 2513 South Hicks Street.
Irwin, Hugh, 1907 Ellsworth Street.
Irwin, Ida, 2121 North Sixteenth Street.
Irwin, Isaac, 2068 North Dauphin Street.
Irwin, James, 1522 Cambridge Street.
Irwin, James, 2141 North Daggatt Street.
Irwin, James, 1912 Pt. Breeze Avenue.
Irwin, James, 1215 Ellsworth Street.
Irwin, James, 2126 Fitzwater Street.
Irwin, James, Jr., 774 Martin.
Irwin, James, Jr., 1225 South Bonsall Street.
Irwin, Dr. J. A., 12019 South Broad Street.
Irwin, James G., 1917 East Wishart Street.

Irwin, James H., 2011 Arch Street.
Irwin, James M., 2263 North Lambert Street.
Irwin, James M., 6220 Race Street.
Irwin, Dr., J. W., 1918 Vine Street.
Irwin, Jeremiah S., 909 Huntington Street.
Irwin, John, 1410 South Seventy-first Street.
Irwin, John, 1221 North Howard Street.
Irwin, John, 3804 Wallace Street.
Irwin, John, 3814 Wallace Street.
Irwin, John, 3010 Syndanham Street.
Irwin, John, 2114 Cherry Street.
Irwin, John, 516 South Thirteenth Street.
Irwin, John, 881 Pennock Street.
Irwin, J. H., 2043 North Third Street.
Irwin, J. H., 1423 Ritner Street.
Irwin, J. M., 1929 Bainbridge Street.
Irwin, J. N., 729 North Forty-third Street.
Irwin, J. P., 1742 Columbia Street.
Irwin, J. R., 2308 East Norris Street.
Irwin, J. R., 3119 Norris Street.
Irwin, J. S., 2424 Sepviva Street.
Irwin, J. T., 3010 North Syndanham Street.
Irwin, J. W., 500 Chestnut Street.
Irwin, Joseph, 2625 Oxford Street.
Irwin, J. L., 1907 Ellsworth Street.
Irwin, J. F., 2557 North Bancroft Street.
Irwin, J. R., 1502 North Twelfth Street.
Irwin, J. W., 49 North Twelfth Street.
Irwin, Louis, 3028 North Fifth Street.
Irwin, Michael, 3804 Wallace Street.
Irwin, Nathan B., 5419 Hunters Isle.
Irwin, Paul D., 2010 North Park Avenue.
Irwin, Raymond, 359 Lyceum Avenue, Roxburgh.
Irwin, Richard, 1607 Frankford Avenue.
Irwin, Richard E., 639 Tioga Street.
Irwin, R. T., 424 East Wildey Street.
Irwin, Robert, 2648 Martha Street.
Irwin, Robert, 3622 Harenford Street.
Irwin, Robert F., Care Irwin McBride & Co.
Irwin, Robert H., 415 Sharerwood Street.
Irwin, Robert S., Care A. D. Irwin & Bros.

Irwin, Samuel, 2648 Martha Street.
Irwin, Samuel F., Care L. H. Parker & Co.
Irwin, Samuel W., 14 Market Street.
Irwin, Sophia D., 2011 DeLancey Street.
Irwin, Thomas W., 5825 Arch Street.
Irwin, T. H., 1740 Green Street.
Irwin, Walter G., 4125 Woodland Avenue.
Irwin, William, 2327 North College Avenue.
Irwin, William, 3514 Warren Street.
Irwin, William, 1134 Tree Street.
Irwin, Dr. William, 634 Snyder Avenue.
Irwin, William, 1821 East Albert Street.
Irwin, W. E., 2617 North Colorado Street.
Irwin, W. H., 1419 South Seventy-first Street.
Irwin, W. H., 2043 North Third Street.
Irwin, W. H., 400 North Redfield Street.
Irwin, W. H. H., 2121 North Sixteenth Street.
Irwin, W. J., 1419 South Seventy-first Street.
Irwin, W. J., 1316 Miffin Street.
Irwin, W. J., 2043 North Third Street.
Irwin, W. J., 2243 Wilder Street.
Irwin, W. N., 1817 Orthodox, Frankford.
Irwin, W. P. M., 4717 Springfield Avenue.
Irwin, W. R., 1536 South Hicks Street.
Irwin, W. T., 2517 North Stanley Street.
Irwin, W. W., 2010 North Park Avenue.
Irwin, Wray H., 321 North Sixteenth Street.

PITTSBURGH, PENNSYLVANIA.

Irvin, Albert, 4744 Liberty Avenue.
Irvin, Cleo B., 1013 Pennsylvania Avenue.
Irvin, David S., 5023 Gertrude Street.
Irvin, Edward, 5509 Second Avenue.
Irvin, E. M., 6365 Pennsylvania Avenue.
Irvin, Frank C., 41 Sterling Avenue.
Irvin, George B., 13 Maple Terrace.
Irvin, George F., 1211 Arch Street, Allegheny.
Irvin, George O., 900 Bremsville Avenue.
Irvin, George W., 1327 Warran, Allegheny.
Irvin, Harry B., 41 Sterling, Allegheny.
Irvin, Harry R., 235 Water Street.

Irvin, Henry, 715 Magee Street.
Irvin, Hugh, 181 Shetland Street.
Irvin, J. R., 10 North Diamond E., Allegheny.
Irvin, Jay S., 41 Sterling, Allegheny.
Irvin, Jesse, 1116 Arch, Allegheny.
Irvin, J. E., 504 Smithfield Street.
Irvin, Matthew, 90 Boogs Street.
Irvin, Obediah, 178 Manton Street.
Irvin, Robert M., 7360 Fleury Street.
Irvine, Arch, 436 Seventh Avenue.
Irvine, F. C., Union Station.
Irvine, George F., 617 Liberty Avenue.
Irvine, J. W., 291 Main Street.
Irvine, James, 315 North Elizabeth Street.
Irvine, J. A. M., 291 Main Street.
Irvine, Jay, 720 Kirkpatrick Street.
Irvine, R. W., 291 Main Street.
Irvine, Samuel, 216 Elysian Street.
Irvine, William, 291 Main Street.
Irvine, William Q., 359 East, Allegheny.
Irvine, William T., Wilkinsburg.
Irving, Ira, 129 Steuben Street.
Irving, James, 6300 Penn Avenue.
Irwin, A. M., 6750 McPherson Street.
Irwin, Alexander, 412 Rebecca, Allegheny.
Irwin, A. T., 732 Maryland Street.
Irwin, A. S., 129 Forty-fourth Street.
Irwin, Annie C., Frick Building 621.
Irwin, Annie E., 516 Market Street.
Irwin, Austin J., 736 Winfield Street.
Irwin, Charles, 504 South Linden.
Irwin, Charles, 1310 Adams, Allegheny.
Irwin, Charles A., 94 Forty-fourth Street.
Irwin, Charles C., 411 Rebecca, Allegheny.
Irwin, Charles E., 2101 Bearn, Allegheny.
Irwin, D. King, 6334 Home Street.
Irwin, Edward E., 1 Freemont Place.
Irwin, Edward H., 1224 Juniata, Allegheny.
Irwin, Edward T., 837 Farragut Street.
Irwin, F. J., Union Depot.
Irwin, Frank, 1613 Irwin Avenue, Allegheny.

Irwin, Frank, 2553 Penn Avenue.
Irwin, Frank L., 1613 Irwin Avenue, Allegheny.
Irwin, Frederick, 2815 Carey Avenue.
Irwin, Frederick H., 1218 Webster Avenue.
Irwin, Frederick J., 232 Fifth Avenue.
Irwin, George A., 7445 Finance Street.
Irwin, George B., 141 Smithfield Street.
Irwin, George L., 12 Alpine Avenue, Allegheny.
Irwin, George L., 1402 Washington Avenue, Allegheny.
Irwin, George W., 4 John Street.
Irwin, George W., 416 Seventh Avenue.
Irwin, Gynn, 5463 Black Street.
Irwin, Harry, 1608 Ohio, Allegheny.
Irwin, Harry, 835 Estella Avenue.
Irwin, Harry C., 1224 Juniata, Allegheny.
Irwin Harry C., care of St. Charles Hotel.
Irwin, Harvey F., 536 Winfield Street.
Irwin, Henry J., 621 Frick Building.
Irwin, H. T., Rosedale Foundry & Machine Company.
Irwin, Harry C., 1707 Anott Building.
Irwin, Hugh L., 146 Sixth Street.
Irwin, J. W., 4908 Penn Avenue.
Irwin, J. A., 4744 Liberty Avenue.
Irwin, J. Charles, 5463 Black Street.
Irwin, Dr. J. K., Smith Block.
Irwin, Jacob W., 268 Forty-sixth Street.
Irwin, James, 817 St. James Street.
Irwin, James, 16 Lacock East, Allegheny.
Irwin, James A., 732 Maryland Avenue.
Irwin, James B., 7724 Juniata.
Irwin, James C., 1926 Lithgow Avenue, Allegheny.
Irwin, James E., 7438 Susquehanna.
Irwin, James H., Room 5, 405 Grant.
Irwin, James J., 152 Henderson, Allegheny.
Irwin, James L., Aralon, Pennsylvania.
Irwin, James M., 5159 Butler Street.
Irwin, James S., 411 Smithfield Street.
Irwin, James S., Jr., 411 Smithfield Street.
Irwin, James V., 435 Sixth Avenue.
Irwin, Jane, 2016 Wylie Avenue.
Irwin, John, 132 Henderson, Allegheny.

Irwin, John, 119 Mayflower Street.
Irwin, John, 6407 Penn Avenue.
Irwin, John, 816 Rebecca, Allegheny.
Irwin, John, 5218 Gertrude Street.
Irwin, J. A., 400 Smithfield Street.
Irwin, J. B., 1224 Juniata, Allegheny.
Irwin, J. D., 2072 Lytle Street.
Irwin, J. F., 4 John Street.
Irwin, J. M., 4627 Center Avenue.
Irwin, J. M., 318 Fourth Avenue.
Irwin, J. T., 435 Liberty Avenue.
Irwin, Joseph, 5463 Black Street.
Irwin, Joseph, 245 Carroll, Allegheny.
Irwin, Joseph, 2553 Penn Avenue.
Irwin, Dr. J. C., 802 Penn Avenue.
Irwin, Laurence H., 537 Turrett Street.
Irwin, Lewis L., 237 Fourth Avenue.
Irwin, Mary M., 405 Grant Street.
Irwin, Maude, 826 Federal, Allegheny.
Irwin, Minnie, 537 Turrett Street.
Irwin, Oscar, 133 Pearl Street.
Irwin, Paul S., 1215 Boyle, Allegheny.
Irwin, Paul W., 1408 Keystone Building.
Irwin, R. S., 32 Davis Street.
Irwin, Robert, 31 Diamond Square.
Irwin, Dr. R. J. A., 1823 Webster Avenue.
Irwin, S. Atwood, 1 Mansion Street.
Irwin, Samuel, 1238 Winter, Allegheny.
Irwin, Samuel, 163 Auburn Street.
Irwin, Samuel C., 524 Penn Avenue.
Irwin, Thomas F., 526 Graham Street.
Irwin, Thomas J. B., 3000 Liberty Avenue.
Irwin, Thomas P., 405 Southern Avenue.
Irwin, Thomas W., 1318 Frick Building.
Irwin, Thomas W., 411 Rebecca, Allegheny.
Irwin, W. M., 426 Pennsylvania Avenue.
Irwin, Walter, 417 Liberty Avenue.
Irwin, Walter, 908 Pennsylvania Avenue.
Irwin, William, 245 Dinwiddie Street.
Irwin, William, 504 South Linden Street.
Irwin, William G., 4126 Butler Street.

Irwin, William H:, 625 Collins Street.
Irwin, William H., 2 Wood Street.
Irwin, William H., 708 Cedar Avenue, Allegheny.
Irwin, William Q., 2007 East Avenue, Allegheny.
Irwin, Wylie E., 64 Almeda Street.

SAN FRANCISCO, CALIFORNIA.

Irvine, Nathaniel, 1760 Jackson Street.
Irvine, Thomas, 521 Post Street.
Irvine, Thomas, 155 Lexington Avenue.
Irvine, West, 1162 Golden Gate Avenue.
Irvine, William A., Occidental Hotel.
Irvine, William B., 3721 Twenty-second Street.
Irvine, William H., 1578 Jackson Street.
Irvine, William L., 730 Pine Street.
Irving, Andrew H., 1626 Waller Street.
Irving, Arthur J., 130 Fourth Street.
Irving, Benjamin, 936 Valencia Street.
Irving, George H., 766 Bryant Street.
Irving, Harry A., 810 O'Farrell Street.
Irving, James, 1168½ Church Street.
Irving, James, 766 Bryant Street.
Irving, James, 1502½ Stockton Street.
Irving, James S., 766 Bryant Street.
Irving, Joseph F., 518 Brannan Street.
Irving, Milvin W., 457 Stevenson Street.
Irving, M. Scott, Tennessee and Twenty-second Street.
Irving, Miss Caroline B., Tennessee and Twenty-second Street.
Irving, Samuel, 324 California Street.
Irving, Samuel C., 24 Second Street.
Irving, William F., 1523 Scott Street.
Irwin, Abraham, 830 Capp Street.
Irwin, A. C. (Marysville, California).
Irwin, Charles M., 466 Page Street.
Irwin, Clifford E., 815 Valencia Street.
Irwin, Clyde W., 3239 Twenty-first Street.
Irwin, David, 1501 Scott Street.
Irwin, Edward H., 1356 Geary Street.
Irwin, Elmer, 530 Eddy Street.
Irwin, Elton, 602 McAllister Street.
Irwin, Francis T., 1428 Montgomery Street.

Irwin, Garland J., 530 Eddy Street.

Irwin, Harry J., Berkeley.

Irwin, Harry O., 631 Union Street.

Irwin, Harry S., Otis Elevator Co.

Irwin, James, Lorin, California.

Irwin, James, 522 Stevenson Street.

Irwin, James, 3610 Sixteenth Street.

Irwin, James, 608 Sixth Street.

Irwin, James B., 720 Eighteenth Street.

Irwin, James E., care of Hirsch & Keirer.

Irwin, Jewell, 1806 Laguna Street.

Irwin, Joseph N. H., 123 Ellis Street.

Irwin, Miss Marie, 3857 Clay Street.

Irwin, Woody C., 1500 Kentucky Street.

Irwin, Nicholas, 262 Octavia.

Irwin, Raymond, 3239 Twenty-first Street.

Irwin, T. A., 530 Eddy Street.

Irwin, Thomas, care of Gulf Bag Company.

Irwin, Tobias, 532 Montgomery.

Irwin, Wallace, 1625 Taylor.

Irvin, Charles, Steamer, Valencia.

Irvin, Henry, 5 Bennington Street.

Irvin, James, 446 Chestnut Street.

Irvin, Thomas J., 406 Sutter Street.

Irvin, William B., 214 Grove Street.

Irvine, Alexander, 1012 Fillmore Street.

Irvine, Bros., 263 Fourth Street.

Irvine, Darwin W., 1611 Waller Street.

Irvine, Felix H., 410 Post Street.

Irvine, Henry E., 1059 Broadway.

Irvine, James, 308 Page Street.

Irvine, James S., Alameda.

Irvine, James W., 1111 Steiner Street.

Irvine, J. C. &. Co., 751 Market Street.

Irvine, John, 1170 Mission Street.

Irvine, John, 709 York Street.

Irvine, John, 103 Grant Avenue.

Irvine, John, Jr., 2317 Jackson Street.

Irvine, John C., 3841 Eighteenth Street.

Irvine, Joseph, 1760 Jackson Street.

Irvine, Leigh H., 624 Golden Gate Avenue.

Irwin, William A., 602 McAllister Street.
Irwin, William G., 2180 Washington Street.
Irwin, William H., 1041½ Vallejo Street.

ST. LOUIS, MISSOURI.

Irvan, John, 1225 Morrison Avenue.
Irvan, Aaron, 2609 Allen Avenue.
Irvin, Clarence, 1521 Benton Street.
Irvin, Dearwood, 4135 Westminister Place.
Irvin, Eck, 4135 Westminister Place.
Irvin, Frank, 2509 North Spring Avenue.
Irvin, Frank B., 2730 Tamm Avenue.
Irvin, F. N., 1521 Benton Street.
Irvin, Hattie C., 1705 Gratiot Street.
Irvin, James, 3106 Manchester Avenue.
Irvin, Jasper, 1521 Benton Street.
Irvin, Leslie A., 4135 Westminster Place.
Irvin, Lyman E., 3650 Finney Avenue.
Irvin, Nathaniel R., 4592 Cottage Avenue.
Irvine, Louis C., care of Hotel Montecello.
Irvine, Walter F., 4958 St. Louis Avenue.
Irvine, Robert, 1524 Morgan Street.
Irving, Adolphus, 1113 High Street.
Irving, Charles F., 4283 Finney Avenue.
Irving, Elizabeth M., 5115 Ridge Avenue.
Irving, George A., 2120 Finney Avenue.
Irving, Gordon, 811 Locust Avenue.
Irving, James M., 811 Locust Avenue.
Irving, Jennie, 512 Montrose Avenue.
Irving, John W., 512 Montrose Avenue.
Irving, Josephine, 938 Rutget Street.
Irving, R. M., 811 Locust Street.
Irving, Samuel R., 2710 Lawton Avenue.
Irving, William W., 5115 Ridge Avenue.
Irwin, Almee, 715 North Compton Avenue.
Irwin, Andrew H., 3115 New Ashland-Place.
Irwin, Charles J., care of Irwin & Co.
Irwin, Charles W., 5899 Clemens Avenue.
Irwin, Chauncy F., 5899 Clemens Avenue.
Irwin, Clarence, 3939 Evans Avenue.
Irwin, Clarence E., 421 Oliver Street.

Irwin, Daisy M., 4470 Morgan Street.
Irwin, David L., 1429 North Park Place.
Irwin, Frank, 904 Chestnut Street.
Irwin, George W., 4212 Gratiot Street.
Irwin, Gertrude H., 4147 McPherson Avenue.
Irwin, Grace M., 4147 McPherson Avenue.
Irwin, Henry, 2120 O'Fallon Street.
Irwin, James, 4403 Fyler Avenue.
Irwin, James S., 3200 Oliver Street.
Irwin, James T., 3974 Evans Avenue.
Irwin, James W., care of Irwin & Lane.
Irwin, John B., 220 A South Twelfth Street.
Irwin, John J., care of Irwin & Co.
Irwin, Joseph, 2023 Oliver Street.
Irwin, Dr. Jud D., 803 Pine Street.
Irwin, Dr. J. Max, 536 North Taylor Avenue.
Irwin, L. Beaumont, 3519 Lucas Avenue.
Irwin, Ruth, 3153 Portis Avenue.
Irwin, Ruth, 3670 Finney Avenue.
Irwin, Thomas, 407 North Broadway.
Irwin, Thomas J., care of Carleton Hotel.
Irwin, Wade, 2205 South Tenth Street.
Irwin, Walger, 1519 Clark Avenue.
Irwin, William A., 3911A Sherman Avenue.
Irwin, William H., 5801 Old Manchester Road.
Irwin, William H., 1429 North Park Place.
Irwin, William R., 715 North Compton Avenue.
Irwin, William T., 1016 Market Street.
Irwin, William T., 709 Pine Street.
Irwin, William W., 716 North Compton Avenue.

ST. PAUL, MINNESOTA.

Irwin, Charles M., 45½ The Angus.
Irwin, Hugh, care of J. B. Buckley.
Irwin, John W., Bemidjie, Minnesota.
Irwin, Miss May H., 605 Miss Street.
Irwin, Dr. W. H., 908 Dayton Avenue.
Irwin, I. H., 202 Glencoe Street.
Irwin, Monsier, 348 South Roberts Street.
Irwin, Thomas, 348 South Roberts Street.
Erwin, Andrew, 2417 Pym Street.

Erwin, G. J., 854 Raymond Avenue.
Erwin, L. L., 154 Carroll Street.
Erwin, Miss May, 2417 Pym Street.
Erwin, Robert, 1010 Marshall Avenue.
Erwin, R. W., 154 Carroll Street.
Erwin, W. F., 154 Carroll Street.
Irwin, Dr., Baraboo, Wisconsin.
McDowell, Albert L., 1047 Earl Street.
McDowell, G. D., 559 Marion Street.
McDowell, Gordon, 992 Lincoln Avenue.
McDowell, Miss H. B., 75 Summit Avenue.
McDowell, H. S., care of Pullman Company.
McDowell, J. B., 254 Farrington Avenue.
McDowell, J. R., 600 St. Anthony Avenue.
McDowell, Mrs. Nelly, 992 Lincoln Avenue.
McDowell, Miss Maud, 335 East Seventh Street.
McDowell, R. G., 992 Lincoln Avenue.
McDowell, William A., 1047 Earl Street.
McDowell, William J., 335 East Seventh Street.
Irvin, George P., 667 West Central Avenue.
Irvin, Mrs. Mary, Merchants Hotel.
Irvine, Cecil C., 390 North St. Albans Street.
Irvine, Clover G., 1935 Rondo Street.
Irvine, Eugene R., 343 Iglehart Street.
Irvine, Thomas, 212 Nat'l G. A.
Irvine, H. H., Bank Building.
Irvine, Frank E., 563 St. Peter Street.
Irvine, John B., 508 Globe Building.
Irvine, Mrs. Louise C., 1046 Hastings Avenue.
Irvine, Miss Maybelle, 343 Iglehart Street.
Irvine, Mrs. Minnie L., 390 North St. Albans Street.
Irvine, Robert, 865 Hague Avenue.
Irvine, William H., 908 Dayton Avenue.
Irving, Charles, 760 St. Anthony Avenue.
Irving, Edwin M., Coates Hotel St. Peters Street.
Irving, James, 760 St. Anthony Avenue.
Irving, John, Co-Operative Grocery Company.
Irving, Robert, 1010 Marshall Avenue.
Irving, Thomas, Great Northern Shops.
Irving, William, 1 S. Burcher Avenue, South Park.
Boyd, Alice, 391 Eighth Street.

Boyd, Allen, 402 North Dale Street.
Boyd, Charles, 11 East Jessamine Street.
Boyd, Clara C., 1036 Westminster Street.
Boyd, Edward A., 1036 Burr Street.
Boyd, Essie W., 37 The Buckingham.
Boyd, Frederick E., 2181 St. Anthony Avenue.
Boyd, George B., 291 W. Central Avenue.
Boyd, James, 944 Marshall Avenue.
Boyd, James H., 291 West Central Avenue.
Boyd, John H., 994 Lincoln Avenue.
Boyd, Joseph B., care of W. H. Rhoads.
Boyd, Lavinia, 958 South Robert Street.
Boyd, Leon, 599 Rice Street.
Boyd, L. Benson, Hotel Sherman.
Boyd, Mark M., 1069 Earl Street.
Boyd, Mrs. Mary J., 1069 Earl Street.
Boyd, Oscar E., Merchants Hotel.
Boyd, Reuben S., 542 Westminster Street.
Boyd, Robert S., 705 Farrington Avenue.
Boyd, Thomas J., 337½ Winifried Street.
Boyd, Walter B., 70 West Jessamine Street.
Boyd, William J., 163 Baker Street.

WASHINGTON, DISTRICT OF COLUMBIA.

Irvin, Anna, 1845 Vernon Avenue, S. W.
Irvin, Frank, 620 Pennsylvania Avenue, N. W.
Irvin, James, 1613 O, N. W.
Irvin, John, 10 Patterson, N. E.
Irvin, Joseph, 716 Eleventh Avenue, N. W.
Irvin, Sadie, wid. James, 637 S, N. W.
Irvin, Thomas, 829 Twenty-sixth, N. W.
Irvin, William B., 1729 New York Avenue.
Irvine, Alfred C., 409 New Jersey Avenue, S. E.
Irvine, Daniel L., 311 Twelfth, N. W.
Irvine, Rev. J. E., 1412 Sixth, N. W.
Irvine, Martin E., 917 First, S. E.
Irvine, William J., 205 G, N. E.
Irvine, Benjamin, 754 Harvard, N. W.
Irvine, Alfred C., 2717 Thirteenth, N. W
Irvine, Daniel L., 311 Twelfth, N. W.
Irvine, Edith M., 1505 Caroline, N. W.

Irving, Amos, 331 Wilson, N. W.
Irving, Benjamin, Fifth corner Morrison, N. W.
Irving, C. W., 516 Thirteenth, N. W.
Irving, Henry, 1749 U, N. W.
Irving, Henry C., 410 D, S. E.
Irving, James, 1101 Half Street, Court, N. W.
Irving, Jane, 1602 Twelfth, N. W.
Irving, Jennie E., 311 Wilson, N. W.
Irving, John, 1737 F, N. W.
Irving, John A., 1201 Madison, N. W.
Irving, John E., 627 Eighth, N. E.
Irving, John B., 627 Eighth, N. E.
Irving, John D., 814 Connecticut Avenue, N. W.
Irving, J. Grant, 18 O, N. W.
Irving, Minnie, 1143 First, N. W.
Irving, M. Lee, 917 First, S. E.
Irving, Thomas W., 1621 O, N. W.
Irving, Walter, 620 I, N. W.
Irving, William, 321 A, N. E.
Irving, William, Congress Heights.
Irvins, Allen, 412 Second, S. W.
Irwin, Albert, 2117 Fifth Street, N. E.
Irwin, Anna G., Navy Department.
Irwin, David A., 1300 Pennsylvania Avenue, N. W.
Irwin, F. Louise, 2143 K, N. W.
Irwin, Harry C., 1322 South Capitol.
Irwin, Harvey S., House of Representatives.
Irwin, James, 1613 O, N. W.
Irwin, James H., 23 Third, N. E.
Irwin, Joseph L., 1734 Thirty-fourth, N. W.
Irwin, Mary, 2477, Eighteenth, N. W.
Irwin, Mary B., 317 C., N. W.
Irwin, Richard L., 908 New Hampshire Avenue, N. W.
Irwin, Thomas J., 829 Twenty-sixth, N. W.
Irwin, William M., 1704 Nineteenth, N. W.
Irwin, William N., 904 K, N. W.
Irwin, Anna G., 1101 Seventeenth, N. W.
Irwin, David A., 1300 Pennsylvania Avenue, N. W.
Irwin, Harry C., 1322 South Capitol.
Irwin, W. Paul, 301 Delaware Avenue, N. E.
Irwin, H. Linton, 1825 Second, N. E.

Irwin, Thomas, 1233 Twelfth, N. W.

Irwin, James H., 23 Third, N. E.

Irwin, Thomas, 829 Twenty-sixth, N. W.

Irwin, Joseph L., 1707 Thirty-fourth, N. W.

Irwin, Thomas J., 1420 Kenesaw Avenue, N. W.

Irwin, Mary, 2477 Eighteenth, N. W.

Irwin, William M., U. S. N., 1704 Ninteenth, N. W.

Irwin, Mary B., Nurse Children's Hospital.

Irwin, William N., The Mt. Vernon Hotel.

Irwin, Minnie L., The Mt. Vernon.

Irwin, Rebecca, 1763 Madison, N. W.

Irwin, Susan, 1101 Seventeenth, N. W.

LAWYERS OF THE CLAN.

Irwin & Irwin, Placerville, Califorina.

Irwin, George W., Sanford, Colorado.

Irwin, W. B., Irving, Kansas.

Irwin, S. D., Tionesta, Pennsylvania.

Irwin & Bridges, Aberdeen, Washington.

Irwin & Hardy, Northampton, Massachusetts

Irwin, James M., Moulton, Alabama.

Irwin, J. L. C., Nanford, California.

Irwin, R., Nanford, California.

Irwin, G. M., Colorado Springs, Colorado.

Irvine, Thomas A., Denver, Colorado.

Irwin, John R., Dawson, Georgia.

Irwin, J. T., Jr., Washington, Georgia.

Irwin, S. R., Bloomington, Illinois.

Irwin, G. P., Normal, Illinois.

Erwin, Dore B., Decatur, Indiana.

Erwin, R. K., Decatur, Indiana.

Irwin, R. W., Frankfort, Indiana.

Irvin, William, Indianapolis, Indiana.

Irvin, Walter, Wabash, Indiana.

Irwin & Hultberg, Sioux City, Iowa.

Irwin, W. W., 457 Madison Avenue, Grand Rapids, Michigan.

Irwin, F. C., Belleplaine, Minnesota.

Irwin, H. D., Phœnix Building, Minneapolis, Minnesota.

Irwin, H. B., DeSoto, Missouri.

Irving, W. V., 13 North Pearl, Albany, New York.

Irving, J. J., Binghampton, New York.

Irwin, Charles, Kingston, New York.
Irwin, Roscoe, Kingston, New York.
Irwin, William R., Akron, Ohio.
Irvin, F. Snyder, Circleville, Ohio.
Irwin, D. P., Greensville, Ohio.
Irwin & Japp, Lawton, Oklahoma Territory.
Irvine, Hayes, Bedford, Pennsylvania.
Irwin, Blake E., Brooksville, Pennsylvania.
Irwin, J. M., Hollidaysburg, Pennsylvania.
Irvine, J. J., Chattanooga, Tennessee.
Erwin, J. W., Derby, Vermont.

DOCTORS OF THE CLAN.

Erwin, Douglas, Fidelity, Illinois.
Erwin, O. P., Medora, Illinois.
Erwin, C. H., Adel, Iowa.
Erwin, Ralph, Malone, New York.
Erwin, Alvan O., Bloomingburg, Ohio.
Erwin, C. W., Erwinton, South Carolina.
Erwin, Charles L., Newport Center, Vermont.
Erwin, Francis H., Ashland, Wisconsin.
Erwin, John C., McKinney, Texas.
Erwin, J. E., Milton, West Virginia.
Erwin, M. M., Powder Springs, Texas.
Erwin, Philip O., Big Sandy, Texas.
Erwin, Thomas T., Hempstead, Texas.
Erwin, William, Hearne, Texas.
Erwin, John H., Kaufman, Texas.
Irvin, George, Aledo, Illinois.
Irvin, C. E., Goodwin, Texas.
Irvin, Edgar H., El Paso, Texas.
Irvin, James S., Danville, Virginia.
Irvin, Orlando C., El Paso, Texas.
Irvine, John F., Tolsboro, Kentucky.
Irvine, William P., McKinney, Texas.
Irvine, Alexander, Coopers, West Virginia.
Irvine, J. Sinkler, Ervington, Virginia.
Irvine, Wesley, Royalton, Wisconsin.
Irvine, William P., Mabank, Texas.
Irwin, N. F., Millerville, Alabama.
Irvin, Thomas H., Moulton, Alalbama.

Irwin, Samuel W., New Britain, Connecticut.
Irwin, Thomas L., Jacksonville, Florida.
Irwin, Joseph A., Iuka, Illinois.
Irwin, Charles N., Mount Sterling, Illinois.
Irwin, Edward M., New Athens, Illinois.
Irwin, Went L., Plymouth, Illinois.
Irwin, Oliver H., Sheldon, Illinois.
Irwin, Samuel G., Crawfordsville, Indiana.
Irwin, Albert J., Goshen, Indiana.
Irwin, Vincent J., Springfield, Mass.
Irwin, George W., Detroit, Michigan.
Irwin, John L., Detroit, Michigan.
Irwin, Thomas C., Grand Rapids, Michigan.
Irwin, Alexander F., Minneapolis, Minnesota.
Irwin, Ralph J., Hastings, Nebraska.
Irwin, F. C., Cranford, New Jersey.
Irwin, Frank K., Newark, New Jersey.
Irwin, Rowland C., Binghampton, New York.
Irwin, Samuel B., West Hebron, New York.
Irwin, R. W., Stout, Ohio.
Irwin, Hanis J., Baraboo, Wisconsin.
Irwin, Bernstine S., Mauch Chunk, Pennsylvania.
Irwin, Alexander, Wallis Station, Texas.
Irwin, Alexander W., Fairview, Texas.
Irwin, B. C., Springdale, Pennsylvania.
Irwin, George G., Mt. Holly Springs, Pennsylvania.
Irwin, George H., Lodi, Wisconsin.
Irwin, James Q., Halls, Tennessee.
Irwin, James W., Marrions Mark, Pennsylvania.
Irwin, J. B., Washington, Pennsylvania.
Irwin, J. Kennedy, Washington, Pennsylvania.
Irwin, Lute B., Economy, Tennessee.
Irwin, Robert C., Harrisburg, Pennsylvania.
Irwin, Thaddeus S., Christiana, Pennsylvania.
Irwin, Thomas A., Erie, Pennsylvania.
Irwin, William B., Churchtown, Pennsylvania.
Irwin, William V., Julian, Pennsylvania.
Irving, E. W., Memphis, Tennessee.
Irving, Samuel M., Meems, Virginia.
Irving, Paulus A., Richmond, Virginia.
Irving, Walter W., Milwaukee, Wisconsin.

Irvine, Maj. R. J. C., War Department, Washington, D. C.
Irvin, Capt. Francis G., War Department, Washington, D.C.

MISCELLANEOUS MEMBERS AND CONNECTIONS OF FAMILY.

Irvin, Robert T., Vista, California.
Irvin, Thomas J., 25 Broad Avenue, New York City.
Irvin, Rev. William, D. D., President Union Club, New York City.
Irvin, George W., New York Athletic Club, New York City.
Irvin, James, New York Athletic Club, New York City.
Irvin, Captain Robert J. C., Army and Navy Club, New York City.
Irvine, William, Montauk Club, New York City.
Irving, Alexander D., Union Club, New York City.
Irving, Alexander D., Jr., Union Club, New York City.
Irving, A. H., Jr., Underwriters' Club, New York City.
Irving, Cirtlandt, Society Col. Marr, New York City.
Irving, Henry S., St. Nicholas Club, New York City.
Irving, John, Road Drivers' Association, New York City.
Irving, John D., Coll. Alum. Association, New York City.
Irving, John T., Authors' Club, New York City.
Irving, John, Jr., West Side Rep. Club, New York City.
Irving, Pierre F., Glencoe, Maryland.
Irving, Richard A., Confed. Vet. Camp, New York City.
Irving, Robert Page, New York South Street, New York City.
McKelway, St. Clair, 21 Monroe Place, Brooklyn, New York.
McKelway, George Irvine, 21 Monroe Place, Brooklyn, New York.
McKelway, George H., 104 Columbia Heights, Brooklyn, New York.
Erving, M. Van R., Soc. Col. Marr, New York City.
Erving, John, 37 Wall Street, New York City.
Erving, John L., Sons of Rer., New York City.
Erwin, Charles H., Marine and Field Club, New York City.
Erwin, Professor F. A., 32 Marnly Place, New York City.
Erwin, James S., Lawyer Club, New York City.
Erwin, J. A., Manhattan Club, New York City.
Erwin, Robert G., Manhattan Club, New York City.
Irving, Walter, New York Historical Society, New York City.
Irving, Washington, Short Hills, New Jersey.
Irving, Walter E., 1133 Broadway, New York City.
Irwin, Dudley M., Board of Trade, Buffalo, New York.
Irwin, Edward W., Reform Club, New York City.
Irwin, E. N., U. of P. Club., New York City.
Irwin, Captain J. G., Army and Navy Club, New York City.

Irwin, George W., 32 Liberty Street, New York City.

Irwin, G. M., Road Drivers' Associaton, New York City.

Irwin, Henry, Jr., 187 Montague, Brooklyn, New York.

Irwin, J. B., Union League Club, New York City.

Irwin, John, Arkwright Club, New York City.

Irwin, Dr. J. A., New York Academy of Medicine, New York City.

Irwin, L. H., Cres. Athletic Club, Brooklyn, New York.

Irwin, Robert Easton, 16 Gramercy Park, New York City.

Irwin, S. N., M. D., New York Phy., M. A., Assn., New York City.

Irwin, Theodore D., Yale Club, New York City.

Irwin, William, 1070 Lexington Avenue, New York City.

Irvin, Effingham T., Harvard Club, New York City.

Irvin, Richard, University Club, New York City.

Harris, Mrs. T. E., Green Bay, Wisconsin.

Robinson, Miss Abbey, Green Bay, Wisconsin.

Martin, Mrs. Wilson, Belle Plains, Minnesota.

Clemens, Renaldo, Erie, Pennsylvania.

Irwin, Dr. John, New York City.

Irwin, Mrs. C. K., Milwaukee, Wisconsin.

Irwin, H. A., Le Mais, Iowa.

Wilder, Mrs. Milton, Melrose, Kansas.

Irwin, Wallace, San Francisco, California.

Irwin, Miss Agnes, Cambridge, Massachusetts.

Irwin, Dr. John L., Detroit, Michigan.

Irwin, James, Mt. Clemens, Michigan.

Irwin, Dr. A. J., Goshen, Indiana.

Irwin, Frank, New Haven, Connecticut.

Ware, Mrs. Fred, Sioux City, Missouri.

Holbrook, Mrs., Owama, Missouri.

Wheelock, Mrs. Kate, New York City.

Calhoun, Mrs. W. A., Buffalo, New York.

Tabor, Mrs. William, Albany, New York.

Upton, Mrs. E. L., Albany, New York.

Barnum, Colonel William, Chicago, Illinois.

Irving, Colonel J. B., Chicago, Illinois.

Irwin, Mr. ——, Maywood, Illinois.

Irwin, Frank C., Oak Park, Illinois.

Strong, Colonel William, Kenosha, Wisconsin.

Cowper, Mrs. A., 78 Seeley Avenue, Chicago, Illinois.

Leech, Mrs. N. H., 3810 Elmwood Avenue, Chicago, Illinois.

Valleau, Mrs. Emily W., 5944 Erie Street, Chicago, Illinois.

Palmer, Mrs. Mary W., 112 Madison Avenue, New York City.

Ellis, Mrs. Helen S., "Fox Hill," Bryn Mawr, Pennsylvania.

Bowles, Harry S., Freeport, Illinois.

Reed, Mrs. R., 1303 Scott St., Covington, Kentucky.

Reed, Mrs. George H., 818 Scott Street, Covington, Kentucky.

Irvine, Walter Vail, Cochecton, New York.

Irvine & Green, Redwine, Minnesota.

Irwin, C. W., Belleplaine, Minnesota.

Irwin, D. O., Lake City, Minnesota.

Irwin, G. W., & Son, Oklahoma City, Oklahoma Territory.

Irwin, G. W., Parker, Oklahoma Territory.

Irvine, F. S., Prague, Oklahoma, Territory.

Erwin, G. W., Russell, Oklahoma, Territory.

Erwin, E., Shawnee, Oklahoma Territory.

Marlow & Irving, Braggs, Indian Territory.

Erwin, J. T., Lodi, Indian Territory.

Irwin & Son, Newburg, Indian Territory.

Irvin, D. H., Tishomingo, Indian Territory.

Irwin & Sons, Lexington, Illinois.

Erwin, F. C., Hampton, Minnesota.

Erwin, G. B., Fairbanks, Alaska.

Irvin, C. G., Robbinsdale, Minnesota.

Irvine, Miss Nellie, Kansas City, Missouri.

Upton, Mrs. E. L., "Larchmere," Waukegan, Illinois.

Bunum, Col. William, Lakota Hotel, Chicago, Illinois.

Erving, Mrs. H., 178 Cleveland Avenue.

Irwin, Mrs. John, 370 Wood Avenue, Montreal, Canada.

Irwin, Robert, 50 Beaver Hall Building, Montreal, Canada.

Irwin, Alexander James, Port Colborne, Ontario, Canada.

Irwin, F. Herbert, Mishawaka, Indiana.

Irwin, H. D., 713–715 Phœnix Building, Minneapolis, Minnesota.

Irwin, James P., 137 West Eighteenth Street, Erie, Pennsylvania.

Boyd, Dr. John H., Evanston, Illinois.

Erwin, Dr. F. H., Washburn, Wisconsin.

Irwin, Frank, Goshen, Indiana.

Johnston, Dr. Christopher, 2138 Oak Street, Baltimore,

Irwin, Miss Alice, 300 Union Street Southeast, Minneapolis Minnesota.

Irwin, Mr. J. Holmes, Mifflintown, Pennsylvania.

Irvin, Dr. F. H., Mishawaka, Indiana.

Irwin, Dr. C. S., Elsberry, Missouri.

Irvin, George L., 1702 Park Avenue, Baltimore.

Irvin, Lawrence, 1409 Aisquith Street, Baltimore, Maryland.

Irvin, Patrick H., 24 East Madison Street, Baltimore, Maryland.

Irwin, Mrs., 805 Western Avenue, Allegheny, Pennsylvania.

Irwin, Miss Ida R., Irwin Avenue, Allegheny, Pennsylvania.

Irwin, Miss L. Beaumont, granddaughter of old Dr. William Beaumont, St. Louis, Mo.

Whitney, Mrs. T. D., Buena Park, Illinois.

Strong, Col. W. A., Kenosha, Wisconsin.

McDowell, Miss Mary, 4638 Ashland Avenue, Chicago, Illinois.

Irwin, Mrs. May, Franklin, Pennsylvania.

Green, Mrs. A. H., 2106 Calumet Avenue, Chicago, Illinois.

Irwin, Mr. Dudley M., Sommers Street, Buffalo, New York.

Irwin, Miss Eula, Knoxville, Tennessee.

Maywell, Mrs. M. E., 3980 Lake Avenue, Chicago, Illinois.

Johnston, Mrs. James, 3340 Vernon Avenue, Chicago, Illinois.

Irwin, Mr. C. K., 133 Seventeeth Street, Milwaukee, Wisconsin.

McDowell, Mrs. J. A., 840 West Adams Street, Creston, Iowa.

Irwin, Rev. C. H., 56 Paternoster Row, E. C., London, England.

Irwin, Miss Edith, Royal Terrace House, Kingstown, Co., Dublin, Ireland.

Irwin, Rev. J., Chaplain of South Dublin Union, and Rector of St. James, Dublin, Ireland.

Irwin, Miss H., Derrygore Castle, Ireland, and 5 Newton Mansion, Queen's Club Gardens, West London, England.

Irwin, Mr., Castle Ballinghorn, Co. South, Ireland.

Irwin, Bankers, Wexford, Co. Wexford, Ireland.

CARLISLES OF LOUISVILLE, KENTUCKY.

Carlisle, Ada.

Carlisle, Arnold A.

Carlisle, Edward.

Carlisle, Elizabeth, widow of William.

Carlisle, Emma E.

Carlisle, Francis M., 2006 Tenth Street.

Carlisle, George C.

Carlisle, Horace G., 1522 West Oak.

Carlisle, Levi.

BOYDS AND MCDOWELLS IN ST. PAUL AND MINNEAPOLIS.

McDowell, Mrs. H., Flat 2, 1825 Elliot Avenue.

MacDowell, H. L., 2414 Fourth Avenue, South.

McDowell, Charles, 437 Erie Street.
McDowell, E. H., 1411 Northeast Sixth Street.
McDowell, F. H., 2010 Polk Street.
McDowell, F. G., 2608 Third Avenue, South.
McDowell, George, 2419 Emerson, North.
McDowell, Mrs. Mary, 2608 Third Avenue, South.
McDowell, W. A., 2429 Nicollet Avenue.

MAXWELLS, MCDOWELLS, AND MCELROYS IN CHICAGO.

Maxwell, Albert H., 8354 Kerfoot Avenue.
Maxwell, Mrs. A. M., 4058 Ridge Avenue.
Maxwell, Miss Amy, 5237 Cornell Avenue.
Maxwell, Miss A. C., 3672 Auburn Street.
Maxwell, Archer, 6342 S. Paulina Street.
Maxwell, A. B., 6108 Ellis Avenue.
Maxwell, A. W., 697 West Lake Street.
Maxwell, A. R., 365 Ashland Boulevard.
Maxwell, A. W., 406, 203 Michigan Avenue.
Maxwell, B. W., 8354 Kerfoot Avenue.
Maxwell, Mrs. C. E., 289 Sixty-sixth Place.
Maxwell, Mrs. Carrie, 280 West Ravenswood Park.
Maxwell, Carroll, 699 West Lake Street.
Maxwell, Mrs. Catherine, 73 South Sangamon Street.
Maxwell, Mrs. C. A., 623 Forty-first Street.
Maxwell, C. C., 2716 North Lincoln Street.
Maxwell, C. D., 4049 Ellis Avenue.
Maxwell, C. E., 77 Forty-seventh Street.
Maxwell, C. E., 6224 Madison Avenue.
Maxwell, C. J., 4723 Prairie Avenue.
Maxwell, C. K., 4058 Ridge Avenue.
Maxwell, David, 6637 South Sangamon, Street.
Maxwell, D. G., 538 Cleveland Avenue.
Maxwell, D. H., 73 North Wood Street.
Maxwell, David, 784 Carroll Avenue.
Maxwell, D. L., 3310 Cottage Grove Avenue.
Maxwell, E. G., Grand Pacific Hotel.
Maxwell, E. D., 40 Plum Street.
Maxwell, E. E., 3980 Lake Avenue.
Maxwell, E. L., 18 Walnut Street.
Maxwell, E. E., 188 Emerson Avenue.
Maxwell, Mrs. E. P., 266 Chestnut Street.

Maxwell, Miss E. R., Ellis Avenue Northwest Corner Fifty-third Street.

Maxwell, Eugene, 699 West Lake Street.

Maxwell, Miss Fannie, 1537 North Western Avenue.

Maxwell, Mrs. Frances, 1537 North Western Avenue.

Maxwell, Frank, 62 Eighteenth Street.

Maxwell, F. A., 8354 Kerfoot Avenue.

Maxwell, F. S., 4058 Ridge Avenue.

Maxwell, F. B., William McKinley High School.

Maxwell, Frederick, 3561 Vincennes Avenue.

Maxwell, F. A., 9 Plymouth Court.

Maxwell, F. E., 7000 Princeton Avenue.

Maxwell, Mrs. Frida, 933 Elston Avenue.

Maxwell, Frisbie, 863 West Lake Street.

Maxwell, George, 1764 Thirty-fifth Street.

Maxwell, George, 939 North Lawndale Avenue.

Maxwell, G. A., 2808 South Forty-first Street.

Maxwell, G. H., 1405, 279 Dearborn Street.

Maxwell, G. W., 4425 Armour Avenue.

Maxwell, John, 201 Washington Boulevard.

Maxwell, J. F., 4771 North Clark Street.

Maxwell, J. H., 1498 North Fairfield Avenue.

Maxwell, J. S., 3524 Prairie Avenue.

Maxwell, J. W., 3101 State Street.

Maxwell, J. W., Rear 3676 Vincennes Avenue.

Maxwell, Joseph, 36 North Canal Street.

Maxwell, Joseph, 668 South Sangamon Street.

Maxwell, J. A., 49 Wabash Avenue.

Maxwell, L. W., 5616 Washington Avenue.

Maxwell, L. G., 7702 Stewart Avenue.

Maxwell, Mrs. Maggie, 3954 South Western Avenue Boulevard.

Maxwell, Miss Margaret, 167 South Sangamon Street.

Maxwell, Mrs. Margaret, 12 Crilly Court.

Maxwell, Martin, 3417 Auburn Street.

Maxwell, M. J., 3417 Auburn Street.

Maxwell, Mrs. Mary, rear 892 West Lake Street.

Maxwell, Miss M. E., Hotel Holland.

Maxwell, Mrs. M. J., 4328 Berkeley Avenue.

Maxwell, Mrs. W. M., 2833 Indiana Avenue.

Maxwell, Meyers, 12 Crilly Court.

Maxwell, Miss Nora, 1436 Washington Boulevard.

Maxwell, Mrs. P. O., 3978 Lake Avenue.
Maxwell, Paul, 130 Michigan Avenue.
Maxwell, Mrs. P. E., 2710 Third Avenue.
Maxwell, Ralph, 759 Forty-second Street.
Maxwell, Peter, 4345 State Street.
Maxwell, P. A., 2710 Fifth Avenue.
Maxwell, Mrs. H. R., 13 Carl Street.
Maxwell, H. J., 34 North Fairfield Avenue.
Maxwell, H. W., 395 Ashland Boulevard.
Maxwell, H. W. 1441 North Halsted Street.
Maxwell, Henry, 4723 South Ridgeway Avenue.
Maxwell, H. B,, 365 Ashland Boulevard.
Maxwell, H. F., 1199 Seventy-second Street.
Maxwell, H. M., 217 Ohio Street.
Maxwell, H. R., 73 Warren Avenue.
Maxwell, I. M., 610 West Van Buren Street.
Maxwell, James, 3746 Parnell Avenue.
Maxwell, James, 8757 Superior Avenue.
Maxwell, James, 367 Ashland Boulevard.
Maxwell, James, 7728 Jackson Avenue.
Maxwell, James, 277 LaSalle Avenue.
Maxwell, James, 4449 South Halsted Street.
Maxwell, John, 258 North Ashland Avenue.
Maxwell, John, 106 North Wells Street.
Maxwell, John, 1537 North Western Avenue.
Maxwell, John, 3431 Vernon Avenue.
Maxwell, John, 6511 South Peoria Street.
Maxwell, Ralph, 13 Carl Street.
Maxwell, R. G., 621 Forty-first Street.
Maxwell, Mrs. Reliefe, 699 West Lake Street.
Maxwell, Robert, 20 Kuehl Place.
Maxwell, Robert, 819 West Van Buren Street.
Maxwell, R. F., 468 Fullerton Avenue.
Maxwell, R. F., 1764 Thirty-fifth Street.
Maxwell, R. F., 3205 Armour Avenue.
Maxwell, R. W., 2711 South Halsted Street.
Maxwell, Mrs. S. J., 3105 Calumet Avenue.
Maxwell, Stanley, 5338 Washington Avenue.
Maxwell, Miss S. F., 3417 Auburn Street.
Maxwell, S. A. & Co., 430 Wabash Avenue.
Maxwell, S. A., 430 Wasbash Avenue.

Maxwell, C. E., 430 Wabash Avenue.
Maxwell, E. E., 430 Wabash Avenue
Maxwell, Thomas, 1109 Douglas Boulevard.
Maxwell, Thomas, 301 South Hermitage Avenue.
Maxwell, Thomas, 863 West Lake Street.
Maxwell, T. E., 3948 South Western Avenue Boulevard.
Maxwell, T. H., 392 North Winchester Avenue.
Maxwell, T. H., 374 Lincoln Avenue.
Maxwell, T. J., 3417 Auburn Street.
Maxwell, T. B., 4058 Ridge Avenue.
Maxwell, Warner, 3614 State Street.
Maxwell, W. A., 22½ Walnut Street.
Maxwell, William, 53 Walnut Street.
Maxwell, William, 8333 Mackinaw Avenue.
Maxwell, William, 8231 Exchange Avenue.
Maxwell, William, 103 West Adams Street.
Maxwell, William, 2939 Dearborn Street.
Maxwell, William, 1109 Douglas Boulevard.
Maxwell, W. A., 1316 Sheridan Road.
Maxwell, W. G., 7355 Vincennes Road.
Maxwell, W. H., 175 Rush Street.
Maxwell, W. H., 18 Walnut Street.
Maxwell, W. J., 876 Sixty-third Street.
Maxwell, W. R., 289 Sixty-sixth Place.
Maxwell, W. S., Dr., 176 Twenty-ninth Street.
Maxwell, W. W., 107 Thirty-seventh Street.
McElroy, Alvin L., 1964 Roberts Street.
McElroy, Mrs. Anna J., 12013 Butler Street.
McElroy, Benard, 748 West Twenty-second Street.
McElroy, B. G., 24 North Ada Street.
McElroy, Charles, 206 Sedgwick Street.
McElroy, C. F., 5 Board of Trade Building.
McElroy, Clifton, 1650 North Hoyne Avenue.
McElroy, D. H., 2701 North Forty-fourth Avenue.
McElroy, D. J., 2554 West Harrison Street.
McElroy, Mrs. Dora, 2177 Thirty-eighth Street.
McElroy, Mrs. D. I., 4235 Grand Boulevard.
McElroy, E. A., 41, 209 Adams Street.
McElroy, E. C., 423 West Randolph Street.
McElroy, E. J., 7209 Lafayette Avenue.
McElroy, Mrs. Ellen, 272 Sixty-sixth Place.

Mrs. Ellen, 840 Washington Boulevard.
F. A., 2957 North Fifty-sixth Avenue.
F. E., 11931 Eggleston Avenue.
F. M., 233 Twenty-third Place.
Frederick, 483 Fulton Street.
George, 314 South Center Avenue.
George, 7622 Jackson Avenue.
George, 29 Elburn Avenue.
G. T., 6004 Wabash Avenue.
Gleyen, 1253 Milwaukee Avenue.
H. P., 5949 Aberdeen Street.
Irvin, 219 South Sangamon Street.
James, 4210 Prairie Avenue.
James, 1139 North Halsted Street.
J. E., 901 North Forty-second Avenue.
J. E., 4235 Grand Boulevard.
J. H., 2552 West Harrison Street.
J. M., 7209 Lafayette Avenue.
J. W., 1139 North Halsted Street.
Mrs. Jane, 284 Forty-first Street.
John, 6936 Bishop Street.
John, 6416 Ingleside Avenue.
John, 1203 Lexington Street.
John, 5530 Bishop Street.
John, 10532 Wentworth Street.
Mrs. J. A., 1520 Kenmore Avenue.
J. H., 195 Fifty-fourth Street.
Joseph, 298 Washburn Avenue.
J. A., 1911 Carroll Avenue.
Dr. J. D., 5500 Wentworth Avenue.
J. P., 1911 Carroll Avenue.
Lee, 473 South Fairfield Avenue.
Mrs. M., 1636 West Fifty-first Street.
Mrs. M. A., 147 Eugenia Street.
Mark, 742 West Harrison Street.
Miss M. D., 3847 Langley Avenue.
Miss M. E., 390 Fullerton Avenue.
Mrs. M. E. A., 6203 State Street.
Matthew, 373 West Taylor Street.
Moses, 343 West One Hundred Fifth Place.
Orville, 314 South Center Avenue.

McElroy, Owen, 3614 Fifth Avenue.
McElroy, Owen, 34 Hope Street.
McElroy, Paul, 6200 Monroe Avenue.
McElroy, P. J., 724 Carroll Avenue.
McElroy, P. J., 2552 West Harrison Street.
McElroy, R. J., 1964 Roberts Avenue.
McElroy, Robert, 7234 Woodlawn Avenue.
McElroy, R. H., 604 Pratt Avenue.
McElroy, R. L., 6200 Monroe Avenue.
McElroy, Samuel, 483 Fulton Street.
McElroy, S. H., 430 Warren Avenue.
McElroy, Thomas, 298 Washburne Avenue.
McElroy, Thomas, 10532 Wentworth Avenue.
McElroy, W. B., 221 Adams Street.
McElroy, William J., 7304 Drexel Avenue.
McElroy, William P., 1797 Ninetieth Place.
McElroy, William R., 12013 Butler Street.
McElroy, William R., 314 Forty-fifth Street.
McDowell, Alexander, 6651 Jackson Avenue.
McDowell, Floyd, 144 West Eighteenth Street.
McDowell, Miss Althea, 1442 Monadnock Building.
McDowell, Andrew L., 4537 Champlain Avenue.
McDowell, Arthur C., 1411 Michigan Avenue.
McDowell, A. G., 3212 Lake Park Avenue.
McDowell, Bernard, 3844 LaSalle Street.
McDowell, Miss Bessie, 109 California Avenue.
McDowell, Mrs. Bridget, 1196 Clybourn Avenue.
McDowell, Mrs. Celia, 6451 St. Lawrence Avenue.
McDowell, Charles, 2908 Dearborn Street.
McDowell, C. H., 515 Ogden Avenue.
McDowell, C. N., 580 Racine Avenue.
McDowell, Daniel, 515 Ogden Avenue.
McDowell, D. M., 337 Twenty-fourth Street.
McDowell, Dr. E. B., 477 Forty-fifth Street.
McDowell, E. C., 670 Washburne Avenue.
McDowell, Miss E. V., 639 Fullerton Avenue.
McDowell, Elmer, 1622 West Twelfth Street.
McDowell, Miss Ethel, 188 Washington Boulevard.
McDowell, Mrs. F. M., 437 Center Street.
McDowell, Florence, 5615 South Green Street.
McDowell, Miss Florence, 5740 Princeton Avenue.

McDowell, Frank, 4635 Armour Avenue.
McDowell, F. B., 4746 Vincennes Avenue.
McDowell, F. H., 1612 Wabash Avenue.
McDowell, F. C., 5705 Drexel Avenue.
McDowell, G. J., 5825 West Erie Street.
McDowell, Mrs. Hannah, 6347 Evans Avenue.
McDowell, Harold, 639 Fullerton Avenue.
McDowell, Mrs. Harriet, 6322 Jackson Park Avenue.
McDowell, H. G., 180 North Center Avenue.
McDowell, H. J., 3844 La Salle Street.
McDowell, H. S., 5615 South Green Street.
McDowell, I. J., 1286 West Congress Street.
McDowell, Miss Isabella, 742 West Adams Street.
McDowell, Irvin, 4630 Gross Avenue.
McDowell, James, 2307 Evanston Avenue.
McDowell, James, 121 Stephenson Avenue.
McDowell, James, 2801 Archer Avenue.
McDowell, J. A., 412 Park Avenue.
McDowell, J. C., 5615 South Green Street.
McDowell, J. C., 3643 State Street.
McDowell, J. E., 5547 Lowe Avenue.
McDowell, J. G., 5825 West Erie Street.
McDowell, J. J., 3712 State Street.
McDowell, Miss Jennie, 5615 South Green Street.
McDowell, Miss J. M., 5603 Washington Avenue.
McDowell, John, 5620 South Elizabeth Street.
McDowell, John, 6326 Ellis Avenue.
McDowell, John, 1549 Michigan Avenue.
McDowell, John, 126 Stephenson Avenue.
McDowell, J. A., 349 Warren Avenue.
McDowell, J. H., 679 North Wells Street.
McDowell, J. J., 6451 St. Lawrence Avenue.
McDowell, J. E., 6347 Evans Avenue.
McDowell, J. A., 3110 Indiana Avenue.
McDowell, Mrs. Lulu, 429 Swan Street.
McDowell, Mrs. L. E., 189 Oakwood Boulevard.
McDowell, Malcolm, Jr., 1710 Cornelia Avenue.
McDowell, Miss M. M., 6415 St. Lawrence Avenue.
McDowell, Mrs. Mary, 462 Ogden Avenue.
McDowell, M. S., 5921 South Green Street.
McDowell, M. F., 5716 Union Avenue.

McDowell, John H.
McDowell, John L.
McDowell, John T.
McDowell, Kate W., widow W. P. McDowell.
McDowell, Lucien.
McDowell, Margaret M., widow J. C.
McDowell, Mary A.
McDowell, Mary K., 1208 Morton.
McDowell, Robert C.
McDowell, Robert E., 618 West Broadway.
McDowell, Rufus.
McDowell, R. A., Kenyon Building.
McDowell, Stuart, 422 Belgravia.
McDowell, William H.
McDowell, W. Wallace, 208–5.

L'ENVOI.

Let hope at anchor rest;
   A sea of death rolls all around the world.
And on its rocks, at eventide,
   Are all Hope's navies hurled.

No light-house sends a gleam
   Across that sullen sea no star shines on the strand;
An unknown Pilot, in the dark,
   Guides every ship to land.

INDEX TO "IRVINES" AND THEIR KIN.

CPSIA information can be obtained at www.ICGtesting.com
Printed in the USA
LVOW09s0248130416

483379LV00012B/279/P